World Trade and Payments

LITTLE, BROWN SERIES IN ECONOMICS

Richard E. Caves, CONSULTING EDITOR

World Trade and Payments

An Introduction

RICHARD E. CAVES *Harvard University*

RONALD W. JONES *University of Rochester*

Little, Brown and Company Boston

Library of Congress Catalog Card No. 72–9926

SECOND PRINTING

Published simultaneously in Canada
by Little, Brown & Company (Canada) Limited

PRINTED IN THE UNITED STATES OF AMERICA

To Verna and Bess

Preface

Irritation can provide a sharper spur to textbook writers than avarice. Probably few teachers toil through the preparation of an undergraduate course without some growing conviction that they could improve on the textbooks at hand. Our own pedagogical grumbles underlie two main goals pursued in writing this volume.

Our first goal is related to the theoretical work in the pure and monetary theories of international trade that has accumulated so vastly in the recent past. How much of this material could or should be brought within undergraduate reach? By stressing the basic questions with which theory is concerned and by reconsidering the order in which material is typically presented, we hope to supply the student with some feeling for the structure of international trade models, not just a bundle of ill-related devices and concepts. Many principal issues of pure theory can be exposed in the model of commodity exchange, which is the subject of Part 1. Traditional models of production and specialization are dealt with subsequently (Part 2), with emphasis placed on the new questions that such models allow us to explore. In Part 4 we employ the modern theory of economic policy to link the monetary and income mechanisms of adjustment to the choice of appropriate policies.

Our second goal is related to the descriptive and empirical material that traditionally decorates trade textbooks without really illustrating the uses of economic analysis. We have eschewed the usual trot down the corridors of history in order to link our descriptive material to the analytical framework — tests of hypotheses and current policy problems that theory can enlighten. Indeed, we have risked relatively heavy emphasis on the analysis of present-day issues of international economic policy, hoping to gain more from the motivating power of urgent contemporary issues than we lose from the rapid and unforeseeable changes in the shape of these policy issues. Alas, the exchange-rate movements begun in February 1973 reveal this risk.

We assume that the student has the background in micro and macro theory provided by the typical introductory course. The exposition of theory in the text relies on diagrams and uses no mathematics beyond a small amount of algebra. The use of simple calculus is now standard in a few undergraduate institutions, and for this audience we have provided a set of brief chapter supplements that expose in more analytic detail the basic structure of trade models discussed in the text. Of special importance is the unified treatment of the effects of market and policy changes on a country's welfare, developed in the supplements to Chapters 3, 6, 12, 13, 22, and 25. Instructors can draw on these selectively to fortify the vintage for advanced undergraduate courses or to deepen the coverage of topics they hold particularly important. We emphasize, however, that the text is entirely self-contained without the supplements.

The book covers a conventional full line of topics and can with some additional material serve as the basis for a full-year course at the undergraduate level. We prefer pure theory before monetary and have so arranged the book. Instructors who wish to reverse the sequence can go from Part 1 to Part 4, then return to Parts 2 and 3. Part 1 is a general introduction to both the pure and monetary theory. Teachers offering courses shorter than a year can use various strategies to condense the material presented. Parts 5 and 6 segregate our principal analyses of international capital flows and the relation between trade and growth. These sections can be dropped entirely or only their first chapters assigned. We have arranged our treatment of some theoretical topics so that instructors can bypass more difficult matter by deleting chapters; examples are Chapter 3 on stability, Chapter 9 on the Heckscher-Ohlin model, and Chapter 19 on devaluation and related policies. Finally, a short theoretical course can drop empirically oriented chapters such as 10, 14, 15, 23, and 24.

We have incurred heavy debts for criticisms and suggestions as our chapters have gone through successive rounds of revision. Parts of the book were tried out on undergraduate trade courses at Harvard and Rochester; our students offered many useful suggestions for revision and clarification. Meredith O. Clement and Arnold Collery read and commented upon the entire manuscript. Other colleagues and students who provided suggestions on earlier drafts include Robert Baldwin, Kim Benston, Richard Brecher, Rudy Dornbusch, Steve Easton, Stanley Engerman, Peter Kenen, Elinda Kornblith, Rick Maitland, Wolfgang Meyer, Michihiro Ohyama, and J. D. Richardson. Secretarial services were efficiently provided by Marjorie Adams, Martha Colburn, and Trudy Zimmerman. Catherine Jones offered comments for stylistic improvements and cheerfully provided copious supplies of tea during the lengthy dialogues between authors in Rochester, Cambridge, and London.

Contents

World Trade and Payments

1 Introduction

Unique among the concerns of economics, international trade has always carried a note of romance — the lure of the exotic, the hint of danger. In the tenth century, thousand-camel caravans crossed the Sahara Desert to supply gold, slaves, and fine crafts to the Mediterranean world in exchange for salt, metal goods, and paper. Traders' dreams of bartering for the riches of the Orient spurred the European voyages of discovery from the fourteenth century. Today, supertankers move hundreds of thousands of tons of crude oil at a time from producing to consuming lands at strikingly low cost — and threaten to pollute hundreds of miles of shoreline should they break up at sea.

The romance of international commerce surges through its contact with public policy. British restrictions on colonial trade helped to fuel the American Revolution. After World War II the nations of Western Europe, sickened of the recurrent wars spawned by modern nationalism, sought permanent reconciliation and peace through a trade treaty — removing barriers to commerce through the European Common Market.

In this book we try to provide an understanding of the economic causes and consequences of international exchange. Any branch of economics rests on theoretical concepts and models. The scholar's job is to bring systematic observation and explanation to the chaotic diversity of the world he observes. The Census Bureau records data on about 14,000 classifications of commodities entering into the foreign trade of the United States — about 4,000 for exports and 10,000 for imports. Do we need 14,000 explanations for these trade flows? Could we find one that would cover every bundle of merchandise? Our quest is for the simplest model, or the smallest family of models, capable of answering what seem to be the important questions about patterns of trade, and how public policy should deal with them.

The foreign commerce of nations is one of the oldest branches of economics, and has drawn the attention of some of the greatest economists. Indeed, many of the ideas you will meet in this book can boast of famous ancestors. We owe much of our understanding of money in international trade to the philosopher David Hume (Chapter 16). One of our principal models of international trade and production (Chapter 7) derives from David Ricardo, an English stockbroker with a powerful analytical mind. Yet much of present-day international economics is quite new. A most fruitful model relating trade to factors of production comes from two twentieth-century Swedish economists, Eli F. Heckscher and Bertil Ohlin (Chapters 8 and 9). And our understanding of how trade relates to employment, and how policy can deal properly with both, is a late fall-out of the Keynesian Revolution of the 1930's (Chapters 17–19).

1.1 THE SUBJECT OF INTERNATIONAL ECONOMICS

International economics is somewhat curiously related to the other conventional branches of economics. Public finance, money and banking, or labor economics selects a neatly distinguished group of transactors or markets in the economy for special study. "But," you ask, "doesn't international economics similarly deal with international markets?" It does, and these markets are capable of exact *legal* definition. Sovereign states are ubiquitous, so we can always tell whether the two parties to a transaction are citizens of different countries.

But are international transactions economically unique and readily separated from transactions within nations? Does the Kansas wheat farmer know or care whether the bushel of wheat he sells will be exported? When you buy a handkerchief, do you inspect it closely for a label indicating manufacture abroad? International transactions are of a piece with domestic markets. Ultimately our explanation of international trade must be part of an explanation of each national market.

This intertwining of international and national markets runs through all of international economics. If India decides to train more physicians, the supply of physicians in Britain is apt to increase (through emigration). If the United States raises government spending to increase employment, employment in Canada is almost sure to increase. Hence you should not be surprised that international economics can easily (and usefully) be viewed as "international aspects of supply and demand," or "international aspects of money and finance," or "international aspects of taxation."

Nonetheless, there are even better reasons for treating international trade and payments as a separate field of study. Here are two that we feel are most important:

1. The models we find useful for explaining international trade are simple, but strong and general. They not only explain patterns of international trade, but they also tell much about patterns of production, income distribution, etc., within countries.

2. The policy questions that arise in international exchange differ from those typically discussed within nation-states, and they require a special analytical apparatus. Yet we contend that the *principles* of policy-making should be the same at home and abroad. International economics can at once attack the special questions of international economic policy and show how to couple foreign and domestic policies correctly.

Let us explore these reasons in more detail. Why should we employ separate models to explain international trade and domestic trade? The traditional answer has been that factors of production — labor and capital — in the long run move freely within the national economy, but their mobility between countries is sharply limited. We suppose that labor and capital move freely between New York and California, whenever workers or lenders feel that such a shift will improve their real incomes. If that assumption is correct, the goods traded between the two states, and the effect of that trade on their "native" factor endowments will be less interesting. (California has no natives.) On the other hand, if little movement of labor and capital takes place between, say, Mexico and France, the commodities they trade and their benefit from the exchange become both interesting and important.

The assumption that factors of production are perfectly mobile within countries and perfectly immobile between them is obviously not completely true. Think of the international migrations of the nineteenth century, the outflow of long-term capital from the United States in the last two decades — and the immobility of low-paid labor out of America's Appalachia or Italy's Mezzogiorno! However, probably no assumption used by economists is completely true. We judge our assumptions not only by this absolute standard, but by a relative one: do they yield more useful and accurate results than any alternative assumption? We shall respect tradition — at least through the first three parts of this book — and build our models on the assumption that factors are perfectly mobile within and perfectly immobile between countries.

Yet this traditional way to distinguish models of international trade fails, we feel, to cut the subject down to its barest essentials. Occam's Razor can give a closer shave! The central questions about international trade deal simply with *exchange* between traders in two national markets. We shall argue that the simplest and clearest explanation of trade between nations, and the gains nations derive from trade, requires only a description of the exchange of fixed endowments of goods. The simplification we make, by concentrating first on exchange, is to put aside the details of producing goods. With the essentials set, we can expand our model of trade to include variability in production.

Models of international exchange and production must ultimately explain satisfactorily the trade patterns we observe around us. Throughout this book we will study the ways in which economists have tested their models against the facts of commerce — and the explanations you can draw from these models for features you observe in the international economy. International economists have been slow in showing that their models will work in the field as well as the laboratory. Many textbooks likewise intermingle their theories not with tests and applications, but with historical description of the international economy. A trot down the corridors of history is always entertaining, but it leaves the impression that the theory of international economics offers windy speculation rather than useful and empirically tested models. We hope to convince you otherwise.

We mentioned above a second reason for studying international economics separately: special questions of policy arise in the international economy. Trade takes place between sovereign nations — between us and them. Two governments, with potentially clashing objectives, can apply their policies to the flow of trade between them — and against each other's interests. More profoundly, because of the fear and suspicion of outsiders of even the most saintly mortal we chronically ask whether or not the nation benefits from trading with foreigners. No one asks whether Vermont gains from trading with New Hampshire, or Minneapolis with St. Paul. But the proposition that the United States and France both gain from trading with each other might not win a majority vote — in either country. Rich countries fear that they will suffer from importing the products of low-wage foreign labor. Poor countries dread imports created by foreign high-level technology. A critical role for the theory of international trade, then, is to identify exactly the gains from trade and their indications for economic policy. Our first approach to trade through a simple model of exchange proves particularly helpful for pinning down the gains from trade.

Picking the best (or the best available) economic policy is the job of welfare economics — the branch of our subject that seeks maximum economic welfare. The odor of value judgments always lurks around welfare economics, especially when we ask, "Whose welfare?" International economics takes a flexible approach to this question. Following the tradition of general economics, we often concentrate on the welfare — the maximum real income — of a country's citizens. But our welfare analysis can serve other goals as well. Finding clashes and harmonies between national and world welfare is an important task of this book. We shall also glance at the welfare of groups of countries (such as the European Common Market) and at the welfare of groups of income recipients within a country. Finally, we shall find that governments sometimes foster policies that are difficult (impossible?) to reconcile with their own national economic welfare, such as maintaining a large domestic farm sector. We can identify more costly and less costly ways to achieve such non-economic goals.

A great deal of economic policy-making is concerned with the short run, and with such objectives as full employment and price stability. Especially in a large economy like the United States, where a small share of output is traded abroad, officials often pick solutions for these problems as if the foreign sector mattered not at all. Then, when something goes wrong with the balance of international payments, they react with an *ad hoc* measure. Our models of short-term policy-making in the open economy lay the groundwork for improving on that practice. We shall find that a nation with enough policy instruments — and enough information about their effects — can solve the problem of its balance of payments and achieve its internal objectives of full employment and price stability as well. We saw before that international transactions intertwine with domestic ones. Thus policies must deal with domestic and international short-term problems together.

Countries' interests can clash over short-term policy issues. In 1971 the United States seemed to create an international crisis by refusing to exchange its gold stock for dollars acquired by foreign central banks. This seeming act of aggression was in fact an act of defense. It bore on the problem of countries' sharing the righting of imbalance in their international transactions. Thus, another task for our models of international economic policy is to expose the sources of harmony and conflict among countries. We shall find countries' positions on the exotic question of international reserves become clear once we understand that they relate to this problem of sharing the burden of adjustment.

1.2 THE ORGANIZATION OF THIS BOOK

We have seen that international economics builds models to explain the links between national economic systems ("inter-national economics," indeed) and to show how nations' policies can yield maximum welfare and stability. Our purpose in this book is to explain those models simply but comprehensively and to show how they can be used. We shall apply those models liberally to present-day issues of international economic policy — not from a delusion that those problems will look the same tomorrow as they do today, but because they provide a handy proving ground to turn theoretical concepts and models into an "active vocabulary" for understanding new issues as they arise.

We promised to begin with the simplest model of exchange between nations, and that is the focus of Part 1. The fundamental forces governing equilibrium in international trade can be explained in a model that assumes only that the citizens of two countries hold arbitrary initial stocks of goods that they can barter with each other. In Chapter 2 we shall show how to predict the pattern of trade and measure the gains from trade in this model. In Chapter 3 we shall find that it also answers our questions about the stability of equilibrium in international trade — questions usually met in much more complex settings. In Chapters 4 and 5 we shall explore the links between this simple model of exchange and the adjustment processes and problems of the international economy we observe. Included is an analysis of the balance-of-payments accounts, our standard statistical tool for understanding international transactions.

With the exchange model before us, we are ready to follow the two principal paths taken by international economics — "real" models dealing with production and exchange and "monetary" models dealing with price levels and employment. In Part 2 we shall expand our exchange model to allow for the production of traded goods, and to show the response of production and income distribution to changes in a nation's foreign trade. We shall test the practical explanatory power of these models and notice the problems of expanding them to cover imperfect competition and technological change.

In Part 3 we shall continue with the real or "barter" model of exchange, turning to the effect of tariffs and other controls on trade. We shall identify the effects of these controls and ask in what circumstances they might be desirable, from the nation's point of view. We shall find a major clash of interests, in that the welfare of all countries together would generally be raised by removing all restrictions on international trade, but one country acting alone can often improve its own welfare by maintaining or increasing restrictions. We shall see that nations have staged repeated tariff "disarmament conferences" (such as the Kennedy Round of 1962–1967) in the attempt to skirt this conflict.

In Part 4 we shall turn to monetary aspects of international economics, showing first how we can fit money stocks and prices into our simple barter models. We shall study monetary and income disturbances in the open economy by using two polar models — one assuming all money prices are flexible (except the exchange rate), the other keeping prices rigid and allowing the economy to depart from full employment and utilization of capacity. With these models, we shall show how countries can devise policies to attain their objectives for both their balance of payments and domestic policy. That demonstration in turn will help us to understand the effects of changing an exchange rate (devaluation or revaluation), changing the quantity of international reserves, or allowing the exchange rate to respond freely to market forces.

In the final two parts of the book we shall take up important problems with both real and monetary aspects. In Part 5 we shall deal with the international movement of capital, both in the sense of real productive capacity and financial purchasing power. In Part 6 we shall turn to growth and development, showing how our simple barter model can encompass economic growth, and applying this and other lessons to the special conditions and problems of the less-developed countries.

1.3 THE CHAPTER SUPPLEMENTS

A question that arises in any undergraduate textbook on economics concerns the level of mathematical training that can be expected from the book's audience. The branch of mathematics that finds application repeatedly in economics is calculus (especially differential calculus). Sometimes this is disguised. Any introductory economics course deals with such concepts as marginal revenue, marginal costs, marginal products, and the marginal propensity to consume — often without mentioning that these are each "derivatives" or "partial derivatives" of calculus. When formal calculus is introduced in an economics text, the claim is often made that the book is "self-contained" because it adds a few pages at the end of the book explaining the rudiments of calculus.

The basic decision made in this book is to keep the chapter texts completely free of any formal mathematics other than a sprinkling of high school algebra. This decision helps account for the heavy reliance on diagrams in the theoretical chapters. To satisfy that part of the reading audience that wants a more formal approach to the subject matter, we have added supplements to some of the chapters. For most of these supplements we have assumed a basic knowledge of differential calculus. In one of them (the supplement to Chapter 13) we use matrices and vectors. Others (the supplements to Chapters 5 and 20, for example) expand on topics in the text and use no mathematics.

The supplements are not designed to be read separately from the text, but the text can be read and understood without recourse to the supplements. In this way the book is geared primarily to an undergraduate audience with limited mathematical training, but we also hope to interest students desiring a more rigorous approach to some theoretical issues.

SUGGESTIONS FOR FURTHER READING

Following each chapter of this book is a brief list of suggestions for further reading. We have in mind principally the teacher wishing to assign fuller accounts of some points developed in the chapter, and the student in quest of further enlightenment — or a term-paper topic. Sometimes we shall refer to classic expositions of important ideas in the chapter. In other cases we shall mention fuller contemporary accounts. Many references deal with applications of international economics to empirical explanation and policy-making. To each reference we have appended a few words explaining its content.

We generally avoid citations to competing textbooks, on the theory that their authors should worry about their own advertising. Nonetheless, it may be helpful here to locate our volume (the chapter texts only) in relation to some others in common use:

Kreinin, Mordechai E. *International Economics: A Policy Approach.* New York: Harcourt Brace Jovanovich, 1971. Easier than our book.

Snider, Delbert A. *Introduction to International Economics,* 5th ed. Homewood, Ill.: Richard D. Irwin, 1971. Easier than our book.

Ellsworth, Paul T., with J. Clark Leith. *The International Economy,* 4th ed. New York: Macmillan, 1969. About the same level as our book.

Kindleberger, Charles P. *International Economics,* 4th ed. Homewood, Ill.: Richard D. Irwin, 1968. About the same level of difficulty as our book.

Södersten, Bo. *International Economics.* New York: Harper & Row, 1970. About the same level as our book, but uses more mathematics.

Yeager, Leland B. *International Monetary Relations: Theory, History, and Policy.* New York: Harper & Row, 1966. About the same level, but dealing only with monetary issues.

Staley, Charles E. *International Economics: Analysis and Issues.* Englewood Cliffs, N. J.: Prentice-Hall, 1970. Shorter and harder than our book.

Heller, H. Robert. *International Trade: Theory and Empirical Evidence.* Englewood Cliffs, N. J.: Prentice-Hall, 1968. More narrow focus on pure theory than ours.

Kemp, Murray C. *The Pure Theory of International Trade and Investment.* Englewood Cliffs, N. J.: Prentice-Hall, 1969. Graduate-level text.

Takayama, Akira. *International Economics.* New York: Holt, Rinehart and Winston, 1972. Graduate-level text.

Pearce, Ivor F. *International Trade.* New York: Norton, 1970. Starts off gently, but becomes more difficult than our book.

PART ONE Commodity Exchange and the Balance of Payments

2 A Model of Commodity Exchange

Some patterns of trade need almost no explanation. If you live in the United States and have a taste for coffee, you have your coffee imported from Brazil or some other coffee-growing country because it is not produced in your own country. If such imports were cut off, your level of well-being or "real income" would surely be reduced. If all trade were of this kind — with each country producing commodities desired by all countries but available only locally — there would be little need for the economist either to expound upon the virtues of trade or to explain the pattern of trade. These would be almost self-evident. Indeed, millions of dollars in world trade takes place each year in coffee, chromium, copper, tea, fruits, and other items that Nature has placed in some communities and not in others. But many items in international commerce cannot be described or explained this way. Automobiles, steel, textiles, processed foods, and myriads of other items are produced in a number of countries. What are the reasons for the large volume of international trade in these items?

In searching for an explanation we naturally inquire about costs. Transistor radios are produced and exported from Taiwan and Japan, wool comes from Australia, and butter from New Zealand. In countless examples we can find the source of trade to be the country with the relatively low cost of production. But this explanation masks a more penetrating question: Why are radios cheaper to produce in Japan than in Brazil?

It may be a surprise that we first explain the gains from trade and the pattern of trade in a setting in which commodities are not produced. Without observing production, we can hardly identify the natural costs of obtaining commodities. The world we have in mind consists of only two communities (to avoid the complexities in-

11

volved in many-country trade), each with residents who possess fixed amounts of two commodities. (Call them food and clothing.) Residents in one country may exchange one commodity for another, either with other residents in their own country or residents abroad. Their desire to engage in such trade will be a natural outgrowth of the disparity between residents (and therefore countries) in tastes and initial commodity possessions. The account of trade that can be given in such a simple model will be the basis for more realistic, and complicated models or stereotypes of international trade where commodities are produced and costs are sensitive to technology and resource availabilities. Part 2 of this book is devoted precisely to this aspect of production, costs, and trade.

The model of trade developed in this and the subsequent two chapters in Part 1 is deliberately kept simple in order to highlight some basic features of trade. (1) What advantage do countries gain by importing commodities that are also available at home? (2) What determines whether, on balance, a country will export food or clothing? (3) How are prices determined internationally, and how do they differ from prices that would prevail if countries could not exchange commodities? (4) In what sense is free trade — the lack of man-made obstacles (such as tariffs or quotas) to the importation of commodities — "optimal" from a world point of view? In exploring these questions we shall review or introduce concepts and graphical techniques that you may remember from earlier courses in economics: pure competition; indifference curves; supply and demand schedules; budget lines; offer curves (or reciprocal demand curves); box diagrams; and contract curves. They will each be explained as they are introduced, and applied throughout this book.

2.1 THE GAINS FROM TRADE

The result we are aiming for in this section is absolutely basic: if in the absence of trade the relative prices of the two commodities differ between countries, both countries can gain by exchanging commodities at any price ratio that lies intermediate between the relative prices ruling before trade. Not only must the result be explained, the terms in which it is phrased perhaps need further elucidation.

Relative Prices and the Budget Line

If food and clothing are the only commodities that can be consumed, the *relative* price of food is the quantity of clothing that must be given up in exchange for one unit of food. You are used to prices being conveniently quoted in terms of money: the price of a certain automobile is $2,624. Money has no real role in this model.[1] The ad-

---

[1] The role of money will be mentioned briefly in Chapter 4, the significance of different countries using different currencies will be discussed in Chapter 5, and a more detailed account of monetary aspects of trade will be presented in Part 4, especially Chapter 16.

vantages of money to ease transactions are taken for granted. We exclude money as a store of wealth that can be used to obtain command over commodities. An individual can obtain one unit more food than he possesses in his endowment bundle only by giving up a quantity of clothing of equivalent value. This quantity represents food's *relative* price.

Figure 2.1 illustrates relative prices diagrammatically. Suppose that point *E* represents the community's initial supply (endowment bundle) of food and clothing. That is, the community possesses *OF* units of clothing and *OG* units of food. The straight line through point *E* has been drawn so that its *slope* indicates relative prices. When mathematicians refer to the slope of a line they mean the vertical distance between two points divided by the horizontal — the segment *BO* divided by *OA* in Figure 2.1. They would also point out that the line through *E* has a negative slope — that an *increase* in what is measured on the vertical axis (food) must be matched by a *decrease* in what is measured on the horizontal axis (clothing). Drawing the price line with a negative slope appeals to the economist, for if the slope of line *BEA* is to represent relative prices, *more* of one commodity should be obtained only by possessing *less* of the other. If the word "slope" refers to a vertical distance divided by a horizontal, does the slope of line *BEA* represent the relative price of food or the relative price of clothing? This question is simple, but experience reveals that it is worth thinking through and remembering. The slope of *BEA*, the ratio *BO/OA*, represents the relative price of clothing.

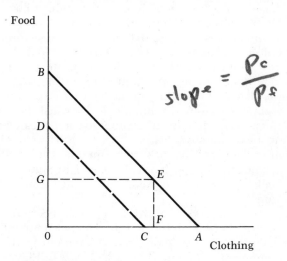

FIGURE 2.1   The Budget Line

The slope of the budget line, *BEA*, which is *OB/OA*, shows the relative price of clothing. Its inverse, *OA/OB*, shows the relative price of food.

Countless times in this book we shall illustrate a *change* in relative prices. If line *BEA* becomes steeper, this implies that the relative price of clothing has gone up. The relative price of the commodity shown on the *horizontal* axis is equal to the slope, which shows the *vertical* distance divided by the horizontal. That relationship is in the nature of price: the relative price of clothing is measured by the amount of food that must be sacrificed to obtain a unit of clothing. This amount, of course, is the inverse of the relative price of food, *OA/OB*.

The dashed line, *DC*, in Figure 2.1 is parallel to *BEA*. Because relative prices are shown by slopes, relative prices are the same along *DC* as along *BEA*. The same would be true of any line parallel to *BEA*. What is special about the line through *E* is that it is the *budget line*. All points on *BEA* have the same value as the endowment point, *E*. For example, *OB* units of food are equivalent in value to *OA* units of clothing because the relative price of clothing is *OB/OA*. If the community should start with bundle *E* and be able to exchange commodities at the relative prices shown by *BEA*, then any point on *BEA* could be consumed. In Figure 2.1 line *BEA* only shows what consumption bundles are possible, it does not show which bundle would be demanded. To determine this bundle, we must specify the community's tastes or preferences.

Indifference Curves

Indifference curves expressing preferences or tastes concerning the two commodities, food and clothing, most readily apply to the individual. Consider the bundle of food and clothing shown by point *A* in Figure 2.2 — quantity *OD* of clothing and *OF* units of food. As long as both commodities yield satisfaction, any consumption bundle northeast of *A*, such as *H*, must be preferred to *A*, and any bundle with less of both commodities than *A*, such as *I*, must be less desirable than *A*. To proceed, suppose one unit of food is deleted from the consumption basket at *A* — leading to the lower level of satisfaction that would be obtained from the bundle *J*. Then ask how much extra clothing must be given to the individual to compensate for the loss of this unit of food. Suppose this quantity is *JB*. If so, the individual is indifferent to the choice of consuming bundle *A* or bundle *B*. *A* and *B* lie on the same indifference curve, labeled y_0 in Figure 2.2. (Throughout the book the symbol "*y*" indicates "real income," "utility," or "satisfaction.")

The foregoing remarks establish that indifference curves are negatively sloped: A sacrifice in the quantity of one commodity consumed must be balanced by the appropriate increment in the quantity of the other commodity. The indifference curves in Figure 2.1 are also bowed in toward the origin, reflecting the common assumption that the marginal rate at which individuals are willing to substitute more of one commodity for less of another changes along an indifference

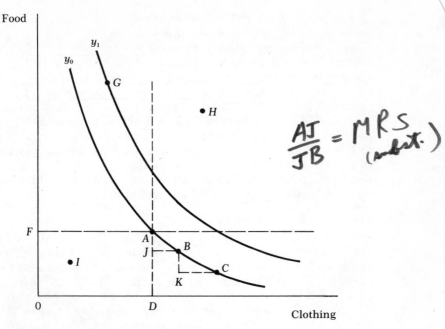

FIGURE 2.2   Indifference Curves

> The bowed-in shape reflects diminishing marginal rates of
> substitution. All points on indifference curve y_1 are preferred
> to any point on indifference curve y_0.

curve. The ratio AJ to JB in Figure 2.2 shows the *marginal rate of
substitution* between food and clothing in moving from A to B. The
ratio BK to KC is smaller, showing that the further sacrifice of food
involved in moving from B to C must be accompanied by an even
larger increment in clothing to keep the individual on indifference
curve y_0. As the consumer has less and less food, each unit has greater
value to him, while each additional unit increment of clothing will
raise his satisfaction less the more clothing he possesses. That is,
the *marginal rate of substitution*, as indicated by the slope of the
indifference curve, diminishes along the curve y_0 as more clothing is
substituted for food.

The indifference curve, y_0, is one of many that could be drawn.
Indeed, the "commodity space" is filled with these curves. Another is
curve y_1, further out from the origin, and therefore indicating a higher
level of real income than does curve y_0. For example, point G is preferred to point A. If the individual initially possessed the bundle of
food and clothing indicated by point A, and were allowed to exchange
some clothing for food so that he could consume point G, he would

clearly improve his well-being. As we shall illustrate, international trade can bring about precisely this kind of gain.

Using indifference curves for a community of individuals (say a country) as well as for any single individual would be extremely convenient. Under strict assumptions this can be done — e.g., if all individuals have identical tastes and initial endowments of food and clothing.[2] We have decided to assume in this book that *community* preferences may be represented by a set of nonintersecting indifference curves. Later we shall point out some of the implications of this assumption. Here we state explicitly that such an assumption is made in full awareness of its abstraction from reality and is justified by its facilitation of all our subsequent discussions of the welfare effects of trade, commercial policy, and growth.

Trade Benefits Both Countries

Reinterpret Figure 2.2 now as a set of indifference curves for the home country, and A as the aggregate bundle of food and clothing available to that community in the absence of any possibility of exchanging goods with other nations. The slope of the indifference curve at A, the marginal rate of substitution, reflects that community's relative evaluation of the two commodities and would thus reflect as well the price of clothing in terms of food. At no other price would the community be content to consume food and clothing in the proportions indicated by point A. This price ratio is illustrated explicitly in Figure 2.3 by the line AB, tangent to the home country's indifference curve, y_0, which runs through the home country's endowment bundle, E. Suppose, now, that the home country is offered a different price ratio at which food and clothing can be exchanged, such as shown by the slope of line CED. It could then offer to export GE units of clothing, which have the same value as FG units of food. Such trade would allow it to consume the bundle, F, on the indifference curve, y_1, which is higher than the original curve, y_0, passing through the endowment bundle. Because the y_1 curve is tangent to line CED, it clearly represents the highest level of satisfaction that the home country could obtain by trades along CED. In such a manner we can prove that the opportunity to trade at relative prices that differ from those in isolation at home must improve real incomes at home.[3]

But is such trade feasible? Could the home country obtain the desired food imports from abroad? Figure 2.4 illustrates a case where

---

[2] A discussion of this issue can be found in Paul A. Samuelson, "Social Indifference Curves," *Quarterly Journal of Economics,* 70 (February 1956): 1–22.

[3] Here we have only considered the case in which the relative price of food offered to the home country is lower than the price shown at E. However, the symmetry of the case should convince you that if the home country were offered a relative clothing price lower than line AEB (shown by a line through E flatter than AEB), it could also reach a higher indifference curve than y_0.

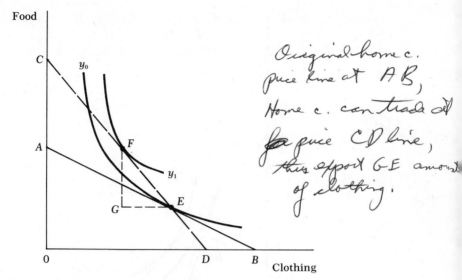

FIGURE 2.3   The Trade Triangle for the Home Country

The home country originally consumes its endowment bundle, E, at relative prices shown by line AB. If it could trade at prices shown by line CD, it could export GE units of clothing to obtain FG units of food, thus consuming the bundle shown by F and improving its real income to the level shown by the y_1 indifference curve.

the foreign country would, at the same price ratio as shown by line CED in Figure 2.3, be willing to export amount FG of food to the home country. In Figure 2.4 the foreign country's endowment point is E^*, and through that point line $C^*E^*D^*$ has been drawn parallel to line CED in Figure 2.3, thereby showing the same relative commodity prices. Along budget line $C^*E^*D^*$ the foreign country's most desired consumption point is F^*. It would be willing to export E^*G^* of food (equal to FG in Figure 2.3) in exchange for G^*F^* imports of clothing. Notice that if the foreign country could not engage in trade, it would evaluate food and clothing by its marginal rate of substitution at E^*, shown by the slope of line $A^*E^*B^*$. But this slope is different from the slope of AEB in Figure 2.3. The relative price of food and clothing that is illustrated in Figure 2.3 by CED and in Figure 2.4 by line $C^*E^*D^*$ lies intermediate between the low price of clothing in the home country before trade (shown by the slope of AEB in Figure 2.3) and the high price of clothing in the pre-trade situation in the foreign country (shown by the slope of $A^*E^*B^*$ in Figure 2.4). This justifies the basic result that we stated at the beginning of this section. A divergence in the relative price of commodities in the two countries

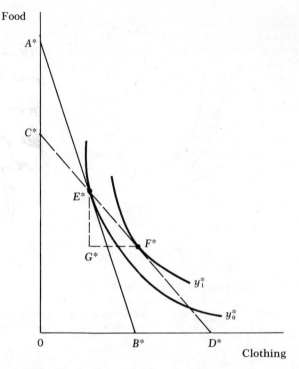

FIGURE 2.4   The Trade Triangle for the Foreign Country

The foreign country, originally consumes its endowment bundle, E^*, at relative prices shown by line A^*B^*. If it could trade at prices shown by line C^*D^*, it could export E^*G^* units of food to obtain G^*F^* units of clothing, thus consuming the bundle shown by F^* and improving its real income to the level shown by the y_1^* indifference curve.

before trade indicates a mutual potential gain from trade for *both* countries at a common intermediate price ratio. No "exploitation" is involved. Although world total supplies of food and clothing are un-altered throughout (by the fixed-endowment assumption of the ex-change model), a redistribution of each commodity from the country in which it is cheaper to the country in which it is valued more highly increases the welfare of each country.

2.2 THE OFFER CURVES AND FREE TRADE EQUILIBRIUM

The diagrammatic argument presented above illustrates the possi-bility that each country can gain by trading at relative prices (terms

Offer Curve

of trade) that differ from those that would rule in the absence of trade. Indeed, Figures 2.3 and 2.4 showed more than this. The common terms of trade given by the slope of line *CED* in Figure 2.3 or line $C^*E^*D^*$ in Figure 2.4 allowed commodity markets to be cleared. By "cleared" we mean that the home country's import demand for food exactly balanced the foreign country's export supply of food at the same terms of trade. Similarly, the home country's exports of clothing (to pay for its food imports) matched the demand for clothing imports in the foreign country. The "offer curve," to be discussed now, builds on this presentation and allows us to survey all possible terms of trade (relative prices) and to distinguish those (usually one) that lead to market equilibrium from those that do not. We shall begin by concentrating on the home country.

markets "cleared"

Offer curve Defined

The Offer Curve

Figure 2.3 is a good starting point. The home country's commodity endowment point, *E*, is fixed. The home country would choose to consume this endowment bundle at terms of trade shown by the slope of line *AEB*, which is tangent to the indifference curve, y_0, at *E*. For any other price ratio, such as shown by line *CED*, the home country would prefer to exchange one commodity for another to obtain a consumption bundle that differs from its endowment bundle. It chooses to trade, because by so doing it can reach a higher level of satisfaction than would be obtained if it consumed its endowment bundle and refrained from trade. The *offer curve* for the home country is the locus of all points such as *E* and *F* in Figure 2.3, each of which would be selected for consumption at appropriate terms of trade.

The possible shape of the offer curve is illustrated in Figure 2.5 by curve *RER'*. The price ratio that would rule at home if there were no opportunity to trade is shown by line 1, tangent to the indifference curve through *E*. Line 2, passing through *E*, shows the consumption possibilities if the home country can exchange commodities at a lower relative price of food than would exist in isolation. The home country responds to this lower price by demanding more food (at *A*) than it did previously (at *E*). Line 3 illustrates an even lower relative price for food, which further stimulates the demand for food (at *B*) compared to its level at higher food prices (at *A* or at *E*). If the relative price of food on world markets should exceed the price in isolation, as shown by line 4, less food would be consumed than at *E*, and more clothing. Line 4's optimal consumption bundle is point *C*, where an indifference curve is tangent to line 4.

The following properties of the home country's offer curve have been illustrated in this presentation:

1. Each point on the offer curve corresponds to terms of trade that make the consumption point on the offer curve equal in value to the initial endowment bundle, *E*. At each point on the offer curve an in-

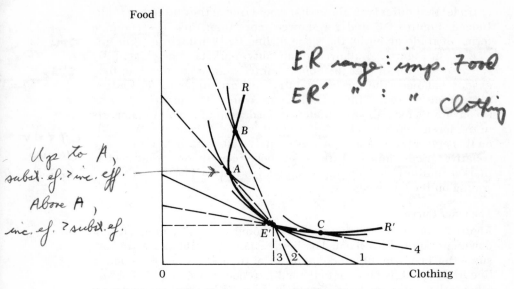

Handwritten notes:

ER range: imp. food
ER' " : " clothing

Up to A,
subst. ef. > inc. ef.
Above A,
inc. ef. > subst. ef.

FIGURE 2.5   The Home Country's Offer Curve

> The home country's offer curve is *RER'*. Each point on the
> offer curve reflects a point of tangency between a budget
> line through the endowment point, *E*, and an indifference
> curve.

difference curve is tangent to the budget line passing through *E* and
the point on the offer curve.

2. The home country imports food and exports clothing only if the
relative price of food is lower in world markets than it would be at
home in isolation (no trade). In Figure 2.5 the home country imports
food in the range *ER* of the offer curve and would attempt to import
clothing in the range *ER'*.

3. The home country's consumption bundles for points on the offer
curve away from *E* all represent higher levels of satisfaction than
does point *E*. These higher levels of satisfaction are the gains from
trade.

4. If the home country imports food, a decrease in the relative price
of food (an improvement in its terms of trade) will result in an increase in food imports. This is illustrated by the movement from *A* to
B in Figure 2.5.[4]

[4] Although a decrease in the relative price of imports leads to an increase in
the quantity of imports along the offer curve, a decrease in the relative price of
exports may or may not lead to a fall in the quantity of exports. Chapter 3 will
pursue this possible asymmetry in the response of demand to changes in the
terms of trade. Figure 2.5 illustrates that a fall in clothing's relative price from
line 3 to line 2 would increase clothing exports (from *B* to *A*), while a further
fall in price to line 1 would decrease clothing exports (from *A* to *E*).

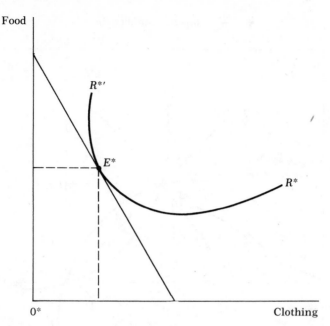

FIGURE 2.6   The Foreign Country's Offer Curve

Free Trade Equilibrium: The Consumption Box Diagram

The preceding account developed and described the offer curve for the home country. The offer curve for the foreign country would not be identical, for we have assumed that tastes and endowments differ from country to country. But it would display the same general features — the four properties described previously. The curve is exhibited in Figure 2.6.

Economists developed the *consumption box diagram* for putting both offer curves in the same diagram, allowing an explicit portrayal of the equilibrium terms of trade and quantities exported and imported from each country. This diagram is presented in Figure 2.7 and described below.

The key to the "box" aspect of the diagram is the assumption of the exchange model that each country's endowment of food and clothing is fixed. That assumption implies that the world totals are fixed as well, and these totals provide the dimensions of the box. Concentrate, first, on the home country's offer curve, RER', passing through its endowment point, E, and showing alternative consumption bundles that would be chosen at various terms of trade by reference to the southwest consumption origin, "O." The foreign offer curve, $R^*E^*R^{*'}$, is similarly represented, except now with reference to the north-east corner, "O^*." (Rotate the diagram 180° and the foreign offer curve

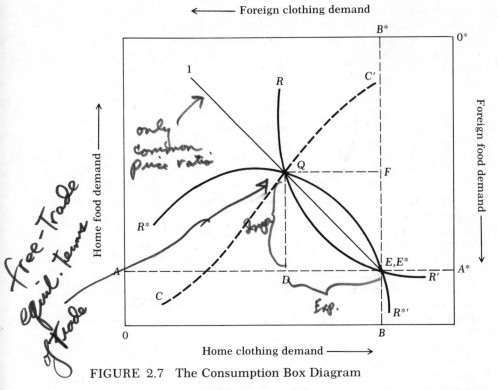

FIGURE 2.7   The Consumption Box Diagram

The dimensions of the box represent the world total endowments of food and clothing. The home country's offer curve,
RER', is drawn relative to the southwest "*O*" origin; the foreign country's offer curve is drawn relative to the northeast
"*O**" origin. Free trade equilibrium is shown by point *Q*; the
equilibrium terms of trade by the slope of line 1.

will assume the more familiar shape of Figure 2.6.) The endowment
points, *E* and *E**, have been "lined up," so that the home country's
endowment of food, say, is *OA* and the foreign country's endowment
of food is *O*A**. These add to the vertical dimension of the box.

Any point in the box represents four quantities. Relative to the home
country's "*O*" origin it shows a possible consumption bundle of food
and clothing at home. Subtract these from the totals available in the
world and the remaining food and clothing is shown by the same point
as a possible consumption bundle for the foreign country, relative to
the northeast "*O**" origin. The two offer curves intersect at *Q*, and the
slope of the line from the mutual endowment point through *Q* (line 1)
shows the *free-trade equilibrium terms of trade*. Point *Q* is the only
point lying on both countries' offer curves, and therefore line 1 shows

the only common price ratio at which markets will be cleared.[5] Each country's consumption of each commodity can be shown by Q: The home country consumes amount AD of clothing and BF of food. The remainder, A^*D of clothing and B^*F of food are consumed abroad. Furthermore, exports and imports are also explicitly shown: the home country exports DE units of clothing in exchange for QD units of imports of food. Both commodity markets are cleared and the value of each country's import demand is equal to its exports.

The offer curve has sometimes been called the reciprocal demand and supply curve (or, for short, the reciprocal demand curve). This longer name reveals that in the home country, for example, the demand for imports is shown by the vertical distance above the endowment point and, at the same time, export supply is shown by the horizontal distance to the left of the endowment point. Later we shall concentrate on trade flows by deleting the sides of the box and retaining the dotted lines through E and E^* as the axes. That is, the new "trade" origin becomes the endowment point and trade flows are measured to the left and above that point.

To keep the appearance of the box diagram uncluttered we have not shown explicitly the underlying indifference curves for each country. These rise from the southwest "O" origin for the home country and descend from the northeast "O^*" origin for the foreign country. We know that for either country there is an indifference curve tangent to the budget line through the endowment point for each point on the offer curve. Indeed, the offer curve was constructed by this means. Because point Q lies on *both* countries' offer curves, each country must have an indifference curve tangent to the same line (1) at Q, and therefore these two indifference curves must be tangent to each other. There are other points in the box at which common tangency holds. These points are indicated by the dotted CQC' curve, which is called the *contract curve*. The mutual gains from trade, and the sense in which free trade is "optimal" from a world point of view, are both revealed by the contract curve.

We shall focus on these issues in Figure 2.8. Three indifference curves, y_0, y_1, and y_2 have been drawn for the home country. The corresponding indifference curves for the foreign country that are tangent to these are the curves y_2^*, y_1^*, and y_0^* respectively. Curves y_0 and y_0^* reflect the levels of real income in the home and foreign countries if there were no trade, and each country must consume its endowment bundle. The offer curves are not drawn, but if they were, they would intersect at point Q, and the slope of EQ represents the equilibrium free-trade relative price of clothing. Both countries gain by trade: The home country increases its real income from y_0 to y_1 and

[5] Of course the E or E^* point shows the offer curves intersecting as well. But there is no common price ratio at which *both* countries would demand the consumption bundles designated by this point.

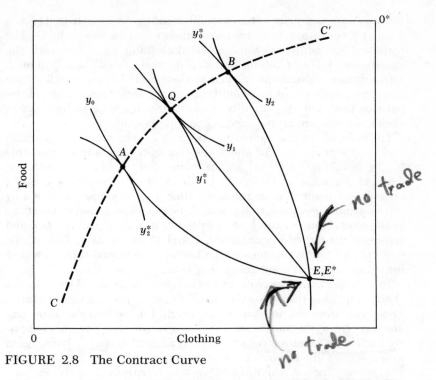

FIGURE 2.8 The Contract Curve

> The CC' curve is the contract curve — the locus of all points where an indifference curve of the home country is tangent to an indifference curve of the foreign country. Point Q represents free trade equilibrium.

the foreign country increases its real income from y_0^* to y_1^*. The price ratios that would rule in each country in isolation are shown by the respective slopes of the y_0 and y_0^* indifference curves at the endowment point E or E^*. The fact that these differ (by assumption) means that the relative valuation that each country places on the two commodities would not be the same in the absence of trade. The opportunity to trade at a common price ratio allows welfare in both countries to rise although the world supplies of food and clothing remain unchanged. One reason for studying the exchange model is that it reveals the basic nature of the gains from trade independently of any additional gains that can be derived if trade, by reallocating the world's resources, increases world outputs.

Points A and B in Figure 2.8 share a property possessed by the free-trade point Q. From any point *on* the contract curve improving the welfare of *both* countries is impossible. From any point *off* the contract curve both countries *can* be made better off — witness the move from E to Q. But can A and Q (or B and Q) be compared? Only by judging the relative worthiness of the two countries. Economists traditionally shy away from such interpersonal (or intercountry) comparisons. The point stressed by the advocates of free trade is *not* that it results in *the* best distribution of the world's commodities, but that it is *one* of the best, because it achieves one of the allocations that cannot be improved upon by one country without simultaneously hurting the other.[6]

2.3 THE PATTERN OF TRADE AND COMPARATIVE ADVANTAGE

Indifference curves, budget lines, box diagrams, and offer curves have been useful in establishing that both parties to the international exchange of commodities can gain by trade even if no new commodities are created. More familiar tools, demand and supply curves, are useful in revealing the pattern of trade. In our previous diagrams we showed that with the opening of trade the home country became a clothing exporter and food importer. This pattern of trade followed from our assumption that if the two countries could not trade, the relative evaluation, or price, of clothing would be lower at home than abroad.[7] This assumption, in turn, must rest upon a comparison of the balance between supply and demand in each country separately.

Figure 2.9 illustrates the supply and demand curves for one of the commodities, food, in each country. The supply curves are vertical, showing the fixed endowments of food in each country — invariant to any change in prices. Demand, of course, is sensitive to price. In this model of exchange, where one commodity is traded for another and money has no role as a store of value, the relevant prices are *relative* prices. On the vertical axis we show the ratio of the price of food to the price of clothing, as if each price could be measured by an outside monetary unit. But such a unit would cancel out in the ratio (p_F/p_C), which shows how much clothing must be given up to obtain a unit of

[6] At this point perhaps we should remind the reader of our strong assumption that indifference curves can be drawn for the individuals that make up the community. To see how strong this is, suppose that in the absence of international trade intranational exchange of commodities would exist between residents at home. Some individuals would then be net sellers of food. If, with the opening of international trade, the relative price of food falls compared to its autarkic value at home (as we have assumed in our diagrams), these net food sellers would be hurt (their "terms of trade" would deteriorate). We have avoided comparing their loss of real income with the gains of the net buyers of food. One way of pursuing this issue is to ask if the net gainers can compensate the net losers.

[7] Ken-ichi Inada, in "A Note on the Heckscher-Ohlin Theorem," *Economic Record*, 43 (March 1967): 88–96, has argued that a country may export the commodity that, in isolation, would be relatively more expensive at home. However, his argument rests upon several equilibrium price ratios in one of the countries before trade, a possibility we rule out by assumption.

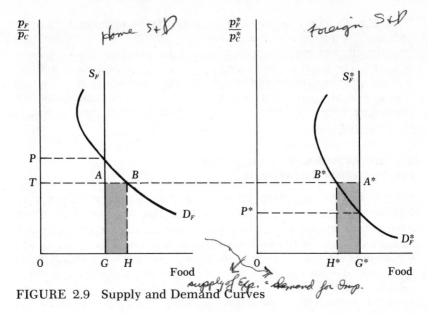

FIGURE 2.9 Supply and Demand Curves

Supply and demand for food in the home country is shown at left, and for the foreign country at right. Before trade, the relative price of food is lower in the foreign country (P^*) than at home (P). With free trade a common intermediate terms of trade (T) is established, with the foreign country exporting B^*A^* of food. Home imports (AB) equal foreign exports (B^*A^*). The shaded areas represent the exchange between countries in clothing, and these are also equal.

food.[8] Asterisks have been added to the price ratio on the foreign country's vertical axis, to suggest that their monetary unit may be different (pounds, say, instead of dollars), although once again only the ratio of clothing to food is relevant.[9] The shape of the demand curve is consistent with the general properties of offer curves discussed in connection with Figure 2.5. In particular, if a country's demand for food exceeds its own supply (such as in the range ER of the home country's offer curve in Figure 2.5), a decrease in food's relative price must stimulate demand.[10]

[8] Suppose the home country's monetary unit is the dollar. Then p_F is $ per unit of food and p_C is $ per unit of clothing. Dividing, we obtain (p_F/p_C) as the number of units of clothing required to purchase a unit of food.

[9] The use of the asterisk to denote variables in the foreign country has been borrowed from Murray C. Kemp, *The Pure Theory of International Trade*. Englewood Cliffs, N. J.: Prentice-Hall, 1964. We have employed this notation in previous diagrams.

[10] The so-called law of downward-sloping demand seems violated for relatively high prices of food in Figure 2.9. As mentioned in Footnote 4, the potential supply of exports need not rise as price rises. This point is pursued in Chapter 3.

If international exchange is prohibited, each country must rely on its own endowment. The market-clearing relative price of food in the home country, P, is higher than that abroad, P^*. If all barriers to the mobility of commodities are dismantled (including the natural barrier of transportation costs), this price discrepancy is a signal for consumers at home to purchase food in the foreign country's market. The relative price of food falls at home and rises abroad. A common price ratio, the terms of trade, T, will be established at which the home country's excess (import) demand, AB, balances the exports (B^*A^*) forthcoming from the foreign country. Free trade creates a single world market in commodities, and the equilibrium world terms of trade could as easily have been illustrated by Figure 2.10, which shows equality between world demand $(D_F + D_F^*)$ and world supply $(S_F + S_F^*)$.

There are two commodities in this model, not one. And yet we have picked just one of them, food, to illustrate the pattern of trade and the free-trade terms of trade. What about clothing? If the world market for food is cleared, so must be the world market for clothing. The reasoning is basic: there is only one market, in which food is exchanged for clothing. Return to Figure 2.9. At terms of trade T the home country's demand for food imports, AB, balances the foreign country's supply of food for export, B^*A^*. Therefore the shaded areas must be equal as well. The area of the rectangle $ABHG$ shows the import demand for food at home, AB, multiplied by food's relative price, AG. This area is the home country's offer of clothing to pay for food. The area $B^*A^*G^*H^*$ represents the foreign country's demand for imports of clothing. In each country exports are the means of payment for imports. At the terms of trade that clear one commodity market, ~~Market Clearing~~

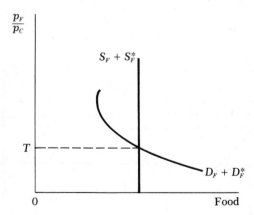

FIGURE 2.10   World Demand and Supply

The terms of trade, T, are determined by the equilibrium between the world's demand for food $(D_F + D_F^*)$ and the supply of food $(S_F + S_F^*)$.

the other is cleared as well, and the value of imports in each country equals the value of exports.

A slight variation in the use of the supply-demand apparatus more clearly reveals *why* food is relatively more expensive before trade in the home country. Notice that in Figure 2.9 the foreign endowment of food is larger than the home endowment (OG^* exceeds OG). This endowment difference may reflect only the larger size of the foreign country, in which case we might also expect its endowment of clothing to be larger. And the absolute size of countries also affects the position of the demand curves; other things being equal, the demand curve for any commodity will lie further to the right the larger the country. To circumvent this problem of size, consider supply-demand diagrams showing *relative* quantities on the horizontal axis. In Figure 2.11 the relative supply curves are vertical because the endowments of each commodity are fixed. We have shown the ratio of food to demand for clothing increasing with a fall in the relative price of food.

Figure 2.11 sets the stage for the question: Why does the home country import food and export clothing? Because the home country possesses *relatively* less food and demands *relatively* more food at any price ratio than does the foreign country. Pretrade price ratios depend upon the comparisons between both relative supplies and relative demands. We have stacked the deck, as it were, by letting both supply and demand differences conspire to cheapen food abroad. We can easily visualize situations in which the home country would import food even if its taste patterns were biased toward clothing (in the sense of a lower D_F/D_C than D_F^*/D_C^* at any comparable price ratio). All that would be required is that the home country's supply

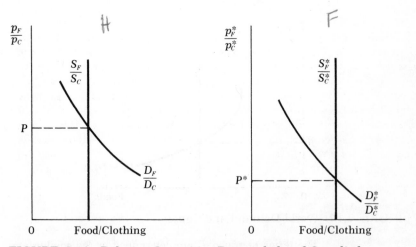

FIGURE 2.11 Relative Quantities Demanded and Supplied

bias (in the sense of S_F/S_C being smaller than S_F^*/S_C^*) be more pro- *Taste*
nounced. Alternatively, taste differences between countries may be *Differences*
greater than relative supply differences, in which case they would
dictate the trade pattern.

All this has put demand and supply differences on the same footing
as determinants of the trade pattern. At this stage of the argument
this equality is appropriate. However, much of the development of
trade theory has been based on the (sometimes implicit) assumption
that typically in the real world countries differ more profoundly in
their production patterns than in their taste patterns. Thus much of *Supply*
the discussion in Part 2 will center on the factors in the background, *Differences*
such as dissimilar technologies or differences in factor resource
availabilities, that lead to relative *supply* differences between countries. However detailed those arguments become, they eventually ✓
reduce to a consideration of the comparison between relative demands and relative supplies at common price ratios. We shall speak
of a country possessing a *comparative advantage* in a commodity
if, before trade, that commodity is *relatively* cheaper in that country
compared to the price ratio abroad. In the exchange model, comparative advantages depend both on supply and demand differences between countries.

2.4 THE EXCHANGE MODEL AND INTERNATIONAL ECONOMICS: RETROSPECT AND PROSPECT

To review what we have set out in this chapter it may be useful to
expound more deliberately the assumptions underlying the exchange
model. In commenting upon these assumptions we can, as well, preview the extensions that will be explored in subsequent chapters.

The Nature of the Market

Pure competition is assumed to characterize all commodity markets.
This assumption is almost all-pervasive in the literature of trade
theory, and will be retained in most of the simple trade models, with
an explicit exception in Chapter 11. Pure competition requires each
participant in the market to treat commodity prices as though they
were beyond his influence. We will often speak loosely of two countries trading with each other. But this is only shorthand for describing
a situation in which many competitive buyers and sellers in one
country interact with those in another. With competition prevailing
in the market, equilibrium is characterized by a market price at which
aggregate demand equals total supply.

The Nature of Supply

The feature of production that distinguishes Part 1 from Part 2 of
this book is that in this and the following two chapters of Part 1 the
quantity of any commodity produced in either country is assumed to

Part 1 differs from Part 2: Part 1 involves no change in commodity prices.

30   COMMODITY EXCHANGE AND THE BALANCE OF PAYMENTS

be completely independent of changes in any commodity prices. Clearly this assumption is not an appeal to realism. Rather, the assumption is made because many issues in the theory of international trade do not depend upon the variability of production in any intimate way. Readers should be warned that in discussing the theory of exchange first, and only then (in Part 2) turning to issues that centrally involve the details of producing commodities, we are departing from the procedure adopted by most texts on international economics. We believe that this allows an easier exposition of the basic ideas without any loss in generality. Because of the assumption that production patterns do not respond to prices, we have spoken of the commodity *endowments* possessed by each country.

One other feature of the endowment setting of this model should be noticed: It is not as simple as we could have made it, for we assume each country is endowed with positive fixed supplies of *both* commodities. Alternatively we might have assumed that the home country only possesses clothing and the foreign country food.[11] However, that would make the nature of the pretrade equilibria in each country (as shown by prices P and P^* in Figure 2.11) difficult to describe and guarantees that the pattern of trade is dictated solely by the contrast between endowments in the two countries. If both countries initially possess both commodities, as we have assumed, the pattern of trade remains to be determined by differences both between the endowment patterns in the two countries and between their taste patterns. This stance reemerges in Part 2, where we shall discuss the Heckscher-Ohlin trade model.

The Nature of Demand

Underlying the demand behavior assumed in the exchange model is the *budget constraint* that states that all income is derived from the endowment bundle (or, in future accounts, the value of goods and services produced) and that all such income is spent currently on commodities. This simple assumption will be adhered to in Chapter 3 and much of our account of the pure theory of trade in Part 2. But there will be places where we wish to modify it — indeed, where the brunt of the discussion depends directly on an alteration of this form of the budget constraint. Thus in Chapter 22 we shall analyze the effect of periodic payments (transfers) from one country to another, such as the reparations payments that some countries have had to make after a war or the remittances that immigrants may send back

[11] The trade model associated with David Ricardo typically has each country producing only one commodity, and thus might appear to be a more simple setting than we wish to discuss here. However, in the Ricardian model each country would produce both commodities in the pretrade situation, and specialize its production pattern to just one commodity only as a consequence of market forces as trade is opened up. The Ricardian model is discussed in Chapter 7.

to the old country. Secondly, and perhaps more importantly, countries may desire to spend more than their incomes (from whatever source) or, conversely, to engage in international lending by spending less than their current incomes. These considerations — having to do with hoarding and dishoarding, saving and dissaving — are directly relevant to a discussion of macroeconomic policy questions in an international setting. They will receive much more detailed coverage in Part 4 where we shall discuss balance-of-payments problems and in Part 5 in our account of foreign investment. The basic significance of such a departure from the assumption that all income is currently spent is discussed in a preliminary fashion in Chapter 4, where in other respects the assumptions of the exchange model are retained.

The purpose of the present chapter was to present a "stripped-down" model of commodity exchange between countries, abstracting from many of the complicated, but interesting, features of actual international trade in an attempt to get to the heart of questions dealing with the pattern of trade and the gains from trade. The key to the benefits from trade is the possibility of purchasing commodities abroad at prices lower than at home. Because the appropriate "price" in this analysis is "relative" price, foreigners can play this game as well. If pretrade price ratios differ between countries, each country has a comparative advantage in selling one commodity and can benefit by importing the other. Basic considerations of supply differences and demand differences between countries determine the commodity in which each country possesses a comparative advantage. The remarks made in this chapter about both the gains from trade and the pattern of trade will carry through in all our subsequent accounts of these issues. In that respect the exchange model is central to more realistic accounts of trade.

SUGGESTIONS FOR FURTHER READING

Marshall, Alfred. *The Pure Theory of Foreign Trade.* London: School of Economics and Political Science, 1930. Originally written in 1879, this classic investigates various shapes of offer curves.

Meade, James. *The Stationary Economy.* London: Allen and Unwin, 1965. Chapters 1–4 present the exchange model.

Supplement to Chapter 2:
The Equations of Exchange Equilibrium

The justification for this supplement lies less in the necessity of proving remarks made in Chapter 2 than it does in the desirability of introducing the reader to the notation and structure of the formal models that will be developed in many supplements of this book.

For notation, we shall use D to refer to demands and x to production. Thus D_F

signifies the home country's demand for food, and x_C^* the foreign country's production of clothing. The asterisk is used, as in the text, to symbolize foreign variables. The word "production" needs elaboration. In Part 1 we assume that the current production of commodities is completely insensitive to price. That is why they are referred to as commodity "endowments." In Part 2 we will break from this assumption, and thus adopting the same notation here for commodity "endowments" as will be used later for production seems desirable. The price of commodity j is denoted by p_j if a monetary unit of account is used for the home country, or p_j^* if the foreign country uses a different unit of account. In our two-commodity, food and clothing example, the home country's prices will be p_F and p_C. The relative price of food is p_F/p_C, and because this, the "terms of trade," is prominent in the real models of trade, we shall use the simple p (in the home country) and p^* (in the foreign country, if prices are different) to denote the terms of trade. We have already adopted this notation for Figures 2.9 and 2.11.

The use of equations in the text is not completely forsaken. For this reason a different numbering scheme is required for the supplements. Thus 2.S.4 refers to the fourth equation in the supplement to Chapter 2.

We shall start the account of the exchange model by pretending that prices in monetary units have meaning. The budget constraint for this model states that for each country the value of aggregate demand must be restricted to, and equal, the value of the endowment bundle. Thus:

$$p_C D_C + p_F D_F = p_C x_C + p_F x_F \tag{2.S.1}$$

$$p_C^* D_C^* + p_F^* D_F^* = p_C^* x_C^* + p_F^* x_F^*. \tag{2.S.2}$$

Assume that in a trading context the home country will import food. Then rewriting these two equations to highlight, on the left-hand side, the country's demand for imports and, on the right-hand side, the corresponding supply of exports becomes convenient:

$$p_F(D_F - x_F) = p_C(x_C - D_C) \tag{2.S.3}$$

$$p_C^*(D_C^* - x_C^*) = p_F^*(x_F^* - D_F^*). \tag{2.S.4}$$

To discuss the terms of trade in a model in which all barriers, man-made or natural, to the free transport of a commodity from one country to another are removed, divide both sides by p_C and p_C^* respectively and remove the asterisk from all prices to obtain:

$$p(D_F - x_F) = (x_C - D_C) \tag{2.S.5}$$

$$(D_C^* - x_C^*) = p(x_F^* - D_F^*). \tag{2.S.6}$$

The symbol, p, is the relative price of food.

Suppose the terms of trade, p, clear the world market for food. That is, the home country's excess demand, $(D_F - x_F)$, equals the foreign country's excess supply, $(x_F^* - D_F^*)$. In such a case it is obvious from equations 2.S.5 and 2.S.6 that the world's clothing market must be cleared as well: $(D_C^* - x_C^*)$ will equal $(x_C - D_C)$.

One consequence of this phenomenon is that free trade market equilibrium can be expressed either by the statement that world demand and supply are equal for food (as in 2.S.7) or for clothing (as in 2.S.8):

$$D_F + D_F^* = x_F + x_F^* \tag{2.S.7}$$

$$D_C + D_C^* = x_C + x_C^*. \tag{2.S.8}$$

If the budget constraints, in equations 2.S.5 and 2.S.6, are always satisfied, 2.S.7 implies 2.S.8 or vice versa. Oddly enough, neither market-clearing equation is typically used in the literature of the pure theory of trade. Rather, they are replaced by the equivalent statement that in free trade equilibrium the value of the home country's imports equals the value of the foreign country's imports. This balance-of-payments equilibrium condition, in equation 2.S.9, follows from the two budget constraints 2.S.5 and 2.S.6 and either 2.S.7 or 2.S.8.

$$p(D_F - x_F) = (D_C^* - x_C^*). \tag{2.S.9}$$

This form is illustrated by the equilibrium free trade price ratio in Figure 2.7. The home country's imports of food $(D_F - x_F)$, which in Figure 2.7 are shown by distance QD, divided by the foreign country's imports of clothing $(D_C^* - x_C^*)$, the distance QF in Figure 2.7, equal the free trade equilibrium relative price of clothing, $1/p$. The equivalent condition, equation 2.S.7, is shown explicitly in Figure 2.10. An alternative form of equation 2.S.8 is the statement that the shaded areas of Figure 2.9 are equal.

This redundancy in stating equilibrium conditions is two-sided. On the one hand it reveals that the model is more simple than a mere scanning of equations might reveal: there is only one market, and if world demand for clothing balances the world endowment at specified terms of trade, then the food market must be cleared as well. *Market Clearing* Furthermore, each country's demand for imports would, at that market-clearing terms of trade, equal the other country's demand for imports. On the other hand, it implies that there are several ways to describe the same equilibrium: the food market is cleared, the clothing market is cleared, or the home country's demand for imports equals, in value, the foreign country's demand for imports. Saying the same thing in three different ways can be confusing. That they are the same should be kept in mind when in Chapter 3 we describe the conditions for market stability.

To summarize: once the budget constraints are put in terms of relative prices (as in equations 2.S.5 and 2.S.6), free trade equilibrium is given by any of the three subsequent equations. Either a commodity market is in world balance or the terms of trade equate the value of each country's demand for imports. Supplies are fixed, but demands depend on prices. In Chapter 3 we shall pursue this problem by specifying more clearly the determinants of demand.

3 The Exchange Model: Stability, Demand, and Applications

The introduction to the model of international exchange provided in Chapter 2 dwelled upon market equilibrium. If a country cannot trade, consumption is limited to the quantity of each commodity in its endowment bundle, and relative prices measure the relative evaluation (marginal rate of substitution) of commodities when local demand and supply balance. Free trade, on the other hand, expands consumption possibilities for both countries by allowing each to consume more or less of a commodity than is possessed locally. This is accomplished through the competitive market, and we illustrated in Chapter 2 how common terms of trade can balance one country's imports and the other country's exports, with both countries made "better off" as a consequence of trade.

This attention to market equilibrium disguises an important question: If prices respond to market forces — rising if demand exceeds supply — will market imbalances disappear? That is, does the market push prices to their equilibrium levels? This is the question of market *stability*, and we shall open our discussion in this chapter with illustrations, based on the consumption box diagram and offer curves, both of stable and of unstable equilibria. Later in the chapter we shall comment upon the significance of stability both for applying the exchange model and for questions important to policy-making officials.

In the course of this discussion it will become apparent that the response of demand to a change in relative prices is the crucial issue in the stability analysis.[1] Partly for this reason we shall in-

[1] Recall that in the exchange model supplies of commodities are completely insensitive to price changes. In Chapter 6 we shall reexamine the stability question in the context of·a model in which production responds to prices.

34

vestigate demand behavior more intensively than in Chapter 2, making explicit use of the *elasticity of import demand* along the offer curve. Indeed, a criterion can be established, in terms of these elasticities, for a stable international market. As well, we shall report briefly on several empirical attempts to measure import demand elasticities in world markets.

We shall conclude the chapter with a brief survey of the uses of the exchange model, indicating applications of this model and extensions of the model to include production that are used in subsequent parts of this book.

3.1 THE PROBLEM OF MARKET STABILITY

To inquire about market stability we must consider, at the outset, the pressure of market forces on relative prices (the terms of trade) when the market is *not* in equilibrium. Figure 3.1 reproduces the offer curves and consumption box diagram shown in Figure 2.7, but adds a new terms of trade line (2) through the endowment point (E, E^*). The market is out of equilibrium at such prices. Home demand for clothing and food is shown by point V (thus FK clothing and IA food are demanded), while foreign demand is indicated by W (O^*J of clothing and O^*H of food). The relative price of food shown by line 2 is too low to allow commodity markets to be cleared. World demand for food exceeds the aggregate quantity of food in the two countries' endowments by amount IH. Because clothing is exchanged for food, this market imbalance is reflected as well in an excess of world clothing over demand by amount KJ. At the prices shown by line 2, excess food demand, IH, has the same value as excess clothing supply, KJ.

The postulate adopted here about price behavior when the competitive market is out of equilibrium is both natural and basic: the relative price of a commodity rises if world demand exceeds world supply. Thus in a world of flexible prices food must go up in value relative to clothing. The terms of trade line 2 swings counter-clockwise toward the equilibrium line 1. The free-trade equilibrium position is point Q, which is stable.

The same construction, but with different underlying taste patterns, leading to differently shaped offer curves, can illustrate an unstable equilibrium point. This construction is the "shoe-lace" diagram made famous almost a century ago by the English economist, Alfred Marshall.[2] It is depicted in Figure 3.2 where, for simplicity, we have deleted the sides of the box and have concentrated, instead, on the "trade" axes through the common endowment point, now labeled O_T (the "trade" origin). Line 1 shows, as before, market-clearing terms of trade, with point Q measuring (rightward) the home country's exports of clothing balanced by the foreign country's imports, and also measuring (downward) the home country's excess demand for food,

[2] A. Marshall, *The Pure Theory of Foreign Trade*. Published privately, 1879, and reprinted by the London School of Economics and Political Science, 1930.

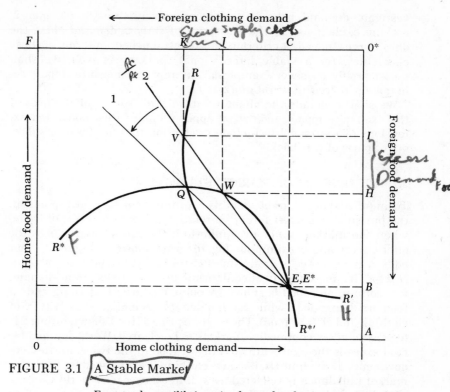

FIGURE 3.1   A Stable Market

Free trade equilibrium is shown by the intersection of the home country's offer curve (*RER′*) and the foreign country's offer curve (*R*E*R*′*) at *Q*. At terms of trade shown by line 2 world demand for food exceeds world supply by *IH*, and world supply of clothing exceeds world demand by the equivalent value, *KJ*. Market forces drive the relative price of food up to its equilibrium value, as shown by line 1.

balanced by foreign exports. If the relative price of food should be pushed down from its equilibrium value, as illustrated by terms of trade line 2, the home country's demand for food imports would increase (point *V* on the home offer curve, $O_T R$, lies above point *Q*). But notice that the foreign export supply of food increases by a greater extent (point *W* on the foreign offer curve, $O_T R^*$, lies above *Q* and also above *V*). That is, a world excess supply of food of amount *AV* exists at terms of trade line 2, depressing the relative price of food. The effect of market disequilibrium on prices forces further reductions in the relative price of food, moving the terms of trade line clockwise from the original equilibrium. Point *Q* represents an unstable equilibrium.

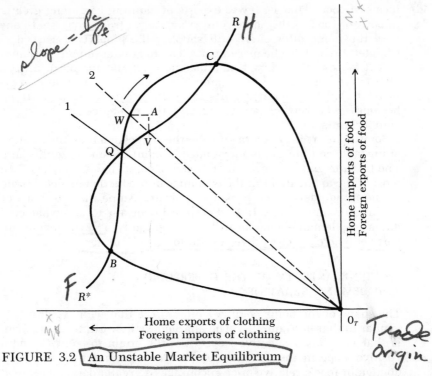

FIGURE 3.2 An Unstable Market Equilibrium

The terms of trade shown by line 1 represent an unstable equilibrium at point Q. For the nearby terms of trade shown by line 2, world excess demand for clothing (WA) is matched in value by a world excess supply of food (AV), causing a rise in the relative price of clothing away from the equilibrium terms of trade, line 1.

You may notice that the two countries' offer curves intersect more than once in Figure 3.2. Besides meeting at point Q, they intersect at B and C. Furthermore, both equilibrium points B and C are stable.[3] Consider point C. The home country's offer curve, $O_T R$, starts out from the O_T origin with a negative slope, as initially greater import demand must be met by greater export supplies. Even before point Q is reached, however, an even greater volume of imports is matched by a smaller volume of exports. This phenomenon is made possible by the fact that moving from Q, say, to V and C corresponds to the home country's export commodity, clothing, becoming more expensive in

[3] Their stability can be seen by applying the same argument as was used with reference to point Q in Figure 3.1. More directly, we have just shown that the disequilibrium terms of trade line 2 is forced to move in a clockwise direction toward point C.

terms of food. That is, fewer exports of clothing command greater imports of food as the home country's terms of trade improve. In any case the home offer curve still satisfies the property described in Chapter 2 whereby cheaper imports lead to greater imports. Because QVCR is positively sloped, it must intersect the foreign country's offer curve northeast of Q (at point C in Figure 3.2).[4] The same argument, based on foreign imports of clothing expanding as clothing becomes relatively cheaper, suggests the existence of the stable equilibrium point B.

Some comfort may be drawn from the suggestion that any position of unstable equilibrium is surrounded by points of stable equilibrium. The fact remains, however, that unstable points like Q may exist. In most of the applications of the exchange or production model of trade in the remainder of the book we wish to assume that positions of equilibrium are stable. It is therefore important to ask what conditions on demand behavior will ensure stability. The concept of import demand elasticity proves useful to this discussion.

3.2 THE ELASTICITY OF THE OFFER CURVE AND DEMAND BEHAVIOR

The shape of the home country's offer curve that we have drawn is similar to that in Figure 3.3. The characteristic worth focusing upon is that $O_T R$ has a negative slope from the origin to point C, and a positive slope in the CBR section. In the first stretch ($O_T AC$) a reduction in food's relative price encourages a greater demand for food and, as well, increased outlays to obtain these food imports. These outlays are measured not in any monetary unit but in units of clothing exported. In the second stretch (CBR), a drop in the relative price of food again leads to a greater demand for food imports, but proportionally less than the drop in price. We know this because the quantity of clothing required as exports to pay for the imports of food becomes less as more food is demanded. This must mean that the lowered requirement of clothing to pay for each unit of food (represented by the fall in food's relative price) must outweigh the greater requirement of clothing to pay for the increased volume of food imported. In short, the total outlay required for the purchase of any commodity is represented by price times quantity demanded. If quantity demanded increases less than proportionally to a price fall, total outlay (in our case represented by clothing exports) decreases.

[4] This feature of equilibrium positions — with an unstable equilibrium (point Q) always flanked by stable equilibria (points B and C) — is treated more extensively in works on advanced economic theory. In international trade models, the reader might look at E. Sohmen, "Demand Elasticities and the Foreign Exchange Market," *Journal of Political Economy*, 65 (October 1957): 431–36, and the comments by Harry Johnson and J. Bhagwati, "Notes on Some Controversies in the Theory of International Trade," *Economic Journal*, 70 (March 1960): 74–93, for an application to the problem of changes in the foreign exchange rate.

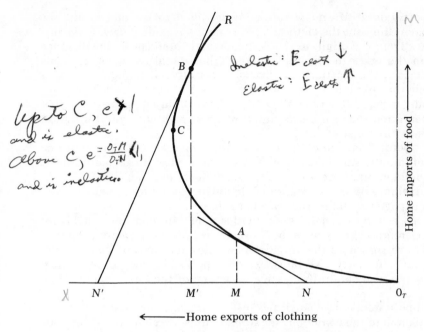

Handwritten annotations on figure:

Inelastic: E close ↓
Elastic: E rise ↑

up to C, $e > 1$ and is elastic.
above C, $e = \frac{O_T M}{O_T N} < 1$, and is inelastic.

←————Home exports of clothing

FIGURE 3.3 The Elasticity of the Home Offer Curve

IMPORT DEMAND

At any point on the home country's offer curve, $O_T R$, the elasticity of the offer curve is the ratio of the distance from the origin to the horizontal intercept of the perpendicular and the distance from the origin to the horizontal intercept of the tangent. Thus the elasticity of the offer curve at A is $O_T M/O_T N$, greater than one, while at B it is $O_T M'/O_T N'$, less than one.

Demand *elasticity* is introduced to allow a comparison between the price change and the corresponding change in demand. The elasticity of a country's import demand (or of its offer curve) is defined as the percentage increase in imports demanded resulting from a one per-cent drop in the relative price of imports. The frequent reference to this elasticity justifies a label. Let ϵ represent the elasticity of the home country's demand for imports along the offer curve (and ϵ^* represents the elasticity of the foreign country's offer curve). If ϵ is greater than one, import demand is said to be *elastic*, if less than one, *inelastic*. Thus the offer curve $O_T R$ in Figure 3.3 is elastic from the origin to C, and inelastic for lower prices of food (the stretch CBR).

There is a handy formula for the value of ϵ at any point on the home country's offer curve. The formula is illustrated in Figure 3.3, and a proof is provided in the supplement to this chapter. For any point (such as A or B in Figure 3.3) drop a perpendicular to the export axis and draw a tangent to the offer curve. The perpendiculars meet the export axis at M and M' respectively, for points A and B, and the tangent lines hit the clothing axis at points N and N'. Divide the distance from the origin to the perpendicular intercept by the distance from the origin to the tangent line's horizontal intercept, and this ratio is ϵ, the elasticity of the home country's demand for imports along the offer curve. Thus at point A, ϵ is given by the ratio O_TM/O_TN, while at point B, ϵ is O_TM'/O_TN'. This formula confirms our earlier observation that ϵ exceeds unity in the stretch O_TC, and falls short of unity in the stretch CBR.

At point C on the offer curve a perpendicular and a tangent line would be the same, and therefore ϵ equals one. At this point import demand is said to be *unit elastic*. A small change in price leads to an equivalent change in quantity demanded, so that total outlay (clothing exports) would neither rise nor fall.

This rule for computing elasticities along an offer curve holds for the foreign country as well. However, recall that foreign exports of food are shown on the *vertical* axis. Therefore for any point on the foreign offer curve we must extend a perpendicular to the vertical axis and also obtain the vertical intercept of the line tangent to the point.

Import demand elasticity is useful in deriving a more precise statement of the conditions for stability in world commodity markets. In Figure 3.1 the stable equilibrium at point Q reveals that if one or both offer curves is elastic, the market must be stable. In order to illustrate an unstable equilibrium it was necessary, in Figure 3.2, to draw *both* countries' offer curves (at Q) inelastic. With these observations in mind we can prove that a market free trade equilibrium will be stable under certain conditions.

The Marshall-Lerner Stability Condition

The home country's offer curve, O_TQR in Figure 3.4, cuts the foreign country's offer curve, O_TQR^*, from below. That is, the line tangent to the home country's offer curve, NQ, is steeper than the line tangent to the foreign country's offer curve, QN^*, at point Q. The equilibrium at Q is stable, as opposed to the intersection in Figure 3.2 at Q where the foreign offer curve was steeper than the home offer curve. Stability thus rests upon a comparison of the slopes of the offer curves at the free trade equilibrium point. This can easily be translated, by our elasticity formulae, into the classic Marshall-Lerner condition: when

$$\epsilon + \epsilon^* > 1,$$ (3.1)

the market is stable.

With NQ steeper than QN^*, we have:

$$\frac{QM}{NM} > \frac{N^*M^*}{QM^*}.$$

It is useful to notice that QM equals O_TM^*, QM^* equals O_TM, and to re-

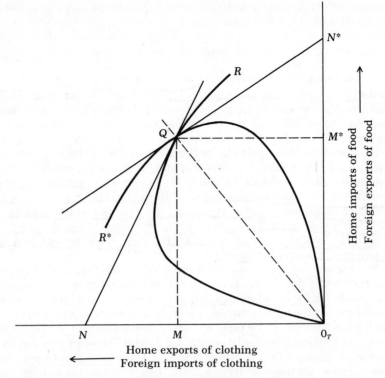

FIGURE 3.4   Proof of the Marshall-Lerner Conditions

The free trade equilibrium point Q is stable, requiring the home country's offer curve O_TQR to cut the foreign country's offer curve, O_TQR^*, from below at point Q. Given the elasticity formulae, whereby ϵ is given by O_TM/O_TN and ϵ^* by O_TM^*/O_TN^*, stability (NQ being steeper than QN^*) requires the Marshall-Lerner conditions: $\epsilon + \epsilon^* > 1$.

write NM as $O_TN - O_TM$ and N^*M^* as $O_TN^* - O_TM^*$. Thus the stable equilibrium at Q reveals that:

$$\frac{O_TM^*}{O_TN - O_TM} > \frac{O_TN^* - O_TM^*}{O_TM}.$$

This inequality is preserved if we divide both numerators by O_TN^* and both denominators by O_TN. Thus:

$$\frac{O_TM^*/O_TN^*}{1 - O_TM/O_TN} > \frac{1 - O_TM^*/O_TN^*}{O_TM/O_TN}.$$

The reason for making these substitutions becomes obvious when you recall that the elasticity of the home country's offer curve at point Q, ϵ, equals $O_T M / O_T N$, and the elasticity of the foreign country's offer curve at Q is $\epsilon^* = O_T M^* / O_T N^*$. That is,

$$\frac{\epsilon^*}{1 - \epsilon} > \frac{1 - \epsilon^*}{\epsilon}$$

becomes the stability criterion. Both offer curves are inelastic at Q, so that both ϵ and ϵ^* are less than unity. This allows us to crossmultiply and simplify (by canceling the $\epsilon\epsilon^*$ term). The Marshall-Lerner condition for the stability of the free trade equilibrium,[5] expression 3.1, emerges.

This condition is important. In the form in which it is expressed in equation 3.1 it is useful in formal applications of the model, which will appear again and again in the supplements. At a more intuitive level it confirms our previous observations that the market must be stable if either offer curve is elastic, as well as the illustration in Figure 3.4 that even if response of import demand in both countries is inelastic, stability is still assured if the *sum* of the import demand elasticities is greater than one.

The concern that we have expressed about conditions that assure the stability of the market is entirely appropriate. The market in internationally traded commodities can have unstable equilibria. If so, we would expect that if the forces of supply and demand are to operate, such equilibria would be rare. An unstable equilibrium is like an egg that can theoretically be balanced on its end. The egg *can* balance in such a position, but any jiggling will move it to a different, and more stable, position on its side. The egg can be propped up, and equilibrium can be "propped up" in world markets if, say, governments interfere by *fixing* prices. Governments rarely interfere in commodity markets, but often in *currency* markets. As we find in Chapters 4 and 5, the pattern of demand and supply for a country's currency may be quite similar to, because it is derived from, the market for its imports and exports. Countries may attempt to *peg* their exchange rates because they fear an underlying instability in the market for foreign exchange that would lead to wide swings in currency values as a consequence of any small jiggle in the market.

The foregoing account of stability has been discussed in terms of offer curves. It may help to reinterpret the argument in terms of familiar supply-demand diagrams. In Chapter 2 our dual depiction of free trade equilibrium — either in terms of offer curves or a world demand-supply balance for one of the commodities — should indicate that market stability can be analyzed by aggregating the two countries' demand and supply curves for food. Figure 2.10 did this in illustrating a unique, stable, free trade equilibrium (at terms of trade, OT). By contrast, Figure 3.5, which is based on the offer curve diagram, Figure 3.2, illustrates an unstable equilibrium price of food,

---

[5] A. Marshall, *The Pure Theory of Foreign Trade*. Abba Lerner, *The Economics of Control*. New York: Macmillan, 1946.

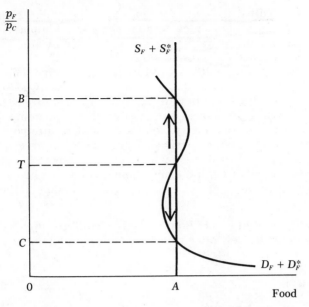

FIGURE 3.5 Supply, Demand, and an Unstable Equilibrium

The equilibrium price ratio shown by T is unstable. This diagram is based on the same demand-supply behavior as Figure 3.2.

OT. For a slightly lower price of food than OT, supply exceeds demand, forcing price even lower toward the stable equilibrium price, OC. Similarly, if food's relative price should lie slightly above OT, world demand for food would exceed world supply, driving price upward to the stable equilibrium level, OB.

Clearly the instability of price ratio OT in Figure 3.5 rests upon the positive slope of the world demand curve for prices near OT. We have argued on several occasions that the demand for the import commodity behaves in the standard fashion — price rises lead to reductions in quantity demanded. The demand for the export commodity, however, may rise or fall with an increase in its price. This asymmetry is important in international trade, for the commodity that is imported by one country is exported by the other, and stability hinges upon the aggregate response to a price change of both importers and exporters. This merits a closer investigation of the effects of a rise in price on demand.

Substitution and Income Effects

A change in price changes quantities demanded for two reasons. First, there is a tendency to consume more of the commodity that is now cheaper. This is shown by a movement along the indifference curve and is called the *substitution effect*. Secondly, a change in price can change real incomes. A fall in the price of imports improves the real income of importers. Any change in real income affects demand. This is called the *income effect*. (TOT effect)

These two strands — the substitution and income effects — are brought together in Figure 3.6. Suppose the community possesses the endowment bundle E and initially faces the terms of trade shown by the slope of line 1 through E. The most preferred consumption point is A, at which the community exports clothing and imports food to attain the level of satisfaction shown by indifference curve y_1. A fall in the relative price of food is shown by the new steeper budget line 2, which also passes through the endowment point, E. The community reacts by consuming point B, the most preferred point on line 2. This move, from A to B, can be decomposed into two parts:

1. The move from A to C. Point C, where indifference curve y_1 has a slope given by the new price ratio (y_1 at C is parallel to line 2), would

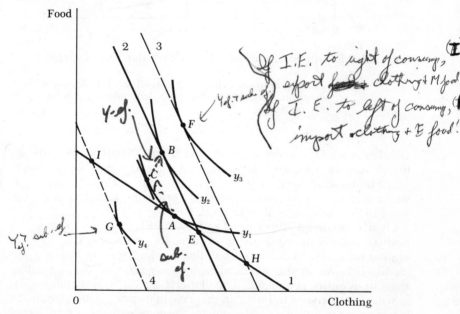

FIGURE 3.6　Substitution and Income Effects

Consumption is initially at A with terms of trade shown by line 1 and E the endowment point. Food is imported. A fall in food's relative price rotates the budget line around point E to line 2, leading to increased consumption of food (point B). The change in demand from A to B can be decomposed into the substitution effect — the move from A to C — and the real income effect — the move from C to B.

be chosen if the community were forced to remain on the same indifference curve, y_1, attained in the initial situation. Consumers must respond to a lowering of the relative price of food by substituting food for clothing in consumption. The move from *A* to *C* is the substitution effect of the price change.

2. The move from *C* to *B*. Demand for both food and clothing would rise if consumers were initially at point *C* and then, at the new prices, an increase in income allowed them to move to budget line 2. This rise is the income effect.

As shown in Figure 3.6, the substitution effect and the income effect conspire to increase the consumption of food. These effects oppose each other in affecting the demand for clothing, however. As clothing's relative price rises, the move from *A* to *C* (the substitution effect) entails a cutback in clothing demand. But the community exports clothing, and thus benefits when the relative price of clothing rises (i.e., its terms of trade improve). On this account it demands more clothing — the move from *C* to *B*. As the diagram has been drawn, the substitution effect on clothing demand is more powerful than the income effect — less clothing is consumed at point *B* than initially at point *A*.

Both substitution and income effects obviously depend upon the taste pattern and upon the fall in food's relative price. But the income effect in addition depends upon the initial trade situation or, what is the same thing, the relationship between the consumption point and the endowment bundle. Two endowment bundles, *H* and *I*, alternative to *E*, have been indicated in Figure 3.6, and it is instructive to analyze the income effect of the same price change in each alternative situation.

Consider point *H*. In the initial situation, with prices shown by the slope of line 1, the community would again consume *A*, but it would import more food than if its endowment bundle were shown by *E*. As a consequence, a fall in the relative price of food would more substantially improve real incomes than previously — the new budget line 3 goes through point *H*, allowing indifference curve y_3 to be attained. Consumption of both commodities is greater at *F* than it was at *B*. The substitution effect of the price change is the same, but the income effect is more powerful — so much so that the community ends up (at *F*) actually consuming more of the commodity (clothing) that has risen in price.

If the endowment bundle had been point *I*, the country would export instead of import food. At price line 1 it would still consume point *A*. But a fall in food's relative price — of the same magnitude as previously considered — would rotate the budget line through *I* to line 4. The community is made worse off by the change in price — real income falling to the level indicated by the y_4 indifference curve. The substitution effect is still indicated by the move from *A* to *C*. The income effect now *reduces* the demand for food (from C to G), and this actually outweighs the substitution effect so that less food is demanded at G than at A, despite the drop in food's relative price.

This much attention has been devoted to decomposing the effect of a change in the terms of trade on demand because the role of income effects is crucial to stability and to other issues that will be dealt with subsequently. We have established that income and substitution effects run counter to each other in affecting the demand for the exported commodity. Reconsider, now, the free trade equilibrium at terms of trade OT in Figure 3.5. The substitution effect of a fall in the relative price of food will encourage greater food demand in both countries and, on this account, lead to a downward sloping world demand for food curve. And it will increase the real income of the country importing food, thus increasing world food demand even further through this income effect. But real income has fallen in the food exporting country. This income effect works in the opposite direction to the income effect in the importing country and to both countries' substitution effects. Figure 3.5 illustrates the case where, in the neighborhood of the terms of trade OT, the income effect of the net exporter outweighs all the other effects that increase the demand for food as price falls. Thus the world demand curve is positively sloped in this region, and the free trade equilibrium established by price OT is unstable.

The Marshall-Lerner conditions are phrased in terms of elasticities of import demand in the two countries. The discussion surrounding Figure 3.5 centered upon each country's demand for one of the commodities, food. These must be related, for Figure 3.5 merely presents the same information about demand behavior as does the offer curve illustration, Figure 3.2, in a different manner. To link up these two approaches you should notice that if demand for imports is inelastic, less will be spent on imports as the relative price of imports falls. That is, fewer exports will be given up, which implies that in the exporting country local demand for the exported commodity rises as the relative price of exports rises. Thus inelasticity in the offer curve for imports implies a positively rising demand curve for exports. Market instability can be traced either to a strong income effect in the exporting country or to small values of demand elasticities for imports. They are the same.

Empirical Estimates of Import Demand Elasticities

In proceeding from the theoretical elasticities to real-world measurements, the economist runs into many difficulties, which we can only hint at. Let us concentrate on attempts to measure the elasticity of demand for imports, ϵ and ϵ^*. How can the influence of changes in the terms of trade be filtered out when imports are affected by many disturbances, such as changes in employment levels and tariff rates? How does one allow for the varying periods of time people require to adjust their plans and purchases when the relative price of imports changes? Because of these and other problems, economists are reluctant to bet heavily on the predictive accuracy of the elasticities they have estimated.

Calculations of the price elasticity of a country's demand for imports usually measure price by the movements of an index of import prices compared to the country's domestic wholesale price index. If the goods it exports enter heavily into the wholesale price index, this price variable will reflect changes in its terms of trade, and the estimated elasticity should correspond to the ϵ's used above. One study estimated an elasticity of 1.1 for the United States' demand for all imports. Another presented estimates for a group of countries, including Canada (1.5), Japan (0.7), Belgium-Luxembourg (1.0), Denmark (1.7), and Norway (0.8).[6] Statistical criteria allow us to place some confidence in these estimates, all of which are safely above the critical value of 0.5 needed to satisfy the Marshall-Lerner stability condition. They are not "awfully high," however, and for some countries we find no indication at all of a statistically significant response of the demand for imports to their relative price.

No wonder some economists have doubted the ability of price movements to painlessly adjust the international economy. On the other hand, many "elasticity optimists" feel that the price elasticities of import demand that we have quoted probably underrepresent the response of international trade to changes in relative prices. Part of their argument rests on problems of statistical method. One of their points, however, is that in real life a country is typically a small part of the trading world, and so faces a relatively elastic offer curve of the rest of the world. Therefore they make estimates of another elasticity, the elasticity of substitution. This is not the same as our ϵ's, but does indicate the response of demand to relative price. Actual measures of the substitution elasticity in international trade are often calculated for a country's exports by relating their share of the world market (or some part thereof) to their relative price, i.e., an index of the country's export prices relative to the export prices of other countries.

A study undertaken at the International Monetary Fund suggests that substitution elasticities are quite high for the manufactured exports of any of the industrial countries to the rest of the industrialized world. If we allow about two years for the response of a country's export share to a change in its relative price, the elasticity is approximately 3; if we observe the adjustment for four years, it rises to 5.[7]

---

[6] M. E. Kreinin, "Price Elasticities in International Trade," *Review of Economics and Statistics,* 49 (November 1967): 510–16; H. S. Houthakker and S. P. Magee "Income and Price Elasticities in World Trade," *Review of Economics and Statistics,* 51 (May 1969): 111–25.

[7] H. B. Junz and R. R. Rhomberg, "Prices and Export Performance of Industrial Countries, 1955–63," *IMF Staff Papers,* 12 (July 1965): 224–69.

In a general way, the evidence presented here on the values of elasticities confirms the existence of stability in international exchange. Their more practical uses lie in providing countries' policymakers with information about the effects on trade of a devaluation of the country's currency, a change in its general level of prices, and the like. We will return to these matters in Part 4.

3.3 SOME APPLICATIONS OF THE EXCHANGE MODEL

Much theoretical work on international trade is based on the model of exchange described above or the extension of the model to include the response of production to relative prices (to be discussed in Part 2). The technique is that of *comparative statics*. This technique involves, first, a description of an initial world trade equilibrium, either by the use of offer curves or demand-supply diagrams. Next, a change in one or more of the determinants of supply or demand and establishment of a new equilibrium are assumed. This new equilibrium is then "compared" with the old in order to determine the effect of the underlying change on the terms of trade, the volume of exports and imports, the level of real incomes in each of the countries, and the like.

Such a standard procedure is only feasible in a free market if the equilibria are stable. This can be illustrated by imagining that in Figure 3.5 the world supply curve shifts slightly to the left. Perhaps some of the foreign country's endowment of food is accidentally destroyed.[8] At a previously existing equilibrium terms of trade, OT, there would now be an excess demand for food. The new equilibrium point, after the supply curve shifts slightly to the left, would show a slightly lower relative price of food. But the market is unstable, and it would be incorrect to infer that p_F/p_C would fall. Instead, the excess demand that is created for food at OT would drive up the price of food. In brief, comparative statics must involve a prior assumption that markets are stable.

To consider an explicit example of this technique, suppose that taste patterns abroad change so that at any price ratio more of the home country's export commodity, clothing, is demanded abroad, and less food (so that aggregate spending abroad remains unchanged). This change is illustrated in Figure 3.7 by an outward shift of the foreign country's offer curve from $O_T R^*$ to $O_T R^{*\prime}$. Initially point Q represents the free trade equilibrium, with the terms of trade shown by the slope of line 1, home exports of clothing by distance $O_T A$, and home imports of food by $O_T C$. Real income at home is indicated by the indifference curve, y_1. The change of tastes abroad shifts the foreign offer curve to $O_T R^{*\prime}$. At the old terms of trade, for example, their demand for clothing has increased from point Q to point F.

---

[8] We are ignoring here the fact that such a shift in endowments would also cause the demand curve to shift. In future applications this factor must, and will, be taken into account.

TOT Slope = $\frac{P_C}{P_F}$

Change in taste by For. c.

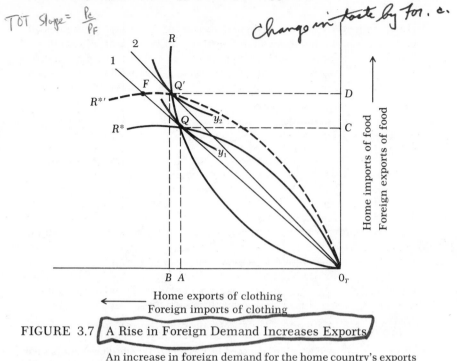

FIGURE 3.7 A Rise in Foreign Demand Increases Exports

An increase in foreign demand for the home country's exports shifts the equilibrium free trade point from Q to Q'.

The relative price of clothing will therefore rise and, in a stable market, a new equilibrium will be reached at Q'. Consider the effects of this change in tastes:

Results

1. The terms of trade have improved for the home country. The relative price of clothing rises to the slope of line 2.
2. The home country's level of well-being has risen, as indicated by the move to the higher indifference curve, y_2.
3. Imports of food to the home country have increased by CD.
4. Foreign imports of clothing have also increased, by amount AB.

No doubt all these results seem self-evident. Yet conclusion 4 depends on an assumption that was implicit in the home country's offer curve, $O_T R$. Figure 3.8 repeats the same exercise, except that the home country's offer curve is *inelastic* between the two equilibria. As a consequence an increased foreign demand for clothing actually results in a lower foreign consumption of clothing. The inelasticity in the home offer curve has caused the relative price of clothing to rise to such an extent that in spite of the change in foreign tastes toward clothing, less clothing is consumed abroad. The home country, of course, benefits from the improvement in its terms of trade. But

2.) Inelastic Home Offer Curve

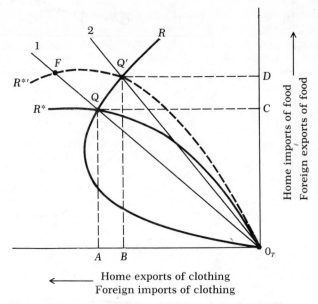

FIGURE 3.8   A Rise in Foreign Demand Reduces Exports

An increased demand by foreigners for clothing reduces their imports of clothing if the home offer curve is inelastic between Q and Q'.

notice that this benefit is now reflected in increased home consumption of *both* commodities.

A different application of comparative statics involves a presumed change in one or both countries' endowment bundles. Unfortunately this change affects the dimensions of the box and shifts the trade origin, making the use of offer curve analysis more cumbersome than in the case of a change in tastes. Supply and demand curves can be employed more simply for this application.

For example, suppose the home country's endowment of its export commodity, clothing, should be enlarged. It is perhaps tempting to show the effect of such a change on relative prices by considering a diagram showing a world demand curve and world supply curve of clothing, with a rightward shift in the supply curve leading to a reduction in the price of clothing. But such a change in the home country's endowment bundle causes incomes at home to change and therefore the demand curve for clothing (and food) to change as well. If the only change in endowments is in clothing, it is, paradoxically, easier to take advantage of the fact that in a two-commodity world there is only one market by concentrating on a supply-demand diagram for food — the commodity that has *not* experienced a change in supply.

Figure 3.9 illustrates the case. There has been no shift in the world supply of food, but there has been a rightward shift in demand. The source of this shift is the increased income experienced by the home country as its endowment of clothing rises. Thus the relative price of food increases from *OT* to *OT'*. In terms of clothing, any increase in the world's endowment of clothing must depress the relative price of clothing.

This result is not at all surprising. But notice that the effect on welfare in the home country is in doubt. On the one hand its real income increases as its endowment bundle expands. On the other hand, its terms of trade deteriorate, which, by itself, would reduce real incomes at home. The dominant effect depends very much on demand elasticities and the effect of a change of incomes on demand, as expressed by the home country's *marginal propensity to import* — the fraction of any "dollar's" worth of extra income that would be channeled into imports at constant prices. This income effect at initial prices dictates the extent of the rightward shift in the demand schedule in Figure 3.9. The elasticities, if low, indicate that a substantial deterioration in the terms of trade is required to clear the food market.

We do not intend to pursue this matter here, not because it is uninteresting, but because it is dealt with explicitly in a later chapter (25)

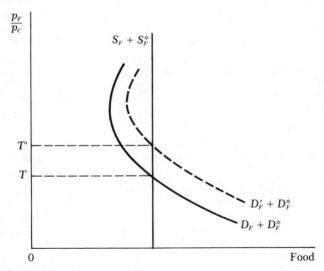

FIGURE 3.9   A Change in Endowments

The home country's clothing endowment increases, shifting its demand curve for food to the right. Therefore the relative price of food rises from *OT* to *OT'*.

on growth and trade. Economic growth involves increases in production and consequent changes in prices. The induced terms of trade effect of expansions in supply must be taken into account in appraising the welfare significance of growth. This example is presented here primarily to indicate that the simple model of commodity exchange goes a long way in revealing the potentially conflicting forces at work in such phenomena as growth. It is a mistake to underestimate the cutting-power of demand and supply analysis in exposing the essential ingredients of many problems in economics, especially in international economics.

3.4 SUMMARY

Market equilibrium suggests a balance in commodity markets between the quantity that net demanders wish to purchase and net sellers wish to supply. Its usefulness in indicating where prices settle depends upon the stability of the market. In much of this chapter we have analyzed the causes of instability and discussed the conditions sufficient to prevent it. An explicit formula, the Marshall-Lerner condition, was developed, stating that the market is stable if the sum of the elasticities of demand for imports in the two countries is greater than one. This condition indicates that instability depends upon inelasticity of demand. By probing more deeply into demand behavior we found that inelasticity in demand for imports is synonymous with a positively sloped demand curve for exports. In this situation the income effects of a change in the terms of trade outweigh the substitution effects so that as export prices rise, the community actually demands more of its export commodity. One country's inelasticity of import demand is not enough to produce instability. A decomposition of demand response into substitution and income effects revealed that both countries' substitution effects and the importer's income effect all contributed to increased demand for the commodity whose relative price falls in the market.

Comparative statics is an exercise devised by economists to compare equilibrium positions, when the old equilibrium is disturbed by a change in the determinants of supply or demand. Only if the market is stable will such a shift in world demand or supply force the terms of trade to the new equilibrium value. If the conditions for stability are met, but demand elasticities are rather low, the terms of trade must change drastically to accommodate a shift in demand or supply. A country's policy-makers may wish to resist the implied wide variation in prices and the consequent changes in real incomes, especially if the market in question represents the monetary aggregates of exports and imports — the market for foreign exchange. Chapters 4 and 5 explore this issue more explicitly, but a full review of the pros and cons of allowing the free market to determine the relative price of a country's currency must await our macroeconomic approach to such questions in Part 4.

Applications of comparative statics are found throughout the book. In this chapter we have suggested how the free trade equilibrium is altered by a change in tastes or a change in endowments. Such changes are at the core of the theoretical discussion of international factor movements in Part 5 and of growth and trade in Part 6. Furthermore, the techniques developed here — of shifting offer curves or shifting demand and supply schedules to compare one equilibrium position with another — will be applied in Part 3, where we shall discuss commercial policy.

Looking backward, this chapter has rounded out our description of free trade equilibrium in Chapter 2 by considering disequilibrium market behavior and shifts in equilibrium positions. Two key assumptions have been retained: Market prices respond to supply and demand; and aggregate spending is limited to the income derived from the commodity endowment bundle. Each assumption is relaxed in Chapter 4 where we shall analyze balance-of-trade deficits and surpluses and nonprice adjustments that the economy may be forced to make in the face of market disequilibrium.

[handwritten margin notes: Two key Assump.'s in this chpt.: (1) (2) These are relaxed in ch. 4.]

SUGGESTIONS FOR FURTHER READING

Johnson, Harry G. and Jagdish Bhagwati, "Notes on Some Controversies in the Theory of International Trade," *Economic Journal*, 70 (March 1960): 74–93. In pages 89–93, the authors discuss how an unstable equilibrium is flanked by two stable equilibria.

Marshall, Alfred. *The Pure Theory of Foreign Trade*. London: School of Economics and Political Science, 1930. The original discussion of elasticity and stability in offer curve diagrams.

Meade, James. *The Stationary Economy*. London: Allen and Unwin, 1965. Chapter 4 gives some simple exercises with offer curves.

Supplement to Chapter 3: Elasticities, Stability Expressions, and Real Incomes

In Chapter 3 we promised a proof of the elasticity formula illustrated in Figure 3.3. This formula is followed by an algebraic proof of the Marshall-Lerner condition for market stability that does not rely upon such a graphical measure of elasticity. We shall then show how to develop an analytic expression for the change in a country's level of real income. This technique provides the basis for much of our succeeding formal analysis of welfare changes in later supplements. It also allows us to develop a condition for market stability that is equivalent to the Marshall-Lerner condition but is more explicit in pointing out possible sources of instability. The supplement concludes with an analytical treatment of a comparative statics problem considered in Chapter 3.

THE ELASTICITY OF THE OFFER CURVE

Let M denote home imports of food, shown on the vertical axis in Figure 3.3, and X, measured right to left, home exports of clothing. The home country's elasticity of demand for imports along the offer curve, ϵ, is the relative change in the quantity of imports demanded (dM/M or, to use a more convenient notation, $\hat{M}$) divided by the relative change in the price of imports (which is X/M). Thus:[1]

$$\epsilon = -\frac{\hat{M}}{(\widehat{X/M})} = -\frac{\hat{M}}{\hat{X} - \hat{M}} = \frac{1}{1 - \hat{X}/\hat{M}} = \frac{1}{1 - \dfrac{dX}{dM}\cdot\dfrac{M}{X}}.$$

Referring to point A in Figure 3.3, dX/dM, the inverse of the slope of the offer curve, is MN/AM, while M/X is distance AM divided by O_TM. Thus the elasticity of the offer curve at point A is, by substitution, O_TM/O_TN.

AN ALGEBRAIC PROOF OF THE MARSHALL-LERNER CONDITION

$p = \dfrac{p_F}{p_C}$

The world excess supply of food is the foreign country's supply of food for export (which can be written as M^*/p where M^* is the foreign import demand for clothing and $1/p$ is the price of clothing in food units) less the home country's food import demand, M. The world market for food is stable if a rise in food's price, p, from an initial equilibrium value creates an excess world supply of food That is, stability requires:

$$\frac{d(M^*/p)}{dp} > \frac{dM}{dp}.$$

Divide the denominator of both sides by the initial food price, p. Divide the numerator of the right-hand side by M and the numerator of the left-hand side by M^*/p, which in the initial equilibrium equals M. Making use of our circumflex notation for *relative* changes, we can state that the market is stable if:

$$\frac{(\widehat{M^*/p})}{\hat{p}} > \frac{\hat{M}}{\hat{p}}. \tag{3.S.1}$$

But by definition ϵ equals $-\hat{M}/\hat{p}$ and the foreign elasticity of demand for imports, ϵ^*, equals $-\hat{M}^*/(\widehat{1/p})$, which is equivalent to $\hat{M}^*/\hat{p}$. Because the inequality in 3.S.1 can be rewritten as:

$$\frac{\hat{M}^* - \hat{p}}{\hat{p}} > \frac{\hat{M}}{\hat{p}},$$

the Marshall-Lerner condition, 3.S.2, follows by substitution of the expressions for ϵ and ϵ^*:

$$\epsilon + \epsilon^* > 1. \tag{3.S.2}$$

CHANGES IN REAL INCOMES

Our analysis throughout is based on the assumption that a community's level of satisfaction or real income depends upon the bundle of commodities it

---

[1] The relative change in a ratio, such as $(\widehat{X/M})$, is the difference between the relative changes in the numerator and denominator.

can consume. For our two-commodity example we can state this formally as:

$$u = u(D_F, D_C).$$

The symbol, u, represents some arbitrary index used to measure utility or the level of welfare. Differentiate this expression to obtain:

$$du = \frac{\partial u}{\partial D_F} dD_F + \frac{\partial u}{\partial D_C} dD_C.$$

which states that when the amounts consumed are altered utility changes by an amount that depends upon the marginal utility of a commodity (e.g., $\partial u/\partial D_F$ for food) multiplied by the change in the quantity of it consumed. The arbitrariness of the utility index can be removed by dividing both sides of this equation by the marginal utility of clothing:

$$\frac{du}{\partial u/\partial D_C} = dD_C + \frac{\partial u/\partial D_F}{\partial u/\partial D_C} dD_F.$$

The left-hand term is positive only if utility has increased. Furthermore, it is a measure of the change in utility expressed in units of clothing (the "utils" cancel out). Call this change in real income in clothing units "dy". The right-hand side can be simplified by noticing that the coefficient of "dD_F" is the *marginal rate of substitution*, the amount of clothing that must be added to compensate for a loss of one unit of food along an indifference curve. But in a market equilibrium this amount corresponds to the relative price of food, p. Thus, equation 3.S.3 can be derived as the basic expression for a change of real income:

$$dy = dD_C + pdD_F. \tag{3.S.3}$$

Equation 3.S.3 reveals that any change in the consumption bundle affects real incomes. The budget constraint, written here as equation 3.S.4,

$$D_C + pD_F = x_C + px_F \tag{3.S.4}$$

reveals that the *source* of any change in real income must reside either in a change in the endowment bundle or a change in the terms of trade. Differentiate equation 3.S.4 to obtain

$$dD_C + pdD_F + D_F dp = dx_C + pdx_F + x_F dp.$$

Subtract $D_F dp$ from both sides, and use expression 3.S.3 for dy to obtain equation 3.S.5:

$$dy = -(D_F - x_F)dp + (dx_C + pdx_F). \tag{3.S.5}$$

This basic expression for the change of real income in the home country provides the following breakdown:

1. The term $-(D_F - x_F)\,dp$ is the *terms of trade effect* already encountered in Chapter 3. Assume the home country is a net importer of food and let M, as before, denote $(D_F - x_F)$. If the terms of trade deteriorate for the home country, dp is positive and real income at home falls by Mdp, an amount proportional to the volume of imports.

2. The term $(dx_C + pdx_F)$, the price-weighted sum of any change in the home country's endowment bundle, enters directly into the measure of a change in real income. However, as the case in Chapter 3 in which the endowment of

clothing increased at home revealed, any change in endowments may disturb the equilibrium value of the terms of trade, so that both expressions in equation 3.S.5 may have to be considered.

We turn, next, to an alternative form of the market stability condition. In this analysis no change in endowments is involved, so that at home dy is given by $-Mdp$ and in the foreign country dy^* is merely *plus Mdp*.

AN ALTERNATIVE STABILITY CONDITION

In Figure 3.5 the price ratio OT represented an unstable equilibrium because the world demand curve for food was positively sloped at that point. In order to ensure that a market equilibrium is stable it is necessary that

$$\frac{dD_F}{dp} + \frac{dD_F^*}{dp} < 0.$$

We proceed by investigating formally the effect of a change in price on quantities demanded. Let the home country's demand for food depend upon the terms of trade and real income:

$$D_F = D_F(p,y). \tag{3.S.6}$$

Differentiating reveals that

$$dD_F = \frac{\partial D_F}{\partial p} dp + \frac{\partial D_F}{\partial y} dy,$$

which is the decomposition into a substitution term, $(\partial D_F/\partial p)dp$, and an income term, $(\partial D_F/\partial y)dy$, mentioned in the text. The *marginal propensity to consume* food (which we call α_F) is the fraction of an increment of income which would be channeled into increased food consumption at constant prices. α_F is the term $p(\partial D_F/\partial y)$, a pure number. With dy given by $-Mdp$, the expression for dD_F/dp can be written as in equation 3.S.7.

$$\frac{dD_F}{dp} = \frac{\partial D_F}{\partial p} - M\frac{\alpha_F}{p}. \tag{3.S.7}$$

The breakdown in the quantity of food demanded abroad is given by analogy:

$$\frac{dD_F^*}{dp} = \frac{\partial D_F^*}{\partial p} + M\frac{\alpha_F^*}{p}. \tag{3.S.8}$$

Add these two terms together and require, for stability, that their sum be negative:

$$\frac{\partial D_F}{\partial p} + \frac{\partial D_F^*}{\partial p} - M \cdot \frac{\alpha_F}{p} + M\frac{\alpha_F^*}{p} < 0. \tag{3.S.9}$$

This inequality confirms that the only term on the left-hand side that is positive, and thus contributes to instability, is the exporting country's income effect.

At this point we introduce another elasticity concept. Let $\bar{\omega}$ denote the effect of a one percent rise in the relative price of food upon the relative reduction in the quantity of food demanded when real income is held constant. That is,

$$\bar{\omega} \equiv -\frac{p}{D_F}\frac{\partial D_F}{\partial p}.$$

$\bar{\omega}^*$, the substitution elasticity of demand for food abroad, can be defined in analogous fashion. Then the inequality in equation 3.S.9 can be rewritten as in expression 3.S.10:

$$\frac{D_F}{D_F + D_F^*}\bar{\omega} + \frac{D_F^*}{D_F + D_F^*}\bar{\omega}^* > \frac{M}{D_F + D_F^*}(\alpha_F^* - \alpha_F). \qquad (3.S.10)$$

This form of the stability condition is in many ways more revealing than the Marshall-Lerner condition. The left side, a weighted average of each country's substitution elasticity of demand, must be positive. If the right side is negative, stability is assured. The right side *is* negative if the importer's (home country's) marginal propensity to consume food is greater than the exporter's. A rise in the relative price of food redistributes real income from the home country (which imports food) toward the foreign country. Instability would require the foreign country's reaction to its rise in real income, as represented by α_F^* in the food market, to exceed the home country's marginal propensity to consume food, α_F. This discrepancy can never exceed unity if both marginal propensities are positive. And the expression $\alpha_F^* - \alpha_F$ is premultiplied by a *fraction*, $M/(D_F + D_F^*)$, which represents the ratio of world trade in food to world consumption. If international commerce is a small part of total demand, this term is small and the world market is likely to be stable. In any case, a sufficient condition for stability is that the left-hand side — the weighted average of substitution elasticities — exceeds unity.

COMPARATIVE STATICS

$p = \dfrac{p_F}{p_c}$

Equation 3.S.11 is the market equilibrium condition:

$$pM = M^* \qquad (3.S.11)$$

the world terms of trade equates the value of import demand in the two countries. Suppose that the home country's endowment of clothing increases, and a new equilibrium terms of trade is established. Retaining our circumflex notation for relative changes, equation 3.S.12 must hold:

$$\hat{p} + \hat{M} = \hat{M}^*. \qquad (3.S.12)$$

The change in foreign imports of clothing, $\hat{M}^*$, is $\epsilon^*\hat{p}$. The change in the home country's imports is represented by a movement along the offer curve $(-\epsilon\hat{p})$ plus a shift of the offer curve. Formally,

$$\hat{M} = -\epsilon\hat{p} + \frac{1}{M}\frac{\partial M}{\partial x_C}dx_C.$$

The term $\partial M/\partial x_C$ refers to the impact at constant prices of an increase in the home country's endowment of clothing on imports of food. This must refer to the home country's demand for food because food endowment is unaltered, and therefore $\partial M/\partial x_C$ is $1/p$ times α_F, the $1/p$ term being introduced to make the units correspond. But α_F, the home country's marginal propensity to consume food, is its *marginal propensity to import.* Call this m. Then:

$$\hat{M} = -\epsilon\hat{p} + \frac{1}{pM}m\,dx_C.$$

At constant terms of trade, growth in the clothing endowment increases demand for food, and therefore demand for imports.

Solving for the change in the terms of trade by substituting into equation 3.S.12 is now easy. This yields:

$$\hat{p} = \frac{1}{\Delta} \cdot \frac{1}{pM} m \, dx_c \qquad (3.S.13)$$

where
$$\Delta \equiv \epsilon + \epsilon^* - 1 > 0.$$

The symbol Δ has been introduced to capture the Marshall-Lerner expression, the sum of import demand elasticities less unity, which must be positive. The conclusion is not surprising: An increase in the home country's clothing endowment must raise the relative price of food (i.e., lower the relative price of clothing).

A glance at the expression for the change in the home country's real income, equation 3.S.5, reveals that the expansion in the home country's endowment of clothing, the commodity it exports, is a mitigated blessing. This expression reduces to:

$$dy = -pM\hat{p} + dx_c.$$

The direct effect of growth (dx_c) is beneficial, but the indirect effect, $-pM\hat{p}$, is harmful. Equation 3.S.13 links the two effects, and by substitution dy is given by equation 3.S.14:

$$dy = \left\{ \frac{\epsilon + \epsilon^* - (1 + m)}{\Delta} \right\} dx_c. \qquad (3.S.14)$$

We have considered the effect on welfare in the home country of growth in its endowment of the export commodity. Our analysis, culminating in equation 3.S.14, suggests that such growth may actually lower real income. This would follow if the sum of import demand elasticities exceeded unity (which we require for stability), but not the value $(1 + m)$. We do not pursue this result here, for it is discussed at greater length in Chapter 25 in the treatment of the effects of growth on trade. But it was convenient to demonstrate both the general applicability of the exchange model and the way in which a comparative statics problem in the theory of international trade can be formally analyzed. It also reveals the significance in such a formal analysis of establishing the precise conditions for market stability.

4 Trade Imbalance and Adjustment Processes in the Exchange Model

A country's balance of trade measures the difference between the value of its exports and the value of its imports. The account of the simple exchange model in the preceding two chapters stresses positions of equilibrium in which all commodity markets are cleared and each country has a zero net balance of trade. Such a model allows a clear introductory view of the determinants of the pattern of trade, stemming from inter-country differences in supply and demand, and the gains to be derived from trade if each country attaches different relative evaluations to commodities. In this chapter we use the exchange model to explore imbalances between exports and imports and possible sources of adjustment or finance. We will introduce new elements in the balance of payments, such as international capital and/or monetary flows, and will discuss a possible role for the exchange rate linking home and foreign currencies.

4.1 DISEQUILIBRIUM IN THE EXCHANGE MODEL: AN ILLUSTRATION

We can simplify the exchange model by letting the home country's endowment bundle be composed only of clothing, and the foreign country's bundle only of food. In Chapter 2 we established the requirements for the home country to be a clothing exporter. With our focus now on disequilibrium behavior, we may assume that the home country is a clothing exporter because it cannot obtain food except by trade.

Figure 4.1 contains a pair of offer curves appropriate for this situation. The home country has quantity OA of clothing in its endowment

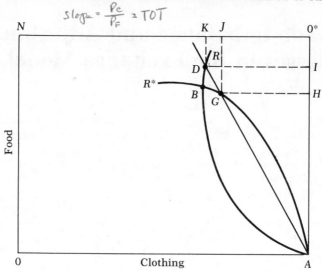

FIGURE 4.1   Disequilibrium Shown by Offer Curves

> The ray *AGD* illustrates a disequilibrium terms of trade. The
> home country demands bundle *D* relative to its consumption
> origin (*O*) and the foreign country demands bundle *G* relative
> to its consumption origin (*O**). There is excess world demand
> for food (*IH*) coupled with excess world supply of clothing
> (*KJ*).

bundle, and the foreign country has *O*A* of food. Demands for food
and clothing are measured from the southwest *O* origin for the home
country and from the northeast *O** origin for the foreign country.
The foreign offer curve is *AR**. Suppose that initially the home offer
curve (not drawn) had intersected *AR** at point *G*, making line *AG* the
equilibrium terms of trade line. The offer curve *ABR* for the home
country is the *new* locus of export supply and import demand at home
after a presumed shift in the home country's taste pattern from
clothing to food. The new equilibrium terms of trade would be shown
by a ray from *A* through the intersection of the two offer curves at *B*
(not drawn). The relative price of clothing shown by the slope of ray
AGD is, in the new situation, *not* an equilibrium terms of trade. The
home country's demand for food, *AI* (corresponding to point *D* on its
offer curve) plus the foreign country's demand for food, *O*H* (corresponding to point *G* on the foreign offer curve) exceeds the world
supply of food, *O*A*, by the amount *IH*. An excess world demand for
food at terms of trade shown by the ray *AGD* must, of course, be reflected in an equivalent excess world supply of clothing. This is
shown by *KJ*, the excess of the home country's endowment of clothing,
NO*, over the sum of the home country's demand for food, *NK*, and

the foreign country's demand for food, O^*J. KJ and IH have the same value at these disequilibrium prices.

Because we are exploring adjustment to market disequilibrium, we may translate the box diagram in Figure 4.1 into diagrams of the world demand-supply imbalance in each market (Figures 4.2 and 4.3). The disequilibrium terms of trade shown by the ray AGD in Figure 4.1 is translated into OA for the relative price of clothing in Figure 4.2 and the reciprocal of this, OL, for the relative price of food in Figure 4.3. At these prices the excess world demand for food $(D_F + D_F^*)$ over world supply (the foreign country's endowment, shown by the vertical S_F^* curve) in Figure 4.3 has the same value as the excess world supply of clothing (shown by the home country's vertical S_C curve) over world demand $(D_C + D_C^*)$ in Figure 4.2. This excess world supply of clothing, KJ in Figure 4.2, has a value in food units of KJ times the relative price of clothing, (OA), or the area $BGJK$. This equals distance HI in Figure 4.3.

The disequilibrium outlined in this section corresponds to that in the account of market stability in Chapter 3. The offer curves in Figure 4.1 (or the downward sloping world demand curves in Figures 4.2 and 4.3), show that the Marshall-Lerner conditions for stability are satisfied, and that *if prices adjust to market forces* the terms of trade will shift against the home country until markets are cleared. That is, the excess supply of clothing will force the relative price of clothing down until demand and supply are equated in each market. In Figure 4.1 the terms of trade line would shift to a ray from A through B, the point of intersection between the offer curves.

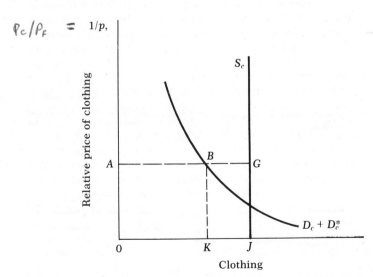

FIGURE 4.2   World Demand and Supply for Clothing

$P_F/P_c = p,$

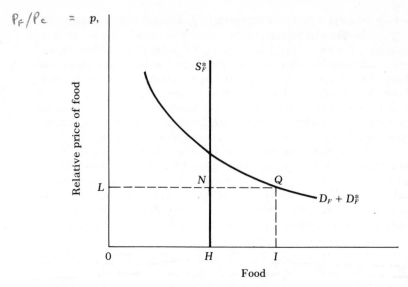

FIGURE 4.3   World Demand and Supply for Food

4.2 POSSIBLE ADJUSTMENT PATTERNS WITH STICKY COMMODITY PRICES

Unfortunately, prices do not always respond to market pressures. In this section we explore possible alternative patterns of market adjustment. We must first define sticky prices. We assume that the local-currency denominated price of the commodity in each country's endowment remains fixed. In the notation introduced in Chapter 2, we assume that p_C and p_F^* (hereafter described as $\bar{p}_C$ and $\bar{p}_F^*$) are constant.

   We now introduce a new concept — the rate of exchange between the currency unit of one country and that of the other. The symbol, r, denotes the price of foreign exchange (the foreign exchange rate) in the home country. Suppose the home country's currency unit is the dollar, and the foreign country's unit of account is the pound sterling. Then the price of foreign exchange to the home country is the number of dollars that must be given up to obtain one pound.[1] Our assumption of sticky prices for commodities in the currency of the country where they are obtained implies, for food, a fixed pound price, $\bar{p}_F^*$. The price of food in dollars, of relevance to the home country's consumers, would then be given by p_F equal to $r\bar{p}_F^*$. The exchange rate, r, translates pound prices to dollar prices. It does so for clothing as well, so that $\bar{p}_C$ equals $r p_C^*$. Our assumption about fixed commodity prices is in

[1] For example, using the United States and the United Kingdom, r went from \$2.80 in the early 1960's to \$2.40 in 1967 to \$2.60 in 1971.

this case that p_c remains constant. The pound price of clothing facing consumers in the foreign country would be given by p_c^*, equal to $\bar{p}_c/r$.

In the disequilibrium situation illustrated in section 4.1 the home country faces a potential balance-of-trade deficit. It wishes to import *AI* units of food (Figure 4.1), but the foreign country wishes to import only *GH* units of clothing, which have a value, in food units, of *AH*. If each nation's demand is satisfied at these disequilibrium prices, the home country would have a trade deficit — an excess of imports over exports, which may be measured in the following ways: by *IH* in food units; by *KJ* in clothing units; by *IH* times $\bar{p}_F^*$ in foreign currency units; or by *IH* times $r\bar{p}_F^*$ in local currency units.

Consider what such an assumption entails. For the home country it means that at the disequilibrium prices inventories of clothing are piling up — at a rate shown by *KJ* in Figure 4.1 or 4.2. This is perhaps more plausible than the alternative assumption whereby consumers are forced to consume a quantity of clothing greater than they demand at these prices. For the foreign country, however, it would imply that inventories of food (beyond current "output" levels shown by *O*A* in Figure 4.1's production box) are sufficient to handle the world excess demand for food shown by *HI*. This we assume. We are supposing that aside from current endowments, each country has accumulated sufficient inventory levels for sellers to supply excess demand at least temporarily.[2]

Market forces or deliberate policy can cope with commodity markets that are out of line and trade deficits and surpluses in several ways.

Changes in the Exchange Rate

Although we have assumed rigidity in commodity prices denoted in the currency of the supplying country, a change in the exchange rate offers an alternative means of changing the terms of trade. Notice that the price of one commodity in terms of another is equal to the ratio of money prices when both are quoted in the same currency units. Thus p, the relative price of food, is given either by $r\bar{p}_F^*/\bar{p}_c$, where both numerator and denominator show prices in home currency units, or by

$$\frac{\bar{p}_F^*}{(\bar{p}_c/r)},$$

where both numerator and denominator show foreign currency

---

[2] The reader may wonder if these inventories affect demand. To make our assumptions explicit, we assume at this stage of the argument that aggregate demand in each country equals the value of the *current* endowment bundle. Thus in Figure 4.1 each country's demand lies on ray *AGD* emanating from each country's endowment point, *A*. For more details see R. W. Jones, "Stability Conditions in International Trade: A General Equilibrium Analysis," *International Economic Review*, 2 (May 1961): 199–209.

prices. In either case, even with the home price of clothing and the foreign price of food rigid, the terms of trade, p, move directly in proportion to the exchange rate, r.

Introducing the exchange rate allows a different description of the disequilibrium in section 4.1. There we stressed that commodity prices were out of line. Specifically the relative price, p, of the home country's import commodity, food, was too low, resulting in an excess demand for food imports into the home country. Alternatively, the price of foreign exchange in the home country, r, is too low, resulting in an excess demand for foreign exchange. The home country's export commodity, clothing, has been too high-priced in world markets. That is, the home country's currency is overpriced — an r too low for equilibrium implies a $(1/r)$ too high, and $(1/r)$ is the price of the home country's currency evaluated in units of foreign exchange.

If the exchange rate can be changed, the trade imbalance in Figure 4.1 can be eradicated; r can be raised, raising p by a proportional amount until the equilibrium point B in Figure 4.1 is attained. The initial trade deficit in the home country can be ascribed to an overvalued home currency, and the proper prescription involves a rise in the exchange rate, r,[3] which can be accomplished under either of two institutional regimes. If exchange rates are free to fluctuate in the market, the excess demand for the foreign country's currency, which is the counterpart of the import surplus in the home country, raises r just as excess demand for any commodity puts upward pressure on its price. This is described as a *depreciation* of the home country's currency. If exchange rates are pegged by governmental action, the level of the peg can be changed. In our example, a deliberate policy move to raise r can be employed. This is described as a *devaluation* of the home country's currency. In Chapter 19 we will discuss in more detail the use of devaluation as an instrument of macroeconomic policy.

Flexibility in commodity prices (or price levels in models with even more commodities) and flexibility in exchange rates are direct substitutes. Such a formal similarity in our simple models should not be allowed to disguise a major real-world difference between the two. Because commodity prices are often sticky in the real world, a country whose exports are overpriced in world markets (leading to a trade deficit) may alter its exchange rate more easily than aim a deflationary policy directly at commodity prices.

In the adjustment mechanisms that follow we assume that the ex-

---

[3] Notice that the stability of the underlying offer curve analysis implies as well that an increase in r will wipe out the trade deficit. In Chapter 5 we derive demand and supply curves for foreign exchange from the underlying demand and supply curves for commodities. Since the latter depend on the terms of trade, p, and since the rigidity of $\bar{p}_C$ and $\bar{p}_F^*$ implies that r and p move in direct proportion to one another, it is easy to see how demand and supply diagrams for commodities can be translated into demand and supply diagrams for foreign exchange. The details are set forth in Chapter 5.

change rate, as well as p_C and p_F^*, are fixed. Alternative routes to adjustment must be found.

2. Changes in Output and Employment

Here: p_C, p_F^* and r are assumed, Fixed.

The word "employment" in this discussion of the exchange model requires explanation. We have been assuming that in each period of time a country (or rather its inhabitants) receives a specific endowment of commodities, reserving until Part 2 an explicit treatment of production. However, it is useful at this point to fudge our endowment assumption a little, a procedure made easier by this chapter's assumption that each country possesses an endowment of only one of the two commodities. If commodities are in fact produced, the proper allocation of resources will not be a problem. We may even assume that each country has a given *labor* endowment, and that labor can be transformed into food output abroad and clothing output at home at a constant ratio.[4]

With all prices and the exchange rate fixed, the disequilibrium for the home country implies, as we have seen, that inventories of clothing pile up during each period. Producers of clothing in the home country may respond by cutting production and thus throwing some of the labor force out of work. Does this clear markets and lead to a balance of trade? And, if so, how much unemployment or output loss is entailed?

Role of Inventories' Adjustment

Figures 4.2 and 4.3 can be used to explore these issues. Let us assume that no changes occur in the foreign country. It only produces food, and is assumed to have sufficient inventories of food to supply the world excess demand (*HI* in Figure 4.3) in the short run. Labor abroad is fully employed, foreclosing the possibility of increased production abroad. If prices are fixed, and foreign spending is limited to the amount earned in *producing* food, neither foreign production nor demand for either commodity will change. The adjustment must take place in the home country.

In the market for clothing in Figure 4.2, *KJ* initially represents the rate at which inventories are piling up in each period. For convenience call this quantity of clothing β. Producers' first reaction may be to cut by amount β the quantity of clothing produced. Will this clear the clothing market? It will shift the S_C supply curve to the left by β (so that S_C becomes *BK*), but it will also shift the demand curve for clothing leftward. This result follows because we now assume that the home country's residents spend in the aggregate only the value of income earned in production. As production falls,

---

[4] The assumption of a simple technology whereby labor can be converted into commodities at a constant rate is adapted from the discussion of the Ricardian model in Chapter 7. However, in the Ricardian model labor can be taken out of one productive sector and employed in another. Here we are aiming at a different result: when labor is thrown out of work in one sector there is no other outlet for employment.

so does demand, still leaving an excess supply of clothing after production falls by β. Of course the D_C curve shifts to the left by less than β, because some of the reduced spending in the home country affects food consumption. Thus the excess supply gap is reduced, but not eliminated, by a cutback of scale β in production of clothing.

How far must this process go? If clothing producers are reluctant to pile up inventories, production of clothing must be cut back until the market is cleared. To pursue this matter, turn to the illustration of the world market for food in Figure 4.3. The foreign supply curve, S_F^*, remains fixed during this adjustment process, while world demand shrinks because D_F is shifting to the left. Therefore we need to ask how much of a leftward shift in D_F is required to clear the food market. This is amount HI, equal to the area $BGJK$ in Figure 4.2, which is $(1/p)$ times β.[5] Therefore home incomes must fall by a sufficient amount to lower home demand for food by β/p. Let ΔY denote the required drop in home incomes when these incomes are expressed in units of clothing. The marginal propensity at home to import food has been labeled m, and by definition,

$$m = p\,\frac{\cdot \Delta D_F}{\Delta Y},$$

(The insertion of "p" on the right-hand side converts the change in the demand for food into clothing units to make m a pure number.) Because prices remain fixed, the only effect on demand is through income changes. From this definition of the marginal propensity to import, m, it is clear that the required fall in home incomes and output is ΔY equal to p/m times the required fall in D_F, which, in turn, was β/p. Thus incomes must fall by:

$$\Delta Y = \frac{1}{m}\cdot \beta,$$

which is a multiple, $(1/m)$, times the initial excess supply of clothing.[6]

It may seem that we have started with one question — how much must clothing production be cut in order to clear the *clothing* market — and ended up with an answer to a different question — how much must clothing production (and therefore home incomes) be cut in order to clear the world's *food* market. But these questions are the

---

[5] Recall that at the disequilibrium prices the value of the excess world demand for food (p_F times HI in local currency units) equals the value of excess world supply of clothing ($p_C \cdot \beta$).

[6] The appearance of a "multiplier," in this case the reciprocal of the marginal propensity to import, may sound familiar to readers who have heard of the standard Keynesian macroeconomics multiplier. They are related, but are not the same, as Chapter 17 will make clear. Notice that we used the simple budget constraint: all earned income is spent. This is not the basic Keynesian assumption, as we point out in Section 4.4.

same, for if all earned income is spent in each country, and one commodity market is cleared, the other must be also. This was one of the lessons of Chapter 2.[7]

In Chapter 2 we also discussed the gains to be obtained from trade by the home country. These gains seem less likely to occur if trade results in unemployment in the clothing industry. Of course we have been discussing trade in the context of sticky prices, which are not market clearing prices. We may construct examples in which non-equilibrium trade is worse than no trade at all. Consider a very general case in which a country produces many commodities, but all domestic prices are sticky — at least on the down-side. Furthermore, fix the exchange rate at an absurdly overvalued level — sufficient to price all the country's commodities out of world markets. That is, suppose r is pegged so low that every domestic p_j divided by r is higher than the cost of producing commodity j abroad. (p_j/r is, of course, the foreign currency price of the home country's output of commodity j). Unemployment at home would be rife, and trade at such prices would clearly not be superior to no trade. In Chapter 2 the gains from trade occurred when prices were flexible and equilibrium was reached.

The exchange model in this disequilibrium context has been used to point out that if all prices are sticky the market may adjust to disequilibrium by cutting back output and employment in the deficit country. The trade deficit means that goods that cannot be sold abroad are piling up at home, and production cuts may be the only means of achieving balance in international accounts. The government may try to prevent unemployment by raising clothing production to the initial level OJ (Figure 4.2). Such a policy — stockpiling the excess clothing — may cure the unemployment problem but will not cure the trade deficit. Therefore, policy conflict may arise between maintaining full employment at home and balance in international accounts.

If, through the stockpiling scheme or other means, full employment levels of output are maintained at home, we still must cope with the trade deficit.

3. Temporary Financing of the Deficit

In the disequilibrium situation portrayed in Figure 4.1 the foreign country surrenders IH amount of food to the home country without a

---

[7] In the clothing industry the supply curve has shifted to the left by amount β/m. The marginal propensity to consume clothing at home is $(1 - m)$. Thus demand for clothing has been reduced by $(1 - m)$ times the change in income, β/m. The *excess* supply of clothing has been reduced by

$$\frac{\beta}{m} - (1 - m) \cdot \frac{\beta}{m}.$$

But this is just β, the initial excess supply. Excess supply has been wiped out.

compensating import of clothing. The home country is willing to export the volume KJ of clothing in exchange, but this is not demanded by residents of the foreign country. How, then, is the home country's deficit, IH, to be financed? Once again we are stretched beyond the confines of the simple exchange model, for if the foreign country will not accept clothing in exchange for food, something else must be given up that it will accept. The most obvious possibilities are assets owned by residents or the government of the home country and acceptable to residents or the government (or banks as financial intermediaries) in the foreign country; for example, the currency of the home country, previously accumulated stocks of the foreign country's currency held by the home country, or perhaps gold stocks held by the home country. Later we shall discuss these possibilities in detail. The difficulty faced in the exchange model, when the quantity of imports demanded exceeds the quantity of exports that foreigners are willing to accept in exchange, can be surmounted temporarily by financial reserves held by the deficit country and desired by the surplus country.

Although a country's deficit can be financed in such a manner in the short run, the home country's reserves of assets acceptable to the foreign country may be limited. And the limits do not end there. The commodity markets are still not cleared. To prevent unemployment the government in the home country may be stockpiling KJ of clothing (Figure 4.2).[8] But the foreign country's inventories of food are decreasing, and if it originally had no excess capacity (we assumed all its labor force was already devoted to food production), this situation cannot continue for long. Clearly there would be pressure for a rise in price, and in real life prices are less apt to be sticky when market pressures call for increases than they are on the downside. Any increase in the absolute price of food abroad would directly alter the relative price of food to clothing even if the price of clothing in the home country does not fall. Such a movement in the terms of trade would tend to restore commodity market equilibrium.

Another force is working on market prices when the home country is surrendering gold or foreign exchange to finance its import surplus: changes in the money supply have a direct impact on prices. This monetary mechanism will be examined at length in Part 4. The expansion in the foreign country's monetary base, as a consequence of its receipts of gold or currency to match its export surplus, exerts upward pressure on prices abroad. Several variations of the "quantity theory of money" could point to this result. Also, the outflow of money from the home country could prove deflationary at home.

All this takes us beyond the explicit assumption in this section that commodity prices are fixed. It suggests the pressures that can build up in the market, making it difficult to adhere to the assumption of fixed prices. There is one more possibility, however, whereby without

---

[8] In a more realistic setting the government could be employing home labor in activities other than clothing production.

changing any commodity prices or levels of employment the commodity markets adjust so that they are cleared at the original disequilibrium terms of trade.

4. International Borrowing and Lending

Consider the demand and supply curves in Figures 4.2 and 4.3. At relative price OA for clothing and OL for food, markets are not cleared. We have previously examined one possible way of clearing markets at these prices, which involved only changes in the home country. The supply of clothing was cut (through production layoffs) and the demand at home for both commodities was reduced by the concurrent fall in home incomes. If taste patterns at home differ from those abroad, any loans that are negotiated between the two countries will, if expenditures adjust to the loans, affect the composition of aggregate world demands. That is, reduced spending in one country and a comparable increase in the other could, if tastes differ, shift the $(D_C + D_C^*)$ curve to the right and the $(D_F + D_F^*)$ curve to the left until both markets are cleared without any changes in prices.

Suppose that consumers in the home country have a stronger preference for the commodity they produce (clothing) than consumers abroad have. Any transfer of purchasing power to the home country, in the form of a loan from the foreign country, would expand home demand for clothing by a greater amount than foreign demand for clothing would be cut. Similarly, aggregate demand for food would decline, because the cut in demand abroad would be more severe than the expansion in demand at home. Then international lending could clear commodity markets that would otherwise be out of line.

Notice that the required direction of the loan depends upon the comparison of taste patterns in the two countries and not upon the fact that the home country faces the trade deficit. Our using international borrowing and lending to clear commodity markets may seem contrived, but in Chapter 22 we will establish more precise conditions for the direction of the loan, asking what the effect of a loan is on commodity markets, the terms of trade, and/or the balance of payments. A transfer of purchasing power through international capital movements can affect the world composition of demand and thus either restore equilibrium or exacerbate disequilibrium in commodity markets.

4.3 THE TRADE BALANCE, SAVINGS, AND INVESTMENT: A FUNDAMENTAL IDENTITY

We have dwelled upon possible reactions of market forces or policymakers to commodity prices that are frozen away from their market-clearing levels. We pointed out the ways in which a market disequilibrium, and the concurrent piling up of inventories of goods, would find expression in an imbalance in the trade account. In this section we relate the trade imbalance both to inventory accumulation or de-cumulation and to the possible spread between aggregate spending and income levels, stating some basic national income account-ing relationships for the simple economy in the exchange model.

National income, or national product, is represented by Y, which is composed of several categories. In general these would correspond to consumption expenditures, C, investment expenditures, I, and gov-ernment spending, G. In this discussion G is zero. But we must take account of the facts of international trade by acknowledging that some of the national product is shipped abroad as export, X, which is not included in the home country's consumption, C, or investment, I; and some local consumption (and, in a more general model, invest-ment) is produced abroad and not at home. That is, the value of imports, M, must be netted out of $C + I$ in order to obtain only that part produced in the home country. Putting all these together we ob-tain as the basic national income and product relationship for our open economy:

$$Y = C + I + X - M.$$

The reader may be puzzled by our inclusion of the investment term I. Our simple model excludes real capital accumulation in the form of plant and equipment or new residential construction. These are the large categories in any nation's "investment." Recall, however, that the I category also includes accumulation of inventories, which were prominent in our previous account of trade in a disequilibrium situa-tion. The community's level of savings, S, is by definition the excess of aggregate national income, Y, over consumption spending, C:

$$S = Y - C.$$

Substituting this relationship for S in the previous definition of Y we obtain our basic accounting equation, which links a country's trade account balance, $X - M$, to its excess of savings over investment:

$$X - M = S - I.$$

Recall the basic nature of the equilibrium of exchange in the pre-ceding two chapters. All income was spent, so that the level of sav-ings, S, was always zero. In addition, we concentrated on positions of free trade *equilibrium*. With all commodity markets cleared, there is no accumulation or decumulation of inventories, so that invest-ment, I, is also zero. The expression above tells us that for such equilibrium states the trade account must be in balance — exports must equal imports. Equilibrium in commodity markets, at terms of trade given by the intersection of the two countries' offer curves, implies a balance between imports and exports.

In the previous sections of this chapter prices were frozen at a disequilibrium position — one in which the home country's export commodity, clothing, was overpriced. This led to a positive accumulation of inventories at home — a positive I — which was the counterpart of the home country's import deficit. Thus even when a country plans to spend on commodities a value just equal to its income (so that S is zero), a trade deficit (or surplus) can arise if uncleared markets lead to inventory increases or decreases.

This source of imbalance in the trade account — inappropriate prices resulting in markets not being cleared — should be sharply distinguished from the other possible explanation of a trade deficit or surplus — an imbalance between a community's aggregate spending and its income. It is often said that some countries are trying to "live beyond their means." In the international sphere a country can spend more than the value of what it produces only by running a trade deficit — an excess of imports over exports.

If a community's savings or dis-savings are so intimately linked with its balance of trade, it is clearly important to deal with models in which allowance and explanations are made for savings behavior. The exchange model's budget constraint — all incomes are spent — stands in the way of an analysis of a country's balance-of-trade difficulties, except where markets are out of line. As a prelude to our discussion of problems of "external balance" in Part 4 we turn briefly in the next section to some of the basic influences on a country's savings pattern, which may help explain trade deficits or surpluses.

4.4 OVERSPENDING AND UNDERSPENDING: A PREVIEW OF AGGREGATE SAVINGS BEHAVIOR

The complexity that can be built into the analysis of a community's aggregate savings behavior is almost without limit. Our objective in this preview is not to be complex or complete. Instead, we discuss three alternative, but not necessarily exclusive, explanations that could account for a departure from the basic budget constraint of the exchange model in Chapters 2 and 3.

Savings Are Related to Incomes

No instructor of a first course in economics today fails to stress the importance of income levels in determining savings. An individual's and community's level of savings will rise as income increases. At low levels of income, savings may be negative and rise with income until a "break-even" level is reached, beyond which savings are positive. That is, a rise in incomes leads to an increase in spending, but of a smaller amount than the increase in incomes. Thus the gap between income and expenditure — savings — grows with income. This is a basic tenet of the simple Keynesian model, and it has definite implications for models of international trade. These are pursued in Chapter 17.

If savings are linked to income levels, a theory of income determination becomes possible. Notice the contrast with the pure model of exchange. There incomes represent the value of the commodity endowment bundle, or, in this chapter's extension, the full employment level of income. In the Keynesian model income levels may be trapped below the full-employment level, inviting a government to use monetary or fiscal weapons to alter income levels. Any policy-induced change in levels of income will, if savings and imports are linked to incomes, affect the balance of trade.

Savings Are Related to Interest Rates

In most societies savings yield a return — represented by or approximated by the market rate of interest. Changes in interest rates change the amount that individuals are willing to borrow, if they are spending in excess of incomes, or to lend, if they are holding expenditures below the level of incomes. If securities such as bonds are traded on the international market, a country may encourage savings at home and attract savings from abroad by raising interest rates. This could allow for, and balance, a trade deficit.

An underdeveloped country may wish to plan for a period in which total expenditures at home exceed its ability to earn income. The implied excess of imports over exports could be financed over a number of years by an appropriately high rate of interest on the country's securities to obtain the necessary loans from abroad. The monetary authorities in a country plagued by a trade deficit may attempt to raise interest rates relative to other countries to attract foreign capital to balance its import surplus.

That such international capital movements are significant is well documented in Chapter 5's discussion of the balance of payments generally and the experience of the United States over the past decade specifically. Parts 4 and 5 contain a thorough discussion of the role of international capital movements. Our more prosaic and abstract argument at this point merely suggests that the extent of international borrowing or lending, which affects the extent of allowable trade deficits and surpluses, is linked, at least in part, to interest rates.

Savings Are Undertaken to Balance Money and Asset Markets

It is possible to view savings as a means of accumulating assets, thus focusing our attention on the underlying relationship between the desired level of asset holdings and current levels of income or expenditure.

To simplify, suppose that the only asset is money. This is a simple world with no bonds or opportunities to amass wealth in any tangible form. People demand money only because commodity transactions are made easier by the use of money. Because of the lack of unique correspondence between the time expenditures are made and pay-checks received, a typical individual wishes to hold a level of money balances, which varies proportionately, say, with the value of his expenditures. If that level of money balances is achieved, we assume he satisfies the exchange model's version of the budget constraint: all income is spent — savings are zero.

Now imagine that something disturbs this balance between his demand for money and his actual stock of money. Some institutional change (e.g., being paid monthly instead of every other week) may raise his demand for money balances. How can his stock of money be raised to match his increased demand? Only by saving — by temporarily cutting his expenditures back below the level of current income in order to accumulate the necessary funds. The same kind of argument would work in reverse if the individual should receive extra money. If money balances are higher than the stocks required for transactions purposes, the excess is not thrown away. It is spent. Thus temporarily the level of expenditures could exceed the level of income in an effort to run down excess money balances.

Such behavior involves a two-tiered explanation of savings. If money (or asset) markets are in equilibrium, savings are determined by current levels of activity. In our version above we used the simple exchange-model form of the budget constraint — savings are zero. However, if the stock demand for money is thrown out of line with supply, that disequilibrium position calls forth a temporary alternative savings pattern. Savings or dis-savings take place in order to right the imbalance in the money (asset) market, but these are temporary measures. Once the accumulation or decumulation of money achieves its aim in bringing stocks in line with demand, savings revert to their old level (zero in our example).

This is only a sketchy explanation of a phenomenon that has important implications for trade deficits and surpluses and the mechanisms whereby a disequilibrium in the trade account can be righted. A country may be running a trade deficit. If this involves a loss of money abroad to finance the deficit, spending at home may be reduced as inhabitants attempt to restore the level of money balances. The deflationary effect on prices at home and the simultaneous inflationary effect abroad may encourage the price movements that will rid the country of the trade deficit. A more leisurely and complete account of this kind of mechanism will be provided in Part 4 (especially Chapter 16).

4.5 SUMMARY

This chapter is a bridge between the pure model of commodity exchange equilibrium of Chapters 2 and 3 and most of the remainder of the book. By concentrating initially on a position of market disequilibrium with rigid commodity prices we were forced to consider ways in which a country's trade deficit could be financed or adjusted. We introduced the potential role of the foreign exchange rate, commodity or currency reserves, and international capital flows. We also introduced the possibility that a country's resources would be thrown out of employment as a consequence of trade if prices and the exchange rate result in over-valued exports. Direct government interference in markets provides one means of maintaining full employment, but at the cost of aggravating the trade deficit. More subtle policy strategies for coping simultaneously with internal and external balance are considered in Part 4.

The fundamental national income accounting identity equates a country's export surplus, $X - M$, to its excess of savings over investment, $S - I$. In the first sections of this chapter we showed that disequilibrium commodity markets, and the resulting unintended changes in inventories, which are part of a nation's investment (I), thus find reflection in a trade imbalance. In section 4.4 we explored various reasons for a nation's savings not being zero (as it is in the exchange model form of the budget constraint). Savings may depend upon income levels, or interest rates — both at home and abroad — or be linked to underlying imbalances in the nation's money or asset markets. Any or all of these considerations may explain why some nations "overspend" and thus find themselves in balance-of-payments difficulties.

This chapter concludes our account of the pure model of exchange. Part 2 presents a more complete analysis of the role of production, which was only briefly discussed in this chapter. Of more immediate interest, in the next chapter the foreign exchange market and the balance of payments are discussed, not primarily in the context of a two commodity model of exchange, but rather in the more complex real-life setting in which many different types of international transactions take place.

SUGGESTIONS FOR FURTHER READING

Johnson, Harry G. "Toward a General Theory of the Balance of Payments," *Readings in International Economics,* eds. Caves and Johnson. Homewood, Ill.: Richard D. Irwin, 1968. Pursues in detail the meaning of balance-of-payments deficits.

Jones, Ronald W. "Stability Conditions in International Trade: A General Equilibrium Analysis," *International Economic Review,* 2 (May 1961). Provides an explanation of trade deficits and surpluses corresponding either to savings behavior or to market disequilibrium.

Pearce, Ivor F. *International Trade.* New York: W. W. Norton, 1970. Chapter 4 discusses the spending income relationship using box diagrams.

5 The Foreign Exchange Market and the Balance of Payments

The foreign exchange rate — the price of foreign currency — connects nations' systems of prices. Are American goods expensive in Europe? Are cameras cheap in Hongkong? These everyday questions cannot be answered without knowing the exchange rates between the currencies of the countries involved. In Chapter 4 we saw that adjustment of the exchange rate is one way to correct a disequilibrium. In this chapter we examine the market forces that determine the exchange rate.

The exchange rate is the price that prevails in the market for foreign currency. In that market, many types of international transactions occur. Most transactions involve exchanging something for money, and most international transactions take place between parties who reckon in different national monetary units. Thus, most international dealings require at least one party to the transaction to make a trip to the market for foreign exchange. (Exceptions would be pure barter exchanges or gifts of goods and services.)

We shall show how the forces of demand and supply governing the market for foreign exchange relate to the simple barter exchange model presented in Chapters 2 and 3. The transactions in actual exchange markets, however, are far more varied than the exchange of clothing for food in our barter model. Exploring some properties and functions of the exchange market (section 5.2), we turn to the statistical records that countries keep of these transactions — their balance-of-payments accounts. Much of international economics (but especially the topics covered by Parts 4 and 5 of this book) involves the effect of one class of international transactions on another, or the effect on both of a common force. The balance-of-payments accounts are the tool that we use to understand these processes. In particular, the payments accounts help us to diagnose the state of the foreign exchange market — a preoccupation of policy-makers in a world where balance-of-payments problems are prevalent. In the final section of this chapter we relate the payments accounts to the problems of measuring external imbalance and applying appropriate remedies.

5.1 BARTER EXCHANGE AND THE MARKET FOR FOREIGN CURRENCY

In Chapter 4 we defined the exchange rate r as the price of foreign currency. Let us translate the notation for foreign and domestic prices into a numerical example. The foreign country's currency is the pound sterling, and its export good (food) sells for £1 per unit. The home country's currency is the dollar, and its exported clothing sells for $5.20. The exchange rate is $2.60 per pound sterling. Then we calculate the price of imports for each country as follows:

Home country $\quad p_F = rp_F^*$ $\qquad\qquad$ $\$2.60 = 2.60 \cdot \pounds1$

Foreign country $\quad p_C^* = \dfrac{1}{r}p_C$ $\qquad\qquad$ $\pounds2 = \dfrac{1}{2.60}\cdot\$5.20.$

The exchange rate is the immediate link between the money prices of domestic and foreign goods. The direct effect of a fall in the price of foreign exchange, then, is the same as that of an improvement in the home country's terms of trade. As we saw in Chapter 4, one way to correct a disequilibrium in the terms of trade is to make a suitable change in the exchange rate.

To demonstrate the relationship of the foreign-exchange market to the barter model of exchange presented in Chapters 2 and 3, we need to establish the implications of equilibrium in barter exchange for the foreign-exchange market. In order to purchase a unit of imported food in the numerical example above, the home-country consumer (United States) must first demand £1 (supply $2.60) in the foreign-exchange market. The foreign national (United Kingdom) must supply £2 (demand $5.20) in order to import a unit of clothing. The demand for imports thus raises a demand for foreign exchange, and its supply results from foreigners' demand for home-country exports. The demand and supply curves in the exchange market rest on the real forces determining the country's imports and exports respectively.

More specifically, equilibrium in barter exchange implies equilibrium in the foreign-exchange market. Barter equilibrium, we know, requires that the markets for traded goods be in equilibrium, and that people stay within their budget constraints — spending only their incomes. Suppose that the terms of trade (p_F/p_C) were 1/2, as in our numerical example. Barter equilibrium could prevail if, for example, 100 units of clothing are exported in exchange for 200 units of food. The *home* currency values of exports and imports would then both be $520 (equals $100 \cdot \$5.20$ or $200 \cdot \$2.60$). The *foreign*-currency values would both be £200 (equals $100 \cdot £2$ or $200 \cdot £1$). But the foreign-currency value of imports is exactly the total quantity of foreign exchange demanded to purchase them, and the foreign-currency value of exports the quantity of exchange supplied by foreign subjects in paying for them. In our barter model, with only merchandise trade taking place, exchange equilibrium implies equilibrium in the foreign-currency market.

Now, what happens if the price of foreign exchange is reduced slightly — say, to $2.40? We can isolate the effect of this disturbance only by assuming that the domestic money price of each country's export good retains its previous value.[1] Then the exchange-rate reduction improves the home country's terms of trade, lowering the relative price of imports from 0.5 ($2.60/$5.20) to 0.46 ($2.40/$5.20). From Chapter 3 we know that this improvement in the terms of trade will, if the conditions for stability are met, create an excess demand for the home country's imports and an excess supply of its exportables. But this is the same as saying that the foreign-currency value of imports potentially exceeds the foreign-currency value of exports. The reduction in the price of foreign exchange thus creates an excess demand for it.

Choosing sterling as "foreign exchange" was entirely arbitrary. From the British viewpoint, the dollar is the foreign currency. Their willingness to supply sterling for the purchase of United States exports is the mirror image of their desire to acquire dollars for that purpose. Likewise, the home-country demand for sterling mirrors American willingness to supply dollars. The reduction in the price of sterling, which was shown in the previous paragraph to create an excess demand for it, could have been viewed as a rise in the sterling price of dollars, creating an excess supply of dollars. *There is really just one currency market* in which sterling and dollars exchange for each other, just as in the barter exchange model (of Chapter 2) there was really only one market in which clothing exchanged for food.

Thus the barter exchange model and the market for foreign exchange are related by two central propositions: (1) Equilibrium in barter exchange implies equilibrium in the foreign-exchange market. (2) A reduction in the price of foreign exchange creates an excess demand for it, if barter exchange is stable so that an improvement in the terms of trade would create an excess demand for imports.

[1] By assuming domestic price levels to be predetermined, we do not mean to imply that domestic prices are *sticky* in the sense explored in Chapter 4. Rather, because the exchange rate is a relationship between nations' money price levels, we lack the information for determining it unless we know those levels.

This analysis of the exchange market has been restricted to the simple barter model. The complexities encountered in real exchange markets fall into three groups.

1. Many transactions require exchange purchases or sales. Beyond the confines of the exchange model, we witness not just the exchange of clothing for food but the financing of trade in innumerable commodities. Furthermore, international transactions also include services such as ocean shipping, tourist expenditures, and insurance and related commercial services. The exchange market also facilitates an important class of transactions involving international flows of capital. In order to record these transactions and understand their collective effect on the exchange market, nations keep statistics called balance-of-payments accounts. In section 5.3 we learn how these accounts are assembled, and how one might expect the transactions they record to affect the market for foreign exchange. We shall see that they can be classified generally as giving rise to either a demand or a supply of foreign exchange. We shall often find it useful to refer to an exchange market as illustrated in Figure 5.1, where the supply and demand curves for foreign exchange (sterling) indicate that the market would be in equilibrium at an exchange rate of $2.60 per pound sterling.

2. The exchange market performs several functions. The exchange market handles not one commodity, "sterling," but many currencies. Furthermore, it deals not only in "spot" exchange but also in currencies for delivery in the future.

3. Maintaining exchange-market equilibrium is a major policy problem. Because the exchange market is the crossroads of all international transactions, it registers excess demands (or supplies) resulting from any class of international transactions, not just imbalances in trade flows (discussed in Chapter 4). Hence we associate *external balance* generally with equilibrium in the exchange market, and imbalance with disequilibrium. Countries often fix their exchange rates, or let them vary only within narrow limits. Yet an exchange rate need not be consistent with equilibrium in the foreign-exchange market just because the government declares that it shall be the prevailing rate. In Figure 5.1, the equilibrium rate of $2.60 is higher than the rate of $2.40 (the dollar-sterling rate from 1967 to 1971). In order to sustain a rate of $2.40, a government must have some means of making it prevail. Otherwise, market excess demand (equal to ab in Figure 5.1) would raise it to $2.60.

When someone speaks of "the exchange rate," you must know how he is defining it — r or $1/r$ in our notation. In some countries, including the United States, people habitually speak of the exchange rate as the price of foreign currency (r, or $2.60, in the previous example). Other countries, such as Britain, quote the foreign price of home currency (for them, $2.60). There is no "right" way; one must simply

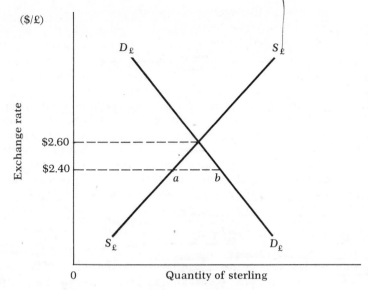

FIGURE 5.1   Market for Foreign Exchange

> U.S. citizens demand foreign exchange (sterling) in order to purchase foreign goods and services. Foreigners supply sterling (i.e., demand dollars) in order to purchase U.S. goods and services.

get the concept straight each time it is used. The British practice has an important advantage. When a country *devalues* its currency, it reduces the foreign-currency price, and $1/r$ falls; *revaluation* increases the foreign price of home currency. The *de-* and *re-* prefixes correspond to the direction of change in $1/r$, whereas one must remember that a devaluing country *raises* the home-currency price of foreign exchange.

5.2 THE FOREIGN EXCHANGE MARKET

The currencies of a number of leading countries are traded within and among financial centers (such as New York, London, Paris, Zurich). Many traders take part at each center, and the centers are in continuous touch with each other. Hence the market for any currency closely matches the economist's model of pure competition.

In New York, the major banks deal in foreign exchange for their customers' convenience, buying exporters' proceeds and supplying the currencies needed by importers. They also deal "wholesale" in foreign exchange at two levels. First, they buy and sell among themselves through brokers who secure commissions for their services. A bank does not hold large inventories of currencies, and must go into the market to even out its position when demand and supply among its customers for a currency fail to balance. Finally, New York banks maintain trading relations and foreign-exchange balances with leading banks in other centers, and exchange is easily bought and sold across national boundaries through *cable transfers,* which cause a deposit lodged in a foreign bank to change hands.[2] Other traders are also present — the agencies of large foreign banks, specialized dealers in foreign bank notes, and out-of-town banks that manage their customers' exchange needs through the brokers or with their New York "correspondent" banks. Even a currency with an official fixed price is normally allowed to fluctuate within small limits, and so exchange rates in this market are in continuous motion.

Exchange rates in different financial centers are kept nearly identical by *arbitrage.* Arbitrage is a general term in economics for buying something where it is cheap and selling where it is dear. If the price of Swiss francs in New York falls below that in London by more than the (small) cost of transaction, it pays to buy in New York and sell in London: this is foreign-exchange arbitrage. It tends to continue until the difference disappears. Arbitrage also keeps consistent exchange rates among the many traded currencies. Disregarding transactions costs, suppose that you buy $1000 worth of sterling in New York, sell it in Paris for German deutsche marks (DM), then sell the DM for dollars in Frankfurt. If you wind up with either more or less than $1000, the exchange rates were not consistent. If a profit was made, you (and other arbitragers) will continue the transaction until the market rates are driven into consistency. If you made a loss, you went around the circuit the wrong way; the opposite series of purchases and sales would have yielded an arbitrage profit. Such transactions are called *triangular arbitrage.* Subject to the limits of transactions costs, they maintain consistency among the bilateral "cross rates" connecting all the world's internationally traded currencies.

Arbitrage or no arbitrage, you might still wonder how the foreign-exchange market copes with the large number of independent currencies represented by the hundred-plus trading nations of the world. Is there an active market in every country for the currency of each nation with which it trades? The answer is no: in any center of foreign-exchange trading most of the business is done in only a few foreign currencies. This does not necessarily imply that the market is imperfect, or that it discriminates against the smaller trading countries. Rather, it demonstrates the convenience to all parties of picking a few leading currencies and using them as the basis for invoicing most international trade. The United States dollar and the pound sterling are the world's principal *vehicle currencies.* The citizens of any country can readily manage most of their international

[2] For a more detailed description, see Alan R. Holmes and Francis H. Schott, *The New York Foreign Exchange Market* (New York: Federal Reserve Bank of New York, 1965).

transactions by conversions between their own currency and dollars or sterling. All currencies remain linked through the vehicle currencies. The number of exchange transactions, the size of currency inventories, and thus the costs of international transactions are thereby reduced.

Forward Exchange Markets

Trading in the foreign-exchange markets includes not only currencies for immediate delivery — *spot exchange* — but also *forward exchange,* currencies to be delivered on a specified date. Forward contracts generally mature in thirty, sixty, ninety, or more days from the date of execution. A market in forward exchange exists principally because persons committing themselves to future transactions involving foreign currencies want to know now what these commitments will be worth at maturity in their home currencies. Thus, a United States importer of British goods may be obliged to pay the shipper in sterling ninety days hence. If the price of sterling falls in the interim, say because the pound is devalued, his profits from the importing transaction are increased. But if the price of sterling rises, his profits are reduced or wiped out. He may wish to avoid taking his chances on either of these outcomes. A possible solution for him, of course, would be to purchase spot sterling now and hold it for ninety days. That would eliminate the exchange risk, but it would tie up his capital and perhaps cost him interest. A better solution, potentially, is to *cover* his future payment by a forward purchase of sterling. That is, he enters a contract to pay a specified number of dollars ninety days hence in exchange for the sterling he will need. The dollar cost of his future payment is thus made certain. Other transactors in the forward market are those who expect to receive sums fixed in foreign currency, and who wish to avoid the risk of unexpected changes in the home-currency value of the proceeds. This group would include exporters who are taking deferred payment from their foreign customers, and the holders of foreign short-term securities, such as British Treasury bills.

The price of forward exchange is set by competition among these traders as well as by *speculators* in foreign exchange. The traders previously described take part in the forward market in order to cover their exchange commitments, i.e., so that their foreign-exchange payments and receipts will be equal at a future date. A speculator, by contrast, is willing to take an *open position,* committing himself to a future net sale or purchase of exchange. If he has sold forward, he must buy in the spot market on the agreed date in order to cover his commitment. He takes a chance on what will happen to the spot market by that time. Suppose that the price today of ninety-day forward sterling is $2.597. If the spot price ninety days hence is $2.612, the speculator earns 1½ cents on each pound sterling that he buys forward. Like the importer whose obligation may be covered by the exchange he sells forward, he ties up no capital in the contract. On the day his contract matures, he simply pays $2.597 for each pound sterling he has purchased forward, and simultaneously sells it spot for $2.612.

The forward market thus allows people with differing expectations about future exchange rates and differing attitudes toward risk to improve their expected future positions. We consider its significance in detail in Chapter 24.

5.3 THE BALANCE-OF-PAYMENTS ACCOUNTS

A nation's balance-of-payments account is a statistical record of all transactions taking place between its residents and the rest of the world. This record is vital to understanding the disturbances and adjustments impinging on the market for foreign exchange, and thus it is watched closely by policy-makers charged with sustaining external balance. The payments accounts also provide the starting point for any serious study of international transactions. You will find a firm grasp on their construction necessary for understanding many of the relations discussed in this book, especially those in Parts 4 and 5.

The Accounting Framework

Broadly speaking, every transaction has two sides. We buy something, and pay for it. Or we sell something, and receive compensation. The accounting rules tell us how to classify and record each side of every transaction. Here is the key rule:

Record as a credit (+) any transaction resulting in a receipt from the rest of the world. Record as a debit (−) any transaction resulting in a payment to the rest of the world.

The receipt and the payment appear with signs opposite to those of the transactions giving rise to them; they are the "other sides."

Thus the sale of an export is classed as a credit, because the foreign buyer is obligated to make payment to us in some form. What might that form be? First, a United States export valued at $5 might be compensated through barter by the shipment of an import also worth $5. Then the export is recorded as a $5 credit, the import — the compensation obtained for it — as a $5 debit. Second, an American export of merchandise valued at $10 might be shipped as a personal gift, say by an American of Italian origin to a relative in Italy. We record the export as a $10 credit in the United States accounts. In fact it gives rise to no receipt, other than the relative's good will. But to complete the double-entry system we must concoct a "debit" side to the transaction, and so we make up the category "unilateral transfers to foreigners," and enter the corresponding debit of $10. Third, and more typically, suppose that an export of $15, recorded as a credit,

simply results in a transfer of $15 in United States funds from the
Danish purchaser to the American exporter. The compensation takes
the form of a drawing down of Danish holdings of United States
currency, and is recorded as a $15 debit. Fourth, suppose that an
export valued at $20 to Great Britain again results in a cash pay-
ment, but that this time an American exporter decides to accept
payment in British pounds sterling valued at $20. The compensating
transaction this time is an increase in United States holdings of
foreign currency, recorded as a $20 debit. The payments accounts
after these four transactions have been recorded would appear as
follows:

Debits (−)		Credits (+)	
Merchandise imports	−5	Merchandise exports	+50
Unilateral transfers to foreigners	−10		
Reduction in foreign holdings of U.S. currency	−15		
Increase in U.S. holdings of foreign exchange	−20		
	−50		+50

We can construct a parallel series of transactions resulting in payments abroad. An American tourist's consumption of food and lodg-
ing in a foreign country is classed as a debit, because it results in a
payment to the rest of the world. We call his purchases an import of
tourist services and class it as a debit of, say, $10; if foreigners (tem-
porarily, at least) accept dollars in payment, the corresponding credit
item is an increase of $10 in foreign holdings of United States cur-
rency. An American investor purchases common shares worth $20
in a Japanese corporation; he pays by requesting his United States
bank to draw down its holdings of Japanese yen by $20 worth, debit-
ing his dollar checking account for the cost of the yen. These two
transactions appear as follows:

Debits (−)		Credits (+)	
Imports of services	−10	Increase in foreign holdings of U.S. currency	+10
Imports of securities	−20	Reduction in U.S. holdings of foreign exchange	+20
	−30		+30

Now suppose that the examples we have mentioned are the only
international transactions taking place between our country and the
rest of the world during one period of time. What do they imply about
the market for foreign exchange? In fact, United States holdings of
foreign exchange are unaltered in total value: one transaction decreases our holdings by the equivalent of $20, and another increases
them by the same amount. Foreign holdings of United States dol-

lars, however, are decreased by $5, being raised $10 by one transaction but reduced $15 by another. This reduction *might* drive up the price of the dollar in the world's foreign-exchange markets. *The fact that every transaction has two sides in the accounting system in no way implies that demand and supply for foreign exchange will be equal.*

Countries often wish to keep their exchange rates fixed. If the commercial transactions already enumerated are driving up the foreign price of the dollar, some foreign government would feel forced to sell an equivalent amount of dollars to keep its own currency from depreciating. This sale itself does not enter into the United States balance of payments unless it is made to an American wishing to reduce his holdings of foreign currency. In that case it would appear as a reduction in United States holdings of foreign exchange (a credit), offset by a reduction in foreign holdings of dollars (a debit). If the sale is made by the foreign government to a foreign national, the transaction merely shifts United States liabilities from foreign official to foreign private holders.

Until August 15, 1971, a foreign government using the United States dollar as a reserve currency to stabilize its exchange rate could recoup its supply of dollars by selling gold to the United States Treasury. This transaction would enter the United States payments accounts with the import of monetary gold appearing as a debit (like any other commodity import). The increase in official foreign holdings of United States currency represents the credit item.

These examples should supply a basic understanding of how the double-entry bookkeeping system works. Now we can see how these transactions are aggregated with the many other possible types into a summary of the nation's international transactions. Transactions are sorted not only into those resulting in receipts and those resulting in payments, but also "horizontally" into those having different significance for the country's national income and national wealth.

The Current Account

The first important class of transactions is called the *current account.* It lumps together sales and purchases of currently produced goods and services and thus relates to the country's current national income. Specifically, it includes transactions that either yield national income or result from its expenditure. Its first major category includes exports and imports of merchandise: all movable goods sold, given away, or otherwise transferred between domestic and foreign ownership. Exports and imports of services also enter the current account. They involve current outputs and expenditures, but no movement of goods across national boundaries. Some of the important international service transactions are:

1. Transportation services comprise freight and insurance charges for the international movement of goods and also the expenditures of tourists on international travel to and from the country. When Ameri-

can imports arrive in foreign ships, or American tourists cross the Atlantic on a foreign airline, the transaction results in a payment and is recorded as a debit in the United States balance of payments.

2. Tourist services include all expenditures by a country's citizens when they are outside its borders (including those for travel once abroad). The expenditures of foreign tourists within the United States are classed as an export of tourist services, and appear as a credit.

3. Business and professional services make up a diverse class of international transactions. International trade in the services of management consulting firms, engineering firms, and the like is brisk. A newly booming service import of the United States results when business firms ship statistical data abroad to Korea, Ireland, and elsewhere to be recorded on tapes for automatic data processing back in the United States. This and other purchases of business services are recorded as debits in the United States balance of payments.

4. An important class of international receipts results from the services produced abroad by the United States' capital stock. The interest or dividends earned by American capital abroad appear as credits. Conversely, earnings of foreign capital "working" in the United States are classed as debits. We must distinguish these payments for the *services* of capital, which appear in the current account, from international movements of the capital itself. The latter are considered below.

The current account finally includes unilateral transfers, gifts, and donations, public and private. As we saw before, these transactions are fictional, but useful and indeed vital to the double-entry system of bookkeeping. The United States government offers economic and military aid to some countries abroad, and American citizens also on balance remit gifts and contributions to foreign countries. These donations naturally appear as debits. (The goods or funds given away comprise the corresponding credit.)

The balance on goods and services is the point of juncture between the international payments statistics and national-income accounts. Gross national product, the chief measure of a nation's economic output, consists of goods produced at home for consumption, investment, governmental use, and for export. The statisticians measure these flows of goods, however, not as they are *produced* but as they are *purchased*. Hence the expenditure flows include all imports as they pass into these final uses, and the imports must then be subtracted to secure the desired measure of domestic production. The import total is ordinarily shown as a subtraction from exports, thus:

$$GNP = C + I + G + (X - M).$$

The term in parentheses, under current United States income definitions, is the balance on goods and services. In the national-income accounts it is called "net exports of goods and services."

The current-account balance in the payments statistics is closely related to the concept of "net foreign investment" appearing in the national accounts. After we subtract from the balance on goods and services the value of output donated abroad by governments and households, we have in the current-account balance a measure of the net increase in United States claims on foreigners — i.e., the net payments due the United States for goods and services sold abroad. These net claims — "net foreign investment" — appear in the national-income accounts as a component of gross investment of the United States.[3]

The Capital Account

We just saw that a country's net sales abroad (adjusted for donations) must equal its increase in net claims on foreigners. The *capital account* of the balance of payments displays the details of this change in net claims or assets. It records the net trade between domestic and foreign citizens in various financial claims. The balance of trade in these financial claims then must equal the net change in United States claims on foreigners.

If we think of understanding balance-of-payments accounting as traversing a golf course, the capital account has most of the sand traps. The main one is semantic, and relates to the nature of capital. For this and many other purposes we think of capital as liquid purchasing power, not embodied in machines or products. To export capital thus is to ship purchasing power abroad, where it is put to use (and presumably earns for the lender dividends or interest that will later appear in the current account). The receipt for exported purchasing power is an imported bond or share, representing a claim on that future income stream. We learned how this transaction must appear in the accounts: the import of securities is a debit, giving rise to a payment, and is thus treated just like the acquisition of an asset in the balance sheet of a firm. The transfer of balances into foreign hands represents the corresponding credit. But this import of securities is commonly called a *capital export*, because liquid purchasing power is sent abroad. We face the seeming paradox that a commodity export appears as a credit, a capital export as a debit, in the international accounts. But the paradox is not real, and you can keep the accounting of capital flows straight if you remember that an export (import) of capital is an import (export) of securities, and that international flows of securities and goods are accounted in directly similar ways.

The capital account contains three principal types of transaction:

1. *Direct investment* occurs when the residents of one country acquire or increase control over a business enterprise in another country. When IBM starts a new subsidiary in Europe, an outflow of

---

[3] See tables in the annual National Income Issue of the *Survey of Current Business*, appearing each July. The current-account balance and net foreign investment in fact differ by United States acquisition of Special Drawing Rights, a form of international-reserve asset to be discussed in Chapter 20.

direct investment is recorded in the United States balance of payments equal to the value of the equity that IBM acquires in the subsidiary (and, of course, to the outflow of equity capital involved in starting it). If an American buys shares in a foreign company that do not give him control of it, however, the flow is classed as one of portfolio rather than direct investment.

2. *Long-term portfolio investment* involves international transactions in securities with an original term to maturity greater than one year. An American purchase of the bonds of a Canadian provincial government, giving rise to a payment, would count as a capital outflow.

3. *Short-term capital flows* involve securities with original terms to maturity of less than a year. A foreign purchase of United States Treasury bills would count as a capital inflow, giving rise to a receipt. We also include as short-term capital flows international shifts in the control of liquid funds. Thus, an increase in United States citizens' holdings of foreign exchange, giving rise to a payment, counts as a capital outflow. This statistical practice makes sense because of both the balance-of-payments accounting system and our concept of capital. British pound notes can be thought of as "securities," giving us a claim on United Kingdom goods and services, just as surely as British Treasury bills. And these banknotes can be acquired for an outflow of our own liquid capital, if we wish, instead of income-yielding securities. (It is often useful to think of cash as a security that offers no interest yield except for its convenience in effecting transactions.)

In both the current and capital accounts we record "balances" as differences between corresponding subtotals of credits and subtotals of debits. By the accounting rule, a preponderance of credits (or receipts) makes the balance positive. A positive balance is also commonly referred to as "favorable" or "active." A balance with a preponderance of debits is negative by the accounting rule, and is called "unfavorable" or "passive." Notice the gravitational pull of the semantics! The receipts side owns all the good words, and has done so ever since the eighteenth-century mercantilists made a national virtue of "storing up treasure" and selling abroad more than one bought. Although economists from Adam Smith on have proclaimed that economic welfare depends on the goods available for the nation's use and not ultimately on the cash earned from selling produce abroad, they have never conquered this linguistic outpost of mercantilism. We shall try to use terms that are as nearly neutral as possible.

Compiling and Presenting
the Payments Accounts

When government statisticians assemble the record of a nation's international transactions, they of course do not observe directly the two sides of every transaction. Errors creep in for two reasons: some transactions are valued incorrectly, so that the quantity recorded for one side of the transaction fails to equal that for its compensation; or a transaction is omitted entirely. An American professor may give a lecture in Canada, depositing his fee in his American checking account. The fee turns up (initially, anyhow) as an increase in United States holdings of Canadian currency — a debit; but the statisticians do not ascertain that the professor has exported professional services, and this credit item goes unrecorded. Likewise, errors occur in the valuation of transactions. Consider such a commodity as bananas, which are auctioned only after they have passed the United States Customs officer. When their entry is recorded, no one knows what their market value will be. A guess is put down. If it fails to equal the payment ultimately made for the bananas, an error will enter the payments statistics. The statistician measures each class of transactions as best he can. Because of these and other errors, the sum of credit and debit items will not be equal. He simply inscribes an item, "Errors and unrecorded transactions," equal to this difference.[4]

In Table 5.1 we present a condensed account of the United States balance of payment for the years 1961 to 1971. It shows some features of the nation's international position. Exports of goods and services usually exceed imports, but this relationship has reversed lately. Military transactions, dominated by purchases abroad by the United States armed forces, are a large outflow. The income from American investments abroad is quite large and rising, but the balance of all other services (dominated by tourist expenditures) shows a net outflow. Net private donations abroad are a growing item, net government economic and military aid a fairly large but static one. The United States has been a heavy exporter of capital, but in some years also receives large inflows of foreign capital. The entry for errors and omissions reveals a large and fluctuating volume of unrecorded net debit items.[5] At the bottom appear two estimates of the "balance" of United States international transactions. We now turn to the problem of detecting imbalance from these data.

5.4 PAYMENTS ACCOUNTS AND POLICY TOWARD THE EXCHANGE MARKET

Under the Articles of Agreement of the International Monetary Fund (1946), the principal trading nations agreed that they would keep exchange rates among themselves fixed at declared par values and change them only in the event of a "fundamental disequilibrium." Yet, as we illustrated in Figure 5.1, an arbitrarily fixed exchange rate may not clear the market for foreign exchange at any one time.

---

[4] For a description of the compilation of the United States balance-of-payments statistics, see U.S. Bureau of the Budget, Review Committee for Balance of Payments Statistics, *The Balance of Payments Statistics of the United States: A Review and Appraisal* (Washington, 1965).

[5] Many economists think that the swings in unrecorded transactions probably reflect undetected movements of short-term capital.

TABLE 5.1   United States Balance of Payments, 1961–1971 (billions of dollars)ᵃ

Transaction	1961	1962	1963	1964	1965	1966	1967	1968	1969	1970	1971
Merchandise trade balance	5.6	4.6	5.2	6.8	4.9	3.9	3.9	0.6	0.7	2.1	-2.9
Exports	20.1	20.8	22.3	25.5	26.4	29.3	30.7	33.6	36.5	42.0	42.8
Imports	-14.5	-16.2	-17.0	-18.6	-21.5	-25.5	-26.8	-33.0	-35.8	-39.9	-45.6
Military transactions, net	-2.6	-2.4	-2.3	-2.1	-2.1	-2.9	-3.1	-3.1	-3.3	-3.4	-2.9
Travel and transportation, net	-1.0	-1.2	-1.3	-1.1	-1.3	-1.4	-1.8	-1.6	-1.8	-2.0	-2.2
Investment income, net	3.6	4.1	4.2	4.9	5.3	5.4	6.0	6.2	6.0	6.2	8.0
Other services, net	0.1	0.1	0.2	0.2	0.3	0.3	0.4	0.3	0.5	0.6	0.7
Balance on goods and services	5.6	5.2	6.0	8.6	7.1	5.3	5.2	2.5	2.0	3.6	0.7
Private remittances	-0.7	-0.7	-0.8	-0.9	-1.0	-1.0	-1.3	-1.2	-1.3	-1.4	-1.5
U.S. Government grants	-1.9	-1.9	-1.9	-1.9	-1.8	-1.9	-1.8	-1.7	-1.6	-1.7	-2.0
Balance on current account	3.1	2.5	3.2	5.8	4.3	2.4	2.1	-0.4	-0.9	0.4	-2.8
U.S. Government capital flows, net	-0.9	-0.9	-1.2	-1.3	-1.5	-1.5	-2.4	-2.1	-1.9	-2.0	-2.4
Long-term private capital flows, net	-2.2	-2.6	-3.4	-4.5	-4.6	-2.6	-2.9	1.2	-0.1	-1.5	-4.1
Balance on current account and long-term capital	0.0	-1.0	-1.3	0.0	-1.8	-1.6	-3.2	-1.3	-2.9	-3.0	-9.3
Nonliquid short-term private capital flows, net	-1.2	-0.6	-0.8	-1.7	-0.2	-0.1	-0.5	0.2	-0.6	-0.5	-2.5
Errors and omissions, net	-1.1	-1.2	-0.5	-1.1	-0.5	-0.4	-1.0	-0.5	-2.6	-0.3ᵇ	-10.2ᵇ
Net liquidity balance	-2.2	-2.8	-2.6	-2.7	-2.5	-2.1	-4.7	-1.7	-6.1	-3.9	-22.0
Liquid private capital flows, net	0.9	0.2	0.6	1.2	1.2	2.4	1.3	3.3	8.8	-6.0	-7.8
Official reserve transactions balance	-1.3	-2.6	-1.9	-1.5	-1.3	0.2	-3.4	1.6	2.7	-9.8	-29.8

Source: U.S. Department of Commerce, Office of Business Economics, *Survey of Current Business*, 51 (June 1971): 30–31; 52 (March 1972): 43.
ᵃ Data for components may not add to totals or balances because of rounding errors.
ᵇ Includes allocation of Special Drawing Rights.

We would generally expect some disequilibrium — fundamental or not.

The methods countries use to deal with external imbalance are closely bound up with the problems of measuring imbalance in the payments accounts. In this section we set forth the conventional way of measuring imbalance and relate it to the strategies available for dealing with imbalance in the exchange market.

Measuring Exchange-Market Imbalance

Return to Figure 5.1 and consider the problem faced by the United States — or Britain — if it desires to keep the exchange rate at $2.40. An excess demand for sterling of *ab* appears at this price. Its counterpart is an excess supply of dollars. The first method used by countries to preserve a fixed exchange rate is simply to stand ready to buy or sell foreign currency at the "official" price, thus satisfying excess demand or sopping up excess supply. For this purpose nations hold *international reserves* — assets that they can either use directly to meet an excess demand for foreign exchange, or indirectly to procure currencies for this purpose. The prevalence of this method of pegging the exchange rate explains the usual approach to measuring imbalance in international payments.

This approach depends upon the distinction between *autonomous* and *accommodating* transactions.[6] Autonomous transactions are undertaken for ordinary commercial motives. They may frequently be influenced by the exchange rate, but they are not intended to affect the rate, or the state of the foreign-exchange market. Accommodating transactions are undertaken to preserve or enforce a price in the market for foreign exchange, and not ordinarily to pursue commercial profit. Broadly speaking, accommodating transactions are intended to keep the exchange rate at the official level. If we want our payments imbalance to indicate the size of the exchange-market disequilibrium, we should shoot for a measure of accommodating transactions.

Suppose that the United States were to finance its exchange-market deficit (*ab* in Figure 5.1) by supplying this amount of sterling from reserves held by the government. This accommodating change in her reserves would provide the United States with an exact measure of the imbalance in the exchange market. But what of the imbalance, in this same case, from Britain's point of view? The American exchange-market deficit is exactly Britain's exchange-market surplus. Yet, because we assumed that United States reserves finance the imbalance, Britain's reserves do not change. Something *does* change from the British viewpoint, however: her short-term liabilities to foreign (i.e., United States) monetary authorities are reduced. Thus the imbalance (surplus) from Britain's viewpoint is measured by the decline in her official liabilities, just as the American deficit is mea-

[6] These terms are suggested by J. E. Meade, *The Balance of Payments*. London: Oxford University Press, 1951, chap. 1.

sured by the decline in United States official assets. A general lesson
lies behind this example. The transactions that accommodate a country's external imbalance are measured not just by the change in its
own reserves; we must also net out any change in stocks of its own
currency held as international reserves by other countries.[7]

One of the measures of external balance used by the United States
(and shown in Table 5.1), the *balance of official reserve transactions,*
indicates the net change in the country's international reserves. It
includes net changes in the United States holdings of monetary gold,
for indeed the United States has traditionally held most or all of its
international reserves in gold rather than in foreign currencies. It
also includes any change in United States borrowing rights with the
International Monetary Fund; we shall explore the fund's operations
in Chapter 20.

Although the balance of official reserve transactions is a logical
measure of external imbalance for the United States, estimating the
disequilibrium in the foreign-exchange market, it is not the only
measure in use. The supplement to this chapter explains the other
measures now employed. After we have considered the alternative
ways a country has of maintaining external balance, the appropriate-
ness of other statistical concepts will be clear.

Policies for Exchange-Market Balance

Chapter 4 included a preliminary survey of the sources of external
imbalance and the policies that might finance or correct it. These
policies are important for their abilities to rectify the underlying
source of trouble — the inappropriate prices or the under- or overspending that cause imbalance. However, they often have a direct
effect upon the exchange market. With our knowledge of balance-of-
payments accounting and the relation of the exchange market to
underlying economic forces, we can interpret the relation of these
policies to the sources of disturbance.

When we discussed the short-run financing of a deficit in section
4.2, we found that many kinds of assets might be sold by a country
wishing to finance a deficit. These include of course the international
reserves that permit the "accommodating transactions" mentioned
above. But a government can finance an exchange-market imbalance
by other means as well. It could use monetary policy to raise the   (1)
interest rate yielded by short-term securities (either the government's
or those of the private sector). If these higher yields tempt foreign
purchasers, the country enjoys a capital inflow that provides extra

[7] Another important conclusion of this argument is that it takes only one
country to have a fixed exchange rate in a two-country world. If A's government stands ready to buy and sell unlimited quantities of B's at a posted
price, B's exchange rate is fixed whether B approves or not. More generally,
in a world of n countries fixed exchange rates will prevail if $n - 1$ of the countries actively peg the external values of their currencies. In practice, the
United States has served for the past two decades as the passive nth country,
with most other countries stabilizing their currencies against the dollar.

supplies of foreign exchange to the market. A government can thus finance a deficit privately as well as by the direct means of using its international reserves. (The implications of this possibility for defining the balance-of-payments surplus or deficit and measuring "accommodating transactions" are taken up in the supplement.) Either way, it reduces the country's net worth in order to permit an excess of purchases from abroad over foreign sales.

Some policies dealing with the exchange market are direct alternatives to others that initially strike elsewhere in the economy. The exchange rate, we now see, is the link between the money price and cost structures of different countries. Excess demand in the exchange market may be attacked directly by changing the exchange rate: devaluing (lowering the price of) the domestic currency, or letting it depreciate in response to forces in the exchange market. But monetary policies designed to change the country's domestic price level would tend to have the same effect. In Figure 5.1, for instance, the imbalance would be directly eliminated by raising the price of sterling from $2.40 to $2.60. However, deflation of the United States price level would have a potentially equivalent effect of shifting both the supply and demand curves for foreign exchange downward until they intersect (and the exchange market is cleared) at a price of $2.40. This is illustrated in Figure 5.2, which reproduces Figure 5.1 but adds

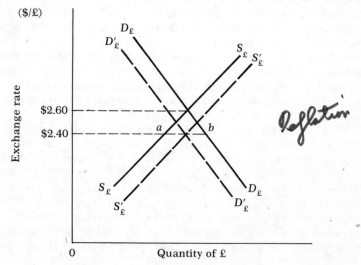

FIGURE 5.2 Effect of Price-Level Change on Exchange Market

Deflating the domestic price level makes foreign goods dearer, shifting foreign-exchange demand to the left. It makes home goods cheaper to foreigners, shifting supply of exchange to the right.

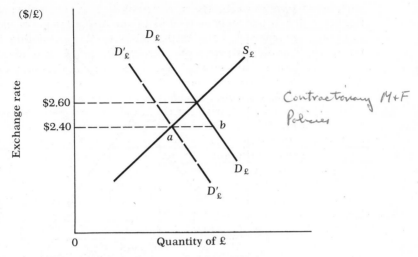

FIGURE 5.3 Effect of Reduction in Overspending
on Exchange Market

> When total spending is cut, part of the reduction falls on im-
> ported goods, shifting demand for foreign exchange to the
> left.

the dashed-line demand and supply schedules $S'_£$ and $D'_£$ to show the
effect of deflation as an alternative way to eliminate exchange-
market disequilibrium.

In Chapter 4 (section 4.4) we noticed various ways in which citizens
could over- or underspend their incomes — causing external deficits
or surpluses. The most direct way to attack an imbalance from this
source is by policies affecting the level of spending, rather than the
foreign-exchange market directly. Figure 5.3 illustrates the effects
of this strategy on the exchange market. Assume that the disequilibrium at the exchange rate of $2.40 is due only to overspending by the
United States. Then a policy curtailing the overspending would reduce the demand for imports and thus shift the demand for foreign
exchange back to the dashed-line position of $D'_£$.

Finally, countries often try to deal with external imbalance by imposing controls that somehow lop off quantity *ab* from the amount
of exchange that people are permitted to purchase and use. The most
comprehensive device is *exchange control*, whereby the government
preempts the exchange market, requiring its citizens to sell it their
earnings from the sale abroad of goods, services, etc.[8] The foreign

---

[8] This preemption is necessary because most buyers would if necessary pay
more than the going exchange rate for foreign currency, a reflection of the
intramarginal consumers' surplus derived from international transactions.
Exchange control frustrates traders' natural bent to bid up the price when the
available supply is less than *Ob*.

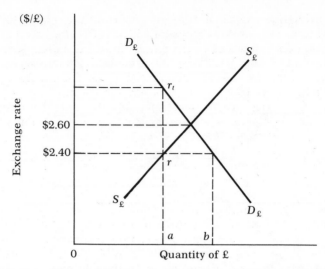

FIGURE 5.4   Effect of Exchange Control on Exchange Market

To enforce $2.40 exchange rate, government acquires Oa foreign exchange and denies access to would-be buyers of ab.

$(5)(\ell)$

Taxes

currency is then resold to customers chosen by the government. In Figure 5.4, it acquires only Oa, and so must refuse would-be purchasers of amount ab. Of course, buyers can be kept from the exchange market by other controls as well. A tax or surcharge imposed on international transactions might be sufficient to cut the exchange demanded to Oa. As Figure 5.4 shows, this would require trade taxes with the average effect of raising the price of international transactions by the fraction $r_t r/ra$.

Our knowledge of what lies behind the foreign-exchange market of course leads us to wonder how these controls relate to the source of difficulty. If a price disequilibrium causes the trouble, controls may be simply an inefficient and selective way of making foreign goods more costly. If a deficit is due to overspending, controls may curb expenditure on imported goods; but frustrated spending on imports does not automatically become saving. The relation between internal and external balance in Chapter 4 shows that controls on the exchange market could easily be frustrated in their objectives.

5.5 SUMMARY

Most countries create their own currency units, and most international transactions involve money. Hence transactors must use the exchange market, where currencies are swapped for one another.

The exchange market is thus an important crossroads for international transactions and a focus for policies affecting external balance. This market can relate to the simple model of barter exchange developed previously. Barter exchange equilibrium implies equilibrium in the market for foreign exchange. Furthermore, if the underlying barter exchange is stable, a (small) reduction in the price of foreign exchange creates an excess demand for it. In general, the demand for foreign exchange derives from the desire to make purchases abroad, and the supply from foreigners' desire to make purchases from the home country.

Real exchange markets are competitive. Rates in markets are kept in line with one another by arbitrage. Traders cut the costs of currency conversion by using widely traded currencies, especially the dollar and the pound sterling, as vehicles for transactions not involving either United States or British traders. The market for forward exchange allows relief from uncertainty about the future home-currency value of receipts or payments denominated in foreign exchange.

The balance-of-payments accounts provide our basis for understanding changes in the foreign-exchange market. They rest on an accounting convention that records as a credit (+) any transaction resulting in a receipt from foreigners, and as a debit (−) any transaction resulting in a payment to the rest of the world. The receipt and the payment respectively give rise to the other side of the double entry. Although we identify two sides to each transaction the market demand and supply for foreign exchange may not be equal.

International transactions are divided into the current account, covering transactions in currently produced goods and services, and the capital account, covering transactions in securities or claims on streams of future income. The current account includes merchandise trade, transportation services, tourist services, business and professional services, and donations (or unilateral transfers). The principal capital-account transactions are direct investment, long-term portfolio investment, and short-term capital flows. Statisticians can record most flows in the balance of payments with only approximate accuracy. The item "errors and unrecorded transactions" covers the net discrepancy in their measurements.

Conceptually, we should measure imbalance in the exchange market from the net quantity of accommodating transactions undertaken to keep the exchange rate from changing (distinguished from autonomous transactions, not intended to affect the rate). This is basically the same as the change in a country's international reserves — if it deals with external imbalance solely by financing its deficit or surplus.

The exchange market registers the effect of policies designed to correct external imbalance. Some policies, however, operate directly on the sources of imbalance (surveyed in Chapter 4); others immediately affect the exchange market.

SUGGESTIONS FOR FURTHER READING

Aliber, Robert Z., ed. *The International Market for Foreign Exchange*. New York: Praeger, 1969. Chapters on markets in different countries.

Cohen, B. J. *Balance-of-Payments Policy*. Harmondsworth, England, and Baltimore: Penguin, 1969. More detail on exchange markets and payments accounts.

Devlin, David T. "The U.S. Balance of Payments: Revised Presentation," *Survey of Current Business,* 51 (June 1971): 24–57. Latest changes in United States statistical presentation.

Henning, Charles N. *International Finance*. New York: Harper, 1958. Includes information on methods and instruments used in actual financing of trade.

Holmes, Alan R., and Francis H. Schott. *The New York Foreign Exchange Market*. New York: Federal Reserve Bank of New York, 1965. Describes institutions and traders.

Meade, J. E. *The Balance of Payments*. London: Oxford University Press, 1951. Analytical basis for measuring "balance."

United States Bureau of the Budget, Review Committee for Balance of Payments Statistics. *The Balance of Payments Statistics of the United States: A Review and Appraisal*. Washington: Government Printing Office, 1965. Last official appraisal.

Supplement to Chapter 5:
Statistical Measures of Balance
in United States Payments Accounts

In this supplement we will describe three concepts of "balance" now employed in the international payments accounts of the United States. The balance-of-payments statistical presentations vary greatly from country to country, but most countries employ a concept at least similar to one of those used by the United States. Hence the provincialism of this discussion is less than its face might indicate.

In section 5.4 we discussed the rationale for the *balance of official reserve transactions,* which is also called the *balance of official settlements.* This concept is simple in principle, but complicated in practice for a nation such as the United States whose currency is a *reserve currency,* meaning that foreign monetary authorities hold their international reserves (partially) in that currency and use it to stabilize the external values of their own currencies. Reserve currencies are a convenience to monetary authorities, as are *vehicle currencies* for private international transactors. The United States dollar and the pound sterling are both the principal vehicle and reserve currencies.

The United States has "backed" the dollar holdings of foreign monetary authorities by agreeing to sell gold at a fixed price. Thus, when the United States runs a deficit, foreign nations may either increase their dollar holdings or cash these in for gold. Thus changes in the United States gold stock are a component of the balance of official reserve transactions. Hence this balance consists of:

1. changes in short-term claims on the United States held by foreign monetary authorities (often as short-term United States Government securities rather than cash);

2. changes in the United States' stock of monetary gold; and

3. changes in the United States' net position with the International Monetary Fund (to be explained in Chapter 20).

These net flows indicate a United States deficit on official reserve transactions when they involve an increase in liabilities to foreign monetary authorities, loss of monetary gold, and rise in net indebtedness to the IMF. For shorthand we shall describe these transactions as "financing" the deficit; we shall also say that these balancing items are put "below the line" when the balance is struck.

At first glance, the balance of official reserve transactions seems to fill our need for a measure of accommodating transactions, and thus for an indicator of the state of the exchange market. Serious doubt enters, however, when we recall the message of sections 4.2 and 5.4: a nation can finance its deficit, adjust it in various ways, or attempt to suppress it. Should we say that a country's external payments are in balance when a deficit is merely being suppressed? When it is being adjusted by measures that can only sweep it temporarily under the rug? Alas, the neat (and useful) distinction between autonomous and accommodating transactions crumbles when we recognize that the autonomous group can bend to public policy, with foreign-exchange demand and supply curves shifted as in Figures 5.2–5.4. Because of this problem, other concepts of external imbalance, which look beyond immediate conditions in the market for foreign exchange, have been suggested.

Consider one policy measure that can readily adjust an external imbalance: changing the interest rate. In the past decade capital flows among the industrial countries have become highly sensitive to differences in nations' rates of interest. Thus a government can attract a capital inflow, and relieve an excess demand in the market for foreign exchange, by raising its interest rate. Easier monetary policy expels capital and combats an incipient exchange-market surplus. Monetary policy thus can substitute in the short run for changes in international reserves. However, some economists would argue, the capital attracted is strictly short-run, and the game cannot be played forever. Hence, they say, our list of accommodating transactions should include international movements of private capital that we think are typically affected by changes in monetary policy designed to attain external balance.

This line of reasoning leads to another concept of external balance, now included in the United States' payments statistics as the *net liquidity balance*. It measures imbalance by the change in reserves (as does the balance of official reserve transactions) plus the net flow of liquid short-term capital. Suppose that a deficit exists in the balance of official reserve transactions, measured by an outflow of reserves. A *larger* deficit would exist in the net liquidity balance if a net *inflow* of liquid short-term capital occurred. The reasoning behind the net liquidity balance holds that an inflow of this capital is apt to reflect the efforts of monetary authorities to reduce the loss of international reserves. Hence the true size of the deficit is better measured by the size of this inflow plus the actual loss of reserves.[1]

Which is the better concept, the official settlements or the net liquidity balance? If flows of liquid short-term capital swung from month to month only in

Net Liquidity Balance

---

[1] For more details see David T. Devlin, "The U.S. Balance of Payments: Revised Presentation," *Survey of Current Business,* 51 (June 1971): 24–57. You should take warning that the net liquidity balance is quite new to United States statistics. It displaces a previous "gross liquidity balance," which was similar statistically but depended on a much different (and less satisfactory) rationale.

response to policy measures — if they had been entirely "accommodating" — the net liquidity balance would claim the prize. But no class of private transactions is ever completely accommodating, because it will reflect unrelated shifts in private decisions. If we want to measure external balance in the context of the policy measures taken to deal with it, we should watch both balances.

A third concept of balance advocated by some economists is the basic balance. It now appears in the United States payments statistics (see Table 5.1) as the "balance on current account and long-term capital," and this title accurately describes the classes of transactions that it treats as autonomous. It measures imbalance by changes in reserves (the official-settlements balance), and also by a group of transactions including capital movements that are short-term but not highly liquid, and the measure of errors and unrecorded transactions (the swings of which are thought to reflect short-term capital flows). In Table 5.1 these classes of transactions are entered after the balance on current account and long-term capital has been struck.

The rationale for the basic balance is not so closely connected to the foreign-exchange market as are those for the official-settlements and net liquidity balances. It claims to measure the imbalance in stable components of international transactions — flows of goods, services, and long-term capital. It treats the rest as "balancing items," not just because they can be influenced by policy in order to secure balance in the exchange market, but also because they may be more volatile. A proponent would argue that the exchange market cannot balance *in the long run* unless the components of the basic balance are in approximate equilibrium; he insists that these are the only truly autonomous transactions if we take the long view.[2]

The case for the basic balance has merit. The statistics certainly show that short-term capital flows are volatile for the United States, as they are for other countries. Yet to treat the basic balance as our principal measure of disequilibrium, short-term capital movements must be both volatile and free of long-term trends. If a country undergoes a substantial (if irregular) net inflow or outflow over a decade, short-term capital is hardly a transitory component of its international transactions. The basic balance, like its sisters, conveys useful information but cannot be our only tool when we analyze a country's external balance.

BALANCE IN UNITED STATES
INTERNATIONAL TRANSACTIONS

A useful way to appreciate the differences among the three concepts of balance just outlined is to return to Table 5.1 and trace their movements over the 1960's. The balance on current account and long-term capital showed no significant imbalance to 1965, but then deteriorated through 1971. Its signal was one to heed, for it reflected the deterioration of the current account due to the Vietnam War and the boom of 1966–1969 in the domestic economy. Both the net liquidity and official-settlements balances signaled substantial deficits through the early 1960's. No great swings in liquid private capital flows occurred during these years, and so both measures reflected "accommodating

---

[2] For a defense of the basic balance, see Hal B. Lary. *Problems of the United States as World Trader and Banker*. New York: National Bureau of Economic Research, 1963, appendix A.

transactions" narrowly defined: the continued acquisition of dollars by foreign monetary authorities and drain from the United States gold stock.

From 1966 the pattern grows more complex. A series of large but irregular inflows of liquid capital to the United States began, reflecting higher interest rates, an attraction (1968, especially) of foreigners to the United States stock market, and the application of some controls to curb capital outflows. These inflows did *not*, however, primarily reflect tight money policy adopted to improve the external balance, although the Federal Reserve at some times was constrained by the fear of capital outflows from making monetary policy as easy as it would have liked. Thus the liquidity balance showed heavy deficits in 1967 and 1969, whereas the official-settlements balance displayed a surplus in 1968 and 1969. In 1970 and 1971 the previous short-term inflows drained out once more, and the official-settlements balance swung into massive deficit.

This brief sketch suggests that the evolution of the United States payments deficit in the 1960's can hardly be grasped without referring to each of our three concepts of imbalance. None by itself reveals either the sources of an imbalance or the effect of the nation's choice among financing, suppressing, and adjusting it.

PART TWO The Theory of Trade and Production

6 Trade with Production Variable

The hallmark of our exchange model discussed in Part 1 is the complete lack of response of a nation's outputs to any changes in the market. A more unrealistic assumption would be difficult to make in discussing economic affairs. And yet such an assumption demonstrated well the nature of trade and especially the gains from free trade for each participating community. Our concluding discussion in Part 1 of the huge variety of transactions that enter each country's balance of payments and represent either a demand for or supply of foreign exchange underlines the need for a more careful analysis of the response of a country's pattern of production to changes in world market prices and sales possibilities.

Part 2 of this book is devoted to a thorough analysis of the production side of an economy. As such it will reveal how the gains from trade discussed in Part 1 are even further enhanced by the market-determined shift of resources in response to new trading opportunities. In addition, several new questions arise: (1) What role does the level of technical knowledge in the two countries play in determining the pattern of trade? (2) How important are the wide differences in nations' endowments of the basic factors of production, labor, capital, and land? (3) In turn, what is the effect of free trade on the distribution of income — on wages, on profits? These are important questions in the extensive literature on international economic affairs. In coming to grips with them we shall delve especially deeply into two simple prototypes of production: in Chapter 7 we shall explore the early classical model of international trade introduced by David Ricardo, while in Chapters 8 and 9 we shall discuss the more modern theory associated with two Swedish economists, Eli Heckscher and

Bertil Ohlin. This latter theory, which has been the primary vehicle for most theoretical contributions in the past thirty years, allows us to examine more thoroughly the bases for the positions of comparative advantage that dictate the pattern of commodity trade among nations. Our discussion of production in Part 2 will be concluded in Chapters 10 and 11, in which we shall both examine the empirical relevance of the Ricardian and Heckscher-Ohlin accounts of trade and take account of more far-reaching recent explanations of the peculiarities of the international pattern of trade.

This chapter is a prelude to these more detailed accounts. Here the focus is on the consequences of having resources respond to market prices. As will be seen, the exchange model needs little qualitative alteration in adjusting to variable production, thus justifying the time spent on the more simple model of exchange in Part 1.

6.1 THE PRODUCTION-POSSIBILITIES SCHEDULE

Economics would become totally uninteresting if a community could produce as much as it desired of all goods and services. That it cannot do so reflects both the basic limitation of resources, natural and man-made, and the quality of technological knowledge that guides the transformation of resources into final commodities. The production-possibilities schedule (or "transformation" schedule as it will sometimes be called) shows the maximum amount of one commodity that can be produced given the quantities of all other commodities also produced. An illustration of such a schedule is the TT' curve, in Figure 6.1, for a simple economy capable of producing only two commodities, which we again call food and clothing. For example, if clothing output is distance OG, the maximum amount of food that can be produced is AG.

In Figure 6.1 several properties of production have been illustrated. First, such a schedule suggests that some points of production, e.g., D, are beyond the productive capacity of this community. If with time the resource base should expand, or if better techniques of production are envisaged, then point D could eventually be produced. Secondly, and closely related, is the negative slope of the TT' schedule. To produce more food than is shown by point A, some current production of clothing must be sacrificed and some resources transferred out of clothing into the food industry. Thirdly, notice that the community can produce at point C. Such a point would, of course, be inefficient in the sense that the TT' schedule shows that from point C one can move in a northeasterly direction and produce more of both commodities. If the community does not use all of its available resources, a point such as C is quite possible. For example, during the depression in the early 1930's most industrial countries faced severe unemployment of labor and capital equipment. Perhaps less obvious is the

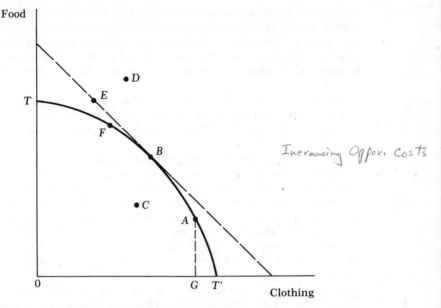

FIGURE 6.1   The Production-Possibilities Schedule

> The bowed-out curve *TT'* shows the maximum amount of food that can be produced for each amount of clothing, subject to the constraints of technological knowledge and a fixed resource base. The slope shows the opportunity costs of producing clothing, which increase as more clothing is produced.

possibility of the combination of production shown by *C* even *with* full employment of all resources. Point *C* might represent the outcome of an arbitrary across-the-board decision to employ exactly 68 percent of every factor of production in the clothing industry, with the remaining 32 percent producing food. Such a decision would take no account of the fact that some resources are especially productive in one sector and not in the other or, more generally, of the fact that techniques of producing clothing are qualitatively different from those used in food production. An economic answer lurks behind the question of allocating the community's resources most efficiently. As explained in the next section of this chapter, the forces of competition ensure that society's production of commodities is efficient, in the sense of lying along the production-possibilities curve.

The *TT'* schedule has been drawn bowed out from the origin, reflecting the so-called law of increasing costs. This bow reflects the assumption that the *opportunity costs* of obtaining an additional unit of a commodity increase as more of that commodity is produced. Consider clothing production, as shown initially at point *F*. The slope of the TT' curve at F shows the sacrifice in food production that is required to produce an additional unit of clothing. This is clothing's opportunity cost — the cost (at the margin) of an extra unit of clothing, *not* in dollars, *not* in labor or material costs, but in terms of the quantity of the other desired final commodity, food, that must be foregone in order to release the resources required by the unit expansion in the clothing industry. Notice how this (marginal) opportunity cost of producing clothing has risen when production of clothing expands to the level shown at B. That is, TT' at B has a greater absolute slope than at F.

What accounts for this general relationship whereby the opportunity cost of any commodity expands as its output increases? Some factors, e.g., highly skilled labor especially trained to produce clothing, may be already employed in clothing production at F and cannot be obtained from further reductions in food output to reach point B. Alternatively, the supply of the best grade of fertile land may increasingly be used up by the time B is reached, necessitating the use of poorer land for food production in moving to F. Elements of this phenomenon — the variability in the aptitude of factors in each occupation — are almost always present in the real world to help account for increasing costs. Nonetheless, as Chapter 9 will illustrate for the highly simplified case in which any factor of production in one occupation has the same potential skill as its counterpart employed in another, increasing opportunity costs can prevail because different sectors of the economy can best utilize labor and capital in different proportions.

The phenomenon of increasing costs may not be universal over the entire range of production possibilities. Figure 6.2 illustrates this for the range BC. In this region attempts to increase clothing production meet with ever-diminishing sacrifices of food as clothing's output is expanded. We speak of decreasing costs here — perhaps they result from such "economies" of large scale production for clothing that foregone food production becomes lower instead of higher. We shall return to this possibility in Chapter 11. Until then we shall assume that transformation schedules are never bowed in toward the origin.

Reconsider the situation in Figure 6.1. If this economy cannot engage in the international exchange of commodities, the production-possibilities schedule is also the consumption-possibilities schedule; the community can only consume what it produces. The opportunity to trade commodities at fixed world prices, however, opens a new range of consumption possibilities. For example, if the world terms of trade are shown by the slope of the dashed line (literally the relative price of clothing is given by the negative of the slope of line EB), the country would maximize its income by allocating resources so as to produce at point B. To see this, notice that a line with the same slope through any other production point, such as A or F, would lie below the line through E and B. If trade is possible at these world

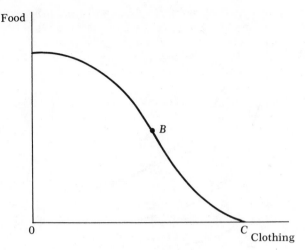

FIGURE 6.2   Decreasing Opportunity Costs $(B \to C)$

> The transformation (production-possibilities) curve is bowed in between *B* and *C*. In this range an increase in clothing production is accompanied by a decrease in the opportunity costs of producing clothing.

prices, the dashed line in Figure 6.1 becomes the community's consumption-possibilities schedule, which is clearly superior to curve *TT'*. For example, point *E* could be consumed at these prices, and this is a consumption bundle lying outside of the possibility of producing along *TT'*. This discussion of the *gains* to be had from trade is picked up in section 6.3. First we must show how competition ensures that (1) production takes place *on* the production-possibilities schedule, and that (2) market prices reflect the community's opportunity cost ratio, as illustrated in Figure 6.1 by the tangency between the price line and *TT'* at *B*.

6.2 THE EFFICIENCY OF PURE COMPETITION

To understand how competition favors the efficient allocation of resources we must investigate the requirements for the community's bundle of outputs to lie on the production-possibilities schedule instead of below it. For this purpose we must review some basic principles of production theory. Again a simplified model in which only two commodities, food and clothing, are produced will be useful. We shall also simplify by assuming that each commodity can be produced with only two factors, say labor and capital.

Figure 6.3 shows three arbitrarily chosen *isoquants* for the food industry. Each point in the diagram represents a quantity of labor

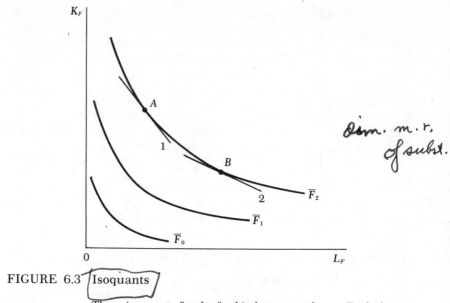

Dim. m. r. of subst.

FIGURE 6.3 Isoquants

Three isoquants for the food industry are shown. Each shows combinations of labor and capital that produce the same quantity of food.

(L_F on the horizontal axis) and the quantity of capital (K_F on the vertical axis) employed in producing food. Associated with each such bundle of inputs is the technologically determined, corresponding level of food production, F. An *isoquant* is a locus of input bundles all of which yield the same level of output. Thus both points A and B in Figure 6.3 are associated with the level of food output, $\bar{F}_2$. A lower level of production, $\bar{F}_1$, can be produced with correspondingly smaller inputs of labor and capital, as shown by the $\bar{F}_1$ curve.

You will no doubt notice that the isoquants resemble in appearance the indifference curves shown in Chapter 2. Along an indifference curve real income, or utility, is constant, whereas the level of production is fixed along an isoquant. Both types of curve are bowed in toward the origin. For indifference curves this curvature reflected the diminishing marginal rate at which one commodity can be substituted for another in keeping constant the level of consumer satisfaction. Similarly, along an isoquant the rate at which labor can be substituted for capital with no sacrifice in output changes as more labor-intensive techniques are employed. The slope of the $\bar{F}_2$ isoquant at A, for example, shows how much capital can be removed from F production when one additional unit of labor is employed and output is kept constant. The slope of the $\bar{F}_2$ isoquant at B shows that as this substitution of labor for capital proceeds, labor becomes less productive in the sense that less capital can be taken off the job when another unit of labor is added. The law of diminishing marginal rate of substitution between factors in production is illustrated by the fact that tangent line 2 at B is flatter than tangent line 1 at A.

Of course labor and capital are also devoted to producing clothing. So as better to understand what is required for these resources to be allocated efficiently between the food and clothing industries, we shall illustrate, in Figure 6.4, a case in which labor and capital are *not* optimally allocated. Suppose food production employs the resources shown by A and clothing production employs the labor and capital mix shown by D. As drawn, the food isoquant at A is steeper than the clothing isoquant at D. This is a signal of *inefficiency* in resource allocation. To show this notice that line AB has been drawn parallel to ED and is of the same length. Therefore if the labor and capital inputs assignments are changed so that point B represents the inputs into food production and point E the inputs in clothing, the same total bundle of labor and capital is employed in the two sectors jointly. But B lies on a higher food isoquant than $\bar{F}$, and E represents a greater clothing output than any point on the $\bar{C}$ isoquant. Therefore the reallocation of resources (from A to B and from D to E) raises outputs of all commodities without using overall any more labor or capital.

From this account it is clear that only if resources are allocated to

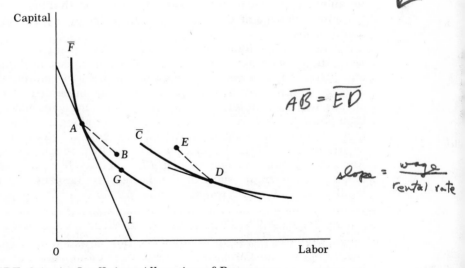

$\overline{AB} = \overline{ED}$

$slope = \dfrac{wage}{rental\ rate}$

FIGURE 6.4   An Inefficient Allocation of Resources

If the food industry employs capital and labor as shown by bundle A and the clothing industry employs bundle D, resources would be allocated inefficiently. Points B and E add up to the same total resource base as A and D, but yield higher outputs of both food and clothing.

each sector, so that the marginal rate of substitution between capital and labor (the slope of the isoquant) is the same in all sectors, will production be efficient.[1] This is precisely what pure competition and flexible prices in the nation's factor markets ensure. Firms in each industry choose factor combinations that produce a given level of output at minimum cost. Just as a consumer minimizes the cost of obtaining a given level of real income by choosing a point where his indifference curve is tangent to his budget line, so does a cost-minimizing firm select its most economical input bundle by going to the point of tangency between an isoquant and a constant factor cost line. Figure 6.4 can be used to illustrate this. The slope of line 1 was chosen to reflect the ratio of the wage rate to the rental on capital equipment. Therefore, any point on line 1 will represent the same total outlay by the firm on factors as does any other point on line 1. Now consider any other factor bundle that would yield the same output, e.g., point G. Such a point must lie on a higher constant-cost line than does A, and therefore will represent a higher cost of producing the same quantity of food.

If firms in both industries face the same wage rate for labor and the same rental on capital equipment, the marginal rate of substitution between labor and capital in each industry is set equal to the common wage/rental ratio, and the two are therefore equal. In such a manner competition in a nation's factor markets ensures that the conditions for an efficient allocation of resources are met, so that the community's production point does lie along the efficient production-possibilities locus.

But does competition also require the "best" point to be chosen along the transformation curve? Yes — as you can see in Figure 6.5, an illustration of a competitive equilibrium for a community not engaged in trade, whose taste patterns can be illustrated by a series of community indifference curves. Competition in factor markets has been shown to require production somewhere along TT'. Two indifference curves have been illustrated in Figure 6.5. Satisfaction is clearly maximized (in the absence of trade) by producing at point A. Any other production point along TT', such as B, yields less real income. Consider the slope of the dashed line tangent to both the indifference curve and transformation schedule at A. Our previous

---

[1] You may notice the similarity between this argument and our account in Chapter 2 of the efficiency of free trade involving equal marginal rates of substitution along indifference curves. Indeed, in Figure 2.7 a consumption box diagram was used to illustrate the "best" points along curve CC' — "best" because any other allocation of commodities between individuals *not* on CC' (e.g., point E in Figure 2.7) makes both individuals worse off than they could be at a point on the CC' contract curve (e.g., the free trade point Q). A "production box" diagram could similarly be constructed to isolate all efficient resource allocations, i.e., those that entail equal marginal rates of factor substitution in the two sectors.

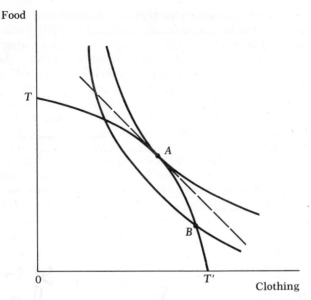

FIGURE 6.5 The Optimal Production Point for a Closed Economy

> An economy not engaged in trade can produce and consume
> anywhere along *TT'*. Point *A*, where an indifference curve
> is tangent to the transformation curve, represents a higher
> level of welfare than any other point (e.g., *B*). The slope of
> the common tangent at *A* shows the relative price of clothing.

account of the exchange model in Chapter 2 showed that the marginal rate of substitution in consumption is set equal to the ratio of commodity prices. The slope of the dashed line in Figure 6.5 shows the ratio of the price of clothing to the price of food. But what about production? Recall that the marginal cost for a competitive firm is, in equilibrium, set equal to the market price of the commodity produced by the firm. This equality holds for clothing and food producers alike. Therefore the ratio of the price of clothing to the price of food is equal, in competitive markets, to the ratio of their marginal costs of production. The slope of the transformation curve equals the ratio of marginal costs in the two industries. It shows the amount of food that must be sacrificed at the margin in order to release sufficient capital and labor to produce an extra unit of clothing.

6.3 PRODUCTION AND THE GAINS FROM TRADE

It is tempting to think that the source of the gain from trade resides in the community's opportunity to shift its resources into the production of commodities in which it has a comparative advantage. This cannot be the only source, for in Part 1 we often remarked on the mutual gains from trade in a model in which no alterations in production were allowed. And yet the opportunity to alter the pattern of production in the face of market conditions abroad that differ from those at home must involve an additional source of mutual benefit from trade. For the two-commodity case this can easily be illustrated for the home country by referring to Figure 6.6.

(1)   If the home country is not allowed to engage in international trade, its consumption possibilities are restricted to points on its TT' schedule, and of these the best is shown by point E where indifference curve y_0 is tangent to the TT' schedule. The pretrade relative price of clothing is shown by the slope of line 1. Suppose with the

(2)   opening of trade, world prices are shown by the slope of line 2. With

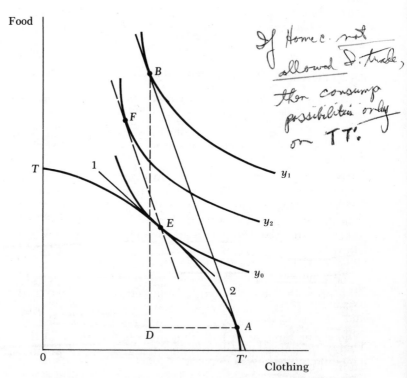

If Home c. not allowed D. trade, then consump possibilities only on TT'.

FIGURE 6.6   The Trade Triangle in the Home Country

With free trade prices shown by the slope of line 2, production at home takes place at A and consumption at B. BDA is the trade triangle — the community exports DA units of clothing in exchange for imports of BD units of food.

clothing relatively expensive abroad, resources flow from food production into the clothing industry until local marginal costs equal world prices, at A. Line 2 shows the new expanded locus of consumption possibilities, and the most desired consumption bundle is point B. At these prices the community desires to export DA of its clothing output in exchange for BD imports of food. BDA represents the trade triangle.

The gains from trade are shown by the increase in real income in moving from curve y_0 to the higher curve, y_1. If resources had been frozen into their occupations at point E the country would still have gained from trade — the consumption point moving from E to F on curve y_2. The movement from F on y_2 to B on y_1 shows the extra gains to be had from trade when production is allowed to change from E to A. That is, the total gain from trade can be decomposed into (1) the gain attributable to consuming at prices different from original home prices — the movement from E to F in consumption, and (2) the gain attributable to the shift of resources that moves production from E to A, thus raising incomes and allowing consumption to expand from F to B.

6.4 FREE TRADE EQUILIBRIUM

World prices are determined by supply and demand in both countries. In a free trade equilibrium the home country's import demand for food must be matched by the foreign country's willingness to export the same quantity of food. If the price line 2 in Figure 6.6 is to reflect an *equilibrium* price ratio, the trade triangle, BDA, must have its mirror image in the foreign country. That is, production and consumption decisions abroad must be as shown in Figure 6.7. The foreign country also has gained from trade — the movement from E^* to B^* entailing a rise in real incomes abroad from level y_0^* to y_1^*. Foreign exports of A^*D^* of food match home imports of BD. The slope of A^*B^*, the foreign country's free trade consumption-possibilities locus, is, of course, the same as the slope of BA in Figure 6.6.

Offer curves can also illustrate an equilibrium of trade between these two countries. Recall from Chapter 2 that along the horizontal axis of an offer-curve diagram we showed the home country's exports and the foreign country's imports, and along the vertical axis the home country's imports, which are the foreign country's exports. That is, the axes show the quantities *traded*, and as prices vary this is a bit difficult to show in Figures 6.6 and 6.7 because both consumption *and* production respond to a change in the terms of trade. To construct the offer curves shown in Figure 6.8 we must collect, for each terms of trade, the demand for imports and supply of exports for each country. The demonstration of equilibrium, stability, and gains from trade then proceeds much as in the diagrammatic discussion of the exchange model presented in Chapter 2. Thus line 2 in Figure 6.8

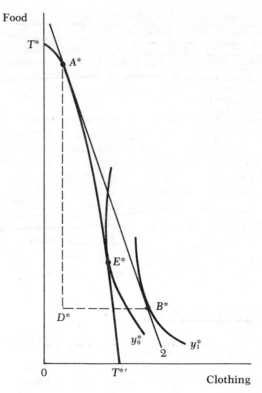

FIGURE 6.7   The Trade Triangle in the Foreign Country

> The slope of line 2 is the same as in Figure 6.6. Trade is
> balanced as the foreign country's trade triangle, $A^*D^*B^*$,
> matches the home country's BDA in Figure 6.6.

shows the equilibrium free trade price ratio, and O_TA and O_TB reflect the dimensions of the trade triangles in Figures 6.6 and 6.7.

In Chapter 3 we discussed the *elasticity* of a community's offer
curve: the percentage response of the quantity of imports demanded
to a 1 percent rise in the price of imports. If production responds to
price changes, the size of these elasticities becomes greater. Not
only would an increase in the price of imports cut down the total home
demand for importables, it would as well shift some resources into
production of importables and *both* of these responses cut down the
net demand for imports.[2] Recall from Chapter 3 our argument about
stability: sufficiently high values for the elasticities of the offer
curves ensure a stable market. This chapter's more realistic model of

___

[2] This is proved formally in the supplement to this chapter.

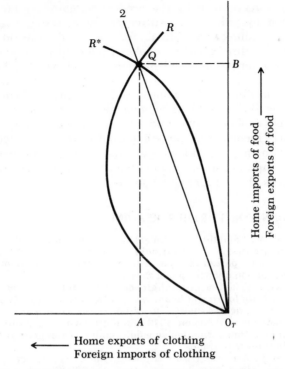

FIGURE 6.8   Free Trade Equilibrium Shown by Offer Curves

The home country's offer curve, $O_T R$, intersects the foreign country's offer curve, $O_T R^*$, at point Q. The slope of line 2 shows the free trade terms of trade. It is the same as the slope of lines 2 in Figures 6.6 and 6.7. The trade triangle, QAO_T, is the same as in the previous two diagrams.

trade with production variable yields values for import demand elasticities more likely to satisfy the stability conditions than in the exchange model where demand was the only variable component of a change in imports.

6.5 SUMMARY

This chapter both extends the discussion of the equilibrium of trade that was presented for a model of pure exchange in Part 1 and introduces the more detailed accounts of production and comparative advantage in Part 2. If a nation's resources can be reallocated in response to prices in the world market that differ from pretrade domestic prices the discussion in Part 1 of the consumption gains from trade is reenforced by the production gains. If markets are characterized by purely competitive behavior, resources adjust to maximize the value of the national income at ruling world prices.

The following three chapters explore in detail two basic models of the theory of international trade. Having already probed the reasons for trade and the nature of the free trade equilibrium, we can then concentrate on different questions, e.g., the sources of comparative advantage as they reside in technological or factor resource differences between countries and the realignment in the internal distribution of income that can be expected as a consequence of trade. In the last two chapters in Part 2 we shall then subject these models of trade to empirical scrutiny and allow for noncompetitive and dynamic sources of comparative advantage.

SUGGESTIONS FOR FURTHER READING

Jones, Ronald W., "Stability Conditions in International Trade: A General Equilibrium Analysis," *International Economic Review*, 2 (May 1961): 199–209. The first part of the article discusses the breakdown of consumption and production changes along the offer curve.

Leontief, Wassily, "The Use of Indifference Curves in the Analysis of Foreign Trade," *Quarterly Journal of Economics*, 47 (May 1933): 493–503; reprinted American Economic Association, *Readings in the Theory of International Trade*. Philadelphia: Blakiston, 1949, Chap. 10. An early exposition showing how to combine transformation schedules and indifference curves to illustrate equilibrium with trade.

Meade, James E. *A Geometry of International Trade*. London: Allen and Unwin, 1952. Meade develops an alternative diagrammatic method of drawing offer curves, with the use of "trade indifference" curves.

Supplement to Chapter 6:
The Elasticity of the Demand for
Imports When Production Is Variable

In section 6.4 we found that with production responsive to market prices the elasticity of the home country's offer curve (demand for imports) exceeds the value that we computed for the exchange model. Here we shall provide a formal proof. Define η as the (positive) elasticity of demand for imports in the home country if production remains unchanged as the price of imports rises. This is the same term as ϵ in the supplement to Chapter 3. Define e as the home country's elasticity of supply of exports assuming that consumption does not respond to changes in relative prices. We shall prove that the elasticity of the home country's demand for imports when both consumption and production changes are incorporated, an elasticity which we label ϵ, is given by the *sum* of η and e:

$$\epsilon = \eta + e. \tag{6.S.1}$$

That is, the elasticity of demand for imports along a nation's offer curve is the sum of (1) the elasticity of demand for imports ignoring production changes, and (2) the elasticity of supply of exports ignoring consumption changes.

In proving this assertion we shall also establish the effect of a change in the terms of trade on the home country's real income. Indeed, the story can begin here, for it is clear that the effect of a price change on the demand for importables must take into account the effect of a price change on real income, because real income is a determinant of demand.

In the supplement to Chapter 3 we established that the change in the home country's real income, dy, is shown by equation 6.S.2:

$$dy = -Mdp + (dx_C + pdx_F). \tag{6.S.2}$$

To repeat the notation, x_C and x_F are the quantities produced of the two commodities (the endowments in Part 1), while M represents the quantity of food imported by the home country and p the relative price of food. The first term on the right-hand side of equation 6.S.2, $-Mdp$, is the terms of trade effect: any rise in the price of imports reduces real income by an amount that is proportional to the volume of imports. The second term, $\{dx_C + pdx_F\}$, shows the change at initial prices in the value of production. For movements along the offer curve in the exchange model of Part 1, both x_C and x_F were fixed so that this term disappeared. Small price changes in this chapter's model change x_C and x_F along the transformation curve. Suppose p rises. The production of food increases, and that of clothing falls. The slope of the price line initially equals the slope of the production-possibilities curve in a competitive market. For example, notice point B in Figure 6.1. But this equality implies that

$$\frac{dx_F}{dx_C} = -\frac{1}{p},$$

$\qquad\qquad\qquad\qquad\qquad\qquad\qquad\qquad\qquad\qquad p = \dfrac{P_F}{P_C}$

or, the same thing,

$$dx_C + pdx_F = 0.$$

Although the effect of the reallocation of resources along the transformation locus on the community's real income cannot be ignored for large price changes (as, for example, in the comparison of the pretrade and free trade equilibria), it can for small changes. Therefore for small movements along the offer curve in this general model with production variable, the change in real income is given by 6.S.3:

$$dy = -Mdp. \tag{6.S.3}$$

With this result in hand we can easily decompose the elasticity of demand for imports along the offer curve, ϵ, into the two components shown in 6.S.1. For $M = D_F - x_F$, and for small price changes the change in D_F is precisely what it would be in the exchange model because the production changes do not affect real incomes. Now e is defined as:

$$e \equiv \frac{(1/p)}{X} \cdot \frac{dX}{d(1/p)},$$

where X is the volume of exports $(x_C - D_C)$, and by definition D_C is assumed constant in computing the elasticity of export supply. Because $(1/p)$ is just $-\hat{p}$, e is equivalently given by

$$-\frac{p}{X}\frac{dx_C}{dp}.$$

In a balanced trade equilibrium,

$$X = pM,$$

and because $dx_C + p\,dx_F$ equals zero, dx_C is just $-p\,dx_F$. Therefore

$$e = \frac{p}{M} \frac{dx_F}{dp}.$$

Finally, notice that by definition,

$$\epsilon \equiv -\frac{\hat{M}}{\hat{p}} = -\frac{p}{M}\frac{dD_F}{dp} + \frac{p}{M}\frac{dx_F}{dp}.$$

This equation completes the proof of 6.S.1.

The rationale for decomposing ϵ as in equation 6.S.1 lies in the fact that the demand for imports reveals behavior of both consumers (their demand for the imported commodity) and producers (their production of the imported commodity). The reactions of consumers and producers to a change in the terms of trade depend on different considerations, and it is therefore useful to isolate each influence in the movement along the offer curve.

7 The Ricardian Trade Model

The possibility that the quantities of commodities that a country produces may respond to changes in market prices was suggested in Chapter 6 in an overview of the theory of trade with production. Now it is time to fill in some necessary details on the manner in which productive resources are converted into commodities. This chapter, and the following two chapters, deal intensively with highly simplified models of production. In particular, in this chapter we shall explore one of the earliest models of trade, associated with the work of David Ricardo.[1]

Ricardo is often credited with originating the doctrine of comparative advantage already encountered in our model of pure exchange (Chapter 2). There we showed that countries could mutually benefit from trade if the *relative* prices of commodities differed between countries in the absence of trade. Each country would gain by exporting the commodity that was valued relatively lower at home. Ricardo believed that relative prices would differ without trade because of their linkage to differing real costs of production. Essentially these were labor costs; hence he argued that each country would gain by exporting that commodity in which comparative (labor) *costs* were lower. With the details of the structure of production filled in, the doctrine of comparative advantage becomes the doctrine of comparative costs.

[1] David Ricardo. *The Principles of Political Economy and Taxation.* New York: Penguin, 1971, chap. 7.

7.1 THE RICARDIAN LABOR THEORY OF VALUE IN A CLOSED ECONOMY

In the simplest version of the Ricardian model commodities are exchanged for each other within a country according to the amounts of labor required to produce them. Labor is treated as the only factor of production requiring remuneration and it is assumed to be homogeneous in quality, so that wage rates in all occupations within the country are similar. Labor requirements per unit of output in the prevailing technology are assumed to be invariant with the scale of production. Let a_{LC} and a_{LF} represent these fixed labor-per-unit-of-output coefficients in the clothing and food industries in the home country. Then if, say, twice as many man-hours are needed to produce a unit of food as to produce a unit of clothing, the price of food must be double that of clothing. In general, the *relative* price of food, p_F/p_C, would equal a_{LF}/a_{LC}.

Constraints on the aggregate outputs of clothing and food are imposed by the size of the existing labor force (L) and the prevailing state of technical knowledge, as given by the a_{LC} and a_{LF} input-output coefficients. We shall assume that the size of the labor force is constant. In particular, we shall rule out either the possibility that labor can emigrate to, or immigrate from, abroad, or that the quantity of labor offered for hire varies with the wage rate. This latter proviso can easily be relaxed, but we shall simplify the following account by assuming that L is fixed. Furthermore, with prices flexible, we shall assume full employment of the given labor force. This finds explicit expression in equation 7.1:

$$a_{LC}x_C + a_{LF}x_F = L. \qquad (7.1)$$

Outputs of clothing and food are shown by x_C and x_F respectively. Therefore the sum of the two industries' total demand for labor is shown by the left-hand side of the equation.

The production possibilities for such an economy are shown in Figure 7.1. If all available labor is employed in the clothing industry, L/a_{LC} units of clothing can be produced. Alternatively, the maximum output of food is given by L/a_{LF}. The straight-line transformation schedule connecting these two endpoints has the equation 7.1. Its slope (or rather the negative of its slope) is a_{LC}/a_{LF}, and this constant equals the relative (or "comparative," or "opportunity") cost of obtaining a unit of clothing, expressed in terms of the quantity of food that must be sacrificed in shifting sufficient labor to yield an additional unit of clothing.

Two indifference curves, illustrating the taste patterns in the home country, are also shown in Figure 7.1. Point E is clearly the optimal consumption point for the home country (assuming it must rely on its own productive resources and cannot engage in trade). The slope of the indifference curve at E, which is also given by $-a_{LC}/a_{LF}$, indicates the relative price of clothing at this no-trade equilibrium point.

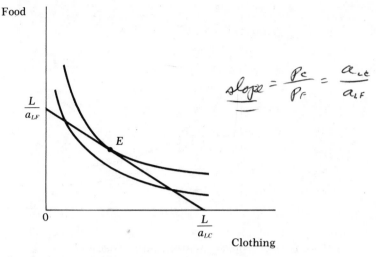

FIGURE 7.1   The Ricardian Transformation Schedule

> The home country's transformation schedule in the Ricardian
> model is the straight line through E. The opportunity cost of
> clothing is shown by the slope of the transformation schedule,
> and equals the ratio of labor coefficients, a_{LC}/a_{LF}.

It is useful to compare the determination of the Ricardian pretrade
equilibrium with that of the pure exchange model discussed in Chapter 2. Figure 7.2 facilitates such a comparison. The transformation
curve in the exchange model can be thought of as the right-angled
segment BEA in Figure 7.2, with the corner, E, representing the endowment bundle. The pretrade price ratio in the exchange model
does not reflect opportunity costs, but is shown by the slope of the
home country's indifference curve through point E. In a sense the
Ricardian straight-line transformation schedule and the exchange
model's right-angled curve represent polar opposites. The smoothly
bowed-out opportunity cost curve illustrated in Chapter 6 is an
intermediate case.

This comparison is also revealed in the difference between relative
supply and demand curves in the two cases. Recall our discussion
in Chapter 2 of the way in which the ratio of demands and supplies
depends upon the price ratio. Figure 7.3 illustrates the pretrade
equilibrium for the model of exchange. Quantities are given by the
endowment bundle. The relative demand curve then determines the
pretrade relative price of food, OA. By contrast, Figure 7.4 illustrates
the pretrade equilibrium in the Ricardian model. Only at the relative
price of food given by a_{LF}/a_{LC}, or OA in Figure 7.4, will both food and
clothing be produced. In the exchange model the supply curve is
vertical, and local demands determine the price ratio. In the Ricardian
model the supply curve is horizontal, and the pattern of demand

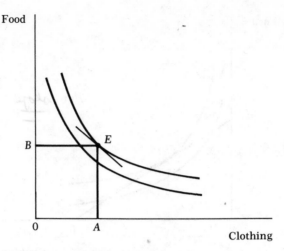

FIGURE 7.2   The Transformation Schedule
             for the Exchange Model

The home country's transformation schedule in the exchange
model (Part 1) is the right-angled broken line *BEA*, with point
E the endowment bundle. Pretrade price ratios are shown by
the slope of the indifference curve passing through *E*.

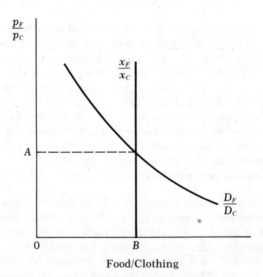

FIGURE 7.3   Relative Demands and Supplies
             in the Exchange Model

With endowments fixed, the pretrade price of food, *OA*, is
shown by the intersection of the relative demand curve with
the vertical relative supply curve.

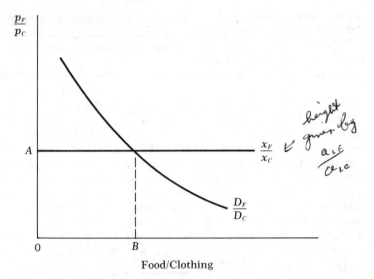

FIGURE 7.4   Relative Demands and Supplies
in the Ricardian Model

> The supply curve is horizontal, with height OA given by the
> ratio of labor costs, a_{LF}/a_{LC}. Demand determines pretrade
> quantities produced and consumed in equilibrium, in the
> ratio OB.

determines only the pretrade composition of outputs. Pretrade prices
depend only upon labor costs.

The hallmark of the labor theory of value for a closed economy is
the intimate connection between commodity prices and labor costs.
When the economy is opened up to trade, however, this view of the
determinants of prices will no longer be adequate.

7.2 THE PATTERN AND GAINS FROM TRADE IN A RICARDIAN MODEL

In a model of this simple character there are nevertheless several
ways in which the description of the foreign country's economy could
differ from that of the home country. First, the foreign country may
not be of the same size, in the sense of having the same quantity of
labor, L^*, available for employment. As we shall see, this difference
will not affect the pattern of trade in a free trade equilibrium. Secondly, tastes may not be the same. Again, in the Ricardian model
this difference does not affect the pattern of trade, in sharp contrast
to the model of pure exchange studied in Chapter 2. There we saw
that the pattern of trade depended both on endowment differences
and taste differences between countries. Finally, the technological

relationship between labor and outputs may differ between countries. For the Ricardian model this difference is crucial, and is not only a matter of more efficient techniques in one country; it also may reflect a better trained labor force.

Suppose, initially, that each country has the same labor coefficient for the production of a given commodity. Food and clothing exhibit the same technology abroad and at home. The transformation schedule for the foreign country would look much like that which was portrayed for the home country in Figure 7.1. The position of the transformation schedule would depend on the country's size, as measured by L^*, but the slope for both countries would be the same. Furthermore, as long as each country consumes some of each commodity, tastes can differ between countries in any manner, and relative commodity price ratios would still be identical between countries before trade is opened up. And, as we discussed in Chapter 2, neither party gains from trading unless pretrade price ratios between countries differ. Thus in order to explain the presence of trade in the Ricardian model, we must assume that technologies differ between countries.[2]

But what if the home country, say, has uniformly superior technology in both commodities? If the home country's labor force can produce a unit of output of either commodity with ten percent fewer man-hours than would be required abroad, pretrade commodity price ratios would still be identical between countries. In Figure 7.1 a ten percent reduction in both a_{LC} and a_{LF} would shift the transformation schedule uniformly outward by ten percent — an effect equivalent to having a ten percent larger work force. Thus no trade would be induced even though technologies differ.

Ricardo assumed, and we shall maintain this assumption for at least the next few chapters, that whereas commodities may be traded internationally, factors of production such as labor cannot cross territorial borders. This, of course, is a starkly unrealistic assumption. However, the view that factor (e.g., labor) mobility is much greater within a country than between countries is expressed in the double-edged mobility assumptions of this model: within countries labor is not impeded from moving from region to region or industry to industry. This mobility supports the assumption of a common internal wage rate. Between countries labor refuses to move or is prevented from moving, even if wage rates differ internationally. For this reason price ratios between commodities that are internationally traded cannot be simply explained by the labor theory of value. As will be shown, this explanation would entail comparing home man-hours with foreign man-hours, and if wage rates differ such a comparison would not indicate price ratios.

[2] This assumption should be borne in mind in considering the Heckscher-Ohlin model in the next two chapters where we shall assume that technology is identical in the two countries, and that the rationale for trade is in ingredients not present in the Ricardian model.

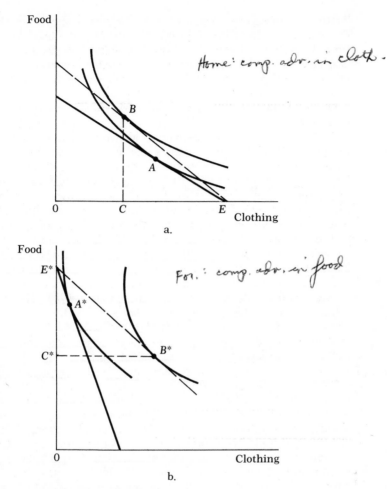

a.

b.

FIGURE 7.5   Free Trade Equilibrium

> Pretrade equilibrium at home is shown by point A in the
> upper diagram; abroad it is shown by A^* in the lower diagram.
> Equilibrium terms of trade are illustrated by the slope of the
> dashed line for each country. The home country produces at
> E and consumes at B; the foreign country produces at E^* and
> consumes at B^*.

Let us assume that technologies differ between countries, but not
uniformly, so that, say, the labor cost of producing clothing (relative
to the man-hours required per unit of food production) is lower in
the home country than abroad. That is, assume the inequality shown
in 7.2:

$$\frac{a_{LC}}{a_{LF}} < \frac{a_{LC}^*}{a_{LF}^*}. \tag{7.2}$$

With reference to the transformation schedule shown in Figure 7.1, this inequality implies a flatter schedule for the home country than for the foreign country and a lower pretrade relative price for clothing. The assumed technological difference between the two countries shown by the inequality 7.2 is a statement of the home country's comparative advantage in producing clothing. With trade opened up between countries, the home country must export clothing and import food.

Free trade equilibrium between the two countries is illustrated in Figure 7.5. The argument is the same as that sketched in Chapter 6, except that now each country's production-possibilities schedule is linear. This linear schedule has severe consequences for the pattern of production. The dashed lines in Figure 7.5 have the same slope, indicating the world free trade relative price of clothing. That this world price ratio clears markets is shown by the equality of the home country's exports of clothing, CE, and the foreign country's imports of clothing, C^*B^*. Similarly, food imports of BC in the home country equal the foreign country's exports of E^*C^*. The analysis is exactly equivalent to that given in the model of pure exchange in Chapter 2 *if* the (commodity) endowment points are E and E^*. This Ricardian solution is special because in each country all (labor) resources are drawn into production of the export commodity. That is, with free trade each country specializes *completely* in the commodity in which it has a comparative advantage, and that commodity is selected solely by reference to relative (and invariant) labor cost ratios. That each country gains from trade is obvious by inspection of Figure 7.5. The level of real income for the home (foreign) country at point B (B^*) is higher than in isolation at A (A^*). The argument is familiar from earlier chapters. A country gains from trade if it is offered different terms of trade from those prevailing at home in isolation. And, as we discussed in Chapter 6 (see Figure 6.6), the gains from trade when resources can shift into the commodity in which that country possesses a comparative advantage are greater than in the exchange model.

7.3 THE EFFECT OF SIZE

We previously suggested that the size of the home country compared to the foreign country was unimportant. For determining the composition of exports and imports this suggestion is correct. The trade pattern depends only upon the comparison of the relative labor coefficients in the two countries. But comparative size does influence the value of the equilibrium terms of trade. In fact, if one country is much larger than the other, the type of equilibrium situation portrayed in Figure 7.5, namely a free trade price ratio lying strictly between the cost ratios in each country, may need to be altered. The equilibrium terms of trade may be identical to those originally prevailing in the large country, implying that the large country does not gain by engaging in free trade!

To see how this phenomenon may occur, consider again the situation in Figure 7.5. In isolation the home country consumes the bundle shown by point A. At any world relative price for food lower than the price ratio shown along the transformation schedule, the home country would concentrate its resources exclusively on clothing and rely entirely on imports to satisfy its demand for food. Furthermore, because food would, in such a case, be cheaper in world markets than initially at home, and because real income at home would rise (e.g., the dashed budget line in Figure 7.5 is superior to the transformation curve), substitution and income effects would both conspire to increase the home country's demand for food over the amount shown at A. But if the foreign country is, by comparison, small, it may be incapable of supplying all of the home country's demand for food. This incapability would occur if OE^* in Figure 7.5 fell short of the home country's pretrade demand for food. But even if that is not the case, the foreign country may be unwilling to export such a large quantity of food; at any terms of trade the foreign country's desired exports of food equal its production minus its own demand for food. And its desired exports may not satisfy the home country's demand for food. The only way out of this impasse is for world prices to settle at a level that will allow some home production of food to augment the quantity imported. The world price ratio must settle at the ratio of labor costs for the two

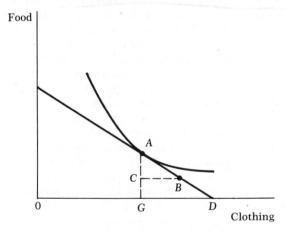

FIGURE 7.6   Trade Equilibrium at Home Country Prices

If the home country is relatively large, the equilibrium terms of trade may settle at the home country's cost ratio. If at these prices the foreign country exports AC units of clothing, home production moves to point B and consumption remains at the pretrade point, A. Specialization in clothing production is incomplete.

commodities in the home country and the home country will not gain from trade.

This situation is shown in Figure 7.6. In the pretrade state the home country consumes and produces at point A. Suppose that at these prices the foreign country would be willing to export AC of food to the home country, but no more. Then world prices must reflect the cost ratio between commodities in the home country, and with trade its consumption remains at A and production shifts to point B. The home country does not become completely specialized in its export commodity, although it does shift some of its resources in that direction.[3] This situation could alternatively be shown by the offer curves of the two countries.

7.4 OFFER CURVES FOR THE RICARDIAN MODEL

Geometrically, the striking feature of the Ricardian model is its linear transformation curve. Offer curves combine information about demand and production because they express net demands and supplies of imports and exports. It should not be surprising, therefore, to find that the offer curves for the Ricardian case consist partly of linear segments, in contrast to the offer curves drawn for the exchange model or for the model in Chapter 6 in which production exhibits increasing opportunity costs.

The linear segments in Figure 7.7 reflect for each country the relative labor costs of producing each commodity; OH for the home country has slope $-a_{LC}/a_{LF}$ and OF for the foreign country has slope $-a_{LC}^*/a_{LF}^*$. Concentrate for the moment on the behavior of import demands for terms of trade strictly between these cost ratios. For such prices we have shown that the home country devotes all its labor resources to the production of clothing and the foreign country to the production of food. Thus for terms of trade in this range the analysis proceeds exactly as in the case of fixed commodity endowments in Chapter 2, with the further simplification that each country is "endowed" (by virtue of the resource response to world prices) with only one commodity. For the foreign country the stretch BQR^* and for the home country AQR therefore possess the characteristics described for the exchange model. As shown in Figure 7.7, the free trade equilibrium price ratio is given by the slope of line 1, with the home country exporting OG units of clothing in exchange for the equivalent value of OJ imports of food.

The significance of the linear segments is brought out by the case

[3] This possibility, that the equilibrium world terms of trade coincide with the pretrade ratio of one of the trading countries, is repeatedly suggested in the writings of Frank Graham. For example, see his *Theory of International Values* (Princeton: Princeton University Press, 1948). His argument was usually centered on the case of many countries. He criticized the "classical" view that the terms of trade would not correspond to the internal cost ratio in any country, a situation that he described as leading to a "limbo" terms of trade.

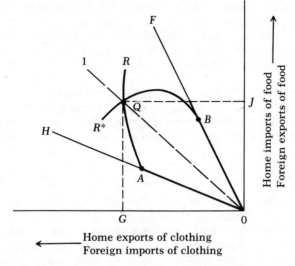

FIGURE 7.7   Offer Curves in the Ricardian Model

Each country's offer curve consists of a linear segment (*OA* for the home country and *OB* abroad) along which specialization in production is incomplete and a curved section (*AR* at home, *BR** abroad) along which specialization is complete.

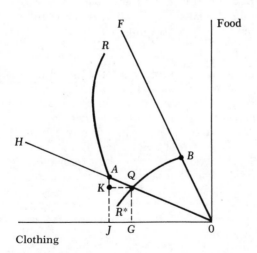

FIGURE 7.8   Free Trade with Incomplete Specialization

The foreign country's offer curve, *OBQR**, intersects the home country's offer curve, *OQAR*, at *Q*, with terms of trade the same as the cost ratio at home. The home country consumes *AJ* units of food, obtaining *KJ* as imports and producing the remainder, *AK*, at home.

in which the home country is substantially larger than the foreign country and, as a consequence, the equilibrium terms of trade settle at the ratio of labor costs in the home country. Figure 7.8 provides an illustration. The free trade equilibrium is at Q, and the home country exports OG units of clothing in exchange for QG units of food. But demand for food in the home country is greater than this, AJ. Therefore the difference, AK, must be provided at home. With the terms of trade shown by line OH, the home country channels some, but not all, of its labor resources into clothing, the remaining labor producing food.

7.5 WAGE RATES AND THE FACTORAL TERMS OF TRADE

So far little has been said about the determination of wage rates, either in the pretrade closed economy, or in the free trade open economy. With trade, food and clothing are shipped between countries and the same price must be paid for either commodity at home and abroad. The relative price of food, p_F/p_C, has been referred to as the terms of trade. More accurately we should call it the *commodity terms of trade*, in order to distinguish it from another ratio of prices — the ratio of wage rates in the two countries. This ratio is known as the *factoral* terms of trade. The nomenclature may seem odd, for by assumption labor cannot cross the frontier in response to more attractive employment opportunities abroad. Nonetheless, it is instructive to see the effect, in this Ricardian model, of the free exchange of commodities on the position of labor at home in comparison with workers abroad. With labor the only paid factor of production in either country, the factoral terms of trade reflect the distribution of gains from trade between countries.

In any economy wage rates are closely linked to productivity. This relationship is exact in a model in which we assume that competition exists. Begin the argument by considering the general relationship between costs and prices in the home country. In a competitive equilibrium the unit costs of producing any commodity cannot fall short of that commodity's market price. The reason is simple: if unit costs in food production, say, were less than the price of food, the consequent profits would signal new entrants into the food industry. By enlarging food output, we would drive down the price of food; increasing the demand for labor would cause the wage rate to be bid up. This process, whereby new firms are attracted to the food industry, would continue until unit costs are raised enough to equal price. Unit costs can, however, exceed price, even in a competitive equilibrium. You may wonder what entrepreneur in his right mind would continue producing food if it is priced lower than the labor costs of production. In our competitive model the answer is "none." Therefore local food production would be zero. For an economy engaged in trade food can be obtained from abroad instead of being produced at home. Indeed, in many of our illustrations in this chapter world

terms of trade were established at which the home country produced
no food and the foreign country no clothing.

When speaking of "prices" we have most often had in mind "relative price" — the quantity of one commodity that must be given up in
exchange for one unit of the other. In analyzing production and factor
returns it is frequently more convenient to refer to absolute prices,
as if there were a common unit of account or money. For example,
we shall refer to the wage rate at home as w, and by this mean dollars, say, per man-hour. An expression like w/p_F would get rid of the
nominal currency unit of account and denote food units per man-hour.
With this in mind consider the *competitive profit conditions* shown
in equations 7.3 and 7.4:

$$a_{LC}w \geqq p_C \qquad\qquad (7.3)$$

$$a_{LF}w \geqq p_F. \qquad\qquad (7.4)$$

These equations state formally our argument in the preceding paragraph. A competitive equilibrium must be characterized by an equality between unit cost and price if production is carried on. Unit cost
can never be less than price in a competitive equilibrium. Unit costs
may exceed price, but only if all producers leave the industry. A
similar set of conditions would, of course, apply to the foreign country, except that wage rates abroad, denoted by w^*, need not be the
same as at home, although with trade the price of either commodity
will be identical in the two countries.

Labor's physical "productivity" is measured in each industry by the
inverse of the labor coefficient. For example, $1/a_{LC}$ is the number of
units of clothing that can be produced with an input of one man-
hour.[4] If this is multiplied by the price of clothing, to obtain $p_C \cdot 1/a_{LC}$,
a measure is derived of the "value" of labor's productivity in clothing.
Thus equations 7.3 and 7.4 can be reinterpreted as saying that the
wage rate must equal the value of labor's productivity in any industry
in which labor is employed, and be equal to or exceed the value of its
productivity in any industry that must shut down.

These remarks suggest that wage rates are linked both to commodity prices and to physical productivities. Therefore a comparison
between home and foreign wage rates must as well involve a comparison in labor productivities in the two countries and the commodity
terms of trade. Suppose a free trade equilibrium is attained at terms
of trade lying strictly between the cost ratios of the two countries so
that the home country specializes in clothing production and the foreign country in food. Then at home,

$$a_{LC}w = p_C,$$

while abroad,

$$a_{LF}^*w^* = p_F.$$

---

[4] Because the input coefficients, a_{LC} and a_{LF}, are assumed to be constant,
$(1/a_{LC})$ denotes both labor's "average product" and "marginal product."

Dividing these two we obtain equation 7.5:

$$\frac{w}{w^*} = \frac{(1/a_{LC})}{(1/a_{LF}^*)} \cdot \frac{p_C}{p_F}.$$ (7.5)

The ratio of wage rates, w/w^*, is the factoral terms of trade. The ratio of commodity prices, p_C/p_F, is the commodity terms of trade (expressed now as the relative price of the home country's export commodity, clothing). Equation 7.5 suggests that an improvement in the home country's terms of trade (an increase in p_C/p_F) must raise the wage rate at home relative to the wage rate abroad by a factor of proportionality given by the ratio of home to foreign labor productivities in the commodities in which labor is employed.

This relationship between the factoral terms of trade and the commodity terms of trade is illustrated by the upward sloping portion of the locus drawn in Figure 7.9. It only holds for commodity terms of trade that lead the home country to produce clothing and the foreign country to produce food:

$$\frac{a_{LC}}{a_{LF}} \leqq \frac{p_C}{p_F} \leqq \frac{a_{LC}^*}{a_{LF}^*}.$$

Two horizontal stretches have been drawn as well, and these indicate

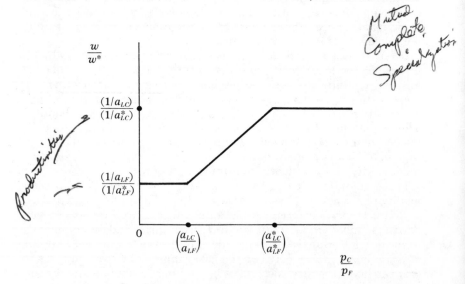

FIGURE 7.9   The Factoral Terms of Trade

The ratio of home to foreign wage rates must lie between the bounds set by the comparison between home and foreign labor productivity in food and the ratio of productivities in clothing. If the home country specializes in clothing and the foreign country in food, an improvement in the home country's commodity terms of trade must directly improve the home country's factoral terms of trade.

that if the commodity terms of trade force both countries to produce the same commodity, the ratio of their wage rates will be given by the ratio of their labor productivities in that same commodity. For example, in Figure 7.8 the relative price of clothing on world markets settled at the cost ratio in the home country, a_{LC}/a_{LF}. With equilibrium at point Q in Figure 7.8 the home country was forced to devote some of its own labor to food production, so that

$$a_{LF}w = p_F.$$

The foreign country, of course, was specialized to food production, so that

$$a_{LF}^* w^* = p_F.$$

Dividing these two yields:

$$\frac{w}{w^*} = \frac{(1/a_{LF})}{(1/a_{LF}^*)},$$

which is the ratio of the productivity of home labor in the food industry to foreign labor in the food industry. Any higher relative price of food (or lower p_C/p_F) would find both countries specialized in food production and thus the same relationship holding between wage rates.[5]

Are wages at home higher or lower than abroad? This question points to the major advance which David Ricardo made in extending the analysis of earlier writers. It had long been conceded (e.g., by Adam Smith) that if each country had an *absolute advantage* in the production of a commodity, both countries should specialize and exchange. Absolute advantage entails a direct comparison of the absolute man-hours required per unit of output in the two countries. Thus suppose a_{LC} is less than a_{LC}^*. Then the home country is said to possess an absolute advantage in clothing production. If, in addition, a_{LF}^* should be less than a_{LF}, the foreign country would have an absolute advantage in food production. In such a case arguing that the foreign country should stick to what it does best, i.e., produce food, and leave all clothing production to the home country seemed reasonable. One of Ricardo's outstanding achievements was showing that even if one country has an absolute advantage in *both* commodities, that country should still concentrate its resources in the commodity in which its absolute advantage is relatively superior — i.e., in which it has a *comparative* advantage. It should rely on the other country to supply its needs of the other good. Of course we need not prove Ricardo's assertion here — that has already been done. The argument for the gains from trade and the pattern of trade has never had

---

[5] Of course such a high relative price for food would entail no clothing being produced anywhere, and thus is unrealistic. However, the horizontal stretches in Figure 7.9 do indicate the bounds within which the factoral terms of trade must lie.

recourse to comparing direct labor costs in a single industry — e.g., a_{LC} and a^*_{LC}.

Suppose the foreign country possesses an absolute advantage in *both* commodities. Trade, along the lines of comparative advantage, is still mutually profitable. Figure 7.9 can be used to reveal that w/w^* must, in this case, fall below unity, whatever the commodity terms of trade. The home wage rate, w, relative to the foreign, w^*, can never exceed the home superiority in the commodity in which the home country has a comparative advantage. Thus technical superiority of one country's labor in all lines does not preclude mutually gainful trade, it instead guarantees a higher wage rate to the more efficient labor.

7.6 THE RICARDIAN MODEL AND WORLD GAINS FROM TRADE

We have often demonstrated in the preceding pages that each country gains from trade, at least if the free trade price ratio differs from that prevailing before trade. Therefore the world as a whole must gain. To conclude this chapter's treatment of the Ricardian model we shall present a simple diagram to illustrate the potential gains from trade from a world point of view.

The concept of a transformation schedule, or production-possibilities schedule, is familiar as applied to an individual country. What we propose here is somehow to *add* the two countries' transformation curves to show the production possibilities with free trade for the world as a whole. This is shown by the solid broken line in Figure 7.10, *ABC*, with the stretch *AB* depicting the home country's transformation schedule and *BC* showing the foreign country's transformation schedule. To trace out the world production-possibilities locus consider all conceivable world terms of trade. For very high food prices, both countries would specialize in food. Thus *OA* in Figure 7.10 is the sum of the two countries' vertical intercepts in Figure 7.5. As p_F/p_C is reduced, it eventually reaches the home country's cost ratio, given by a_{LF}/a_{LC}. For such a price ratio the foreign country must remain specialized in food, but the home country can produce anywhere along its own transformation schedule. In Figure 7.10 point *B* represents the world output combination when the home country specializes in clothing and the foreign country in food. World production would be fixed at point *B* for any lower values for p_F/p_C until this price ratio reaches the cost ratio for the foreign country, a^*_{LF}/a^*_{LC}. At such a price ratio the foreign country can commence production of clothing. The distance *OC* in Figure 7.10 corresponds to maximal world production of clothing.

From the world point of view, schedule *ABC* in Figure 7.10 represents the best locus of production that can be obtained. What is the worst? Clearly if unemployment is allowed in each country, or if the best techniques available for production in each country are ignored,

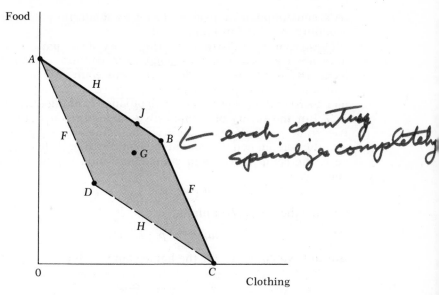

FIGURE 7.10 The World Transformation Schedule

The locus *AJBC* shows the maximal world outputs of food and clothing that can be obtained with free trade. With no trade allowed, world outputs would lie somewhere in the shaded area.

any point within *OABC* is possible. But suppose production in each country is constrained to lie on that country's transformation schedule. From the world point of view the worst pattern of production would assign the foreign country production of clothing, in which it has a comparative *dis*advantage, before the home country is allowed to produce any. Thus the dashed curve *ADC* in Figure 7.10 shows the inner locus of possible world production. For example, at point *D* the home country specializes in food and the foreign country in clothing. In general, the requirement that each country fully utilizes its resources given its own technology only ensures that world production lies somewhere in the shaded area in Figure 7.10. The discipline of free trade ensures that world production lies on the outer locus *ABC*. By contrast, if no trade took place and each country produced at *A* and *A** in isolation in Figure 7.5, world production would be shown by an interior point, *G*, in Figure 7.10.

Point *B* in Figure 7.10 shows world output when each country specializes completely in producing the commodity in which it has a comparative advantage. Point *B* will in fact represent production if demand conditions yield a free trade equilibrium price ratio strictly between the cost ratios in each country, e.g., line 1 in Figure 7.7. But this need not be the outcome. In Figure 7.8 the world terms of trade settled at the home country's cost ratio and part of the home country's consumption of food was met by domestic production, corresponding to point J in Figure 7.10.

These remarks illustrate that the theory of comparative advantage does not necessarily tell us what each country *will* produce. The locus *ABC* in Figure 7.10 allows the home country to produce food, in which it has a comparative disadvantage (e.g., at point J, or anywhere along *AB*) or the foreign country to produce clothing (anywhere along *BC*). But the theory of comparative advantage *does* state that with free trade you will never observe the home country producing food *and* the foreign country producing clothing. For if this were to be the case, the competitive profit conditions would involve, for the home country,

$$a_{LF}w = p_F; \ a_{LC}w \geqq p_C,$$

and, for the foreign country,

$$a_{LC}^*w^* = p_C; \ a_{LF}^*w^* \geqq p_F.$$

But this would imply, for the home country, that

$$\frac{a_{LC}}{a_{LF}} \geqq \frac{p_C}{p_F},$$

and, for the foreign country, that

$$\frac{a_{LC}^*}{a_{LF}^*} \leqq \frac{p_C}{p_F}.$$

These conditions violate the assumption made in inequality 7.2 that the home country has a comparative advantage in producing clothing. Free trade thus rules out any combination of both countries' producing the commodity in which they have a comparative *disadvantage* and therefore any point in Figure 7.10's shaded area.[6] Comparative advantage picks out the best locus of world outputs. Demand conditions then choose from among these the actual pattern of production.

7.7 SUMMARY

The Ricardian model is both the oldest and simplest model of trade in which the details of production are fully incorporated. It is typically the first model presented in a trade course to introduce the gains from trade, the pattern of trade, and other features of a free trade equilibrium. In this book we have instead introduced these concepts in a model of pure commodity exchange in Part 1, because the Ricardian

[6] For extensions of this argument, see R. W. Jones, "Comparative Advantage and the Theory of Tariffs: A Multi-Country, Multi-Commodity Model," *Review of Economic Studies*, 28 (June 1961): 161–175. In this article it is shown that condition 7.2, which can be rewritten as $a_{LC}a_{LF}^* < a_{LC}^*a_{LF}$, can be generalized to yield the optimal comparative advantage assignment of commodities to countries as that which *minimizes* the product of the labor coefficients.

very Imp.

model has some special features that will not carry through in our more general treatment of trade models with production in Chapters 8 and 9. We list these briefly in order to summarize this chapter.

1. The pattern of trade is dictated solely by the "supply side." In particular, the home country must export clothing and import food if the invariant labor productivity in clothing in the home country is relatively higher than abroad. This assumption was embodied in inequality 7.2. In more general models (including the exchange model) both supply and demand differences contribute to the relationship between pretrade commodity price ratios in the two countries and therefore to the pattern of trade.

Ricardian Model

Assump.

2. If the world terms of trade lie strictly between the cost ratios in the two countries, each will specialize completely in the production of one commodity (clothing in the home country and food abroad). This severe shift of resources is not characteristic of the models of trade to be considered next, in which a country might engage in trade while supporting an import-competing industry.

3. The gains from trade might mistakenly be considered to hinge directly upon the transfer of (labor) resources into the commodity in which a country possesses a comparative advantage. This view is erroneous because it neglects the consumption gains derived from a country's ability to consume at *different* prices from those prevailing before trade. Thus even if labor were frozen in its pretrade occupations in the Ricardian model, trade would be beneficial. The movement of resources in response to different world prices is the source of *additional* (production) gains from trade. The exchange model was designed to establish this point.

4. The Ricardian model assumes a difference in the relative technology in one country and another. A more general view, as we shall see, explicitly incorporates the effect of nonlabor factors of production on labor productivities, costs, and the pattern of trade.

Assump.

SUGGESTIONS FOR FURTHER READING

Becker, Gary, "A Note on Multi-Country Trade," *American Economic Review*, 42 (September 1952): 558–568. Provides a geometrical technique for adding offer curves for several countries in a Ricardian model.

Elliott, George, "The Theory of International Values," *Journal of Political Economy*, 58 (February 1950): 16–29. Discusses the two country, many-commodity case.

Graham, Frank. *The Theory of International Values.* Princeton: Princeton University Press, 1948. Many numerical examples of the many-commodity Ricardian case.

Jones, Ronald W., "Comparative Advantage and the Theory of Tariffs: A Multi-Country, Multi-Commodity Model," *Review of Economic Studies,* 28 (June 1961): 161–175. The extension of Ricardian theory to higher dimensional cases.

Ricardo, David. *The Principles of Political Economy and Taxation.* New York: Penguin, 1971. Chapter 7 is the classic source, with the example of England and Portugal producing wine and cloth cited in most textbooks.

8 The Heckscher-Ohlin Model: A Preliminary View

In the history of economic doctrine the Ricardian model of trade, described in the preceding chapter, stood basically unchallenged until the advent of the "modern" theory of trade, in the first third of this century. The two prominent names associated with this new theory are both Swedish: Eli Heckscher and Bertil Ohlin.[1] Between the times of Ricardo and Heckscher and Ohlin much was done to extend and expand the basis for a trade model laid down by Ricardo. Indeed, much of the intervening work, developed especially by John Stuart Mill and Alfred Marshall, was concerned with such questions as the determination of the equilibrium terms of trade through offer curve analysis, which we developed separately in our treatment of the model of pure exchange in Part 1.[2]

The basic point of departure for the Heckscher-Ohlin theory is the inclusion of more than one factor of production in the relevant technology for each country. Once this is allowed it is possible to introduce a new way in which the basic setting in one country could differ from that in the other and thus to consider an alternative explanation for the pattern of trade. In the Ricardian model two countries could differ:

[1] E. Heckscher, "The Effect of Foreign Trade on the Distribution of Income," *Ekonomisk Tidskrift*, 21 (1919): 497–512; reprinted American Economic Association, *Readings in the Theory of International Trade*. Philadelphia: Blakiston, 1949, chap. 13. B. Ohlin. *Interregional and International Trade*. Cambridge: Harvard University Press, 1933.

[2] See especially J. S. Mill. *Principles of Political Economy with Some of Their Applications to Social Philosophy.* 1848. Alfred Marshall. *The Pure Theory of Foreign Trade.* 1879. Reprinted by London School of Economics and Political Science, 1930.

1. in technology,
2. in taste patterns, and
3. in the size of the productive labor forces.

As we discussed in Chapter 7, the difference between countries that was crucial in explaining the pattern of trade was the first, the difference in levels of technology. By adding more factors of production, the Heckscher-Ohlin model introduces the possibility of a fourth kind of difference, namely, that the proportions in which a country is endowed with its factors of production vary from country to country. The modern theory asserts that countries usually export those commodities that intensively use the particular factors of production found locally in relative abundance.

Our purpose in these next two chapters is to explore the implications of this fourth kind of difference. To highlight this new feature we shall assume that the basic technology available in each country is the same, thus obviating the one source of comparative advantage found in the Ricardian model. From the very outset this assumption sets the Heckscher-Ohlin model apart from the Ricardian model: it approaches reality by adding to the number of productive factors, but simplifies by neglecting differences in technological know-how. Each model thus becomes a vehicle for alternative, and separate, explanations of trading patterns. In Chapter 10 we shall test each prototype against observed real-world behavior.

Our discussion of the Heckscher-Ohlin model of trade is broken down into two chapters. The present chapter presents the Heckscher-Ohlin model with a strikingly simple assumption as to the nature of technology. Recall our discussion of the smoothly bowed-in isoquants in Chapter 6, embodying the assumption that the proportions in which capital and labor are combined in production can and will change if market conditions (factor prices) change. That is the kind of technology assumed in the general treatment of the modern theory we shall provide in Chapter 9. In our present treatment we assume that only one combination of capital and labor can be employed in a particular industry. This assumption is not only more simple, it corresponds as well to the Ricardian assumption of fixed labor coefficients.

8.1 THE RELATIONSHIP BETWEEN OUTPUTS AND FACTOR ENDOWMENTS

We shall start our exposition along the same lines as the Ricardian model. In particular, in Chapter 7 we showed that the size of the country's labor force, coupled with the given technology's fixed labor requirements per unit of each output, constrained the production possibilities for the economy to lie along a straight line — the transformation schedule shown in Figure 7.1. In this simplified Heckscher-Ohlin model labor is not the only productive agent whose supply is fixed for the economy. Let us assume there is another such factor — capital — in fixed supply and denoted by K. The description of the technology must now encompass not only the labor input-output coefficients but also the quantity of capital required in each industry to produce a unit of output, a_{KC} and a_{KF}.

The economy's aggregate demand for each factor of production, shown on the left side of inequalities 8.1 and 8.2, cannot exceed the total factor availabilities in a competitive equilibrium:

$$a_{LC}x_C + a_{LF}x_F \leq L \tag{8.1}$$

$$a_{KC}x_C + a_{KF}x_F \leq K. \tag{8.2}$$

As in the Ricardian case illustrated in Figure 7.1, the labor constraint defines a linear combination of outputs that will fully employ the available supply of labor. A combination of outputs below this line would leave some labor unemployed. The output combinations that use up all the available supply of capital also lie on a straight line. But would this line be steeper or flatter than the labor constraint? Its slope depends upon a simple characteristic of the home country's technology that we have yet to discuss — a comparison of the labor/capital ratios required in each industry. Let us assume that factor requirements differ from industry to industry, and that, for concreteness, clothing is labor-intensive. By labor-intensive we mean that the ratio of labor to capital employed in clothing exceeds the corresponding ratio in the food industry. Formally, we assume:

$$\frac{a_{LC}}{a_{KC}} > \frac{a_{LF}}{a_{KF}}. \tag{8.3}$$

With this assumption, we can see that the line showing the capital constraint in Figure 8.1 is flatter than the line showing the labor constraint. The algebraic manipulation is simple. But consider the economic meaning. The slope of each line shows the opportunity cost of obtaining another unit of clothing (in terms of the sacrifice of food) if the factor associated with that line were the only restriction on outputs. Thus in the Ricardian model the slope of the labor constraint was given by (minus) a_{LC}/a_{LF}. Because by assumption clothing is labor-intensive, the labor constraint must be relatively more binding upon the production of clothing than is the capital constraint. That is, if capital were the only scarce factor, expanding clothing production would be cheaper (in terms of foregone food production) than if labor were the only scarce factor.

The inner locus of the two lines in Figure 8.1 (shown by the shaded portions) is the home country's transformation schedule. From the vertical intercept to point A along this locus labor is not fully employed. Similarly, for outputs of clothing exceeding the level shown at A there is an excess supply of capital. The rigidity of the technology implies that only the output combination shown by A will fully utilize both factors of production. For this reason we had to include the inequality signs in expressions 8.1 and 8.2.

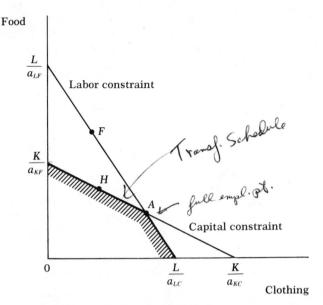

FIGURE 8.1 The Transformation Schedule
in a <u>Fixed-Coefficients</u> Heckscher-Ohlin Model

The transformation schedule is the heavy line formed by
the inner locus of the labor and capital constraints on output.
The line showing the labor constraint is steeper because it is
assumed that <u>clothing is labor-intensive</u> compared with food.

This diagram, and especially the combined full-employment point
shown by A in Figure 8.1, will be the focus of our attention in much of
what follows. But notice the hidden assumption embodied in the way
we have drawn this diagram. We have assumed that the relative
availability of the labor and capital endowments makes full employment of both factors technologically *possible*. That is, the lines
intersect (in the positive quadrant). Our assumption that the two
commodities require factors in different proportions (inequality
8.3) only tells us that these lines have different slopes. It does not
say anything about the intersection of these nonparallel lines. Thus
consider the situation shown by Figure 8.2. Here the economy possesses an absolute redundancy of capital. (For realistic examples it
would be better to think of a model in which land, instead of capital,
is the other factor of production.) The rental on capital goods must be
driven to zero, and the analysis of such a case proceeds *exactly* as
in our discussion of the Ricardian model in Chapter 7! If both goods
are produced, they are exchanged for each other in the ratio of their
labor contents.

Now consider a diagram in which factor supplies, instead of commodity outputs, are represented along the axes. In Figure 8.3 the

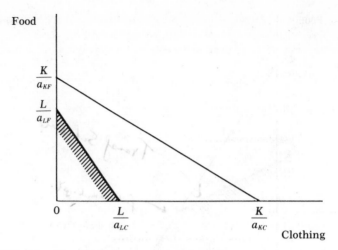

FIGURE 8.2   The Transformation Schedule
with Absolute Redundancy of Capital

> If capital is overly abundant relative to labor, the labor con-
> straint (heavy line) is the transformation schedule.

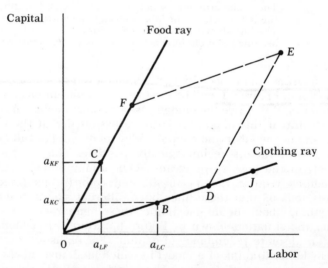

FIGURE 8.3   Factor Endowments Determine
Full-Employment Outputs

> If the capital-labor endowment point is shown by point E,
> only the combination of OD units of clothing and OF units
> of food can lead to full employment of both factors. These
> output levels correspond to point A in Figure 8.1.

horizontal axis measures labor units. Along this axis we have indicated the values for the labor input coefficients per unit of clothing, a_{LC}, and for food, a_{LF}. Similarly, along the vertical axis, which measures capital units, we have shown the capital/output figures, a_{KC} and a_{KF}. Thus point *B* shows the labor and capital required to produce one unit of clothing. Because the input-output coefficients are fixed, technology exhibits *constant returns to scale,* and by this we mean that if all inputs into any industry are increased in the same proportion, output of that industry will rise by the same proportion. For example, the point on the clothing ray that is twice as far from the origin as *B* (point *J*) represents two units of output of clothing. With this in mind we can easily see that the clothing ray is a kind of ruler along which values of clothing production can be read. Similar remarks, of course, can be made about the food ray. The crucial assumption about technology is embodied in inequality 8.3 — clothing is labor-intensive. This makes the clothing ray flatter than the food ray in Figure 8.3.[3]

Suppose we know in advance that clothing production is shown by distance *OD* and food production by *OF* (approximately a value of $x_C = 1.6$ and $x_F = 1.8$). In each industry both labor and capital are required for such production, as shown by points *D* and *F*. The aggregate labor and capital demands of the economy are shown by point *E*, where *FE* is parallel to *OD* and *DE* is parallel to *OF*. Parallel in each case, and also equal. Thus to clothing's demand for factors, shown by *OD,* must be added food's demand for factors, shown by *OF*. But *OF* is equal in length and direction to *DE*, so that point *E* represents aggregate demands for labor and capital.

By this technique any output combination in Figure 8.3 can yield the required total factor demand. Now work this backward. Suppose the economy's *endowment* point is shown by point *E*. If both factors are to be fully employed, clothing output must be *OD* and food output *OF*. This output combination is the only one that will clear the factor markets. For example, suppose that clothing production were to be reduced along the clothing ray from *OD*. No conceivable expansion of food production could exactly absorb the resources released by this cutback in clothing, for clothing releases a greater quantity of labor per unit of capital than can be absorbed by the food industry.

Obviously Figure 8.3 is linked directly to Figure 8.1. Point *A* in Figure 8.1 shows the only combination of outputs at which both factors are fully employed. If the (L,K) endowment bundle underlying the transformation schedule in Figure 8.1 corresponds to *E* in

---

[3] No significance should be attached to Figure 8.3's depiction of a_{LC} exceeding a_{LF} or a_{KF} exceeding a_{KC}. Either of these relationships could be altered by an appropriate redefinition of the units in which clothing is measured (e.g., going from single units to dozens). But such change of units cannot alter the fact that the capital/labor *ratio* in food is greater than in clothing.

Figure 8.3, then the outputs OD of clothing and OF of food in Figure 8.3 correspond to the coordinates of point A in Figure 8.1.

8.2 COMPARATIVE ADVANTAGE AND THE HECKSCHER-OHLIN THEOREM

In pursuing our discussion let us assume, unless otherwise indicated, that each country can technologically achieve full employment of both factors. Alternatively phrased, the capital/labor endowment ratio exceeds the capital/labor requirements in clothing and falls short of the fixed capital/labor ratio utilized in food. Thus the transformation schedule is given by the shaded line in Figure 8.1 instead of Figure 8.2. For the home country it is redrawn in Figure 8.4.

The pretrade equilibrium is shown by a point where an indifference curve for the home country is tangent to the transformation schedule. The word "tangent" is perhaps ill-advised, for, as Figure 8.4 illustrates, the highest indifference curve attainable without trade in the home country may be at the (interior) corner of the transformation schedule. In such a case both factors are fully employed, outputs and consumption are shown by point A in Figure 8.4, and the pretrade price ratio is shown by the slope of the indifference curve at A. Indeed, the situation is reminiscent of the pretrade solution for an exchange model, with its right-angled transformation curve.

With trade, the production pattern need no longer correspond to point A. If p, the relative price of food, is very low (represented by a

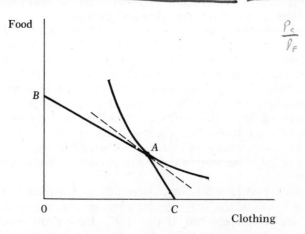

FIGURE 8.4   The Home Country's Transformation Schedule

> The pretrade equilibrium at home is at point A, the point along the BAC transformation schedule where the greatest real income is attained. The pretrade relative price of clothing is shown by the dotted line tangent to the indifference curve at A.

price line steeper than *AC* in Figure 8.4), the home country would devote its resources only to clothing production, at point *C*. (Of course some capital would therefore be underutilized, but the value of national income would be higher than at the full-employment point, *A*.) If the price corresponds to the slope of *AC*, production could take place anywhere along *AC*. For price ratios between the slopes of *AC* and *BA*, production remains frozen at *A*. As *p* rises to the level shown by the slope of *BA*, production is once again indeterminate between *B* and *A*. Any higher relative price of food would drive the home country to specialize completely in food production (at *B*).

The price-output response just described is depicted by the stepped supply function in Figure 8.5. The two crucial values for p_F/p_C correspond to the ratio of labor coefficients used in the two industries (as shown by the inverse of the slope of *AC* in Figure 8.4) and the ratio of the capital coefficients (the inverse of the slope of *BA* in Figure 8.4). Between these two points *p* is in the range where production remains fixed at *A* in Figure 8.4. Notice what a blend this simple Heckscher-Ohlin model is of the exchange model with its vertical supply curve and the Ricardian model that exhibits a horizontal relative supply curve.

Figure 8.4 illustrates a pretrade equilibrium for the home country at the corner-point, *A*. This is consistent with Figure 8.5, which portrays the demand curve (the locus of relative demands, D_F/D_C) intersecting the supply curve at a point on the vertical rise of the step function. Thus *OH* in Figure 8.5 represents the home country's pretrade relative price for food.

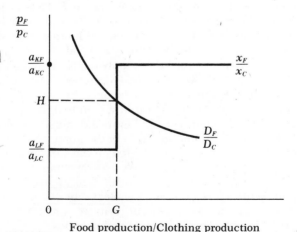

FIGURE 8.5   Relative Demands and Supplies in the Home Country

The relative supply curve is the broken step function, x_F/x_C. The pretrade relative price of food at home is *OH*, determined by the intersection of the relative demand and supply curves.

Suppose the foreign country is more *capital-abundant* than the home country. Because scale by itself does not matter, clearly what we mean by capital abundance involves comparing the relative capital/labor endowment ratios in the two countries. Formally, our assumption about the two countries' mix of endowments is given by inequality 8.4:

$$\frac{L}{K} > \frac{L^*}{K^*}, \tag{8.4}$$

which states that the home country is relatively labor-*abundant*. The inequality in 8.3 states that clothing is relatively labor-*intensive*. These concepts should not be confused. The latter is a statement about the technological difference between commodities; the former is a statement about factor endowment differences between countries. The consequence of such a difference in factor endowments for the shape of the supply curve, and thus ultimately for pretrade price ratios and the pattern of trade, can most easily be seen by referring back to Figure 8.1. Because scale by itself is unimportant for this question, assume that the foreign country has the same size labor force as well as identical technology as the home country. Therefore its labor constraint line in the output space of Figure 8.1 would be identical to that of the home country. If the foreign country is capital-abundant, its capital constraint locus must lie further out from the origin (although maintaining the same slope) than the home country's capital line in Figure 8.1. This position implies that the intersection of these two lines for the foreign country would lie along the labor constraint line, northwest of A, e.g., at F. That is, its transformation curve, shown in Figure 8.6, would show at the point of the "kink" a greater output of food, the capital-intensive good, and a lower output of clothing, the labor-intensive good.

Translate this difference into the supply curve. With reference to Figure 8.5 the heights of the horizontal stretches must be the same for both countries, reflecting, as they do, only the technology shared by both countries. However, the point at which both factors are fully employed in the foreign country (F in Figure 8.6) must reflect a *higher* ratio of food to clothing production than in the home country. That is, the *length* of the lower horizontal stretch on the supply curve for the foreign country (Figure 8.7) must be greater than for the home country. Compare OG^* in Figure 8.7 with OG in Figure 8.5.

This conclusion is a basic one for the Heckscher-Ohlin model, and deserves to be rephrased in a general form. We have demonstrated that under the assumption of identical technologies

at any common price ratio consistent with full employment of both factors in both countries, the capital-abundant country must produce a relatively greater amount of the capital-intensive commodity than does the labor-abundant country.

(1)
H-O Thm.   (a) In terms of Factor Constraints
            (b) In "   " D+S (Relative Curves)

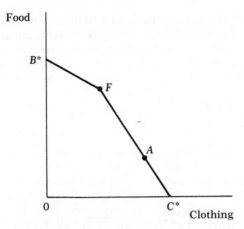

FIGURE 8.6   The Foreign Country's Transformation Schedule

The broken line, B^*FC, is the foreign country's transformation schedule under the assumptions that technology is common between the two countries, the size of the labor force is identical, but the foreign country has a larger supply of capital. The home country's transformation curve has its kink at point A.

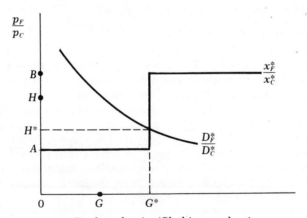

Food production/Clothing production

FIGURE 8.7   Relative Demands and Supplies in the Foreign Country

The vertical stretch of the relative supply curve in the foreign country lies further to the right than in the home country. Thus OG^* exceeds OG (which is the same as in Figure 8.5). If demands are similar in the two countries, the pretrade price of food abroad, OH^*, must be lower than at home (shown by OH, which is taken from Figure 8.5).

Notice furthermore that if demand patterns are identical between countries,[4] such a biased difference in the supply curves would imply that the foreign country has a lower pretrade price of food, relative to clothing, than does the home country. That is, OH^* in Figure 8.7 is lower than OH in Figure 8.5. In this instance the following statement, known as the _Heckscher-Ohlin theorem,_ would be satisfied:

> _The capital-abundant country has a comparative advantage in (and exports) the capital-intensive commodity._

We can easily see that the Heckscher-Ohlin theorem may not be satisfied if demand patterns differ between countries. If tastes in the capital-abundant country are sufficiently biased toward consumption of the capital-intensive commodity, its relative price before trade may be higher than in the labor-abundant country. This is an old phenomenon encountered in the exchange model in Chapter 2. In general, prices depend upon both demand and supply. The essence of the Heckscher-Ohlin theorem is its statement about the bias on the supply side imparted by differences in relative factor endowments. Trade patterns ultimately depend on the diversity between countries' taste patterns compared to the dissimilarity in countries' production structures — especially, in this case, in their factor endowments.

8.3 FACTOR PRICES AND COMMODITY PRICES: THE FACTOR PRICE EQUALIZATION THEOREM

In our discussion of the determinants of factor prices in the Ricardian model we already displayed in equations 7.3 and 7.4 the link between commodity prices and factor prices that is brought about by competition in the market. Each inequality in 7.3 and 7.4 refers to the balance, between unit cost and price, that must be struck in each industry in a competitive equilibrium. Price cannot settle at a level higher than unit costs, because new firms would then be attracted to the industry, pushing up costs and lowering price. These competitive profit relationships hold no matter how many factors are engaged in each industry. In particular, the inequalities shown by 8.5 and 8.6 are relevant to the Heckscher-Ohlin model:

$$\begin{cases} a_{LC}w + a_{KC}r \geqq p_C & (8.5) \\ a_{LF}w + a_{KF}r \geqq p_F. & (8.6) \end{cases}$$

The wage rate is denoted by w and the payment for the use of a unit of capital by r. Once again the equality sign must hold for any industry that actively produces in a competitive equilibrium. If unit costs exceed price, that industry must shut down.

In the Ricardian model we observed that in each country only one

[4] We assume, as well, that relative demands depend only upon relative prices.

FACTOR - PRICE EQUAL. THEOREM

terms of trade would allow both industries to operate — that price ratio that reflected the ratio of constant labor coefficients in the two commodities. Here this situation is less restricted. Consider Figures 8.5 and 8.7 (or, alternatively, 8.4 and 8.6). Notice that either country can be incompletely specialized (i.e., can produce both commodities) if the terms of trade lie between (or are equal to) the labor cost ratios (a_{LF}/a_{LC}) and the capital cost ratios (a_{KF}/a_{KC}), which by our assumption are identical between countries. From this we conclude that if some of both commodities are *consumed* in a free trade equilibrium, the terms of trade must lie in this range. Therefore in a free trade equilibrium an inequality can never be observed in 8.5 or 8.6.[5] Let us take advantage of this by rewriting these as equalities:

$$a_{LC}w + a_{KC}r = p_C \qquad (8.7)$$
$$a_{LF}w + a_{KF}r = p_F. \qquad (8.8)$$

In a Free Trade Equilibrium

Observe, further, that we need not have picked on the home country; exactly the same relationship must hold for the foreign country *in a free trade equilibrium:*

$$a_{LC}w^* + a_{KC}r^* = p_C \qquad (8.9)$$
$$a_{LF}w^* + a_{KF}r^* = p_F. \qquad (8.10)$$

The input-output coefficients, a_{ij}, are not starred because we have assumed identical techniques in use at home and abroad. And the p_j are not starred because we assume that commodities are freely traded between countries and that transport costs are negligible.

One of the most fundamental propositions in the Heckscher-Ohlin trade model becomes available to us when we compare the home country's competitive profit conditions, 8.7 and 8.8, and the foreign country's competitive profit conditions, 8.9 and 8.10:

> *If both countries have the same input-output coefficients, and if free trade forces both countries to face the same commodity prices, they must have the same wage rates and the same rentals on capital equipment.*

(2) FPE Thm.

This is the *factor price equalization theorem.* Should we find it surprising? There is no world market in labor and capital. By assumption no factor of production can cross national boundaries to compete directly with its counterpart in the other country. And we have assumed that countries differ in their natural endowments of labor and capital. We might reasonably presume (as we shall examine below) that in the labor-abundant country wages would be lower than in the capital-rich country. Assuming this presumption is true if no

---

[5] A warning is appropriate here. In the more general Heckscher-Ohlin model to be considered in Chapter 9, it *is* possible that with trade one industry will be forced to close down, because unit costs exceed price, despite the assumption of identical technologies in the two countries.

trade takes place, we may assert that free trade in commodities overwhelms such differences and indirectly ensures that the same factor of production earns the same return in either country, despite the presumed lack of direct competition. That is, establishing a common market in commodities ensures that factor prices are, through this indirect force, completely equated as between countries.

But perhaps we are getting ahead of the story. We have stated, but not proved, the factor price equalization theorem. Return to the competitive profit conditions, 8.7 and 8.8, for the home country, and notice the structural similarity between these conditions and the full-employment conditions shown in equations 8.1 and 8.2. Assuming both factors are fully employed, 8.1 and 8.2 state that the array of input-output coefficients, the a_{ij}, links the *physical* variables of the model — the output levels of clothing and food — to the factor endowments, labor and capital. Figure 8.3 was used to show that one endowment point (E) determines uniquely the composition of output (OD of clothing and OF of food), if industries differ in their capital/labor requirements. Similarly, 8.7 and 8.8 state that the array of input-output coefficients links the *financial* variables of the model — the factor returns, w and r — to the commodity prices, p_C and p_F.

This analogy is carried through in Figure 8.8, which relates financial variables in the same manner that Figure 8.3 relates the physical variables. The labor coefficients in the two industries are indicated by point B. If labor were the only cost involved in production, and if the wage rate were set at unity, the prices (equal to unit costs) of clothing

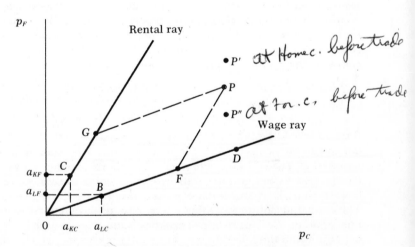

FIGURE 8.8   Commodity Prices Determine Factor Prices

If point P represents the common free trade prices of clothing and food in the two countries, wage rates are equalized at home and abroad at level OF and rentals on capital equipment are commonly given by OG.

and food would be shown by the coordinates of point *B*. If the wage rate were to be four times as large, so would both commodity prices, and this would be shown by the coordinates of point *D* (that is, $4a_{LC}$ for p_C and $4a_{LF}$ for p_F). In other words, using the distance *OB* as the unit indicator for wage rates, any point along the wage ray would indicate the labor costs of producing both commodities. Of course in this Heckscher-Ohlin model capital costs must be reckoned with as well. The rental ray is constructed in the same manner as the wage ray, with *OC* representing a level of $r = 1$. Thus if the wage rate and rental rate are known, both labor and capital costs per unit of output can be computed (along the *w* ray and *r* ray respectively). To find unit costs of production these must be added. Thus if the wage rate is given by *OF* (i.e., *w* equal to around $2\frac{1}{2}$) and the rental by *OG* (i.e., *r* equal to around 2), commodity prices are shown by the coordinates of point *P* since costs of production equal competitive prices. *OF* in labor costs are added to *FP* (equal to *OG*) in capital costs to obtain point *P*. The logic of the construction is identical with that used earlier to explain how each industry's demands for the two factors combine to yield total factor demands in Figure 8.3.

The factor price equalization theorem is derived from the observation that if commodity prices are given (say by point *P* in Figure 8.8), and techniques differ between industries (shown by the fact that the wage ray and rental ray have different slopes), there is a unique wage rate (*OF*) and rental on capital goods (*OG*) at which the competitive profit conditions are satisfied. Therefore if the foreign country has the same technology as the home country (i.e., the same wage ray and rental ray, with the same unit scale, given by the a_{ij}), and if there exists a free trade equilibrium in which commodity prices are equated between countries (i.e., *P* shows commodity prices both at home and abroad), the wage rate must be identical between countries, and so must the rental on capital. The fact that the capital/labor endowment ratios and/or taste patterns may differ as between countries has no bearing on this result.

Examine this latter statement more carefully by means of Figures 8.5 and 8.7. Although taste patterns were assumed there to be identical in the two countries, factor endowments were not, and this ensured that the relative price of the capital-intensive commodity (food) was lower before trade in the capital-abundant (foreign) country (i.e., *OH** in Figure 8.7 was lower than *OH* in Figure 8.5). The free trade price ratio, shown by the slope of *OP* in Figure 8.8, lies between *OH** and *OH*. Therefore before trade the point representing commodity prices at home lay above the ray *OP*, and the point representing commodity prices abroad would lie below ray *OP* in Figure 8.8. But these positions imply that before trade the wage/rent ratio at home must have been lower than the ratio prevailing abroad. This condition follows readily from Figure 8.8. For example suppose that the pretrade prices in the home country are represented by *P'* and in the foreign country by *P''* in Figure 8.8, where, for convenience, we have kept the price of clothing the same throughout. (Remember that without monetary variables introduced explicitly into the model, the theory deals only with relative prices.) Endowment differences cause differences in pretrade factor prices, but free trade in commodities wipes out any such differential.

The factor price equalization theorem is a strong result. Casual observation reveals that a factor of production such as labor does not earn the same return in the United States as it does in Japan or Brazil. Some economists have therefore rejected the Heckscher-Ohlin model. In Chapter 10 we shall discuss extensively tests of these models of trade, but a few remarks here may be appropriate. All economic models abstract from the complexity of the real world — abstraction is in the nature of theory. This chapter's preliminary version of the Heckscher-Ohlin model is especially simple: countries are assumed to differ only in their relative supplies of capital and labor. This difference tends to make the relative price of the capital-intensive commodity (food) relatively low before trade in the capital-abundant country (the foreign country in our example). But free trade in commodities wipes out this commodity price differential and, in this model, removes as well the bias that factor abundance imparts to factor prices. The assumption of identical productive techniques is obviously significant. Without it, no presumption of trade equalizing factor returns remains. Other complications could also disrupt the theorem: transport costs or tariffs may interfere with the equalization of commodity prices between countries; other factors of production may impart regional differences in basic factor productivities and market returns. Or, as we will demonstrate in Chapter 9, actual techniques (input-output coefficients) employed in the two countries may differ even though a general knowledge of technology is commonly shared. This difference as well will destroy the factor price equalization argument.

Some important propositions of the Heckscher-Ohlin model do *not* depend upon the assumption that technology is identical at home and abroad. We shall turn to these in the next section. But notice that to the extent that they are independent, one might reject the factor price equalization argument, which does assume identical technologies, without necessarily rejecting other characteristics of the Heckscher-Ohlin model that do not depend upon this assumption. This distinction is rarely remembered by economists anxious to attack the Heckscher-Ohlin model.

8.4 APPLICATIONS OF THE HECKSCHER-OHLIN FRAMEWORK TO A SINGLE COUNTRY: THE STOLPER-SAMUELSON THEOREM AND THE RYBCZYNSKI THEOREM

The graphical apparatus set up in Figures 8.3 and 8.8 is useful in showing the similarity of the relationship between factor endowments and commodity outputs on the one hand to that between commodity prices and factor prices on the other in this preliminary (fixed-coefficients) version of the Heckscher-Ohlin model. This *duality* feature, as it is sometimes called, can be probed more deeply in asking the following two questions concerning physical and financial variables in any one country:

1. If commodity prices change, how are factor prices affected?
2. If a country's factor endowment bundle grows, how are full-employment levels of output affected?

The Stolper-Samuelson Theorem[6]

An increase in the relative price of a commodity increases the real return to the factor used intensively in its production.

There is more to this proposition than may readily be apparent. If the price of clothing rises, and clothing is labor-intensive, the theorem states not only that the wage rate rises, it also asserts that wages rise by a proportionally *greater* extent than the price of clothing. Therefore a week's wages buy more clothing or more food than before: workers are better off in a *real* sense because wages rise more than any commodity price.

Figure 8.9 is designed to prove this result, and is merely a redrawing of the essential features of Figure 8.8. In the initial situation commodity prices at home are shown by the coordinates of point P. The wage rate is given by distance OF and the rental on capital by OG. Suppose the price of food remains constant but that the price of clothing rises, as shown by the move from P to P'. Because clothing is produced by more labor-intensive techniques than food, clothing costs (equal to price) can rise relative to food costs only by increasing wages (and reducing rents to keep the price of food from changing). Wages rise from OF to OH and rentals fall from OG to OI. But more can be said: the relative rise in wages is FH/OF, which obviously exceeds the percentage rise in the price of clothing, PP'/JP. By similar triangles, FH/OF equals LH/NL. But LH equals PP' and NL is less than JP. The proof is complete.

The Rybczynski Theorem

The result obtained by Rybczynski in 1955 points to the uneven effect of the growth in one factor on the composition of commodity outputs.[7]

[6] Wolfgang F. Stolper and Paul A. Samuelson, "Protection and Real Wages," *Review of Economic Studies*, 9 (November 1941): 58–73; reprinted American Economic Association, *Readings in the Theory of International Trade*. Philadelphia: Blakiston, 1949, chap. 15.
[7] T. M. Rybczynski, "Factor Endowments and Relative Commodity Prices," *Economica*, N.S. 22 (November 1955): 336–41. See also R. W. Jones, "Factor Proportions and the Heckscher-Ohlin Theorem," *Review of Economic Studies*, 24 (October 1956): 1–10. The graphical proofs used above are obtained from R. W. Jones, "Duality in International Trade: A Geometric Note," *Canadian Journal of Economics and Political Science*, 31 (August 1965): 390–93.

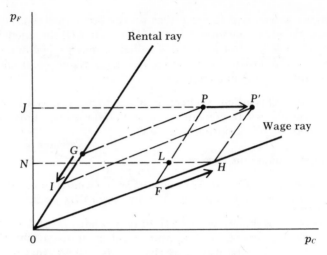

FIGURE 8.9 The Stolper-Samuelson Theorem

An increase in the price of labor-intensive clothing is illustrated by the move from P to P'. This move causes wages to rise from OF to OH and rents to fall from OG to OI. The relative rise in wages, shown by the ratio FH/OF, exceeds the relative rise in the price of clothing, PP'/JP.

In Figure 8.10 a country's labor force grows, with no balancing increase in its capital stock, by the movement from E to E'. In order to maintain full employment of both productive factors we must expand the output of the labor-intensive clothing industry from OD to OI. Indeed, the relative rise in the output of clothing, DI/OD, exceeds the relative rise in the labor force, EE'/JE. (DI/OD equals QI/NQ. QI equals EE' but NQ is less than JE.) Rybczynski cared more that although no factor supply has been reduced, one of the commodity outputs must decline. Alternatively stated,

An increase in the endowment of just one factor of production must cause the industry using the other factor intensively to decline.

The key to this result lies in the observation that with an expanded labor force and no change in techniques, the labor-intensive clothing industry can only expand if it obtains capital (and labor) from the other sector of the economy, because the overall supply of capital is unchanged. Thus food production must contract.

Both the Stolper-Samuelson and Rybczynski theorems are special cases of a general investigation of the effect of endowment changes on outputs and of commodity price changes on factor prices. Obviously the same diagrams can be employed to consider the effect of less extreme endowment or price changes. The supplement to this

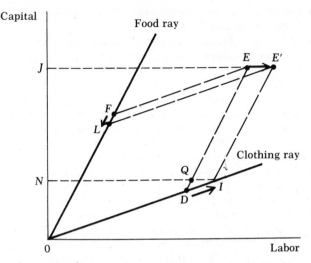

FIGURE 8.10 The Rybczynski Theorem

An increase in the home country's endowment of labor, with no corresponding increase in its capital stock, shifts the endowment point from E to E'. This shift causes the labor-intensive clothing industry to expand from OD to OI and the capital-intensive food industry to *decline,* from OF to OL.

chapter investigates the more general case. These results are essential building blocks in our further investigation of commercial policy (especially Chapter 13) and growth and trade (especially Chapter 25).

8.5 SUMMARY

The Heckscher-Ohlin model of trade differs from the Ricardian model in involving more than one factor in the production process, whose role in limiting outputs and affecting unit costs and prices must be accounted for. To concentrate on this feature, the Heckscher-Ohlin model assumes identical technology between countries when exploring the pattern of trade and the consequence of trade for the returns to productive factors. The special assumption made in this chapter's preliminary account of the Heckscher-Ohlin model is that productive techniques, as reflected in the input-output coefficients, are not only identical between countries but also independent of factor prices.

A number of results have been obtained in this simple model, and to summarize these results we should focus upon the strong relationships between commodity outputs and factor endowments, on the one hand, and factor and commodity prices, on the other, that are implied by the shared technology. These relationships are illustrated in Figures 8.11 and 8.12.

Figure 8.11 indicates that with clothing assumed to be labor-intensive and input-output coefficients fixed, the higher is the labor/capital endowment ratio, the greater must be the ratio of full-employment clothing production to food production. Thus the home country's higher labor/capital endowment ratio shown by OB in Figure 8.11, compared with OA for the foreign country, ensures the supply bias in establishing positions of comparative advantage that was discussed in section 8.2. The home country's output of clothing, OD in Figure 8.11, must exceed that of the foreign country's OC.

If this bias on the supply side that is generated by intercountry differences in factor endowments is not outweighed by an offsetting and greater difference in demand patterns, the home country will, with free trade, export labor-intensive clothing. That is, if supply differences dictate the comparison of pretrade commodity price ratios, the Heckscher-Ohlin theorem holds: the labor-abundant country exports the labor-intensive commodity. The pretrade relative price of clothing could be OA in the home country in Figure 8.12 and OC abroad. This price reflects as well a lower wage/rent ratio at home (OD compared with OF abroad in Figure 8.12). On the other hand, demand in the labor-abundant home country could be so

Note; upward slope explained by Rybczynski Theorem

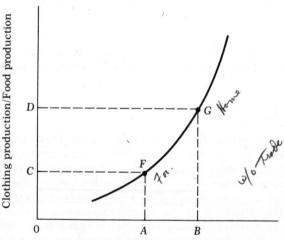

FIGURE 8.11   The Relationship between Outputs and Endowments

The upward sloping curve (drawn under the assumption that clothing is labor-intensive) shows, for any labor/capital endowment ratio, the unique clothing/food production ratio maintaining full employment. If technologies are identical between countries, points F and G can illustrate the endowment and output configurations at home (G) and abroad (F).

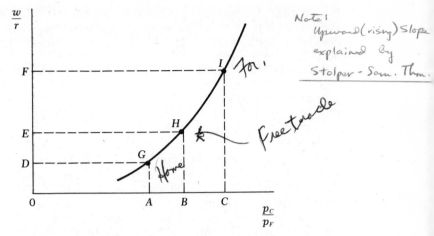

Note!
Upward (rising) Slope
explained by
Stolper - Sam. Thm.

for:

Freetrade

Home

FIGURE 8.12   The Relationship between Factor Prices
and Commodity Prices

>The upward sloping curve shows that any commodity price
>ratio implies a unique factor price ratio. If the relative price
>of labor-intensive clothing is lower in the labor-abundant
>home country before trade, the wage/rent ratio must be
>lower at home (compare G for the home country with I
>abroad). Free trade leads to an intermediate value for the
>terms of trade and equalizes factor prices (point H).

biased toward consumption of labor-intensive clothing that, before
trade, clothing is more expensive at home. This would be illustrated in
Figure 8.12 by having OA represent the pretrade price of clothing
abroad and OC at home. In such a case the Heckscher-Ohlin theorem
would be invalidated — the labor-abundant home country would
export food, which is capital-intensive.

Exception
due to
Taste
Patterns

   To continue with this exceptional case, notice that if the pretrade
price ratio in the home country is OC (Figure 8.12), the labor-abundant country is also the (pretrade) high wage country. Furthermore,
suppose we introduce an *alternative* definition of factor abundance,
whereby the home country is deemed to be labor-abundant only if
before trade it is the country with the lower wage/rent ratio. Then
according to Figure 8.12 the labor-abundant (low-wage) country is
the country in which the labor-intensive commodity is cheaper before
trade, and therefore the labor-abundant country would export the
labor-intensive commodity. With this revised definition of factor
abundance, the Heckscher-Ohlin theorem would seem always to
hold. This would reflect Figure 8.12's strong relationship between
commodity and factor price ratios.

   Definitions of factor abundance, like all definitions, are neither
correct nor incorrect — they are a matter of choice. We prefer the
one given earlier, whereby the home country is deemed labor-abundant only if its labor/capital endowment ratio is higher than abroad.

Notice that this concept is easier to use for any empirical test of the nature of trade flows, as we shall discuss in Chapter 10, because it does not hinge upon the value of variables (wage/rent ratios) in a non-observable pretrade situation.

Whatever the pattern of trade, Figure 8.12 also illustrates the factor price equalization theorem. With free trade a common "intermediate" price of clothing is established in world markets — OB in Figure 8.12. This common price drives each country's wage/rent ratio to the same value — shown by OE.

We have made use of the fact that our assumptions guarantee positive slopes for the two curves drawn in Figures 8.11 and 8.12. But another feature of these curves has not been mentioned. Notice that they are both rather steep.[8] For example, in Figure 8.11 the increase in the clothing/food output ratio that is involved in going from OC to OD is greater than the underlying increase in the labor/capital endowment ratio from OA to OB. In a similar vein, in Figure 8.12 the proportionate increase in p_C/p_F in going from OA to OB is associated with a magnified (greater than proportionate) increase in the wage/rent ratio. This relationship illustrates a general feature of the model that finds specific application in the Stolper-Samuelson theorem and the Rybczynski theorem discussed in section 8.4. In the supplement to this chapter we will provide a formal algebraic proof of these relationships.

SUGGESTIONS FOR FURTHER READING

A consideration of the fixed coefficients case is found in the following two sources. A more extensive set of readings on the Heckscher-Ohlin theory is provided at the end of Chapter 9.

Jones, Ronald W., "Duality in International Trade: A Geometrical Note," *Canadian Journal of Economics and Political Science*, 31 (August 1965): 390–93. Discusses the analogies between Figures 8.3 and 8.8.
Meade, James E. *The Stationary Economy*. London: Allen and Unwin, 1965, chap. 11. Discusses the case of fixed technical coefficients.

Supplement to Chapter 8:
The Fixed-Coefficients Model: A Formal Analysis

The basic structure of this simplified version of the Heckscher-Ohlin model is provided by equations 8.1 and 8.2, the full-employment conditions, and 8.5 and 8.6, the competitive profit conditions. Of course similar relationships hold in

---

[8] Quite aside from the fact that the curves are steep (i.e., inelastic) is the fact that they are drawn concave upward. As could easily be checked, upward concavity is a consequence of our assumption of fixed coefficients. But it is not a property of the model that is of much economic interest, so we shall refrain from discussing this feature.

the foreign country. In this supplement we shall develop some of the formal
properties of the model that were discussed in the text. We shall start by reproducing here the full-employment pair, 8.S.1 and 8.S.2, with the inequalities
now removed, because we shall assume that both factors are indeed fully
employed:

Assumptions:
(1)

$$a_{LC}x_C + a_{LF}x_F = L \qquad (8.S.1)$$

$$a_{KC}x_C + a_{KF}x_F = K. \qquad (8.S.2)$$

We also reproduce the competitive profit conditions:

$$a_{LC}w + a_{KC}r = p_C \qquad (8.S.3)$$

(2)

$$a_{LF}w + a_{KF}r = p_F. \qquad (8.S.4)$$

The technology, given by the array of a_{ij} coefficients, is constant. From the
full employment equations we can link changes in factor endowments to the
required changes in outputs. From the competitive profit conditions we can
associate changes in commodity prices with changes in factor prices. Because
the general form of all four equations is the same, let us initially work just
with one of them, say the full employment condition for labor, equation 8.S.1.

(3) Fixed Coeff. Technology

Differentiate this condition totally to obtain:

$$a_{LC}dx_C + a_{LF}dx_F = dL.$$

It proves convenient to use relative, instead of absolute, changes; a ^ over a
variable indicates the relative change in that variable. For example, $\hat{L}$ is dL/L,
the relative increase in the country's labor supply. Thus the expression above
can be written as:

$$\frac{a_{LC}x_C}{L}\hat{x}_C + \frac{a_{LF}x_F}{L}\hat{x}_F = \hat{L}.$$

The term $a_{LC}x_C/L$ refers to the fraction of the labor force used to produce
clothing. Call this λ_{LC}. We define λ_{LF} similarly. With labor fully employed, these
two fractions add to unity. Applying the same reasoning to the capital con-
straint we obtain the following pair of relationships among *relative changes*
in endowments and full-employment levels of output:

(4)
Let $\lambda_{LC} = \dfrac{a_{LC}x_C}{L}$

$$\lambda_{LC}\hat{x}_C + \lambda_{LF}\hat{x}_F = \hat{L} \qquad (8.S.5)$$

$$\lambda_{KC}\hat{x}_C + \lambda_{KF}\hat{x}_F = \hat{K}. \qquad (8.S.6)$$

Each of these equations states that the relative change in the endowment of
a factor of production must be matched by a positive weighted average of
relative output changes. For example, if the output of the clothing industry
rises by 8 percent, and that of food by 3 percent, the capital stock must rise by a
number (like 5 percent) trapped between these two figures.

This example illustrates the *magnification effect*.[1] Suppose that the labor
endowment expands more than the capital supply so $\hat{L} > \hat{K}$. Then the magnification effect states that the labor-intensive commodity will expand relatively
more than either factor, and the capital-intensive commodity will grow, if at

---

[1] The term "magnification effect" was introduced in R. W. Jones, "The Structure of
Simple General Equilibrium Models," *Journal of Political Economy,* 73 (December 1965):
557–72, from which much of the material in this supplement and the supplement to
Chapter 9 is drawn.

all, at a smaller rate than either factor. If:

$$\hat{L} > \hat{K}$$

then

$$\hat{x}_C > \hat{L} > \hat{K} > \hat{x}_F.$$

There are two, separate, facts to notice about this ranking. First, the labor-intensive commodity, x_C, has expanded more than the capital-intensive commodity, x_F. Second, in this chain of ranking the output changes are the extreme changes, since each endowment change is a positively weighted average of (and therefore is trapped between) each output change. Indeed, if $\hat{K} = 0$, $\hat{x}_F < 0$, which illustrates the Rybcyznski theorem.

Perform a final exercise on the full-employment equations of change. Subtract equation 8.S.6 from equation 8.S.5 to obtain:

$$(\lambda_{LC} - \lambda_{KC})\,\hat{x}_C + (\lambda_{LF} - \lambda_{KF})\,\hat{x}_F = (\hat{L} - \hat{K}).$$

Then observe that the coefficient of $\hat{x}_F$ is just $-(\lambda_{LC} - \lambda_{KC})$ because $\lambda_{LF} = 1 - \lambda_{LC}$ and $\lambda_{KF} = 1 - \lambda_{KC}$. Finally introduce the notation $|\lambda|$ for $\lambda_{LC} - \lambda_{KC}$. This yields:

$$(\hat{x}_C - \hat{x}_F) = \frac{1}{|\lambda|}(\hat{L} - \hat{K}). \qquad (8.S.7)$$

(5) The sign of $|\lambda|$ indicates the labor-intensive commodity. We chose the notation, $|\lambda|$, for $(\lambda_{LC} - \lambda_{KC})$, because the determinant of factor-allocation coefficients in 8.S.5 and 8.S.6, which is

$$\lambda_{LC}\lambda_{KF} - \lambda_{KC}\lambda_{LF},$$

can be written as $(\lambda_{LC} - \lambda_{KC})$ by substituting $(1 - \lambda_{KC})$ for λ_{KF} and $(1 - \lambda_{LC})$ for λ_{LF}. But directly by definition,

$$\lambda_{LC}\lambda_{KF} - \lambda_{KC}\lambda_{LF} = \frac{x_C x_F}{LK}(a_{LC}a_{KF} - a_{KC}a_{LF}).$$

Therefore $|\lambda|$ is positive if and only if the first commodity is labor-intensive. Because $|\lambda|$ is the difference between two fractions, it must itself be a fraction, which confirms the magnification effect illustrated in Figure 8.11. Because $1/|\lambda|$ is larger than one, any increase in the labor/capital endowment ratio implies a greater relative increase in the output ratio.

This argument also follows for the competitive profit equations 8.S.3 and 8.S.4. Differentiating the first of these,

$$\frac{a_{LC}w}{p_C}\hat{w} + \frac{a_{KC}r}{p_C}\hat{r} = \hat{p}_C.$$

We need to interpret the coefficients of $\hat{w}$ and $\hat{r}$. They are the distributive shares of each factor in the clothing industry. Thus $a_{LC}w/p_C$, which we shall relabel θ_{LC}, is the fraction of each dollar's worth of clothing that is paid out as wages. Because in a competitive equilibrium all excess profits are squeezed out, $a_{KC}r/p_C$, or θ_{KC}, capital's distributive share in the clothing industry, is one minus labor's distributive share.

In this fashion the equations of change associated with the competitive profit conditions can be written as in 8.S.8 and 8.S.9:

$$\theta_{LC}\hat{w} + \theta_{KC}\hat{r} = \hat{p}_C \qquad (8.S.8)$$

$$\theta_{LF}\hat{w} + \theta_{KF}\hat{r} = \hat{p}_F. \qquad (8.S.9)$$

Each of these equations simply states: if factor prices change, the consequent change in each commodity price must be a positive weighted average of the relative factor price changes. The weights in each case reflect the importance of that factor in unit costs — as expressed by its distributive share.

Because the structure of 8.S.8 and 8.S.9 is similar to that of 8.S.5 and 8.S.6 we would expect to find the magnification effect again. As an extreme case, suppose there is a pure price inflation, with $\hat{p}_C = \hat{p}_F$. Clearly both factor prices must increase in the same proportion. This increase can easily be checked by referring to Figure 8.8 and moving point P along the ray from the origin. Consider a case in which the commodity price *ratio* changes, and for concreteness assume that $\hat{p}_C > \hat{p}_F$. The magnification effect reveals that if clothing is labor-intensive, the wage rate will rise by relatively more than either commodity price, and the rental on capital goods by less. If:

$$\hat{p}_C > \hat{p}_F,$$

then

$$\hat{w} > \hat{p}_C > \hat{p}_F > \hat{r}.$$

Stolper–Sam., Thm.

In this ranking each commodity price change is trapped between the relative factor price changes, because, as equations 8.S.8 and 8.S.9 state, each $\hat{p}_j$ is a positive weighted average of $\hat{w}$ and $\hat{r}$. Once again the extremely basic feature of technology — two factors are combined to produce one output — leads to this magnification effect.[2]

Commercial Policy implications

In section 8.4 we gave a special case of this ranking in our discussion of the Stolper-Samuelson theorem. If a tariff or other disturbance raises the relative price of labor-intensive clothing ($\hat{p}_C > \hat{p}_F$), the wage rate must rise by a greater relative amount than any commodity price — labor unambiguously benefits from such a change.

Finally, adopt the procedure used previously in subtracting the two full-employment equations of change. Applied now to the competitive profit equations of change 8.S.8 and 8.S.9, this procedure yields:

(7)

$$(\hat{w} - \hat{r}) = \frac{1}{|\theta|}(\hat{p}_C - \hat{p}_F). \qquad (8.S.10)$$

$|\theta|$ can be defined as $(\theta_{LC} - \theta_{LF})$, which is equivalent to the determinant of distributive share coefficients in 8.S.8 and 8.S.9, $\theta_{LC}\theta_{KF} - \theta_{LF}\theta_{KC}$. $|\theta|$ must be a fraction, and the sign of $|\theta|$ depends upon factor intensities. Because

$$|\theta| = \frac{wr}{p_C p_F}(a_{LC}a_{KF} - a_{KC}a_{LF}),$$

it will be positive when $|\lambda|$ is positive, namely when the clothing industry is labor-intensive. If clothing is labor-intensive, we have shown that x_C must employ a greater fraction of the labor force, λ_{LC}, than it does of the capital supply, λ_{KC}, and that labor's distributive share in x_C, θ_{LC}, must exceed its share in x_F, θ_{LF}. Thus our assumption that clothing is labor-intensive confirms, because $1/|\theta|$ is greater than unity, our drawing the w/r response as a magnified reflection of any change in p_C/p_F in Figure 8.12.

This breakdown of the structure of the Heckscher-Ohlin model with fixed input-output coefficients will find ready application in our more general treatment in Chapter 9 in which each a_{ij} is sensitive to the prevailing factor prices.

---

[2] Despite the wide intuitive appeal of a technology in which many factors (here two) combine to produce one output, there are exceptions involving joint production. A stark example: two commodities (wool and mutton) may be produced from one factor of production (sheep). In such cases the role of factors and commodities in the magnification effect is reversed.

9 The Heckscher-Ohlin Model: A General Treatment

Allows Variable Input Coeff.

Having developed the structure of the Heckscher-Ohlin model in Chapter 8, we now turn to a more general account in which the productive techniques actually adopted in any economy are capable of responding to a change in market circumstances. If wage rates rise, we assume that in all industries capital is substituted for labor. As we shall see, this assumption of factor substitutability allows for a more flexible response of outputs to changes in the terms of trade. Full employment now becomes possible for many output combinations. Furthermore, the model exhibits a wider variety of results with variable input coefficients than with fixed coefficients, including the possibility that countries will actually utilize techniques that differ from each other even though they share a common knowledge of technology. In this respect the general form of the Heckscher-Ohlin model can, in circumstances to be spelled out below, closely approximate the Ricardian model.

9.1 THE CHOICE OF TECHNIQUES IN PRODUCTION

The concept of an *isoquant* has already been discussed in Chapter 6. Of special importance here is the *unit isoquant* showing combinations of labor and capital that can produce *one* unit of output. Figure 9.1 illustrates both the type of unit isoquant implicitly assumed in Chapter 8 (the right-angled, dashed isoquant) and the isoquant allowing techniques to vary with factor prices. If the ratio of wages to rents is shown by the absolute value of the slope of line 1, costs are minimized by choosing the input-output coefficients at point A. Should wages rise relatively more than rents (as indicated by line 2), we may

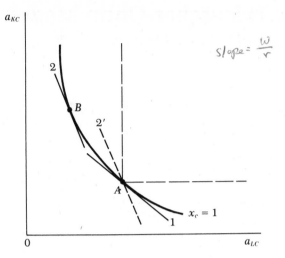

FIGURE 9.1   The Unit Isoquant

> The bowed-in curve shows combinations of capital and labor for producing one unit of clothing. Two alternative wage/rent ratios are indicated by the (absolute value of) slopes of lines 1 and 2. Technique A is chosen with line 1, while unit costs are minimized at B if the wage/rent ratio rises to the slope shown by line 2. With fixed coefficients, input coefficients remain frozen at A.

assume that less labor and more capital will be employed per unit of output as shown by point B. In the fixed-coefficient case in Chapter 8, the choice of techniques would remain frozen at A (line 2' is parallel to line 2). Figure 9.1 illustrates the choices available in the clothing industry. In a similar fashion we could draw a unit isoquant for food production.

Figure 9.2 shows explicitly the dependence of factor proportions upon factor prices. It reveals the same kind of assumption about factor proportions as we made in Chapter 8: food is more capital-intensive than clothing. But now it is vital to compare both factor proportions at the *same* wage/rent ratio. If the wage/rent ratio is shown by OA, the capital/labor ratio in the food industry, OC, exceeds that chosen in the clothing industry, OB. We do not deny that food can be produced with less capital-intensive techniques than clothing. Point G on the food factor-proportions curve is lower than point H. But point G would only be adopted at a lower wage/rent ratio, OF, and if this prevailed, clothing producers would shift to an even lower capital/labor ratio (point I). When we assume that the technology dictates that food is the capital-intensive industry, we mean that a_{KF}/a_{LF} would exceed a_{KC}/a_{LC} at a wage/rent ratio common to both industries.

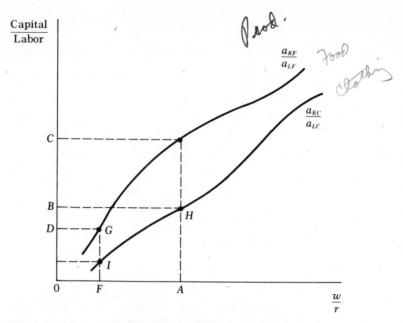

FIGURE 9.2   Factor Proportions are Dependent upon Factor Prices

Each upward sloping curve shows how capital/labor ratios adopted in an industry depend upon the prevailing level of the wage/rent ratio. The curve for the food industry lies above that for the clothing industry, reflecting our assumption that food is the capital-intensive industry. Food *could* be produced by more labor-intensive techniques than clothing (compare points G and H), but not at a common wage/rent ratio.

Throughout this chapter we shall assume that the two factor-proportions curves shown in Figure 9.2 do not cross each other. No previous assumption about technology guarantees this, and no a priori reason can be given to justify it. Indeed, in Chapter 10 we shall explore the implications for the Heckscher-Ohlin model of allowing these curves to cross. This is the *factor-intensity reversal* phenomenon, which questions some empirical tests of the Heckscher-Ohlin model.

9.2 THE TRANSFORMATION SCHEDULE AND THE RELATIONSHIP BETWEEN OUTPUTS AND ENDOWMENTS

Allowing factor proportions to vary continuously with changes in wage/rental ratios leads, as we shall show, to a smoothly bowed-out transformation schedule. Figure 9.3 contrasts this shape with that found in previous models. The exchange model and the Ricardian

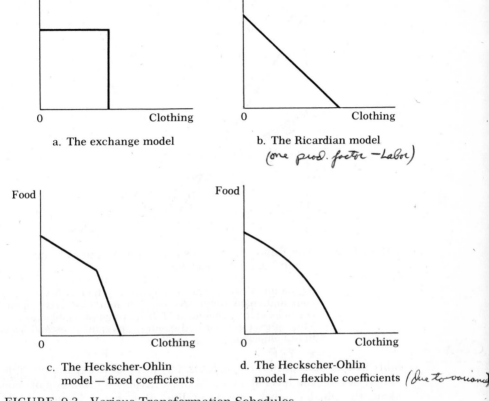

a. The exchange model

b. The Ricardian model
(one prod. factor —Labor)

c. The Heckscher-Ohlin
   model — fixed coefficients

d. The Heckscher-Ohlin
   model — flexible coefficients *(due to variance)*

FIGURE 9.3   Various Transformation Schedules

model yield the polar opposites of zero flexibility in production and infinite substitutability between food and clothing at a given ratio. The Heckscher-Ohlin model, allowing two productive factors instead of one (as in the Ricardian model), leads to a bowed-out schedule which, if coefficients of production are variable, reflects a smooth reallocation of resources between food and clothing.

To show this smooth reallocation we shall build upon the previous chapter's construction of the production-possibilities schedule. Suppose the home country fully employs both labor and capital at some initial set of factor and commodity prices. As Figures 9.1 or 9.2 suggest, the input-output coefficients are chosen with reference to this wage/rent ratio. If these coefficients were frozen at their initial values, the transformation schedule would look like Figure 8.1, with full-employment production at *A*. For convenience this has been reproduced as the shaded broken line in Figure 9.4. With no flexi-

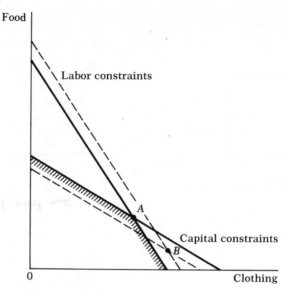

FIGURE 9.4   The Endowment Constraints on Outputs Change
When Factor Prices Change

At the initial wage/rent ratio, point A is the full-employment
combination of outputs. As the wage/rental ratio rises, labor-
coefficients in each industry fall, and capital coefficients rise.
This shifts the labor and capital constraint lines and leads
to full employment at point B.

Construction of Bowed-Out PPF :

bility in the input-output coefficients, any attempt to expand clothing
output beyond the level shown at A must involve a reduction of food
along the shaded labor constraint line. But this reduction would
leave some capital unemployed, driving down the rental on capital
equipment. Now assume some flexibility in input-output coefficients.

(Say, in response to P_C/P_F rising) As w/r rises, both industries economize on their use of labor. Similarly, capital, now cheaper, is used more lavishly. Thus the labor
constraint line in Figure 9.4 shifts outward (its vertical and horizontal intercepts are L/a_{LF} and L/a_{LC} respectively and labor coefficients are reduced) and the capital constraint line inward. They now
intersect at point B, suggesting that with flexibility in the a_{ij} coefficients, full employment of both factors can be maintained as clothing
production expands from point A, and with less sacrifice of food
output. That is, point B lies outside the old shaded broken-line transformation schedule.[1]

[1] The reader may wonder why we have drawn the new factor constraint
lines parallel to the original ones in Figure 9.4. They are only parallel under
highly special circumstances. We mean only to establish that point B lies
within the cone southeast of A formed by the original full-employment lines
through point A.

This process could be continued to yield a smooth transformation schedule running through *A* and *B*. But the argument just presented does not really establish that the production-possibilities locus is bowed out from the origin. Fortunately a simple line of argument can be used to establish this property. Consider the two points *A* and *B* on the transformation curve drawn in Figure 9.5. At each of these both factors are fully employed. At *A* the two industries are using factors in some given proportions. Suppose we keep these proportions fixed, but exactly halve the totals of labor and capital employed by each industry. Because of the constant-returns-to-scale nature of the technology, such a halving of the resource base would cut by exactly 50 percent the output of each industry. This output combination is shown by *D*. Now let the released resources (one-half of the total labor force and one-half of the capital stock) be used by industries exactly in the proportions that would be adopted at *B*. That is, the combination of outputs shown by point *E*, representing half the production totals shown by *B*, can be achieved with this remaining 50 percent of the communities' resources. In this way we can produce points *D* and *E*, whose total output is shown by point *C*, halfway on the straight line segment joining *A* and *B*.

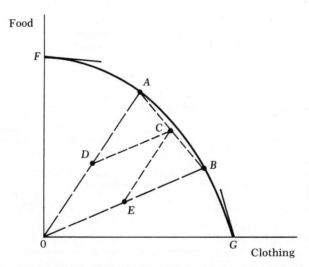

FIGURE 9.5   The Transformation Schedule Is Bowed Out
              from the Origin

If half the community's resources are allocated to industries as at point *A*, and the remaining half as at point *B*, constant-returns-to-scale technology assures aggregate output at *C*. But a better allocation of resources can yield a higher output. Therefore the production-possibilities schedule is bowed out from the origin.

Have we inadvertently proved too strong a result? Must the transformation schedule between A and B in Figure 9.5 be the linear segment connecting them? The answer is no. We have only demonstrated that point C *could* be produced. But producing clothing and food in this "mixed" fashion — using partly the techniques appropriate at A and partly those appropriate at B — would be inefficient. From our previous argument centered on Figure 9.4 we can see that each industry uses more capital-intensive techniques at B than at A — if, as we have assumed, clothing is the labor-intensive commodity.[2] Therefore if factor proportions are chosen to lie between those used at A and B, the economy's total output bundle will be greater than shown by the AB line segment. Because A and B were chosen arbitrarily, this argument confirms that the full-employment locus of competitive outputs must be smoothly bowed out from the origin.

With each fixed endowment bundle of labor and capital we thus associate a bowed-out transformation curve showing full-employment levels of output. This production-possibilities locus will shift to a new position if there is a change in the aggregate resource base. If the community's resource levels expand, the transformation schedule shifts outward. If the expansion is uniform, say an increase of 50 percent in both the labor supply and the capital stock, the transformation schedule is itself uniformly shifted out by 50 percent. In a constant-returns-to-scale world, we need a change in underlying endowment proportions to alter the shape of the locus of outputs. A change in endowment proportions twists the transformation schedule.

Compare the shapes of the transformation schedules in the capital abundant foreign country and the labor abundant home country. Pick a point on each country's transformation schedule where the slopes are the same, e.g., points A and B in Figure 9.6. Then point B on the foreign country's curve will correspond to a higher relative production of capital-intensive food than point A on the home country's curve. That is, the foreign transformation curve is steeper than the home curve along any ray from the origin.

This assertion as to the effect of factor endowments on the shape of the transformation schedule follows directly from our discussion in Chapter 8. Because the commodity price ratio is reflected in the slope of the transformation schedule, equal slopes at A and B in Figure 9.6 imply that each country is facing the same commodity and factor prices and thus using the same input-output coefficients. In such circumstances Figure 8.11 illustrated that the capital abundant country must produce a higher proportion of the capital intensive commodity.

---

[2] Because the total supplies of labor and capital are fixed and fully employed, an expansion of the labor-intensive industry must entail a change of techniques toward more capital-intensive processes in each industry.

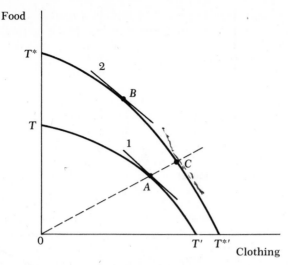

FIGURE 9.6   The Home (TT') and Foreign ($T^*T^{*\prime}$)
Transformation Schedules

> If the foreign country is capital-abundant (and larger), and
> food is capital-intensive, the foreign country will produce a
> greater food/clothing output ratio than at home at any com-
> mon commodity price ratio (e.g., as shown by the slopes of
> lines 1 and 2).

9.3 SUPPLY CURVES AND COMPARATIVE ADVANTAGE

The bias imparted to production by differences in factor endowments
is easily illustrated in a diagram showing relative quantities produced against relative prices. Figure 9.7 parallels Figure 9.3 in
reviewing the shapes of the supply curves in the models considered
thus far. Only in the Heckscher-Ohlin model with flexible input-
output coefficients will a rise in the relative price of food coax out
smoothly increasing quantities of food. For the home country this
smooth increase is shown in Figure 9.7d, in conjunction with the
transformation curve shown in Figure 9.5. If the relative price of
clothing lies between the slopes of the lines tangent to the transformation schedule at the corner points F and G in Figure 9.5, the
home country will produce both commodities, and as p_F/p_C rises
production smoothly adjusts toward greater relative output of food.
For sufficiently low values of p_F/p_C — below OG in Figure 9.7d —
all resources are devoted to the clothing industry. Similarly, a relative
price of OF or higher for food in Figure 9.7d results in zero output for
clothing. Compare the shape of this relative supply curve with the
completely vertical curve for the model of pure exchange, the perfectly horizontal curve in the Ricardian model, and the rising step

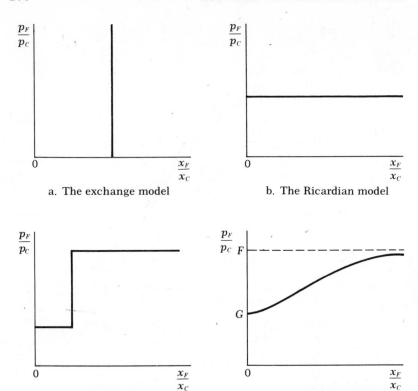

FIGURE 9.7   Various Relative Supply Curves

For the range of relative food prices from OG to OF in 9.7d, both commodities are produced and full employment prevails.

function in the Heckscher-Ohlin model with fixed input-output coefficients.

The home country's relative supply curve has been reproduced in Figure 9.8 to facilitate comparison with the dashed, foreign country supply curve. It also slopes upward for an intermediate range of price ratios (the range G^*F^* in Figure 9.8). Outside this range the foreign country would specialize completely in clothing (for p_F/p_C below OG^*) or food (for p_F/p_C above OF^*). The foreign curve lies below the home curve, reflecting that if both countries produce commodities in the same proportions, the relative cost of the capital-intensive commodity must be lower in the more capital-abundant country. The foreign curve lies to the right of the home curve. This was shown in Figure 9.6: at any common price ratio the capital-abundant country produces relatively more of the capital-intensive commodity. This was also

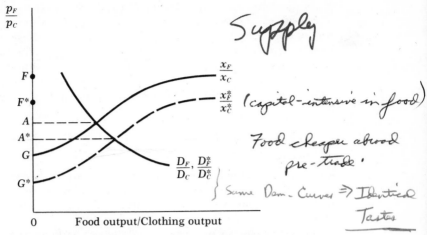

Supply

$\frac{x_F}{x_C}$

$\frac{x_F^*}{x_C^*}$ *(capital-intensive in food)*

Food cheaper abroad pre-trade.

$\left.\right\}$ *Same Dem. Curves ⇒ Identical Tastes*

FIGURE 9.8   Pretrade Equilibrium at Home and Abroad

> The rising relative supply curve for food at home lies above (or to the left of) the foreign supply curve. The position of the curves reflects the bias in production imparted by the capital-abundant foreign country's comparative advantage in producing capital-intensive food. If both countries have identical relative demand curves, food will be relatively cheap abroad ($OA^* < OA$) before trade.

illustrated in Figure 8.11 — a high L/K leads to a high ratio of clothing to food production.

In Figure 9.8 we have illustrated the case in which both countries have identical taste patterns. Therefore the Heckscher-Ohlin theorem — the more capital-abundant country exports the capital-intensive commodity — is vindicated. The relative price of capital-intensive food is lower in the pretrade foreign equilibrium (OA^*) than at home (OA), and therefore with trade each country exports the commodity requiring more intensive use of its more abundant factor.

However, our former warnings about the Heckscher-Ohlin theorem still hold. If the taste pattern in the capital-abundant country is heavily biased toward the consumption of the capital-intensive commodity, this commodity might prove to be more expensive before trade. In Figure 9.8 this would indeed be the case if the D_F^*/D_C^* curve intersected the x_F^*/x_C^* curve far enough to the right so that A^* exceeds A.

Theorem Imp.

Imp. — an Exception

9.4 THE FACTOR-PRICE EQUALIZATION ARGUMENT

Recall how we proved in Chapter 8 that commodity trade will equalize the reward a factor in one country earns and what that same factor abroad receives. We first found that if either country wished to consume both food and clothing in the free trade equilibrium, the terms of trade must lie within certain bounds in order to allow for production of both commodities.[3] Remember that these bounds were identical in the two countries. Thus unit costs in equilibrium *equal commodity prices, as* shown in Chapter 8 by equations 8.7 and 8.8 for the home country and 8.9 and 8.10 for the foreign country. For convenience the home country's pair is reproduced here as 9.1 and 9.2:

$$a_{LC}w + a_{KC}r = p_C \qquad\qquad (9.1)$$

$$a_{LF}w + a_{KF}r = p_F. \qquad\qquad (9.2)$$

Identical fixed-coefficients technology assured the same array of input-output coefficients, a_{ij}^*, abroad as at home. Free trade leads to the same commodity prices p_C and p_F. Therefore factor prices were equalized.

The same kind of argument holds when coefficients are flexible *if the terms of trade settle at a level that allows each country to produce both food and clothing.* This is a big proviso. As Figure 9.8 revealed, in some ranges of food's relative price the home country's food industry is driven out of competition (the range G^*G). At other prices, the foreign country could not compete in clothing (the range F^*F).[4] This feature is essential to the Heckscher-Ohlin model, and in section 9.5 we shall pursue the question of specialization in production. For the moment assume that the terms of trade with free trade settle at a level that allows each country to produce both commodities. If wages and rents are equalized between the two countries, so will be the input-output coefficients, because technical knowledge is assumed to be the same and each a_{ij} depends only upon the wage/rent ratio. Therefore unit costs for each commodity would be equal in each country. Now argue in the other direction. If countries face the same commodity prices with free trade, they must have the same wages and rents.[5]

We shall turn now to the possibility that one or both countries will be forced to specialize in production. For the industry that is forced to shut down, unit costs would exceed international price, and one of the

---

[3] Recall that these bounds were set by the relative labor costs for the two commodities, on the one hand, and the relative capital costs, on the other. Thus:

$$\frac{a_{LF}}{a_{LC}} \leq \frac{p_F}{p_C} \leq \frac{a_{KF}}{a_{KC}}.$$

The ratio of capital costs is higher because, by assumption, food is capital-intensive.

[4] Of course for the terms of trade to lie in either of these ranges demand schedules would have to differ from those shown in Figure 9.8.

[5] A formal proof is provided in the supplement to this Chapter. As discussed in Chapter 10, in the case of factor-intensity reversals there is no presumption of factor price equalization.

equalities in 9.1 or 9.2 or the equivalent in the foreign country would be disrupted and, along with it, the argument for factor price equalization.

9.5 SPECIALIZATION IN PRODUCTION

The possibility that one country may be driven to specialize completely was implicit in Figure 9.8. Of course the demand pattern shown in Figure 9.8 precluded this outcome; familiar offer curve analysis has shown that the equilibrium terms of trade must lie between the pretrade price ratios of the two countries, OA^* and OA in Figure 9.8. But with different demand patterns, specialization could occur. Indeed, if factor endowment proportions differ enough between countries, OF^* in Figure 9.8 could lie below OG. In such a case at least one country *must* be completely specialized. The kind of diagram illustrated in Figure 9.2, relating factor proportions to factor prices, is especially revealing for the question of specialization. These curves are reproduced in Figure 9.9. They reflect only the technology common to both countries. But factor endowment proportions, which differ between countries, delimit whatever range of the curves is relevant. Suppose the home country's factor endowment capital/labor ratio is OA. Then the wage/rent ratio at home must be trapped between OD and OE. To see this, consider a wage/rent ratio at home higher than OE, say OH. Firms in *both* the clothing and the food industries would, in such a case, demand a higher proportion of capital per man for production than is available in the home economy. Such an excess demand for capital can therefore not be met, rentals would rise (and wages fall), and this process must continue until the wage/rent ratio is driven down within the range DE. If both factors are to be fully employed, the wage/rent ratio must adjust so that factor proportions required in the two industries "straddle" the endowment ratio. Similarly, if the higher capital/labor endowment ratio abroad is given by OB, the foreign wage/rent ratio must lie between OF and OG. This position allows a common overlap, FE, and factor prices between countries may be equal in this range. But if the foreign capital/labor endowment ratio lies at OC instead of OB — even further removed from the proportions available to the home country — the foreign wage/rent ratio must lie in the range HI. In such a case there is no overlap between the factor prices that could prevail at home and abroad. Free trade in commodities would not suffice to drag the wage/rent ratio in the capital-abundant foreign country down to the level that could prevail in the home country.

As useful as Figure 9.9 is, by itself it cannot tell us where each country's wage/rent ratio will settle with free trade, because it tells us nothing directly about commodity prices, and the equilibrium commodity terms of trade depend both upon supply and demand. Offer curve analysis, as described in Chapter 6 for the case (applicable here)

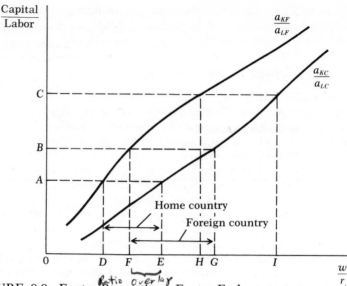

FIGURE 9.9   Factor Proportions, Factor Endowments,
and Factor Prices

> *AO* represents the home country's endowment proportions
> of capital to labor. Given the technology shown by the upward
> sloping curves, the home wage/rent ratio must lie in the range
> *DE*. If the foreign capital/labor endowment ratio is *OB*, the
> foreign wage/rent ratio must lie in the range *FG*. The overlap,
> *FE*, is the only range in which factor price equalization be-
> tween countries could occur.

in which production takes place along a bowed-out transformation
curve, does reveal, however, that the free trade terms of trade will
lie between the pretrade price ratios in each country.

9.6 A SUMMARY OF THE HECKSCHER-OHLIN THEORY
AND A COMPARISON WITH THE RICARDIAN MODEL

A number of propositions have been developed within the framework
of the Heckscher-Ohlin theory. Some of these have little to do with
the pattern of trade. Instead, they refer to the consequences for a
single country of a change either in endowments or in commodity
prices. They do not rely upon an assumption of a common pool of
technical knowledge in the two countries. Instead, they only assume
that a country possesses two productive factors (labor and capital
have been our examples) which are combined in different proportions
to produce two commodities (food and clothing) and that technology
exhibits constant returns to scale. The latter, of course, implies
that a doubling of all inputs into any productive process will cause

outputs to double as well. We begin our summary with these propositions: (1) The transformation curve must be bowed out. If input-
output coefficients are fixed, the transformation schedule consists
of two line-segments such as in Figure 9.3c. Full employment of both
labor and capital can only be obtained at the kink in the schedule.
The relative supply curve is the broken step-function illustrated in
Figure 9.7c. If input-output coefficients respond to factor prices, the
transformation schedule is smoothly bowed out, as in Figure 9.3d,
both factors of production are fully employed everywhere, and the
relative supply curve is smoothly upward sloping, as in Figure 9.7d. (3)
(2) The Rybczynski theorem:

Rybc. Theorem

> *An increase in the endowment of one factor* at constant prices
> *will increase the output of the commodity that uses that factor
> intensively and* reduce *the output of the other commodity.*

This proposition is the same in the fixed and variable coefficients
cases because at constant commodity and factor prices the input-
output coefficients remain constant in either case. (3) The Stolper-
Samuelson theorem:

(4)
Stol.-Sam. Theorem

> *An increase in the relative price of a commodity will drive up
> the return to the factor used intensively in producing that
> commodity by a greater relative amount.*

This proposition holds whether or not factor proportions respond to
factor price changes.

It is meaningless to compare these last two results with the Ricardian model, for they depend intimately on the requirement of two
factors of production for each productive process.

The two basic propositions in the Heckscher-Ohlin theory that
deal with the results of trade depend heavily upon the assumption
that both countries share a common knowledge of technology. These
are: (1) The Heckscher-Ohlin theorem:

> *The relatively capital-abundant country exports the capital-
> intensive commodity,*

and (2) The factor price equalization theorem:

> *Free trade in commodities equalizes the returns earned by the
> same factor in the two countries.*

In our preceding discussion we have explained these theorems
and pointed to instances in which one proposition or the other may
fail to hold. To review that material we may think of two alternative
cases, differing primarily in the extent of the dissimilarity between
factor endowment proportions between countries. The first of these is
illustrated by the two transformation schedules shown in Figure 9.10.
The foreign country has a slightly higher capital/labor endowment
proportion than does the home country, tilting its transformation

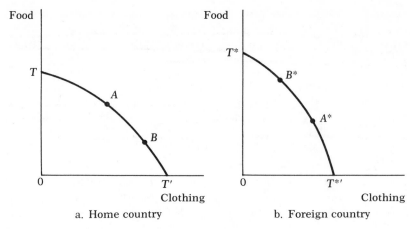

FIGURE 9.10   Home and Foreign Transformation Schedules:
Factor Endowments Fairly Similar

> For any ray from the origin the home country's transfor-
> mation schedule is flatter than the foreign country's. If
> pretrade production is at A at home and A* abroad, the
> capital-abundant foreign country exports capital-intensive
> food. But this Heckscher-Ohlin theorem is reversed if (B, B*)
> represent pretrade production and consumption patterns.
> With trade, both countries can be incompletely specialized,
> in which case the factor price equalization theorem holds.

schedule so that for any common ratio of food to clothing produced
in the two countries the opportunity costs of producing labor-intensive
clothing will be higher abroad. If A and A* represent pretrade consumption and production at home and abroad respectively, the
relative price of clothing would be lower at home. With trade the
Heckscher-Ohlin theorem would hold: the capital-abundant foreign
country would export capital-intensive food. On the other hand,
demand in each country might be biased toward the commodity that
uses intensively the factor of production in which that country is
more plentifully endowed. This demand bias works counter to the
production bias and could produce pretrade points B and B*. With
TT' steeper at B than is T*T*' at B*, the home country will export
capital-intensive food. The Heckscher-Ohlin theorem would not be
satisfied.[6]

The transformation schedules in Figure 9.10 exhibit a wide range
of the terms of trade (slopes) at which both countries could be incompletely specialized. If the equilibrium free trade price ratio settles in

----

[6] Recall our comment in Chapter 8 that relative factor abundance could be
defined by comparing pretrade factor price ratios. If so, the labor-abundant
(low wage) country in both of these examples exports the labor-intensive
commodity. The wage/rent ratio in the foreign country at B* is lower than in
the home country at B.

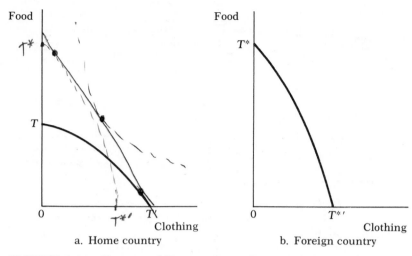

FIGURE 9.11   Home and Foreign Transformation Schedules:
Factor Endowments Much Different

> The labor-abundant home country's transformation sched-
> ule is flatter everywhere than the foreign country's trans-
> formation schedule. Factor prices can never be equalized
> with trade but the Heckscher-Ohlin theorem must hold:
> the capital-abundant country exports the capital-intensive
> commodity.

this range, the factor price equalization theorem must hold.[7] Both of
these results — that the Heckscher-Ohlin theorem may be invalidated, and that factor prices could be equalized with trade, were
characteristic of the case of fixed coefficients in Chapter 8.

Contrast this case with another in which the foreign country is so
much more capital-abundant than the home country that its transformation curve is steeper at every point than the home country's
transformation curve is at any point. How much larger must the
foreign capital/labor endowment ratio be to produce this result?
Figure 9.9 illustrates the answer. If the home endowment proportions are at *OA*, a foreign ratio shown by *OC* would suffice.[8] This case

---

[7] It may be interesting to notice that if the pretrade points *B* and *B** obtain
in each country, so that the Heckscher-Ohlin theorem is invalidated, the
factor price equalization theorem *must* hold! Free trade production in the
home country would lie between *B* and *A* and abroad between *B** and *A**.
Specialization in each country must be incomplete. For details, see N. Minabe,
"The Heckscher-Ohlin Theorem, the Leontief Paradox, and Patterns of Economic Growth," *American Economic Review*, 56 (December 1966): 1193–
1211.

[8] Of course somewhat lower ratios would do as well. Notice that the closer
the two industries are in the proportions in which they use factors, the more
narrow is the range of possible wage/rent ratios and therefore the more similar
can endowment proportions be still to have the foreign transformation curve
everywhere steeper than the home curve.

is illustrated in Figure 9.11. Two conclusions emerge. First, the factor price equalization theorem can never be satisfied — no common commodity terms of trade will allow both countries to be incompletely specialized. Secondly, the Heckscher-Ohlin theorem must hold: the home country must export labor-intensive clothing. Advocates of the Heckscher-Ohlin explanation of trading patterns find their case strengthened precisely in those cases in which the factor price equalization result cannot be obtained!

Finally, observe how closely the second case (Figure 9.11) approximates the Ricardian model. Although transformation schedules are not linear, at least one country, and perhaps both, must specialize completely with free trade. Furthermore, although both countries share a common pool of technical knowledge, the input-output coefficients actually used can never be identical between countries because factor prices are not equalized. What the Heckscher-Ohlin model has added to the Ricardian model is a reason for differences between countries' actual input-output coefficients or factor productivities. This reason resides in their different endowments of labor and capital.

9.7 POSSIBLE EXTENSIONS

These past two chapters have analyzed in some detail the standard Heckscher-Ohlin model of trade with two productive factors and two commodities. This discussion, coupled with our earlier analysis of demand in Part 1, will form the basis for a number of applications later in the book. In closing this chapter we shall remark briefly upon several modifications or extensions that may add realistic features to the basic model.

(1) The Possibility of Factor-Intensity Reversals

Factor-intensity reversals will be discussed in Chapter 10. They point to the fact that in one country food may be more capital-intensive than clothing, but that in another country the opposite ranking may be found. For example, in the United States food may be produced by more highly capital-intensive techniques than clothing, but more labor-intensive methods may be used in a country such as Japan. In terms of our diagrams, factor-intensity reversals would be illustrated in Figure 9.9 if the two curves crossed each other.

(2) Complications in the Pattern of Demand

Suppose laborers and capitalists have different taste patterns. Changes in the commodity terms of trade will alter factor prices and the distribution of income, thus giving more weight to one set of taste patterns and less to the other. It would no longer be possible to draw a set of community indifference curves without prior knowledge of the manner in which, in the background, the distribution of income is being altered. This problem has been analyzed elsewhere.[9] Here it is just mentioned as an extension of the Heckscher-Ohlin model that can readily be handled although it does introduce complications.

(3) Different Technologies in the Two Countries

Suppose the clothing and food unit isoquants differ from one country to another. One simple case to investigate would involve the foreign country, say, having a uniformly superior technology, in the sense that any bundle of capital and labor could produce, for example, a ten percent higher output of either commodity in the foreign country. This case would leave intact much of the analytical apparatus developed in this chapter — e.g., the curves in Figure 9.9. The general case, of nonuniform differences, is more difficult to handle, but it can be done.[10] We shall have occasion later, in Chapter 25, to investigate a situation in which a nonuniform change takes place in the general manner in which factors are combined to produce commodities.

(4) Nonconstant Returns to Scale

Two departures from the assumption of constant returns to scale technology can be made. In the case of increasing returns, there is a payoff to large size. To the extent that some industries exhibit lower unit costs with larger scale use of resources, we might argue that large countries will have a comparative advantage in such industries. Obviously many qualifications would have to be made to this simple argument. In addition, we may question the compatibility of our assumption of pure competition with the existence of increasing returns. These topics will be picked up in Chapter 11.

Diminishing returns to scale, whereby a doubling of capital and labor does not yield as great a relative increase in output, sometimes betrays the fact that not all factors of production have been taken into account. A process may use land or natural resources, as well as capital and labor, and these may not be as expandable as production increases. This possibility leads us to the next kind of extension.

(5) The Possibility of Many Factors and Many Commodities

Any theory that restricts to a small number (here two) the factors and commodities being analyzed is obviously open to criticism that what

---

[9] See Harry G. Johnson, "Income Distribution, the Offer Curve, and the Effects of Tariffs," *Manchester School of Economics and Social Studies*, 28 (September 1960): 215–42.

[10] An early treatment is given by R. Findlay and H. Grubert, "Factor Intensities, Technological Progress, and the Terms of Trade," *Oxford Economic Papers*, N.S. 11 (February 1959): 111–121, and a recent review of some of the results is provided in R. W. Jones, "The Role of Technology in the Theory of International Trade," *The Technology Factor in International Trade*, ed. R. Vernon. New York, 1970.

holds for two may not hold for seventeen. A true multi-factor, multi-commodity model of production clearly lies beyond the scale of analysis we wish to examine here. We can consider briefly, however, the effect on the simple Heckscher-Ohlin model of having more commodities than factors or vice versa.

Suppose that in each country there is a third factor, land, used only in the production of food. If the home country should be better-endowed with land, this would, by itself, tend to confer upon it a comparative advantage in producing food. And this influence could even be stronger than the opposite bias imparted in our earlier assumptions that the capital/labor ratio in food is higher than in clothing and the foreign country is capital-abundant. The Heckscher-Ohlin theorem, if it focused only on capital and labor, might incorrectly predict the pattern of trade.

This leads to a basic point. In explaining the network of world trade some commodity flows are relatively easy to describe. Coffee is grown in Brazil and imported to the United States. Bolivia produces more tin than is desired for local consumption. Many countries have strong comparative advantages in some items because they possess the quantity and quality of resources specifically required in their production. The Heckscher-Ohlin model, with its assumption that all (both) commodities require all (both) factors, represents a step upward in sophistication in attempting to describe trade patterns.

We have already dealt with a model in which there are more commodities than factors — the Ricardian model. This asymmetry typically led to the result that a country would specialize in only one commodity. In a Heckscher-Ohlin world we expect a similar result: trading countries will typically produce no more commodities than the number of factors in existence.

(6) **Factor Mobility**

The Heckscher-Ohlin model follows the Ricardian model in assuming that labor could not move internationally, but there was a single labor market internally. This assumption is applied to capital as well as labor.

Within a country there may not be perfect competition for the same factor. This statement is not the same as pointing out that factors may be noncompeting because they have different skills — opera singers and university professors should be treated as different factors. Rather, barriers to entry (e.g., because of unions) or natural obstacles (high transport costs, preference for living in certain localities, etc.) may allow several factor returns to be maintained for the same factor, depending upon industry location and the like. We will discuss this phenomenon in Chapter 13 where we shall see that a country's commercial policy could be used to try to adjust for internal distortions in factor markets.

In many instances substantial movement of factors of production has taken place across national boundaries — labor migration to the

United States in the late 19th century or to West Germany or Israel in the post–World War II years, or, with capital, the extensive investment by British capitalists in American and Canadian productive activity in the last century, or the return flow of American capital to Europe at the current time. These are only some of the more obvious examples of international factor mobility. This subject will receive much more detailed investigation in Part 5.

This list of possible extensions to the basic Heckscher-Ohlin model could be expanded. But where does this leave the model? Some empirical observations are made in Chapter 10. Consider, here, only the theoretical usefulness of the model. The Ricardian model is ideally suited to pointing out the gains from trade. This, we saw earlier, could be accomplished as well in a model of pure exchange. As a model for explaining the pattern and nature of trade it is deficient in resting its whole case on arbitrary differences in technology. The Heckscher-Ohlin model took the necessary step forward in indicating that many factors combined to produce commodities, and that information on the pretrade structure of commodity prices, a necessary ingredient in explaining trade patterns, required knowledge of the availabilities of broad categories of factors such as labor and capital in different countries. As some critics of the Heckscher-Ohlin theory argue, many other considerations may affect the pricing structure, but as long as factor endowments differ worldwide as much as they seem, they cannot be ignored in the explanation of the structure of prices. Throughout our discussions of comparative advantage — in the exchange model, the Ricardian model, and the two versions of the Heckscher-Ohlin model — we have stressed the simplicity of looking at local demand and supply conditions for an ultimate understanding of the nature of trade. The Heckscher-Ohlin model is a sophisticated but still simple account showing how factor endowments and technology combine to influence the supply side of the market.

SUGGESTIONS FOR FURTHER READING

Heckscher, Eli, "The Effect of Foreign Trade on the Distribution of Income," reprinted American Economic Association, *Readings in the Theory of International Trade.* Philadelphia: Blakiston, 1949, chap. 13. This article originally appeared in Swedish: *Ekonomisk Tidskrift,* 21 (1919): 497–512. It discusses the effect of trade on factor prices in a nonmathematical, nongeometric format.

Johnson, Harry G., "Factor Endowments, International Trade and Factor Prices," *The Manchester School of Economic and Social Studies,* 25 (September 1957): 270–83; reprinted Johnson, *International Trade and Economic Growth.* Cambridge: Harvard University Press, 1958, chap. 1. Discusses the Heckscher-Ohlin model with emphasis on Figure 9.2.

Jones, Ronald W., "Factor Proportions and the Heckscher-Ohlin Theorem," *Review of Economic Studies,* 24 (October 1956): 1–10; reprinted ed. Jagdish Bhagwati. *International Trade.* Baltimore: Penguin, 1969, chap. 4. Emphasizes alternative definitions of factor abundance and comments upon the meaning of the Heckscher-Ohlin theorem.

Ohlin, Bertil. *Interregional and International Trade.* Cambridge: Harvard University Press, 1933. Together with the Heckscher article this book forms the basis for the modern theory of trade.

Rybczynski, T. M., "Factor Endowment and Relative Commodity Prices," *Economica,* N.S. 22 (November 1955): 336–41. A statement and proof of the Rybczynski theorem, using production box diagrams.

Samuelson, Paul A., "International Factor-Price Equalization Once Again," *Economic Journal,* 59 (June 1949): 181–97; reprinted ed. Stiglitz. *The Collected Scientific Papers of Paul A. Samuelson,* vol. 2. Cambridge: MIT Press, 1966, chap. 68. A restatement of Samuelson's factor-price equalization theorem.

Stolper, W. F., and Samuelson, P. A., "Protection and Real Wages," *Review of Economic Studies,* 9 (November 1941): 58–73; reprinted ed. Stiglitz. *The Collected Scientific Papers of Paul A. Samuelson,* vol. 2. Cambridge: MIT Press, 1966, chap. 66. The original statement of the Stolper-Samuelson theorem.

Supplement to Chapter 9:
The Variable-Coefficients Model: A Formal Analysis

In this supplement we shall extend the formal model developed in the supplement to Chapter 8 to the case in which input-output coefficients respond to factor prices. We shall be interested only in small changes in which the home country actively produces both commodities so that the competitive profit conditions are satisfied with equalities. We also assume full employment of both labor and capital. For convenience the pair of full-employment equations and competitive profit conditions, cited in equations 8.S.1–8.S.4, are reproduced below:

$$a_{LC}x_C + a_{LF}x_F = L \qquad (9.S.1)$$

$$a_{KC}x_C + a_{KF}x_F = K \qquad (9.S.2)$$

$$a_{LC}w + a_{KC}r = p_C \qquad (9.S.3)$$

$$a_{LF}w + a_{KF}r = p_F. \qquad (9.S.4)$$

Full-Empl. brace applies to (9.S.1)–(9.S.2); *Competitive Profit* brace applies to (9.S.3)–(9.S.4).

We shall proceed as in the supplement to Chapter 8 to differentiate 9.S.1–9.S.4 totally and to put the results in terms of relative changes. This leads initially to:

$$\lambda_{LC}\hat{x}_C + \lambda_{LF}\hat{x}_F = \hat{L} - (\lambda_{LC}\hat{a}_{LC} + \lambda_{LF}\hat{a}_{LF}) \qquad (9.S.5)$$

$$\lambda_{KC}\hat{x}_C + \lambda_{KF}\hat{x}_F = \hat{K} - (\lambda_{KC}\hat{a}_{KC} + \lambda_{KF}\hat{a}_{KF}) \qquad (9.S.6)$$

$$\theta_{LC}\hat{w} + \theta_{KC}\hat{r} = \hat{p}_C - (\theta_{LC}\hat{a}_{LC} + \theta_{KC}\hat{a}_{KC}) \qquad (9.S.7)$$

$$\theta_{LF}\hat{w} + \theta_{KF}\hat{r} = \hat{p}_F - (\theta_{LF}\hat{a}_{LF} + \theta_{KF}\hat{a}_{KF}). \qquad (9.S.8)$$

Recall that each factor allocation coefficient, λ_{ij}, represents the fraction of the country's endowment of factor i that is used to produce commodity j. The distributive-share coefficient, θ_{ij}, indicates what fraction of total costs in the jth industry is spent on the ith factor. The "hat" notation again represents relative changes. For example $\hat{r}$ is merely dr/r. Equations 9.S.5–9.S.8 generalize to the case of variable coefficients the corresponding set 8.S.5, 8.S.6, 8.S.8, and 8.S.9 for the fixed-coefficients case. In the latter all the $\hat{a}_{ij}$ terms disappeared because each a_{ij} was a constant. Now account must be taken of (1)

Special Case: Fixed Coeffs.

the weighted average of the changed intensity with which an input is used in the two industries (with the weights given by the fraction of the aggregate supply of that factor used in that industry), and (2) the weighted average of the changed intensity with which the two inputs are used in an industry (with the weights provided by distributive factor shares).

Our assumption about technology is that there is a smoothly bowed-in unit isoquant for each industry that is common to both countries. Furthermore, of the available techniques firms choose the one that minimizes unit costs with reference to the prevailing factor prices. This is shown graphically in Figure 9.1 for the clothing industry. Point B, for example, is chosen when the wage/rent ratio is shown by the slope of line 2. That is, the slope of the factor cost line, $-w/r$, is set equal to the slope of the isoquant, da_{KC}/da_{LC}. Or,

$$w\,da_{LC} + r\,da_{KC} = 0. \qquad \} \text{ under Cost-Min.}$$

Put in relative terms this implies:

$$\theta_{LC}\hat{a}_{LC} + \theta_{KC}\hat{a}_{KC} = 0. \qquad (9.S.9)$$

Similarly, in the food industry,

$$\theta_{LF}\hat{a}_{LF} + \theta_{KF}\hat{a}_{KF} = 0. \qquad (9.S.10)$$

Each of these expressions states that if the labor coefficient is increased, the capital coefficient must be reduced along the unit isoquant. The distributive share weighted average of these changes in input-output coefficients indicates the change in unit costs. At a point of cost minimization this change must be zero; all cost reductions from altering techniques along the unit isoquant must already be taken if the chosen techniques minimize costs.

These conditions directly simplify the competitive profit equations of change, 9.S.7 and 9.S.8. They become identical to equations 8.S.8 and 8.S.9 for the fixed-coefficients case:

$$\theta_{LC}\hat{w} + \theta_{KC}\hat{r} = \hat{p}_c \qquad (9.S.11)$$

$$\theta_{LF}\hat{w} + \theta_{KF}\hat{r} = \hat{p}_F. \qquad (9.S.12)$$

Each commodity price change must be a weighted average of the relative factor price changes. From this we can easily reestablish the *factor price equalization theorem*. If two countries have the same technology, and if free trade wipes out any difference between commodity prices in the two countries, factor prices must be equalized as well. To see this, interpret the relative changes shown in 9.S.11 and 9.S.12 as relative differences between countries. With free trade erasing intercountry differences in commodity prices, $\hat{p}_C = \hat{p}_F = 0$, and therefore $\hat{w} = \hat{r} = 0$. That is, factor prices are equalized. Notice that to obtain this result we had to assume that each country produces both commodities.

In a similar fashion the magnification effect linking relative price changes must also remain valid. To repeat, suppose prices change for the home country, with the relative price of labor-intensive clothing rising. If:

$$\hat{p}_C > \hat{p}_F$$

then

$$\hat{w} > \hat{p}_C > \hat{p}_F > \hat{r}.$$

This leads once again to the Stolper-Samuelson proposition that if the relative domestic price of the labor-intensive commodity can be raised, labor unambiguously benefits.

Equation 9.S.9 is the first of two relationships that link the response of the two input-output coefficients in the clothing industry to factor price changes. It reflects the tangency associated with a point of cost minimization. The second relationship focuses on the extent to which techniques will change as a consequence of a change in market conditions, and reflects the curvature of the isoquant. It is important to know whether an increase in the wage/rent ratio results in a large, or a small, alteration in the capital/labor ratio. The *elasticity of substitution* between capital and labor, which for the clothing industry we denote by σ_C, refers precisely to this extent of variability in techniques. σ_C is defined as the percentage increase in the capital/labor ratio in the clothing industry that is associated with a one percent increase in the wage/rent ratio. The relative increase in the capital/labor ratio in clothing is $(\hat{a}_{KC} - \hat{a}_{LC})$ and in the wage/rent ratio is $(\hat{w} - \hat{r})$. Therefore, by definition of σ_C,

$$(\hat{a}_{KC} - \hat{a}_{LC}) \equiv \sigma_C(\hat{w} - \hat{r}). \qquad (9.S.13)$$

It is a simple step to combine 9.S.9 and 9.S.13 to solve individually for $\hat{a}_{LC}$ and $\hat{a}_{KC}$ as functions of the relative factor price change, $(\hat{w} - \hat{r})$. The solutions are shown in 9.S.14:

$$\hat{a}_{LC} = -\theta_{KC}\sigma_C(\hat{w} - \hat{r})$$

$$\hat{a}_{KC} = \theta_{LC}\sigma_C(\hat{w} - \hat{r}). \qquad (9.S.14)$$

These solutions for changes in the input-output coefficients in the clothing industry are of the same form as those for the food industry — merely replace C with F in the subscripts of 9.S.14.

From our earlier discussion of the transformation schedule it is clear that equations 9.S.5 and 9.S.6 will not reduce to as simple a form as the competitive profit equations of change. For we know that even if endowments remain unchanged ($\hat{L} = \hat{K} = 0$ in 9.S.5 and 9.S.6), full-employment output levels can range the entire length of the production-possibilities locus. To probe further, examine the bracketed expression $(\lambda_{LC}\hat{a}_{LC} + \lambda_{LF}\hat{a}_{LF})$. Suppose the wage/rent ratio rises. We know that this will cause *both* industries to use less labor-intensive techniques. Therefore this expression must be negative, and have the same effect on outputs as would an increase in the total supply of available labor. If industries slough off labor, full employment can be maintained only by having an expansion in the output of the labor-intensive industry. We have already obtained, in equations 9.S.14, an explicit solution for each $\hat{a}_{ij}$ in terms of the factor price change and characteristics of the technology (distributive shares and elasticities of substitution). Therefore it is a simple matter to substitute 9.S.14 (and the analogous solution for the $\hat{a}_{iF}$ in the food industry) into 9.S.5 and 9.S.6 to obtain:

$$\lambda_{LC}\hat{x}_C + \lambda_{LF}\hat{x}_F = \hat{L} + \delta_L(\hat{w} - \hat{r}) \qquad (9.S.15)$$

$$\lambda_{KC}\hat{x}_C + \lambda_{KF}\hat{x}_F = \hat{K} - \delta_K(\hat{w} - \hat{r}) \qquad (9.S.16)$$

where

$$\delta_L \equiv \lambda_{LC}\theta_{KC}\sigma_C + \lambda_{LF}\theta_{KF}\sigma_F$$

$$\delta_K \equiv \lambda_{KC}\theta_{LC}\sigma_C + \lambda_{KF}\theta_{LF}\sigma_F.$$

The details of the δ's are not as important as the general concept that each δ_i is positive, implying that an increase in the wage/rent ratio, by causing each industry to use labor more sparingly and capital more intensively, has an effect on outputs that is similar to an increase in the labor supply and a reduc-

[margin annotation:] $\sigma_d = \dfrac{\dfrac{\ell\left(\frac{x}{c}\right)}{x/L}}{\dfrac{\ell\left(\frac{w}{r}\right)}{w/r}}$

tion in capital. This is what was portrayed graphically in Figure 9.4, in the movement of outputs from point A to point B.

Subtract 9.S.16 from 9.S.15. Using the terminology of Chapter 8 leads to 9.S.17:

$$(\hat{x}_C - \hat{x}_F) = \frac{1}{|\lambda|}(\hat{L} - \hat{K}) + \frac{(\delta_L + \delta_K)}{|\lambda|}(\hat{w} - \hat{r}). \qquad (9.S.17)$$

If clothing is labor-intensive, $|\lambda|$ is a positive fraction, $\lambda_{LC} - \lambda_{KC}$. Finally, substitute the relationship between a relative commodity price change and a relative factor price change (equation 8.S.10) to obtain:

$$(\hat{x}_C - \hat{x}_F) = \frac{1}{|\lambda|}(\hat{L} - \hat{K}) + \sigma_S(\hat{p}_C - \hat{p}_F) \qquad (9.S.18)$$

where

$$\sigma_S \equiv \frac{\delta_L + \delta_K}{|\lambda||\theta|} > 0.$$

This equation, which states explicitly how either endowment changes or price changes can alter the composition of outputs, can summarize much that has been portrayed graphically in Chapter 9. Notice that because δ_L and δ_K are positive, and because both $|\lambda|$ and $|\theta|$ have the same sign, σ_S must be positive. σ_S shows how relative outputs change along the transformation curve as relative prices change. It is the elasticity of substitution along the transformation curve. It suggests what Figure 9.8 illustrated, that an increase in the relative price of food must increase the relative output of food if, as assumed along transformation curves, endowments are held constant. Because the commodity price ratio is identified with the slope of the transformation curve, it supports the demonstration in Figure 9.5 that the transformation curve is bowed out from the origin.

Finally, notice how at constant commodity prices outputs respond in a magnified fashion to any change in factor endowments, because $|\lambda|$ is a positive fraction. This property was used in Figure 9.8 to show that if the home country was labor abundant, it would produce a higher output of the labor-intensive commodity than the foreign country if they faced the same terms of trade. The magnification effect linking endowment changes with the composition of outputs remains as described in Chapter 8 if commodity prices are held constant.

10 Testing the Ricardian and Heckscher-Ohlin Models of Trade

We have now explored two models of international trade and production. Each selects assumptions about production and deduces their implications for the pattern of trade, the terms of trade, and the payments to factors of production. Why two models? In building theoretical models, the goal of scientists is to make theory as simple as possible, consistent with providing the answers they need. They would not have two models if one would do. Certainly we should not need separate models if both could be deduced from identical assumptions about the real economic world. The Ricardian and Heckscher-Ohlin models' explanations and predictions seem to differ on many important points, because their respective sets of assumptions are not equivalent. But if they rest on different views about "reality," which one is right? Can we determine that one set of assumptions fits reality better than the other? Does one set fit one part of the world, while the other surpasses it elsewhere?

In the first section of this chapter we shall consider the empirical differences in these two models, and ask what is needed to test or confirm a theoretical model. Then we shall take up successively the applications of the Ricardian and Heckscher-Ohlin models.

10.1 ASSUMPTIONS AND PREDICTIONS IN MODELS OF TRADE

No model literally describes reality, accounting for every sparrow's fall, or every price's rise. Model-building is always a process of strategic simplification. For models of economic behavior and economic welfare we try to leave out (or aggregate) actors and connections in the economy that are of no great importance for its performance, in order to concentrate on those that are. Both the Ricardian and Heckscher-Ohlin models, as typically presented and used by economists, omit many features of the world about us — monopoly, price rigidity, and other imperfections in markets; the effect of advertising on consumers' behavior; the effect of inflation on tomorrow's expected prices; failures to use the most efficient techniques of production; and many more. Our two models differ critically in their simplifications, however, on one point: Heckscher-Ohlin allows for two (or more) factors in the production of each good; Ricardo assumes that only one factor (labor) can be put into alternative lines of production. We must choose the one whose starting point gives us the more valuable results.

On first thought, you might say that Heckscher-Ohlin wins hands down. Are there not many factors of production in the world — butchers, bakers, candlestick makers; tongs and turret lathes? And does this model not yield a rich harvest of predictions, e.g. of how changes in the terms of trade will alter the outputs, techniques of production, and factor prices? True, but one cannot be certain without checking the facts that these extra complexities of the Heckscher-Ohlin model are warranted by its usefulness. For instance, we can easily construct a description of complex reality for which the Ricardian model is a more fruitful simplification than is Heckscher-Ohlin: The world contains many factors of production, but the broadly used factors — labor and capital — are employed in nearly the same proportions in every line of production. Hence changes in relative output volumes induce no significant shifts in factor prices. Furthermore, production functions are not the same everywhere. Florida enjoys a comparative advantage in orange-growing because of abundant sunshine — an unproduced, unmarketable gift of nature — and not because of her capital-labor endowment. The United States west coast may require fewer tangible resources to produce aircraft because much of the work can be done out of doors. The United States has recently become a major exporter of coal, perhaps not because she has so *much* land overlying coal deposits, but because the deposits lie nearer the surface in thicker seams, and hence require less capital and labor to work than those of other countries. Each of these traits makes production functions appear to differ from place to place.[1]

In this world the Ricardian model is still a valid and useful description of a nation's production possibilities. The simple labor

---

[1] Defenders of Heckscher-Ohlin might argue that we should simply subdivide our factors of production more finely, so that we measure the nation's factor endowment not just in quantity of land, or even quantity of coal land, but rather in grades of coal land. This is logically possible, but it quickly threatens to make the model hopelessly cumbersome and tautological. And it does not work for differences in climate or environment that cannot be traded on the market.

coefficients of Chapter $7 - a_{LC}$ and a_{LF} — are stable measures of production technology, and their predictions about patterns of trade are unaffected by the terms of trade, the capital stock, and the like. Although the Heckscher-Ohlin description of the productive apparatus is richer, we cannot automatically assume that it is more accurate.

On the other hand, if the assumptions underlying the Heckscher-Ohlin model are correct, the Ricardian analysis would fail. The labor coefficients would vary with factor prices. Or if, as in Chapter 8, the labor coefficients are fixed but labor collaborates with capital in different proportions from industry to industry, we will rob ourselves of important predictions about the effects of trade on factor prices if we concentrate only on the labor coefficients. The simpler model proves inaccurate and incomplete.

We have referred often to criteria for judging a model — the correctness of its assumptions, the fullness and accuracy of its predictions, etc. How should one choose the better model? Economists argue heatedly over this question, so the following position will not win the agreement of all. A model's value ultimately depends on its predictive power — the accuracy with which it deduces empirical outcomes from its assumptions about reality.[2] A fundamental prediction of the Heckscher-Ohlin model, what we called the Heckscher-Ohlin theorem, holds that a nation that is well endowed with capital will export capital-intensive goods; if this prediction should fail to hold, the model's stock would plummet. Thus the success of our models in explaining real-life phenomena is a fundamental test.

It is not the only test, however. Suppose our model has explained the patterns of trade of the United States and Germany. We now wish it to tell us the future trade pattern of Korea, as economic development proceeds, or of Yugoslavia, as she expands her currently restricted trade with the West. Is our model applicable? This question is vital, and can be answered only by testing the "fit" of the model's assumptions to the economic characteristics of the Korean or the Yugoslav economy. No model has been tested by economists in every setting. A fruitful model, as judged by its predictions, works somewhere, or sometime. We now need to determine its "realm of validity," the economic phenomena to which it can be applied. When we contemplate using a model to answer a question, we need to know not only that it has given the right answer to a similar question, but also that the scene of its former success matches that where we would now apply it.

---

[2] Economists often use the word "prediction" to include more than the activities of the weather-man. As an exercise, a weather forecaster could try to "predict" the weather a year ago today from the information that was available a year ago yesterday. Then he could check the actual weather a year ago today against his "forecast," to judge the performance of his model. In short, prediction and explanation use the same basic scientific activity to verify the effect that a model suggests should flow from stipulated causes.

The problem of the aptness of assumptions cuts even deeper than this. We can build a model using the assumption that the moon is made of green cheese. We test one of its predictions, and it works. We have not yet tested, or perhaps cannot test, other predictions that we can extract from it. Should we draw complete confidence from the first predictive success, discounting the possibility of a fluke? Or should we send an astronaut (astromouse?) to verify the assumption directly? In practice, the testing of predictions from a model and the verifying of assumptions used to build it are complementary rather than substitute activities.[3]

Although assumptions and predictions both matter, economists who have used the Ricardian and Heckscher-Ohlin models have been largely concerned with testing their predictions. Their tests range from checking a model's predictions against historical experience to performing sophisticated statistical exercises. As we survey some of the tests, we shall see that they raise teasing questions about the aptness of the assumptions underlying these models, and sometimes about the logic of their construction. They also give us a basis — the only basis we have — for declaring that one model delivers superior performance.

10.2 EVIDENCE ON THE RICARDIAN MODEL

The Ricardian model predicts that countries should export products with low domestic labor requirements. Equivalently, they should specialize in goods for which their labor productivity — output per worker — is relatively high. In this form the prediction was tested by Sir Donald MacDougall on data for United Kingdom and United States exports and productivity for 1937.[4] He calculated the ratio of British to American exports for each of twenty industry groups, and also the ratio of United States to British output per worker. British exports were typically low where American labor productivity was relatively high. MacDougall's ratios for the individual industries fell into the following ranges:

[3] One vital type of prediction that we want from a model concerns the choice of economic policies. Whether policy *A* will make the nation better off can seldom be tested by putting *A* into force and checking the temperature on a welfare thermometer. If we adopt *A* on the basis of our theoretical model, we should know both that *A*'s behavioral predictions about the world have proved accurate, and that *A*'s assumptions seem consistent with the situation at hand.

[4] "British and American Exports: A Study Suggested by the Theory of Comparative Costs," *Economic Journal*, 61 (December 1951): 697–724, reprinted in American Economic Association, *Readings in International Economics* (Homewood, Ill.: Richard D. Irwin, 1968). Recent, similar studies are Robert M. Stern, "British and American Productivity and Comparative Costs in International Trade," *Oxford Economic Papers*, 14 (October 1962): 275–96; and Bela Balassa, "An Empirical Demonstration of Classical Comparative Cost Theory," *Review of Economics and Statistics*, 45 (August 1963): 231–38.

United States/United Kingdom output per worker	United Kingdom/United States exports
More than 2.0	0.12 to 1.0
1.4 to 2.0	2.0 to 18.0
Less than 1.4	11.0 to 250.0

Several incidental results of his study shed light on the Ricardian model and its predictive power.

The export ratio that MacDougall used was for United States total exports to all countries but the United Kingdom, and for total United Kingdom exports to all countries but the United States. Why did he exclude their mutual trade — only a small fraction of the total for each? The answer is that the United States tariff, its height varying from sector to sector, intercepts the British exports in varying degrees, and thus blunts the effect of British productivity differences. Likewise, the British tariff imposes a barrier of variable height to United States exports. In the rest of the world, however, both exporters generally face the same tariffs.[5] Those tariffs curb both countries' exports, but should not distort the ratio of United Kingdom to United States exports of a single product. Including their mutual trade in the calculations would distort the influence of comparative costs by injecting the influence of the differing United States and United Kingdom tariff structures.

MacDougall stressed values of the ratio of United States to United Kingdom productivity greater than or less than 2.0, because he found wages in the United States then to be about double those in Britain. If American labor is twice as productive but gets paid twice as much as British workers, money costs of production should be the same in the two countries. For productivity ratios higher than 2.0, the United States should enjoy an *absolute* advantage in a product, being able to produce it for lower money costs. Where the United States productivity advantage fails to offset the wage differential, British production should enjoy an absolute advantage. What about cases in which the productivity differential just offsets the wage differential, so that neither United States nor United Kingdom producers enjoy a significant cost advantage? Some economists have concluded that the export ratio ought to be about 1.0 in that case, and have tried to explain why on average it was not. Yet a moment's thought about demand and country size, in the model of Chapter 7, quickly tells us that we can predict nothing a priori about the sharing of an export market between two countries when neither has a cost advantage.

[5] Actually, the United Kingdom in her overseas territories often faced lower tariffs due to an arrangement called Imperial Preference (see Chapter 15). These tariffs were lower in the same proportion for all goods, however, and should not have thrown off the test. MacDougall noticed that in 1937 United States tariffs generally offset Britain's productivity advantage, where one existed, over protected United States industries.

Suppose that one is diversified in resources and factor endowment, and can easily supply most of its needs, whereas the other's resources are limited and specialized, making it dependent on imports. The second country might then be the larger trader if their sizes, costs, and all other factors were constant. Thus the force of reciprocal demand may explain MacDougall's finding that in 1937 the United States exported less than the United Kingdom of products in which the American productivity advantage just offset the wage disadvantages.

One critic of MacDougall's study has argued that he erred in comparing labor productivities with market shares directly. Instead he should have made sure that advantages in labor productivity were reflected in advantages in export prices. MacDougall's data in fact do not reveal any link between United States and United Kingdom labor productivities for various goods and the relative prices charged for them on export markets. Hence we should not trust his finding of a link between exports and productivities.[6] When we consider the Ricardian model of Chapter 7, this objection appears clearly incorrect. When America and Britain are exporting the same product, they must presumably be selling it at the same price. One could have a productivity advantage, and hence a larger market share, but in a purely competitive market this would not yield a lower price. MacDougall's original hypothesis thus correctly set forth the predictions of the Ricardian model.

We cannot yet judge whether the Ricardian model works better than any competitor, but we can say that it works, i.e., that American and British trade patterns have been found broadly consistent with its predictions. One way to test explanations like these is to ask whether they can be improved greatly by making the model a bit more elaborate. The success of the Ricardian model in reducing the determinants of trade patterns (on the cost side) to one fundamental force — labor productivity — would be depreciated if we could explain trade patterns much more fully by taking a few other simple forces into account.

One candidate that has been tested is difference in a country's wages from industry to industry. The Ricardian model assumes that the labor market, like all others, is purely competitive. Hence a single wage would prevail in all industries in a country. (Wages might vary with skill, of course; the Ricardian model assumes that we can ignore this facet of reality.) Economists have often noticed that wages vary from industry to industry, although by much less than does average labor productivity. Thus a nation's labor market certainly pulls industry wages toward a common level. Still, differences in wages due to imperfect labor markets might influence trade among countries.

[6] Jagdish Bhagwati, "The Pure Theory of International Trade: A Survey," *Economic Journal*, 74 (March 1964): 10–17.

Suppose that labor productivity did *not* differ from industry to industry. Then wage differences, not productivity differences, ought to govern production costs and patterns of specialization and trade. Testing this proposition is simple enough: we need only ask whether wages are lower in a country's export industries than in those that compete with imports. Several studies[7] have shown that, if anything, wages are higher in countries' export industries. Hence they could hardly contribute to explaining comparative advantage. But why should wage differences run in the opposite direction? One possible answer is that these studies have often taken little or no account of skill differences in the labor forces producing exports and import-competing goods. If a country's exports require more highly skilled labor than its import-competing goods, we should expect average wages in the export industries to be higher. We shall refer to this possibility again.

One does not, then, improve the power of labor productivities to explain trade patterns by taking inter-industry wage differences into account. Instead, suppose that we allow for differences in the quantity of capital employed from industry to industry. Here we approach a direct test of the Ricardian model against the more complex Heckscher-Ohlin, for indeed the latter declares that we should explain trade patterns by labor, capital, and perhaps other factors, rather than just labor alone.

10.3 TESTING THE HECKSCHER-OHLIN MODEL: HISTORICAL PATTERNS

Applications of the Heckscher-Ohlin model of trade have taken two forms. It has proved a useful framework for the broad-brush interpretation of patterns of trade and their long-run evolution. And it has been put to a formal test parallel to MacDougall's investigation of the Ricardian model. In this section we study the usefulness of the Heckscher-Ohlin model as a guide to understanding historical patterns.

Ohlin's great book, *Interregional and International Trade* (1933), contained not only the ideas underlying the model presented in Chapters 8 and 9, but also many historical examples and illustrations. He found that the wheat-growing nations of Europe could be divided into two groups, the exporting (or self-sufficient) countries with low population densities (ratios of labor to land), and the importing countries with high densities of population. On first glance we might think it paradoxical that exporting countries like Russia or Rumania would achieve low wheat yields per acre, importing countries like Denmark or the Netherlands much higher yields. Yet Ohlin

---

[7] E.g., Irving B. Kravis, "Wages and Foreign Trade," *Review of Economics and Statistics*, 38 (February 1956): 14–30.

pointed out that his theory leads us to expect just this: in importing countries where wheat is expensive and land scarce, large quantities of other factors (labor, capital) should be employed per unit of land, and achieve high yields; in exporting countries where wheat would be cheap, and land abundant, the land was worked "extensively" by a few cooperating factors, and yields were correspondingly low. Such facts reflected both the influence of factor endowments (land and labor) on trade, and also the interrelation between factor prices and the input mixture. Ohlin also illustrated the effects of varying ratios of capital to land. In the Baltic countries, capital was scarce and interest rates high during the 1920's. Exploitation for export of timber lands in these countries often involved the building of sawmills, even where the abundant wood was of inferior quality better suited for woodpulp. The reason, he suggested, was that pulp mills are necessarily much larger and more capital-intensive than sawmills, and thus ill-suited to the prevailing factor prices.

The Heckscher-Ohlin model also helps to explain changes over time in a country's pattern of trade. In her early stages as an exporter of manufactures, Japan specialized in goods requiring large quantities of unskilled labor — inexpensive textiles, cheap toys, and other simple manufactures. One of her traditional specialties, silk, is particularly labor-intensive. In recent years, however, Japan's advantage has shifted toward manufactures requiring large quantities of skilled labor — cameras, electronic instruments, automobiles — and her advantage in manufactures intensive in unskilled labor has to some degree been lost to such countries as Korea, Hongkong, and India.

This model of trade can even assist in explaining political change. The English Reform Bill of 1832 provided for more popular representation in the House of Commons and reduced the power of the landed aristocracy. The new commercial and industrial classes, who benefited, included the owners of capital employed in producing Britain's rapidly growing exports of manufactures. Thus the reform increased the political power of factors of production — labor and capital — employed intensively in producing exports, and reduced the power of land engaged in the import-competing production of grain. Clearly the stage was set for a policy change that would increase the price of exports relative to that of imports — and import-competing production. As we found in Chapter 8 (sec. 8.3), the removal of a tariff would bring about just this shift. Hence, some observers have suggested, the famous repeal of the Corn Laws (1846) may have reflected political-economic forces rather than the intellectual triumph of liberal free-trade sentiment.[8]

The trade of the United States over the past century reveals an important trend that is explained by the Heckscher-Ohlin model. A

[8] For these and other examples, see Charles P. Kindleberger, *Foreign Trade and the National Economy*. New Haven: Yale University Press, 1962.

century ago, the United States was, compared to its principal trading partners, rich in natural resources. Over the years some American natural resources — forests, metallic ores — have been partially depleted and other nations have been drawn into world trade to supply these primary products. These facts would lead us to expect that "land" — natural resources in general — has gone from being the abundant to being the scarce factor in the United States endowment, and that American trade has switched from predominantly exporting resource-intensive products to principally importing them.

Some calculations by Jaroslav Vanek confirm this trend. How is the natural-resources content of trade flows measured? This cannot be done directly. Agricultural land varies too much in topography, climate, etc., to be measured by total acreage. And the natural resources available to produce metals and minerals can hardly be tallied except by the outputs themselves. Therefore Vanek proceeded indirectly by measuring for various years the value of the products of natural resources embodied in United States exports and in the goods produced in the United States in competition with imports. Sure enough, the value of resource products embodied in the typical bundle of United States exports fell from nearly twice that required (at home) for the production of goods competing with our imports, in 1870, to a level about three-fourths of the requirements for imports in 1955.[9] One can say that the United States' trade pattern has changed toward the export of products using factors other than natural resources intensively, and toward the import of resource-intensive products.

Factor Endowments and Multilateral Trade

The cases discussed in this section have in one way contrasted sharply with the theory presented in Chapters 8 and 9. The theoretical model is most easily grasped if we stick to two countries, commodities, and factors of production; in practice, Nature persistently presents us with at least three factors and many more commodities and countries. The formal theory grows very complicated when we allow for many entities, but some feeling for its application in more complex situations is still desirable. One useful application, in a world with more than two countries, concerns not the trade pattern but the bilateral balances of trade that might develop between pairs of countries.

Consider the problem first as purely theoretical. Suppose we identify three regions in the trading world that can be ranked by their endowments of land, labor, and capital in the fashion shown below:

[9] Jaroslav Vanek, "The Natural Resource Content of Foreign Trade, 1870–1955, and the Relative Abundance of Natural Resources in the United States," *Review of Economics and Statistics*, 41 (May 1959): 146–53.

Relative factor supply	Region A	Region B	Region C
Ample	Labor	Land	Capital
Moderate	Land	Capital	Labor
Scarce	Capital	Labor	Land

Each region trades numerous commodities with the others under purely competitive conditions. These patterns of factor abundance imply something about bilateral trade balances among these countries. Region *A* is rich in labor but *B* is poor. Hence *B*'s demand for imports of the goods in which *A* specializes will be strong, the comparative disadvantage of their domestic production being great. But the converse should not hold: *A*'s maximum disadvantage lies in capital-intensive goods, but *B* is only moderately well endowed with capital. Hence, other things equal, *A* is likely to have a trade surplus with *B*. The situation for bilateral trade between *A* and *C* is the reverse: *C*'s endowment is suitable for specialization in the capital-intensive goods *A* is most likely to import, yet *C* is moderately well endowed with labor and hence may not be equally receptive to *A*'s exports. *A* is likely to have a trade deficit with *C*. Notice that *A*'s predicted surplus with *B* and deficit with *C* is consistent with overall balance for *A*, her total exports equaling total imports. When we find, by the same reasoning, that *B* is likely to run a surplus on bilateral trade with *C*, it is clear that this model is also consistent with overall trade balance for *B* and *C* as well.

Karl-Erik Hansson, who set forth this schema, proposed that it explains rather well the pattern of bilateral trade balances observed among major trading areas, up to World War I. Equate region *A* with the tropics, well suited to export resource-intensive products requiring unskilled labor but relatively little capital. Equate region *B* with the United States and the other temperate regions settled by European emigrants. Equate region *C* with the European countries. Trade balances between these regions were relatively stable and agreed closely with the theoretical prediction.[10] This is a casual "test" of the theory, but it does illustrate the richness of the Heckscher-Ohlin theory for explaining historical patterns.

10.4 TESTING THE HECKSCHER-OHLIN THEOREM: UNITED STATES TRADE AND FACTOR ENDOWMENT

If this factor-proportions model seems to explain broad patterns and trends in international trade, it should also stand up to close statistical scrutiny of its chief hypothesis: that nations export products that use intensively their abundant factors, and import goods that require large quantities of their scarce factors. W. W. Leontief set out to test this by calculating the capital and labor required to produce a million dollars' worth of United States exports, and a million dollars' worth of goods directly competitive with United States imports. For each industry, such as automobiles, he measured the capital and labor required per unit of output — not just in the auto assembly process itself, but also in the steel, rubber, glass, etc., industries that supply inputs to the automobile industry. Noting the average composition of United States exports in 1947, he then computed the capital and labor needed to produce a million-dollar bundle of typical exportable goods. From the composition of United States imports that year (excluding items not produced in the country such as coffee and bananas), he estimated the capital and labor required to produce a million dollars' worth of replacements for these imports at home.

The United States seems obviously endowed with more capital per worker than any other country. Therefore, Leontief reasoned, the Heckscher-Ohlin theorem predicts that United States exports will require more capital per worker than do United States import-competing goods. But his figures showed that import-replacements demand 30 percent *more* capital per worker than exports; the United States trade pattern is that of a labor-rich country! (His results appear in Table 10.1.) Concerned that his findings might simply stem from distortions in the United States trade pattern just after World War II, he repeated the calculation using the average composition of exports and imports in 1951. As section 2 of the table shows, the greater capital-intensity of import-competing goods was reduced substantially but still remained. A recent repeat of the test (section 3 of Table 10.1) again yielded the paradoxical result, almost as strong as ever. This curious disease proved contagious. Similar calculations for Japan, to all appearances the most labor-rich industrial country, revealed its exports to be more capital-intensive than its import-replacements. India's exports to the world at large proved relatively labor-intensive, but her exports to the United States proved more capital-intensive than goods with competing imports from America. Canada provided relief by being more capital-intensive in her exports than in her import-competing goods — Canada would appear to be a relatively capital-rich country — but the same capital-intensity marked Canada's bilateral exports to the apparently capital-richer United States.[11] Paradoxes abounded!

These failures of a simple and highly plausible hypothesis sent economists scurrying — both back to the theoretical model and forth

---

[11] The conclusions drawn from bilateral trade patterns here and in the balance of this chapter depend on certain assumptions. Broadly speaking, they follow if each country's output of one class of goods is not identical to outputs of similar goods produced elsewhere. This assumption makes sense for industrial goods; we examine it further in Chapter 11.

TABLE 10.1 Domestic Capital and Labor Requirements
per Million Dollars of United States
Exports and Competitive Import Replacements

Factor	Exports	Competitive imports	Ratio of imports to exports
1. U.S. production structure in 1947 and average composition of trade in 1947:			
Capital	$2,550,780	$3,091,339	
Labor	182	170	
Capital per man-year	$14,010	$18,180	1.30
2. U.S. production structure in 1947 and average composition of trade in 1951:			
Capital	$2,256,800	$2,303,400	
Labor	174	168	
Capital per man-year	$12,977	$13,726	1.06
3. U.S. production structure in 1958 and average composition of trade in 1962:			
Capital	$1,876,000	$2,132,000	
Labor	131	119	
Capital per man-year	$14,200	$18,000	1.27

Sources: W. W. Leontief, "Factor Proportions and the Structure of American Trade: Further Theoretical and Empirical Analysis," *Review of Economics and Statistics*, 38 (November 1956): 392, 397; Robert E. Baldwin, "Determinants of the Commodity Structure of U.S. Trade," *American Economic Review*, 61 (March 1971): 134.

to the statistical evidence. Here we review some of the principal qualifications and subsidiary tests.

Effectiveness of United States Labor

Leontief himself suggested that the explanation of his results might lie in the superior efficiency of American labor. Perhaps United States workers were three times as effective as foreign labor, in the sense that *with the same amount of capital* they could turn out three times as much. The apparent abundance of capital per worker in the United States could then be an illusion, in that the *effective* United States labor force would be thrice the number of workers actually employed. Of the possible explanations for this alleged superiority, Leontief believed that superior American entrepreneurship and *(k)* economic organization increased effectiveness of labor. This explanation has found few takers. It is not easily tested empirically, but the evidence we have fails to support it.[12] American entrepreneurship may indeed excel, but why should it be much more adroit at coaxing extra output from labor than from capital? If organizational superiority simply made *all* American factors more productive than their foreign counterparts, the effective capital-richness of the United States economy should be unaffected. We would still expect, following Heckscher-Ohlin, that United States exports should be capital-intensive relative to import-replacements.

(2) **Consumption Patterns**

Theorists quickly pointed out that Leontief's results were not *necessarily* inconsistent with America's capital-rich position, although they clashed with the Heckscher-Ohlin theorem. As we found in Chapter 8, the prediction that a capital-rich country will export capital-intensive goods rests entirely on a model of productive factors and costs, and not on demand. At given terms of trade, a nation's factor endowment might bias it toward capital-intensive exports. Yet the tastes of its consumers might run so strongly toward capital-intensive goods that these would be in excess demand. The country would then export labor-intensive goods, although it could and did produce large quantities of capital-intensive products.[13] Does the United States possess a sweet tooth for capital-intensive goods? Apparently not. Studies show that the way consumers divide their outlays among various goods differs little from one industrial country to another, so the Heckscher-Ohlin assumption that tastes are similar appears to be correct. Furthermore, as incomes per capita rise, people spend more on services, which are seldom capital-intensive in production.

(3) **Labor Skills**

Several critics of Leontief's results worried whether he had taken account of enough distinctions among factors of production. Should

[12] Mordechai E. Kreinin tried to test Leontief's conjecture by asking multinational companies to compare the labor time required per unit of output in their United States factories with that in their European plants. From their replies he concluded: "A realistic factor by which to multiply the number of United States workers in order to allow for the difference in effectiveness is $1\frac{1}{3}$ or at most $1\frac{1}{4}$, but not 2 or 3." See his "Comparative Labor Effectiveness and the Leontief Scarce-Factor Paradox," *American Economic Review*, 55 (March 1965): 131–40.

[13] The proposition that a capital-rich country produces large quantities of capital-intensive goods is sometimes called the weak version of the Heckscher-Ohlin theorem, the proposition that its exports are more capital-intensive than its imports the strong version of the theorem. The strong version obviously requires an assumption about demand conditions in order to prove valid, the weak version is less informative but needs no such assumption.

we be concerned with a nation's abundance of "labor," "skilled labor," "plumbers"? How far need we subdivide a broadly defined factor of production into its distinguishable components? The answer depends somewhat on the problem we are trying to solve, but ultimately on the ease and speed with which one factor can be turned into another, e.g., a salesman retrained to be a plumber. If the transition is easy and quick, we expect workers to move between the two occupations to equate the wages received in them, and the economy's structure of production and trade to be influenced not by the relative quantities of the two, but by the aggregate supply.

Plumbers and salesmen apart, skilled labor in general probably cannot be created readily and quickly from unskilled labor, so that a nation's endowment of labor skills can help to determine its trade pattern. The United States possesses a rich endowment of skills in its labor force, relative to other countries. Hence, Leontief's paradox might be resolved if we took account of skilled and unskilled labor separately. Indeed, this maneuver helps somewhat to explain the paradox. Several studies have now shown that United States exports require large proportions of skilled labor, United States import-competing industries large quantities of unskilled labor.[14]

Another way to look at the role of labor skills is to recognize that the education and training of the nation's work-force represent capital. A man who invests six months in acquiring a skill creates capital, as does a man who spends six months building a machine. Leontief did not include the value of this "human capital" in his calculations. Indeed it cannot be valued directly, like the machines and buildings owned by a manufacturer, because skilled workers are not bought and sold — only their services. But if we value labor skills indirectly by capitalizing the extra income they yield to the skilled worker over the wages of the unskilled, this component of capital suffices to reverse Leontief's paradox.[15]

(4) Research and Development

Somewhat related to the role of skilled labor is the influence of research and development in United States exports. "Research" itself demands much skilled labor. We know that industries that carry on significant amounts of research in the United States tend strongly to be net exporters, and so typical United States exports are much more "research intensive" than the typical goods competing with imports. Hence the role of research in the exporting activities in part explains the intensive use made of skilled labor in export pro-

---

[14] See Robert E. Baldwin, "Determinants of the Commodity Structure of U.S. Trade," *American Economic Review.* 61 (March 1971): 126–46.

[15] Peter B. Kenen, "Nature, Capital, and Trade," *Journal of Political Economy* 73 (October 1965): 437–60.

duction.[16] It confirms our previous finding that the United States exports products intensive in skilled labor and imports products that (if produced at home) would demand large quantities of scarce unskilled labor (and perhaps scarce capital).

(5) **Tariffs**

Several critics have urged that Leontief's findings are distorted by the influence of United States and perhaps foreign tariffs. Recall the way in which Leontief calculated his typical bundle of import-competing products: by taking the actual composition of United States imports and using these percentages to assign importance to the individual lines of import-competing production. Suppose that the United States tariff were systematically designed to protect domestic industries requiring large quantities of unskilled labor. High tariff rates on such products would preclude most imports of them, and labor-intensive industries would hence carry very small weights in determining the average capital-labor requirements of import-competing production. The Heckscher-Ohlin theorem predicts trade patterns from factor endowments only on the assumption that market forces are given free play and are not blocked by tariffs or other impediments. Hence we cannot fairly test it without allowing for their influence.

Some evidence indeed suggests that the United States tariff protects most heavily industries requiring large quantities of labor, especially unskilled. If we identify and weigh the import-competing industries not by actual flows of imports, but by the mix of imports that the United States would purchase if these tariffs were removed, the average capital-intensity of import-competing production would fall.[17] Hence the tendency of American tariffs to conceal the import-competing character of labor-intensive industries helps to explain Leontief's paradox.

(6) **Natural Resources**

We saw that Leontief's test may have oversimplified in failing to distinguish between skilled and unskilled labor, as components of the United States factor endowment. The test has also been criticized

[16] Donald Keesing, "The Impact of Research and Development on United States Trade," *The Open Economy: Essays on International Trade,* ed. P. B. Kenen and R. Lawrence. New York: Columbia University Press, 1968, pp. 175–89. It is also possible to view research, like skills, as creating a form of capital — knowledge — which Leontief failed to value in toting up the capital requirements of various industries. If this intangible capital belonging to each industry were valued by capitalizing the extra profits it generates, the capital-intensity of the exporting industries would be significantly increased. Notice that using research resources to create knowledge does not differ in principle from creating capital by using them to build machines, or instill labor skills.

[17] Baldwin, pp. 130, 139. The significance of the United States tariff is discussed in Chapter 14.

for omitting natural resources. In section 10.3 we found that the United States' trade pattern has changed over the long run as the country's natural resources have grown increasingly scarce. One might say that the United States exports goods requiring large quantities of its abundant capital *and* labor, importing goods that (if produced at home) would require large quantities of scarce natural resources. Indeed, it was found that the natural-resource products embodied in a million dollars' worth of United States exports were barely over half of those contained in the equivalent volume of import-replacements.

Granting this important role for natural resources, should they throw off Leontief's test, which was based solely on the relative proportions of capital and labor? If the United States is well endowed with capital, should that not bias it toward exporting capital-intensive and importing labor-intensive goods, whatever the pull of natural resources? Not necessarily. Outputs requiring substantial inputs of natural resources might not be typical in their requirements of capital and labor. The production functions for resource-intensive goods might systematically require larger inputs of capital per man-year, at any factor prices, than goods without significant resource content. That "affinity" of natural resources for capital could explain Leontief's computations that mark United States import-replacements as relatively capital-intensive.[18]

Factor-Intensity Reversals

An exotic but important problem with Leontief's test lies in the possibility that a theoretical assumption essential to the Heckscher-Ohlin theorem may be violated in practice. This assumption, mentioned in Chapter 9, is that one (of two) commodities would be produced by labor-intensive methods, compared with the other, for any common ratio of factor prices. That is, factor-intensity rankings never reverse when factor prices change. There is no a priori reason for this assumption to be valid, yet the model's conclusions change greatly if it fails to hold.

The assumption would fail in a situation where we can find one wage/rent ratio at which commodity 1 is labor-intensive relative to commodity 2, but others at which its efficient production is capital-intensive. The pair of unit isoquants in Figure 10.1 illustrates this assumption. (This figure should be compared to Figure 9.1.) If wage/rent ratios are low, as shown by the absolute values of the slopes of the isoquants at A and B, product X_1 is labor-intensive. However, for considerably higher wage/rent ratios, such as the one indicated by the slopes at C and D, cost-minimization entails that X_1 be produced by

[18] W. P. Travis and others have pointed out that this argument would fail if factor prices were in fact equalized between countries. The evidence that the factor price equalization theorem fails in practice seems compelling, however. For discussion, see Baldwin, pp. 128–29.

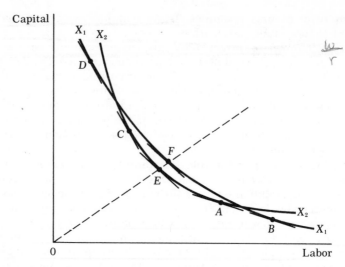

FIGURE 10.1   Factor-Intensity Reversal

At wage-rent ratio shown at E (or F), X_1 and X_2 use capital and labor in same proportions. At higher ratios, X_1 is capital-intensive (D lies above C). At lower ratios, X_1 is labor-intensive (B lies below A).

capital-intensive techniques. This being the case, the assumption of smooth substitutability between capital and labor suggests that at an intermediate factor price ratio (shown by the slopes at E and F) X_1 and X_2 will exhibit identical capital/labor ratios. When X_1's production is labor-intensive in one country and capital-intensive in the other, a price ratio p_1/p_2 can correspond to quite different wage/rent ratios in the two countries, and the factor price equalization theorem no longer holds.

More important for the Leontief test, the Heckscher-Ohlin theorem also no longer necessarily holds. When we hypothesize that the labor-rich country enjoys a comparative advantage in the labor-intensive commodity, the capital-rich country in the capital-intensive commodity, we quickly realize that when a factor-intensity reversal has occurred *these are the same commodity*. In Figure 10.1, points A and B might describe the factor combinations used to produce X_2 and X_1 (respectively) in the labor-rich country, points C and D the combinations used by the capital-rich country. Suppose that the labor-rich country exports its labor-intensive commodity, X_1.[19] If the capital-rich country were also to adhere to the theorem and export its capital-intensive good, that would also be X_1. In a two country model, they cannot both export the same good. Hence, where a factor-in-

---

[19] Recall that point B indicates a more labor-intensive technology than does point A, and D a more capital-intensive one than C.

tensity reversal has occurred, one of the two countries must show a "Leontief paradox."

What can we make in practice of the possibility of factor-intensity reversals? A reversal could potentially explain a paradoxical result for the United States — or for Japan. But, with an embarrassment of riches, we have both! One can only examine the evidence directly to see if intensity reversals seem to afflict an important group of internationally traded commodities. Economists differ on the answer to this question, and one can say only that substantial reversals are possible. For example, Michael Hodd found a reversal in the trade flows between Britain and the United States: each country exports capital-intensive goods to the other.[20]

That still leaves us with the list of paradoxes mentioned at the start of this section — United States, Japan, Canada, etc. Seiji Naya has argued, however, that recognition of some intensity reversals, along with the role of natural resources, allows us to unscramble the whole omelet.[21] He shows that one major resource-intensive sector — agriculture — is indeed subject to reversals of its capital-labor ratio between countries. Rice is raised in the United States using elaborate mechanical equipment, in Japan by large quantities of hand labor. Japanese agriculture is less capital-intensive than most other sectors of the Japanese economy, whereas American agriculture — and this surprises many people — is more capital-intensive than much of American manufacturing.

This apparent reversal of factor intensities between "agriculture" and "other sectors" helps to reconcile the plentiful paradoxes found by applying Leontief's method to various countries. Labor-intensive Japan exports goods that are more capital-intensive than are her import-replacements. But Japan is a heavy importer of foodstuffs, and these imports would be labor-intensive if produced in Japan instead. Hence they weight her trade toward a relative labor-intensity of imports, and we can say that Japan's imports would be much more capital-intensive if her lack of natural (agricultural) resources did not compel her to import so much food. Likewise, Canada's exports to the United States were found more capital-intensive than her imports from the United States, although Canada is an international borrower and hence should be the less capital-rich of the two countries. But Canada's exports to the United States are heavily weighted by resource-intensive products other than agricultural.[22] Hence we can say that Canada exports relatively capital-intensive goods, despite her relative shortage of capital, because of the dominant role

[20] Michael Hodd, "An Empirical Investigation of the Heckscher-Ohlin Theory," *Economica*, 34 (February 1967): 20–29.

[21] Seiji Naya, "Natural Resources, Factor Mix, and Factor Reversal in International Trade," *American Economic Review*, 57 (May 1967): 561–70.

[22] Actually, Canada's agriculture is quite capital-intensive. If she did export much farm produce to the United States, this conclusion would probably not change.

of her abundant natural resources — exploited by capital-intensive methods.

Finally, the United States resembles Japan in being short of natural resources, and her imports of nonagricultural resource-intensive goods pull up Leontief's measurement of the capital-intensity of American import replacements. The United States is a net agricultural exporter, but her agriculture is capital-intensive; if we deleted agricultural output from the lists of American exports and imports and repeated Leontief's computation, we would find the labor-intensity of the remaining exports even greater than it is when we include agriculture.[23] Thus we can say that America's scarcity of nonagricultural natural resources pulls United States trade toward capital-intensity of imports, whereas her agricultural net-export status cuts against the Leontief paradox.

How does it all come out? Is the Leontief paradox lost? When we add up the influence of labor skills, natural-resource scarcities, and United States tariffs excluding labor-intensive imports, they seem to reverse the conclusion that United States trade is *dominated* by export of the produce of abundant labor and the import of goods that require large quantities of scarce capital. Furthermore, it seems possible to explain away the paradoxical findings for other countries in the same fashion. But in restoring the toppled Heckscher-Ohlin theorem to its throne, we have robbed it of much of its empirical simplicity: two factors of production are not enough, and the absence of factor-intensity reversals between countries cannot be assumed. Perhaps the empirical predictions of the Ricardian model, less rich but less complex, should not be thrust aside lightly.

10.5 SUMMARY

The Ricardian and Heckscher-Ohlin models rest on differing factual assumptions. Both drastically simplify reality; we cannot tell without testing their predictions empirically which does a better job of capturing the central forces governing international trade.

Ricardo's model predicts that countries will export large quantities of goods in which they enjoy high labor productivity. MacDougall and others confirmed this for British and American exports and productivities. Differences in wages between industries within a country could throw the Ricardian prediction off, but were shown not to do so.

The Heckscher-Ohlin model explains historical patterns of trade and their changes. Ohlin himself found trade patterns and factor-intensities of production that confirm the predictions of his model. The model also helps to explain changes in trade over time: the United States' growing scarcity of natural resources is mirrored in the changing natural resource-intensity of her imports and exports.

[23] In Table 10.1, the ratio of capital requirements per man-year in 1958/1962 would rise from 1.27 to 1.41.

When three countries or regions are taken into account, the model successfully explains bilateral trade balances between them.

W. W. Leontief sought to test the Heckscher-Ohlin theorem on United States trade, but made the paradoxical discovery that this capital-rich country exports relatively labor-intensive goods. Efforts to explain this paradox have advanced as possible bases for reconciliation:

1. The high effectiveness of American labor.
2. The possibility that the United States is a heavy consumer of capital-intensive goods.
3. The high skilled-labor requirements of American exports.
4. The importance of research and development for American exports.
5. The restriction of labor-intensive imports by American tariffs.
6. The influence of scarce natural resources on the capital-labor requirements of traded goods.
7. The possibility that factor-intensity reversals disrupt the test.

The last five factors all help to explain away the paradox, and to reconcile the results of similar tests performed on the trade of other countries.

SUGGESTIONS FOR FURTHER READING

Baldwin, Robert E. "Determinants of the Commodity Structure of U.S. Trade," *American Economic Review* 61 (March 1971): 126–46. Sophisticated summary and extension of evidence on the "Leontief paradox."

Hansson, Karl-Erik. "A General Theory of the System of Multilateral Trade," *American Economic Review* 42 (March 1952): 58–68. Application of Heckscher-Ohlin model to bilateral trade patterns of major regions.

Kindleberger, Charles P. *Foreign Trade and the National Economy*. New Haven: Yale University Press, 1962. Evidence on relation of trade to various traits of the national economy.

Kravis, Irving B. "Wages and Foreign Trade," *Review of Economics and Statistics* 38 (February 1956): 14–30. Evidence that export industries do not depend on low-wage labor.

Leontief, W. W. "Domestic Production and Foreign Trade: the American Capital Position Re-examined," *Economia Internazionale* 7 (February 1954): 3–32; reprinted in American Economic Association, *Readings in International Economics*. Homewood, Ill.: Richard D. Irwin, 1968, chap. 30. Original statement of the "Leontief paradox."

MacDougall, Donald. "British and American Exports: A Study Suggested by the Theory of Comparative Costs," *Economic Journal,* 61 (December 1951): 697–724; reprinted American Economic Association, *Readings in International Economics*, chap. 32. Statistical test of Ricardian model.

Ohlin, Bertil. *Interregional and International Trade*. Cambridge, Mass.: Harvard University Press, 1933. Besides presenting the basic Heckscher-Ohlin model, contains many empirical observations supporting it.

Vanek, Jaroslav. "The Natural Resource Content of Foreign Trade, 1870–1955, and the Relative Abundance of Natural Resources in the United States," *Review of Economics and Statistics*, 41 (May 1959): 146–53. Influence of natural resources on capital-labor intensity of United States trade.

11 Imperfect Competition and Technology in International Trade

In this chapter we shall continue the investigation begun in Chapter 10 of the predictive power of the theory of international trade. We shall turn from testing the principal theories of international specialization to generating some new theories. The forces of imperfect competition and technological change discussed below simply revise or extend the assumptions underlying the model of production and exchange. We shall see what conclusions flow from these altered assumptions and how well they explain actual patterns of specialization and trade.

11.1 IMPERFECTIONS IN COMPETITION

The theory of international trade usually assumes that goods are produced and sold under conditions of perfect competition, although many industries in real life, especially in manufacturing, mining, and some services, obviously match the assumption rather poorly. A model does not depend on the literal accuracy of its assumptions, of course. The purpose of building theoretical models is to abstract from the inessential clutter of reality in order to focus on forces of broad underlying importance. For many purposes, the assumption of pure competition does not do excessive violence to reality. That is, many economists feel that the behavioral predictions and the welfare judgments devolving from models that assume pure competition often perform reasonably well when tested. We would not disagree. However, a lot of behavior in the international economy does reflect departures from pure competition. In this section we consider some of the traits of markets where competition is imperfect and show their effects on international trade.

Introductory courses in economics usually present three models of market structures other than the purely competitive. A monopolist is the sole seller of a product that has no close substitutes. The model of monopolistic competition assumes a large number of sellers, none large enough to detect the influence of his pricing decision on the average price in the rest of the market. Nonetheless, each seller's product differs enough from those of his rivals that (unlike the pure competitor) he faces a downward sloping demand curve. Finally, the sellers in situations of oligopoly are few enough that each takes some account of his rivals' possible responses to his actions. Although oligopoly is harder to describe in simple, deterministic, theoretical models, it is a common market structure in the industrial economy. Within the national economy, scale economies, product differentiation, and other forces conspire to permit markets to be dominated by a few sellers. They employ collusive behavior — not always successfully — to wrest from their market some of the excess profits it would yield to a pure monopolist.

These noncompetitive elements in national markets influence international trade in many important ways. They affect the international division of labor, making the bundle of goods and services that a country exports differ from what we might expect in purely competitive markets. They distort price relations from those that competitive markets would determine. In this section we shall consider in turn what economic theory and the available factual evidence reveal about these influences.

A. Competition in National and International Markets

Important products are often produced by only a few sellers in a country. In the United States, the significant producers of automobiles, aluminum, or flat glass can all be counted on the fingers of one hand. One of the virtues of international exchange is that competition with foreign producers decreases the ability of domestic firms with potential monopoly power to cause misallocation of resources. A gain in economic welfare arises from putting a domestic monopolist into international competition — a gain independent of the welfare benefits from exchange that we discussed in Chapters 2 and 6.

One source of welfare gains from international competition can be illustrated in Figure 11.1, which presents the factors governing the price set by a profit-maximizing monopolist. Total domestic demand for the product is shown by demand curve D, and the corresponding marginal revenue curve is MR. The monopolist's long-run marginal costs are indicated by MC. In the absence of competition from abroad, the profit-maximizing seller would choose the output that equates marginal cost to marginal revenue. Corresponding to this, he would

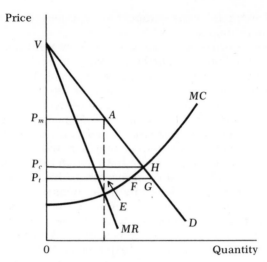

FIGURE 11.1   Influence of Import Competition
on Domestic Monopolist

> Monopolist would charge P_m without import competition,
> but now faces world price P_t. Consumers' surplus increases
> by *AEG* (net); were domestic industry competitive, gain
> would be only *FHG*.

charge price OP_m for output P_mA. Suppose his market is not sheltered
from import competition, however. The simplest way to depict external competition is to suppose that the product is produced competitively and sold at a market equilibrium price P_t in the outside world.
If our country's national market is too small to influence this world
price, the supply of imports becomes perfectly elastic at the world
price P_t and can be shown as P_tG. The monopolist, unprotected
against import competition, now becomes a price-taker, and can
only sell the output that will maximize his profits at the world price
P_t. That output is P_tF. The country would consume P_tG, importing FG.

Figure 11.1 allows us to illustrate the change in consumer welfare
that results from eliminating the monopolist's sheltered position in
the domestic market. The net utility of purchasing a product at any
given price, such as P_t, is (under certain assumptions) reflected in the
triangular area lying under the demand curve and above P_tG. That
is, this area measures the greatest sum that consumers would be
willing to pay for the privilege of consuming quantity P_tG of the
product, above its actual cost (P_tG times OP_t). With import competition setting price P_t, this "consumers' surplus" is VP_tG. But when
the sheltered monopolist sets price P_m, it is only VP_mA. The gain in
consumer welfare, area P_mAGP_t is not the same as the gain in national
welfare, however. Part of it comes at the expense of profits for the

monopolist: he loses unit profits of P_mP_t on sales of P_mA, so his position is worsened by the area P_mAEP_t, and this loss must be offset against the gain to consumers.[1] A net gain remains, however, measured by the triangle AEG, and one can argue that a smaller gain would have resulted if the product had been sold competitively before the introduction of trade into the sheltered home market. To prove that point, we need to make the strong assumption that the total cost of producing any given output would have been the same for a domestic competitive industry as for the monopolist. The monopolist's marginal cost curve, MC then becomes the equivalent of a domestic supply curve. Supply and demand in a sheltered market would have been equated at price OP_c, with quantity P_cH produced and sold domestically. By analogy to the case of the monopolist, we can see that the gross gain in consumers' surplus is now P_cHGP_t. But part of this gain, again, represents a transfer away from the profits or "surplus" earned by firms in the competitive domestic industry.[2] That surplus is reduced by the amount of area P_cHFP_t, leaving a net gain of HGF. This is included in AEG, the net gain when a monopolized market is open to trade, and thus is smaller.

Competition in a market seems to increase when it is opened to imports. But the same sort of gain can arise if a formerly sheltered monopolist now sells as a net exporter on a competitive world market. Figure 11.2 reproduces the basic elements of Figure 11.1, but the world price P_t is now raised so that it lies above point H. If the country can buy as much as it wishes at P_t without driving up the external price, it can also sell as much as it wishes abroad without driving that price down. And, indeed, with the country's market opened to trade the monopolist will become a net exporter. Without the protection of trade barriers he cannot charge a price higher than P_t at home. But at P_t he will profit by supplying not only the quantity P_tC demanded by the home market, but also exports of CD. Once again a net social

[1] Offsetting gains in consumers' welfare dollar for dollar against losses in monopoly profits may seem unethical. Each measures personal real income, however. If we object to valuing them equally, it is because we disapprove ethically of the income distribution associated with the monopolist's sheltered position in the market. In analyses of this sort, one usually assumes that one dollar's worth of income is as good as any other, no matter to whom it goes. This assumption is tantamount to supposing either the income distribution has been made socially optimal through the adjustment of taxes or that society has no preferences about it.

[2] We make the usual assumption that normal profits — the opportunity cost of capital — are included in the supply curve of the competitive industry (or the long-run marginal cost curve of the domestic monopolist). The area above MC and below P_cH is then a pure surplus, consisting of rents that accrue to the firms (or to factors of production that they employ) because intramarginal units of output are selling for more than their minimum supply price (opportunity cost). Notice that, when the domestic price falls from P_c to P_t, part of the gain in consumers' surplus is measured by the triangle HGF, which corresponds to no net loss to producers, and thus represents a net social gain.

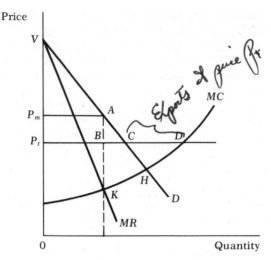

FIGURE 11.2   Influence of Export Opportunities
on Domestic Monopolist

> Monopolist would charge P_m without export opportunities.
> Exposed to trade, he charges world price P_t and exports CD.
> Consumers' surplus increases by ABC (net).

gain accrues, measured by areas ABC (a net increase in consumers' surplus) and BDK (a gross gain in the producer's surplus, which may or may not offset his loss of P_mABP_t).[3]

B. International Oligopoly: Cartels and Dumping

The preceding analysis illustrates the potential effect of international competition on monopoly in a sheltered domestic market, but it rests on the rather extreme assumption that there is only one seller in the home market but enough sellers for pure competition in the world at large. The fewness of sellers of a product results from traits of the product and of its production that do not vary much from country to country. If its sellers are few in one country, they are likely to be few in all regions. This means that oligopoly at home is likely to be matched by oligopoly abroad: if domestic sellers recognize the interdependence of their pricing decisions in the home market, they may recognize their interdependence in the world market. International oligopoly has many possible consequences. In this section we consider two of them: international cartels and "dumping."

---

[3] Once again, we can compare the gain that would accrue from trade if the domestic industry had been competitive. The no-trade equilibrium would have yielded the price and quantity indicated by point H. The net welfare gain from trade of CDH is less than that in the monopoly case, $ABC + BDK$.

1.) Cartels

Cartels can be defined with varying degrees of formality. We shall define them loosely as agreements among firms to divide markets among themselves, fix prices, exclude would-be competitors, or otherwise try to increase joint monopoly profits. Such agreements can operate either within nations or across their boundaries. They have long been illegal under the antitrust laws of the United States, and since World War II their legality in the industrial nations of Europe has been greatly circumscribed. Likewise, the operation of international cartels is best documented for the period between World Wars I and II, a fact that may reflect a subsequent decline in their strength and importance.[4] Most international cartels seem to have tried to divide markets among producing firms, to eliminate rivalry for customers. A common pattern was to allot each producer (or national group of producers) its home market and divide up the rest of the world — markets with no production, or production by non-members — among the parties. Industries such as those producing chemicals might divide the manufacture and sale of various individual products among themselves or agree to license patents on new discoveries only to each other. These arrangements, when successful, both raised prices around the world and made them differ from one national market to another.[5] Prices were sometimes rigid, because cartels' arrangements were not tight enough to permit continuous adjustment to keep a price at the monopolistic profit-maximizing level. And breakdowns of understanding sometimes led to the collapse of cartels into price warring and predatory practices.

In their effects on international trade, cartels apparently not only increased the degree of monopoly in domestic markets but also thwarted adjustments of production among countries in ways indicated by comparative advantage. A complete profit-maximizing cartel would rationally concentrate production in its most efficient units, sharing the total profit among its members. But this was seldom done internationally. Hence the probable effect of international cartels on the allocation of resources in the world economy has been to restrict the total quantity employed in the cartelized industry and also distort the pattern of production among countries.

The international cartel is used by sellers in different countries to curb rivalry among themselves. Its use suggests that oligopolistic sellers may find collusion with their foreign rivals more difficult than with their domestic rivals. In domestic markets where sellers are few, competition often appears to be restricted by "tacit collusion."

---

[4] See George W. Stocking and Myron W. Watkins, *Cartels in Action* (New York: Twentieth Century Fund, 1946); idem, *Cartels or Competition?* (New York: Twentieth Century Fund, 1948), especially chap. 4.

[5] For several years after 1928 tungsten carbide was sold by Krupp in Europe for about $50 a pound, by General Electric in the United States for a list price of $453 a pound. General Electric's manufacturing cost was quoted as $8 a pound. See Stocking, *Cartels or Competition?*, pp. 132–33.

That is, through recurrent contact and experience sellers become adept at gauging each other's reactions and, without any formal collusion, can push the commitment of resources in their market toward that which a profit-maximizing monopolist would choose. For many reasons this tacit collusion will occur more easily within national markets than between sellers in different countries. Cultural differences and increased difficulties of communicating play an important part. The local markets served are likely to differ in many qualitative ways, and with them the general strategies sellers use in serving them. Transport costs and tariffs tend to make sellers less sensitive to the actions of their foreign than their domestic rivals.

Thus, oligopolists are likely to be more collusive with their domestic rivals, and more competitive in dealing with foreign rivals. If we take this statement as a hypothesis about oligopoly markets, it explains several important patterns of business behavior affecting international trade. One likely pattern occurs when domestic oligopolists facing rising import competition refuse to meet the lower price charged for the imports. If the imported product is a close substitute for their own and sells for a lower delivered price, this refusal of course costs them a significant share of the domestic market. They may suffer this erosion rather than enter into price competition because of the imperfect collusion among themselves. Every price change, especially one downward, raises the possibility that misunderstanding will occur and price warfare break out. For example, the steel industry in the United States has often been charged with maintaining list prices that are inflexible and insensitive to imports as well as to other competitive pressures. If "import discipline" affected the pricing behavior of domestic oligopolists, you would expect prices of domestic steel products to rise slowly where competing imports are large or where the prices of comparable foreign steel items rise slowly. But one statistical study of the prices of forty-six steel products in the mid-1950's found no such influence.[6] More recently the steel producers have responded to their foreign competition in a different fashion: demanding that the government curb imports by means of quantitative restrictions. Although import competition is generally a good anti-monopoly device, oligopolies sometimes refuse to respond to its pressures.

Another important result of oligopoly in international markets is dumping. Dumping occurs when producers sell abroad at prices that regularly yield them less net revenue (after payment of transportation costs, tariffs, etc.) than do sales of comparable goods in their home market. Notice that this could not occur in a purely competitive market. A pure competitor sells his entire output at a price dictated to him by the market. If he can choose between two markets, one yielding higher returns per unit sold than the other, he will dispose

[6] Lawrence B. Krause, "Import Discipline; the Case of the United States Steel Industry," *Journal of Industrial Economics*, 11 (November 1962): 33–47.

of his whole output in the higher-price market. A profit-maximizing seller with some monopoly power, however, will not necessarily behave in this way. Consider the domestic monopolist illustrated in Figure 11.3. His situation closely resembles that of the monopolist described in Figure 11.2, in that he can profit by selling abroad at the world price P_t. Figure 11.3 illustrates again the price that would maximize monopoly profits in the home market without foreign sales (P_m) and the price prevailing in the world market (P_t), which we again take to be purely competitive. But now different prices can be charged in the home and foreign markets, perhaps because a tariff protecting the home market keeps goods sold cheaply abroad from being re-imported and undercutting the higher domestic price. A monopolist maximizes profits by setting a price that equates his marginal cost to the marginal revenue he can earn in each of his markets: if the marginal revenues were not equal, he should shift sales from the lower to the higher until they are equalized. In Figure 11.3 the marginal revenue from foreign sales is equal to the world price P_t, because that price is unaffected by the monopolist's level of exports. The monopolist hence will sell in the domestic market at

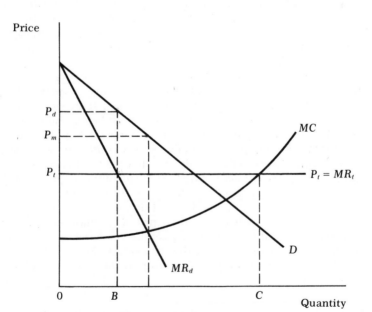

FIGURE 11.3   "Dumping" and Discrimination
between Domestic and Foreign Markets

Monopolist faces demand curve D at home, world price P_t. If he can charge separate prices at home and abroad, he sets P_d and P_t respectively, selling OB at home and BC abroad.

price P_d, which equates marginal revenue derived from the domestic market (MR_d) to that earned from foreign sales (MR_t). If his total production is OC, his marginal cost (MC) is equated to the common value of marginal revenue, and profits are maximized. Exports are BC, domestic sales OB. Notice that this discrimination between the domestic and foreign markets has caused a higher price to be charged in the domestic market than if no trade were occurring (P_d exceeds P_m). In Figure 11.2, however, where we assumed that the seller could not discriminate between his domestic and foreign markets, we found that the introduction of trade brought a lower price for the domestic market.

We introduced the model of dumping in the context of oligopoly in domestic and international markets, yet explained it on the assumption of pure monopoly at home and pure competition abroad. These assumptions, however, merely push to the limit a difference between home and foreign markets that we suggested before — domestic oligopolists are likely to recognize their interdependence more fully than sellers based in different countries. This difference implies that the individual seller will view the demand curve he faces in the home market as less elastic than the demand he faces abroad: if he cuts prices he expects his domestic rivals to follow, but he assumes that sellers abroad are less likely to react. That difference in elasticities of demand in home and foreign markets predicts that sellers will prefer a higher price at home.[7]

The evidence seems to suggest that dumping occurs in many industries, and at the hands of producers in many countries. For instance, a recent disclosure that Japanese color television sets were being sold in the United States at prices much below those in Japan prompted a boycott by irate Japanese customers![8] A survey taken before World War II of pricing by seventy-six United States exporting firms found that forty-six of them received lower net prices on their foreign than their domestic sales, and only nine captured higher proceeds abroad.[9] Dumping appears to grow more prevalent when producers suffer a reduction in demand that leaves them with excess capacity. Then they will cut foreign prices, perhaps to levels that cover their marginal but not their average costs, while maintaining prices at home to avoid spoiling that market. As Figure 11.3 showed, excess capacity is not necessary for dumping, but it often provides an extra incentive.

[7] Figure 11.3 is a special case of the model of discriminating monopoly because foreign demand is assumed perfectly elastic. For a treatment of the general case see Joan Robinson, *The Economics of Imperfect Competition.* London: Macmillan, 1933, chap. 15.

[8] *Business Week,* March 6, 1971, p. 41.

[9] United States Temporary National Economic Committee, *Export Prices and Export Cartels,* Monograph No. 6. Washington: Government Printing Office, 1940, chaps. 5 and 6.

Dumping presents an odd problem for economic policy. It favors the foreign consumer over the domestic one. You might expect governments, concerned with the welfare of their citizens, to try to keep their exporters from dumping. Yet the importing countries typically outlaw or discourage dumping. Their justification is that dumping is unfair to domestic producers, or that temporary dumping might be used to drive native firms out of business.

C. **Product Differentiation**

Another imperfection in actual markets is called product differentiation. The outputs of different producers of the same class of goods — brands of gasoline, typewriters, wristwatches, etc. — are similar in function and compete closely with each other. Nonetheless, consumers detect differences that make competing brands less than perfect substitutes. In their eyes brand *A* may differ from brand *B* in physical traits, images or attitudes created by advertising, etc. Consumers hold diverse views on the relative merits of *A* and *B*, and a small cut in the price of *A* will not pull all the customers away from *B*. Differentiation can occur even when the number of sellers is large enough that no one is conscious of the effect of his actions on the other individuals. This market structure is described by the model of *monopolistic competition.* Differentiation can also occur, however, when sellers are few: *differentiated oligopoly.* In general, product differentiation reduces the sensitivity of sellers to each other's pricing decisions. The chances that a rival will react to one's own price reduction are reduced, because its impact on his share of the market will (ceteris paribus) be smaller when product differentiation is present. Differentiation also makes varying the product itself a competitive strategy: rather than cut the price, one can offer a better product at the same price.

In order to explore the effects of product differentiation in international trade, we should compare the sensitivity of one brand to another. Not all rivals' products will be equally good substitutes for one's own. A Lincoln may be a close substitute for a Cadillac, but a Volkswagen may not. Often product varieties may be arranged in a chain of substitutes. Varieties *A* and *B* are good substitutes for each other, *B* and *C*, *C* and *D*, etc.; but products located far apart on the chain are not close substitutes. Now suppose that, before international trade is permitted to occur, we observe in the home country such a chain of producers *A*, *B*, *C*, ... *N* of a product; and in the foreign country the same (general) product is produced by another chain of producers *A**, *B**, *C**, ... *N**. The two economies now are opened up to international trade.

If differentiation were not present, we would expect cost and demand conditions to produce a net flow of trade. If the home country were the net exporter, some producers abroad (the least efficient, presumably) would leave the industry and free their factors of pro-

duction for other uses, while in the home industry new producers
would enter, old ones expand, or both. With differentiation, however,
we must ask how the two chains of substitutes will relate to each
other after trade is opened. The chains may join end-on. That is, the
home country's varieties N, M, L, . . . may be relatively close substitutes for the foreign country's A*, B*, C*, . . . , but goods at the opposite ends of the two chains may be poor substitutes. For example, the
ranking of the varieties in both countries may run from the relatively
costly and high-quality (A and A*) down to the relatively cheap and
low-quality (N and N*). But because levels of income per capita in
the foreign country are lower than at home, the *absolute* quality level
of the top-quality foreign varieties may about match that of the cheapest home varieties. If with the opening of trade the home country
enjoys a cost advantage in the sense of comparative cost, the foreign
producers competed out of business will be those at the head of the
chain A*, B*, C* . . . .

An alternative possibility is that the two chains of substitutes,
rather than joining at the ends, will overlap throughout. A* proves
to be a good substitute for A and B, B* for B and C, etc. The effects of
introducing trade in this case may differ dramatically from the previous one. Even if the home producers again enjoy a cost advantage,
the prevalent downward-sloping demand curves may preclude their
driving more than a few foreign producers from the market. More
important, some foreign varieties will appeal to home consumers, so
that some imports of the product will occur even if costs and demand
conditions in general equilibrium favor the home producers enough
that net exports occur. Thus, product differentiation can explain two-
way flows of products in the same general class.[10] Furthermore, as
the chain of substitutes becomes more tightly interlaced, each producer (in either country) finds himself facing closer rivals than before, implying a flatter demand curve for his product. He must behave
more nearly like a pure competitor than before, and inefficiencies
associated with prices in excess of marginal cost may be reduced.

A powerful test of the importance of product differentiation in
international trade has been provided by the formation of the European Economic Community, which has removed all tariffs among its
member countries (original members are France, West Germany,
Italy, Netherlands, Belgium, and Luxembourg). When tariff protection is wiped out in purely competitive markets, one expects hitherto
protected industries to be competed down. A country will find its net
exports of a product group rising, if it enjoys a comparative advantage, or its net imports rising, if it is at a comparative disadvantage.
Yet two studies have found no such increases in net trade balances.
Instead, each Common Market country's exports to its partners rose

---

[10] *Can,* not *must.* In the previous instance of the chains of substitutes
joining at their ends, no reason emerged for the occurrence of imports as well
as exports.

in most product groups, rather than rising in some and falling in others. *Net* exports or imports changed little while gross exports rose all around, suggesting a large increase in the interpenetration of markets.[11] This story is consistent with our second model of product differentiation, in which countries' product chains become interlinked, and liberalization raises exports all around. But it is not consistent with any likely description of the world in which product differentiation is assumed to be absent.

Differentiation may affect the volume of trade between countries in other ways as well. For example, the tastes of citizens in different countries for a good, such as washing machines, may depend on their average level of income per capita. In rich countries, housewives and others may value their time highly, and therefore be willing to pay for time-saving convenience in their home appliances. Among differentiated varieties of washers, then, they would prefer elaborate automatic equipment that requires little time or attention from its user. Countries with lower incomes, placing a lower value on household labor, would desire less elaborate and costly varieties that require more labor input from the user. Thus there would be broad physical similarities among the varieties preferred in all high-income countries, other broad similarities among those chosen in middle-income countries, and so forth.

Now consider the world distribution of the production of these differentiated varieties. The producer of differentiated consumer goods always enjoys an advantage over import competition in his home market because differentiation reflects the traits of the national culture and life style. The domestic producer and his employees understand this background and use it to guide the "styling" of their product. The foreign producer either is guided by a different cultural heritage, or must incur costs or run risks in guessing what product traits will attract foreign consumers. The real costs of production may run against a local producer, of course, and "comparative disadvantage" might offset his advantages in supplying the differentiated variety of goods wanted by the home market. But the differentiated producer enjoys an advantage in serving the home market that is denied to the maker of undifferentiated goods.

Let us put together the propositions of the last two paragraphs. Producers of differentiated goods are likely to be strong in their home markets. The goods the home markets desire will depend on the citizens' level of income per capita. These propositions imply several predictions about international trade in differentiated goods. First, production is likely to be widespread among countries. International trade in these goods may occur, but the tendency for production to

---

[11] Bela Balassa, "Tariff Reductions and Trade in Manufactures," *American Economic Review,* 56 (June 1966): 466–73; Herbert G. Grubel, "Intra-Industry Specialization and the Pattern of Trade," *Canadian Journal of Economics and Political Science*, 33 (August 1967): 374–88.

concentrate in the most efficient locations will be blunted — even without tariff protection. Second, home producers are likely to succeed in catering to "majority" tastes among their citizens, but foreign producers may find numerous pockets of "minority" tastes — odd sectors of the culture, outer reaches of the income distribution, and the like — attracted to their product varieties.[12] We often hear this proposition in everyday life, when people view imports (of differentiated goods) as "specialty" or "unusual" items. Third, countries with similar levels of income per capita and similar cultures may swap large volumes of differentiated goods with each other. Their varieties will appeal to each other's consumers, and their chains of substitutes will tend to interlock in the pattern of A, A^*, B, B^*, etc., that was described above.[13] Tests of this final proposition have turned up largely negative results. Later in this chapter we shall discuss some of the reasons.

11.2 TECHNOLOGY FACTORS AND TECHNOLOGICAL CHANGE

We have explored the possible determinants of patterns of trade in the framework of long-run general equilibrium. Economists often use this technique of assuming forces that shape the economic world and deducing their full effects in the absence of any other change or disturbance — even when their goal is to explain the changing and growing economic universe. Theorizing is by nature a process of abstracting from inessentials. Ignoring the continuing stream of changes in order to isolate the effects of one of them may reveal the essentials we want. But, again, it may not. Some persistent features of international trade may depend on continuing economic growth and change. In this section we examine several hypotheses about the influence of economic change on patterns of trade. They all revolve around technology or technological change, so we follow convention in calling them "technology factors" in international trade. What makes them logically distinctive, however, is their emphasis on continuous disturbances and dynamic imbalances in the world economy.

A. **Innovation and Technological Gap**

A new product is developed, or a new production process embodied in a novel kind of capital equipment. The innovating firm tests its discovery on the market — presumably the market closest and best known

---

[12] The United States appears to enjoy a comparative advantage in producing elaborate consumer durables, countries like Japan and Italy in simpler versions of the same products. See Louis T. Wells, Jr., "Test of a Product Cycle Model of International Trade: U.S. Exports of Consumer Durables," *Quarterly Journal of Economics*, 83 (February 1969): 152–62.

[13] For a somewhat similar argument see Staffan Burenstam Linder, *An Essay on Trade and Transformation*. Uppsala: Almqvist & Wiksell, 1961, chap. 3.

to it. This is generally its home or local market. If the innovation proves profitable, the firm looks for wider markets, perhaps in foreign lands. The country's exports grow. If the innovation's success is repeated abroad, the rest of the world's reciprocal demand curve for the innovating country's goods shifts outward. The home country's imports become relatively cheaper, and some factors of production switch from producing goods that compete with imports and toward production of the novel good. The innovator's profits from foreign sales bring additional gains from trade to the home country.

The innovation, unless completely protected by patents, is likely to bestir imitators. If the innovation is first placed on the home market, domestic competitors will be the first to feel the threat to their sales, and hence the first to take defensive action. When the innovation becomes an export item, imitation is also likely abroad. If foreign producers can also match the innovation, the shift of the foreign reciprocal demand curve described above may be largely temporary. The home country's innovative gains disappear as successful imitation takes place abroad.

In this story innovation is only a one-shot disturbance to the circuits of international trade. However, some countries may regularly prove to be fertile sources of innovation. Their export lists would always contain new products that have not yet been successfully imitated elsewhere. We would have to explain their trade, then, not solely by their factor endowments or Ricardian productivity advantages, but rather in part as "technological gap" exports. Do some countries enjoy special talents as innovators? For the United States, the answer may be yes. The argument goes as follows.

Innovation, whether by the toolshed tinkerer or the corporate research laboratory, is the purposive activity of someone who perceives a "need" and finds a way to fill it. Needs are judged by the economic benefits from the innovation, which in turn govern the size of the potential profit awaiting the innovator. Most innovations seem to be labor-saving, as the fork-lift truck that reduces the labor involved in moving and stacking things. That is, most innovations seem to cut the quantity of labor used in a production process, relative to the quantity of capital, at any factor prices. The biggest payout to labor-saving innovations, however, comes where labor is most expensive, and where its price is expected to continue to rise. The United States, as the country with the highest labor cost, thus seems to offer the strongest incentive to the labor-saving innovation. In the nineteenth century, economic historians have argued, the scarcity and dearness of labor made the United States a fruitful source of mechanical inventions. Coupled with an abundance of labor skills (invention itself requires a high proportion of skilled labor) and congenial cultural traits, American inventive dominance has continued. Thus a significant proportion of the United States' exports probably consists of "technological gap" trade. If United States inventiveness ever dried up and the cycle of imitation ran its course, the country's terms of trade would probably deteriorate and her level of income per capita fall relative to other countries.

The United States is of course far from being the only source of innovations. The role is also filled by countries with abundant skilled scientific labor, such as Great Britain, or by those afflicted with raw-material shortages and thus conscious of the usefulness of synthetic materials, such as Germany. The empirical evidence, however, is particularly clear for the United States. Industries making the strongest research effort (measured, for instance, by research and development expenditures as a percentage of sales) account for 72 percent of the country's exports of manufactured goods, but only 39 percent of the nation's total sales of manufactures.[14] Furthermore, one statistical study for 24 countries confirms the link between innovation and high labor costs. For each country an index of the "newness" of its manufactured exports was calculated. Innovation was found to be related to level of national income per capita, and high income per person is ordinarily associated with relatively costly labor.[15]

Consider the implications of the technological gap for world trade in a group of products like plastics or man-made fibers. Each group represents innovations, some new, some decades old. You would expect the highly industrialized countries, best suited and motivated to innovate, to enjoy the largest shares of world exports in new products belonging to such a group. As products age, however, their manufacture spreads to countries that are not themselves innovators, but that ultimately hold a comparative advantage. You would expect the United States to export a larger share of its production of new products not yet imitated abroad than of older products — except for goods so new that their use has not begun abroad. Finally, because many countries give heavy tariff protection to their domestic fiber and plastics industries, the portion of a product's total world production entering into trade should fall as the product ages, and more imitators produce their domestic requirements behind tariff walls. A study by G. C. Hufbauer of synthetic materials in international trade confirms each of these predictions.[16]

B. Product Cycle

The technological gap is a somewhat unsatisfactory explanation of dynamic trade patterns. Why is the gap so many years, no more, no less? The theory explains the elimination of the gap but not its per-

[14] W. Gruber, D. Mehta, and R. Vernon, "The R&D Factor in International Trade and International Investment of United States Industries," *Journal of Political Economy*, 75 (February 1967): 20–37.

[15] G. C. Hufbauer, "The Impact of National Characteristics and Technology on the Commodity Composition of Trade in Manufactured Goods," *The Technology Factor in International Trade*, ed. Raymond Vernon. New York: National Bureau of Economic Research, 1970, pp. 184–89.

[16] G. C. Hufbauer, *Synthetic Materials and the Theory of International Trade*. Cambridge: Harvard University Press, 1966, chap. 6.

sistence. For a better performance in this role we can turn to a closely related model of the "product cycle."[17] The model of the product cycle suggests that changes occur in the input requirements of a new product as it becomes established in markets and standardized in production. These changes may shift the cost advantage from one country to another.

Someone has invented and marketed the radio. Again, we suppose that it cannot readily be imitated by producers in either the domestic or foreign markets. At the start its market success is uncertain. The new product does not automatically appeal to many customers. Its manufacture is small-scale. Production techniques are likely to be novel and to require large inputs of skilled labor. "Mass production" is unsuitable because of both the small market and technological uncertainties. The good must be produced near its market, because the producer needs a quick feedback of information in order to improve its performance, reliability, and general appeal. Hence the innovator's home market will be the first served.

When the product is established at home, it will enter into international trade as the innovator tests foreign markets. Furthermore, the location of production may start to shift. Whereas production in the pilot stage may require much skilled labor, standardization and general consumer acceptance allow for mass production. This demands lesser labor skills, and yet may be no more capital-intensive. Furthermore, as the product grows standardized and its market becomes more competitive, the pull of cost advantages on the location of production grows stronger. While it remains a monopolized novelty, demand is likely to be price-inelastic. If it enjoys success, innovative profits can be earned even if production costs are not minimized in the short run. As the product matures and becomes standardized, imitative competition is likely to arise and make the demand facing the individual producer significantly more elastic. Costs start to tell. Unless the country where the innovation first becomes established has an ultimate comparative advantage, production will spread or shift to other countries as the product matures.

Once again, this model helps to explain changes in production and trade in new product lines, such as electronics. The United States has been a principal innovator, but production has also spread (with a lag) to countries such as the United Kingdom and Japan. Again, the export performance of American producers is better for new products than for those approaching maturity. Furthermore, for goods whose manufacture is spreading abroad we observe a shift from processes heavily dependent on skilled labor to automatic assembly processes using relatively more capital and unskilled labor.[18]

---

[17] Raymond Vernon, "International Investment and International Trade in the Product Cycle," *Quarterly Journal of Economics*, 80 (May 1966): 190–207.
[18] Seev Hirsch, *Location of Industry and International Competitiveness*. Oxford: Clarendon Press, 1967, chap. 4.

The product cycle, as an explanation of changes in production and trade, involves shifts in patterns of consumption as well as in the technology of production. As a consumer good matures, it is said to pass from being a luxury to being a necessity. But "necessity" is a relative term, and what people (or countries) at one level of income per capita view as necessary may remain strictly a luxury to those less well off. As production standardizes, a good will become cheaper relative to other goods. This force and the general growth of incomes per capita broaden the international market for a good as it matures. We suggested above that the local production of differentiated consumer goods is likely to depend on the size and character of the local market. Then the spread of production among countries would reflect its rate of passage into the "necessity" class — how fast consumers accept it, and how well off they must be to count it a necessity.

C. Scale Economies

In the "pure theory" of international trade, where long-run equilibrium is reached in purely competitive markets, economies of scale in the national production of a good can be readily taken into account. Indeed, as you saw in Chapter 6, they make little difference for conditions of equilibrium in the exchange model. But their innocence is lost when we also inject into the theory some other complexities of the real world.

By economies of scale we mean a reduction in the real unit cost of production of a good as the quantity produced increases. This definition encompasses several types of economies.

Economies to the Firm or to the National Industry? We usually measure the scale economies of the piece of equipment, the plant, or perhaps the multiplant firm. Economies to the firm may explain the presence of monopoly in a national or regional market where only one or a few firms can produce at scales that exhaust the available economies before the market is glutted. On the other hand, scale economies may depend on the size of the national market but not necessarily on the sizes of plants serving it. A small national economy may mean thin and inefficient transactions channels, short production runs for some goods, or fixed costs that must be spread over small volumes. Then the small market may suffer from higher costs, whether or not the number of firms serving it is small.

Static Economies or Dynamic Economies? We traditionally suppose that economies of scale relate to output per period of time. For example, a high-volume assembly line achieves lower unit costs than low-volume custom production of the same product. But because experience usually teaches something, unit costs may depend on (decrease with) the cumulative total volume of production rather than the rate of output. Low unit costs then favor the old producer, rather than the big producer. In activities such as airframe (i.e., aircraft) assembly, producers expect to benefit from a "learning curve" that expresses the rate at which unit costs fall as the cumulative output rises.

Keeping these distinctions in mind, we can notice some effects of scale economies. The productivity of the small country in particular may suffer from (static) diseconomies of small scale. Consider first the effect of tariff protection, imposed either by the small country itself or by its trading partners. Figure 11.4 shows the long-run average cost curve for a product, at the small (home) country's factor prices. Its shape is commonly suggested by empirical evidence: severe cost disadvantages for small scales, but costs approximately constant beyond some output (OM). DD represents the national demand curve for the product. Suppose that the world price of the product is P_2, so that its production at home is inefficient at any scale, but that for political reasons a tariff is used to establish a domestic industry. If the country were large enough to demand at least OM at a price equal to long-run average cost, a tariff of P_1P_2/P_2O would suffice. But the small country with demand DD requires the higher level of protection P_3P_2/P_2O to establish home production. The loss of consumers' surplus per unit consumed is greater than for the large country. Looked at another way, a world price of P_1 is needed to

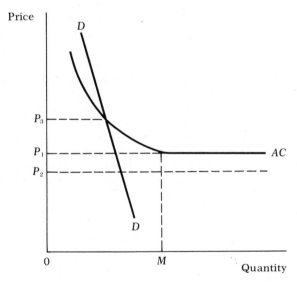

FIGURE 11.4 Economies of Scale in the Small National Market

P_2 is world price, AC is average cost curve. Small country (demand level DD) requires tariff of P_3P_2/P_2O to start domestic production. Large country would need only P_1P_2/P_2O.

make this industry competitive for resources in a large country, a price of P_3 in a small country.[19]

The small nation is also likely to suffer from the tariffs imposed by other countries. Suppose that the rest of the world sets a tariff so that the foreign price (including tariff) is greater than P_1, but that home-country producers after paying the tariff would receive only P_2. The home country is potentially an efficient export producer under free trade. But foreign tariffs not only prevent it from producing at efficient scale (more than OM) for the world market, but also confine it to producing (if at all) at an inefficiently small scale for the home market. One study has suggested that many Canadian manufacturing industries are placed in the position shown in Figure 11.4 by the joint influence of Canadian and United States tariffs. The real cost of the two tariffs has been estimated at 10.5 percent of Canadian GNP, with no less than half of this burden due to the United States tariff![20]

This argument suggests that a small country's problems with scale economies disappear in a world of free trade. Then it is no longer confined to small-scale production of its exportable goods, and its disadvantage reposes only in nontraded items. But forces other than tariffs may restrict its large-scale exports. Jacques Drèze has argued that many goods are effectively differentiated between national markets — not just consumer goods styled to national tastes but all sorts of goods for which national standards exist and differ (electrical sockets and voltages, pipe diameters, etc.). Product differentiation, as we suggested above, thus may prevail quite broadly among similar goods in the international economy. The small country cannot achieve efficient scale by producing them for its home market, and pervasive differentiation impedes its access to foreign markets (unless its producers take the risk in building factories to produce strictly for export). Its best way out of the dilemma, Drèze suggests, may be to specialize in exporting undifferentiated intermediate goods — steel, glass, nonferrous metals, wood products, and the like. He finds that Belgium indeed does this, importing differentiated goods and producing relatively few consumers' goods specially styled to national tastes.[21] Another implication of these forces is that the export trade of large industrial countries will, other things equal, be inflated by the presence of many "specialty" items (whether industrial or consumer goods). The large country may hold no cost advantage, but its large

[19] Actually, when costs are falling, so that marginal cost lies below average cost, production in the home country can be justified when the world price is less than P_3. See W. M. Corden, "Monopoly, Tariffs and Subsidies," *Economica*, 34 (February 1967): 50–58.

[20] R. J. Wonnacott and Paul Wonnacott, *Free Trade Between the United States and Canada: the Potential Economic Effects*, Harvard Economic Studies, vol. 129. Cambridge: Harvard University Press, 1967, chap. 15.

[21] J. Drèze, "Quelques reflexions sereins sur l'adaptation de l'industrie Belge au Marché Commun," *Comptes rendues des Travaux de la Société Royale d'Economie Politique de Belgique*, no. 275. 1960.

market supports domestic output, and the "availability" of these goods in turn increases its trade.[22]

Dynamic scale economies or "learning by doing" can influence the location of production through the advantage gained by the first producer. The learning curve helps explain the "technology gap" in the spread of production of new goods. Whether or not it explains the delay, however, depends on the ease with which the fruits of experience can be transferred from country to country. Does a late-coming producer start in the same state of ignorance as the pioneer, or can he acquire most of the wisdom that has accumulated by the time he starts? If the latecomer can profit from others' mistakes, there is a case for waiting while others make them. If experience does not travel between countries, however, welfare may be raised by public policies designed to promote a head start in areas of new technology. These urgent and unresolved questions of economic policy turn on the mechanisms by which technology is transferred internationally — the export of new capital goods, the licensing of new techniques, the international corporation, and so forth. We shall return to them in Chapter 23 when we consider foreign direct investment.

11.3 SUMMARY

In this chapter we modified the assumptions previously used to explain international specialization and trade, taking into account imperfections in competition and the forces of technology and technological change.

When the domestic market is dominated by a monopolist, opening it to the competition of imports conveys greater benefits to the nation than when the domestic industry is competitively organized. The same is true when export opportunities are opened for the domestic industry: the gains are greater when domestic production is initially monopolized. If production of one good is highly concentrated in one country, it is likely to be in other countries as well. Oligopolies in different countries tend to form cartels, dividing markets among themselves and distorting the allocation of world production away from its most efficient pattern. Oligopolists find it harder to collude with their foreign than with their domestic rivals. This fact helps to explain "dumping" — selling abroad for net revenues per unit less than those obtained in the home market.

Product differentiation affects trade in diverse ways, depending on the interlinking of substitute varieties of a good produced at home and abroad. When products are differentiated, countries may both import and export the same goods. Furthermore, the domestic producer always enjoys an advantage from knowing the differentiated tastes of his home market, so the extent of international specializa-

---

[22] See Hufbauer, "The Impact of National Characteristics," pp. 199–206. The "availability" concept was originally suggested by Irving Kravis.

tion is less than it would be if differentiation were absent and costs alone controlled the location of production.

"Technology" factors in international trade direct our attention to the fact that long-run adjustments in trade patterns are always occurring, and the patterns of trade we observe reflect long-run disequilibria. A portion of American exports may persistently consist of "technological gap" trade, new products that could be efficiently produced abroad (by the test of long-run comparative advantage) but whose production has not yet spread. The "product cycle" helps to explain the timing of the spread of production of new goods — as they mature their input requirements shift from skilled labor toward unskilled labor used in assembly-line processes. Scale economies, reflecting production technology, affect the location of production in both static and dynamic ways. Because tariffs are generally present, scale economies create disadvantages for the small nation; it may be unable to produce efficiently for its home market, yet foreign tariffs may preclude production at an efficient scale for export. Dynamic scale economies ("learning by doing") give an advantage to the first or the older producer where the benefits of experience cannot be fully transmitted to the new producer.

SUGGESTIONS FOR FURTHER READING

Baldwin, R. E., and J. D. Richardson, eds. *Selected Topics in International Trade and Finance: A Book of Readings.* Boston: Little, Brown, 1973. Part I contains important papers on the "new theories" of international trade.

Grubel, Herbert G. "Intra-Industry Specialization and the Pattern of Trade," *Canadian Journal of Economics and Political Science,* 33 (August 1967): 374–88. Indirect evidence of imperfect competition in trade.

Hufbauer, G. C. "The Impact of National Characteristics and Technology on the Commodity Composition of Trade in Manufactured Goods," *The Technology Factor in International Trade.* New York: National Bureau of Economic Research, 1970, pp. 145–231. Extensive statistical test of theories discussed in this chapter.

Johnson, Harry G. *Comparative Cost and Commercial Policy Theory for a Developing World Economy.* Stockholm: Almqvist and Wiksell, 1968. Theoretical extension of models discussed in this chapter.

McLachlan, D. L., and D. Swann. *Competition Policy in the European Community.* London: Oxford University Press, 1967. Part 2 gives evidence on cartel behavior in recent years.

Vernon, Raymond. "International Investment and International Trade in the Product Cycle," *Quarterly Journal of Economics,* 80 (May 1966): 190–207. Model of effects of product innovation on trade and investment.

PART THREE The Theory and Practice of Commercial Policy

12 The Theory of Tariffs

Free trade implies that countries do not interfere with the importation and exportation of commodities. If natural costs of transport can be ignored, free trade implies that commodities can be obtained for the same price in all countries. The early parts of this book pointed to the mutual gains obtainable to all countries undertaking trade. However, for hundreds of years countries have felt impelled for a variety of reasons to erect barriers to the exchange of goods and services across national borders. Part 3 of this book is devoted to exploring the nature of such impediments, the motivation behind their use, and the recent history of commercial policy, especially in the United States, Western Europe, and the countries in the Soviet Bloc.

Perhaps the most important weapon of commercial policy has been the tariff. A tariff is a tax on foreign trade; it makes foreign commodities more expensive at home than abroad, both for domestic consumers and producers. Tariffs alter the allocation of resources, change both domestic and world prices, and redistribute income both among countries and among productive factors within a country.

This chapter analyzes the tariff in the simple two-country, two-commodity, two-factor model of trade developed in Part 2. We shall begin with the simple case of a country that levies a tariff but is too unimportant in world markets to affect world prices thereby. In section 12.2 we shall investigate the possible effect of a tariff on a country's terms of trade when a country's commercial policy can affect world prices. Not surprisingly, a country may then improve its terms of trade by the exercise of commercial policy. In section 12.3 we shall investigate the domestic welfare effects of a tariff and develop the concept of the "optimum tariff." We shall conclude with an appraisal of tariffs with respect to the efficiency of the world's allocation of resources.

In Chapter 13 we shall broaden the theoretical discussion to consider several arguments in favor of tariff intervention. We shall also show that other forms of policy — e.g., consumption or production taxes — sometimes entail fewer distortions in the economy than would tariffs. Chapters 14 and 15 turn to practical issues of trade policy for the United States and other industrial countries, including regional arrangements such as the European Economic Community.

12.1 THE TARIFF FOR A SMALL COUNTRY

A tariff drives a wedge between domestic prices and world prices of a country's imports. If the country is too small to affect world prices, as we assume in this section, the domestic price of imports rises by the full extent of the tariff. Figures 12.1–12.3 illustrate the way in which a tariff shifts resources into the import-competing industry, and shifts demand away from imports. On both counts a tariff reduces a small country's imports.[1]

The effect of a tariff on production is easier to analyze than is the effect on demand. As Figure 12.1 illustrates, a tariff levied by a small country raises the relative price of imports (of food) by the full extent of the tariff. The world terms of trade are given by the slope of line 1; the posttariff relative *domestic* price ratio by the slope of line 2. The protection provided by the tariff shifts resources and outputs toward the domestic food industry — from point A to point B. Notice that the aggregate value of production at world prices has been reduced. Measured in units of food, the value of production is OF before the tariff, but OD after resources have been coaxed into producing more food. This is a signal that a small country does itself harm by the imposition of a tariff.

The analysis of the change in demand has been broken down into two steps. In Figure 12.2 we illustrate the effect of a tariff on the consumption of importables under the assumption that production possibilities are rigid — given by the exchange model's right-angled TAT' transformation schedule. The original free trade equilibrium is shown by the production point at A, the world terms of trade by line 1, and consumption by point G. The indifference curve, y_0, is the

---

[1] We shall always assume that the tariff rate is quoted on an ad valorem basis. This means that the domestic price of imports, say p_F, equals a multiple, $(1 + t)$, of the world price, p_F^*. The tariff rate is sometimes quoted as a percentage of the foreign price — e.g., 100 t might be 28 percent. For a tariff rate, t, the wedge separating home and foreign prices would rise if the foreign price rises. A different kind of tariff is the *specific* tariff — a rate quoted in absolute dollars per physical unit (e.g., $2.10 a ton). If t' denotes this amount, p_F would equal $(p_F^* + t')$. An inflation of world prices would in such a case leave the absolute tariff wedge unchanged (and diminish its relative significance).

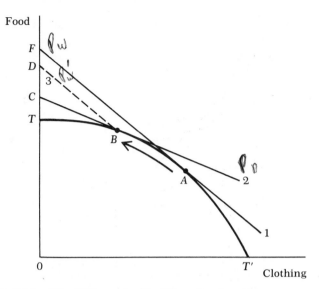

FIGURE 12.1   The Effect of a Tariff on Production

The initial free trade prices are shown by line 1, production is at *A* and national income, measured in units of food, is *OF*. A tariff on imports of food raises the domestic relative price of food as shown by line 2. Resources are shifted into food; production moves to point *B*. At world prices national income in food units has been reduced to *OD* (line 3 is parallel to line 1).

highest attainable given budget line 1. The small home country imports *GK* units of food in exchange for *KA* units of clothing as exports. A tariff on food raises the domestic relative price of food — this rise is shown by the slope of the flatter line 2 (3 or 4). If the community could stay on indifference curve y_0 it would alter its consumption pattern from *G* to *H*. This change would illustrate the *substitution* effect. A rise in food's relative price (behind the tariff wall) would cause consumers at home to reduce food consumption in favor of an increased demand for clothing. But as we warned in Chapters 2 and 3, there is also an *income* effect, shown here by the move from *H* to *J*, on the lower indifference curve, y_1.

This point is tricky, so we must go through the argument carefully. The dotted ray from the origin, *ONJH*, shows the various consumption bundles that would be chosen if incomes changed but relative prices remain fixed at the ratio shown by lines 2, 3, or 4 — the posttariff domestic price ratio.[2] We have shown the posttariff consumption point, *J*, as the intersection between the ray *ONJH* and the line 1

[2] This curve is called an *income-consumption* locus, and we have assumed it is a ray from the origin because we assumed earlier in the book that the

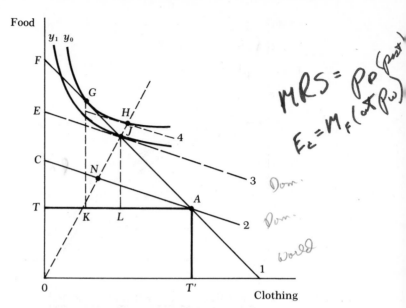

FIGURE 12.2 The Effect of a Tariff on Consumption
in an Exchange Model

Production remains at A on the right-angled TAT′ transformation schedule. A tariff raises the relative domestic
price of food to line 2 (parallel to lines 3 and 4). Food consumption falls by the substitution effect (from G to H) plus
an income effect (from H to J). Distance EC measures the
tariff revenue in terms of food. The trade triangle shrinks
from GKA to JLA.

through the production point (A) whose slope indicates *world* prices.
J is the consumption point because demand equilibrium requires
that (1) the marginal rate of substitution at home equals the domestic (posttariff) price ratio (this requirement is satisfied by all
points on ONJH), and (2) the amount of clothing the domestic economy is willing to export equals its demand for imports of food *at world
prices* (this requirement is satisfied by all points on line 1).

As Figure 12.2 illustrates, the home country is harmed by levying a
tariff—it ends up on a lower indifference curve at J than it could
obtain with free trade at G. This result is basic, for it suggests that if a
country is too small to affect world prices by its own commercial
policy, the best tariff is a zero tariff. As Chapter 13 discusses, other
considerations may warrant an active commercial policy for a small
country.

ratio of quantities demanded depends only upon the relative domestic price
ratio.

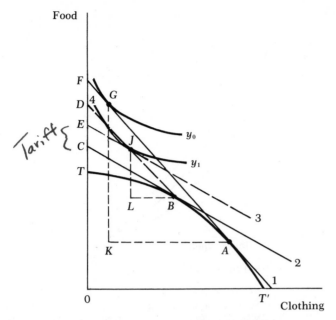

FIGURE 12.3 The Effect of a Tariff on Imports

> A tariff raises the domestic relative price of food (shown
> by lines 2 and 3) above the fixed world price (shown by lines
> 1 and 4). Domestic production of food rises from A to B.
> Domestic consumption of food falls from G to J. The trade
> triangle shrinks from GKA to JLB.

A nation's imports reflect both its demand for the importable commodity and its domestic production of that same commodity. Figure
12.1 was designed to show how a tariff encourages a greater production of importables. Figure 12.2 kept production fixed in order to
highlight the effect of a tariff in cutting demand for importables.
These two strands are brought together in Figure 12.3. The free trade
equilibrium production and consumption points are represented by
points A and G respectively, with the slope of line 1 indicating the
fixed relative world price of clothing to food. A tariff on food raises
the relative domestic price of food and encourages greater local
production. This effect is shown by the move from A to B, where line 2
shows posttariff domestic prices. Line 4 is parallel to line 1, and shows
combinations of clothing and food that have the same value at world
prices as does the production point, B. The home country's consumption bundle after the tariff must lie somewhere along line 4; specifically it must rest at J where indifference curve y_1 has a slope equal to
the *domestic* price ratio (line 3 is parallel to line 2). The home country's demand for imports has been reduced from GK to JL — a combination of greater production and lessened demand for food. But

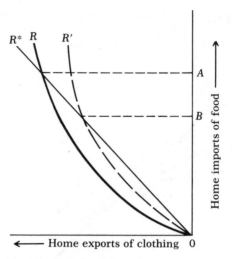

FIGURE 12.4   Tariffs and the Offer Curve

The ray OR^* indicates the fixed world terms of trade — unaffected by the tariff of a small country. OR is the home country's offer curve with free trade. A tariff causes the offer curve to shrink toward the origin — to OR'. At the given world terms of trade the demand for food imports is reduced from OA to OB.

the tariff has lowered real income from the y_0 curve to y_1. Not only is the value at world prices of aggregate production less with the tariff (compare OD with OF), the consumption point along budget line 4 represents a less than optimal bundle because domestic prices (the slope of line 3) are distorted away from world prices (the slope of line 4).

This loss of real income may seem all the more noteworthy because with a tariff the home country receives tariff revenue which, we assume, is passed on to consumers.[3] Evaluated at the relative domestic price of food, the value of incomes earned in production after the tariff is distance OC in Figure 12.3. The tariff revenue is CE, and the budget line appropriate to domestic consumers is line 3, which lies *outside* the transformation curve (by the amount of the tariff revenue). However, the best point along line 3 (point J) is inferior to the best point (G) along the pretariff budget line 1, in which there was no tariff revenue.

[3] We could alternatively have assumed that the government retains the tariff proceeds to spend as it wishes. But this assumption would complicate the analysis by forcing us to compare the private sector's spending pattern (as indicated by the indifference map) with that of the government. Instead, we shall assume that individuals receive in "lump-sum" fashion the proceeds of the tariff revenue — and treat these proceeds like any other income.

Figure 12.4 illustrates a tariff shifting the tariff-levying country's offer curve toward the origin. A small country faces fixed world terms of trade. The net effect of the tariff is, as we have shown, to reduce the quantity of imports demanded, from *OA* to *OB* in Figure 12.4. This result would hold for any given world terms of trade, as indicated by a comparison of the tariff-ridden offer curve, *OR'*, with the free-trade offer curve, *OR*.

12.2 THE EFFECT OF A TARIFF ON WORLD AND DOMESTIC PRICES

The analysis of the case of a country too small to affect world prices is essential in understanding the more general situation in which one country's commercial policy can disturb world commodity markets. The foreign offer curve is no longer the ray *OR** as in Figure 12.4, incorporating the assumption of fixed world prices. We show in Figure 12.5 the foreign offer curve *OR**, which shows that a lowering of clothing's relative price increases foreign imports of clothing. Once

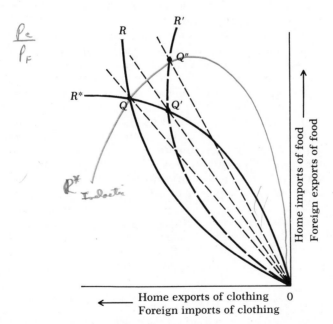

FIGURE 12.5   A Tariff Improves the Terms of Trade

> The free trade equilibrium is at point *Q*, with the relative price of clothing shown by the slope of *OQ*. A tariff in the home country shifts the offer curve from *OR* to *OR'*, with the new equilibrium at *Q'* and the relative price of clothing shown by the slope of *OQ'*. The home country has improved its terms of trade.

again a tariff levied by the home country shifts its offer curve inward from *OR* to *OR'*. But the reduction in home demand for food imports, which this shift represents, now causes the relative world price of food to fall in order to clear markets. This fall is shown by a swing in the world terms of trade from ray *OQ* to *OQ'* in Figure 12.5.

A country can use a tariff to improve its terms of trade. It acts like a seller of a commodity who finds himself with some monopoly power. By controlling supply, he can exercise some influence over price. Just as a tariff reduces the home country's import demand at given world terms of trade, so does it reduce the quantity of exports supplied. Looked at in this way, a tariff is a means of forcing up the relative price of a country's exports on world markets. An improvement in the terms of trade means both a reduction in the world relative price of imports and an increase in the relative price of exports — they are the same thing. We should remember that although the government of the tariff-levying country can act like a monopolist, we still assume that private firms are numerous enough to act competitively.

If a tariff depresses the relative world price of imports, the price behind the tariff wall — the *domestic* relative price of imports — cannot rise by the full extent of the tariff. This relation points to a conflict in the motives lying behind the use of a tariff. Tariffs often aim to protect local import-competing industries. Their concern is to raise the domestic price of the commodities they produce. If the foreign offer curve is infinitely elastic — the case illustrated by *OR** in Figure 12.4 — the domestic relative price of food rises by the full extent of the tariff. The foreign curve *OQ'QR** in Figure 12.5 is elastic, but the tariff does depress the relative world price of food to some extent. If the foreign offer curve had been inelastic, the world terms of trade would have improved by a greater amount. Imagine drawing a foreign offer curve in Figure 12.5 so that it passes from the origin through *Q''* and *Q* (instead of *Q'* and *Q* as drawn). In such a case the shift in the home offer curve as a consequence of the tariff would have lowered food's relative price in world markets to the level indicated by *OQ''*.

There remains the curious possibility that a tariff might depress the relative world price of a country's import commodity to such an extent that the *domestic* price of imports falls as well.[4] In our example, the relative price of food could fall by a greater amount than the tariff

Metzler
Paradox

[4] The argument that a tariff may fail to raise the price of the protected commodity behind the tariff wall is found in Lloyd Metzler, "Tariffs, the Terms of Trade, and the Distribution of National Incomes," *Journal of Political Economy,* 57 (February 1949): 1–29; reprinted eds. Caves and Johnson, *Readings in International Economics.* Homewood, Ill.: Richard D. Irwin, 1968, chap. 2. This result was recently challenged by Bo Södersten and Karl Vind in "Tariffs and Trade in General Equilibrium," *American Economic Review,* 58 (June 1968): 394–408. A rejoinder, defending Metzler, is contained in R. W. Jones, "Tariffs and Trade in General Equilibrium: Comment," *American Economic Review,* 59 (June 1969): 418–24.

itself. The important feature of such a possibility is that the tariff fails to protect the import-competing sector of the economy. Instead, it would drive resources toward the export sector. Yet this is just the case in which a tariff leads to a large gain in the world terms of trade.

The precise conditions required for a tariff to fail to protect need not concern us here.[5] Needless to say, they require a low foreign elasticity of demand. Disturbances such as tariffs require large price adjustments when response to price changes (which is what elasticities measure) is low.

12.3 TARIFFS AND DOMESTIC WELFARE:
THE OPTIMUM TARIFF

If a country can improve its terms of trade, it is better off. This message of our analysis of the exchange model (in Part 1) was reinforced in Part 2, where we discussed production changes. However, this message needs severe qualification if the terms of trade improvement is engineered by commercial policy. Suppose the home country were to levy ever higher tariffs on imports of food. Each tariff hike improves its terms of trade. But eventually the tariff can become so high that all trade is wiped out, and at this point the home country is certainly not better off than it was in the initial free trade situation. In Chapter 2 we demonstrated the gains from free trade compared with no trade. Clearly an improvement in the terms of trade cannot be the sole index of the effect of a tariff on domestic welfare.

Figure 12.6 illustrates the point. Free trade is shown by the intersection of the offer curves OR and OR^* at Q. Line 1 shows the free trade terms of trade, with the equilibrium point Q shown by the tangency of indifference curve y_1 to line 1. Suppose a tariff shifted the home offer curve to OR', intersecting OR^* at point Q'. The home country would improve its terms of trade (a ray from the origin to Q' is steeper than line 1). And yet the home country is no better off — it remains on indifference curve y_1. The tariff has improved the terms of trade by cutting the volume of trade, and the latter has a deleterious effect on welfare.

The reasoning is basic: a tariff separates the home and foreign relative prices of food. The foreign (world) price indicates to the home country the *cost* of obtaining another unit of food. The domestic price indicates to the home country the *value* of obtaining another unit of food, because domestic prices reflect marginal rates of substitution along the home indifference curve. With a tariff wedge, the value of an extra unit of food at home thus exceeds the cost of obtaining it, so that an increase in food imports would increase welfare. But working this the other way, a reduction in imports must lower

[5] They are developed in the supplement to this Chapter.

welfare by cutting back purchases where value exceeds cost. At Q' the terms of trade are superior to those at Q (which improves welfare), but the volume of imports is lower (which harms welfare). At Q' is the point where these two effects just balance.

Figure 12.6 also shows that a lower tariff rate, such as that leading to offer curve OR'', can improve welfare. Indeed this lower tariff is the *optimal tariff*, for indifference curve y_2, tangent to the foreign offer curve OR^*, is the highest that can be reached by any tariff policy. In effect the home country's choice of a tariff implies a choice among all the points on the foreign offer curve. Q'' is the best point for the home country.

There is a formula for the optimal tariff rate. It is instructive to derive this formula by means of the offer curve diagrams, because such a derivation illustrates the distinction between world terms of trade and domestic prices that is represented by the tariff. Turn to Figure 12.7. A tariff that shifts the home offer curve so that it cuts

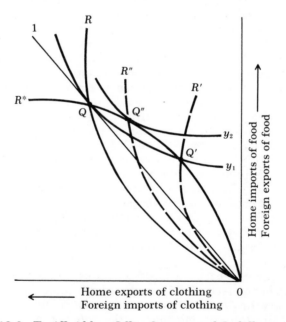

FIGURE 12.6 Tariff-ridden Offer Curves and Indifference Curves

> Point Q is the free trade equilibrium, with terms of trade shown by line 1. A tariff that shifts the offer curve to OR', with the new equilibrium at Q', improves the terms of trade but lowers the volume of trade. The home country is no better off than at Q with free trade. The optimal tariff shifts the offer curve to OR''.

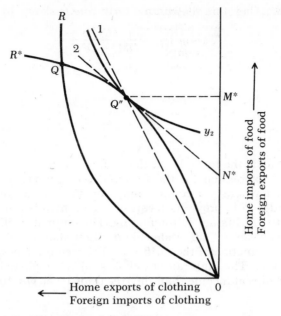

FIGURE 12.7   The Optimal Tariff Rate

> The optimal rate of duty is the tariff that shifts the home
> offer curve so that it intersects OR^* at point Q'', where in-
> difference curve y_2 is tangent to OR^*. ~~Line 1 shows the
> world terms of trade and line 2 the domestic price ratio.
> Therefore the tariff rate, t, is~~ ON^*/N^*M^*. Since the elasticity
> of the foreign offer curve at Q'' is $\epsilon^* = OM^*/ON^*$, it follows
> that the optimal tariff rate is $t = 1/(\epsilon^* - 1)$.

OR^* at point Q'' is optimal. The world terms of trade would be indicated by the slope of line 1 through Q'' and the origin. Specifically,
the world relative price of food is $Q''M^*/OM^*$. Call this p^*. The domestic price ratio is indicated by line 2, tangent to indifference curve y_2.
This shows a higher relative price of food, $Q''M^*/N^*M^*$. Call this p. If
t represents the tariff rate,

$$p = (1 + t)p^*.$$

But p/p^* equals OM^*/N^*M^* or $(1 + ON^*/N^*M^*)$. Therefore the tariff
rate is shown graphically by the distance ON^* divided by N^*M^*.

    In Chapter 3 we illustrated how the elasticity of demand for imports
along an offer curve can be shown by drawing a tangent to the offer
curve and extending a perpendicular line to the export axis. The
elasticity of the foreign offer curve at Q'', ϵ^*, is given by the ratio of

OM^* to ON^*. Therefore the optimal tariff rate is shown by

$$t = \frac{ON^*}{N^*M^*} = \frac{ON^*}{OM^* - ON^*}$$

$$= \frac{1}{\dfrac{OM^*}{ON^*} - 1}$$

$$= \frac{1}{\epsilon^* - 1}.$$

This equation is the formula for the optimal tariff rate.

The final expression for the formula is less important than the concept that whereas a country may benefit from levying a small tariff in order to improve its terms of trade, there is a limit beyond which higher tariffs are self-defeating. The optimal tariff is not the tariff that chokes off all trade. Figure 12.8 shows real income or welfare as a function of the tariff rate. The free trade position has a zero tariff rate. The high rate, t_1, chokes off all trade and leads to a lower level of real income than the free trade level, OA. In Chapter 2

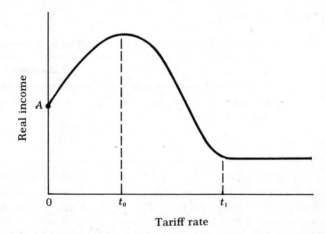

FIGURE 12.8   Domestic Welfare Depends upon the Tariff Rate

Free trade leads to a level of real income indexed by OA. For a country with some influence on world prices, a tariff can improve its terms of trade and lead initially to a gain in real income. Rate t_0 is the optimum tariff. Higher rates of duty cost more in foregone opportunities to import than is gained by a lowering of import prices. Rate t_1 cuts off all imports, and leads to a level of real income identical to that of the no-trade state, which is lower than the free trade level, OA.

this was our basic point about the gains from trade. The rate t_0 is the optimal tariff.

Throughout this discussion we have assumed that the foreign country passively allows the home country to pursue whatever commercial practices it pleases while it retains a policy of free trade. This assumption overlooks the very real possibility of retaliation by the foreign country in the form of its own tariff. Any foreign tariff worsens the terms of trade for the home country. If the foreign country does retaliate because of a tariff levied at home, it is no longer clear that the home country can benefit. Many outcomes of such a tariff war are possible. As we shall relate in Chapter 14, much of the tariff history of the major trading nations for the past forty years has been characterized by multilateral attempts to reduce tariff barriers, in full awareness of the dangers of escalation when a single country pursues an active commercial policy on its own.

12.4 TARIFFS AND THE EFFICIENCY OF FREE TRADE

Supporters of the free trade doctrine point to the loss in *world* efficiency entailed by a tariff. Although the tariff-levying countries might gain, others stand to lose *more*. This argument focuses upon the dead-weight loss introduced by the *distortion* that a tariff creates between prices in one country and another. To probe further, we shall consider the argument in two stages: the effect of a tariff on world production, and the effect of a tariff on world consumption possibilities given the levels of production.

A tariff on food in the home country raises the relative price of food above its level in the foreign country. This higher price is reflected in a difference in the slopes of the two countries' transformation curves. Figure 12.9 superimposes the point showing production on the foreign transformation schedule — drawn upside down — upon the point showing production at home. The production point is Q, and the tariff wedge separating relative prices at home and abroad causes price line 1 at home to be flatter than price line 2 abroad. The point 0^* shows posttariff world outputs of food and clothing relative to the axes through 0. If the tariff were removed, resources in each country would be shifted into the commodity in which that country possesses a comparative advantage — clothing at home and food abroad Points A and B represent possible free trade production points. The slope of TT' at A equals the slope of $T^*T^{*\prime}$ at B, and if B were to be superimposed upon A, total world outputs would expand from 0^* to C.

One consequence of a tariff, therefore, is a reduction of world outputs below the free trade level. But from a world point of view this is not the only consequence. Recall from the exchange model of Chapter 2 our discussion of the box diagram and the contract curve (Figures 2.7 and 2.8). For convenience the box is reproduced as Figure 12.10.

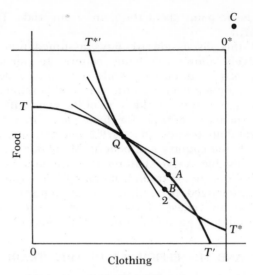

FIGURE 12.9   A Tariff and World Production

Point Q represents production at home and abroad. The foreign transformation schedule, $T^*T^{*'}$, is upside down so that total world production is shown by O^*. The home country's tariff on food imports leads to a higher relative price of food at home (shown by line 1) than abroad (shown by line 2). If the tariff is removed, both countries would face the same price ratio, e.g., the common slope at A and B. If B is superimposed upon A, total world production expands from O^* to C.

With a tariff the home country's offer curve, EAR, shifts to intersect the foreign country's offer curve at B. In Figure 12.10 we have drawn the indifference curve for the foreign country through B (y_0^*), with foreign prices shown by the slope of line 2, and the indifference curve for the home country through B (y_0), with a higher domestic relative price of food as indicated by the slope of line 1. Because prices differ at home and abroad, point B lies off the contract curve, CC', which is the locus of all points where a home indifference curve is tangent to a foreign indifference curve. The dead-weight loss entailed by the tariff finds reflection in the fact that a point such as D is available where, with the same world totals of food and clothing, both countries could be better off than at B. A tariff redistributes income between countries, but it is an inefficient device.

The two arguments illustrated in Figures 12.9 and 12.10 reinforce each other. Figure 12.10 shows the world welfare loss of moving off the contract curve for any *given* levels of world outputs, while Figure 12.9 shows how a tariff *reduces* world outputs.

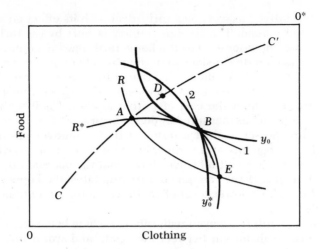

FIGURE 12.10 The Tariff Pulls Consumption
off the Contract Curve

> The dimensions of the box are the (assumed) fixed world
> outputs of food and clothing. Point *B* represents consump-
> tion in each country with a tariff on food at home, causing
> line 1 to be flatter than line 2. *B* is inefficient from a world
> point of view because it is off the contract curve. A point
> such as *D* allows each country's welfare to be improved
> over that at *B*.

12.5 SUMMARY

Tariff theory has both "positive" and "normative" aspects. The
positive aspects are the effects of a tariff on prices, consumption,
production, and trade. Proceeding first with a "small" country's
tariff we found that resources are shifted into the import-competing
sector of the economy and demand is drawn away from the imported
commodity. On both counts the country's demand for imports falls
at the given world terms of trade. This was expressed in the tariff-
ridden offer curve, which shrinks in toward the origin compared
with the free trade offer curve. If a country is large enough for its
actions to influence world prices, the contraction in import demand
induced by the tariff will lower the country's relative price of imports
and thus improve its terms of trade. We had to settle for a more ambiguous result concerning the relative domestic price of imports.
Typically a tariff is "protective," because it raises the local price
of the dutiable item, but if foreign response to price changes is sufficiently inelastic, the relative world price of imports could fall by more
than the tariff itself. In that case a tariff on food would, paradoxically,
lower the relative price of food behind the tariff wall.

The "normative" aspects of a tariff deal with its effect on welfare at home and abroad. The foreign country is hurt by the tariff — its terms of trade deteriorate. For the home tariff-levying country, however, there is more to consider than the possible improvement in the terms of trade. Once the domestic price of imports is higher than the world price, any further tariff increases may reduce imports of a commodity for which the cost of purchase abroad is less than the valuation at home (as measured by domestic prices). This loss in trade volume must be set against a terms of trade improvement in measuring the net benefits of a tariff. The extreme case of a tariff sufficiently high to choke off all trade shows that the optimal tariff must fall short of this. If the foreign country retaliates, the home country may end up with a lower level of real income than it obtained with free trade.

A tariff is an inferior way to redistribute income between countries. It introduces a distortion between domestic and world prices, and causes world outputs to settle at a suboptimal level while pushing consumption off the contract curve for any given levels of output. In this sense a tariff is a *second-best* instrument from a world point of view. Other means of redistributing income internationally, e.g., a direct gift from the foreign country to the home country, might allow both countries to emerge with a higher level of real income than with a distortionary tariff. This "second-best" concept has wider applicability to other arguments for tariffs, as we shall see in Chapter 13.

SUGGESTIONS FOR FURTHER READING

Jones, Ronald W., "Tariffs and Trade in General Equilibrium: Comment," *American Economic Review*, 59 (June 1969): 418–24. A brief analysis of basic tariff theory.

Metzler, Lloyd, "Tariffs, the Terms of Trade, and the Distribution of National Incomes," *Journal of Political Economy*, 57 (February 1949): 1–29. A more extensive account of tariff theory, concentrating on the effect of tariffs on domestic prices.

Supplement to Chapter 12:
Real Incomes, Prices, and the Tariff

REAL INCOMES AND THE OPTIMUM TARIFF

Recall from the supplement to Chapter 3 the basic expression for the change in the home country's level of real income, dy, in terms of the domestic price-weighted sum of consumption changes. This equation was 3.S.3, reproduced here as 12.S.1:

$$dy = dD_C + pdD_F. \qquad (12.S.1)$$

This expression needs no modification in the case of tariffs, for it rests on the simple notion that real income depends only upon the quantities of each commodity consumed and the relative valuation at the margin of one commodity in terms of another, as reflected in the *domestic* relative price of food, p.

The home country's budget constraint informs us of the source of a change in real incomes. But with a tariff we can write the budget constraint in terms of either domestic or world prices. It is instructive to look at each in turn.

In terms of domestic prices aggregate spending at home, $D_C + pD_F$, is limited to the value of income, which is derived both from income earned in producing commodities, $x_C + px_F$, and from the proceeds of the tariff revenue, which depends upon the home country's quantity of food imports, M, the foreign relative price of imports, p^*, and the tariff rate, t, and is the product of these three terms. Thus:

$$D_C + pD_F = x_C + px_F + tp^*M. \tag{12.S.2}$$

Figure 12.3 illustrated this form of the budget constraint with all items measured in food units instead of clothing units. With posttariff consumption at J, the aggregate value of incomes at domestic prices was OE, the value of incomes earned in production was shown by OC, and CE was the tariff revenue.

Consider, now, a small change in the tariff rate. This change leads to changes in prices, the consumption bundle, and production so that:

$$dD_C + pdD_F + D_Fdp = dx_C + pdx_F + x_Fdp + d(tp^*M).$$

Shift D_Fdp to the right-hand side to obtain 12.S.3:

$$(dD_C + pdD_F) = -Mdp + (dx_C + pdx_F) + d(tp^*M). \tag{12.S.3}$$

Notice that the left-hand side is, by the definition given in equation 12.S.1, the increase in the home country's real income, dy. Furthermore, the expression $dx_C + pdx_F$ on the right-hand side must vanish because the slope of the transformation schedule, dx_F/dx_C, must equal the negative of clothing's relative price, $1/p$.[1] Thus 12.S.3 can be simplified as 12.S.4:

$$dy = -Mdp + d(tp^*M). \tag{12.S.4}$$

That is, the sources of any real income gain to the home country are to be found in (1) a change in the domestic relative price of imports, dp, where any decrease in this price will raise real incomes at home by a factor given by the volume of imports, M; and (2) any increase in the tariff revenue, $d(tp^*M)$.

Expenditure and income are related by *world* prices. The domestic relative price of food, p, is given by $(1 + t)p^*$, and substituting this quantity into equation 12.S.2, noticing that M is given by excess food demand, $D_F - x_F$, results in equation 12.S.5:

$$D_C + p^*D_F = x_C + p^*x_F. \tag{12.S.5}$$

This equation states that at *world* prices the value of the home country's consumption bundle exactly equals the value of its production bundle. This equality was illustrated in Figure 12.3 by the fact that the posttariff consumption bundle, J, and production bundle, B, both lay on line 4 whose slope, $-(1/p^*)$, indicated the world terms of trade. Differentiate 12.S.5 to obtain:

$$dD_C + p^*dD_F = -Mdp^* + (dx_C + p^*dx_F)$$

Add and subtract pdD_F on the left-hand side and pdx_F on the right-hand side. This yields

$$(dD_C + pdD_F) + (p^* - p)dD_F = -Mdp^* + (dx_C + pdx_F) + (p^* - p)dx_F.$$

---

[1] See the supplement to Chapter 6 for a more complete account.

As already explained, $dD_C + pdD_F$ is the definition of the increase in real income at home, and $dx_C + pdx_F$ vanishes if resources are allocated at the optimal point along the transformation schedule. Since the change in imports, dM, is equal to $dD_F - dx_F$, the entire expression reduces to 12.S.6:

$$dy = -Mdp^* + (p - p^*)dM. \qquad (12.S.6)$$

It is difficult to overestimate the importance of the breakdown represented by equation 12.S.6 in understanding the welfare significance of tariffs. The first term, $-Mdp^*$, is the terms of trade effect, now stated in terms of world prices. Any policy that depresses the relative price at which the home country can purchase its imports in the world market will favorably affect welfare at home by an amount proportional to the volume of imports. But if trade is impeded, as it would be if a tariff exists, the second term, $(p - p^*)dM$, must also be taken into account. $p - p^*$ is the tariff wedge — it is the discrepancy (tp^*) between the relative domestic price of imports and the world price of imports. This second term indicates that any increase in the home country's level of imports must increase real income if the cost of obtaining imports in the world market (as shown by p^*) falls short of the relative value of imports in the local market (as shown by p). Any policy pursued by the home country that restricts imports entails a welfare loss if a tariff wedge has raised the domestic (relative) price of imports over the world level. This loss is directly proportional to the extent of the tariff rate.

The optimal tariff is found by setting dy equal to 0 in equation 12.S.6. (In Figure 12.8 $dy = 0$ at the optimal tariff rate t_0.) Replace $(p - p^*)$ by the equivalent expression, tp^*:

$$Mdp^* = tp^*dM.$$

Dividing both sides by p^*M, and recalling our use of the "hat" notation to express relative changes (e.g., $\hat{M}$ is defined as dM/M), we can express the optimal tariff as:

$$t = \frac{1}{\hat{M}/\hat{p}^*} \cdot \qquad (12.S.7)$$

The foreign offer curve remains stationary. Therefore if $\hat{M}$, the relative change in the home country's import demand, could be linked to $\hat{M}^*$, the relative change in foreign import demand, the expression for the optimal tariff given by equation 12.S.7 could be translated into an expression involving ϵ^*, the elasticity of import demand along the foreign offer curve.

The relationship between M and M^* is simple — it is given by the equilibrium condition 12.S.8 that states that at world prices the value of the home country's imports is equated to the value of foreign imports (or home country exports).

$$p^*M = M^*. \qquad (12.S.8)$$

Taking relative changes in 12.S.8 yields equation 12.S.9.

$$\hat{p}^* + \hat{M} = \hat{M}^*. \qquad (12.S.9)$$

Therefore $\hat{M}/\hat{p}^*$ equals $\hat{M}^*/\hat{p}^* - 1$. But $\hat{M}^*/\hat{p}^*$ is merely the definition of ϵ^*, the elasticity of the foreign country's demand for imports along its offer curve.[2]

---

[2] This elasticity formulation was introduced in Chapter 3. Because $1/p^*$ is the relative price of the foreign country's imports (clothing), ϵ^* is defined as *minus* $\hat{M}^*$ divided by $\widehat{1/p^*}$, which is equivalent to *plus* $\hat{M}^*/\hat{p}^*$.

From this we see that the formula for the optimum tariff given in 12.S.7 can be rewritten as in 12.S.10:

$$t = \frac{1}{\epsilon^* - 1} \cdot \tag{12.S.10}$$

In Chapter 12 we geometrically proved the same expression. The formula needs to be interpreted carefully. It seems to state that if the foreign offer curve is inelastic, ($\epsilon^* < 1$), the tariff should be negative. This interpretation of the relationships underlying the formula would be incorrect. Reconsider equation 12.S.6. If the foreign offer curve is inelastic, an increase in the tariff would cause home imports to rise. The terms of trade improve for the home country, and with ϵ^* less than one, foreigners offer more food for export. (Imagine a foreign offer curve passing through points Q and Q'' in Figure 12.5.) On both counts dy in 12.S.6 must be positive. The home country should raise its tariff until it reaches the elastic stretch of the foreign offer curve. Only then will a favorable movement in the terms of trade be countered by an unfavorable cutback in the volume of imports.

THE IMPACT OF TARIFFS ON WORLD AND DOMESTIC PRICES

Assume that the tariff level is initially at zero.[3] The expression for the sources of a real income change in equation 12.S.6 then reduces to the terms of trade effect:

$$dy = -M dp^*.$$

Our first task is to derive a solution for the effect of a small increase in the tariff rate upon the world relative price of food, p^*. The basic equilibrium relationship in the market, equating at world prices the value of imports in the two countries, was given in 12.S.8. From this equation the equation in rates of change was developed in 12.S.9. The foreign offer curve relates $\hat{M}^*$ to the change in the terms of trade, $\hat{p}^*$. Explicitly,

$$\hat{M}^* = \epsilon^* \hat{p}^*. \tag{12.S.11}$$

The expression for $\hat{M}$ is more complicated. A change in the tariff rate shifts the home country's offer curve. Therefore $\hat{M}$ will exhibit a mixture of such a shift as well as move *along* the home country's offer curve. Specifically, we may write $M = M(p^*, t)$ and decompose the rates of change as in 12.S.12:

$$\hat{M} = -\epsilon \hat{p}^* + \beta dt, \tag{12.S.12}$$

where β, defined literally as $1/M \cdot \partial M/\partial t$, is the shift in the home country's offer curve at given world terms of trade. One of our primary objectives is to develop an explicit expression for β to guarantee that it is negative. In Figure 12.4 we argued that an increase in t would reduce imports at given world terms of trade.

Substituting 12.S.11 for $\hat{M}^*$ and 12.S.12 for $\hat{M}$ into 12.S.9 yields the following solution for the effect of a tariff on world terms of trade:

$$\hat{p}^* = \frac{1}{\Delta} \beta dt \tag{12.S.13}$$

where

$$\Delta = \epsilon + \epsilon^* - 1.$$

---

[3] A more general treatment is provided in R. W. Jones: "Tariffs and Trade in General Equilibrium: Comment," *American Economic Review*, 59 (June 1969): 418–24.

The expression, Δ, captures the Marshall-Lerner condition for market stability discussed in Chapter 3. If we assume the market to be stable, the sum of import demand elasticities must exceed unity and Δ must therefore be positive.

Home prices are linked to foreign prices by the tariff rate: $p = (1 + t)p^*$. Taking relative changes in these terms and equating yields 12.S.14:

$$\hat{p} = \hat{p}^* + dt. \qquad (12.S.14)$$

With the solution for the terms of trade change, $\hat{p}^*$, given by 12.S.13 we may substitute to obtain the solution shown in 12.S.15 for the change in the relative domestic price of imports, $\hat{p}$:

$$\hat{p} = \frac{1}{\Delta}(\Delta + \beta)dt. \qquad (12.S.15)$$

Although Δ is positive, we have argued (and will subsequently prove) that β is negative. This argument underscores the doubts we expressed in the text that an increase in t must protect the import-competing industry.

To develop an explicit expression for β, the shift in the home country's offer curve as a result of a tariff, we shall examine more closely the determinants of the home country's demand for imports, M, which is the difference between its total demand for food, D_F, and local production of food, x_F. As discussed in Chapter 3, D_F depends upon the *domestic* price ratio, p, and real income, y. Thus:

$$D_F = D_F(p, y).$$

Taking small changes we obtain:

$$dD_F = \frac{\partial D_F}{\partial p} dp + \frac{\partial D_F}{\partial y} dy.$$

The term $\partial D_F/\partial p$ refers to the substitution effect of an increase in food's domestic relative price on demand assuming real income is constant. We may put this into elasticity notation by defining $\bar{\eta}$ as:

$$\bar{\eta} \equiv -\frac{p}{M} \frac{\partial D_F}{\partial p}. \qquad (12.S.16)$$

Thus defined, $\bar{\eta}$ must be positive. The term $\partial D_F/\partial y$ is related to the marginal propensity to import, m. Adjusting for units,

$$m \equiv p \frac{\partial D_F}{\partial y}. \qquad (12.S.17)$$

Introducing $\bar{\eta}$ and m into the breakdown of dD_F we obtain:

$$dD_F = M(-\bar{\eta}\hat{p} + \frac{m}{pM} dy). \qquad (12.S.18)$$

The change in real income, dy, is linked to the change in the terms of trade; the relative change in the domestic price ratio, $\hat{p}$, is linked to the change in the terms of trade and the change in the tariff rate by 12.S.14. Thus the change in D_F can be rewritten as:

$$dD_F = -M[(\bar{\eta} + m)\hat{p}^* + \bar{\eta}dt]. \qquad (12.S.19)$$

Turning to the supply side, the change in the production of importables, dx_F, is connected to the change in the production of exportables, dx_C, by the domestic price ratio, because the slope of the transformation schedule, dx_F/dx_C, equals $-(1/p)$, clothing's relative price facing local producers. Recall the definition of e in Chapter 6 as the home country's elasticity of supply of exports under the assumption that demand is constant:

$$e \equiv \frac{(1/p)}{(x_C - D_C)d(1/p)} \frac{dx_C}{.} \tag{12.S.20}$$

Having just established that dx_C equals $-pdx_F$ and noticing that $(x_C - D_C)$, the home country's supply of exports, must equal the value of its import demand, pM, we may obtain:

$$dx_F = M e\hat{p}.$$

Finally, substituting 12.S.14 for the change in domestic prices results in:

$$dx_F = M(e\hat{p}^* + edt). \tag{12.S.21}$$

We now have the ingredients for expressing the change in import demand as the difference between dD_F and dx_F. Thus:

$$\hat{M} = -[(\bar{\eta} + e + m)\hat{p}^* + (\bar{\eta} + e)dt]. \tag{12.S.22}$$

Compare this with 12.S.12 to prove that the breakdown of the elasticity of demand for imports along the offer curve is:

$$\epsilon = \bar{\eta} + e + m. \tag{12.S.23}$$

The expression for the *shift* in the offer curve, denoted by β in 12.S.12, is, by comparison with 12.S.22, revealed to be:

$$\beta = -(\bar{\eta} + e). \tag{12.S.24}$$

This confirms our argument in Chapter 12 that at constant world terms of trade an increase in the tariff constricts imports both by encouraging resource allocation toward the import-competing sector, and by cutting back on demand for the imported commodity through the substitution effect.

We may now develop an explicit criterion for the paradoxical-sounding case in which a tariff so depresses the terms of trade that the relative domestic price of imports falls as well. Substitute the expression for β in 12.S.24 into the expression for $\hat{p}$ in 12.S.15 to obtain:

$$\hat{p} = \frac{1}{\Delta} \{\epsilon + \epsilon^* - 1 - \bar{\eta} - e\}dt.$$

This can be simplified by noticing that the elasticity of the home country's offer curve (as shown by 12.S.23) consists of the two substitution terms, $\bar{\eta}$ and e, plus the home marginal propensity to import. Therefore the solution for $\hat{p}$ is:

$$\hat{p} = \frac{1}{\Delta} \{\epsilon^* + m - 1\}dt. \tag{12.S.25}$$

The verbal argument in Chapter 12 suggested that a tariff could fail to protect if the foreign import demand elasticity, ϵ^*, were sufficiently small. Equation 12.S.25 reveals that the critical value for this elasticity is $(1 - m)$ or, more simply, the home country's propensity to consume its export commodity.

13 The Political Economy of Tariffs

Commercial policy is often employed for reasons unrelated to the optimal tariff. Any interference with free trade disturbs factor and commodity prices and outputs, and some groups may gain from these alterations, despite possible losses to the community as a whole. In addition, some arguments for controlling trade take us beyond our static model of trade into questions of welfare over time and the macroeconomic effect of the tariff. This chapter surveys the major arguments for trade intervention made over the years. A nation's stance in its commercial policy is rarely simple, often resting upon several arguments for interference in free trade.

At the end of this chapter we take notice of the fact that many items of commerce are not final consumer goods but raw materials and intermediate goods. Tariffs on intermediate goods make us distinguish between nominal tariffs on final consumer goods and the implied "effective" tariffs on their assembly within the nation's borders.

13.1 THE TARIFF AS A DEVICE FOR RAISING REVENUE

Long before the progressive income tax and other sophisticated instruments were devised to provide governments with necessary revenues, the government agent at the port of entry typically extracted his toll on the inflow of merchandise from abroad. Any tariff rate that is not so high as to be prohibitive is a source of revenue. Although modern industrial states rarely rely on customs duties as a source of revenue, less developed regions often do.

The relationship between a tariff's impact on real income and on tariff revenue is expressed in Figure 13.1. A zero tariff yields no

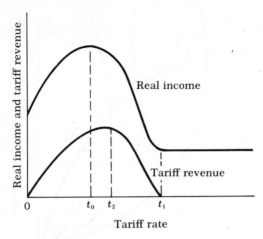

FIGURE 13.1   Tariff Revenue and Real Income

The curve showing tariff revenue reaches a peak at a higher
rate of tariff than does the curve showing real income.

revenue. Tariff rate t_1 is assumed to be prohibitive, so that higher
rates of duty as well yield no revenue. In the diagram we assume that
revenues rise continuously, reaching a peak for rate t_2, and, as imports dwindle evermore, fall continuously to zero at rate t_1. The
crucial point to notice is that the revenue-maximizing rate, t_2, exceeds the optimal tariff rate, t_0. An algebraic proof is provided in the
supplement to this Chapter. Figure 13.2 provides the geometric argument. The tariff rate underlying the home country's OR' offer curve is
the optimal tariff rate. A home indifference curve is tangent to the
foreign offer curve at Q'. A slightly higher tariff rate shifts the home
offer curve to OR'', intersecting the foreign offer curve at Q''. Because
line $Q'A$ is tangent to OR^* at Q', point Q'', also on the foreign offer
curve, OR^*, lies fairly close to line $Q'A$. But the home indifference
curve at Q'' is flatter. Therefore the tangent line, $Q''B$, has a higher
vertical intercept: OB exceeds OA. These vertical intercepts, in turn,
measure the tariff revenue in food units. (If the home country had no
tariff, its budget line would pass through the origin.) A tariff rate
exceeding the rate that maximizes real income can lead to a higher
tariff revenue.

That these two critical rates are not equivalent underscores the
point that pursuing commercial policy for revenue purposes is not
optimal strategy. Thus if at current tariff levels an increase in the rate
of duty would lower tariff revenues, the current levels are too high
for optimal welfare.

It is well at this point to recall that for a small country that cannot
influence the world prices of what it buys and sells, the optimal tariff
rate is zero. A tariff to raise revenue must then be rationalized by other

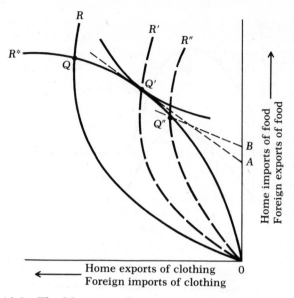

FIGURE 13.2   The Maximum Revenue Tariff and the Optimal Tariff

The optimal tariff is shown by OR', with an equilibrium at Q' and tariff revenue (measured in food units) equal to OA. A slightly higher tariff rate, underlying the offer curve OR'', leads to an equilibrium at Q'' with a higher tariff revenue, OB. The optimal tariff rate is lower than the rate that maximizes tariff revenue.

arguments, e.g., the ease of collection on international commerce as compared with local sales or income taxes.

13.2 TARIFFS AND THE DISTRIBUTION OF INCOME

The American steel industry is one among many that feel threatened by foreign competition. What attitude toward tariffs or other protective devices would you expect from a steelworker especially trained in tasks that have little application outside the steel industry? Or from the owner of a specialized item of machinery that cannot be used for any other purpose than making steel? Productive factors that are tied to one industry or occupation are very much affected by trade and commercial policies. Special interests and specific factors employed in import-competing industries will usually favor trade restrictions.

If protection favors inputs specific to import-competing production, a counter-argument for free trade can be mounted by factors tied to the nation's export industries. The logic is there, but the argument is less obvious. We might not recognize that dismantling barriers to imports encourages prices and production in the export sectors.

The Heckscher-Ohlin theory developed in Chapters 8 and 9 incorporated a different assumption about the nature of productive factors. There were no laborers in the steel industry who through training and experience had acquired skills for that industry but not for others. A laborer is a laborer. He earns the same return in all sectors of the economy, and no barriers prevent his switching jobs from one industry to another. If one sector of the economy stands to lose by a change in commercial policy, the other sector must gain, and we might assume that unimpeded factor flows between industries assure that each factor could benefit if the change in policy benefits the community as a whole. As our earlier discussion of the Heckscher-Ohlin theory revealed, however, changes in relative commodity prices get transmitted into magnified changes (in opposite directions) in the returns to the productive factors. One factor gains from trade and the other loses.[1]

The Heckscher-Ohlin theory thus provides a germ of truth for the so-called pauper labor argument, which states that laborers in a high-wage (capital abundant) country are hurt by competition from low-paid labor abroad. The crude version of the pauper labor argument overlooks the fact that foreign low wages tend to go hand-in-hand with high capital costs, and both factors contribute to unit costs of commodities. Nonetheless, the Heckscher-Ohlin theory points to the fact that free trade and the importation of labor-intensive commodities in a labor-scarce country alleviates the local relative shortage of labor and depresses real wages below their pretrade value.[2]

The preceding argument has left out of account the proceeds of the tariff revenue. Recall our assumption that these proceeds were redistributed to the private sector. The section of the population that loses real factor income may be compensated out of the proceeds of the tariff revenue. Once the possibility of internal redistribution is admitted, the argument for a tariff shifts back to our argument in Chapter 12 about the optimal tariff for the community as a whole. Income redistribution can supplement the desired commercial policy so that losses to factor incomes are made up in other ways. Even if a country is concerned about the internal distribution of income, the best policy in principle is to maximize the entire community's real income by means of the optimal tariff, and then employ other policy measures (taxes, transfers) to distribute this income as seems most appropriate.

This income redistribution need not come out of the tariff revenue.

---

[1] See especially the discussion of the Stolper-Samuelson theorem in Chapter 8.

[2] Recall from Chapter 12 the possibility that a tariff may fail to protect. If the foreign import demand elasticity is sufficiently low, the domestic price of imports may fall when a tariff is levied. If these imports are labor-intensive, local wages may be lowered by a tariff.

Consider a country too small in world markets to influence its terms of trade. For such a country free trade is optimal, and there are no tariff proceeds to distribute. Compared with the pretrade situation, the scarce factor loses by free trade, as its return in the market place must be driven down.

13.3 TARIFFS AND ALTERNATIVE POLICY MEASURES FOR SPECIAL OBJECTIVES

A tariff is not the only kind of policy-imposed distortion of prices, the allocation of resources, and demands. For example, if we want to encourage production in an industry deemed vital to national security, a protective tariff could do the job. But "better" means may be available. In this section we shall consider several arguments that have been made for tariff protection for some specific objective (other than the maximization of the community's real income), and contrast the tariff with other forms of impediments.

A tariff creates a spread between foreign prices and domestic prices, but leaves domestic consumers and producers facing the same prices. A tariff, then, stands in contrast to a *consumption tax,* which raises prices to consumers over that faced by producers (whether at home or abroad), or to a *production tax,* which also creates a spread between the prices confronting the consumer and the domestic producer. (The same kinds of remarks can be made about consumption or production *subsidies.*)

We can illustrate the differing effects of these tax (or subsidy) devices by considering possible objectives of government policy that can be secured by more than one fiscal strategy. Suppose, first, that the government opts for greater production of importables than the free trade level. There may be a desire to increase production of importables because labor seéms to benefit from the training received there. Or producers in the import-competing industry may claim that they must be protected against unfair foreign competition. Alternatively, the nation may desire to become more self-reliant in the production of importables in case trade in the future is interrupted. Whatever the reason, consider the situation in Figure 13.3. World prices are shown by the slope of line 1, with free trade production shown by point A, along the transformation curve TT', and consumption by point B. Suppose, furthermore, that the country is so small that no change in its own policy can affect the world terms of trade.

A tariff on imports of food can shift resources into the import-competing sector to raise production from OI to OJ, where OJ is the government's desired level of production of food. The domestic relative price of food rises, as shown by line 2. The new production point is at C and the consumption point is at E, with tariff revenue given by FG in units of the import commodity and the marginal rate of

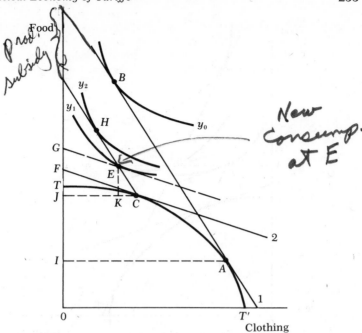

Food *(handwritten: Prod. subsidy)*

y_2

B

y_1

H

y_0

(handwritten: New Consump. at E)

G

F

T

J

E

K C

2

I

A

1

0

T'

Clothing

FIGURE 13.3 Tariffs vs. Production Subsidies to Achieve a Production Goal

> Free trade production is at A and consumption at B. If OJ level of food production must be undertaken, a tariff that raises food's relative price at home to line 2 is sufficient. Consumption is then at E. A production subsidy could yield the same result for producers, but at a lower cost in welfare. Consumption is at H.

substitution along indifference curve y_1 at E reflecting the domestic price ratio. Trade has been restricted — imports of food, EK, are equal at world prices to exports, KC, of clothing. This illustration of the effect of a tariff exactly matches Figure 12.3.

Line HEC in Figure 13.3 has been drawn parallel to line 1 and there-fore reflects the world terms of trade. Now suppose that instead of an import tariff the government had subsidized import-competing pro-duction allowing resources to be shifted from the free trade point, A, to point C on transformation curve TT'. The subsidy exactly offsets the higher costs of producing food at C compared with world prices. Consumers, however, are allowed to purchase commodities on the world market. Because line HEC, showing *world* prices, cuts indif-ference curve y_1 at E, consumers can reach the higher indifference curve, y_2, at H. If the government's goal has been to raise the produc-tion of food to OJ, it can achieve this goal by a tariff, but could also

(handwritten margin: Imp.)

(handwritten bottom: Subsidized Prod.)

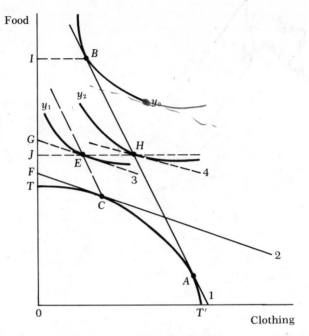

FIGURE 13.4   Tariffs vs. Consumption Taxes
to Achieve a Consumption Goal

Free trade production is at *A* and consumption at *B*. The
target restriction on consumption of food is indicated by *OJ*.
A tariff accomplishes this restriction by shifting production
to point *C* (with the tariff-ridden prices shown by lines 2 and
3) and consumption to point *E*. A consumption tax at a
higher rate allows production to remain at *A*, restricts consumption of food to *OJ*, and yields a higher level of real income at point *H*.

achieve it at a *smaller* sacrifice in welfare by a direct production
subsidy. Using commercial (tariff) policy to achieve a production goal
is inefficient compared with an approach directed expressly at producers without distorting choices for consumers as well. Of course the
community as a whole has still suffered the welfare loss in going from
y_0 to y_2 in order to support production levels of food at *OJ*.[3]

A different situation is pictured in Figure 13.4. In a free trade
equilibrium the world terms of trade are shown by the slope of line 1.
Production takes place at point *A* on the transformation curve *TT'* and
consumption is shown by *B* with real income for the community indicated by y_0. Thus with free trade the country would choose to con-

[3] This analysis can be found in W. M. Corden, "Tariffs, Subsidies, and the
Terms of Trade," *Economica*, N.S. 24 (August 1957): 235–42.

sume amount *OI* of importables. Suppose, now, that the government wishes to restrict consumption of food below this level, say to *OJ*. Although "food" may be a bad illustration, suppose it is a "luxury" item and if this country is relatively poor but developing, government planners may feel that the private sector should be overruled and consumption of "food" restricted.

A tariff on imports can restrict consumption of importables below the free trade level. In Figure 13.4 the tariff that reduces consumption of food to level *OJ* is illustrated. The relative domestic price of food is raised by the tariff, as shown by the slopes of lines 2 and 3. Resources are attracted to the protected industry, as shown by the movement along the transformation schedule from *A* to *C*. The tariff revenue is shown by *FG* in food units, and consumption behind the tariff wall is shown by point *E*. With world prices assumed fixed, the tariff has imposed a welfare loss, shown by the movement of the equilibrium consumption bundle from indifference curve y_0 to indifference curve y_1.

However, a *consumption tax* can reduce consumption of food from *OI* to *OJ* without such a drastic loss in the community's welfare. A tariff reduces consumption of food, as the government intends, but also attracts resources into the production of food, involving a needless extra welfare loss. This loss could be avoided by replacing the tariff with a consumption tax, which raises the price of food facing consumers but leaves producers to compete at world market prices. Production returns to its free trade level, shown by *A*. The required level of the consumption tax is determined by the slope of the indifference curve at *H*, where the world terms of trade line 1 intersects the government-imposed ceiling on consumption of food (shown by line *JH*). Such a tax limits consumption of food to *OJ*, as before, but welfare is only reduced from y_0 to y_2 instead of from y_0 to y_1.

Arguments for tariffs are often aimed at altering the production or consumption pattern of a free trade regime. Heeding the pleas of special consumer or producer interests involves a loss in welfare to the nation as a whole. But the tariff affects both consumption and production; using it to alter either makes this loss larger than necessary. A more efficient instrument is a production tax or subsidy to change production or a consumption tax or subsidy if the government wishes to control consumption. In each case the instrument should be used that works most directly on the objective.[4]

---

[4] Other examples and a more detailed discussion of the material in this and the following section can be found in H. G. Johnson, "Optimal Trade Intervention in the Presence of Domestic Distortions," *Trade, Growth, and the Balance of Payments*, R. E. Baldwin et al. Chicago: Rand McNally, 1965. See also J. N. Bhagwati, "The Generalized Theory of Distortions and Welfare," *Trade, Balance of Payments, and Growth: Papers in International Economics in Honor of Charles P. Kindleberger*, eds. J. N. Bhagwati et al. Amsterdam: North Holland, 1971, chap. 4.

13.4 DOMESTIC DISTORTIONS AND POLICY INTERVENTIONS

The price distortions we have considered all take the form of government-imposed wedges between the prices faced by different groups. But distortions may reflect not tax wedges but built-in features of the economy whereby prices do not accurately reflect marginal opportunity costs in production and/or marginal social rates of substitution in consumption. In such cases it has been argued that free trade is not an optimal policy, even leaving aside the optimal tariff argument. Instead, a government should impose tariffs or subsidies on trade to counter the inaccuracy of market prices as indicators of social benefits or costs.

Consider the possibility that the domestic price ratio is distorted from the slope of the production possibilities schedule. To be specific, suppose clothing's relative price at home is higher than the opportunity costs of producing another unit of clothing, measured in foregone production of food. Production of clothing might be controlled by a monopolist who charges a price exceeding marginal costs. Alternatively, production of clothing may be subject to external economies that accrue as the industry expands but are not perceived by individual firms. If clothing production should expand, firms would find clothing productivity rising even though they do not anticipate it. Market prices would then overstate opportunity costs.

Figure 13.5 illustrates such a case. The no-trade equilibrium is at A, with the domestic relative price of clothing, shown by the slope of line 1, exceeding the true marginal opportunity costs of producing clothing, as shown by the slope of the TT' schedule at A. The possibility of free trade at a price ratio different from that ruling at home need not involve gains from trade! Suppose that in world markets clothing is cheaper than at home but more expensive than it would be at A if there were no distortion. That is, suppose a line showing international prices is steeper than the TT' schedule at A but flatter than line 1. Trade then forces resources at home out of clothing and into food, so that production takes place at point B.

With world prices shown by the dashed line BC in Figure 13.5, free trade could involve consumption at a point such as C, which clearly lies on a *lower* indifference curve (not drawn) than does the pretrade point, A. Notice that in terms of opportunity costs the home country has a comparative advantage in producing clothing (the slope of TT' at A is flatter than the slope of the dashed line showing world prices). And yet because of the distortion, trade has encouraged a shift of resources in the wrong direction, out of the commodity in which the home country has a comparative advantage. This shift leads to an argument in favor of tariff protection. A prohibitive tariff returns consumption to point A and thus represents a gain for the home country. But other policies can do even better. If producers of clothing are sufficiently subsidized (or if food is sufficiently taxed), production

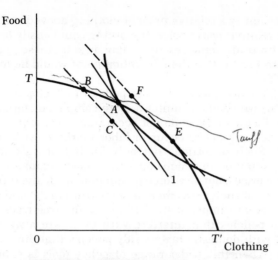

FIGURE 13.5   Free Trade with Distortions in Production
May Lead to a Welfare Loss

The pretrade equilibrium at *A* reflects a distortion in production that makes the relative price of clothing (shown by
line 1) exceed the opportunity costs of clothing (shown by
the slope of *TT'* at *A*). If the world clothing price lies between these two figures, free trade could lead to a production point *B* and consumption point *C* that is inferior to no
trade. A production subsidy could eliminate the distortion
and lead to consumption at *F*.

could be coaxed to point *E* and consumers allowed to purchase at
world prices to reach, say, point *F* where an indifference curve (not
drawn) is tangent to the dashed world price line *EF*. Once again a
policy of *trade* intervention is inferior to an alternative tax-subsidy
policy aimed directly at the source of the distortion, which lies in
production, not trade. This latter policy avoids the consumption loss
entailed by forcing consumers to trade at prices different from world
prices.

The situation described in Figure 13.5 is somewhat extreme. It is
characterized by a world price ratio lying between the domestic price
ratio and the domestic opportunity cost ratio, which leads the home
country to shift resources away from the commodity in which it has a
comparative advantage.[5] Despite the domestic distortion that raises

[5] In Figure 13.5 we have illustrated the case in which the home country is
harmed by trade. But line *BC* might have been flatter (although still not as flat
as *TT'* at *A*) and could have cut the indifference curve through *A*. In such a
case trade would improve real income despite the shift of resources away from
clothing, in which the country has a comparative advantage. The production
loss could be outweighed by the consumption gains from trade.

the home country's relative price of clothing above local opportunity costs, the relative *world* price of clothing could easily be higher still so that with trade some resources flow into increased production of clothing. In Figure 13.5 the production point would lie to the right of A along TT'.

In our later discussion of trade policy in developing regions (see Chapter 26) we shall encounter a more complex distortion, in which returns in factor markets do not accurately represent productivities. This is especially apt to occur in labor markets, with some sectors unionized. Such distortions not only hit industries unevenly, thus creating a situation in which opportunity costs again are not equated to domestic prices, but also force production inside the transformation schedule. In all such cases there is some truth in the notion that trade impediments can improve welfare above the free trade level. However, such policies that interfere with trade are always inefficient compared with domestic tax-subsidy policies that directly affect the distortion. When this wider range of policy tools is explicitly available, the only way in which trade impediments can be the most useful weapon is if the foreign terms of trade can be affected by a restriction of trade. That is, the optimal tariff argument is the only exception to a policy of free trade. And this argument is irrelevant for a country too small to affect world prices and must even be modified for large countries if there is a danger of retaliation.

13.5 DYNAMIC ARGUMENTS FOR PROTECTION

In this and the following section we shall consider briefly some of the arguments that have been raised for protection that stretch beyond the confines of the trade model that we have developed in Parts 1 and 2.

A nation that enters into trade generally finds its productive resources reallocated. Some industries suffer contraction in the face of foreign competition. In itself this fact does not support a protectionist stand. Just as some industries are bound to lose, others, in which the country has a comparative advantage, will gain. Nonetheless it is sometimes argued that certain industries will *in the future* be able to compete successfully if protection now grants them a chance to develop. This is the so-called *infant industry* argument for protection.

The first doubt about this proposition is that the "infant" may never grow up. Even if present protection leads to cost reductions as the industry expands, protection is not worthwhile if the industry could never compete on world markets. The argument only becomes feasible if the tariff or subsidy can eventually be dismantled and a genuine comparative advantage be established for that industry.

But even assuming that the infant does grow up, the whole project may not have been worthwhile. For during the course of protection there has been a real loss on both the consumption side and in terms of foregone alternative production which, by assumption, had greater value at world prices. Any future gains must not only be discounted back to the present, but must also be set against the more immediate real income loss to the community for the period in which the industry is protected.

Suppose that even on such a calculation net gains may be had from developing the industry. Why won't this be apparent to the entrepreneurs? Business firms often make investments, the returns to which are spread out over future periods. That is, most investments involve a trade-off between present costs and future benefits, and if undertaken reflect an assessment that the present value of the benefits exceeds the costs. The argument for sheltering an industry during its growth is certainly weakened if prospective gains consist in economies of scale (average costs reduced with expansion of output) that are perceived by the firm.

The germ of truth in the infant industry argument applies when the eventual gains from establishing the industry cannot all be recouped by those who have made the initial investments. Some form of externality must be present. To take an example from the setting of under-developed countries, workers gain by the skills learned during industrialization. These skills, deemed a gain to the community, can be transferred to other industries. That is, the entrepreneurs in a particular sector may undergo costs of training the labor force that are subsequently lost to them if that labor moves to other occupations.[6] If so, it is maintained that protection should be given to offset these losses. Once again, tariff protection may not be the best instrument. The situation calls for a change in production, but not in consumption. A tariff introduces a consumption loss that would not result from a production subsidy.

Another argument sometimes raised in favor of protection is that it may encourage foreign investment in home markets. (We shall postpone to Part 5 an appraisal of this goal.) A tariff can affect the pattern of investment. If a country is initially importing a commodity, a protective tariff wall forces foreign firms either to cut prices, lose sales, or, alternatively, try to produce the commodity directly in the home market and thus avoid the tariff. Such "tariff-factories" are not rare, as evidenced, for example, in the number of automobile assembly plants located in Argentina, Brazil, South Africa, and other countries which do not possess a comparative advantage in automobile production.

Finally, consider the perhaps paradoxical argument that tariffs should be imposed in order to force reductions in trade impediments in other countries. This is a tariff "for bargaining purposes." The ob-

---

[6] Notice, however, that it is possible to argue that if laborers are aware of the value of skills learned in an industry, competition will drive wages in that industry below wage rates prevailing elsewhere in the economy.

jective is not to maintain a tariff, but rather to use it as a weapon in future negotiations. The most obvious recent example was the pronouncement on August 15, 1971 by President Nixon of a 10 percent surcharge on all dutiable items. A clear indication was given at the time that the surcharge could be negotiated away, and it was.

13.6 THE TARIFF AS AN INSTRUMENT OF MACROECONOMIC POLICY: A PRELIMINARY VIEW

A number of arguments in favor of tariff protection have been presented and, except for the optimum tariff argument, we have found that a tariff is always less desirable than some other instrument of domestic policy. But two of the major arguments that have been used, currently and in the past, have not been discussed. It is often said that tariffs can strengthen a country's balance of payments and raise domestic employment. Here we deal with these issues only cursorily, to emphasize that they present problems outside the scope of our model and must await satisfactory treatment in Part 4.

Consider the argument for employment. This argument is not the same as that presented in section 13.2 whereby a country that levies a tariff on labor-intensive imports could improve the real incomes of its laborers. Here the issue is employment, and the argument is that a tariff can save or create new jobs in a country's import-competing industries by diverting home spending away from imports to local industries. What is left out is the question of employment in a nation's export industries, which problem would become more aggravated if foreign countries respond to such "beggar-thy-neighbor" attempts to export a nation's unemployment problem by raising tariff levels against the home country's exports.

The difficulty in appraising the employment argument now is that our model assumes that prices are sufficiently flexible to guarantee full employment. Furthermore, we have assumed that all income is spent, so that aggregate demand cannot be insufficient *unless* commodity markets and/or the exchange rate are out of line so that a country's desired spending abroad exceeds foreign demand for the home country's exports. This is the thin edge of the wedge. If market prices are sticky and markets not cleared, demand for the *home* country's products may be insufficient.

The employment argument and the balance of payments argument are intertwined. If a tariff that shifts spending from imports to home goods is always matched by an equivalent fall in exports so that trade is balanced, there is very little left of the employment argument. In our models a balance of trade was an equilibrium condition, and unless a different model is specified it will not be possible adequately to appraise the argument that a tariff can create an export surplus and raise employment.

13.7 EFFECTIVE PROTECTION

Actual production processes are rarely as simple as our two-factor theory has assumed. In particular, commodities at various stages of fabrication are outputs of some productive activities and inputs into others. Flour to make bread, spun yarn to make clothing, sheet steel to make automobiles — these are only a few examples of interindustry flows in what economists call "intermediate commodities." A large volume of international trade in these intermediate commodities has encouraged the development of a new concept in analyzing a country's commercial policy, that of the "effective rate of protection." It takes account of the fact that the "nominal" tariff applied to imports of a commodity does not by itself indicate the impact of protection for the domestic industry producing that commodity if it utilizes imported inputs that are subject to duty. The domestic industry "adds value" to the imported inputs, and the effect of protection on this "value added" is the key indicator of how protection affects resource allocation.

Take an example: suppose the free trade price of clothing on world markets is $1.00, and to produce a unit of clothing a country imports $.40 worth of spun yarn from abroad. The domestic industry then creates an additional $.60 worth of value added. Now suppose a 40 percent "nominal" tariff is levied on clothing imports, raising their domestic price to $1.40, and a 10 percent tariff is applied to imports of spun yarn, raising their cost to $.44 per unit of clothing behind the tariff wall. The domestic producer now receives as value added per unit of clothing $.96, the difference between $1.40 and the $.44 he spends as outlay on imported cloth. This difference represents an increase of 60 percent over the original value added ($[1.40 - .44]/.60$). The tariff structure has yielded a 60 percent "effective rate" of protection to domestic clothing producers, whereas the "nominal" rate on clothing imports was only 40 percent. This example illustrates the kind of "escalation" that can be built into a nation's tariff structure if commodities at a lower level of fabrication or processing (steel, yarn) are charged lower duties than more finished items (automobiles, clothing).

The ingredients in the effective tariff rate emerge from this example. The rate attempts to measure the percentage by which value added can increase over the free trade level as a consequence of a tariff structure. Let the fixed free trade price of imports of the *final* good be denoted by p_j^*. With a tariff at rate t_j on these imports, the domestic price becomes $(1 + t_j)p_j^*$. Suppose the productive process uses an imported intermediate good, i, with fixed world price, p_i^*. If a tariff at rate t_i is applied to imports of this intermediate good, its price behind the tariff wall is $(1 + t_i)p_i^*$. We also need to know how much of the intermediate good is required per unit of final output. Let this be denoted by a_{ij}, and assume it is fixed. Then at free trade world prices the value added per unit of final output is

$$v_j^* = p_j^* - a_{ij}p_i^*.$$

Compare this with value added at domestic posttariff prices, v_j:

$$v_j = (1 + t_j)p_j^* - a_{ij}(1 + t_i)p_i^*.$$

The effective rate of protection by definition is

$$\frac{v_j - v_j^*}{v_j^*} = \frac{t_j p_j^* - t_i a_{ij}p_i^*}{p_j^* - a_{ij}p_i^*}.$$

Finally, divide both numerator and denominator by the world price of the final commodity, p_j^*, and let θ_{ij} denote the *share* of the intermediate commodity in a dollar's worth of final output at free trade prices. That is, θ_{ij} is $a_{ij}p_i^*/p_j^*$. The effective rate of protection provided to the final commodity is thus:

$$\frac{t_j - \theta_{ij}t_i}{1 - \theta_{ij}}.$$

In our numerical example t_j was .40, $t_i = .10$, and θ_{ij} was .40. The effective tariff rate was 60 percent, although the nominal rate was only 40 percent.

In a recent study made for the World Bank, Bela Balassa computed the nominal and effective rates of duty for selected industry groups in seven developing countries. Some of the computations are rather startling. For example, in Chile in 1961 the nominal rate of duty on processed food was 82 percent.[7] This may sound high, but compare it with the calculated effective rate, 2,884 percent! Computations of effective rates have been used in bargaining sessions when tariff schedules are negotiated. It is useful for all parties to know which local productive activities receive especially favored rates of protection. The nominal rates are less helpful than effective rates in providing this information.[8]

13.8 SUMMARY

The basic theory of tariffs set out in the preceding chapter focused on the gain which a country may obtain if it has some monopoly power on world markets and can improve its terms of trade by levying a tariff. This gain provided the key valid argument for tariffs. In this chapter we surveyed a number of other arguments for protection.

---

[7] These figures are from Balassa and associates, *The Structure of Protection in Developing Countries.* Baltimore: John Hopkins University Press, 1971, p. 54.

[8] We have already remarked that effective rates of protection are higher than nominal rates for processes in which nominal tariffs on outputs are higher than tariffs on intermediate good imports. Let e denote the effective rate. Then the formula can be rewritten as $(1 - \theta_{ij})e + \theta_{ij}t_i = t_j$. This states that the nominal rate is a weighted average of the effective rate and the tariff on inputs.

These ranged from the desire to raise real wages by protecting labor-intensive imports or controlling production or consumption levels in certain industries to encouraging "infant" industries to develop, sheltered in early years from foreign competition.

In all the cases we studied we found that tariffs could help achieve any of these aims. But in each case a superior set of policies could also satisfy these objectives at a lower welfare cost. For example, if an industry seems to need a minimal home market, a tariff can be levied. But levying a tariff involves a consumption loss represented by the distortion between world and domestic prices. A production subsidy can achieve the same production goal and allow consumers to buy at world prices. The basic point is that tariffs interfere with *trade*, whereas the stipulated target or source of distortion often resides in production alone or consumption alone.

In the final section we introduced the concept of the effective rate of protection. This highlights the complexity in productive activity that exists in the real world. Domestic productive processes often rely on imported raw materials and intermediate products, and a tariff structure allocates resources more in line with the effective rates of protection on these processes than with the nominal rates on the end products.

SUGGESTIONS FOR FURTHER READING

Black, John, "Arguments for Tariffs," *Oxford Economic Papers,* N.S. 11 (June 1959): 191–208. A discussion of various arguments for protection.

Corden, W. M., "Tariffs, Subsidies, and the Terms of Trade," *Economica,* N.S. 24 (August 1957): 235–42. A lucid treatment of alternative protective devices.

Grubel, H. G. "Effective Protection: A Non-Specialist Guide to the Theory, Policy Implications, and Controversies," *Selected Topics in International Trade and Finance: A Book of Readings,* ed. R. E. Baldwin and J. D. Richardson. Boston: Little, Brown, 1973. Part II.A. An introduction to the issues in effective protection.

Johnson, Harry G., "Optimal Trade Intervention in the Presence of Domestic Distortions," *Trade, Growth and the Balance of Payments,* R. E. Baldwin et al. Chicago: Rand McNally, 1965. A general discussion of trade taxes and production and consumption subsidies, relying heavily on diagrammatic analysis.

Stolper, Wolfgang, and Samuelson, Paul A., "Protection and Real Wages," *Review of Economic Studies,* 9 (November 1941): 58–73. The analysis of the effect of a tariff on wages and rents.

Supplement to Chapter 13:
Tariffs, Distortions, and Welfare

In this supplement we shall continue the algebraic account of the tariff initiated in the supplement to Chapter 12. In particular, we shall provide a more formal proof of the fact that the maximum revenue tariff exceeds the optimal tariff. We shall also continue our analysis of the welfare effect of a small change in the tariff rate. Finally, a broader analysis of the tariff, making use of matrix algebra, allows an easy overview of the question of gains from trade and commercial policy.

THE MAXIMUM-REVENUE TARIFF

In the supplement to Chapter 12 we expressed the home country's budget constraint in terms of domestic prices (see equation 12.S.2). When differentiated, this expression led to an expression for the change in real income, in terms of the change in the domestic price ratio and the tariff revenue. This equation was 12.S.4, which is reproduced below as equation 13.S.1:

$$dy = -Mdp + d(tp^*M). \tag{13.S.1}$$

Consider this expression in conjunction with Figure 13.1. The optimal tariff rate is t_0, and we know from the optimal tariff formula (equation 12.S.10) that near t_0 the foreign offer curve must be elastic. This means that the tariff must be "protective" in the sense of raising p with a small further increase in t. Thus the $-Mdp$ term in 13.S.1 is negative in the neighborhood of the optimum tariff, where dy equals zero. As a consequence, $d(tp^*M)$ must be positive. That is, at rate t_0 in Figure 13.1 the curve plotting the tariff revenue against the tariff rate must be positively sloped. Tariff revenue reaches a maximum at the higher rate, t_2.

DISTORTIONS AND REAL INCOMES

The distinction between domestic and foreign prices is crucial in any discussion of the tariff. In section 13.4 a further distinction was made — between domestic prices received by producers and the slope of the community's production-possibilities schedule. A distortion on the production side can raise the home country's relative price of clothing above its social opportunity costs, as illustrated at point A in Figure 13.5. Expressed in terms of food's relative price we have *three* different terms: p^*, the relative price of food on world markets; p, the relative price of food facing domestic consumers and producers; and p_T, the opportunity costs at home of producing food, as given by the slope of the transformation schedule.

We start with the home country's budget constraint expressed in world prices:

$$D_C + p^*D_F = x_C + p^*x_F. \tag{13.S.2}$$

Differentiating we obtain:

$$dD_C + p^*dD_F = -Mdp^* + \{dx_C + p^*dx_F\}.$$

Add and subtract pdD_F on the left and p_Tdx_F on the right. We now have:

$$(dD_C + pdD_F) + (p^* - p)dD_F = -Mdp^* + (dx_C + p_Tdx_F) + (p^* - p_T)dx_F.$$

This equation can be simplified in two respects: (1) the expression $\{dD_C + pdD_F\}$ is, by definition, the improvement in real income at home; (2) the expression $(dx_C + p_Tdx_F)$ is zero because p_T is, by definition, the slope of the transformation curve. With these simplifications we obtain:

$$dy = -Mdp^* + (p - p^*)dD_F + (p^* - p_T)dx_F. \tag{13.S.3}$$

In our first treatment of distortion, represented in Figure 13.5, free trade increased food production from A to B when the world relative price of food, p^*, was lower than the domestic opportunity cost, p_T. Thus for small changes, the $(p^* - p_T)dx_F$ term in equation 13.S.3, being negative, illustrates the production loss. However, the consumption gain in moving to free trade is picked up by the $(p - p^*)dD_F$ term. As illustrated in Figure 13.5, the world relative price of food, p^*, is higher than the domestic price, p, and trade reduces food demand, D_F. Thus the term $(p - p^*)dD_F$ is positive.

In the alternative case (not shown diagrammatically) the world relative price of food was lower than the domestic price, despite the fact that the latter was distorted below food's opportunity cost at home. That is, p^* was less than p_T and, because trade shifted resources away from food, $(p^* - p_T)dx_F$ was positive. Nonetheless, an export subsidy or a subsidy directly on the home production of clothing could further cut back food production and thus yield increased production gains until p_T finally rises to the world price level. Suppose an export subsidy had been used. It would create a wedge between home and foreign prices so that p is smaller than p^* (the home country's export commodity is relatively cheaper abroad). A switch at this point away from an *export* subsidy to a subsidy on the *production* of clothing raises p, reduces D_F, and involves a further consumption gain represented by $(p - p^*)dD_F$. The optimal policy in the case of a production distortion is a production subsidy, *not* a trade subsidy.

Throughout our discussion of distortions we have concentrated upon the case of a small country that cannot affect world prices. Thus the terms of trade effect, $-Mdp^*$ in equation 13.S.3, vanishes and we only had to consider the effect of a tariff in altering demand for the importable commodity where domestic and world prices differ and for production where world prices and opportunity costs are separated. As equation 13.S.3 reveals, the analysis of the large country case superimposes upon this effect the terms of trade argument.

TARIFFS, GAINS FROM TRADE, AND WELFARE: A GENERAL ANALYSIS

We wish to compare welfare or real income of an economy in two situations, in which prices, quantities traded, and trade restrictions may differ by more than "a small amount." There is no restriction on the number of commodities produced or consumed at home or abroad. For notation we use x as the *vector* of quantities produced at home, D as the *vector* of quantities demanded or consumed, p as the *vector* of prices ruling in the home country, and p^* as the *vector* of prices ruling abroad.[1] Not all commodities need be produced at home, so that in the vector $x = (x_1, x_2, \ldots, x_n)$ some entries may be zero. Similarly, not all commodities produced need be demanded locally, so that in the vector $D = (D_1, D_2, \ldots, D_n)$ some entries may also be zero. The two situations we wish to compare are denoted by a single prime and a double prime. Thus in the initial situation home prices are given by the vector $p' = (p_1', p_2', \ldots, p_n')$. This vector may or may not represent a situation in which some international trade takes place. In the second situation prices have altered at home to $p'' = (p_1'', p_2'', \ldots, p_n'')$. Let the vector E represent the home country's set of *excess demands*. Thus:

$$E \equiv D - x. \tag{13.S.4}$$

[1] The analysis in this section rests heavily upon Michihiro Ohyama, "Stability and Welfare in General Equilibrium." Ph.D. Thesis, University of Rochester, 1972.

An element E_i in the vector E is positive if commodity i is imported at home, it is negative if i is exported, and is zero if high transport costs or tariffs result in no international exchange of the ith commodity.

The basic criterion with which welfare in the double-prime situation is contrasted to welfare in the single-prime situation involves a comparison of the value of aggregate demand in each, when the prices used for the evaluation are in both instances those of the double-prime situation. Thus welfare is deemed to have risen if

$$p''D'' - p''D' > 0. \qquad (13.S.5)$$

This inequality states that if the initial bundle of goods consumed (D') could have been purchased in the double-prime situation, the community is assumed to have increased its real income.

This assumption is illustrated for the two-commodity case in Figure 13.S.1. The fact that the consumption bundle in the single-prime situation, D', lies below the line showing prices in the double-prime situation (and supporting demand, D'') is taken as a sufficient criterion for establishing that point D'' represents a higher level of welfare. Clearly if indifference curves do not intersect, point D' must lie on a lower indifference curve than point D''.

Equation 13.S.4 states that the vector of excess demands equals the vector of total demands minus the vector of production. Turning this equation around it states that demand equals excess demand *plus* production. Making this substitution for both the single-prime and double-prime situations in the improvement in welfare criterion, 13.S.5, yields the inequality in 13.S.6 as an equivalent expression:

$$p''(E'' - E') + p''(x'' - x') > 0. \qquad (13.S.6)$$

Prices at home in the double-prime situation will differ from prices abroad

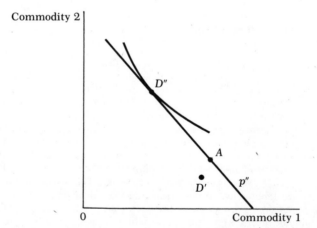

Commodity 2

D''

A

D'

p''

0   Commodity 1

FIGURE 13.S.1   The Welfare Criterion for Two Commodities

Two alternative consumption bundles are illustrated: D' and D''. The prices ruling when D'' is consumed are shown by line p''. The welfare criterion whereby situation double-prime is superior to situation single-prime is shown by the fact that D' lies below line p'', which means $p''D'' - p''D' > 0$.

for any traded commodity that is subject to a tariff, an export tax, or a subsidy in the home country. Let the matrix T'' represent these taxes and/or trade subsidies. T'' is a *diagonal matrix,* all of whose elements are zero except the diagonal terms. The entry, t_i'', in the ith row and column of T'' represents the tariff rate on imports of commodity i if t_i'' is positive, or the import subsidy on commodity i if t_i'' is negative. This means that for any commodity, i,

$$p_i'' = (1 + t_i'')p_i^{*''},$$

where $p_i^{*''}$ is the world price of commodity i. This can be summarized in matrix notation by making use of the identity matrix, I, whose off-diagonal elements are all zero, and with "ones" all along the diagonal. Thus:

$$p'' = (I + T'')p^{*''}. \tag{13.S.7}$$

The home country's budget constraint states that the value at world prices of aggregate excess demand is zero, both for the double-prime and single-prime situations:

$$p^{*''}E'' = 0 \tag{13.S.8}$$

$$p^{*'}E' = 0. \tag{13.S.9}$$

Furthermore, if the single-prime situation refers to the pretrade situation at home, each element of the vector E' would have to equal zero because in equilibrium local demand would have to be balanced by local sources of supply.

All the ingredients are now at hand to transform the welfare criterion, 13.S.6, into an explicit listing of the sources of an improvement in real incomes. To proceed we merely need to substitute the relationship shown in 13.S.7 between domestic and world prices into the first term in 13.S.6. Thus

$$p''(E'' - E') = (I + T'')p^{*''}(E'' - E').$$

This expression, in turn, equals

$$p^{*''}E'' - p^{*''}E' + T''p^{*''}(E'' - E').$$

But notice that by 13.S.8, $p^{*''}E''$ vanishes. This statement of the budget constraint at world prices applies as well to the single-prime situation (shown by equation 13.S.9), and thus allows us to add $p^{*'}E'$ (equal to zero) to the expression above. Thus rewritten it becomes

$$-(p^{*''} - p^{*'})E' + T''p^{*''}(E'' - E').$$

Substitute this expression for $p''(E'' - E')$ back into 13.S.6 to obtain 13.S.10 as the basic welfare criterion:

$$-(p^{*''} - p^{*'})E' + T''p^{*''}(E'' - E') + p''(x'' - x') > 0. \tag{13.S.10}$$

Each of the three terms in 13.S.10 should be familiar from our earlier discussion:

1. The term $-(p^{*''} - p^{*'})E'$ is the terms of trade effect. If the two primed situations represent different trading equilibria very close to each other, and if only one relative price (because only two commodities) exist, it is shown by the $-Mdp^*$ term, say, in 13.S.3. Our general expression states that the community's welfare improves to the extent that the world price falls for any commodity imported ($E_i' > 0$), or rises for any commodity exported ($E_i' < 0$).

2. The term $T''p^{*''}(E'' - E')$ measures the change in the volume of trade for all commodities for which domestic prices, p'', differ from world prices, $p^{*''}$.

The term $T''p^{*''}$ is the tariff wedge. Returning again to the case in which only two commodities are traded, and the two situations are very close to each other, this term reduces to the $(p - p^*)dM$ term in equation 12.S.6. It states in general that real income is improved if the level of imports rises for any commodity worth more at home (as indicated by p'') than it costs to obtain in world markets (as indicated by $p^{*''}$).

3. The term $p''(x'' - x')$ must in any case be greater than or equal to zero. It shows the change in real income attributable to the change in production. In the absence of distortions, x'' is the point on the transformation schedule that maximizes the value of output at domestic prices when these are given by p''. Therefore the value of any other production possibility, say x', at these prices p'' must be less. If the single-prime and double-prime situations are very close together in the two-commodity model, this term reduces to $dx_C + pdx_F$. As we argued in Chapter 6 and subsequently, this reduction approaches zero as an expression of the equality between the domestic price ratio and the slope of the transformation schedule.

This line of reasoning has been useful in comparing two states of trade, differing from each other in prices — perhaps as a result of changes in tariffs. It is also useful in comparing a state of trade (in the double-prime situation) with the pretrade situation. In such a case each element in the vector E' goes to zero. The welfare criterion, 13.S.10, then assumes the special form:

$$T''p^{*''}E'' + p''(x'' - x') > 0. \qquad (13.S.11)$$

Because the production term, $p''(x'' - x')$, must be nonnegative, as we have just argued, this criterion yields a powerful result. Suppose that a complex mixture of tariffs and trade subsidies exists. Is the community better off than with no trade? The question needs to be raised because an export subsidy by itself can reduce welfare at home — this is akin to giving something away. The term $T''p^{*''}E''$ represents the *net* tariff-and-subsidy revenue to the home government. The criterion reveals that regardless of the pattern of subsidies, if this *net* revenue is positive, trade must be superior to no trade.[2]

This analysis has stopped short of considering the effect of distortions or consumption taxes (or subsidies) or production taxes (or subsidies). But the same method of analysis can be applied to these cases as well. The results would point in the same direction as those obtained in the "calculus" approach earlier in this supplement.

---

[2] This result is attributable to Ohyama, "Stability and Welfare in General Equilibrium."

14 Trade Control from an International Viewpoint: United States Policy and Trade Liberalization

A country can gain from imposing a tariff if the terms of trade turn in its favor, but it inflicts a loss on the rest of the world greater than its gain, and thus lowers income for the world as a whole. Countries seem to recognize this clash between national and world interests, and have made multilateral efforts to remove their controls on trade. In this chapter we shall examine the world's interest in and pursuit of freer trade. In the first section we shall consider theoretically the clash between national and international interests in trade policy; we shall also show how to measure the effects of removing a tariff on welfare. In the rest of the chapter we shall apply these concepts to the trade policy of the United States and to America's role in international efforts to reduce trade controls.

14.1 WORLD WELFARE AND TRADE WARFARE

A tariff reduces world welfare, as we saw in section 12.4, because it moves the trading equilibrium off the contract curve. Suppose that the home country (in a two-country trading world) imposes a tariff. What can the foreign country do? Should it follow its fighting instincts, and retaliate with a tariff of its own? Can it restore an efficient trading equilibrium, on the contract curve?

The problem is illustrated in Figure 14.1, which slightly modifies Figure 12.6. Make the home country's initial tariff optimal from its national point of view. Its optimal tariff shifts its offer curve from OR to OR', raising its welfare from community indifference curve y_1

271

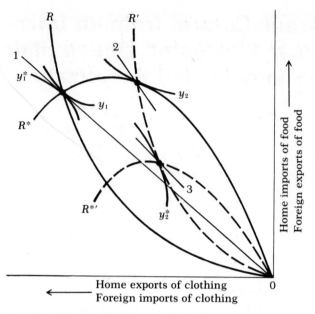

FIGURE 14.1   Effect on Welfare of Tariff Imposition and Retaliation

Home country's tariff shifts its offer curve from OR to OR', raising its income to y_2. The foreign country may then retaliate, shifting its own offer curve from OR^* to $OR^{*'}$; it thus obtains income level y_2^*, which leaves it and the home country both less well off than with free trade.

to y_2. The foreign country's welfare, indifference curve y_1^* in the initial free trade situation, must be reduced.[1]

One course open to the foreign country is to bribe the home country to remove its tariff. Putting the trading partners back on the contract curve would raise world welfare. Could it also raise welfare for the foreign country, taking into account the cost of the bribe? The home country would reject any bribe leaving it worse off than income level y_2, gained when it imposed the tariff. The foreign country must become worse off than in the initial free trade situation. But it could indeed pay a bribe this large and still be better off than if the tariff remains.

---

[1] The lower level of welfare abroad would be represented by an indifference curve tangent to the price slope (2), which measures world terms of trade after the home country has imposed its tariff. This indifference curve (not shown to avoid cluttering the diagram) must correspond to a lower level of welfare than y_1^*.

The foreign country will not use a bribe, though, if a better alternative is available. It will consider retaliating with its own tariff. The home country's tariff-ridden offer curve is now OR', and so the foreign country's best retaliatory action is to impose a tariff that would secure the best possible trading point on OR'. Its highest attainable indifference curve is y_2^*, tangent to OR'. Hence its best retaliatory tariff would shift its offer curve from OR^* to $OR^{*'}$, moving the world terms of trade from slope 2 to slope 3.

Should the foreign country offer the bribe to return to free trade, or should it retaliate? There is no general way to tell. Welfare level y_2^* might be either higher or lower than what the bribe could achieve.[2] Retaliation thus might look like the best policy.

The trouble with retaliation is that the trade warfare can continue for additional rounds — the home country increasing its tariff in response to the foreign country's retaliation, and so forth. Each round will reduce world welfare. The parties eventually reach a set of tariffs from which neither can improve his position by a further increase, halting the cycle. But at no stage must they see the folly of their ways and return to free trade.[3] In the real-life world of many countries, the problem may be even worse, because the effects of one country's tariff increase may be diffused enough that it does not expect retaliation, or does not easily identify it. And a general treaty of tariff disarmament involves finding acceptable terms not for two but for many countries. When we study international efforts at trade liberalization, later in this chapter, we shall find ample evidence that countries do not expect to benefit by unilaterally removing their tariffs. Hence a concerted multilateral effort is necessary to move toward welfare-maximizing free trade.

Tariffs on Individual Products, Welfare, and Revenue

As we take up the story of international efforts at trade liberalization, we will need a simple technique for showing the effects of changing the tariff on a single product on the economic welfare of producers

---

[2] The home country will certainly reject any bribe that leaves it worse off than community welfare level y_2 — its initial gain from the optimal tariff. Thus the best the foreign country can do via a bribe is to achieve a trading point on one of its own higher indifference curves, and on the home country's curve y_2. The foreign country's alternative strategy of imposing its own optimal tariff yields indifference curve y_2^*. Curve y_2^* might or might not represent a higher level of welfare than any point on the home country's curve y_2 — it depends on whether or not the two intersect. Only if they do, is bribing the home country back to free trade the better immediate strategy. We are neglecting, however, the effects of any further tariff increases by the home country, to be considered next.

[3] For a more extensive analysis, see Tibor Scitovsky, "A Reconsideration of the Theory of Tariffs," *Review of Economic Studies,* 9, no. 2 (1942): 89–110; reprinted American Economic Association. *Readings in the Theory of International Trade* (Philadelphia: Blakiston, 1950); and Harry G. Johnson, "Optimum Tariffs and Retaliation," *Review of Economic Studies,* 21, no. 2 (1954): 142–53.

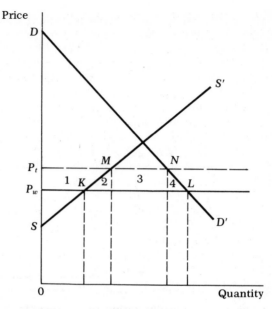

FIGURE 14.2   Effects on Welfare and Government Revenue
of Tariff on Individual Product

Domestic demand is DD', domestic supply SS', world price
P_w. Imposing tariff P_tP_w/P_wO leaves world price unchanged,
raises domestic price to P_t, and causes a welfare loss (net)
measured by triangular areas 2 and 4.

and consumers and the government's tax revenue. This technique
employs ordinary supply and demand curves, not to depict the forces
of general equilibrium (as in previous chapters) but to concentrate
on one market that we suppose to be a small part of the national
economy.[4]

Figure 14.2 illustrates the method. The nation is a net importer of
the product, and a small purchaser of it on the world market. Hence
the world price is not affected by its purchases, and it can take any
desired quantity at price P_w. The horizontal line extending from P_w is
thus the supply curve for imports. The demand curve for the product
is DD'. The supply curve, SS', shows the domestic output at various
prices.

If no tariff is in force, price P_w prevails in the domestic market.
Domestic producers supply quantity P_wK, and imports KL, of the total

---

[4] We call this type of analysis *partial equilibrium,* and it assumes that the
market we are examining is small enough that changes in its ruling price do
not perceptibly shift demand or supply curves anywhere else in the economy.

amount P_wL consumed. Suppose that a tariff is imposed at rate P_tP_w/P_wO. The world price cannot fall, and hence the domestic price (after payment of the tariff) must be elevated by the full amount of the duty to P_t (if any imports are still purchased). At this higher price, domestic supply is enlarged to P_tM, total consumption reduced to P_tN, and imports shrink to MN.

Because the world price is fixed, the nation as a whole must lose by imposing the tariff. Figure 14.2 shows how the effect is spread among consumers, domestic producers, and the government. The total welfare that consumers derive from any given commodity can be measured by what they would pay rather than do without the good entirely. For reasons explained in introductory texts on economics, this is approximated by the area under the demand curve and above the market price line. In Figure 14.2 this "consumers' surplus" under free trade is measured by the triangular area beneath the demand curve and above P_wL; when the tariff is imposed, it shrinks to the area above P_tN, and consumers lose an amount of welfare measured by the trapezoidal area P_wLNP_t.

A tariff likewise affects domestic producers' welfare. The area under the supply curve depicts the opportunity cost of factors of production (including normal profit to producers). Sometimes increases in output encounter diminishing returns, and as in Figure 14.2 the supply curve acquires an upward slope. Then some factors employed in the industry earn more than the opportunity cost of their services, and a "producers' surplus" results.[5] It is measured by the area above the supply curve. Thus, when free trade prevails and the ruling price is P_w, domestic producers enjoy the surplus triangular area SKP_w. When the tariff is imposed, the surplus rises to SMP_t. Thus domestic consumers lose and producers gain from the imposition of a tariff.

Before weighing these effects against one another, we must count one more: the tariff revenue collected by the government. After the tariff is imposed, the government gathers P_wP_t on each unit of imports. The tariff yields total revenue of $P_wP_t \cdot MN$, the area labeled 3 in the diagram. What significance does it have for welfare? We can suppose either that the government hands the revenue back to the consumers, or that it provides public services just as valuable to them (at the margin) as is their private consumption. Either way, government revenue is dollar for dollar as good as surplus to the consumers.

Now we can compare the welfare effects of a tariff on domestic interests. Consumers lose an amount equal to the sum of areas 1 + 2 + 3 + 4. Producers' surplus increases by area 1. Government

---

[5] The concept of producers' surplus is subject to serious qualifications. See E. J. Mishan, "What is Producer's Surplus?" *American Economic Review*, 58 (December 1968): 1269–82.

revenue grows by area 3. Thus the net loss to the country from imposing the tariff is areas 2 + 4. Area 4 is often called the "deadweight loss" of consumers' surplus due to the imposition of a tax. Area 2 depicts the excess real cost of securing output $P_tM - P_wK$ from domestic sources rather than from imports. This type of analysis suffers from neglecting the effects on other markets of this tariff through the terms of trade. However, it shows clearly (if roughly) the distribution of a tariff's welfare effects. We shall use these tools later in this chapter, and in Chapter 15. First, the tariff policies of the United States provide background to international efforts to liberalize trade.

14.2 UNITED STATES TARIFF POLICY AND THE RECIPROCAL TRADE AGREEMENTS PROGRAM

The United States' Trade Agreements Act of 1934 is to a large degree the cornerstone of international efforts to reduce tariffs. It also divides the tariff history of the United States, ending detailed control by Congress of America's tariff rates. The last gasp of congressional tariff-making was the Smoot-Hawley Act of 1930, which inflated rates so that the average dollar's worth of dutiable American imports paid a tariff of 53 cents. No wonder the United States' share of world trade dropped from 16 to 11 percent in the next five years.[6] The world total also declined, as international trade shriveled in the face of the Great Depression of the 1930's.

The combined effect on United States exports of the depression and of retaliatory increases in other countries' tariffs prompted a major shift in trade policy in 1934. Congress authorized the President to negotiate agreements with foreign trading partners to lower tariffs hampering American exports. In return, United States tariffs would be cut on selected goods exported by the partner. The President could offer to cut the rates of duty set by the Smoot-Hawley Act up to 50 percent. By 1940 the United States had entered into bilateral trade agreements with 20 partners, thereby setting a ritual for these accords. Each country bargains for tariff reductions on tariffs constricting its exports. Nations judge the equivalence of their concessions by the value of *existing* trade to which they apply.

Do these features make much sense in terms of economic welfare? Not if the importing countries are small purchasers of the goods on which they grant tariff concessions. When a small country lowers a tariff on a competitively produced import, the exporting countries get no benefit. They gain only if the world price rises, which requires that the importing company be large enough to influence the world price significantly. The small country cutting tariffs benefits only

[6] On the origins of the trade-agreements program, see Don D. Humphrey. *American Imports*. New York: Twentieth Century Fund, 1955, chaps. 5, 6.

itself. Furthermore, as we saw in Chapter 12, its benefit depends on the amount of extra trade due to the lowered tariff (as well as on the size of the reduction), not on the quantity of imports that previously clambered over the barrier.

If we assume that the tariff-cutting importer is large enough to influence his terms of trade, however, the reciprocal trade agreements make some sense. A tariff reduction now raises the world price of the imported good, benefiting the exporter. The size of this benefit depends on the initial volume of trade (as well as on the size of the tariff concession). This terms of trade gain to the exporter is a loss to the importer unless his tariff was higher than optimal. The importer might not be a net gainer from cutting a single tariff (even though the world is). But the importer's terms of trade loss on one product can be offset by his gain as an exporter, when a reciprocal agreement is signed. And these gains and losses are more likely to cancel if each party cuts tariffs on the same initial volume of trade.[7]

The United States and its trade-agreement partners tended to pick for liberalization goods for which each was the other's principal supplier. This choice was also consistent with tariff disarmament, because the reduced tariffs applied to imports from all sources, not just from the partner. Suppose the United States and Brazil grant each other tariff concessions on coffee and automobiles, respectively. Each is a large importer, so their increased purchases raise the world prices of both goods. Both gain from lower trade barriers (see Figure 14.2). Because the prices (ex tariff) of each party's imports and exports move in the same direction, the change in their terms of trade should be small. The United States may also import coffee from Colombia, and Brazil may import some autos from Britain. Then the United States feels it has given away uncompensated benefits by paying a higher world price for Colombian coffee, Brazil by paying more for British autos. The United States and Brazil minimize these "spillover benefits" by cutting tariffs only on goods imported mainly from the partner country. Regrets over spillover benefits came to inhibit bilateral trade agreements and ultimately led countries to multilateral tariff bargaining, where these benefits could be taken into account.

Congress has authorized the President to enter into tariff-cutting agreements only for limited periods. The authority was repeatedly renewed between 1934 and 1967, then allowed to expire. In some of

Elements of monopoly and product differentiation in individual product markets, discussed in Chapter 11, probably contribute to causing the prices of a country's imports ex tariff to rise when the tariff is reduced. A study of United States tariff reductions in the 1950's found that nearly half of the price effects took the form of increased external prices, rather than reduced prices (including tariff) to domestic consumers. See M. E. Kreinin, "Effect of Tariff Changes on the Prices and Volume of Imports," *American Economic Review*, 51 (June 1961): 310–24.

these renewals the executive gained additional authority to cut tariffs. Suppose that a tariff rate had been bargained down each time by the maximum permitted by law. The rate today would be only 8.5 percent of the Smoot-Hawley rate prevailing in 1934. Indeed, average United States tariff rates have fallen substantially. The average dollar's worth of dutiable imports paid around 50 cents in customs duties in 1934, but little more than 10 cents in recent years. A spurious force explains at least half of the decline, however. Many American tariff rates are defined by statute as *specific* rates — so many cents per pound, or dollars per bale. (Rates stated as a percentage of the foreign wholesale value of the article are called *ad valorem* rates.) The money prices of nearly all imported articles have risen substantially since the Great Depression, but the dollar values of the specific duties have remained the same (except, of course, for trade-agreement reductions); hence the incidence of most specific rates has declined by at least one-half. Still, negotiated cuts in statutory rates have lowered trade barriers substantially, for both the United States and other industrial countries.

Since World War II United States commercial policy has acquired many protectionist exceptions, letting some groups of import-competing producers win their freedom from foreign competition.[8] The exceptions divide into two types — those offering a general safety net for producers dislodged by import competition, and those designed to assist particular groups.

The most important general exemption has been the *escape clause*, which permits a domestic industry believing it has been injured by import competition due to a trade-agreement concession to petition the United States Tariff Commission for relief. One expects that a lower tariff will injure import-competing producers. Some resources will no longer be able to earn as high returns as they can in other uses. This is the market's signal that they should move. Before 1962 the escape clause accepted the *fact* of increased imports as an indication of injury. Injured producers did not need to show a connection between increased imports and the tariff concession: the trade agreement might be signed in 1935, the influx of imports begin in 1955. The only remedy, when the Tariff Commission found that injury had taken place, was a recommendation that the President raise the tariff. In the Trade Expansion Act of 1962, however, injury was redefined as the sustained failure of resources displaced by increased imports to earn their opportunity cost, or to be transferred to other

---

[8] For further information, see Peter B. Kenen. *Giant Among Nations.* Chicago: Rand McNally, 1963, chaps. 3, 4; Stanley D. Metzger. *Trade Agreements and the Kennedy Round.* Fairfax, Va.: Coiner Publications, 1964; L. B. Yeager and D. G. Tuerck. *Trade Policy and the Price System.* Scranton, Pa.: International Textbook Co., 1966.

uses. Instead of increasing the tariff, the government can provide adjustment assistance to retrain workers, aid businesses to increase their efficiency, switch to other lines of production, and the like. The new approach seems both fair and efficient. Relocating factors of production after a tariff cut is costly, and indeed some factors may lose permanently from freer trade. The benefit goes to other factors and to consumers generally (in the form of enlarged consumers' surplus). Hence consumers — as taxpayers — should help the displaced factors to meet the cost of adjustment so the nation can enjoy a higher real income.[9]

Special protective provisions have also sheltered some sectors of the United States economy from import competition. Important among these is the National Security Amendment, which blocks action to decrease or eliminate any duty if the President determines that such actions "threaten to impair the national security." Preserving an industry essential for the national defense could surely justify interference with the market mechanism. As we saw in Chapter 13, however, the efficient way to maintain a socially needed level of output is to subsidize production rather than to restrict imports; a needless loss of consumers' surplus results from trade restrictions. Another important exemption from trade liberalization is given to agriculture. The United States, like most other countries, does not let supply and demand determine the prices of many domestic farm products. Imports are kept out in order to hold these prices above the world level.

In recent years, special protectionist measures have often taken the form of import restrictions other than tariffs. We shall consider their significance in section 14.4.

14.3 GATT AND MULTILATERAL TRADE LIBERALIZATION

Since World War II nations have agreed on tariff reductions largely through multilateral negotiations under the aegis of the General Agreement on Tariffs and Trade (GATT). GATT has fostered large tariff cuts and helped to settle serious disputes over commercial policy. Its vital role is now clouded by a dubious future. In this section

---

[9] In fact the proportion of escapes through the escape-clause has been small both before and after the important changes of 1962. Over the years 1948–1962, the Tariff Commission recommended relief (or divided evenly on its recommendation) in 41 out of 113 completed investigations; the President rolled back the tariff concession in only 15 of these. During 1962–1969, with the revised criteria in effect, the Commission recommended relief in only 3 of 29 cases. Not much adjustment assistance has been given. For a survey of recent cases see T. W. Murray and M. R. Edgmand, "Full Employment, Trade Expansion, and Adjustment Assistance," *Southern Economic Journal,* 36 (April 1970): 404–24.

we shall review major provisions of the agreement, and describe multilateral tariff bargaining within its framework.[10]

GATT is a framework of rules for nations' management of their commercial policy. We shall consider its provisions in three areas — discriminatory trade controls, quantitative restrictions, and the settlement of disputes over trade policy.

GATT's most pervasive concern is that trade restrictions not discriminate between supplier countries. Any "advantage, favour, privilege, or immunity" granted in trade with one country "shall be accorded immediately and unconditionally" to like trade with all other GATT members. This provision is both economic and political. Economically, almost all forms of discrimination are inefficient: if A's preference lets B sell to her at a higher (net) price than does C, trade and production could be switched from B to C so that (when all adjustments are made) everybody in A is potentially better off. The political case for equal treatment rests on the likelihood that the victim of a discriminatory tariff will retaliate and raise a tariff against the offender. Discrimination is thus both a cause and an instrument of trade warfare, and is likely to lead to higher restrictions on trade all around.

Another GATT rule is that domestic industry should be protected by tariffs rather than quantitative restrictions (QRs) or other devices controlling the quantity of trade directly, rather than the price at which it takes place. (We shall explore the rationale of this preference in section 14.4.) Like most sweeping provisions in international agreements, this one was hedged with important exceptions. One of these permits QRs to protect domestic agriculture. Another allows their use to safeguard a country's balance-of-payments position. QRs were widely used for this purpose during and after World War II, and many Cassandras feared that this exception gave away the anti-QR rule. The industrial countries were largely weaned away from quantitative controls on trade as post–World War II recovery was completed, although relapses have occurred.

A third function of GATT has been to provide an international forum to mediate disputes over commercial policy. Suppose that for a domestic reason a GATT member raises a tariff and thus harms another member's interests. The plaintiff's complaint is circulated to all members, and any with an interest in the issue can join the subsequent discussions. A bilateral consultation takes place. If it yields an agreement, the decision is circulated to all members (lest third

---

[10] Two major studies of GATT are Gerard Curzon. *Multilateral Commercial Diplomacy: The General Agreement on Tariffs and Trade and Its Impact on National Commercial Policies and Techniques.* London: Michael Joseph, 1964; and Kenneth W. Dam. *The GATT: Law and International Economic Organization.* Chicago: University of Chicago Press, 1970.

parties be injured). If not, a panel of conciliation is appointed to examine the complaint and make recommendations. The offender, for instance, may be urged to offer alternative tariff concessions. As a last resort the plaintiff may be authorized to retaliate, with the GATT members weighing the equivalence of the retaliation to the offense. The worth of this procedure is shown by the squalid tariff history of the 1920's when newly independent states boosted their tariffs, and each increase prompted a cycle of retaliation. The level and complexity of tariffs rose all around. Without GATT's surveillance, similar trade warfare could have occurred after World War II.

Multilateral Tariff Reduction under GATT

GATT evolved from the United States' trade-agreements program of the 1930's. It listed mutual tariff reduction as a major objective. The members of GATT devised a procedure for multilateral tariff bargaining designed to streamline the older bilateral procedure. Six bargaining sessions have taken place since 1947, keyed to the United States President's successive renewals of authority to bargain for tariff concessions.[11] The first five sessions consisted of simultaneous batteries of bilateral negotiations. Each party could match the spillover benefits (defined above) flowing from its own concessions against the incidental benefits gained as a third party from other negotiations. A net loser on spillovers could demand additional compensation. Hence each party could be sure of an equitable deal in both its bilateral negotiations and the incidence of spillover benefits. Thus GATT's bargaining procedure disposed of the inhibition that had threatened to strangle bilateral trade negotiations.

The procedure yielded broad and deep tariff cuts on the first try — at Geneva in 1947. The United States bargained a weighted-average reduction of 18.9 percent in its duties, whereas each of the next four rounds (1940–1962) brought reductions of 4 percent or less. A number of factors caused these multilateral sessions to produce diminishing returns. Many tariff rates in 1947 contained "surplus protection," elevating the price of imports more than enough to allow the competing domestic industry to operate profitably. Successive reductions peeled away the surplus and evoked protests from import-competing producers. Governments heeded the call and grew less willing to bargain. Some countries' tariffs had been whittled to low levels, so that foreign exporters would offer them little for further cuts. Some countries held back from further reductions for fear that they would run out of trading stock. Although the GATT kept its

---

[11] This linkage pays tribute less to the importance of the United States as a trading power than to the uniquely cumbersome character of America's fiscal machinery; other countries can bargain first and secure legislative approval afterward.

members from raising tariffs as bargaining weapons[12] it could not keep the momentum of tariff reduction from running down. Finally, the members of the European Economic Community, having agreed in 1957 to form a common external tariff by a simple compromise, could consent only with greatest difficulty to cut the common tariff on one product but not another.[13] Thus by the early 1960's the old process of item-by-item tariff bargaining, even in the multilateral GATT framework, had apparently run its course.

The last session of multilateral tariff bargaining, the Kennedy Round completed in 1967, departed even further from bilateral bargaining between principal suppliers.[14] The chief industrial countries agreed on the target of an across-the-board 50 percent cut in all tariff rates. They would forego balancing the reciprocal benefits stemming from this overall cut. Each country could propose to except some of its tariffs from the cut — presumably where unacceptable injury to domestic industries would result. Bargaining would proceed over the size of the exceptions lists, rather than over the 50 percent cut itself. Some groups of commodities were handled by special procedures, and bilateral deals were made with some countries not taking part in the 50 percent cut. After prolonged and theatrical negotiations the Kennedy Round was completed successfully in 1967, just before expiration of the United States' bargaining authority. The chief actors agreed to weighted-average tariff cuts of around 35 percent, making the Kennedy Round the most sweeping tariff reduction since the GATT went into effect. But it also left the participants prostrate and dubious about a repetition of this performance. Where do tariffs stand now among the industrial countries? Do they still seriously impede trade? Or, as some assert, are non-tariff barriers now the main blocks to efficient international exchange?

[12] Before World War II, countries commonly increased their tariffs for bargaining. In 1935, for instance, the Union of South Africa introduced a new higher tariff against countries not enjoying preferential arrangements with her, "to increase the Union's bargaining power in its negotiations with other countries for tariff concessions, and, thus, to extend the overseas markets for Union products." See M. H. De Kock. *The Economic Development of South Africa*. London: P. S. King, 1936, p. 121.

[13] The Common Market will be discussed in more detail in Chapter 15. One negotiator described the process of securing agreement from the Community on tariff reductions as "trying to nail a piece of jelly to the wall."

[14] For a brief account of the Kennedy Round see Bernard Norwood, "The Kennedy Round: A Try at Linear Trade Negotiations," *Journal of Law and Economics,* 12 (October 1969): 297–319. Two extensive studies are Ernest H. Preeg. *Traders and Diplomats.* Washington: Brookings Institution, 1970, and John W. Evans. *The Kennedy Round in American Trade Policy: the Twilight of the GATT?* Cambridge: Harvard University Press, 1971.

TABLE 14.1   Comparison of Nominal Tariff Rates Prevailing
after Kennedy Round in United States, European
Economic Community, United Kingdom,
and Japan (percentages)

	Average tariff on dutiable imports[a]			
Product category	*United States*	*European Economic Community*	*United Kingdom*	*Japan*
Mineral products	7.5	5.5	4.8	6.2
Chemical products[b]	9.3	7.6	9.4	10.7
Rubber products	6.0	7.8	7.8	7.5
Hides, furs, leather products	10.4	5.7	13.1	12.7
Wood and cork products	7.1	8.8	7.3	10.1
Pulp and paper	5.5	7.5	13.2	6.4
Textiles	20.1	12.6	16.9	13.6
Footwear and headwear	12.1	12.4	14.7	22.7
Stone, ceramic, and glass products	15.0	8.0	10.3	9.5
Base metals and metal products	6.3	7.0	9.0	7.1
Nonelectrical machinery	6.0	6.4	8.6	10.0
Electrical machinery	7.1	9.1	12.4	10.8
Transportation equipment	3.5	9.9	11.0	13.9
Precision instruments	13.1	8.4	13.5	10.0
Manufactured articles	9.9	8.6	10.8	10.7
All articles	9.6	8.1	10.6	9.5

Source: Ernest H. Preeg. *Traders and Diplomats.* Washington: Brookings
Institution, 1970, Tables 13-1 to 13-4.

[a] Mainly unweighted averages as percentage of delivered value.

[b] Includes reductions contingent on removal by United States of certain
nontariff barriers.

Present-day Levels of Tariffs

Table 14.1 shows the average levels of tariffs on nonagricultural
goods prevailing after all the Kennedy Round reductions come into
effect. Most rates quoted in the table are unweighted averages of the
tariffs on specific goods in the category indicated. An unweighted
average is a poor way, but the best available, to assess the height of a
country's tariff rates. Ideally, we want to weight (i.e., assign importance to) each individual rate by the volume of that good a country
would import under free trade, by the extra trade that would take
place if the tariff were removed, or by the extra real income that
would result from its removal; however, none of these calculations
is simple, and the unweighted average avoids some pitfalls of the

practical alternative measures.[15] The rates shown in the table are relatively low — at least in comparison to rates before World War II. The United States emerges as a higher-tariff region than the European Economic Community, though somewhat below the United Kingdom and Japan.

How much production is inefficiently secreted behind these remaining tariff walls? Countries' experience with the effects on trade of changes in prices and tariffs gives us some notion how trade will expand and production shift when tariffs are cut. One study estimated the effects on trade and welfare in the chief industrial countries of the across-the-board 50 percent tariff cut originally sought in the Kennedy Round.[16] It found that trade in the dutiable articles subject to reduction would ultimately expand by about 14 percent. The long-run welfare gains for these countries were also estimated, using a method like that illustrated in Figure 14.2. The gain for the United States was placed at $149 million annually, the gain for the industrial countries as a group at $326 million. People often observe that welfare gains from tariff reduction lift the national income by quite a small percentage. The point of the observation is unclear: should we forego a gain in real welfare because it is "only" $150 million a year?

These figures probably understate the effects on trade and welfare if the industrial countries were to go all the way and eliminate tariffs among themselves. Free trade ends a substantial administrative cost for both the government that collects and the trader who pays. Depending on the political context, eliminating a tariff may reduce uncertainty for the exporter. Finally, free trade might produce welfare gains different from and larger than those we have measured following small tariff cuts. These other benefits may include greater competitive pressure on domestic enterprise to operate efficiently, and wider choice for consumers when foreign and domestic goods are not identical and tariff reduction makes more varieties available on the market.

What would the United States gain — or lose — from further tariff cuts? The tariff affects America's terms of trade, so that they would deteriorate significantly following unilateral tariff reduction.[17] But that fact merely reminds us of the case for multilateral cuts in tariffs, which benefit consumers without moving the terms of trade much one way or the other.

---

[15] Sometimes tariff averages are calculated using actual imports as weights. This is easy but leads to a systematic downward bias: a high tariff keeps most goods out and lets few in, hence carries a low weight. For a discussion of tariff measurement problems, see Preeg. *Traders and Diplomats.* Appendix A.

[16] B. Balassa and M. E. Kreinin, "Trade Liberalization under the 'Kennedy Round': The Static Effects," *Review of Economics and Statistics,* 49 (May 1967): 125–37.

[17] Giorgio Basevi, "The Restrictive Effect of the U.S. Tariff and Its Welfare Value," *American Economic Review,* 58 (September 1968): 840–52.

Another potential cost of tariff removal by the United States would be harm to some factors of production. We saw in Chapters 8 and 12 that, in a two-factor model, a tariff can benefit the factor used intensively in the import-competing industry even if it harms the nation as a whole. That factor would suffer if the tariff were eliminated and might deserve compensation from the benefits flowing to the rest of the economy. What are the distributive effects of the tariff? Table 14.2 shows tests of several hypotheses about its protective role as of 1972, when reductions negotiated in the Kennedy Round were completed. It covers only the manufacturing sector, rather than the whole economy, but gives some hints about the tariff's effect. For each industry the average levels of both nominal and effective rates of protection were measured (including nontariff barriers). Industries were ranked from the most protected to the least protected, and the

TABLE 14.2   Characteristics of Industries in Relation to
Levels of Protection Given by United States
Tariffs, Nominal and Effective, after
Kennedy Round Reductions

Industry characteristics and tariff measure	*Industries ranked by level of protection*			
	Highest quarter	*Second quarter*	*Third quarter*	*Lowest quarter*
Labor-intensity (measured by payrolls as percentage of all factor payments)				
Nominal	46%	50%	53%	45%
Effective	47%	48%	52%	44%
Level of labor skill (measured by payroll per worker)				
Nominal	$6,000	$6,700	$7,200	$7,100
Effective	$6,000	$6,600	$7,500	$6,900
Size of manufacturing establishment (measured by value added per establishment in millions of dollars)				
Nominal	$1.8[a]	$1.4	$2.2	$3.6
Effective	$1.5[a]	$1.6	$3.2	$2.6

Source: Tariff rates — Robert E. Baldwin. *Nontariff Distortions of International Trade.* Washington: Brookings Institution, 1970, pp. 163–64; other data — United States Bureau of the Census. *1967 Census of Manufactures: Summary and Subject Statistics.* Washington: Government Printing Office, 1971, Table 3.

[a] The "ordnance and accessories" sector has been omitted from this class. The large establishments producing military wares hardly seem relevant to testing the effect of tariff protection.

list was divided into quarters. Then we averaged some traits of industries in these successive quarters:

1. Does the tariff protect labor-intensive industries? We saw (Chapter 10) that one explanation for the "Leontief paradox" is that the American tariff systematically protects labor. We can measure the labor-intensity of industries roughly by the share which payrolls comprise of payments to all factors of production (the industry's value-added). The top two lines of Table 14.2 show that the least protected industries are indeed the least labor-intensive. Beyond the bottom quarter, however, the hypothesis fails: the most heavily protected industries are not very labor-intensive.

2. Does the tariff protect low-skilled labor? Without sheltering labor-intensive industries generally, the United States tariff might nonetheless protect workers with low skills. Low skills command low rewards in the labor market, and we would expect that annual payroll per worker would be small in industries requiring low levels of skill or education. The table shows that indeed the industries paying the lowest wages receive higher protection (both nominal and effective) than others. Freer trade might well harm the least-skilled segment of the labor force, and the nation should certainly consider more active policies to provide them with valuable skills.

3. Does the tariff protect small business? Industries containing many small plants or firms may enjoy high tariff protection, if only because they can be politically effective campaigners for it. Table 14.2 shows that factor payments per establishment — an "input" measure of business size — are considerably lower for industries in the upper half of the tariff ranks than in the lower half. The tariff indeed seems to protect small businesses, and their adjustments problems would require attention if trade were freed.

Is further multilateral trade liberalization in the cards? The pessimist finds fuel for his doubts close at hand. The preference for nondiscrimination embodied in GATT is giving way to widespread interest in discriminatory trading arrangements. As we shall see in Chapter 15, this interest may be either good or bad. Furthermore, trade barriers other than tariffs are now a growing irritant in commercial diplomacy. GATT's members are committed to efforts to reduce them, and this campaign will (and probably should) precede further efforts at tariff-cutting.

14.4 NONTARIFF BARRIERS TO TRADE

Economists often believe tariffs to be less noxious than other trade restrictions. Despite GATT's opposition, many nontariff restrictions on trade remain and new ones are being invented. Their removal was given high priority at the close of the Kennedy Round, because they threatened to grow and undo the laborious work of trade liberalization. The Congress has seriously considered legislation that would trigger quotas on many products if imports gained significantly more of the American market. Nontariff barriers are sure to be a major issue in commercial diplomacy over the coming years. We shall first explore the theoretical significance of nontariff barriers, then survey some of the major types in use.

Theory of Quantitative Restrictions

What is a nontariff barrier? The definition must be somewhat arbitrary. For instance, recalling Chapter 13, we could argue that any domestic tax or subsidy on production or consumption that alters relative prices also distorts the volume of trade. Hence if we call "anything that isn't a tariff but distorts trade" a nontariff barrier, all domestic market distortions are caught in the net. Hence we shall concentrate on one group of distortions — those other than tariffs that directly alter the volume or composition of international trade. Nontariff barriers are most easily understood by comparing them with tariffs. We have picked quantitative restrictions for scrutiny.[18]

The effect of a QR is basically the same as that of a tariff, yet their incidental differences are important. The similarity is shown in Figure 14.3. The supply and demand curves for an imported product are shown by S and D; we omit domestic supply. A quantitative restriction equal to OQ_0 per period of time is imposed. This is an effective restriction, because it is smaller than the free trade flow of imports (corresponding to point F). Imports are bought and sold on competitive markets. Hence we know what prices must prevail inside and outside the country's boundaries: P_t and P_w would clear the domestic and foreign markets respectively, if OQ_0 imports are permitted. We know that a tariff separates the domestic and foreign prices of an import, and that in equilibrium a tariff rate must equal the proportion by which it elevates the internal above the external price. Hence a quota that produces a price distortion of P_tP_w/P_wO is equivalent in its restrictive effect to a tariff of that percentage; we could depict the equivalent tariff by schedule S_t, which lies uniformly above S by that percentage and indicates the domestic price (including tariff) that must be paid for a quantity of imports.

If a quota always has its tariff equivalent,[19] why do import-competing producers often prefer protection by quotas over protection by tariffs? And why do economists often prefer the opposite? One difference is political: a producer group may be able to secure a quota corresponding, say, to a tariff of 150 percent; the general public might

---

[18] For general information on quotas and other nontariff barriers, see Robert E. Baldwin. *Nontariff Distortions of International Trade.* Washington: Brookings Institution, 1970; G. and V. Curzon. *Hidden Barriers to International Trade,* Thames Essays no. 1. London: Trade Policy Research Centre, 1970; W. B. Kelly, Jr., "Nontariff Barriers," *Studies in Trade Liberalization,* ed. B. Balassa. Baltimore: Johns Hopkins Press, 1967, pp. 265–314.

[19] This equivalence is subject to many limitations. See F. D. Holzman, "Comparison of Different Forms of Trade Barriers," *Review of Economics and Statistics,* 51 (May 1969): 159–65.

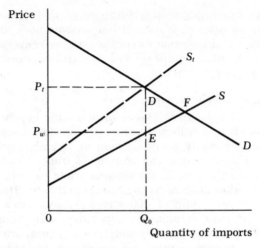

FIGURE 14.3   Comparison of Effects of Tariff
              and Quantitative Restriction

Demand and supply for imports are D and S respectively.
Imposing a quota of OQ_0 drives domestic price up to P_t,
external price down to P_w. Effect is thus equivalent to a
tariff of $P_t P_w / P_w O$.

well consider such a high tariff too greedy and protest, whereas they
cannot easily calculate the tariff equivalent of the quota.

Other differences are purely economic, however. When economic
growth occurs, demand and supply schedules (as in Figure 14.3)
shift steadily to the right. If the quota is constant, the tariff-equivalent
increases steadily, although an ad valorem tariff would stay constant.
A quota destroys the sensitivity of the market to any economic change
that calls for more imports. If demand shifts toward this product (an
upward shift in D), or productivity gains improve its supply (downward shift in S), the optimal quantity of imports increases; a tariff
would permit this increase, but a quota does not. This defect supplies
another reason that import-competing producers value quotas: they
are protected against uncertainty about future economic changes
that would increase the flow of competing imports.

Another difference has to do with the revenue representing that gap
between the foreign and the domestic price. In Figure 14.3, a tariff of
$P_t P_w / P_w O$ would generate for the government revenue measured by
the rectangle $P_t DEP_w$. When imports are limited by quota, no tariff is
ordinarily collected. Yet the privilege of buying abroad at P_w and
selling domestically at P_t is obviously valuable. The government
might auction off licenses to import to the highest bidder. Competitive bidding by would-be importers would wipe out this potential
profit and hand the government the same revenue as if it levied the
tariff-equivalent. On the other hand, the government might give away

import licenses to the domestic importers, in which case they capture the proceeds P_tDEP_w. If it awards the licenses to foreign exporters, their country gains the scarcity rent. Notice that the world welfare cost of the restriction, *DEF*, is the same in each case. The method of administering a quota only redistributes income.

The United States' experience with its quotas on imports of sugar and crude petroleum provides squalid evidence of the effects of dispensing quotas by methods other than auction. The petroleum quotas have generally been worth about half a billion dollars to their recipients, the sugar quotas perhaps half of that. When Cuba's sugar quota was canceled in 1960, a lobbying scramble began as other sugar-producing countries courted the favor of the Congress, especially its key committee members controlling the allocation among exporters. The oil import quotas became mandatory in 1959, and administrative rules of rapidly increasing complexity were set up to allocate them among the various claimants — old international oil companies vs. those newly going abroad, small vs. large, petroleum refiners vs. petrochemical producers, inland vs. coastal refineries. Quotas cannot be traded among users, so the limited imports do not go to those for whom they would have the greatest value. Likewise, the allocation of sugar quotas among the producing nations is just capricious foreign aid; it does not concentrate output in the exporting country with the greatest comparative advantage.[20]

A close relative of quantitative restrictions is the so-called "voluntary" export agreement, whereby the importing country or countries solicit the cooperation of the exporters to restrict the flow of trade, using the threat of tariffs or quotas. An elaborate agreement for the restriction of trade in cotton yarn and textiles, involving 29 countries, took effect in 1962. Under its terms some net importers employ quotas, and the exporting countries restrict shipments to the other importers. Export restriction has been particularly popular in the United States, which has also pressed them upon foreign shippers of steel and non-cotton textiles. This protectionist device is shot through with perversity. People think it is "nicer" for the importing country to secure voluntary control by exporters rather than to impose tariffs or quotas itself. Because exporter restriction is effectively identical to a QR with the quotas given to the exporters, this civility is costly to the importing country. The real income transferred from domestic consumers (P_tDEP_w in Figure 14.3) goes not to the government or domestic importers, but to foreign exporters. Furthermore, getting the exporters to restrict trade forces them to collude with one another and promotes monopolistic restriction of the importer's markets. Thus exporter restrictions probably cost the importing country more welfare than any other way to secure the same reduction of imports.

[20] See D. Cater and W. Pincus, "Our Sugar Diplomacy," *The Reporter*, 24 (April 13, 1961): 24–28; K. W. Dam, "Implementation of Import Quotas: The Case of Oil," *Journal of Law and Economics*, 14 (April 1971): 1–60.

Other Nontariff Barriers

Other nontariff barriers can also be explained by comparing their restrictive incidence to that of an equivalent tariff. Like quotas, they usually differ from tariffs in how much they permit a market to respond to some economic change, or in how they distribute the "profit" from restricting imports and reducing the welfare of consumers.

Exchange Control. We briefly discuss exchange control; used extensively by the less-developed countries, it will be discussed in Chapter 26. Nations using exchange control manipulate the foreign currency made available to their importers instead of controlling the quantities of imports bought. Like a general system of import quotas, exchange control lets a government manage the mix of purchased imports in great detail. The two systems should affect markets somewhat differently, if only because exchange control constrains the value of foreign exchange spent rather than the number of units purchased.

Government Preferences in Purchasing. The members of GATT have rightly given increased attention to nontariff barriers consisting of preferences for domestic suppliers in governmental purchasing. Governments buy hefty shares of the goods and services produced in many countries: in 1965, 17 percent in the United Kingdom, 13 percent in France, 19 percent in Sweden, 18 percent in the United States. A preference for home suppliers on the public shopping list thus can slice the volume of trade substantially. Under our Buy American Act of 1933, a domestic price is not considered unreasonably high if it lies no more than 6 percent above what a foreign supplier quotes; the margin rises to 12 percent if the domestic supplier is a small firm or located in a depressed area, and (since 1962) to 50 percent if the purchaser is the Department of Defense. In addition, the purchasing policies of more than 20 states and many local governments discriminate in favor of "local business." Foreign governments usually do not codify their practices so clearly, but their tariff-equivalents often exceed those of the Buy American regulations.

Administrative and Technical Barriers. Some devices impede trade not by substituting other controls for tariffs but by magnifying the effect of the statutory rates of duty. Most of them create increased transactions costs or uncertainties for the exporter. Some simply inflate the statutory rates of duty. Such a feature of United States tariff administration is the valuation of some imports (benzenoid chemicals, rubber-soled footwear, canned clams, woolen knit gloves) not on the basis of their foreign export value — the usual procedure — but on the basis of the wholesale price of competing goods produced in the United States. This is called the American Selling Price system (ASP). It simply jacks up the nominal tariff rates for these products, because the import-competing industries charge higher prices than do their foreign competitors. A study by the Tariff Commission found that in 1964 the average nominal tariff on benzenoid chemicals was 40 percent on their ASP value but over 65 percent when converted to foreign export value,[21] and over 100 percent on some items.

Another technical and administrative barrier to trade arises from the differing technical standards employed from country to country for electrical voltages, screw threads, chemical strengths, and other traits of manufactured commodities. These standards may not be designed to impede trade, but they can certainly do so when they force the exporter to redesign his product to foreign specifications before he can export it. The protective intent of technical standards surfaces when we witness industrial countries competing to get their national sets of standards adopted by developing countries, in order to give their exporters an advantage over foreign producers designing to different standards.[22]

Efforts are under way among the members of GATT to try to quantify the principal nontariff barriers and bring them into the orbit of multilateral bargaining for freer trade. As we have seen in this section, the concept of the tariff equivalent provides some help for understanding how these barriers impede the flow of trade. Still, their effects are complex, and the scope for clandestine protection (in such areas as government purchasing and customs classification) is broad. Nontariff barriers are not very likely to systematically go upon the bargaining table at a future Kennedy Round.

14.5 SUMMARY

The theory of tariff warfare helps to explain international commercial diplomacy. Although free trade is optimal for the world as a whole, a large country can benefit by imposing its own tariff. Retaliation, however, is apt to leave everybody worse off. From such a situation, multilateral tariff disarmament is an attractive way to share the gains of moving to world free trade. These gains can be illustrated with simple partial-equilibrium demand and supply diagrams.

The United States' Reciprocal Trade Agreements program embodies such an effort at tariff disarmament. It was used from 1934 on in bilateral negotiations to lower duties set by the Smoot-Hawley Act of 1930. Eventually, concern with incidental terms of trade improvements given to third parties impeded these bilateral deals and encouraged the multilateral tariff reductions undertaken periodically

---

[21] Cited by Baldwin, pp. 134–135. These percentages are consistent with the hypothesis that American chemical manufacturers set their prices above world levels by just the margin permitted by the tariff. Let P_t be the domestic price to be determined, t the ad valorem tariff rate, P_w the world price. If the tariff were based on export value, the producer in the home market would set $P_t = P_w (1 + t)$; when it is based on American selling price, however, he chooses price $P_t = P_w + tP_t = P_w/(1 - t)$. If $t = .4$, $P_t = 1.4P_w$ in the case of export value; $P_t = 1.67P_w$ in the case of American selling price.

[22] Robert F. Legget. *Standards in Canada*. Ottawa: Information Canada, 1970, chap. 15.

since World War II. The United States has led the way with these, but American legislation has at times been hamstrung by protectionist features.

The General Agreement on Tariffs and Trade has been the vehicle for multilateral trade liberalization. The GATT tries to avoid discriminatory tariffs. It also encourages tariffs rather than quantitative restrictions when a domestic industry is to be protected. It has helped to keep commercial disputes between countries from escalating. Multilateral bargaining has secured large tariff reductions over the years, and industrial countries' nominal tariffs on manufactures now hover around 10 percent. The United States tariff protects low-skilled workers and small businesses.

Although we can calculate the tariff equivalent of a quantitative restriction, economists generally favor tariffs over QRs on principle. A QR can hide a very high level of protection, and its incidence can rise over time. QRs are used when politically powerful producer groups desire heavy protection. "Voluntary" export agreements are a form of quota administered by foreign sellers, and are particularly costly in welfare for the importing country. Other nontariff barriers to trade include exchange control (used principally by developing countries), domestic preferences in government purchasing, and administrative and technical barriers.

SUGGESTIONS FOR FURTHER READING

Baldwin, Robert E. *Nontariff Distortions of International Trade.* Washington: Brookings Institution, 1970. Analytical survey of United States nontariff barriers.

Baldwin, R. E., and J. D. Richardson, eds. *Selected Topics in International Trade and Finance: A Book of Readings.* Boston: Little, Brown, 1973. Parts II.B and II.C contain many useful papers on current trade-policy issues.

Curzon, Gerard. *Multilateral Commercial Diplomacy.* London: Michael Joseph, 1964. Background and operation of the General Agreement on Tariffs and Trade.

Evans, John W. *The Kennedy Round in American Trade Policy: the Twilight of the GATT?* Cambridge: Harvard University Press, 1971. Detailed study of the Kennedy Round of tariff bargaining.

Kenen, Peter B. *Giant Among Nations.* Chicago: Rand McNally, 1963. Readable survey of United States trade policy up to 1960.

Krause, Lawrence B. "Trade Policy for the Seventies," *Columbia Journal of World Business,* 6 (January–February 1971): 5–14. Appraisal of prospects for trade policy.

Scitovsky, Tibor. "A Reconsideration of the Theory of Tariffs," *Review of Economic Studies,* 9, no. 2 (1942), 89–110; reprinted American Economic Association. *Readings in the Theory of International Trade.* Philadelphia: Blakiston, 1950, chap. 16. Theory of tariff warfare and disarmament.

U.S. Commission on International Trade and Investment Policy. *United States International Economic Policy in an Interdependent World.* Washington: U.S. Government Printing Office, 1971. Volume 1 of papers submitted to the Commission covers many current aspects of trade policy.

15 Trade Control from a Regional Viewpoint: Customs Unions and Soviet Bloc Trade

In the last chapter we explored the case for unrestricted trade from a world viewpoint and reviewed the mutual efforts of countries to remove impediments to trade. Campaigns for trade liberalization are not confined, however, to freeing trade around the world. Groups of nations often try to ease trade restrictions among themselves while leaving them intact against the outside world. In this chapter we shall deal with such efforts at partial liberalization.

Preferential trading arrangements now follow one after another. In 1957 six nations of Continental Europe formed the European Economic Community (EEC), prompting seven others to organize the European Free Trade Area. These two groups are now engaged in a slow and complex process of consolidation. The less-developed countries, especially in Latin America and Africa, have gathered into similar if less far-reaching unions. Nor are preferences a recent discovery: Great Britain and her Commonwealth associates in 1931 agreed to levy lower tariff rates on goods imported from each other — Imperial Preference tariffs (now updated to Commonwealth Preferences).

The economic effects of these arrangements, usually undertaken for both political and economic reasons, raise a number of important questions. Do the participants gain economically? If so, what factors control the size of the gain? Do the outsiders lose? If so, can the world as a whole become worse off? We shall explore the theory of regional trading arrangements in the first two sections of this chapter, then test some of its predictions against the experience of the EEC. We shall also take up a related but distinctive regional group — the socialist block of countries, where trading arrangements are seasoned with the problems of organizing exchange among production ministries outside the market system.

15.1 FUNDAMENTAL EFFECTS OF TRADE PREFERENCES

A group of countries forms a preferential trading arrangement when they place lower restrictions on trade with each other than on trade with the outside world. The members need not be neighbors, but because they often are, we shall also call these "regional arrangements." Likewise, the preferences need not extend to all products traded, but we shall follow common practice in assuming that they generally do. Even assuming that preferences are given on all goods, we can imagine several different arrangements. The following terms for describing them have come into fairly standard usage:

Preferential Trading Club. Members give small tariff preferences — levy slightly lower tariffs — to each other, keeping their original tariffs against the outside world. The Commonwealth Preferences comprise a trading club. Britain's exports to the Commonwealth have recently received preferences of around 7 percent.

Free-Trade Area. Members eliminate tariffs among themselves but keep their original tariffs against the outside world. The European Free Trade Area comes honestly by its name.

Customs Union. Members not only eliminate all tariffs among themselves but also form a common tariff against the outside world.

Common Market. Members proceed beyond the requirements of a customs union to eliminate restrictions among themselves on international movements of factors of production. The European Economic Community, often called "the Common Market," largely fits this definition.

Economic Union. Members proceed beyond the requirements of a common market to unify their fiscal, monetary, and socioeconomic policies. Belgium and Luxembourg formed an economic union in 1921, and the EEC plans ultimately to go most of the distance to economic union.

These preferential arrangements are analytically interesting — and complex — because they both distort and liberalize trade. Trade is freed because some flows face lower restrictions than before. But trade is also distorted because goods coming into a member country pay different tariffs depending on their origin — the external tariff if from outside the group, a preferential or zero rate if from a partner. The distortion amounts to price discrimination — charging or (in this case) paying different prices for identical goods at a given market location. Because of this two-faced character of preferential arrangements, you would guess correctly that they can either improve or worsen the economic welfare of their members or of the world as a whole. In this section we shall analyze the effects of preferences in the simplest possible way, to show how they can either improve or

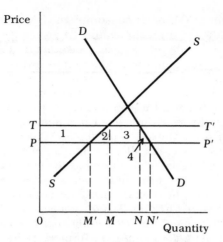

FIGURE 15.1 Welfare Effects of Trade Creation

> PP' is the partner-country supply curve. Tariff removal cuts domestic price from OT to OP, expands imports to $M'N'$, and raises welfare by areas $2 + 4$.

worsen the allocation of resources. In the next section we shall push a short distance into the general-equilibrium analysis of preferential arrangements.

Twenty years ago Professor Jacob Viner first showed that preferences could either improve or worsen allocation, in that they could lead either to *trade creation* or *trade diversion*.[1] Let us suppose that A and B form a customs union, leaving C (the rest of the world) outside. Previously, A produced part of its requirements of good x at home, inefficiently, behind its tariff wall. Partner B is the most efficient producer of x and the sole world exporter. When A abolishes tariffs against B (and all the necessary market adjustments have taken place), A's inefficient x industry is partly competed down, as A's imports from B expand. Trade has been *created*. The gains are the same as if A had eliminated its x tariff completely.

The effects are illustrated in Figure 15.1, which builds on a method of analysis set forth in section 14.1. A's demand and domestic supply curves for x are respectively shown as DD and SS. We suppose that x is produced in B under conditions of perfectly elastic supply, so that an unlimited quantity is available at price OP. A's external tariff is set at the rate PT/OP. Hence, before the customs union was formed, the supply function for imports after payment of tariff was TT'; hence

[1] Jacob Viner. *The Customs Union Issue*. New York: Carnegie Endowment for International Peace, 1950, chap. 4. The exposition in this section draws heavily upon Harry G. Johnson. *Money, Trade, and Economic Growth*. London: Allen and Unwin, 1962, chap. 3.

A produced amount OM of its consumption (ON) of x, importing MN from B. Elimination of the tariff against B now makes PP' the relevant import supply schedule and causes consumption to expand to ON', imports to $M'N'$, and domestic production to shrink to OM'. The four numbered areas in the diagram measure the welfare gain. A's consumers of x enjoy a gain in surplus measured by the whole area $1 + 2 + 3 + 4$, but not all of this is net gain to the country. Area 1 formerly was profit to A's protected producers of x, so this gain to consumers is offset by the loss to producers.[2] Likewise area 3 formerly represented tariff revenue collected by A's government that is now lost when the preference is given to B. If the government was spending its revenues on useful things — parks and schools — there is no presumption that any net social benefit derives from (in effect) giving the revenue measured by area 3 to the consumers of x; therefore we count it as having no net welfare significance. Two triangles remain, both measuring net gains to A. Area 2 formerly represented part of the real cost of securing OM of domestic production; we assume those resources are now put to other uses, so the extra surplus measured by 2 is a net benefit. Likewise, area 4 represents a pure gain in consumers' surplus not subject to any offset. The net benefit is areas $2 + 4$.[3]

Trade diversion, on the other hand, would occur if A's consumption of y was formerly supplied by outsider C, the world's most efficient producer. B can also produce y, however. If B is not too inefficient, the opportunity to sell in A without paying A's tariff may let B undercut C, even though B is less efficient. This situation is shown in Figure 15.2, where A's demand curve for y appears as DD. We suppose that C can supply y at a domestic cost (and price) of P_C, and that this supply is perfectly elastic; likewise, B can supply y at the higher constant cost (and price) of P_B. Before the customs union is formed, A imposes an ad valorem tariff on imports of y equal to $P_C T_C / OP_C$ or $P_B T_B / OP_B$ — they are the same. A would buy from the least costly source after paying the tariff, and hence would import OM_C at price OT_C. Forming the customs union allows B's exports of y to enter duty-free, and A's consumption expands to OM_B. Areas in the diagram are labeled to illustrate the significant effects on welfare. Once again, lowering a tariff (even preferentially) allows a gain to A's consumers of y — areas $3 + 4$. The meanings of these areas match their counterparts in Figure

---

[2] We ignore considerations bearing on the distribution of income in A, supposing that a dollar of income is equally good no matter who receives it. If x were consumed by the poor but deserving and produced by the rich and conniving, we might count the redistribution measured by area 1 as (to some extent) a net gain.

[3] Notice that this benefit would be easily measurable in practice. We need to know only the former tariff per unit — PT — and the increase in imports — $M'N'$ minus MN. The product of these multiplied by one-half approximates areas $2 + 4$. See Harry G. Johnson, "The Gains from Freer Trade with Europe: An Estimate," *Manchester School*, 26 (September 1958): 247–55.

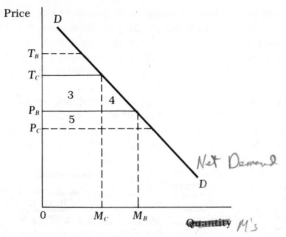

FIGURE 15.2 Welfare Effects of Trade Diversion

P_B indicates pretariff supply price in partner country, P_C pretariff supply price in rest of world. Tariff preference lowers internal price from T_C to P_B. Welfare loss occurs if area 5 exceeds area 4.

15.1: area 3 shows tariff revenue formerly collected on imports from C, its loss offsetting the congruent gain in consumers' surplus; and area 4 depicts a pure gain in consumers' surplus not subject to any offset. A loss occurs, however, in the form of area 5. Formerly areas 3 + 5 measured the total tariff revenue collected on imports OM_C. But now this revenue is lost to A's government, and the part denoted by 5 instead paid by A's consumers to the higher-cost producers of y in B. It is pure social loss.[4] A *net* welfare loss from trade diversion occurs if area 5 is larger than area 4. It need not be, of course: the loss from switching to a less efficient source of supply could be more than offset by the gain from halting a restraint on consumers' spending.

What can we say about the net influence of these forces? If A and B consume and trade many commodities, can we add up the net effect of all the instances of trade creation and diversion that will occur when they form a customs union or free trade area? An accurate prediction would demand a large collection of data. Nonetheless, some rough tests can suggest the chances that trade creation (which must raise welfare) will prevail over trade diversion (which may or may not). For trade creation to predominate, the economies of A and B should be *actually competitive* (before the union) but *potentially complementary* (after it comes into effect). Trade creation requires

[4] No welfare gain for country B is involved, because the resources drawn into the production of y presumably were engaged in other activities where their value productivity was just as high.

protected production, initially, and hence the actual output patterns of the two economies must, due to protective tariffs against each other, look rather similar before they join in a customs union. Thus we stipulate that they should appear actually competitive. However, each member must also be the most efficient producer of goods protected and inefficiently produced by its partner — this condition guarantees trade creation rather than trade diversion. What might the test mean in practice? Consider two preferential arrangements — the European Economic Community and the United Kingdom's Commonwealth Preferences. The EEC includes industrial nations which, before the Community was formed, produced similar lines of industrial goods. The Community hardly contains the most efficient producer of *every* manufacture — hence it allowed some trade diversion — but it surely enclosed ample inefficient production that could be competed down — allowing a significant amount of trade creation. The Commonwealth, on the other hand, includes economically diverse industrial nations, temperate zone specialists in resource-intensive products, and tropical agricultural nations. The extent of competing production was probably small, allowing little trade creation. Furthermore, the Commonwealth may not encompass enough countries of the same type to make the inclusion of the most efficient producer of many lines of goods very likely. Hence the scope for trade diversion seems fairly large. One might hazard the (highly superficial) guess that the EEC could increase welfare more than Commonwealth Preferences could.

Other simple tests for a union's welfare significance can also be used. Higher initial tariffs mean greater potential benefit. Higher initial tariffs enlarge areas 4 in Figures 15.1 and 15.2. If a common external tariff is formed (as in a customs union), the chances of benefit are enlarged if the new common tariff is lower than the previous individual ones — making trade diversion less likely, reducing the distance $P_C T_C$ (in Figure 15.2) and thus cutting the chance that P_B will fall within it. A larger preferential arrangement is more likely to be beneficial. This condition is obvious if we enlarge a hypothetical customs union until it includes nearly all the world's economic activity. With little production taking place outside, there is little chance that the union fails to include the most efficient producer, and hence trade diversion is curtailed.

15.2 DISTRIBUTION OF GAINS AND LOSSES FROM PREFERENCES

These techniques for measuring the welfare effects of trade creation and diversion assume that the country's terms of trade remain unchanged. This assumption underlies the perfectly elastic supply curves for imports employed in Figures 15.1 and 15.2. Were these curves positively sloped, the creation of preferences would worsen the home country's terms of trade with its partner, when that trade expands, or improve them with the outside world, when purchases are diverted to the partner country.

Most preferential arrangements among countries seem to be formed primarily for political reasons. Countries base the decision to form a customs union and select partners on broad diplomatic considerations and not on precise economic motives or calculations. Still, whether intended or not, a preferential arrangement is likely to change its members' terms of trade with the outside world and with each other. The possible results are complex, but we can show some likely outcomes by considering preferential arrangements in the context of general equilibrium.

Let us start with a question that has a simple answer. Suppose that A and B decide to form a preferential arrangement, excluding C (the outside world). What tariff structure will maximize their joint gain from the venture? In the absence of any special market distortions, A and B should clearly adopt free trade with each other and levy the optimum tariff against the outside world. Even if each member's tariff was optimal before, from its own viewpoint, each gains from the expansion of previously restricted trade with the other. If their individual tariffs were not optimal, a further gain accrues from switching to the optimal tariff. Notice that their joint monopoly power in trade could well be greater than that of either separately. If they are sole exporters of a product and each previously calculated his optimal tariff on the assumption that the other's remained unchanged, further monopoly gains should accrue to them from setting their external tariff jointly. Should A and B form a free trade area, making no changes in their former external tariffs, the elimination of internal tariffs is still apt to improve their terms of trade with the outside world. Some trade diversion is the only requirement. The switch of trade away from C, as A and B adopt preferences and increase their mutual trade, has the same effect on C as if A's and B's offer curves to C were shifted inward. (Trade creation, conversely, is a source of gains to members of the preferential arrangement that entails no corresponding loss for the outside world.)

How are the gains from trade creation distributed between the members of a preferential arrangement? The respective sizes of the countries will be one determining force. Suppose that Canada and the United States were to form a free trade area, with the United States being so much larger that its internal relative prices remain unchanged when the two tariff barriers fall, whereas Canada's adjust fully to those in the United States. Although reallocations of resources occur in both countries, those in Canada are *proportionally* much larger. But Canada can trade at United States internal prices without having to pay the United States tariff.

To go beyond this example, we need a formal model of trade among the three countries. Its mechanics become a bit complicated, and so we shall place it in a supplement to this chapter, and report only its general conclusions here. A and B form a customs union, leaving C outside. Suppose that B and C export similar goods, so that they compete with each other in A's market but undertake little direct trade with each other. It then becomes clear that in the customs union between A and B, A discriminates in favor of B and against C. B trades at A's internal prices, whereas C's terms of trade remain affected by the union's — particularly, A's — external tariff.

Suppose first that the union is too small for variations in its trade to change prices in the world at large. A's terms of trade with C are then unaffected by the customs union, and A's domestic prices are likewise locked in place by her continuing trade with C. The opportunity to trade tariff-free at A's internal prices then clearly benefits B. B's exportables — which are A's importables — command higher prices in A's economy when B no longer must pay A's tariff. B's terms of trade improve. A suffers, however, because B's gain comes at the expense of tariff revenue which A formerly collected on trade with B. Thus, when the customs union fails to affect external ("world") prices, B gains and A loses. Trader A could hardly benefit by discriminating in favor of B when he cannot recoup his losses by a higher price to C.

When the customs union covers a large portion of the trading world, however, A can gain in just this fashion. The removal of tariffs between A and B diverts A's trade from C to B and improves A's terms of trade with the outside world. B by itself still gains from the removal of tariffs. A's exports are B's import goods, however, and the improvement in A's terms of trade by diverting trade from C cuts into B's gains, and could wipe them out. Thus the large customs union gains as a whole by diverting trade from the rest of the world, and the outsiders lose. The more the terms of trade improve, the larger are A's gains. B may capture some of the gains, or she may emerge a net loser.

The theory of customs unions is thus a complex business and, worse yet, yields few definite conclusions from every reasonable set of assumptions. Nonetheless, we suggest the following generalizations: (1) Unless the preferential group of countries is quite small, its preferences will divert some trade, turning the terms of trade in its favor. Thus, the outside world will probably be left worse off, unless the members reduce their external tariff. (2) Benefits to members from forming a preferential arrangement may not be divided equally. Indeed, one member may gain and the other lose, even when net benefits are available to the group as a whole.

15.3 PREFERENTIAL ARRANGEMENTS IN PRACTICE: EUROPEAN ECONOMIC COMMUNITY

Customs unions and free trade areas have been popular in the last two decades among both industrial and less-developed countries. The European Economic Community was formed in 1957 by France,

West Germany, Italy, Netherlands, and Belgium–Luxembourg. In 1959, largely in reaction to the EEC, the European Free Trade Area (EFTA) was organized by seven nations on the periphery of Europe: Austria, Denmark, Norway, Portugal, Sweden, Switzerland, and the United Kingdom. Both groups moved to eliminate tariffs among themselves by staged reductions, EFTA finishing the job in 1967, EEC in 1968. The Common Market, in addition, has adopted a Common External Tariff, its rates set (with some exceptions) by averaging the rates for individual products that previously appeared in the member nations' tariff schedules.[5] Interest in such arrangements has also run high among the less-developed nations, although political difficulties have led to some frustration. For instance, eight South American nations plus Mexico have agreed to form a Latin American Free Trade Area, and five Central American countries to create a Central American Common Market. In each case the union is propelled by political and economic objectives, with the latter including the real-income gains described in the preceding section and others, such as economic growth and economies of scale in production for small countries.

In this section we shall review some empirical evidence on the effects of preferential arrangements, in order to illustrate and give perspective to the theoretical concepts presented above.

Trade Creation and Diversion in the Common Market

We saw in section 15.1 that the welfare effects of a preferential arrangement are related to trade creation and diversion. Consider the effect of the Common Market on international trade in manufactures. We cannot simply look at the size of trade flows — external and internal — before and after the EEC was formed. They changed in response to forces other than tariff rates — the growth of national incomes, to take the most obvious. One reasonable way to estimate trade creation and diversion, however, is from changes in the sources of supply of manufactures to the Common Market countries, as Edwin M. Truman has done.[6]

The reduction of internal tariffs, which was 60 percent complete in 1964, should result in some trade creation, reflected in a loss in the share of consumption of manufactures held by domestic producers. Truman found that this reduction, though small, did occur for every country. Trade creation and trade diversion both expand the shares of consumption held by producers in other EEC countries; their shares in fact rose rapidly. Finally, trade diversion results in lost shares for outside producers. However, the shares of many outsiders

---

[5] For an up-to-date description of the EEC, see D. Swann. *The Economics of the Common Market.* Harmondsworth, England, and Baltimore: Penguin Books, 1970.

[6] "The European Economic Community: Trade Creation and Trade Diversion," *Yale Economic Essays*, 9 (Spring 1969): 201–57.

increased despite tariff discrimination! How could that occur, if the theory is correct? The increase probably occurred because the EEC members, while forming their common external tariff (CXT), lowered the area's previous average weights.

What of the distribution of gains and losses from this preferential arrangement? If no *net* diversion of trade occurred, the rest of the world was not harmed, and may in fact have gained. We could restate our findings by saying that tariff reductions by some EEC members in moving to the CXT (as well as in the CXT itself) shifted the EEC's offer curve outward, indeed by more than enough to offset the inward shifting of the preferential removal of internal tariffs. Hence the rest of the world's terms of trade should, if anything, have improved. A study by L. B. Krause, which disagrees slightly with Truman's in finding a small amount of net trade diversion, still concludes that the net injury to the outside world was small.[7]

Those who have studied trade creation in the Common Market find that its form is consistent with but strikingly different from that described in section 15.1. In a model that assumes purely competitive markets for homogeneous products, trade creation calls for the competing down of a domestic industry, or some portion of it (see Figure 15.1). Empirically, we would expect firms in this industry to go out of business, discharging their employees and selling or scrapping their fixed equipment. These resources would then be shunted to other industries in which the country enjoys a comparative advantage. As we discovered in section 11.1, however, the pattern can vary drastically when products are differentiated, or when the output of an industry is diversified. Then the common removal of trade barriers may lead some firms in the x industry of both countries A and B to contract or expire, others to expand; neither industry undergoes a general shutdown, and each expands its exports to the other. Broadly speaking, such a general expansion of (gross) exports to partner countries has characterized trade creation in the Common Market. Furthermore, to avoid conventional trade creation products need not even be differentiated. If an import-competing industry produces not one homogeneous good, but somewhat diversified subproducts, trade creation can mean greater specialization among the firms in individual subproducts, as apparently occurred in the iron and steel producing firms in the Common Market.[8] In this case, at best no resources need incur the costs of transfer from one firm to another. Thus trade creation in practice seems likely to entail smaller costs of

---

[7] Lawrence B. Krause. *European Economic Integration and the United States.* Washington: Brookings Institution, 1968, chap. 2. Another measure of the effects on trade of the Common Market is provided by B. Balassa, "Trade Creation and Trade Diversion in the European Common Market," *Economic Journal,* 77 (March 1967): 1–21.

[8] Michael Adler, "Specialization in the European Coal and Steel Community," *Journal of Common Market Studies,* 8 (March 1970): 175–91.

reallocating resources than the interindustry adjustments emphasized in the model of trade creation with pure competition.

Preferential Arrangements among Developing Nations

Preferential arrangements have been popular among the less-developed countries, where they are often seen as an adjunct to development planning. Development plans often establish import-competing
manufacturing industries behind massive walls of tariff protection.
In the short run these industries are often clearly inefficient, because
they lack a comparative advantage; governments believe, however,
that in the long run their existence will further the country's growth.
Now, one reason for the apparent inefficiency of these sheltered
manufacturing industries is the small scale of markets for their
products in less-developed countries. Empirical evidence suggests
that scale economies are typically unimportant in markets as large
as those of the larger industrial countries; they can seriously hamper
efficient production, however, in the many less-developed countries
with small populations and incomes per capita.

Rather than starting a small inefficient plant in Colombia, Ecuador,
and Paraguay to manufacture (or assemble) farm tractors, why not
form a free trade area and agree to put the tractor plant in one country, a maker of radios in a second, a tire factory in the third? Each
country would gain its industrial sector, yet the disadvantages of
small scale would be mitigated if each plant serves all three markets.
Furthermore, the expansion of trade among them should be balanced.
This goal has been an important motive for both the Latin American
Free Trade Area and the Central American Common Market (where
national markets are hopelessly small). A recent study found that the
nations of the Latin American Free Trade Area, by locating plants of
six important manufacturing industries at the most efficient site,
could save around 10 percent in production costs over a situation in
which every member (or nearly every member) started its own protected production. Further gains would accrue in consumers' benefits
(like area 4 in Figure 15.1).[9]

15.4 TRADE PROBLEMS OF THE SOVIET BLOC

The theory of preferential arrangements can also be applied to the
trade relations of the USSR and its Eastern European neighbors.
These centrally planned economies trade heavily with each other,
because of ideological preferences, restrictions on trade imposed for
military and strategic reasons by the Western countries, and in-
trinsic problems in establishing trade relations between market and
centrally planned economies. The Eastern bloc's principal trading

---

[9] Martin Carnoy, "A Welfare Analysis of Latin American Economic Union:
Six Industry Studies," *Journal of Political Economy,* 78 (July/August 1970):
626–54.

association, the Council for Mutual Economic Assistance (CMEA), is not a preferential area in the same sense as the EEC. Yet both East-West trade and trade among the CMEA nations raise enough problems related to the theory of preferential arrangements to justify reviewing them in its context. Furthermore, they allow us to consider the special problems of external trade in centrally planned economies.

Planning and trading in the CMEA countries are difficult to discuss because the institutions have been changing very rapidly. From a situation in which the price system was not used for valuing alternatives and allocating resources, they have moved over the past decade and a half to one in which the signals of a price system are increasingly heeded. Our discussion will stress the problems they faced in allocating resources and planning trade without resorting to the price system.[10]

The managers of a socialist economy could in principle employ the price system to put resources to their best uses, even if they eschew private ownership of the means of production. Tell the manager of each production ministry or enterprise to expand output whenever its price exceeds marginal cost, contract it when price falls short of marginal cost. Tell the ministry in charge of prices to raise the price of any good, service, or factor of production when its demand exceeds supply, lower it when supply exceeds demand. Resources then would tend to be devoted to their best uses without any elaborate mechanism of central planning. Although the CMEA countries have moved toward using prices for rationing and signaling, they have depended primarily on detailed central planning to allocate scarce resources. In the USSR the mixture of outputs — consumer goods, producer goods, defense — has been chosen by the government, and the retail prices of consumer goods have been set to ration their arbitrary quantities in relation to consumers' demands and purchasing power. Wholesale prices have borne no relation to retail prices and served accounting purposes rather than guiding the mix of inputs and outputs chosen by production units. Those inputs and outputs instead have been set by "material balances": enterprises submit lists of input requirements for the target outputs assigned to them; all inputs and outputs of a physical item are added up centrally, and the enterprises' plans sent back for revision in light of any excess supplies or demands thereby revealed.

International trade has generally been viewed not as an opportunity to benefit the CMEA countries through specialization but rather as a

[10] For a good short account, see F. D. Holzman, "Foreign Trade Behavior of Centrally Planned Economies," *Industrialization in Two Systems: Essays in Honor of Alexander Gerschenkron*, ed. H. Rosovsky. New York: John Wiley, 1966, pp. 237–65. Recent changes are discussed by R. J. Familton, "East-West Trade and Payments Relations," *IMF Staff Papers,* 17 (March 1970): 170–210.

way to fill otherwise intractable excesses of requirements over supplies. Exports are merely the trading stock for securing imports — a piquant contrast to the mercantilistic habits of Western governments, which often treat exports as good per se and imports as a necessary evil. The task of securing these imports has fallen to foreign-trade organizations. They barter for the needed imports whatever domestic outputs are in short-run excess supply. National self-sufficiency has been viewed as a goal and trade as a source of potential disruption to planning. This posture is not wildly unrealistic for the vast and diversified Soviet Union, but it hardly made sense for the small countries of Eastern Europe when they copied the USSR's planning practices. It is no surprise that the foreign-trade turnover of the CMEA countries in 1955 was no more than one-third of expected Western market economies of comparable size and income levels.[11] The planners have been reluctant to invest resources (i.e., make a long-term commitment) in export production, and hence export trade has not seized ultimate comparative advantage, but rather has been a vent for temporary surpluses.

East-West Trade

The CMEA countries have undoubtedly diverted trade toward each other and away from the outside world. In 1948 no CMEA nation carried on more than 30 percent of its trade with other CMEA powers; now the figure is seldom less than two-thirds. This switch results from many forces, including discrimination by the West. Two sets of trade-restricting factors reflect the trading problems of planned economies and hence help to explain this shift.

One set of restrictive forces denies Western buyers the chance to "go shopping" in CMEA markets — obviously a deterrent to trade. Superficially, this restriction arises from the "inconvertibility" of CMEA currencies — meaning that they cannot legally be held by outsiders, and hence cannot be used freely to purchase within the Bloc. Yet this inconvertibility merely reflects the necessities of trade subject to CMEA planning procedures. Prices — the basis on which one shops — have not served (as in a market economy) to value alternatives among Bloc goods. If outsiders shopped on the basis of CMEA countries' internal prices, set for other internal purposes, the resulting trade could be quite inefficient. For instance, the USSR and other CMEA countries have preferred high prices for consumer goods and low prices for producer goods, neither reflecting opportunity costs in production.

The situation is described in Figure 15.3, where we show a transformation function for producer and consumer goods. We suppose that the planners allocate output between these two classes in the

[11] See Frederic L. Pryor. *The Communist Foreign Trade System.* Cambridge: MIT Press, 1963, chap. 1.

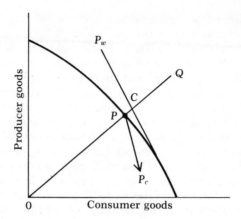

FIGURE 15.3 Effect of CMEA Pricing Practices on Potential Gains from Trade

Production takes place at P. With world prices P_w, the socialist economy would gain from producing consumer goods for export and trading to point C. Internal prices P_c, set to favor producer goods, cannot guide trade because they imply an inefficient specialization in producer goods.

proportion given by line OQ, making no systematic use of international trade (except to meet temporary shortages or dispose of temporary surpluses). The relative prices in Western markets we suppose to be indicated by price slope P_w. It suggests that, by taking full advantage of international trade the CMEA country could export consumer goods, obtaining for final use the producer and consumer goods indicated by point C, superior to bundle P actually produced and used. On the other hand, the internal prices used by the CMEA country, P_c, render producer goods cheaper. If Western traders were allowed to make offers at these internal prices, the CMEA country would export producer goods, and wind up at an inferior point somewhere along PP_c.

Apart from the irrational CMEA internal prices, Westerners could not be allowed to place orders ad lib. without potentially spoiling the planned internal allocations, if planning via material balances allows no production for export in the long run. Hence East-West trade must be effected by the CMEA countries' foreign-trade organizations bargaining as best they can on Western markets, and at Western prices.[12]

In striking such bargains they have suffered from many drawbacks. One is the lack of long-term supplies of potential exports designed to

[12] This section, including Figure 15.3, draws heavily on Holzman, pp. 242–47.

non-CMEA tastes and standards. CMEA managers, operating in a framework of quantitative production targets, have in effect lived in a seller's market and have not been guided by the salability of their goods. Hence CMEA goods (other than homogeneous raw materials) have commanded poorer terms of trade on Western markets than the terms among the CMEA countries themselves. Bargaining with the West has also been complicated by the CMEA's need to secure external balance and to meet periodic quotas on strategic imports. For instance, Western traders have been known to postpone negotiations with CMEA foreign-trade organizations until they knew the latter were under deadline pressures to fulfill their quotas — a timing hardly favorable to CMEA gains from trade. The CMEA countries also apparently hold very small reserves of foreign exchange, and because the Bloc currencies themselves are inconvertible trade must be balanced over the fairly short run.

Trade among CMEA Nations
The CMEA countries seem to have diverted trade toward each other and away from the West. Have they also created a great deal of trade among themselves? On the one hand, you might suppose that integrated region-wide planning would allow these similar, centrally planned economies broad opportunities for exploiting cost advantages and scale economies in locating new productive capacity. On the other hand, arranging trade between sovereign centrally planned economies might be even more complex than arranging it between them and market economies.

Initially, the Eastern European countries copied the planning practices of the USSR, including its self-sufficiency and its emphasis on heavy industry. Even with the political dominance in the area of the USSR (hence references to the "Russian Embassy system of coordination"), only recently have the CMEA countries moved seriously toward coordinating their investment planning and abandoned a purely national approach. They have used numerous intermediate devices. Bilateral trade agreements have served to specify the intrabloc trade pattern in advance. But for a long time these trade agreements lacked integration with production planning. If they could not influence the placement of new productive resources, they could not advance the CMEA's division of labor. Production remained restricted to traditional patterns, and trade served only to vent short-run surpluses. The CMEA apparently promoted much technical cooperation among its members within some industries, and with this cooperation came *intraproduct specialization* in some outputs. But *interproduct specialization* that would give the CMEA nations significantly differing industrial structures came slowly. Only with the round of planning for 1966–1970 was significant intrabloc coordination attempted in drawing up long-term plans, and rough trade and production balances struck for the region as a whole. Perhaps it is no surprise that this coordination would arrive only as the CMEA countries became more interested in efficient planning procedures and the use of prices to test alternatives.[13]

15.5 SUMMARY

Preferential arrangements among groups of countries — trading clubs, free trade areas, customs unions, etc. — are now a popular way to cut tariffs. They can either raise or lower economic welfare, in that they both free trade (among their members) and distort trade (with the outside world). Beneficial trade creation results when protected production is competed down and trade expanded between members. The effects are like those of the nondiscriminatory removal of tariffs. Trade diversion occurs when a preference causes a country to switch its purchases from a more efficient to a less efficient supplier. That switch itself imposes a welfare cost, but it could be offset by a gain for consumers. A union is most likely to benefit the world when a lot of protected production is competed down, when very high tariffs are lowered, and when the union comprises a large portion of the trading world.

A preferential arrangement is likely to shift the terms of trade of each party. The members would maximize their joint welfare by freeing trade among themselves and levying the optimal tariff against outsiders. A member who gives a preference to its partner loses (and the partner gains) if the member's terms of trade with the outside world fail to improve; if they improve, however, the member and the partner may both benefit. Speaking broadly, preferences seem likely to improve their members' terms of trade and welfare and to impose a cost on the outside world.

The European Economic Community seems to have created a good deal of trade and diverted little or none. The absence of diversion may be due to the way the common external tariff was formed by averaging members' previous tariffs. Trade creation in the EEC has been associated with increased intraindustry rather than interindustry specialization in production; we would expect this adjustment where products are differentiated and firms are diversified. Among the less-developed countries an important potential benefit from preferences lies in exploiting scale economies in a larger market.

The regional trading arrangements of the USSR and its neighbors do not take the form of a customs union, but preferences and efforts at trade creation are involved. Trade between planned and market economies is difficult when the former do not employ prices to mea-

[13] For information, see Pryor, chaps. 1, 6, 7; M. Kaser. *COMECON: Integration Problems of the Planned Economies,* 2nd ed. London: Oxford University Press, 1967; H. S. Levine, "The Effects of Foreign Trade on Soviet Planning Practices," *International Trade and Central Planning,* ed. A. A. Brown and E. Neuberger. Berkeley and Los Angeles: University of California Press, 1968, 255–76.

sure the opportunity costs of outputs. The CMEA countries have secured essential imports from the West by barter, exporting temporary surpluses and not committing production in line with long-run comparative advantage. They have diverted trade heavily toward each other, but only recently have they begun to coordinate their planning machinery in order to pursue comparative advantage among themselves.

SUGGESTIONS FOR FURTHER READING

Baldwin, R. E., and J. D. Richardson, eds. *Selected Topics in International Trade and Finance: A Book of Readings.* Boston: Little, Brown, 1973. Part II.D includes papers on several kinds of preferential arrangements.

Denton, G. R., ed. *Economic Integration in Europe.* Reading University Studies on Contemporary Europe, no. 3. London: Weidenfeld and Nicolson, 1969. Evidence on various aspects of trade-preference areas in Europe.

Grunwald, Joseph, M. S. Wionczek, and Martin Carnoy. *Latin American Integration and U.S. Policy.* Washington: Brookings Institution, 1972. Integration among less-developed countries and its effects.

Holzman, F. D., "Foreign Trade Behavior of Centrally Planned Economies," *Industrialization in Two Systems,* ed. Henry Rosovsky. New York: John Wiley, 1966, pp. 237–265. Analytical treatment of problems of foreign trade in a planned economy.

Johnson, Harry G. *Money, Trade and Economic Growth.* London: George Allen and Unwin, 1962. Chapter 3 contains a good simplified treatment of customs-union theory.

Kaser, M. *COMECON: Integration Problems of the Planned Economies,* 2nd ed. London: Oxford University Press, 1967. Problems of trade relations among centrally planned economies.

Krause, Lawrence B. *European Economic Integration and the United States.* Washington: Brookings Institution, 1968. Surveys effects of Common Market on various American interests.

Pisar, Samuel. *Coexistence and Commerce: Guidelines for Transactions between East and West.* New York: McGraw-Hill, 1970. Economic, political, and business aspects of East-West trade.

Swann, D. *The Economics of the Common Market.* Harmondsworth, England, and Baltimore: Penguin, 1970. Describes institutions and rules of European Economic Community.

Supplement to Chapter 15:
Distribution of Gains and Losses from Preferences

Here we shall extend the offer-curve geometry to show how the losses to the outside world (country *C*) when a customs union is formed are related to the distribution of gains between customs-union members *A* and *B*. In our model we assume that *A*, *B*, and *C* trade commodities 1 and 2 in the following pattern:

> *A* exports 2 to *B* and *C*, imports 1 from *B* and *C*
> *B* exports 1 to *A*, imports 2 from *A*
> *C* exports 1 to *A*, imports 2 from *A*.

(It may strike you as odd that B and C do not trade with each other; but for them to do so, when the model includes only two commodities, would imply that one country imports and exports the same product.)

This initial trading situation is shown in Figure 15.S.1, which differs from the equilibrium with reciprocal demand curves depicted in Chapter 2 only by including a third country. OA and OB are the offer curves of countries A and B respectively, based at the origin of the diagram. Because A swaps good 2 for good 1 with both partners, we must somehow add B's and C's offers of 1 for 2, in order to establish the trading equilibrium. Each offer is described as a quantity of 1 exchanging for a quantity of 2, at any given terms of trade. Thus, at terms of trade OT, OO' is B's offer. We can add C's offer at these same terms by placing the origin of C's offer curve at O' (its axes are shown as dashed lines), observing C's offer as $O'P$, and reaching a total of $B - C$ offer of OP. Because OA also passes through point P, OT turns out to be the equilibrium terms of trade.[1]

This construction is consistent with any levels of tariffs being set by A, B, and C. A tariff distorts the country's offer curve, of course, and makes its internal price ratio unequal to the world terms of trade OT. The construction requires that A's tariff be nondiscriminatory, however. Now we shall show what happens if A discriminates, eliminating its tariff against partner B while keeping it against the outside world (C). Figure 15.S.2 reproduces the essentials of Figure 15.S.1, but with the offer curves of A and C deleted. Before the preference is given, A trades good 2 for good 1 with B at terms OT, with the exchange between them described by the vector OP_b (which corresponds to OO' in Figure 15.S.1). A also trades with C along the vector P_bP_a, with P_a indicating A's total trade flow (like P in Figure 15.S.1). By the short line intersecting at P_a we show the internal prices prevailing for country A. So long as A continues to trade with C at terms OT, and A's external tariff remains unchanged, A's internal price ratio is locked in place. (The slope of the line of course indicates that due to A's tariff the relative price of A's export good 2 will be lower internally than on the world market.)

Now we shall assume in Figure 15.S.2 that C is a very large country — or one with a flat transformation schedule — so that the world terms of trade remain locked at OT no matter how much C's trade with A may vary. With A's external tariff also fixed, A's internal prices must not change.[2] These unchanged prices mean that when A eliminates its tariff toward B, B can trade at A's fixed internal prices. Hence the terms of trade line OT_b has a slope equal to that of the internal price slope at P_a. B's offer curve indicates trade between A and B at these terms to point P'_b. Recalling that B's indifference map must show higher levels of real income as we move out along its offer curve, we see that B is now better off than before. A can still trade with C at world terms OT. We can describe A's trade with C, after the preference is granted to B, by a trading vector based at P'_b and parallel to OT. A's trade with C proceeds along this trading line (T_a) until P'_a is reached, where one of A's community indifference curve is tangent to this line representing A's internal prices. There, A would be in overall trading equilibrium.[3] But A is also unambiguously worse off than

---

[1] By starting with alternative terms of trade we could construct an aggregate $B - C$ offer curve consisting of points like P.

[2] They would change, however, if a preference to B should extinguish A's trade with the outside world. We shall ignore this possibility.

[3] Point P'_a is not on A's offer curve, as shown in Figure 15.S.1. We have, implicitly, after allowing B to trade to equilibrium at P'_b, constructed a new offer curve for A from the origin P'_b.

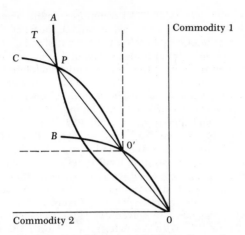

FIGURE 15.S.1   Trading Equilibrium with Three Countries
and Two Commodities

A exports 2 and imports 1 in its trade with both *B* and *C*. *A*'s offer
curve is *OA*, *B*'s is *OB*. For any given terms of trade, such as *OT*, we
can aggregate *B*'s and *C*'s offers by placing the origin of *C*'s offer
curve at *O'*.

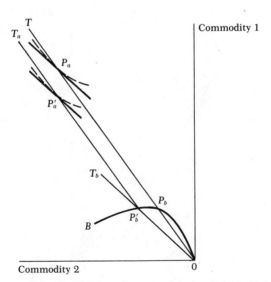

FIGURE 15.S.2   Effects of Customs Union When World Terms
of Trade Fixed

A offers a tariff preference to *B* but continues tariff-ridden trade with
C; terms of trade remain *OT*. Preferential trade moves *B* from P_b to
superior trading position P_b'. *A*, continuing to trade with *C*, winds up
in inferior trading position P_a'.

before the preference was granted. A's community indifference-curve system indicates higher satisfaction as we move up and to the right in Figure 15.S.2; as is shown, P_a must represent a higher level of satisfaction than P'_a.

Thus, when the world terms of trade are given, the country that continues to carry on tariff-ridden trade with the outside world must lose from granting a preference, and its partner must gain. This conclusion would not change if B also granted a tariff preference to A. The removal of B's tariff would shift its offer curve OB outward; but it would not change the fixity of A's internal prices, and hence would merely move point P'_b farther out on line OT_b. B's gains are increased, but A would become even worse off than before! To keep these conclusions in perspective, you should remember that with the world terms of trade OT given, A's optimum tariff is zero.

The distribution of gains changes if we assume that world terms of trade OT are not fixed. When A grants a preference that diverts its trade from C to B, A's terms improve. This diversion is shown in Figure 15.S.3, which resembles Figure 15.S.2 but allows for an improvement (from A's viewpoint) of the terms of trade from OT to OT'. With A's external tariff unchanged, A's internal prices also change in the same proportion, the reduced volume of trade driving up the price of A's export good 2. When A removes its tariff from trade with B, permitting B once again to trade at A's internal prices, the relevant internal prices will reflect this improvement in the terms of trade. Hence the trading line OT'_b has a steeper slope than OT_b, which measures A's *initial* internal prices at P_a. Once again, B trades along OT'_b to an equilibrium point given by

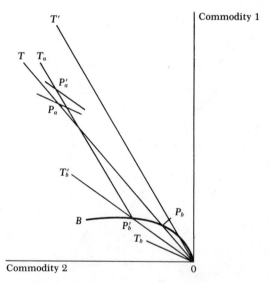

FIGURE 15.S.3   Effects of Customs Union When World Terms of Trade Change

> A's trade preference diverts trade from C and toward B. A's external terms of trade (with C) improve from OT to OT'. A's welfare improves (P'_a preferred to P_a), as does B's (P'_b preferred to P_b).

B's offer curve, and point P'_b is an origin for A's constricted trade with C. This trade takes place along trading vector T_a, which is parallel to the new external terms of trade line OT'. Notice that A's trade with C has contracted, $P'_bP'_a$ being shorter than P_bP_a; this force shifts the world terms of trade from OT to OT'.[4] The distribution of benefits differs from that shown in Figure 15.S.2. First of all, the change from OT to OT' involves a worsening of terms of trade for the rest of the world, thus leaving C worse off than before. B attains a higher indifference curve and thus benefits from A's preference. But A also winds up better off in this case, because the improvement in its terms of trade offsets the cost to A of trade diversion — the favor conferred by letting B trade at A's internal prices.[5] Hence, when the terms of trade are variable, both customs-union partners can benefit directly from discrimination against the outside world.[6]

Other outcomes can be shown by the theory of preferential trading. On the one hand, if A dominates the preferential arrangement politically, and can force its will upon B and C, it maximizes its own welfare not by going to free trade with B, but by adjusting its (optimal but nondiscriminatory) tariff downward for B and upward against C. This action is profit-maximizing for a discriminating monopolist.[7] On the other hand, when B would gain but A lose from a preference, it may pay for B to bribe A to enter into the arrangement. In terms of Figure 15.S.3, the potential terms of trade improvement to OT' might be too small for A to wind up (at P'_a) better off without a bribe, but B's gains (in moving to P'_b) could be large enough to allow B to profit from paying it.

[4] Figure 15.S.3 does not illustrate step-by-step how the new trading equilibrium is determined, but it does show the equilibrium conditions which must prevail when it is reached.

[5] Notice, furthermore, that the terms of trade might even have improved enough to make B worse off; this improvement would involve OT'_b lying above OT, and hence P'_b between P_b and the origin.

[6] The analysis embodied in Figures 15.S.1–15.S.3 draws heavily upon M. C. Kemp. *A Contribution to the General Equilibrium Theory of Preferential Trading,* Contributions to Economic Analysis, no. 61. Amsterdam: North-Holland Publishing Co., 1969, chaps. 2, 4, 8.

[7] Discrimination was considered in partial equilibrium in section 11.1. The general-equilibrium analysis is quite simple; see A. M. Henderson, "A Geometrical Note on Bulk Purchase," *Economica,* 15 (February 1948): 61–9.

PART FOUR Macroeconomic Concerns: Internal and External Balance

16 Adjustments of Money Supply and the Price Level

Hardly any important country lived through the 1960's without experiencing a balance-of-payments crisis. The United States dollar fell into deficit in 1958. In 1962 President Kennedy declared, "I am hopeful that . . . reasonable equilibrium in our international payments can be achieved within the next two years." Four years later President Johnson said, "For 1966, external balance is our goal." In 1972 President Nixon explained sweeping measures he had taken on August 15, 1971: "Our deficit . . . had risen far too high." External balance does not come easily.

Nor does it come without international discord. Germany accused the United States of forcing inflation upon the German people through the country's external surplus, and the United States accused Germany of failing to assist in dealing with the American deficit. In 1964 Great Britain rent the European Free Trade Area by reimposing freshly removed tariffs on imports from her free trade partners, to protect her balance of payments.

A payments crisis exacts its domestic political cost. Professor Richard Cooper's study of less-developed countries revealed that governments are twice as likely to fall in the year following a devaluation, and finance ministers three times as likely to get the sack![1]

External balance thus is neither a casual nor a tractable problem for most countries. True, they usually give it lower priority than the problems of full employment and price stability. Those great domestic

[1] Richard N. Cooper, *Currency Devaluation in Developing Countries*, Essays in International Finance, No. 86. Princeton, N.J.: International Finance Section, 1971, pp. 28–29.

issues get the sustained attention of economic officials in most of the industrial nations, with the balance of payments attracting notice only when a deficit flares up.

The occasional frantic heed that governments pay to external imbalance and the troubles they face in restoring balance lie within Part 4 of this volume. Their plight casts a glitter of paradox over the analysis of the coming chapters, for:

1. Automatic mechanisms of adjustment should *eventually* correct internal imbalance without policy intervention. (Why do they fail to work quickly enough, or why are they not allowed to carry out the job?)

2. External balance is directly related to domestic prices and aggregate demand. Any action a country takes toward these "domestic" variables inevitably touches its external balance as well. (Why then do governments often treat internal and external balance as if they were unrelated?)

The common thread of Part 4 is that we no longer assume that each country's transactors plan, in the aggregate, to spend each period an amount just equal to the money value of their incomes. This assumption enables us to cut through the befogging detail of economic activity and expose fundamental forces in the international economic system. But it does not always hold true. We must draw on new economic models to learn how it is disturbed, and how income and expenditure are brought back into line. These models are old friends from introductory economics texts — macroeconomic analysis and monetary theory, now extended to bring out their implications for the international economy.

16.1 AN OVERVIEW

The models we have developed so far in this book dealt with equilibrium of exchange and production in the international economy. Barter equilibrium was subjected to various disturbances, so we could discover their effect on such variables as the terms of trade or the pattern of specialization. Nonetheless, we have avoided dealing with two kinds of imbalance: disequilibrium in the foreign-exchange market (except for passing notice in Chapter 5); and violation of the budget constraint — overspending or underspending of incomes. To justify ignoring these phenomena, we must now show how these imbalances are corrected — through either market forces or the intervention of public policy.

A close relation exists between equilibrium in the foreign-exchange market — which we shall call *external balance* — and the satisfaction of the budget constraint. We should understand at the start why violation of the budget constraint is apt to involve external imbalance,

and vice versa. For planned income and expenditure to be equal —
i.e., for *internal balance* to prevail:

Income expected from domestic sales plus income expected
from export sales must equal *planned purchases of domestic*
output plus planned purchases of imports.

For the moment, associate external balance with trade in goods and
services, although we know from Chapter 5 that other transactions
can also be involved.

Now suppose that, with external balance prevailing initially,
people decide to increase their aggregate expenditure without any
parallel rise in income. They spend more on both domestic goods and
imports. The change upsets external balance as well as the budget
constraint. On the other hand, suppose that an initial equilibrium is
disturbed by a rise in export sales. Besides displacing external balance, it increases income and disrupts the equality of planned income
and expenditure.

These joint disruptions have afflicted the income circuits of many
countries. In the 1960's, West Germany complained repeatedly that
booming exports were not only causing a surplus in her balance of
payments but were also fueling domestic inflation. And the boom in
domestic expenditure experienced by the United States in the late
1960's not only fed a troublesome inflationary spiral but also caused
imports to exceed exports for the first time in the twentieth century.

Overall Balance and Mechanisms of Adjustment

The first question in this part of our study is: will any automatic
mechanism restore internal and external balance? (For convenience,
we shall refer to internal and external balance together as *overall
balance.*) Introductory courses in economics explain how equilibrium
(or balance) is restored in the market for a product, when it has been
displaced. In Chapter 5 we saw that external balance does correspond
to equilibrium in one market — the market for foreign exchange. The
most direct way to maintain this equilibrium would seem to be allowing the exchange rate to adjust continuously to clear the market.
However, countries usually choose not to employ this method of
maintaining external balance (we explore the merit of this preference
in Chapter 21 below). Hence we shall inquire whether any other
mechanisms can restore a disturbed external balance, when adjustment of the price of foreign exchange is unavailable.

In Part 1 we introduced internal balance simply by assumption,
without invoking any mechanism of adjustment that causes people to
spend their incomes — no more, no less. Yet various mechanisms that
bring about this result have been expounded theoretically and tested
empirically. We shall explore them in the context of two models of
the domestic economy: *the flexible-price economy* and the *rigid-
price economy.*

1. In this chapter we shall develop a model in which all product and factor prices are *flexible* and markets purely competitive. This means that full employment and full utilization of capacity prevail at all times. Internal imbalance can still exist, but it appears as potential inflation or deflation of the general price level. This model is the logical foundation of the "pure" models of exchange and production presented in Parts 1 and 2.

2. In Chapter 17 we shall turn to a world in which all product and factor prices are sticky or *rigid*, and thus fail to change when demand or supply shifts. Markets are not necessarily competitive. Potential internal imbalance is reflected in unemployed workers and equipment, or in unfilled orders.

In both models we explore similar questions about the restoration of internal and external balance after disturbances have upset one or both. Why two models rather than one? Unfortunately, modern industrial economies exhibit both stickiness and flexibility in the movement of prices: rigidity and idle capacity in some instances, flexibility in others, and even unemployment and inflation at the same time. Alas, no workable model can cope with a world in which prices are only *somewhat* flexible. Our best chance for a clear understanding of complex reality lies in grasping these simple models and then applying their conclusions. At the close of Chapter 18 we shall discuss the problems of using the flexible-price and rigid-price models for dealing with partial or temporary rigidity.

Policy for Internal and External Balance

Where does the analysis of these automatic mechanisms of adjustment leave us in selecting policies for internal and external balance? We shall discover automatic mechanisms that would theoretically eliminate external imbalance in conditions of either flexible or rigid prices. Internal balance is also restored following a disturbance when prices are flexible, although some inflation or deflation may be necessary. When prices are rigid, however, income and expenditure do not generally settle at a full-employment level. Empirical evidence tells us that these adjustment processes work. Still, we have only the assurance that eventually they will right the economy — though not the level of employment, with rigid prices. Room certainly remains for applying policy tools to achieve internal and external balance, and we shall turn to this problem in Chapter 18.

We already discovered why any disturbance to internal balance is likely to disrupt external imbalance (and vice versa). The same lesson applies to the effects of policies: almost any policy designed to change the state of external balance affects internal balance as well (and vice versa). This fact upsets our usual simple approach to economic policymaking: take the deficiencies one by one, and devise a policy to correct each. That approach is hardly adequate when any policy designed to affect external balance changes the state of internal balance for better or worse. The ideal approach involves setting policies for internal and external balance simultaneously, so these interdependences can be taken into account. What the economy needs is not "a policy for internal balance and a policy for external balance," but "enough policies to secure internal and external balance together."

Any macroeconomic policy affects both internal and external balance. For the familiar instruments of fiscal and monetary policy, those effects are easy to predict. Foretelling the impact on internal balance of similar policies associated with external adjustments is more difficult.

The difficulty arises partly because devaluation or revaluation is typically a policy of last resort, used by a country after it has failed to cure a persistent external (and perhaps internal) imbalance through what it regards as lesser measures. The United States, for example, struggled with a chronic if changeable deficit for a decade before devaluing in 1971. Devaluation's effect on internal balance represents a particularly touchy problem: it can raise aggregate demand in some circumstances, lower it in others. In Chapter 19 we develop a framework for exploring the internal consequences of devaluation and similar measures aimed (directly) at improving external balance.

In Chapter 5 our preliminary survey of ways to maintain equilibrium in the foreign-exchange market classified the available techniques into those that finance an imbalance and those that promote adjustment in the market. Most of our discussion of policies for external balance in Chapters 18 and 19 will deal with policies for adjustment, i.e., achieving external balance. That leaves hanging the question of financing or eliminating an external deficit. In Chapter 20 we shall explore this in depth by analyzing the demand for international reserves and the controversies over the appropriate form and quantity of these reserves. The inquiry brings out another critical feature of policies for external balance: one country's external deficit is the rest of the world's (net) external surplus. Hence, when one nation acts to eliminate its external imbalance, its trading partners are (to some degree) spared the trouble of acting. We shall see that the arcane and moralistic disputes among nations over the role of gold in international reserves and the quantity of reserves in existence really boil down to issues of who will do the adjusting, and how it will be done.

In the first five chapters of this section we assume that nations choose to maintain fixed foreign-exchange rates, without asking why they do it, or whether they should. Chapter 21 reopens this question by exploring the debate over the relative virtues of fixed and flexible (or market-determined) exchange rates. A full understanding of the issues depends on the preceding discussion of adjustment mechanisms for internal and external balance and the complexities of devising policies to attain both objectives.

16.2 MONEY HOLDINGS, THE PRICE LEVEL, AND INTERNAL BALANCE

In this chapter we present the first of our two models of internal and external balance — the one appropriate to an economy in which all prices are flexible and adjust immediately in each market to eliminate excess demand or supply. All prices save one: we suppose, when we apply this model to the open economy, that the exchange rate is fixed. Meeting this model first in the simple context of a closed economy proves helpful, however. Its elements should be familiar to you from an introductory course in economics as the "quantity theory of money." We want to stress, though, that it is a model of internal — and external — balance as well as a theory of the demand for money.

The model does begin with a hypothesis about the demand for money: people desire to hold cash balances in proportion to their money expenditure. For convenience and safety individuals and businesses hold some cash (or bank deposits) to tide them over the intervals between the receipt of income and the expenditure of the proceeds; these intervals and payments practices vary little over time. People do not let their cash balances get too small — they would risk being unable to make purchases when the need or wish arises. On the other hand, they avoid unduly large cash balances; spare cash can always be used to buy utility-yielding goods and services, whereas cash balances (beyond some level) provide no extra utility in the form of added convenience in making transactions. Hence we suppose that for each household and firm — and thus the economy as a whole — there exists a preferred ratio of cash balances to total money expenditure. This ratio may change; it fell when credit cards were invented. It might also differ from country to country.

Now consider a closed economy with a fixed initial endowment bundle (as in Part 1 of this book) or with a set of production possibilities (as in the Ricardian or Heckscher-Ohlin models of Part 2). We already know, in either case, how relative prices and the level of real expenditure are determined. The country's preferred ratio of cash balances to money expenditure depends on the forces described in the preceding paragraph. Now if we know the money value of the total real expenditure — that is, if the price level is specified — we can calculate the quantity of money demanded. Furthermore, if that is the quantity of money *actually held* in the economy, we can say that cash holdings will be in equilibrium: people will have the cash balances they desire, given the level of money prices and total real expenditure. Notice also that they must be spending just the value of their incomes; otherwise their cash balances would be either building up if they underspend or running down if they overspend. *Monetary equilibrium implies internal balance*.

Now suppose that the cash balances people hold are exogenously increased by ten percent: gold is discovered, or the government finances a deficit by printing more money.[2] Rather than hold extra cash balances, people spend more temporarily. But they cannot succeed in the aggregate. Income and expenditure are given in real terms, and there is no place for the extra cash to go except from hand to hand. What gives way, of course, is the price level. The ten percent excess supply of money (at the initial price level) corresponds to an excess demand for goods, and their prices are bid up. The price level must rise until money expenditures again bear the desired relation to the supply of money that people hold. If that proportional relation stays fixed, the price level must rise by the same ten percent as money supply. Notice that in the new monetary equilibrium real incomes and *relative* prices should be the same as before; nothing has occurred that should alter them.

Our quantity theory of money is thus also a theory about total money expenditure. As we found in Chapter 4 (section 4.4), it is one possible explanation of over- and underspending of incomes. People underspend their incomes (or save) when their actual cash balances are less than the balances they wish to hold; they overspend (dissave) when cash balances are excessive.[3] We can also anticipate the effects of other disturbances. For instance, an increase in productivity that raises the level of real income and expenditure would render cash balances deficient at the initial price level, and temporary underspending would cause the price level to fall. An increase in the cash balances people wish to hold would also prompt them to underspend temporarily, and drive down the price level until it bore the new desired relation to the (fixed) money supply.

16.3 MONETARY ADJUSTMENT AND BALANCE IN THE OPEN ECONOMY

Now we shall extend this model to the international economy, proceeding in stages. The analysis of internal and external balance in the flexible-price economy comes across most clearly if we first take up the country too small to influence the world prices of the goods it exports and imports. To make the analysis explicit, we assume that the small country is completely specialized in the production of its export good (clothing); this assumption is not necessary for the results.

---

[2] Since gold discoveries are rather infrequent, we might notice that this disturbance is functionally equivalent to others that might occur. For instance, people may decide to hold a smaller cash balance in relation to their expenditures (because the credit card is introduced), or a business boom may tempt firms to draw down their liquidity in order to raise investment outlays.

[3] We could explore the speeds of these adjustments by supposing that the rate of under- (over-) spending is proportional to the size of the gap between actual and desired cash balances.

Monetary Adjustment in the Small Open Economy

Consider again the disturbance assumed in the preceding section — a ten percent increase in the country's money supply. Starting from an initial equilibrium (which now includes equilibrium in the foreign-exchange market), this excess supply of money creates an excess demand for all goods — domestically produced clothing and also imported food. Let us suppose that one-half of the extra expenditure falls upon food imports. To buy more food, it is first necessary to buy more foreign exchange. But by our assumption of a fixed exchange rate, the country's monetary authority must stand ready to supply the extra foreign exchange from its reserves, absorbing half of the increase in the money supply. The foreign exchange can then be employed to purchase food from abroad without driving up its price. One-half of the monetary injection is disposed of without any effect on the price level.

What about the other half, assumed to fall on home-produced clothing? You might suppose, following the reasoning of section 16.2, that it would drive up the price level. Any tendency to bid up its price, however, runs afoul of clothing's status as the country's export good. Because clothing is sold abroad at a fixed world price, and the exchange rate is fixed, the domestic price received from export sales is fixed. Because the clothing industry is competitive, any tendency for extra domestic demand to drive up the price simply diverts clothing from export into domestic channels without raising its price. The net impact of the half of the monetary injection expended on clothing is to divert that much clothing away from export markets. The country's foreign-exchange earnings fall (in domestic currency) by the amount of the extra spending on clothing.

Our attention now returns to the exchange stabilization authority. It already acquired half of the monetary injection to finance the extra food imports. But the nation also loses foreign-exchange earnings from clothing exports in the amount of the other half of the injection, and the stabilization authority must make this amount of foreign exchange available to keep its price from rising. The monetary injection is converted into extra consumption with no increase in the domestic price level, and the exchange stabilization authority winds up owning the extra cash balances (and with its international reserves depleted by an equivalent amount).[4]

[4] You may find it helpful to see this example spelled out in more numerical detail. Money expenditure was initially 100 (in domestic currency) and rises by 10. Initially, half of income is spent on imports, so the rate of spending on clothing and food is 50 each. Likewise, the domestic value of clothing exports and food imports is 50 each. Of the monetary injection, 5 is spend on extra food, raising imports to 55. The 5 spent on extra clothing diverts equivalent exports, reducing them to 45. The exchange stabilization fund must make up the difference between the (domestic value of) foreign exchange supplied (45) and demanded (55), and hence purchases the whole initial injection of 10.

Furthermore, the story would not be changed fundamentally if we allowed the small country to produce some domestic goods or services not entering into trade (haircuts), or to be incompletely specialized and produce some food at home. Excess demand for food produced at home, in competition with imports, would not raise its price because that price is locked into place by the competition from imports (and the fixed exchange rate); once again, the excess demand for "importable" goods must spill entirely onto imports. The case of non-traded goods is a bit more complex but leads to no different result. If excess demand falls upon haircuts as well as clothing and food, the price of haircuts can rise temporarily. The increase *must* be temporary, however. The domestic prices of clothing and food are locked in place (as before), and real income stays unchanged. A rise in the money price of haircuts is thus also a rise in their relative price. The higher price cannot persist after the extra cash balances have been worked off (and lodged with the exchange stabilization fund); if it did, people would purchase fewer haircuts than before the monetary disturbance intruded, and the haircut market could not be in equilibrium.

Finally, consider a disturbance imposed on the small country from without, in the form of an increase of prices in the rest of the world by ten percent. Given the exchange rate, the domestic price of its exportable clothing must also be pulled up ten percent. Consumers thus find the prices of home goods as well as imports (food) elevated ten percent. The home-currency cost of their previous bundle of consumption goods increases by ten percent, but their cash balances are unchanged. This creates an excess demand for cash balances, meaning that people temporarily depress their consumption in order to build up these balances to the desired higher level. The demand for imported food falls. Reduced demand for clothing frees more of it for sale abroad. Export earnings rise, import purchases fall, and the excess demand for domestic cash balances generates an equivalent excess supply of foreign exchange. Once again, the exchange stabilization fund must absorb the disturbance, this time by purchasing foreign exchange and disgorging the domestic currency demanded to support the higher level of money expenditures.

You might wish to compare this account of the monetary adjustment mechanism with that given by such classic writers as the philosopher David Hume.[5] He and many other writers supposed that the effect of an increase in a nation's money supply *initially* raises the prices of all home-produced goods in the same proportion. *Then* the dearness of the country's traded goods (relative to foreign goods) worsens the trade balance and drains off the extra money. But telling

---

[5] David Hume, "Of the Balance of Trade," reprinted in *International Finance: Selected Readings,* ed. Richard N. Cooper. Harmondsworth, England: Penguin Books, 1969, chap. 1.

the tale in this form requires assuming that identical traded goods —
cloth produced at home and abroad — can sell at one price in one
country, another price (converted into the same currency) in another.
We would not expect this in purely competitive commodity markets.

Monetary Adjustment in the Two-Country World

Now we can explore fully the effects of monetary disturbances in the
international economy, by moving to a two-country model of the sort
presented in Parts 1 and 2 above. No longer is one country a neg-
ligibly small component of the world economy. Previously, we permitted monetary disturbances at home to be reflected in equivalent
changes in foreign exchange circulating outside its borders. This
foreign exchange is somebody else's currency, yet we have so far
assumed the injection to be too small to influence the price level
abroad. Now we include the foreign country explicitly, assuming that
its citizens also hold cash balances in fixed proportion to their money
expenditures.

Once more, assume an increase of ten percent in the money supply
of the home country. The excess supply of domestic currency translates itself as before into an excess demand for foreign currency and
goods. But now the increase in the demand for the imported good is
substantial enough to drive up its price. To see where the process
ends, we turn to the equilibrium conditions that must hold when the
increase in the home country's money supply has had its full impact.
Real incomes and relative prices must wind up the same as before the
disturbance, both at home and abroad, because nothing has occurred
to change incomes or the relative demands and supplies for food and
clothing. Therefore the *money* prices of both goods must have increased in the same proportion, for otherwise relative prices could
not hold unchanged. If all money prices have risen in the same proportion (call it α), money expenditure must have risen by α percent
in each country. Furthermore, each country could be satisfied with its
cash balances only if these have also risen by α percent. The ten
percent rise in the home country's money supply thus must be equivalent to an α percent rise in the money supply of the world as a whole
(when valued in terms of domestic currency).

How can we calculate α? This fraction must equal the ratio of the
initiating increase in the home country's money supply to the initial
money supply (valued in home currency) of the world as a whole.[6]

---

[6] Let us extend the numerical example of footnote 4 to cover this case. In
the home country, income is initially 100, the desired ratio of cash balances to
expenditure is 0.20, and the initial money supply 20. Make the exchange rate
equal to unity. The foreign country's income initially is 200 (valued in either
currency), its preferred cash-balances ratio 0.10, and its initial money stock
20. Now, as before, an increase of 10 occurs in the home country's money
supply.

In the text we argued that the rise of the world price level, α, must equal

The supplement to this chapter formally demonstrates the reasons for this. Nonetheless, the conclusion is easy to grasp intuitively. Forget national boundaries, and consider only the whole world of our model. The money supply increases. The increase must drive up the prices of all the world's goods in the same proportion.

To see the reason that the existence of separate countries — and currencies — requires no change in this simple reasoning, you should remember the process whereby an increase in home currency becomes increased balances of foreign currency in circulation. The home country's excess demand for traded goods forces its exchange stabilization authority to sell foreign exchange and absorb domestic currency. (Alternatively, the foreign country's exchange stabilization fund could do the same.) The cumulative external deficit for the home country must be large enough to generate the requisite increase in cash balances abroad. You can see from this model that countries would worry about their neighbors' rates of inflation. Furthermore, their reasons for worrying more about inflation in the United States than in Luxembourg are evident.

16.4 MONETARY SYSTEMS IN PRACTICE

Our flexible-price model has been set forth in abstract and simplified terms. Yet it has helped for over two centuries to explain practical economic forces. In this section we sketch briefly its relation to actual monetary systems. In the process, we can judge how closely some of its assumptions fit historical reality.

How closely have a country's international reserves been related to its domestic money supply? Take the case (from section 16.3) of a small country trading in a world where prices outside her borders have suddenly been raised by ten percent. An external surplus, we saw, transmits the increase to the domestic price level. We assumed two things about the link between the trade surplus and the increased money supply: a trade surplus (and increased international reserves) worth one unit of domestic currency raises the domestic money supply by exactly one unit; this relation between the change in reserves and in domestic currency cannot be affected by domestic monetary policy. We shall find that actual monetary systems can be described by their adherence to (or departure from) either or both assumptions.

---

the proportional increase of the world money supply; because the world money supply is 40, $\alpha = 10/40 = 0.25$. Let us see if this is consistent with restoration of the initial equilibrium. The home country's new level of money expenditure would be 125, the foreign country's 250; assuming the cash-balance ratios unchanged, their new desired money stocks would be 25 each, just absorbing the monetary injection of 10. The argument of the text does not depend on the desired cash-balance ratios of the two countries being the same.

Gold Coin Standard

Gold continues to play some role in nations' international reserves — the resources they employ to stabilize the external values of their currencies. Before World War I, however, gold was a firm link between the external balances and internal monetary systems of countries on the "gold standard." Actual practices were quite diverse, so it is useful to look first at an unreal and simplified model, the gold coin standard. Suppose that all money in circulation consists of gold coin — no bank deposits or paper money. Each nation's mint stands ready to convert melted foreign coin — or newly mined gold — into national coin at a nominal cost. Thus, as a country defines the gold content of its national currency unit, it determines its exchange rate against other currencies. An importer faced with the need to make a payment abroad could then ship the appropriate weight of his own coin to be converted into coin of the realm where the debt was owed, if that were cheaper than buying foreign money directly. Suppose a quantity of gold could be converted into £1 worth of British coins or $2.60 of American coins. If the exchange rate (price of sterling) were more than $2.60, and if it cost almost nothing to ship gold between countries, it would be cheaper for the American importer to ship gold when making sterling payments. If it were less (i.e., dollars were more costly in sterling), the British importer would make his payments through gold shipments to the United States. Such movements of specie would keep currencies locked together at their "gold parity" exchange rates. As long as gold could be transferred legally and costlessly, no one would rationally buy foreign currency at any other price.

The operation of a gold coin standard would match both of our key assumptions about monetary adjustments. An excess of receipts over payments would lead to a gold inflow, an equal expansion of the money supply at home and contraction abroad. Notice that no authority need stand ready to stabilize the country's foreign exchange rate. The mint's willingness to coin gold freely would fulfill this function. Furthermore, changes in the money stock would be linked automatically to imbalances in international payments; there is no room for discretionary action by the monetary authorities.

Gold Standard with Fractional Reserve Banking

This simplified gold coin standard has no exact counterpart in monetary history, although a number of countries once accepted the basic conditions for it — free convertibility between paper money and gold or gold coin, and no restriction on the international shipment of gold. These privileges prevailed widely during the heyday of the international gold standard, roughly from 1880 to World War I. But banking systems at this time were neither so simple nor so passive as this description implied. As the Industrial Revolution proceeded, financial systems emerged in which gold was not the principal medium of exchange but rather the reserve against which the banking sector issued a much larger quantity of other forms of money — paper (or fiduciary) currency and bank deposits. This form of "fractional reserve" banking carried two important implications for international monetary adjustments: a change in international reserves (the gold stock) could now cause a much larger change in money supply; and the banks' policy concerning interest rates could now affect the adjustment process. Both traits violate our key assumptions made above.

Under fractional reserve banking a change in the reserve base can cause a much larger change in the total money supply. Suppose that by law or custom banks must keep a reserve of one dollar against every ten of deposits held. If reserves of any one bank increased by one dollar, the system as a whole expands loans and deposits until the total money supply has expanded by ten dollars. This is the maximum expansion if the banking system is "fully loaned up"; if the price of bank credit — the rate of interest — is flexible, as other prices are assumed to be, cash balances like other resources should be fully employed.

In this system international payments disturbances exert a more powerful effect on the money supply than in the absence of fractional reserve banking. What difference does this make? Suppose once more that the disturbance is a ten percent increase in world prices. If our country is small and produces only goods that are traded internationally, their home-currency prices are pulled up by the same percentage. A surplus in the trade balance must occur, however, as citizens cut back expenditure and attempt to build up their cash balances to the level warranted by the new higher value of total money expenditure. With a fractional reserve banking system, a smaller trade imbalance will generate the necessary increase in cash balance — only one-tenth as large, if the banking system's reserve ratio is one-tenth.

Monetary Policy under the Gold Standard

A banking system may make another difference to adjustment under the gold standard through the interest rate and international capital movements. Even before national monetary authorities emerged (such as the Federal Reserve System of the United States), banks were employing discretionary policies to affect the monetary mechanism of adjustment. Suppose that the economy faces recurrent temporary imbalances. Sometimes (say, during a business boom) people try to overspend their incomes and reduce their money balances; at other times they underspend and build up their hoards. In a period of overspending the trade balance runs into deficit and the monetary authority loses gold. With fractional reserve banking, the natural consequence would be deflationary pressure on domestic prices. The banking system, viewing the trouble as temporary, might feel that the deflationary pressure serves no good purpose. It can be averted if the banks raise the interest rate they will pay to borrow from abroad. If capital is mobile internationally, a higher rate attracts loans from abroad, increasing the demand for domestic currency on the foreign exchange market. The capital inflow can offset the trade deficit, and no loss of reserves or monetary contraction need occur. Such a banking policy might be inappropriate if the disturbance is permanent (say, a shift of demand toward imported goods), but could usefully avoid needless adjustments if it is temporary.

To what extent did banking policy avoid adjusting the domestic money supply to the changing international gold reserves between 1880 and 1914? If adjustments are to come about, an increase (decrease) in a country's monetary gold stock must be associated with an increase (decrease) in its money supply. If the banking system intervenes at all, it should raise its interest (or discount) rate when gold reserves decline, in order to prompt the contraction of the domestic money supply. Economic historians have found that European central banks did typically behave this way (especially in England, Germany, and the Netherlands). So far, so good for the gold standard. But one can put the central banks' behavior to a somewhat stricter test. When its gold reserves fell, a bank should not only have raised its discount rate, but also raised it *enough* to force the domestic money base to shrink as well. But this on the average did not happen![7] Interest-rate policy may have protected the banks' international reserves through its effects on international capital flows, but it did not with any regularity force adjustments in the price level upon the domestic economies.

Modern Banking Systems

After World War I a serious effort was made by the major industrial countries to revive the prewar gold standard, and by the mid-1920's most countries had restored links between their gold (or foreign-exchange) reserves and their domestic money supplies. This effort to return to the old rules of the game ran into trouble even at the outset. Important countries, especially Great Britain, tried not just to return to the gold standard, but to return at the same gold parity (exchange rate) as prevailed before the war. But after a long absence the prewar gold parities did not need to represent equilibrium exchange rates. The adjustment mechanism we outlined above will make any gold parity an equilibrium one. If a country going on the gold standard picks too high a price for its currency (in terms of gold and other currencies), it generates an external deficit, gold

---

[7] Arthur I. Bloomfield, *Monetary Policy under the International Gold Standard: 1880–1914*. New York: Federal Reserve Bank of New York, 1959. This study contains a good brief account of banking policy during the supposed heyday of the gold standard.

outflow and deflation of its domestic price level[8] (and perhaps inflation of prices abroad). If prices are truly flexible, deflation is a painless process — they merely need to be bid down. In practice the process was never this easy — Britain's return to the gold standard at the prewar parity brought deflation accompanied by unemployment and labor strife.

The experience of countries during the Great Depression of the 1930's reinforced the twenties' discontent with the gold standard. Too many monetary adjustments were serving no good purpose. Price levels could not be run up and down without exacting serious economic costs — especially unemployment, resulting from deflationary pressure. Central banks today frequently protect domestic monetary conditions from the effect of international disturbances. Technically, we say that they *sterilize* changes in their international reserves. When a payments surplus occurs and the money supply increases, as the exchange-stabilization authorities pay out domestic currency for foreign exchange, the central bank sterilizes by effecting an equal contraction of the money supply. Sometimes sterilization is automatic: the exchange stabilization fund needs only to keep its domestic assets in the form of deposits with the banking system. Sometimes it is discretionary but common. Either way, the *tactical* significance of sterilization in present-day monetary policy is that it sets up a presumption against allowing international monetary adjustments to run their course.[9]

16.5 MONEY AND FINANCIAL ASSETS IN INTERNATIONAL ADJUSTMENT

In the preceding section we glimpsed a role for financial assets in international adjustment, noticing that policy-makers might induce international capital flows to avert a loss (or gain) of monetary gold. Inducing international capital flows is one way to finance a payments imbalance; as we remarked in Chapter 4, it causes the country to borrow abroad to finance an excess of expenditure over income, or lend abroad to finance such an excess abroad.

This policy-induced international flow of capital needs to be related to the holding and adjusting of the economy's financial assets. Now we shall broaden the model presented in sections 16.2 and 16.3, to provide a more fundamental role for capital flows in the adjustment process. Previously we assumed that people desire a specified

---

[8] Of nontraded goods, but perhaps also the prices of traded goods if they have risen out of line with those abroad during a period of disrupted trade.

[9] You should notice the relation between the policy choices discussed in this section and the classification we offered in Chapter 5 of ways to deal with disturbances to the foreign-exchange market. A country that regularly sterilizes changes in its reserves will be expected to finance its imbalances rather than use mechanisms of adjustment.

relation between their cash balances and money expenditures. This assumption explained the effects of any disturbance to the relation between them. Now we allow the financial assets of households to include not only cash (i.e., currency and bank deposits) but also securities. In practice, these securities can be bonds, common stocks, mortgages, various short-term loans, and many others.

We suppose that individuals can hold their wealth in these and many other forms; we could also include real property, and later (Chapter 24) we shall add foreign currencies. The economic model of *portfolio balance* describes a utility-maximizing individual's choice among these assets. He wants the highest possible rate of return on his wealth, but he will accept a lower average return in order to obtain a less risky portfolio. This objective suggests two important features of his choice among assets for his portfolio: some high-return high-risk assets may be skipped, in favor of lower-return but low-risk assets; the portfolio will include several assets, because their individual risks will average out.

At this stage we ignore most features of the portfolio-balance model and employ one of its basic implications. We decrease individuals' portfolio choices to two assets: money, which is convenient in making transactions (and is riskless) but yields no interest; and bonds, which yield fixed interest payments. The portfolio model predicts that, *at a fixed rate of interest*, individuals will hold money and bonds in their portfolios in a definite fixed proportion. (If the interest rate increases, they raise the proportion of bonds, sacrificing at the margin some of the convenience yield of cash balances.)

This prediction of portfolio analysis can now be linked to the hypothesis about the demand for money employed earlier in this chapter: people hold cash balances in a preferred proportion to their level of money expenditure. If money and expenditure are linked by the transactions-demand for cash, and money and bonds by the balancing of portfolio holdings, we derive this hypothesis:

> *At a fixed interest rate, people try to keep their bond holdings in the fixed proportion to their level of expenditure.*

If bonds and money are adjusted in the same way to the level of expenditure, why bring bonds in separately? The main reason is that they can be traded internationally, like commodities. Not every debt instrument enjoys an international market, of course. A mortgage on Mr. Smith's house would be viewed askance by, say, a Middle East oil potentate, who would have no easy way of judging the chances that Smith would make his payments on schedule. However, bonds and other securities issued by large and "mature" corporations and by governments with a record of financial prudence may (as we shall see in Chapter 23) enjoy a brisk international trade. At first we will suppose that bonds, like imports and exports, are freely traded internationally and thus command the same price everywhere. In other words, the interest rate is the same in every country.

We will now take up once more the country too small for its monetary disturbances to influence the world prices of traded goods. Suppose the same initial disturbance as before: its citizens suddenly find themselves holding ten percent more of each financial asset than previously. When only cash assets were involved, we saw that expenditures would be temporarily stretched in order to dispose of the excess; because the small country could not affect world prices, it would simply run a trade deficit equal to the monetary injection. Now, however, the temporary overspending involves net sales of bonds as well as a depletion of cash balances. An excess supply of bonds should depress their domestic price (raise the interest rate). This cannot happen, however, because we assume their price to be set on the world market. Hence the excess supply of bonds is sold abroad, exchanged for a temporary increase in consumption. The adjustment thus occurs very much as if bonds were absent. The difference appears in the balance-of-payments accounts: the trade deficit is financed partly by a net capital inflow (outflow of securities), and only partly by a loss of international reserves. You might say that international trade in securities reduces the strains that disturbances of this sort create for a country's international reserves.

Bonds can affect adjustment, however, even if they are not fully mobile internationally. Suppose now that they are *immobile* internationally — that a bond issued by a business or government debtor in one country has no market outside that country. When individuals (as before) find themselves holding excessive financial assets, they again try to get rid of both money and bonds. But if everyone tries to dispose of bonds, and these cannot be sold outside the country, the price of bonds must fall. Individuals reduce the value of their holdings of bonds, relative to the money value of expenditure. But the reduction comes simply through a decline in unit values — a capital loss. The country does not enjoy a temporary bulge in consumption, as it does when bonds can be sold to foreigners.[10] In this case the trade deficit due to the monetary disturbance will be smaller than the reduction in the value of households' financial assets.[11]

Is the international transfer of assets, as part of the adjustment process, more than a theoretical curiosity? Its worth depends on the amount of financial assets held in a nation's portfolio that enjoy

---

[10] For an interesting account of the theoretical role of bonds in international adjustment, see Tibor Scitovsky, *Money and the Balance of Payments*. Chicago: Rand McNally and Co., 1969, chap. 8.

[11] Neither bonds nor money is traded internationally, in this example, yet their fates are different; the value of bonds falls in relation to goods, but money prices are constant. No paradox is involved, however, because we assume that the exchange rate is fixed. The monetary authorities stand ready to sell foreign exchange at a fixed price, and thus stabilize the value of domestic currency in terms of internationally traded goods. If the exchange rate were determined in the market, this disturbance would drive up the cost of internationally traded goods in money, as well as in bonds.

broad international markets. Some calculations by Tibor Scitovsky
suggest that the proportion may run as low as five percent for the
United States (a large country with a giant volume of internal investment and, hence, financial claims) and as high as fifteen percent for
the Netherlands (a small country and an active foreign lender).[12]

In this section we have developed one role for international capital
movements in monetary adjustment — a role parallel to that of
money in our flexible-prices model. Other roles will emerge in several
later chapters of this book.

16.6 PRICE LEVELS AND EXCHANGE RATES IN PRACTICE

Throughout this book we have tried to show how the models of international economic theory can be put to practical use. We know (from
section 16.4) that the flexible-prices model is a framework for in-
terpreting the systems that nations have used for organizing their
international monetary relations. Does it explain present-day adjustments in the international economy equally well? Unfortunately,
the evidence gives no clear answer. The stability of the relation of
cash balances to money expenditures is hotly disputed among economists concerned with domestic macroeconomic policy. The relation
between monetary changes and external balance, however, has not
been tested fully enough even to generate a controversy!

Price Level, Trade Balance, and Exchange Rate

Much evidence does exist, however, on the mechanism whereby the
trade balance reflects price levels at home and abroad. We saw that
this link is necessary for our model to work: the trade balance must
respond sensitively to monetary disturbances raising one country's
price level relative to foreign prices. During the late 1950's, as the
reconstruction from World War II ended, many industrial nations
relaxed controls over purchases of foreign goods by their citizens.
This freeing of transactions and the availability of a broader range of
goods sharpened price competition among exporting countries and
quickly made it apparent that the movements of nations' export
prices, reflecting the underlying trends of money prices and costs in
their economies, strongly influenced their success in selling exports
on world markets. At current rates of exchange, countries with
relatively slow rates of inflation could frequently offer their exports
at favorable prices and enlarge their market shares.

The data in Table 16.1 reflect this effect. The first column shows
changes in the volumes of manufactured exports sold by several
industrial countries between 1953 and 1961 (ranked in descending
order), and the second column contains changes over the same

---

[12] *Ibid.*, pp. 100–103.

TABLE 16.1   Changes in Prices and Quantities Sold
of Manufactured Exports, Selected
Industrial Countries, 1953–1961

Country	Percentage change in volume of manufactured exports	Percentage change in unit value, manufactured exports
Italy	+346%	−20%
Japan	+282	− 5
Germany	+181	+ 9
France	+117	− 3
Belgium-Luxembourg	+ 87	− 5
United States	+ 31	+21
United Kingdom	+ 30	+14

Source: Bela Balassa, "Recent Developments in the Competitiveness of American Industry and Prospects for the Future," in U.S. Congress Joint Economic Committee, *Factors Affecting the United States Balance of Payments.* Washington: Government Printing Office, 1962, p. 46.

period in the price indexes of their exports. At least when we compare the countries at the top and bottom of the list, there is a clear tendency for fast-rising sales to go with falling prices, slow growth of exports with high price increases. The relation is not tight — we would not expect it to be, because many other forces affect the growth of trade — but it does suggest the power that changes in a country's price level may exert over its trade balance.[13]

The Purchasing-Power Parity Hypothesis

An important proposition about price levels and external balance — one that has been the focus of much empirical research — is the "purchasing-power parity hypothesis." This proposition addresses itself to the relation between the domestic price level and the equilibrium foreign-exchange rate. We know that the equilibrium exchange rate must change if an outside force disturbs the trade balance. Thus, even before stating the hypothesis, we can see that any proposition running from the price level to the exchange rate will also shed light on the adjustment of the trade balance.

The purchasing-power parity hypothesis (or "doctrine," as it is usually called) was first advanced during World War I as a method for locating the equilibrium rate of exchange for a country that had been through a major monetary disturbance — such as that associated

[13] The price indexes used to construct Table 16.1 are really "unit value indexes," which exclude the effect of changes in the mixture of goods sold and improvements in their quality less well than most domestic price indexes.

with a war or a runaway inflation. In such times international trans-actions might be disrupted or distorted by a thousand controls and uncertainties, and the underlying determinants of comparative advantage and the "barter" equilibrium in international trade might change drastically. Any surviving fixed exchange rate might lie hopelessly distant from a value that would equilibrate the foreign-exchange market. As the dust settled, how would you pick a rate to be set during a period of return to normality? The purchasing-power parity hypothesis offered an answer, or rather two related answers.

The *relative* version of the hypothesis provided the following answer. Pick a period in the recent past when conditions were reason-ably normal both at home and abroad, and observe the price of foreign exchange. Calculate the change in the domestic price level since that base period, and divide it by the change in the price level in the rest of the world over the same period. Multiply the base period's exchange rate by this fraction, and the result should approximate the current equilibrium exchange rate. That is, if the price of foreign exchange was $2.00 during the most recent period of tranquility and prices have since gone up twice as much at home as abroad, the new equilibrium rate ought to be $4.00.

The *absolute* version of the hypothesis gets the same result more directly. Calculate the average price today of a standard bundle of internationally traded goods on the domestic market. Calculate the average price today of the same standard bundle in foreign markets, priced in foreign currency. The equilibrium rate should be the price of foreign exchange that equates the values of these two bundles. Thus, if our chosen market basket of traded goods costs $26.00 in the United States and ten pounds sterling in Great Britain, the equilibrium ex-change rate should be $2.60 per pound sterling.[14]

A favorite indoor sport of economists has been thinking up new reasons for the failure of either version of the hypothesis, and at this game any number can win. We shall concentrate on the relative version, because it is both the more popular of the two and the weaker in its implied assumptions — the absolute version is vulnerable to factors that would undermine the relative version, as well as to other forces. Either version surely makes sense in the light of the real theory of international trade and the model of price-level adjustment devel-oped above. In equilibrium the prices of competitively traded goods, converted at the current exchange rate, must be the same in all countries — this justifies the absolute version. The same reasoning

[14] The absolute version of the hypothesis has traditionally been recessive, but recently it was revived as a proposed method for finding an equilibrium exchange rate for the United States dollar. See H. S. Houthakker, "Exchange Rate Adjustment," in U.S. Congress, Joint Economic Committee, *Factors Affecting the United States Balance of Payments*. Washington: Government Printing Office, 1962, pp. 289–304.

warrants the relative version, with the additional proviso that some distortion (such as heavy tariffs in one country) might make the absolute version fail but, if it stands unchanged over time, still allow the relative version to work.

Why might the relative version not work? Tariffs might have changed since the base period — to pick up the point just mentioned — forcing prices inside and outside of the tariff frontier into a different relation to each other. A change might have occurred in the volume of international capital flows, shifting the demand for home or foreign currency on the exchange markets and driving the exchange rate at least temporarily off the parity mark. The rate of real economic growth at home, say, might have run substantially ahead of that abroad. Although differing growth rates could have various effects, a likely one would be to shift the home country's offer curve outward and require deterioration in the terms of trade to bring about equilibrium in exchange (as was explained in Chapter 2); this shift in the equilibrium terms of trade could correspond to a shift in the equilibrium relation between the two countries' money price levels, and hence the exchange rate.

Other difficulties appear when we consider which goods enter into price indexes used to calculate the relative rates of price change at home and abroad. People usually have in mind a broadly based retail or wholesale price index. Such an index will, at the very least, include some commodities that are precluded from trade by heavy transport costs and the like. A retail-price index especially will be weighted with the prices of nontraded services (such as the service of retail distribution). Some economists have pointed to the inclusion of nontraded goods as a source of error in calculating purchasing-power parity exchange rates. Should they be left out? Yes and no, says the theory that we developed above. Suppose that we observe our open economy adjusting to an inflationary injection to its money supply. We learned that the adjustment will involve both overspending on traded goods (but without necessarily raising their domestic money prices) and inflation of the prices of nontraded goods. Any guess we make at the equilibrium rate of exchange *ought* to take account of the inflationary pressures reflected in the markets for nontraded goods, because these signal the extent to which cash balances remain excessive. Remembering that the parity hypothesis addresses disequilibrium situations, we see a strong case for taking nontraded goods into account.

We raised the parity hypothesis, however, not so much to theorize about it as to draw upon the empirical evidence it has generated about price levels and international adjustment. If the hypothesis holds in practice — especially in its relative version — it would support the view that changes in money price levels significantly affect international adjustment. If it should fail dismally, however, we would be left in uncertainty. Does the price-adjustment mechanism really not work? Or does the trouble lie with the theoretical deficiencies of the hypothesis, explored above?

Fortunately, the hypothesis seems to perform reasonably well in tests devised by Leland B. Yeager.[15] Taking the exchange rates of thirty-five countries in terms of the United States dollar in 1937, he calculated the change to 1957 of a United States price index in comparison to the change of a similar index for each foreign country, and multiplied the 1937 exchange rate by this fraction. The answer provided for each foreign country a hypothetical purchasing-power parity exchange rate with the United States dollar as of 1957. By 1957, he reasoned, most of the reconstruction from World War II had been completed and the associated controls relaxed, so that actual exchange rates should lie fairly close to equilibrium rates. Thus his calculated rates could be compared to actual rates to test whether or not the parity hypothesis would predict equilibrium rates over two turbulent decades. In three-fourths of his cases (26 of 35) the actual exchange rate in 1957 was within 25 percent of his calculated parity rate. This performance seems rather good — just how good, it is hard to say — and boosts confidence in the role of price-level adjustments in securing external balance.

16.7 SUMMARY

This chapter has explored monetary mechanisms of adjustment that we might expect to restore and maintain external balance when the money prices of goods and factors of production are flexible. In a closed economy, monetary theory predicts that an increase in cash balances will raise all prices in the same proportion (so long as people wish to hold cash in fixed proportion to money expenditure).

This adjustment process operates in the open economy, but gives very different results. In the small country with a fixed exchange rate an injection of cash balances leads to increased spending on traded goods, but money prices are locked to the world level and cannot rise. The country runs a trade deficit, and the authorities pegging the exchange rate are forced to buy up the whole injection of cash balances. All prices and private cash holdings return to their initial positions — even the prices of nontraded goods, which could have been bid up during the adjustment process. If the open economy is large enough to influence world prices, we conclude that a monetary injection will raise world prices and the world's money supply by the same proportion.

We can compare these theoretical models of monetary adjustment

---

[15] Leland B. Yeager, "A Rehabilitation of Purchasing-Power Parity," *Journal of Political Economy*, 66 (December 1958): 516–30.

to methods countries have used to manage their monetary systems. The classical gold standard matches two central traits of our theoretical model: an external surplus of one unit increases the domestic money supply by one unit, and the banking system cannot alter this link. Fractional-reserve banking violates the first of these traits, however, and most actual monetary systems have given the banking sector some choice about the second. Modern monetary policy usually severs the automatic link between the foreign balance and the money supply, and changes in reserves are sterilized.

The theory of monetary adjustments can be enlarged by recognizing bonds as a financial asset held in a portfolio along with money. If bonds are freely marketed internationally, part of the adjustment to a payments deficit will come in the disposal of bonds to foreigners, reducing the ratio of households' assets to their money expenditure levels and helping to restore expenditure to equality with income. Even if bonds are not traded internationally, efforts of households to overspend their incomes will involve them in a net attempt to sell off bonds domestically. This drives down their prices and thus the *value* of securities relative to expenditure, and also helps to restore equality between expenditure and income (and thus between foreign sales and purchases).

Empirical inquiries have not established the strength and regularity of the relation between cash balances in an economy and its spending on foreign goods. It is clear, though, that a country's price level strongly affects its foreign balance. The purchasing-power parity hypothesis embodies this relation and seems to succeed in predicting the new equilibrium exchange rate when a country's price level has changed drastically during a war or financial turmoil.

SUGGESTIONS FOR FURTHER READING

Balassa, Bela. "The Purchasing-Power Parity Doctrine: A Reappraisal," *Journal of Political Economy,* 72 (December 1964): 584–96. A restatement with theoretical extensions and evidence.

Bloomfield, Arthur I. *Monetary Policy under the International Gold Standard: 1880–1914.* New York: Federal Reserve Bank of New York, 1959. Studies banking policy under the gold standard.

Collery, Arnold. *International Adjustment, Open Economies, and the Quantity Theory of Money.* Princeton Studies in International Finance, No. 28. Princeton: International Finance Section, Princeton University, 1971. Advanced theoretical study of money in open economies.

Mundell, Robert A. *International Economics.* New York: Macmillan, 1968. Chapter 8 provides an advanced model of monetary equilibrium in an open economy.

Scitovsky, Tibor. *Money and the Balance of Payments.* Chicago: Rand McNally and Co., 1969. Chapter 8 develops the role of bonds in international adjustments.

Yeager, Leland B. *International Monetary Relations: Theory, History, and Policy.* New York: Harper & Row, 1966. Part 2 analyzes historical monetary systems in detail.

Supplement to Chapter 16:
A Role for Money in the Trade Model

In this supplement we formally incorporate money into the model of commodity exchange in Part 1. Consider first the home country in the absence of trade. Let E denote the monetary value of expenditures on food and clothing, Y the monetary value of the endowment bundle, Z the demand for money,[1] and Z_0 the supply of money, which, in a closed economy, is assumed to be controlled by the monetary authorities.

The basic assumption about the demand for money is that it is proportional to the monetary value of aggregate expenditure. Thus:

$$Z = k \cdot E, \qquad (16.S.1)$$

where k is the (assumed) constant showing the demand for money per unit of annual expenditure. We should realize that Z and E have different dimensionality. Z is a *stock* whereas E is a *flow*. Z measures the demand for a stock of money to hold at an *instant of time* whereas E measures aggregate demand for commodities *per unit of time*. If the time unit is a month, k will be twelve times larger than if the time unit is a year.

Monetary equilibrium is said to prevail when the demand for money, as given in equation 16.S.1, is equal to the existing stock of money, Z_0:

$$Z = Z_0. \qquad (16.S.2)$$

The role of money emerges when demand and supply for money balances are *not* in equilibrium. Our budget constraint dictated that all income is spent, but this constraint must now be modified in the case of a disequilibrium in the money market. Specifically, if the stock of money held by residents exceeds their demand, we assume that the community attempts to spend more than its income. That is,

$$\text{if } Z_0 > Z \text{ then } E > Y.$$

Alternatively, if money balances are deemed inadequate (because the supply, Z_0, falls short of $k \cdot E$) we assume that individuals attempt to build up their monetary stocks in the only way open to them — by hoarding, or spending less than their incomes.

The rate of hoarding $(Y - E)$ or dishoarding $(E - Y)$ is taken to be proportional to the monetary disequilibrium. Formally, we assume:

$$Y - E = h \cdot (Z - Z_0). \qquad (16.S.3)$$

In this expression hoarding is represented by the excess of income over expenditures, and the (assumed) constant h shows the rate at which the community strives to attain monetary equilibrium. Like k in equation 16.S.1, the value of h depends on the time period over which incomes and expenditures are measured. If this is a month instead of a year, h will be approximately $\frac{1}{12}$ as large. We shall assume that the time unit we choose is short enough that the required adjustment of spending plans, relative to income, to balance the

---

[1] Unfortunately the symbol, M, has been preempted for imports.

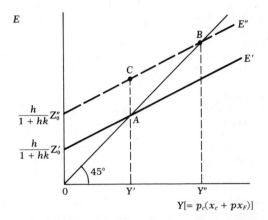

FIGURE 16.S.1   Expenditures, Income, and the Money Supply

> A doubling of the money supply, from Z_0' to Z_0'', leads to a doubling
> in the price level. With fixed quantities of commodities, the monetary
> value of income doubles from Y' to Y''. The expenditure lines have
> the general equation:
>
> $$E = \frac{1}{1 + hk}Y + \frac{h}{1 + hk}Z_0$$

money market takes more than one period. That is, h is assumed to be smaller
than one.

A simple diagram will illustrate the adjustment process in a closed economy.
In Figure 16.S.1 the vertical axis shows the monetary value of expenditures on
commodities, $p_C(D_C + pD_F)$ while the horizontal axis measures the monetary
value of incomes earned in production, $p_C(x_C + px_F)$. (Recall that p denotes the
relative price of food.) The budget constraint equates expenditures with income — shown by the 45° line. If monetary stocks are in balance, the community's equilibrium is shown on this line, e.g., at A. If money markets are not
in equilibrium, the community is attempting to hoard or dishoard. Aggregate
expenditures are then shown by the E' or E'' lines in Figure 16.S.1. To see this,
substitute kE for the demand for cash balances, Z, in equation 16.S.3 and solve
for E to obtain:[2]

$$E = \frac{1}{1 + hk}Y + \frac{h}{1 + hk}Z_0. \qquad (16.S.4)$$

For any amount of monetary stocks, e.g., Z_0', the expenditure curve slopes upward, but less than the 45° line. That is, if Y rises individuals must refrain

---

[2] Note that the time dimensionality of h and k are inversely related, so that the product,
hk, is a pure number. In fact it is a kind of elasticity:

$$hk = \frac{(Y - E)/E}{(Z - Z_0)/Z}.$$

The product hk is the percentage of original expenditure that will go into hoarding as a
consequence of a one percent increase in the demand for money balances.

from spending all their income in order to accumulate larger balances to hold against their increased expenditures. Part of the increase in income will go into hoarding. An increase in the stock of money, say from Z_0' to Z_0'' in Figure 16.S.1, shifts the expenditure curve upward. From an initial equilibrium income level, Y', suppose the money stock doubles from Z_0' to Z_0''. Expenditures initially rise from $Y'A$ (equal to OY') to $Y'C$ (greater than income OY') as residents attempt to work off extra money balances. Prices are forced upward. With x_C and x_F fixed (the commodity endowment bundle), the monetary value of Y increases, serving to raise expenditures even further. Each succeeding rise in prices raises the demand for money balances until the new equilibrium is reached at point B. Income has doubled from OY' to OY'', exclusively through a doubling in the price level. Real income and the *relative* price of food, p, are the same at Y'' as at Y' and the money value of expenditures is again equated to the money value of incomes.

The process of adjustment to a monetary disturbance is somewhat different in an *open* economy. An increase in Z_0 causes the home country to attempt to increase expenditures, as before. But the home country can now obtain more commodities on the world market, and thus runs a deficit in its balance of trade. As world prices of both food and clothing are pressed upward by the monetary expansion in the home country, the foreign country's *demand* for money balances increases, causing a cut in foreign expenditures below their level of income. The home country overspends, the foreign country underspends, and money flows from the home country to the foreign country as an expression of home trade deficits and foreign trade surpluses.

One can easily describe the long-run equilibrium position when this adjustment process has run its course and both monetary markets and commodity markets are balanced:

1. The terms of trade settle at the previous free trade level. When prices have risen sufficiently to restore equality between each country's money stock and its transactions demand for cash, the budget constraints ($E = Y$) underlying the food and clothing demand curves in each country are restored. Therefore commodity markets can be cleared only when the terms of trade, p, settle at their initial level.

2. The price level rises by the percentage increase in the world money supply. Monetary equilibrium in the world as a whole requires:

$$kE + k^*E^* = Z_0 + Z_0^*. \qquad (16.S.5)$$

Now E is equal to p_C times the value in units of clothing of aggregate home spending, $(D_C + pD_F)$. But when commodity markets are cleared in long-run equilibrium, the consumption bundle (D_C, D_F), and the terms of trade, p, regain their initial values. Similarly, E^* is equal to p_C times the unchanged value of $(D_C^* + pD_F^*)$. Therefore the left-hand side of 16.S.5 rises in percentage terms by the rise in p_C (which is equal to the rise in p_F). This rise must equal the percentage rise in $(Z_0 + Z_0^*)$, the world money supply.

3. The money supply in both countries has risen as a consequence of the initial increase in the money supply in the home country. More precisely, the money supply in each country has risen by the *same* relative amount. Consider the home country. Its demand for money balances is kE and in long-run equilibrium this is its money stock, Z_0. But previously we argued that because k is constant by assumption, kE rises by the same percentage as p_C, or the price

level. The same applies to k^*E^* — it also experiences a percentage increase given by the relative increase in world prices.[3]

We have argued that a monetary disturbance will have no long-run effect on the terms of trade and quantities traded. But its temporary effect in general is difficult to describe. With spending increased at home and reduced abroad, relative prices will change, reflecting the different spending propensities in the two countries. This change is like a *transfer* from the foreign country to the home country, and in Chapter 22 we shall analyze in more detail how a transfer affects the terms of trade. Here we need only stress that the transfer is temporary, as are the trade deficits and surpluses. The new monetary equilibrium exhibits balanced trade, the same terms of trade, but a higher price level, as the old.

---

[3] To simplify the exposition we have adopted the assumptions of the exchange model in Part 1. But notice that even if production of food and clothing in each country is free to vary along a smoothly bowed out transformation curve, production patterns depend on the terms of trade. With p the same in the new long-run equilibrium position, so must be the amounts produced in each country. The pattern of price changes *during* monetary disequilibrium, however, need not be the same as in the exchange model.

17 Adjustments of Real Output and Employment

From the flexible-price economy explored in Chapter 16 we move to the other hemisphere — where money prices of products and factors of production in each country are rigid. No longer can changes in money prices help to maintain external or internal balance. Instead, real output and employment become variable. The forces that altered *money* expenditure in the flexible-prices model now change *real* income and expenditure instead.

The rigid-prices model closely resembles the flexible-prices model, despite the critical differences in their assumptions. This resemblance is more apparent when we apply them to open economies than in the closed economy, where students of introductory economics first make their acquaintance. To show this parallelism we shall develop the rigid-prices model in the same stages as we did the flexible-prices model — first for the closed economy, then the small trading country, and finally the two-country world.

Some economists look down on rigid-price models as "the economics of deep depression," rendered obsolete by governments' success in maintaining full employment. But this view is too narrow. Prices may be flexible but only with significant delays, so that the economy acts as if prices were rigid during the periods of adjustment. Or they may resist downward pressures when the economy departs from full employment, even if they are fully flexible upward. These possibilities warn us of the need to understand adjustment in a rigid-price economy, even when most industrial countries are maintaining nearly full employment.

17.1 INCOME DETERMINATION IN CLOSED AND OPEN ECONOMIES

Our rigid-prices model, like its predecessor in Chapter 16, stresses the interdependence of internal and external balance — the way in which the two adjust to any disturbance in the system. Our condition for external balance remains the same as before: equilibrium in the foreign-exchange market. The concept of internal balance must change, however. The logic of the flexible-prices model indicates that all positions of equilibrium (internal and external balance) entail full employment in the economy. The essential finding of the rigid-prices model is that planned expenditure and income can be in balance *without full employment*. We can observe equilibrium in income and expenditure with real income below its ideal level. We reserve the term *internal balance* for situations in which *income equals planned expenditure at a full-employment level of output*.

Equilibrium and Adjustment in the Closed Economy

Let us review the determination of income in the simple Keynesian model of the closed economy, with the aid of Figure 17.1. The upper part demonstrates how we find equilibrium in income and expenditure; it appears in most textbooks on introductory economics. For output and employment to remain unchanged, the total spending that people plan to undertake, when income is at a given level, must equal that flow of income. Some expenditure is independent of the level of income — call it *investment* (we neglect the role of the government). The balance of expenditure on *consumption* depends on the level of income. In Figure 17.1a we illustrate this dependence — the consumption function — with the line $C(Y)$. Thus equilibrium requires that income (Y) equal planned expenditure on consumption (C) and investment (I), or

$$Y = C(Y) + I.$$

This is shown in Figure 17.1a by the intersection of the $C(Y) + I$ with the 45° line. At lower levels of real income, planned expenditure would exceed income — area 1 in the diagram — and income would rise. At higher levels than equilibrium income Y_0, planned expenditure would fall short of income — area 2 in Figure 17.1a — and income would fall. Equilibrium income Y_0 does not need to equal full-employment income Y_F.

The lower half of Figure 17.1 is a different presentation of this equilibrium — one·that we shall use later to illustrate equilibrium in the open economy. Suppose we rewrite our equilibrium condition as

$$Y - C(Y) = I.$$

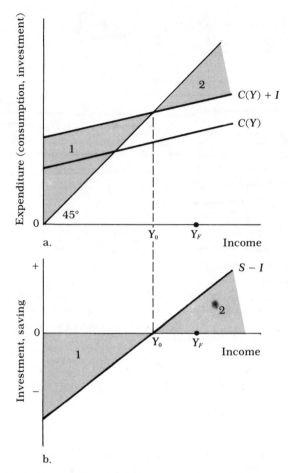

FIGURE 17.1   Keynesian Equilibrium in Closed Economy

Part a gives the conventional depiction of the equilibrium condition $Y = C(Y) + I$. Part b shows the equivalent condition $S = I$. Income equilibrium does not involve full employment.

The left-hand side is *saving* (S), the excess of income over consumption. Now move *investment* to the left-hand side as well:

$$S - I = 0,$$

and we have an equivalent condition for equilibrium in income. The $S - I$ function is in Figure 17.1b. It must slope upward. Investment, which enters with a minus sign, is a constant. Saving is negative at very low income levels, then becomes positive and rises to equal investment at Y_0 (where $S - I = 0$). At higher levels of income, saving exceeds investment. Thus areas 1 and 2 in the lower half of Figure 17.1 have the same significance as their counterparts in the upper half.

We can also recall the effect on this equilibrium of a disturbance, such as a change in the flow of investment (generally, any exogenous component of expenditure). You have surely met this exercise in comparative statics in the guise of "the multiplier," which tells how a continuing injection to expenditure raises income and employment until it is finally offset by increased leakages into saving. The induced increase in income due to this injection is given by the formula

$$\frac{1}{1 - \text{marginal propensity to consume}}.$$

We shall be developing multiplier expressions for the open economy. Hence, let us derive this expression from the equilibrium conditions given above. We noticed that saving must equal investment, i.e., that exogenous injections into the expenditure stream must equal the amount people plan to save — *not* to spend — out of the equilibrium level of income. But if this condition holds for each position of equilibrium, the *changes* in saving and investment between two equilibria must also be equal. Because the change in saving is endogenous and depends on the change in income, we can write

$$\Delta I = \Delta S = s\Delta Y.$$

The multiplier relates the induced change in income (ΔY) to the disturbance, the injection to investment (ΔI). Hence we can derive the multiplier directly as

$$\Delta Y/\Delta I = 1/s.$$

multiplier $\frac{1}{1-b}$

Equilibrium and Adjustment in the Open Economy

What happens to this analysis as we open the economy to trade? The answer is quite simple for the small open economy — too small for changes in its imports to affect total world expenditure. (Compare our definition of the small country in Chapter 16 — too small to disturb external prices.) We amend our condition for equilibrium in income flows, then derive multiplier expressions for income disturbances at home or abroad.

Take the version of the closed-economy equilibrium condition in which planned saving equals investment. The sense of this, we saw, was that it relates the exogenous injections into the income stream to the endogenous leakages out of it. Exports of goods and services (X) are exogenous like investment, because foreign spending on exports in the rigid-price economy is not influenced by income at home. (With rigid prices and excess capacity, foreign sales are not affected by the level of domestic purchases of exportable goods.) Likewise, spending on imports (M) puts income into foreign but not domestic pockets. It comprises a leakage out of the income circuit, like domestic saving. Hence, in the open economy, the equilibrium condition relating injections and leakages in the income stream is:

$$I + X = S + M.$$

Notice that this is *not* a condition for external balance; if we re-arrange the terms of this equilibrium condition, it becomes

$$X - M = S - I$$

i.e., the surplus in the trade balance (a net injection from abroad) must equal the excess of saving over domestic investment (a net domestic leakage).

From this condition for internal balance in the open economy, we can now derive the open-economy multiplier. The changes in injections to and leakages from the income stream, between two positions of equilibrium, must also be equal:

$$\Delta I + \Delta X = \Delta S + \Delta M. \tag{17.1}$$

To proceed further, we need a precise hypothesis about the effect on the foreign sector of any change in income. We also argued that exports in the rigid-price economy would be independent of income. Any category of domestic spending, however, could spill partly onto imports. To make the model as simple as possible, we assume that spending on imports varies, like the consumption of domestic goods, only with the level of income.[1] Hence we can relate imports to income in the same way as saving:

$$\Delta M = m\Delta Y,$$

where m denotes the *marginal propensity to import*.

This permits us to rewrite expression 17.1 as

$$\Delta I + \Delta X = (s + m)\,\Delta Y, \tag{17.2}$$

and the multiplier, when an exogenous change occurs in investment with exports constant, becomes

$$\boxed{\frac{\Delta Y}{\Delta I} = \frac{1}{s + m}\cdot} \quad \text{or} \quad \Delta Y = \frac{1}{s+m}\,\Delta X\,(\text{or}\,\Delta I) \tag{17.3}$$

A change in exports, with investment held constant, has the same effect on income as an equal change in investment. The right-hand side of 17.3 thus can be viewed either as the foreign-trade multiplier — the income change associated with an exogenous disturbance in

[1] This assumption does not preclude imports from entering into investment, government expenditure, or even exports (as when raw materials are imported for processing and sale abroad). But it does rule out *changes* in imports when these exogenous spending categories change.

exports — or simply as *the* multiplier in an open economy. We shall refer to it as the *open-economy multiplier.*

We stressed that the condition for income equilibrium from which we deduced this multiplier does not necessarily imply external balance. Suppose, nonetheless, that external balance prevails when an exogenous increase in exports occurs. Do imports increase by enough to restore external balance? Remembering that $\Delta M = m\Delta Y$,

$$\Delta M = m\Delta Y = m\,\frac{1}{s+m}\,\Delta X = \frac{m}{s+m}\,\Delta X. \qquad (17.4)$$

Because s and m are both positive fractions, the increase in imports has to be smaller than the increase in exports. The multiplier effects of an increase in exports thus cut into the initial improvement in the trade balance wrought by the rise in exports, but the extra imports fall short of the increase in exports so long as additional domestic saving is induced (that is, s exceeds zero). The trade balance is improved permanently by the percentage that domestic saving constitutes of all domestic leakages.[2]

Income adjustments help to restore external balance when a disturbance strikes the foreign sector, but they ordinarily fail to do the whole job. Thus you can see the need for one of the assumptions that underlies the theoretical model of the multiplier in an open economy: the authorities must passively finance a payments deficit or absorb the foreign-exchange counterpart of a surplus in ways that do not affect flows of income and expenditure.

We have touched upon disturbances stemming from investment and from exports, but have not exhausted all the possibilities.[3] Exogenous disturbances can occur in the "endogenous" flows as well. For instance, consumers' tastes might shift toward imports, so that at a given (initial) income level expenditure is shifted toward imports and away from consumption of domestic goods, leaving personal saving unchanged. The reduction in spending on home goods affects the income circuit just like a reduction in investment. If the initial reduction in consumption is $-\Delta C$ (equals ΔM, the change in imports), income falls by

$$\Delta Y = \frac{1}{s+m}\,\Delta C.$$

[2] The improvement in the trade balance is $\Delta X - \Delta M$. By 17.4,

$$\Delta X - \Delta M = \Delta X - \frac{m}{s+m}\,\Delta X = \left(1 - \frac{m}{s+m}\right)\Delta X = \left(\frac{s}{s+m}\right)\Delta X.$$

[3] One omission is the government sector. Taxes on personal incomes, corporate profits, and even real estate are sensitive to the overall level of income. They constitute another endogenous leakage out of the system, like personal saving. (We can think of s in the multiplier formulae as including the tax leakage, which of course would raise its value.) Government expenditure is normally treated as exogenous, although it may depend in the short run on both total income and tax receipts.

Furthermore, an induced fall in imports partly offsets the worsening
of the trade balance caused by the initial shift of expenditure to imports. That shift was ΔM. The cut in import spending induced by the
multiplier response is $m\Delta Y = m\Delta C/(s + m)$. Therefore the *net* worsening of the trade balance is

$$\left(1 - \frac{m}{s + m}\right)\Delta M, \text{ which equals } \left(\frac{s}{s + m}\right)\Delta M.$$

Again, we see that the open-economy multiplier always mitigates
the initial effect of any disturbance to external balance.

We need a diagrammatic interpretation of the open-economy multiplier, to help us with applications of the rigid-prices model here and
in the following chapters. We can build one starting from the lower
half of Figure 17.1, whose axes also serve for Figure 17.2. Again we
measure income on the horizontal axis; Y_F would be full-employment
income. The vertical axis displays (positive and negative values of)
the leakages and injections in the income circuit. In Figure 17.1b
we graphed the condition for equilibrium of income in the closed
economy, $S - I = 0$. Now take the parallel condition for equilibrium in
the open economy:

$$X - M = S - I.$$

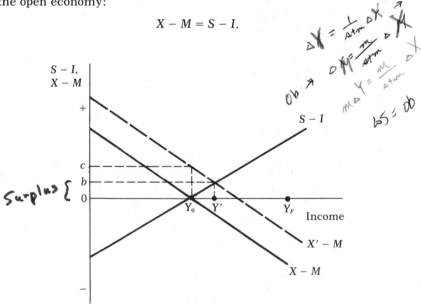

FIGURE 17.2   Effect of Increase in Exports on Income
             and Trade Balance

Income is in equilibrium at Y_0, which satisfies the equilibrium condition $X - M = S - I$. Increase of exports by Oc
raises income to Y' and leaves a residual trade-balance
surplus of Ob.

The $X - M$ schedule in Figure 17.1 shows how the trade balance would change as income increases. Exports represent a constant exogenous flow of expenditure which (for the small country) is independent of income; imports increase with income. Thus, when we subtract imports from exports we get a downward-sloping function. When income is less than Y_0 in Figure 17.2, imports are small and the trade balance $(X - M)$ is positive; when income grows larger than Y_0, increased imports render it negative. The function $S - I$ was already constructed in similar fashion. Saving increases with income; investment, independent of income, is subtracted from it. When income is less than Y_0, saving is less than investment; it exceeds investment for income levels greater than Y_0.

As Figure 17.2 is drawn Y_0 is the equilibrium level of income at which $X - M = S - I$. The schedules intersect on the horizontal axis, indicating that $X = M$ and $S = I$. You know from the previous discussion that this is quite arbitrary, and not necessary for income to be in equilibrium. Suppose now that a disturbance increases exports by an amount Oc. We illustrate this by shifting the $X - M$ schedule upward by Oc, giving us the new schedule $X' - M$. Income, saving, and imports all rise. At income Y' we have $X' - M = S - I$. Notice that external balance no longer exists — rather, there is a trade surplus of Ob, which is less than the initial improvement of Oc, because of the induced increase in imports of bc.

Income Determination in a Two-Country Model

In deriving the multiplier for an open economy, we have so far neglected the ramifications abroad of income and expenditure changes in one country. Yet, historically, that would be a serious mistake. During the Great Depression of the 1930's countries repeatedly used policies to switch domestic expenditure away from imports and toward home goods, in order to raise the utilization of home resources. These switches of course reduced income and employment abroad: one country's reduced imports were another's reduced exports, and the term "beggar-my-neighbor policies" was hung on such expenditure-switching devices. These policies were not only unneighborly, but could fail to raise incomes. At the very least, country A's diversion of expenditure from imports would lower country B's income, and thus B's imports from A. The *net* effect of the switch could be calculated only by subtracting from the multiplier-induced increase in A's income (due to the switch of expenditure to home goods) the induced decrease that would ensue from the fall in A's exports to B. (More likely, B would retaliate against A's action by cutting imports from A by as much as the shrinkage of B's exports to A. In that case, both countries would gain no employment, and could lose some benefits from trade.)

Let us think of the world as a two-country model — the home country and the rest of world consolidated as "the foreign country."

The conditions for equilibrium in income given above must now hold for each country. Using asterisks to denote the foreign nation, we now require equilibrium of income in each country:

$$I + X = S + M \qquad Home$$

$$I^* + X^* = S^* + M^*. \qquad Foreign$$

Put a delta before each variable, and we have the equations governing changes in the two countries' incomes. These relations are not independent, however. The home country's exports are the foreign country's imports, and depend on changes in its income. And the home country's income governs the foreign country's exports. Hence we can rewrite these expressions:

$$\Delta I + m^*\Delta Y^* = s\Delta Y + m\Delta Y \qquad Home$$

$$\Delta I^* + m\Delta Y = s^*\Delta Y^* + m^*\Delta Y^*. \qquad Foreign \tag{17.5}$$

For equilibrium to prevail in both countries, both relations must be satisfied. Formally, to deduce the effects of any given disturbance on income in either country, we must solve the equations numbered 17.5 simultaneously.

That procedure allows us to calculate a variety of multipliers, like expression 17.3 but taking account of repercussions abroad when a disturbance, domestic or foreign, causes domestic income to change. Rather than present these awkward formulae here, we will derive them in a supplement to this chapter. The expressions are less important than a grasp of the directions in which foreign repercussions work.

First, consider the effect of a change in domestic investment, $\Delta Y/\Delta I$. The expression 17.3 showed how the power of investment to "multiply" income is limited by leakages into domestic saving and imports. The import leakage now is not a total loss; it raises income abroad and leads to a *partial* reinjection to the domestic income stream from the increased foreign demand for our exports. Hence the value of $\Delta Y/\Delta I$ when foreign repercussions are taken into account is higher than when they are not.

Before, we could calculate a multiplier for $\Delta Y/\Delta X$ without seeking the source of the disturbance to exports. Because exports depend on income abroad, we must trace the disturbance to the foreign country's expenditure circuit. Expenditure abroad could change (so as to increase our exports) in two ways. A disturbance could increase total expenditure in the foreign country, or it could involve a switch of expenditure from its home goods to its imports (our exports). If an increase of expenditure abroad should fall entirely upon the home country's exports, the multiplier would be the same as for an increase in domestic investment. This exogenous increase in foreign spending on our exports affects both countries' incomes in the same

way as an equal exogenous increase in domestic investment spending. If the increase in total spending abroad should fall initially on
the foreign country's goods, however, the effect on the home country's
income must be weaker, because a leakage into saving abroad occurs
before the increase in expenditure begins to affect home-country
exports.

Suppose that the disturbance abroad involves no change in total
foreign expenditure, but rather a switch from the foreign country's
to the home country's output. Income in the home country still increases, although the effect is less than for disturbances that raise
foreign expenditure. Indeed, income abroad will be reduced.

This two-country model of income determination with rigid prices
is an interesting contrast to the two-country flexible-price model
discussed in section 16.3. There we tried to predict the effect of
monetary disturbances on prices and levels of money expenditure.
Here the focus is upon disturbances to real expenditure and their
effect on the level of real income and employment. A central conclusion from section 16.3 was that an injection into the world's money
supply would lead to the same expansion of world prices and money
expenditure, wherever it occurred. The same conclusion does *not* hold
for the fixed-prices model. Differences between countries in leakage
into saving (i.e., between s and s^*) make a difference: a dollar's
worth of extra investment will raise *world* real income by more if it
occurs in the country with the lower marginal propensity to save.

17.2 THE OPEN-ECONOMY MULTIPLIER IN PRACTICE

Economists trying to predict the effects of actual income disturbances in the world economy have made heavy use of the concepts
developed in section 17.1. Although the assumptions of the rigid-
prices model happily are never completely satisfied, that model
supplies reasonably accurate answers to some questions about
economic behavior.

Measurement of the Open-Economy Multiplier

Estimates of the multiplier are usually made not from simple for-
mulas like those given above but from elaborate statistical models of
the economy. However, these models differ less in the way they depict
the adjustment of income to disturbances than in the amount of detail
they take into account. The leakage into saving, for instance, may be
estimated separately for each class of income recipients, and the
savings of businesses and governments are taken into account.
Domestic investment is not completely exogenous, but responds
somewhat to the growth of income and employment; inventories
respond to short-term disturbances.

Table 17.1 presents the effects of an increase in exports as estimated by the Data Resources model of the United States economy,

TABLE 17.1   Predicted Effects of Increase in United States
             Exports on GNP and Other Variables, 1972–1981
             (amounts in billions of current dollars)

Variable	Year					
	1972	1973	1974	1975	1978	1981
Exports of goods and services	$5.0	5.0	5.0	5.0	5.0	5.0
Imports of goods and services	$0.5	0.8	1.1	1.6	2.8	4.3
Current-account balance	$4.5	4.2	3.9	3.4	2.2	0.7
Gross National Product	$8.8	8.7	10.6	13.3	13.2	12.5
Multiplier[a]	1.8	1.7	2.1	2.7	2.6	2.5
Investment	$1.2	0.7	1.2	2.2	2.0	0.7
Industrial production	1.6%	1.2	1.2	1.4	1.3	1.5
Capacity utilization	1.7%	1.1	0.8	0.8	−0.2	−1.1

Source: Calculations from Data Resources model, courtesy of Professor
Otto Eckstein, Harvard University.
   [a] Ratio in each period of predicted displacement of GNP to assumed change
in exports.

one of those currently used for economic forecasting. The calculations assume that exports of goods and services will increase by $5
billion (about 7 percent) in 1972 and remain in each subsequent
year $5 billion higher than otherwise. The table shows the displace-
ment of imports, gross national product, and other variables in
future years from the values the model would forecast in the absence
of the disturbance. The line showing values of the open-economy
multiplier indicates not an ultimate value, with all consequences of
the disturbance having worked themselves out, but rather the cumulative effect of the disturbance up to the year in question. (In practice,
we are much more concerned with predicting the effects of a disturbance over a few years than with its ultimate consequences.)

The table confirms our theoretical prediction that imports will
rise less than the initiating disturbance in exports, leaving a residual improvement in the current-account balance; after a decade,
however, little of this improvement remains. The open-economy
multiplier (calculated as the ratio of the predicted change in GNP to
the change in exports) rises to 2.7 but then falls off slightly. GNP does
not rise steadily in response to the export disturbance but rather
fluctuates mildly around its upward trend. Some extra investment
takes place, increasing the economy's industrial capacity. Industrial
production rises by slightly more than one percent, but after six years
the extra growth of capacity actually outruns the increase in production, and the portion of capacity utilized falls.

Income Elasticities, Growth, and the Trade Balance

Another practical use of the rigid-prices model is for studying the effects of economic growth on a country's balance of trade. In a world where most countries experience real economic growth, the exports of any country are growing partly because of the expanding demand of its trading partners. Its imports grow at a rate related to the expansion of its own national income. Do these growth processes expand its exports and imports at about the same rate, or does its current-account balance run either to deficit or surplus? For countries maintaining fixed exchange rates but short of policy instruments for keeping the exchange market in balance, this question is important.

The growth of a country's imports is obviously related to the growth of its income and its marginal propensity to import. The marginal propensity, however, is inconvenient to use in this context. Instead, we define the *income elasticity of demand for imports* as the percentage of (induced) change in imports divided by the percentage of change in income. If imports double while income is growing 50 percent, for example, the value of the income elasticity would be two.[4]

Return, now, to the trade balance of a growing country. In a sense, a high income elasticity of demand is hostile to a country's desire to avoid trade deficits. However, its trade balance is threatened not by its own income elasticity so much as by the following possibilities:

1. Its income elasticity is higher than those of the countries that buy its exports. If all grow at the same rate, but the home country has the highest income elasticity of import demand, our trade balance will run to deficit.

2. Its income grows faster than the incomes of its trading partners. If all have the same income elasticities, but our income grows most rapidly, our trade balance will tend toward deficits.

Measurements of income elasticities of import demand show which industrial nations might face asymmetrical income elasticities. Calculating each country's import elasticity is easy enough. To estimate the income elasticity of foreign import demand for its exports, however, we must take an average of those calculated for all of its trading partners. The average is weighted, with the importance of each trading partner's elasticity being proportional to the share that

---

[4] Formally, we can express the income elasticity of demand for imports in various forms:

$$\frac{\Delta M/M}{\Delta Y/Y} = \frac{\Delta M}{\Delta Y} \cdot \frac{Y}{M} = \frac{\Delta M/\Delta Y}{M/Y}.$$

The last of these is particularly interesting, because it reveals the income elasticity to be the marginal propensity to import divided by the average propensity to import.

TABLE 17.2   Income Elasticities of Demand for
Merchandise Exports and Imports,
Selected Industrial Countries

Country	Foreign income elasticity of demand for exports	National income elasticity of demand for imports
Japan	3.55	1.23
Australia	1.18	0.90
West Germany	2.44	1.89
Denmark	1.69	1.31
Italy	2.96	2.25
Netherlands	1.88	1.89
United States	0.99	1.51
United Kingdom	0.86	1.66

Source: H. S. Houthakker and Stephen P. Magee, "Income and Price Elasticities in World Trade," *Review of Economics and Statistics,* 51 (May 1969): Table 1.

it takes of the country's exports. Some comparisons provided by H. S. Houthakker and S. P. Magee appear in Table 17.2. We have ranked the countries starting with Japan, the one with the highest ratio of foreign to domestic income elasticities. If Japan grew at the same rate as other industrial nations, she might run recurrent surpluses in her trade balance. The fact that Japan was not (until recently) a major "surplus country" may be due to an offsetting factor: she has also grown faster than nearly all of her trading partners. At the bottom of the list, with the lowest values of the foreign relative to domestic income elasticities, are the United States and United Kingdom, nations plagued repeatedly with balance-of-payments deficits in the 1960's. For four countries — Australia, West Germany, Denmark, and Italy — the elasticity of export demand exceeds the elasticity of import demand by about the same proportion. Australia's import demand elasticity is much lower than Italy's. But one should not guess that Australia is less deficit-prone from this fact alone; the average foreign income elasticity of demand for Italy's exports seems to be proportionally as large as her own for imports. Thus, if all countries were growing at the same rate, Italy's total trade would be growing much faster than Australia's, but both might run trade surpluses in about the same proportion.

Keep in mind that these conclusions deal only with the rate of growth on aggregate demand, or absorption. They do not take account of the effect of growth on supplies of different types of goods. This matter, which could change our findings considerably, is taken up in Chapter 25.

17.3 MONETARY ADJUSTMENTS AND REAL EXPENDITURE

Up to this point, the discussion of equilibrium in the rigid-price economy is entirely different from the analysis of the flexible-price economy in Chapter 16. There, disturbances had an initial impact on prices or cash balances; here, on real expenditure. There, all adjustments occurred in money prices and money expenditure; here, in real income (or employment) and expenditure. Do these two sets of adjustment mechanisms inhabit separate worlds, with no overlap? The disturbances to real expenditure explored in this chapter could not occur with money prices completely flexible, for employment is then full and real output constant. Adjustments to monetary disturbances, however, can be built into the rigid-prices model, and they indicate important changes in some of the conclusions reached above.

Recall a principal finding (from section 17.1) about the open-economy multiplier. A disturbance occurs in the form of a permanent increase in exports of amount ΔX. Income increases by this amount times the open-economy multiplier. Imports rise by less than exports:

$$\Delta M = \left(\frac{m}{s + m}\right) \Delta X < \Delta X.$$

The multiplier adjustment restores income equilibrium but can leave external imbalance. Likewise, equilibrium in the two-country world need not leave the nations in external balance.

From Chapter 16 we know that, unless the authorities sterilize the effects of any change in their international reserves, the money supply will be affected by any disequilibrium in the trade balance, with a trade surplus being associated with a continuous increase. When the increase in exports first occurs, before any induced rise in imports has been felt, the money supply must be increasing at a rate of ΔX. As the income multiplier works itself out, induced increases in imports cut into this export surplus and constrict the injection of cash balances. But the multiplier mechanism itself, leaving a residual trade surplus, implies that this monetary injection will not be shut off entirely! After income flows have returned to equilibrium — when the multiplier process has worked itself out — the money supply continues to increase, with people's cash balances growing steadily in relation to their level of money expenditure.

If we believe that households keep a constant relation between their cash balances and levels of expenditure — the fundamental behavior pattern explored in Chapter 16 — the open-economy multiplier is not a sufficient explanation of an export injection. Fortunately, it is not difficult to show what further changes in income and imports have to occur if monetary equilibrium is restored after such a disturbance.

As the open-economy multiplier raises employment and real income, following the increase in exports, people hold more money to support their increased levels of money (and real) expenditure. Part of the inflow of cash balances is needed to fill the increased demand for transactions balances. But money expenditure stops rising when the multiplier effects have run their course, and the continuing money inflow ultimately exceeds the increased transactions demand. The excess cash balances should create an excess demand for goods, and thus increased real expenditure.

Let us explore how this happens, sticking to Keynesian income concepts. Consumption continues to depend only on real income. If households find themselves with excess cash balances, they react not with excess demand for consumer goods — the behavior pattern we assumed in Chapter 16 — but rather by putting the unneeded balances into income-yielding securities. Their purchases drive up the price of bonds, which is the same thing as lowering the rate of interest.[5] Business enterprises, noticing the reduced cost of funds, increase their borrowing (issue more bonds) and raise their planned levels of real capital formation. We now have another source of injection into the income stream. The initiating export injection not only raises income and expenditure directly, but it also injects cash balances (beyond the increased demand for transactions purposes), which drive down the interest rate and raise capital formation.

How large might this induced injection of domestic investment be? We can answer this indirectly by first raising another question: by how much must income increase before monetary equilibrium is restored? Clearly, enough so that the injection of cash balances into the system ends, which requires the induced change in imports to equal the initiating change in exports:

$$\Delta M = \Delta X.$$

If imports are governed by a fixed marginal propensity to import (m), households become satisfied to purchase this level of imports only when income has risen by enough that $\Delta M = m \cdot \Delta Y$. This condition reveals the increase in income necessary to restore monetary equilibrium:

$$\Delta Y = \frac{1}{m}\Delta M = \frac{1}{m}\Delta X. \tag{17.6}$$

Part of this results from the income multiplier analyzed above — let us call that part ΔY_k. The rest, ΔY_z, is due to the induced injection of domestic investment which occurs as the interest rate is driven

---

[5] This behavior is not consistent with an assumption we employed in Chapter 16 — that people desire to keep their financial assets in constant proportion to their money expenditure. Which assumption matches actual economic behavior is an empirical question, and the evidence at hand does not provide a firm answer.

down by households' efforts to rid themselves of excess cash balances. Because $\Delta Y = \Delta Y_k + \Delta Y_z$, we can secure an expression for ΔY_z by subtracting the old "open-economy multiplier" from our new expression for ΔY. Thus:

$$\Delta Y_z = \Delta Y - \Delta Y_k = \left[\frac{1}{m} - \frac{1}{s+m}\right]\Delta X = \frac{s/m}{s+m} \cdot \Delta X. \quad (17.7)$$

That is, the excess cash balances must induce enough extra domestic investment spending to raise income by $(s/m)/(s+m)$ times the initiating change in exports. Which part contributes more to the total increase in income? You can see that this depends on whether the domestic leakage into saving — the marginal propensity to save — is greater or less than the marginal propensity to import. In practice s could certainly exceed m, making the monetary adjustment more important than the conventional multiplier. Marginal propensities to import vary greatly from country to country, and in practice are apt to determine the relative sizes of these effects. In a small country, where the marginal propensity to import is usually high, the multiplier looks proportionally more important, even while the *total* change in income due to a given export disturbance ($\Delta Y = \Delta X/m$) becomes smaller.

Figure 17.3, which builds upon Figure 17.2, is a graphical interpretation of this monetary adjustment. The initial equilibrium of income at Y_0 is identical to that illustrated in Figure 17.2, as is the export disturbance of Oc shifting the trade-balance schedule upward to $X' - M$. The income adjustments due to the Keynesian multiplier would raise income to Y_k, and once again leave a residual trade surplus equal to Ob per period of time. The monetary injection corresponding to this surplus raises investment, which is depicted by a downward shift of the $S - I$ curve. That shift must continue until the lowered $S - I'$ function intersects the trade-balance function on the horizontal axis at Y'. Only then, with investment increased by an amount Qd, will internal and external balance both prevail.[6]

Responding to an external disturbance, the multiplier and the monetary mechanism of adjustment complement each other and push income and the trade balance in the same direction. Does this partnership hold for other disturbances? It does, as we can see in the example of an increase in government expenditure. The effect of a change in government spending on income is a familiar application of the multiplier. Not so often noticed, however, is the fact that a change in government expenditure must always be accompanied by a change in the economy's supply of money or securities, simply because a government deficit must be financed. If the budget was balanced initially and government spending increases by ΔG and remains at this higher level, a deficit of ΔG must be financed each period. Either

---

[6] It can be shown that the ratio of the induced increase in investment to the initial increase in exports, $-Od/Oc$ in Figure 17.2, must be equal to s/m.

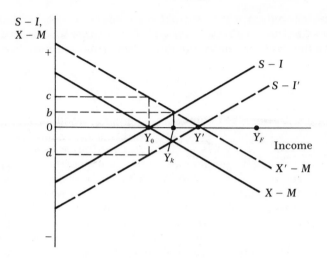

FIGURE 17.3   Effect of Monetary Adjustment on Income
Following an Export Increase

Income is initially in equilibrium at Y_0. Export increase Oc
raises it to Y_k via Keynesian multiplier. Monetary injections
cause further rise to Y'.

the money supply must be increased ("outside money" creation), more
bonds must be placed in the hands of the public, or some combination
of the two must be employed. We shall assume here that the deficit is
financed by increasing the money supply.[7]

The multiplier effects of the rise in government spending increase
income and imports in the ways described before. If we use the simple
open-economy multiplier (neglecting foreign repercussions), income
eventually increases by $\Delta Y_k = \Delta G/(s + m)$. A portion of spending spills
over onto imports, which rise by $\Delta M = [m/(s + m)]\Delta G$. Income flows
could reach equilibrium with an external deficit of this amount occurring each period. But this would not be consistent with monetary
equilibrium. The government, financing its deficit, would be issuing
new money each period at a rate of ΔG, while the payments deficit
was extracting it from the system at the smaller rate ΔM. The public's
cash balances would be steadily increasing.

By this stage you should spot the resemblance of this case to the
preceding one where the monetary injection arose from an increase in
exports. Again, the accumulating money balances must encourage
extra spending and drive up real income by an additional amount,
until the import leakage is large enough to rid the system each period

---

[7] The effects of bond financing would be similar, and would involve the sorts
of adjustment we discussed in section 16.4. The deficit to be financed would
become less than ΔG per period if taxes increase along with real income
following the rise in government spending.

(by ΔM) of the amount of money injected each period through the financing of the government deficit (ΔG). Internal balance is restored at a higher level of income: $\Delta Y = \Delta G/m$. A chronic external deficit prevails, however, so long as the government deficit continues. Monetary adjustments potentially increase the leverage of fiscal policy on income, but at the expense of enlarging the sustained external deficit that results.

As with the effects of an increase of exports, we find that monetary adjustments magnify the effect of the multiplier on real income. Furthermore, they restore external balance when the disturbance does not involve continuous exogenous changes in the money supply. When such changes are taking place, however, monetary adjustments produce an external imbalance sufficient to offset their effect on the domestic money supply.

In these respects our rigid-prices model with monetary adjustments now yields the same conclusions about external balance as did the flexible-prices model of Chapter 16. However, broad differences remain between the two models.

Each model contains a mechanism that restores internal equilibrium after a disturbance. In the rigid-prices model, the equilibrium need not coincide with full employment. Our analysis showed that the monetary adjustment mechanism would cause a different level of real income to be reached from that predicted by the conventional multiplier, but either income-expenditure equilibrium would only accidentally involve full employment. By contrast, the assumptions of the flexible-prices model guarantee that internal balance coincides with full employment.

The second difference lies in the concepts we used to explain the monetary adjustment in the two models. In Chapter 16 we simply assumed that excess cash balances led directly to an excess demand for commodities; here we channeled excess cash balances first into (excess) demand for securities, and only then into increased real expenditure. The analytical difference lies in the way we model households' behavior: do extra cash balances go into consumption, or are they transformed into bonds? The factual evidence does not seem to support either outcome to the exclusion of the other. We must simply keep both possibilities in mind.[8]

17.4 SUMMARY

This chapter dealt with an economy in which product and factor prices are rigid, and resources normally underemployed. Equality of income and planned spending no longer necessarily correspond to

---

[8] Attempts to demonstrate the influence of increases in the domestic money supply on the demand for imports have so far failed to produce significant results. See J. M. Fleming and L. Boissonneault, "Money Supply and Imports," *IMF Staff Papers*, 8 (May 1961): 227–40.

full employment; any level of unemployment can generate an equilibrium income.

The multiplier in the closed economy indicates the change in real income that follows a disturbance to expenditure. We estimate it as change in income necessary to restore equality between the injections into and leakages from the income circuit. In the open economy these leakages include imports as well as saving. Thus the open-economy multiplier becomes $1/(s + m)$, in contrast to the value of $1/s$ in a closed economy. It predicts that an increase of exports will raise income and imports, although the increase of imports will fall short of the initiating rise in exports. The foreign repercussions of a change in domestic expenditure raise the value of the open-economy multiplier. The extra imports induced by our domestic expansion constitute a positive export disturbance abroad and rebound to raise our own exports.

Many empirical applications have been made of these relations between trade and real income. Multipliers can be estimated from complex statistical models of the economy. The income-elasticity of import demand equals the ratio of the marginal propensity to import to the average propensity to import, and reveals some effects of differing rates of economic growth on the trade balance.

The money mechanism of adjustment can operate in the rigid price economy even though the price level is shackled. An increase of exports not only raises domestic expenditure but also increases the money supply (unless monetary policy consciously prevents it). The monetary injection continues until imports rise to equal the higher level of exports. From this we deduce that the open-economy multiplier, allowing for the effect of cash balances on the level of expenditure, must equal $1/m$, which exceeds the value of $1/(s + m)$ that is associated with income adjustments alone. The requirement of external balance for a stable money supply affects the operation of fiscal policy: a permanent increase of government expenditure will now raise real income by more than before, but it will create a larger chronic external imbalance.

SUGGESTIONS FOR FURTHER READING

Duesenberry, J. S., et al., eds. *The Brookings Quarterly Econometric Model of the United States.* Chicago: Rand McNally, 1965. Chapter 11, by R. Rhomberg and L. Boissonneault, provides an elaborate statistical model of the international income linkages of the United States economy.

Fleming, J. M., and L. Boissonneault, "Money Supply and Imports," *IMF Staff Papers*, 8 (May 1961): 227–40. Tests effect of money-supply changes on imports.

Machlup, Fritz. *International Trade and the National Income Multiplier.* New York: Augustus M. Kelley, 1965. Classic work on open-economy multiplier, originally published 1943.

Meade, J. E. *The Balance of Payments.* London: Oxford University Press, 1951. Part II provides a detailed treatment of income adjustments.

Robinson, Romney. "A Graphical Analysis of the Foreign Trade Multiplier," *Economic Journal*, 62 (September 1952): 546–64. Geometric treatment.

Tsiang, S. C. "Balance of Payments and Domestic Flow of Income and Expenditures," *IMF Staff Papers*, 1 (September 1950): 254–88. Enumerates ways in which a balance-of-payments change can disturb income.

Supplement to Chapter 17: Open-Economy Multipliers in the Two-Country Model

Starting from the equilibrium conditions of equations 17.5, we can calculate open-economy multipliers for expenditure disturbances. To compute $\Delta Y/\Delta I$ we solved these two equations simultaneously, setting $\Delta I^* = 0$, eliminating ΔY^*, and expressing ΔY in terms of ΔI. Notice that income flows in the foreign country must be valued in domestic currency. The multiplier now is

$$\frac{\Delta Y}{\Delta I} = \frac{1 + m^*/s^*}{s + m + m^*s/s^*}. \qquad (17.S.1)$$

Comparing equation 17.S.1 with the multiplier that omitted foreign repercussions (17.3), we can see that its value has been increased. When we examine the additions to the numerator and denominator of 17.3, in order to get 17.S.1, we can see that it reduces to $1/s$ (after canceling out m^*/s^*). Because $1/s > 1/(s + m)$, the whole expression in 17.S.1 must exceed 17.3.

What about an increase in the foreign country's investment level? If we express the change in home income in response to a change in investment abroad (setting $\Delta I = 0$), we get

$$\frac{\Delta Y}{\Delta I^*} = \frac{m^*/s^*}{s + m + m^*s/s^*}. \qquad (17.S.2)$$

This is of course smaller than the multiplier when the investment increase occurs at home, because only the import leakage from the foreign country is an injection to home income.

Finally, suppose that an increase in exports results from a switch of expenditure in the foreign country to imports and away from domestic goods. The multiplier in this case is

$$\frac{\Delta Y}{\Delta X} = \frac{1}{s + m + m^*s/s^*}. \qquad (17.S.3)$$

A glance will tell that expression 17.S.3 is the difference between 17.S.1 and 17.S.2, which is just as it should be! The increase in foreign purchases of our exports is equivalent to an increase in investment at home — 17.S.1. And the reduction in spending on domestic goods abroad is equivalent to a *negative* change in investment abroad, which is a subtraction of 17.S.2.

Multipliers for the foreign country are found in similar fashion by solving equations 17.5 for ΔY^* and eliminating ΔY.

Effects on world income are calculated by adding the multipliers for the changes in domestic and foreign incomes that result from a disturbance. (We have already had to express all flows in the home country's currency.) Define the change in world income as $\Delta W \equiv \Delta Y + \Delta Y^*$. Calculate $\Delta Y^*/\Delta I$ (it will be 17.S.2 with each variable lacking an asterisk acquiring one, and vice versa). Put this new expression and 17.S.1 over a common denominator by multiplying their original numerators and denominators respectively by s^* and s. Adding the results, we find

$$\frac{\Delta W}{\Delta I} = \frac{s^* + m^* + m}{ss^* + m^*s + ms^*} .$$

By a similar procedure,

$$\frac{\Delta W}{\Delta I^*} = \frac{s + m^* + m}{ss^* + m^*s + ms^*} .$$

We see that $\Delta W/\Delta I \gtreqless \Delta W/\Delta I^*$ as $s^* \gtreqless s$. This proposition is mentioned in the text of section 17.1.

18 Policies for Internal and External Balance

In economies that depend primarily on the market to allocate resources, policy is naturally aimed at righting "market failures" — setting the market's results right when it fails to achieve social goals. Thus we shall turn to policy for internal and external balance after having studied the market mechanisms of adjustment and their potential for maintaining balance in the open economy.

A knowledge of the properties of market mechanisms of adjustment of course fails to tell us whether — and when — policies should be applied. The monetary mechanism should eventually restore external balance, even if money prices are rigid. But should we always wait passively while it takes its course? That question has no general answer. The answer depends on the costs of transitional imbalances, our ability to predict their near-future course, the availability of policy weapons, our trust in public officials to use these weapons properly, etc. This chapter cannot treat all of these factors. We shall simply suppose that internal and external imbalances occur and ask how policies can treat them.

Our framework for analyzing policies has an affinity for the rigid-prices model of Chapter 17. Without committing ourselves to the empirical proposition that macroeconomic imbalances are due to rigid prices, we nonetheless find that model a fruitful starting point for studying the effects of policy actions. The reason is that full employment is the major target of macroeconomic policy in the domestic economy, and the Keynesian model is designed explicitly to identify policies that will attain it. Our study of adjustment mechanisms showed that any disturbance is apt to produce both internal and external imbalance. The same lesson is central to our study of policy:

every shift of policy affects both balances. We shall show how various combinations of policy instruments can be used to restore overall balance.

The flexible- and rigid-prices models will be reconsidered side by side in the final section of this chapter. There we explore the contemporary dilemma of simultaneous unemployment and inflation and its implications for the open economy.

18.1 ATTAINING INTERNAL AND EXTERNAL BALANCE

We define the two major targets of economic policy as external and internal balance. External balance requires little explanation. It involves equilibrium in the market for foreign exchange, the balance toward which adjustments in the exchange market move. (Countries in practice sometimes pick a specific exchange-market deficit or surplus as a policy target, but we shall neglect that possibility here. In the short run a target of nonzero balance involves no qualitative difference in policy-making from one of zero balance; in the long run it is inconsistent with equilibrium in income flows.)

We equate internal balance with full employment without inflationary pressure. This is not the income equilibrium toward which the economy with rigid prices tends. Depending on the level of exogenous spending, any level of employment can represent equilibrium in the Keynesian model. But for purposes of policy we are interested only in equilibrium achieved at full employment. We will suppose until section 18.4 that a full-employment equilibrium, lacking any excess aggregate demand, also entails no inflationary pressure.

People — including economists — concerned with policy-making usually treat external and internal balance independently. To secure full employment, one plies the standard tools of fiscal and monetary policy: taxes or government expenditure, the money supply, reserve requirements, etc. Rarely in everyday discussion of policy do we recognize that each of these instruments generally changes both internal and external balance — and then the joint influence is often seen as a troublesome side effect.

In this section we will show that these joint influences can be used, by setting policies simultaneously, to achieve overall balance. We pick two standard tools of policy, changes in the level of government spending, and changes in the exchange rate. (Monetary policy and the monetary mechanism of adjustment are taken up in section 18.2.) A change in either instrument affects both internal and external balance:

1. An increase in government expenditure raises aggregate demand and reduces unemployment; a decrease reduces overfull employment or potential inflationary pressure. Changes in government expenditure also affect external balance through the demand for imports: an

r : price of for. currency

increase in expenditure worsens the current-account balance; a reduction improves it.

2. A currency devaluation cheapens domestic goods relative to foreign goods, and thus improves the balance of trade in goods and services (henceforth the trade balance); a revaluation worsens it.[1] Through the trade balance, devaluation also alters total expenditure; the effect is the same as of the exogenous export increases we studied in Chapter 17. An improvement in the balance (due to devaluation) reduces unemployment; a worsening (due to revaluation) reduces inflationary pressure.

r ↑ (devaluation)
X ↑,
U ↓

These policy variables are measured on the axes of Figure 18.1, which allows us to show their joint effect on internal and external balance.[2] The vertical axis measures the exchange rate as the price of foreign currency, r in the notation of Part 1. You must keep in mind that an *increase* in the price of foreign exchange (a movement up the axis) represents a *devaluation*; a cut in the price (movement down the axis) indicates a *revaluation*.

Very Imp.

Assume that full employment prevails at a point such as K, corresponding to government expenditure (G_0, in this case) and the exchange rate r_0. Were we to raise the price of foreign currency (devalue), exports would rise relative to imports, and the contribution of the foreign balance to income would be enlarged. Suppose now that the government wishes to raise public expenditure without upsetting internal balance, say, because more highways are needed. It does not wish to raise taxes (we assume them constant throughout). The increase in expenditure would be inflationary, but this effect can be curbed if the government cuts the price of foreign exchange. Revaluation discourages exports and, by making foreign goods cheaper at home, switches expenditure to imports. The trade balance (B, hereafter) becomes negative, and the government can raise G without disturbing full-employment income. A new combination of policies can thus be found, at a point like c, involving an increase of G and a reduction of r that will preserve internal balance. We can find by this process other combinations of the exchange rate and the government-controlled level of expenditure yielding full employment, and they will lie on a negatively sloped line in Figure 18.1, YY'. Any point on the line represents internal balance — we shall call it the

---

[1] We shall assume (as in Chapter 4) that each nation specializes in its export good, or bundle of export goods. We can then avoid worrying about import-competing goods whose domestic prices change when the exchange rate changes.

[2] This diagram is based on one presented by T. W. Swan, "Longer-Run Problems of the Balance of Payments," *The Australian Economy: A Volume of Readings*, eds. H. W. Arndt and W. M. Corden. Melbourne: Cheshire Press, 1955, pp. 384–95. Reprinted in American Economic Association, *Readings in International Economics*. Homewood, Ill.: Richard D. Irwin, 1967.

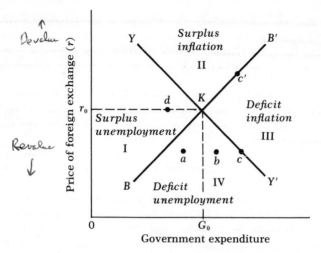

FIGURE 18.1   Policies for Internal and External Balance

YY' shows combinations of the exchange rate and level of
government spending that yield full employment. BB'
shows combinations that yield balance-of-payments equilibrium. Combination K provides overall balance.

"internal-balance schedule" — but every point indicates a different
combination of the exchange rate and government expenditure.
Any point to the right of YY' indicates too much government spending
at the planned level of private expenditure, and thus potential inflationary pressure on the economy. Another way to interpret this imbalance is to say that, at the level of government spending, foreign
exchange is too dear and therefore net sales abroad are too large.
Every point to the left of YY', on the other hand, indicates potential
unemployment.[3]

External balance is affected by the price of foreign exchange, with
B increasing when devaluation occurs (i.e., r increases). But B is
also altered by policies that change the level of expenditure, because
any policy-induced change in expenditure falls partly on imported
goods and services. Assume again an increase in highway expendi-

[3] In getting accustomed to Figure 18.1, you should notice how sharply it
differs from the diagrams usually employed in economic analysis. They ordinarily display the variable on one axis as a function of that on the other:
quantity demanded as a function of price, or consumption as a function of
income. Figure 18.1, however, is more complex. The dependent variables —
the trade balance and aggregate demand — appear on neither axis. Each is a
function of the policy variables shown on both axes. We graph values of
government expenditure and the exchange rate that are consistent with desired levels of the trade balance and aggregate demand, but these levels cannot be illustrated on the axes.

ture. It generates (through the multiplier) an increase in total income, which will be spent partly on foreign goods. The trade balance worsens. To preserve external balance the price of foreign currency must be raised. Exports will be encouraged, and consumers will retrench on imports. A new combination of G and r might give external balance at c'. Many combinations of exchange rate and government expenditure would be consistent with external balance. These will lie along a positively sloped line, BB' in Figure 18.1, that can be called the "external-balance schedule." Below this line, the exchange rate is too low for the current level of expenditure, and the external balance is in deficit. Above, the rate is too high, and an excess of exports over imports will appear.

By now we can see that only one combination of public expenditure and the exchange rate will yield external and internal balance at the same time, namely, the values corresponding to point K at the intersection of the YY' and BB' schedules. Any policy combination off the schedules indicates both external and internal imbalance; any point on one schedule but not at their intersection corresponds to one type of imbalance. We can go farther by identifying the exact economic ills indicated by points lying in the wedges between the YY' and BB' schedules — the "zones of imbalance" marked in Figure 18.1. They are:

Zone I: External surplus; internal unemployment
Zone II: External surplus; internal inflation
Zone III: External deficit; internal inflation
Zone IV: External deficit; internal unemployment

Thus points a and b both indicate a deficit combined with unemployment; c involves an external deficit but full employment.

The diagram also shows us how policy should be employed to correct any imbalance. At point c the deficit calls for devaluation. Yet devaluation alone — which in the diagram would entail a movement vertically from c up to c' on BB' — would be inappropriate. Devaluation would restore external balance but throw the economy into inflation; the foreign balance improves and adds to private spending without public expenditure being reduced. A smaller devaluation, coupled with a cut in expenditure, is necessary to reach point K.

Now consider cases with neither internal nor external balance at the outset. At point a, for example, the deficit and unemployment clearly should be attacked by raising expenditure and devaluing the currency until internal and external balance are both reached at K. At point b, however, the same conditions call for devaluation combined with reduced expenditure. How can this be? As the rising price of foreign exchange improves the trade balance, the foreign net contribution to income rises. If public spending were not reduced, devaluation itself would move the economy vertically from b into Zone III, overshooting internal balance and unleashing inflationary pressures. The mix of policies appropriate for point b is thus qualitatively the same as for c; even if there is unemployment initially, expenditure reduction *may* be necessary to keep devaluation from throwing internal balance into inflation. Comparing cases a and b, we see that in Zone IV devaluation unambiguously helps the economy, but the appropriate direction of change for expenditure depends on whether public spending is initially above or below the level that would yield internal balance at K.

As you might suppose, the same sort of conclusion holds for each other zone of imbalance. In Zone I, for example, expanding government expenditure helps to combat both unemployment and trade surplus. Whether devaluation or revaluation is required, however, depends on the relative size of the two problems. Unlike the expenditure increase, which promotes improvement of both internal and external balance, any change in the exchange rate tends to move the economy toward one target but away from the other. Devaluation or revaluation must be used as a marginal corrective, applied with the appropriate increase of expenditure. Only in special cases like point d will one policy change — increasing expenditure — attain both internal and external balance. Despite the initial surplus no revaluation is needed.

Let us restate the main conclusions drawn from Figure 18.1. (1) Many combinations of policy determining the level of public spending and the exchange rate will yield full employment, and many others will yield external balance, but only one will yield balance in both sectors. (2) Any policy instrument will generally change both internal and external balance. When one form of imbalance exists, one instrument is not enough. "If there is inflationary pressure, deflate!" may be good advice as far as it goes, but without revaluation it will create a new problem of external surplus if none existed before. (3) When there is imbalance in both sectors, one policy instrument can always be found that will move the economy toward both internal and external balance; only in special cases will it alone achieve balance in both. (4) When there is imbalance in both sectors, the appropriate direction of change in the other policy instrument is ambiguous, and cannot be calculated unless we know the correct value of that instrument in conditions of full balance.

We can say in passing that Figure 18.1 is an application of the general theory of economic policy. This theory assumes that all targets in the economy are interdependent, and that each policy instrument affects the attainment of all of the targets. One of its corollaries, illustrated above, is that one normally requires as many policy instruments as one has policy targets. With too few instruments at least one target will be missed, and the economy must usually settle for a "least bad" compromise. For instance, if the country were not free to change its exchange rate, and a rate lower than r_0 prevailed, expenditure would have to be set to yield the "least unpleasant" combination of external deficit and unemployment. Thus, in Figure 18.1 the points *a*, *b*, and *c* all lie on a horizontal line (not drawn) and thus correspond to an exchange rate lower than r_0. Expenditure could be set to preserve internal balance but with a large deficit (at *c*). Public spending could be cut to reduce the deficit slightly at the cost of some unemployment (at *b*), or cut heavily to remove much of the deficit at a heavy cost in unemployment (at *a*). Unless new alternatives can be found, the country must settle for a combination of evils.

r' fixed

18.2 BALANCE WITH FIXED EXCHANGE RATE (*thru I. k-flows*)

The analysis of Figure 18.1 tells us a good deal about organization of economic policy to attain both internal and external balance. We can demonstrate other aspects of this problem of economic policy by considering the following two questions: Will other combinations of policy instruments maintain internal and external balance? Can other important classes of international transactions, besides the trade balance, secure these policy targets?

In fact many instruments of policy can aid in bringing about internal and external balance. So far, only changes in the exchange rate have been used for their primary effect on international transactions. However, many other devices can accomplish the same purpose — namely, causing transactors in the home country, the rest of the world, or both, to switch their expenditures between home and foreign goods. We shall study these alternatives in Chapter 19. Also, in referring to policies that change the level of expenditures we did not survey all policies that might do the job. The main candidates are fiscal and monetary policy. We shall now ask whether it makes any difference which of these is chosen for a role in stabilizing the economy. In the process we shall learn how to manage external balance through international capital flows.

Contrary to the implication of the preceding section, most nations dislike using the exchange rate freely as a policy variable for securing balance. This attitude reflects, and is embodied in, the Articles of Agreement of the International Monetary Fund, which commit IMF members to maintain fixed exchange rates in the absence of "fundamental disequilibrium." A nation can in principle always cure a payments imbalance by inflating or deflating the domestic economy, but only by accident will this policy also serve the short-run needs of internal balance. Can it, however, maintain both internal and external balance by using policies with a broad effect on the domestic economy?

Consider Figure 18.2. Its horizontal axis, identical to that of Figure 18.1, measures government expenditure. On the vertical axis is another variable subject to economic policy — the interest rate. (In practice, many rates of interest persist in financial markets for loans or securities of varying riskiness and lifetime to maturity; we shall

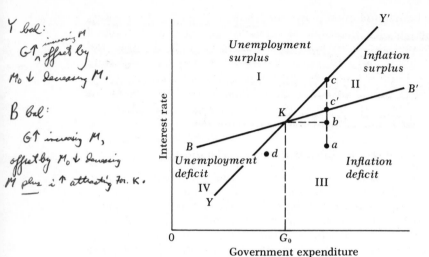

FIGURE 18.2   Effect of Fiscal and Monetary Policy
on Internal and External Balance

> YY' and BB' schedules show combinations of fiscal and
> monetary policies yielding internal and external balance.
> Policy combination K yields balance overall.

abstract from this diversity and suppose a single rate for a single
type of security, such as bonds issued by "sound" corporations.) The
interest rate can be influenced by the authorities through their control
of the money supply, because a shrinkage leaves people feeling short
of cash balances, and lowers the price of bonds and thereby raises the
rate of interest. The interest rate in turn affects expenditure in the
private sector of the economy, principally business investment.
    Internal balance, as before, depends on the right combination of
the two policy instruments.[4] But many "right combinations" can be
found. Starting from point K in Figure 18.2, where full employment is
assumed to exist, suppose that the government desires to raise public
spending. Internal balance can be preserved by a rise in the interest
rate (reflecting a contraction of the money supply). The new internal
balance will lie northeast of K, at a point such as c, reflecting an easier
fiscal policy and a tighter monetary policy. All combinations of fiscal

    [4]When we speak of a change in fiscal policy, alone, we assume that the
interest rate remains unchanged. A rise in government expenditure, and thus
in total income, normally increases the demand for money for transactions.
To keep the interest rate from rising, monetary authorities would have to expand the money supply to meet these transactions needs. Hence, when we
speak of a change in fiscal policy with monetary policy constant, we are holding the interest rate constant but not the money supply.

↑G eff. is offset mainly by M.↓

and monetary policy yielding full employment fall on a line such as YY', which has a positive slope.

What about external balance? Suppose that point K represents initial external balance, and that the same policy changes as before are brought about, in order to observe their effect on external balance. An increase in public spending raises imports, because part of any increase in spending goes to buy goods and services from abroad. The offsetting contraction of monetary policy reduces private spending on both home and foreign goods. The right amount of monetary tightening offsets the worsening of the balance of trade caused by fiscal policy. A new point of external balance can be found northeast of K, and in general the external-balance schedule BB' will have a positive slope. Monetary contraction and fiscal expansion must be plied in opposite directions to sustain external balance, just as to preserve internal balance.

B bal.

But at this stage some worries creep in. Suppose that the marginal propensity to import is constant (say, $m = 0.10$) and does not depend on which group of transactors in the economy does the spending. If total income rises by \$100, due to extra government spending, imports will rise by \$10. But in order to maintain internal balance following such a change, the interest rate must be raised enough to constrict private spending by \$100. Of this reduction \$10 will be taken from imports. The offsetting change in monetary policy required to maintain internal balance equals the change required to maintain external balance, and the internal- and external-balance schedules either coincide or lie parallel to each other! That is to say, either *any* combination of fiscal and monetary policy lying on overlapping YY' and BB' schedules will secure both internal and external balance, or else *no* combination will give both kinds of balance (if the two schedules fail to coincide).

There are various reasons, however, why the slopes of the YY' and BB' schedules should not be identical, and therefore intersect as shown in Figure 18.2. Let us first consider a class of transaction that we have already met in several guises — international capital flows. In the two preceding chapters (sections 16.5 and 17.3), we supposed that people hold a portion of their wealth in interest-yielding securities. Their behavior is governed by a desire to maximize income — through the highest attainable rate of interest (tempered by such considerations as liquidity and exposure to risk). If the interest rate rises, people may save more of their incomes and purchase more securities; they may also shift more of their wealth into securities and out of other assets (such as cash). If the domestic interest rate rises relative to that abroad, domestic and foreign asset holders alike shift their portfolios from foreign toward domestic securities. This increased export of securities is, of course, an inflow of capital and a positive change in the external balance. Thus, we generally expect

↑i Home improves b. of p.

a rise in a country's interest rate to improve external balance through the capital account.[5]

Now return to the effects of a fiscal expansion offset by a monetary contraction. We saw that, if the portion of each dollar of expenditure devoted to imports is fixed, such offsetting shifts affect internal and external balance in the same proportions. Fiscal policy has no direct effect on international capital flows, so long as the interest rate remains constant. But a change in monetary policy does affect these flows. If monetary policy tightens, external balance improves in two ways. Not only are imports reduced, but receipts from abroad increase as capital is pulled into the country by the higher interest rate. The fiscal expansion worsens the balance of payments by increasing imports; a monetary contraction that would maintain internal balance makes an offsetting improvement in net external payments not only by causing an equal cut in import spending, but also by inducing a net improvement in the balance of capital flows. In Figure 18.2, the monetary contraction needed to restore *internal* balance, after an increase in government spending of Kb, is bc. But the monetary contraction needed to restore *external* balance is the smaller amount bc'. The external-balance schedule BB' is therefore flatter than the internal-balance schedule YY'. The two schedules intersect, and, as in Figure 18.1, only the combination of policies indicated by K will ensure simultaneous internal and external balance.[6]

We can complete the analysis of Figure 18.2 by noticing the consequences of an inappropriate policy combination lying off the YY' and BB' schedules. Above YY' monetary policy is too tight for current fiscal policy, and unemployment occurs; below, monetary policy is too easy, and inflationary pressures are experienced. Above the external-balance schedule tight monetary policy both repels imports and attracts capital, provoking a payments surplus; conversely, points below BB' indicate a payments deficit. The four wedges converging on K once more indicate zones of imbalance, with differing combinations of internal and external imbalance. The Roman numerals identify them as in Figure 18.1; for example, Zone II again indicates external surplus and potential internal inflation.

---

[5] For some purposes it is important to distinguish two effects of an increase in the domestic interest rate: (1) all asset holders shift the composition of their portfolios toward domestic securities (what we call a stock-adjustment response); (2) so long as the higher interest rate prevails, asset holders place more of their new savings than before in domestic securities (a *flow* response). We shall neglect the distinction in this chapter but return to it in Part 5.

[6] You should notice the differences between the external-balance schedule in Figure 18.2 and that in Figure 18.1. Each depicts policy combinations leading to zero excess demand in the market for foreign exchange. In Figure 18.1 zero excess demand is secured by balance in the current account (with capital flows assumed nonexistent). In Figure 18.2 points on BB' generally involve an imbalance in the current account offset by an equal and opposite imbalance in the capital account.

Conclusions about the proper direction of change in the policy instruments also can be drawn from Figure 18.2 in the same way as from Figure 18.1. Point *a* lies in Zone III, and a deficit and inflationary pressure call for both a contraction of public spending and a rise in the rate of interest. The same problems at point *b,* however, would be solved by a contraction of fiscal policy alone; monetary policy is already tight enough to secure overall balance once the appropriate change in fiscal policy is made. At point *c'* external balance and inflationary pressure coexist. Fiscal policy must be tightened but monetary policy eased somewhat, in order to keep the fiscal contraction from throwing the balance of payments into surplus as inflationary pressures abate. Notice that we can no longer neatly conclude, as we did from Figure 18.1, that in each zone of imbalance the direction of change for one policy instrument is unambiguous. In Zone III point *a* calls for fiscal contraction, as would any point lying between *b* and *c'.* At point *d,* however, a monetary contraction must be associated with fiscal expansion in order to secure a relatively large improvement in the balance of payments while getting rid of only a relatively small amount of inflationary pressure. In Zone III, and in Zone I as well, the proper direction of change for both instruments depends on the relative sizes of the internal and external disequilibria. But, on the other hand, in Zones II and IV we can tell unambiguously the right direction of change for both instruments. In Zone IV unemployment and payments deficit are always fought by expansionary fiscal policy coupled with a tightening of monetary policy. The rising interest rate combats the restoration of full employment, but does less harm there than the good it does in eliminating the payments deficit; and the interest rate at any point in Zone IV is lower than it must be if balance is secured at point *K.* In the late 1950's and early 1960's, the United States suffered from unemployment combined with an external deficit (Zone IV); some economists urged on the basis of these theoretical considerations that fiscal policy should be eased and monetary policy tightened.[7]

Capital flows, if responsive to monetary policy, thus allow countries to secure overall balance without changing their exchange rates. These flows are the only reason, however, for the different leverages of monetary and fiscal policies on internal and external balance. Recall that, for the YY' and BB' lines to have the same slope, the portion of an expenditure change falling upon imports must be the same whether the change is due to fiscal or monetary policy. Yet this may not be the case. Suppose that government expenditure consists mostly of purchases of domestic goods and the salaries of civil servants, but a substantial share of the flows of private expenditure affected by

[7] Figure 18.2 and much of the analysis surrounding it is drawn from R. A. Mundell, "The Appropriate Use of Monetary and Fiscal Policy under Fixed Exchange Rates," *IMF Staff Papers,* 9 (March 1962): 70–77.

monetary policy is directed to imports. Then equal changes in total expenditure wrought by fiscal and monetary policy affect the balance of trade unequally, and a fiscal easing coupled with a monetary tightening improves the trade balance rather than leaving it unchanged. In that case, the BB' schedule is again flatter than the YY' schedule as drawn in Figure 18.2 — even if capital flows are not sensitive to the interest rate — and fiscal and monetary policy can once more be "played off" against one another to secure financial balance.[8]

18.3 THE STRATEGY OF INTERNATIONAL ECONOMIC POLICY

The major lesson emerging from our analysis is that each policy change affects both balances in the economy. The only sure way for a government to get them both right is to deal with both at once. To reach the real counterpart of the overall-balance point K in our diagram, authorities in charge of policy instrument need to know the exact size of the imbalances and what is being done with other instruments. They must also know the response of the economy to each lever of policy. These requirements imply continual sessions in the cabinet room, so that the department or agency in charge of each policy instrument makes its decisions only with full knowledge of what the others are doing — and all of them working with accurate short-term forecasts of the economy's movements.

As the newspapers constantly remind us, national economic policy is not made so neatly. Monetary authorities may know what actions the fiscal policy-makers are taking, but they may disagree or fail to coordinate their actions. They may differ on the proper targets for the economy: a treasury may be willing to accept a three percent rate of inflation, a central bank may not. The time they need to swing different policy instruments into action may vary, due to political constraints or other factors. Because of these limitations on policy-making, we would take comfort from a method of getting the economy to full equilibrium that is simpler than the simultaneous quest for balance. Is there an easier way to do it? One hopes so.

A candidate is at hand, known as *policy assignment*. Traditionally each policy instrument has been "assigned" to a target. The intelligent layman, asked why a country should devalue its currency, will answer: "To get rid of its international payments deficit." As we saw above, a better answer would be: "To get rid of its international payments deficit, unemployment, or both." Yet, as we contemplate the limits on the formation and coordination of policy, the layman may be right after all. Suppose that authorities setting each policy instrument are told to pursue a single target, ignoring the incidental effects

[8] This case is explored by R. W. Jones, "Monetary and Fiscal Policy for an Economy with Fixed Exchange Rates," *Journal of Political Economy*, 76 (July/August 1968): Part 2, pp. 921–43.

of their actions on other targets. Following our example from section 18.2, we might assign the monetary authorities to maintain external balance, adjusting the interest rate only in regard to the current balance of payments, while the fiscal authorities change public spending only to correct internal imbalance. Figure 18.3, reproducing the principal features of Figure 18.2, shows how this practice would work.

Suppose the initial situation is that shown at point *g*, one of inflationary pressure and a potential payments surplus. The monetary authorities, observing the surplus, lower the rate of interest. If they do so by the appropriate amount the surplus is eliminated at point *h* on the external-balance schedule. Inflationary pressure remains, however, and the fiscal authorities now act, reducing expenditure to secure internal balance at *i*. This action restores the payments surplus in part, and the interest rate is again lowered by the monetary authorities to secure external balance at *j*. You can easily see that this process ultimately converges on full balance at *K*. Each authority's action re-creates a problem for the other, but the problem is smaller each time around.

What if the authorities had drawn different assignments, with the fiscal authorities changing expenditure to secure external balance

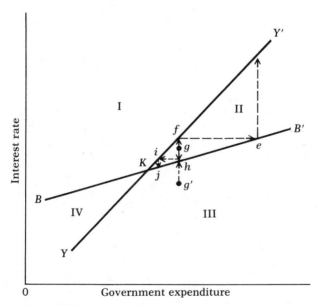

FIGURE 18.3   Effects of Assigning Fiscal and Monetary Policy
to Pursue Individual Policy Targets

Assigning monetary policy to external balance and fiscal policy to internal balance produces stable adjustment path *ghij*. Opposite assignment produces unstable path *gfe* . . . .

and the monetary officials pursuing internal balance? Starting again from point g, the monetary authorities raise the interest rate to combat inflation, gaining internal balance at f. Fiscal policy next attacks the payments surplus by expansionary measures leading to point e. The inflationary pressure is now worse than it was at g, and the interest rate is again raised. This assignment, rather than stabilizing the economy, renders it unstable and forces the authorities to take larger and larger steps in pursuit of their respective targets! Clearly the assignments make a great deal of difference.

This conclusion is not affected by our arbitrary choice of point g (in Zone II) as a starting point. An initial situation of inflation and payments deficit at point g' would yield the same results. If the monetary authorities tried to eliminate the deficit, the interest rate would be raised to bring the system to point h, and the sequence would continue i, j, . . . But if they raised the interest rate to eliminate inflation, the system would come to f and continue on an unstable course. This demonstration does not depend on our assumption that the monetary authorities act first. If this role falls to the fiscal authorities, the first adjustment is horizontal from g. You should be able to show that the same conclusions about stability will then follow.

These lessons about the importance of making the right assignment can also be drawn from Figure 18.1. We reproduce it as Figure 18.4, but with the slope of the external-balance schedule flattened and

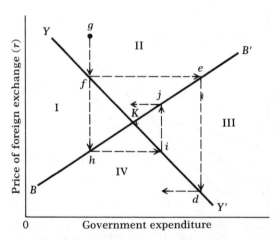

FIGURE 18.4   Effects of Assigning Fiscal Policy and Exchange-Rate Adjustment to Pursue Individual Policy Targets

Assigning exchange-rate adjustment to external balance and fiscal policy to internal balance produces stable adjustment path *gfhij*. Opposite assignment produces unstable path *gfed* . . . .

the internal-balance schedule made steeper. These modifications imply that changes in the exchange rate have a more powerful effect on external balance, in the sense that a larger change in expenditure would be needed to offset them; conversely, the exchange rate has less effect on internal balance. Suppose, as common sense would suggest, that changes in the exchange rate be used to maintain external balance. Start from point *g* in Figure 18.4, which as in Figure 18.3 lies in Zone II and indicates initial inflationary pressure and a potential payments surplus. If first the currency is revalued (exchange rate lowered), to eliminate the surplus, the system is carried to point *h*. In the process inflation is eliminated and some unemployment created, so expenditure is now raised to attain internal balance at *i*. A new payments imbalance emerges, now as a deficit, but smaller than the initial surplus. Devaluation brings the system to *j*. Again, full balance (*K*) will be approached by a decreasing spiral cycling counterclockwise.[9]

Once more, the opposite assignment would produce an unstable policy system. If revaluation were used to correct the inflationary pressure indicated at *g,* it would attain internal balance at *f*. The continuing payments surplus calls for increased expenditure to secure external balance at *e*. This creates worse inflationary pressure than at *g* and forces a revaluation to *d*. Now external payments are massively in deficit, calling for contraction of expenditure. This policy system spins the economy in an expanding clockwise spiral — once again an unstable situation.

If individual tasks are to be assigned to policy authorities, we must find a way to tell what assignments will stabilize the economy and what ones will generate economic instability. Fortunately, a method exists, and a hint about its nature lies in the shift we made in the slopes of the YY' and BB' curves in moving from Figure 18.1 to Figure 18.4. Clearly the slopes of these curves are important. They reveal the ratios of the change in one balance to the change in the other effected by a small change in the respective policy instruments. In flattening BB' we implicitly raised the relative effectiveness of exchange-rate changes for securing external balance, or reduced the "spillover" consequences of such changes for internal balance. Assigning exchange-rate policy to securing external balance yields a stable system if the ratio of the effect of an exchange-rate change on external balance to its effect on internal balance exceeds the ratio of the effects of expenditure policy on external and internal balance. Graphically, this condition requires the slope of the external-balance schedule to be flatter (less) than the slope of the internal-balance schedule (ignoring their difference in sign). The same conclusion would hold for Figure 18.3. The assignment of monetary policy to

[9] You may have encountered this adjustment process before in the so-called *cobweb cycle,* which can occur in markets where the quantity produced responds to changes in price only after a period of time.

secure external balance requires that monetary policy have relatively more leverage on external balance. Graphically, BB' must be flatter than YY'. If fiscal policy has greater leverage on external balance,[10] BB' becomes steeper than YY'.

Our conclusion remains that setting policies for internal and external balance simultaneously, taking the size of both imbalances into account, is the ideal solution. (In terms of Figures 18.3 and 18.4 this means proceeding from g directly to K.) Correct assignment brings the economy eventually into balance, but with wobbles along the way in both the settings of economic policy and the state of the economy.

18.4 INFLATION WITH UNEMPLOYMENT

In this chapter we have treated "full employment" as a readily defined concept. With prices rigid, a lower level of aggregate demand than that yielding full employment puts productive facilities out of work. With a higher level of demand, output cannot be further expanded, and prices tend to increase. Likewise, in Chapters 16 and 17 we developed models of adjustment mechanisms to restore income equilibrium and external balance on the mutually exclusive assumptions that prices are completely flexible or completely rigid.

These clear dichotomies contrast sadly to the economic straits in which most industrial countries now find themselves. Their price levels rise — sometimes by only a percentage point or so annually, sometimes by much larger amounts — no matter how ardent their desires to "stop inflation." Yet unemployment, though normally a low percentage of the labor force, fluctuates a bit from time to time and seems to fall in response to investment booms, big increases in government spending, and the like. Both real income and the price level seem to change when a disturbance occurs in an open economy. We must now decide how to use our flexible-price and rigid-price models to analyze such circumstances. How can policy attempt to deal with them?

Adapting Analytical Tools

To interpret the coexistence of inflation and unemployment, many economists start from the concept of the *Phillips curve,* which formalizes the link between inflation and unemployment and explains it in terms of the behavior of labor and product markets. The concept assumes a short-run relation between the unemployed portion of the labor force and the rate at which money wages rise. Wage increases reflect productivity growth in the economy. They also reflect the pressure of excess demand in the labor market, rising as unem-

---

[10] For example, because capital is not mobile internationally, and fiscal policy affects expenditure flows having a higher import content than those affected by monetary policy.

ployment is lowered. The same relation links the general price level to the utilization of the nation's factors of production: the fuller the utilization, the faster prices creep upward.[11]

When disturbances occur in an economy marked by "Phillips curve" conditions, the resulting adjustments should share some traits of both our flexible-prices and rigid-prices models. Unfortunately, there is no neat way to describe the combination of ingredients. Take the case of an exogenous increase in exports for a country operating close to full employment. Some increase in real income and employment will occur; also, the general price level is driven up — because of both higher consumption spending out of increased real income (the multiplier mechanism) and efforts to dispose of overabundant cash balances. Nothing can be said about the increase in money expenditure, because it depends on the joint effects of extra real income and cash balances (and, sooner or later, people's reactions to rising price levels as well). External balance is restored by the simultaneous effect of both mechanisms. Imports rise from the spending of extra real incomes and also because the prices of domestic goods are higher, causing consumers to purchase more foreign goods. The higher domestic prices and costs reduce the value of exports by driving up their prices or making their production unprofitable.[12] Real output rises less than we would predict from rigid prices, and the price level increases less than we would expect from completely flexible prices (because the volume of transactions increases). External balance will be restored by automatic market forces, but the conditions for internal balance are less obvious.

Managing Economic Policy

How can policy achieve overall balance when inflation and unemployment coincide? A logical approach would be to recognize that we now have three targets, with "internal balance" bifurcated into "full employment" and "price stability." In the earlier sections of this chapter, we implied that a third policy instrument is needed in order to achieve these two domestic goals plus external balance. Indeed, countries have followed this strategy in their experiments with "incomes

---

[11] A common objection to the Phillips curve and its variants is that people will get used to inflation and build it into their economic plans. The United States might be able to get unemployment down to three percent by letting inflation run at five percent annually, say, but sooner or later trade unions would expect the five percent price increase and build it into their wage demands. Once this happened, more than three percent unemployment would be needed to keep inflation at five percent. This objection is quite valid in principle. The problem in practice is uncertainty over the speed with which people build the present rate of inflation into their expectations, and over the safe period for which a government can sustain high levels of aggregate demand in the short run.

[12] For simplicity we assume that the demand for imports and the foreign demand for exports are of greater than unit elasticity.

policy" and other devices to curb inflation through channels other than reducing aggregate demand. The United States started along this course in 1971. Modest success at most has rewarded these efforts. Countries seem condemned to pursuing internal balance, as the least undesirable combination of inflation and unemployment. The internal-balance target might be five percent unemployment with no inflation, or four percent with two percent inflation, or three percent unemployment with five percent inflation. The choice among these becomes a matter of social preferences.

Once that choice is made, the combination selected becomes the single target of internal balance, and the analysis of sections 18.1–18.3 is again broadly appropriate. When trading nations accept different rates of domestic inflation, however, trouble soon comes for maintaining external balance. Consider Figure 18.5, which reproduces the essentials of Figure 18.1. The internal-balance schedule reflects combinations of the exchange rate and government expenditure that will yield the least undesirable combination of inflation and unemployment. The trouble is that overall balance at K cannot be sustained. If internal balance involves an annual increase in the price level and prices abroad remain (for instance) unchanged, the nation's goods in foreign prices grow steadily more expensive at the initial equilibrium exchange rate r_0. To maintain external balance with a higher home price level and the same exchange rate, domestic expenditure must be lowered to offset the deteriorating trade balance. This is true for any point on BB', not just for K: the whole external-balance schedule shifts to the left. By the same token, at any exchange rate the export surplus grows smaller (or the deficit larger) as the price level rises, and a higher level of expenditure is needed to

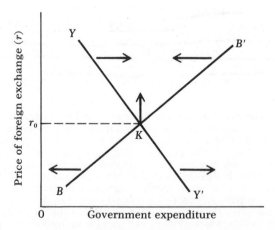

FIGURE 18.5   Internal and External Balance with Inflation at Home

Inflation at home tends to shift YY' to the right, BB' to the left. Equilibrium exchange rate must rise.

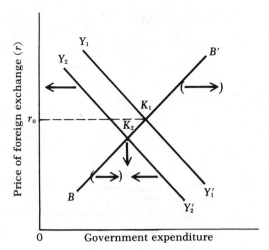

FIGURE 18.6 Internal and External Balance with Inflation at Home and Abroad

Internal-balance schedule Y_1Y_1' corresponds to world inflation rate, and K_1 can be sustained. Internal-balance schedule Y_2Y_2' corresponds to a slower inflation rate, and requires continual revaluation.

sustain internal balance. The internal-balance schedule shifts to the right. It is clear that internal balance, if it encompasses inflation faster than that abroad, requires an upward drift each year in the price of foreign exchange — i.e., depreciation of the domestic currency — in order to sustain full balance.

Figure 18.5 is perhaps excessively dismal in supposing that world money prices remain fixed while inflation continues at home. Yet the options for a single country are not logically superior when inflation is taking place abroad. Figure 18.6 is constructed on the same assumptions as 18.5, except that we now suppose world prices to be rising at a constant rate each year. Now the comparison of this world rate of inflation with the domestic rate underlying the internal-balance schedule becomes important. Let us suppose that they are the same, in the case of internal-balance schedule Y_1Y_1'. Then K_1 is a sustainable point of financial balance. With common internal and foreign rates of inflation, the forces that shifted the balance schedules in Figure 18.5 are absent, so that K_1 can persist. You can see why some economists have argued that a country can maintain external balance through domestic fiscal and monetary policy if it holds its inflation rate a bit below the world rate to cure a deficit or lets it run a bit ahead to eliminate a surplus.[13]

[13] For example, Gottfried Haberler, "Domestic Economic Policies and the United States Balance of Payments," *The Dollar in Crisis,* ed. S. E. Harris. New York: Harcourt, Brace, 1961, pp. 63–72.

Suppose instead that our country desires to hold prices constant, accepting the higher rate of unemployment, while inflation continues as before in the world outside. This would indicate a different internal balance schedule Y_2Y_2' lying to the left of Y_1Y_1'. (A lower rate of inflation requires less total expenditure for any given exchange rate, and hence a lower rate of government outlay.) But financial balance, K_2, cannot be sustained. The instability is the opposite sort to that illustrated in Figure 18.5. As home inflation lags behind the world rate, the trade balance at any exchange rate grows increasingly favorable; expenditure must be cut to sustain internal balance, and Y_2Y_2' shifts to the left just as BB' shifts to the right (arrows in parentheses). Now the price of foreign exchange must fall each year (K_2 would drift downward) if balance is to be maintained.[14] Clearly, in a "Phillips curve" world it is difficult to keep a fixed exchange rate and be out of step with the world rate of inflation.

18.5 SUMMARY

Economic policy can aim at overall balance (full employment and external balance) if enough instruments are available. By setting both the exchange rate and government expenditure simultaneously at the right levels, internal and external balance can be obtained. Any departure entails imbalance in the form of deficit or surplus abroad, inflation or unemployment at home. One cannot jump to conclusions, by observing which of these ills prevail, about the right direction of change for each policy instrument. Each affects both internal and external balance, and before changing one you must observe its standing relative to the level that would produce full balance.

Even if the exchange rate cannot be varied, the adroit use of fiscal and monetary policy can secure both internal and external balance. This is the case if monetary policy affects external balance through changes in international capital flows as well as through the current account. Then a deficit coupled with unemployment is curable by tightening monetary policy while easing fiscal policy: fiscal policy has relatively more leverage on employment and can bring about a net increase in income; the greater leverage of monetary policy on the foreign balance effects a net improvement in the flow of international payments.

This "pure theory" of economic policy requires a lot of information and coordination. A less ambitious approach is to instruct the authorities managing each policy instrument to pursue a single target. They then may approach full balance through a series of moves. Because each policy affects both targets, every time one policy lever is pulled it spoils the balance just achieved by the other policy-making agency.

[14] This analysis is adapted from A. M. C. Waterman, "Some Footnotes to the 'Swan Diagram' — or How Dependent Is a Dependent Economy?" *Economic Record,* 42 (September 1966): 447–64.

If the "assignment" is correct, however, these displacements will be smaller every time around. An incorrect assignment produces larger and larger displacements, and destabilizes the economy. Correct assignment requires instructing each policy-maker to pursue the target on which his instrument has the stronger leverage.

Our policy model assumes that prices are rigid at less than full employment but flexible upward if aggregate demand exceeds the full-employment level. In practice nations often suffer unemployment and inflation at the same time. We describe this phenomenon by means of the Phillips curve, which relates inflation to unemployment. In such conditions, the effect of an increase in exports is adjustment of the sorts described in both the flexible-prices and rigid-prices models. If countries cannot find a policy instrument to allow full employment without inflation, they must choose a least undesirable combination of the two. When inflation occurs in world prices, a country must either choose the same rate of inflation or continuously modify its policies (for example, change its exchange rate). Otherwise, external balance will be lost.

SUGGESTIONS FOR FURTHER READING

Cooper, Richard N. *The Economics of Interdependence: Economic Policy in the Atlantic Community.* New York: McGraw-Hill, 1968. Chapters 1 and 6 discuss policy coordination within and among countries.

Fellner, William, *et al. Maintaining and Restoring Balance in International Payments.* Princeton: Princeton University Press, 1966. Chapters 2, 6, 7, 8, 10, and 13 deal with the choice among policy instruments for internal and external balance.

Meade, J. E. *The Balance of Payments.* London: Oxford University Press, 1951. Parts 3 and 4 provide a classic discussion of the theory of economic policy in an open economy.

Mundell, R. A. "The Appropriate Use of Monetary and Fiscal Policy under Fixed Exchange Rates," *IMF Staff Papers,* 9 (March 1962): 70–77. Pioneer analysis of internal and external balance without exchange-rate changes.

Swan, T. W. "Longer-Run Problems of the Balance of Payments," American Economic Association, *Readings in International Economics.* Homewood, Ill.: Richard D. Irwin, 1968. Chapter 27 demonstrates the joint use of exchange-rate changes and fiscal policy for internal and external balance.

Whitman, Marina v. N. *Policies for Internal and External Balance.* Special Papers in International Economics, no. 9. Princeton: International Finance Section, Princeton University, 1970. An advanced formal survey of the theory of internal and external balance.

19 Currency Devaluation and Related Policy Instruments

On many occasions since World War II industrial nations have been forced to devalue or revalue their currencies. This action almost always came about only when external imbalance had swollen to massive scale — revealed by either a sustained change in international reserves or a scramble for policies to suppress or conceal this disequilibrium. To understand exchange-rate adjustments, therefore, we must study them in the context of the imbalances that bring them about. In Chapter 18 we saw that changes in the exchange rate can be combined with other policies to secure internal and external balance. This chapter complements that finding with a close look at the consequences of devaluation and related policies where both external and internal imbalances exist. Specifically, we shall ask: What are the effects of devaluation when imbalance exists? How do its effects compare to those of other policies used in times of critical external imbalance?

Everything we say about devaluation in the face of a deficit applies in mirror image to the upward revaluation of a currency in the face of a payments surplus. In the grand tradition of the "dismal science" we shall stick to the case of a deficit. In fact, accounting peculiarities apart, one country cannot suffer a deficit without others enjoying surpluses; it becomes an open question who adjusts his exchange rate to right the situation. We shall turn to this problem in Chapter 20, in which we shall take up the international aspects of maintaining internal and external balance.

Economists have used many models to analyze the effects of devaluation. The one we shall employ in this chapter is suitable for a country large enough to influence the world price of its export good.

We can then assume that devaluation cheapens the home country's goods and services relative to those abroad, and thus causes the terms of trade to deteriorate. In a supplement to this chapter we shall briefly explore a model suitable for a country too small to influence the world prices of traded goods; in that setting we can show the effects of devaluation on the home country's market for nontraded goods.

Devaluation affects many variables: it changes consumption patterns, reallocates resources, and shifts both money and real incomes. Hence its full effect on an economy is difficult to forecast or interpret. To isolate the fundamentals, we shall first describe the effects of devaluation in a simple exchange model. Then we can explore in greater depth its relation to internal balance and the prevailing domestic economic policies.

19.1 DEVALUATION AND DISEQUILIBRIUM IN EXCHANGE

A country considers devaluing its currency because of an external deficit, actual or potential. To understand the role of devaluation in curing a deficit, we must specify carefully the sources of the deficit. The simple model of exchange, introduced in Part 1, allows the essential features to be put in sharp relief.[1] It assumes that trading countries start with fixed endowments of goods that are traded competitively. This trade leads to equilibrium values for the terms of trade between the two goods and the quantities exchanged, as was explained in Chapter 2.

Because devaluation affects the terms of trade only through money prices in the two countries, we must also specify the effect on money prices. Here we suppose that each country regulates its money supply to keep the price of its export good constant in terms of its home currency. This is a plausible way to manage internal balance in a model with flexible prices; it is a natural assumption for a rigid-prices model if no import-competing goods are produced at home. The advantage of assuming that the money price of each country's export stays constant appears when we identify the effect of devaluation on the terms of trade. The exchange rate links the money price and cost structures of the two countries. When a nation devalues — cheapens its currency — it also cheapens its goods to citizens of the foreign country and makes foreign goods dearer at home. When we specify that the *home-currency* prices of exports remain constant, we guarantee that the home-currency price of the devaluing country's import good rises by the amount of the devaluation, while the domestic price of its export-

[1] Many approaches have been taken by economic theorists to the analysis of devaluation. This section draws principally upon J. E. Meade. *A Geometry of International Trade*. London: George Allen & Unwin, 1952, chap. 7, and R. W. Jones, "Stability Conditions in International Trade: A General Equilibrium Analysis," *International Economic Review,* 2 (May 1961): 199–209.

able good stays constant. Thus its terms of trade worsen in direct proportion to the devaluation. And in the eyes of the foreign country, our devaluation improves the price of *their* export good by the same proportion as the devaluation.

In this model we can show the effects of devaluation on two types of disequilibrium. These match up to two terms that are used — both frequently and carelessly — to describe payments imbalances.

Overvaluation See notes.

People often say that the currency of a country with a payments deficit is "overvalued." This statement may mean only "I think we should devalue," or "I think we should deflate." Overvaluation can, however, be given an exact meaning in the simple model of exchange. Consider Figure 19.1, which closely resembles Figure 2.7. The sides of the box diagram measure the two countries' endowments of clothing (horizontally), the home country's export good, and food (vertically), which the home country imports. We measure the home country's initial endowment and final consumption bundles from O, the foreign country's from O^*. The endowment points for the two countries, E and E^*, indicate their initial bundles of food and clothing; these coincide, as the construction of the box diagram requires. The home and

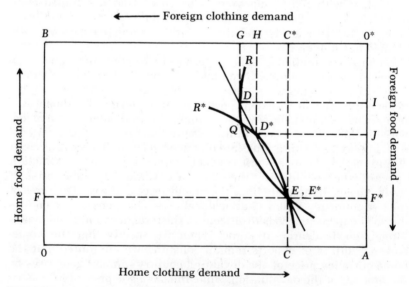

FIGURE 19.1   External Imbalance with Overvaluation, and Effects of Devaluation

Overvaluation is reflected in disequilibrium terms of trade ED^*D, which cause excess world supply for clothing of GH, excess demand for food of IJ.

foreign countries' offer curves are respectively EQR and E^*QR^*. If the terms of trade between clothing and food were equal to the slope of a line (not shown) through E and Q, the trading countries would be in full equilibrium. By our monetary assumption — export prices kept constant in the home currency — the exchange rate would bear the same relation, and the exchange market would be in equilibrium.

Suppose, however, that the home country's currency (and export good) has somehow become "overvalued." The price slope ED^*D indicates a higher relative price for the home country's clothing exports than is consistent with equilibrium, and this price would correspond to too high a price for the home currency.[2] At this exchange rate the home country would wish to consume the bundle of goods indicated by point D, BG of clothing and AI of food. The foreign country, however, would wish to consume the combination indicated by D^*, O^*H of clothing and O^*J of food. Clearly these plans are not mutually consistent. Desired world consumption of the (overvalued) clothing falls short of the available supply by GH; desired consumption of (undervalued) food exceeds supply by IJ.

We shall consider the relation of this disequilibrium to internal spending plans. The value of each country's aggregate planned transactions is equal to the value of its endowment bundle (E and E^*). The trouble lies solely in a price ratio that does not clear commodity markets. Suppose that transactions took place at this disequilibrium price ratio. These transactions could occur, as we explained in Chapter 4, if the sellers of exports in each country let their inventories vary when the quantities demanded in the marketplace are not expected. At terms of trade ED the home country's exporters expect to sell GC^* of clothing abroad, but in fact the foreign country will purchase only HC^*, and so inventories rise by GH. On the other hand, the home country's planned purchases of food exceed the supply by IJ, and the foreign country's inventories (not counted in their initial endowment bundle) fall by this amount. At price ratio ED^*D, the values of GH and of IJ are the same, and either one measures the trade deficit (which is the same as the balance-of-payments deficit) of the home country. For example, valuing imports in terms of exports, we would say that the home country's imports IF^* are worth GC^* of its export good, exceeding actual exports of HC^* by GH.

Devaluation could cure these difficulties by changing the exchange rate so that the price ratio becomes a slope connecting points E and Q. The home country's terms of trade deteriorate until external balance occurs. Income and expenditure plans become consistent, and internal balance is achieved as well. The overvaluation of the home country's goods is eliminated. The size of the necessary change in the exchange rate and in the terms of trade is determined by a pair of old friends from Chapter 3, the elasticities of the offer curves. There

[2] We explored this disturbance in Chapter 4; compare Figure 4.1.

we saw that the exchange market was stable if the sum of the home
and foreign offer-curve elasticities was greater than unity: $e + e^* > 1$.
Now the devaluation will improve the trade balance only if that
condition is fulfilled. The higher these elasticities, the smaller is the
devaluation needed to eliminate any disequilibrium.

Overspending   *See notes*

A feature of the external imbalance due to "overvaluation" is that
each country plans to spend exactly its income — in our model, its
initial endowment bundle. But we could also imagine an external
imbalance due to difficulties of an opposite sort. A trade deficit adds
to the expenditure, or absorption of goods and services, that a country
can attain during a period of time. A country could be "living beyond
its means" without overtaxing its endowment bundle if its expenditure plans were based not on its real income (i.e., the endowment
bundle) but on that plus the accustomed trade deficit. Such a deficit
can be built into expenditure plans because of the method by which
a country with a fixed exchange rate maintains the external value of
its currency. Thus, until its reserves are exhausted, a deficit country's
foreign-exchange authority can make planned overspending possible
by paying the equivalent amount of exchange each period.

Figure 19.2 illustrates such an imbalance. It is essentially the same
as Figure 19.1, with home and foreign endowment bundles measured
from origins O and O^* respectively. The endowment points again
coincide at E, E^*, but now we suppose that both countries are accustomed to a deficit in the home country's trade balance that regularly
transfers to it an amount of clothing equal to EG. (Shifting commodity
endowments from the foreign to the home country necessarily involves moving to the right or upward from point E.[3]) From point G,
the offer curves GQR and GQR^* show the quantities of goods that the
home and foreign countries respectively would be willing to trade at
various terms. The terms of trade and exchange rate corresponding
to GBQ thus represent a provisional equilibrium of exchange if we
ignore the overspending. There is not necessarily any overvaluation,
as in the previous case (Figure 19.1). But there is overspending measured by the built-in payments deficit of EG.

All this is quite mysterious without an explanation of how this
built-in deficit might occur, and what it means for internal balance.
Suppose that citizens of the home country have decided to decrease
their cash balances in order to increase their consumption by EG
(valued in clothing). The government, which we have supposed keeps
the price of clothing constant in domestic currency, does so by selling

---

[3] There is no special significance to measuring the built-in deficit in terms
of the home country's export good. If, instead, the deficit were equal to EB
of its imported good, the analysis would lead to the same conclusions. In general, a transfer of any combination of the two goods leading to a point on line
GB will have the same consequences.

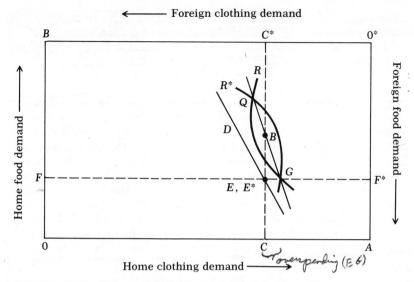

FIGURE 19.2 External Imbalance with Overspending,
and Effects of Devaluation

Overspending is reflected in net resource transfer to the
home country of *EG,* the trade deficit. To restore balance
spending must be cut by *EG;* devaluation is needed if *ED*
is flatter than *GBQ.*

its inventories. The foreign country is willing to donate an equal
quantity of clothing from its endowment bundle to rebuild the home
government's inventories. Although these institutional arrangements
sound bizarre, they differ from common practice under fixed exchange rates *only* in that governments hold foreign exchange and not
goods. The intergovernmental transfer of clothing, described here,
plays the same role as a decrease in official holdings of foreign exchange, which diverts inventories held abroad when a country has a
payments deficit. In our example, after a period of trading, expenditure at home exceeds income by the transfer *EG,* and in the foreign
country falls short of it by the same amount. The trade *deficit* is *EG*
because "commercial" trade from point *G* to consumption point *Q* is
balanced, taken by itself. Commodity markets are in equilibrium, but
cash balances of the home country's private sector are being decreased in order to inflate consumption.

Devaluation *may help* to cut overspending. The central point is the
overspending itself. If it were stopped, and the transfer of *EG* ex-
tinguished, would devaluation still be necessary? As overspending
of *EG* in the home country falls, we cut back our spending on both
our exportable clothing and our imported food. The cutback of imports

is governed by our marginal propensity to import, m. Conversely, the increase in expenditure abroad, once EG is no longer siphoned out of the foreign endowment bundle, increases our exports in a proportion governed by the foreign marginal propensity to import, m^*. If $m + m^*$ should add up to one, the cut in overspending would eliminate the deficit by itself, and no devaluation would be needed. If $m + m^* < 1$, however, our trade balance would improve by a smaller amount. Some devaluation would still be needed in order to restore external balance, as in the case described in Figure 19.1. We drew Figure 19.2 with line GBQ, the equilibrium terms of trade with overspending, steeper than ED, the equilibrium line with no overspending. This difference in slopes implies that the sum of marginal propensities is less than one, and devaluation will still be needed; but GBQ could be flatter, so that wiping out the transfer would require the home country to increase the value of its currency. In any case, if devaluation is called for, the elasticities of the offer curves come into play, just as in Figure 19.1. The more the sum of their elasticities exceeds one, the smaller is the required devaluation.

19.2 DEVALUATION, SPENDING, AND OVERSPENDING

Devaluation can apparently occur in the face of diverse economic disturbances. Overvaluation can result from inflation of prices at home, or deflation abroad. Overspending can reflect many disturbances in domestic or foreign income circuits that cause the home country's transactors to spend more than their incomes. We know from the simple models of Chapter 18 that devaluation can be coupled with a change in government spending (or some other instrument) to yield full financial balance. But we also know that countries often fail to manage such effective coordination. Devaluation thus frequently occurs when internal balance is not tightly managed.

This internal imbalance raises two problems for the analysis of devaluation. First, how does devaluation affect aggregate spending? Second, will its effect on spending impair or amplify its effect on external balance — the immediate target?

Devaluation and Income

Suppose that devaluation occurs in a country whose economy is described by the rigid-prices model of Chapter 17, with some unemployment and thus room for expansion of output. What happens to income, and how does it affect the size of the devaluation needed? This question was implicitly answered in Chapter 18, when we considered Figure 18.1. Let us make that analysis explicit, and use it in answering the second of the two questions just raised.

Figure 19.3, which closely resembles Figures 17.2 and 17.3, allows us to isolate the effect of devaluation on income. Starting once again from the condition for internal balance, we shall construct the trade-

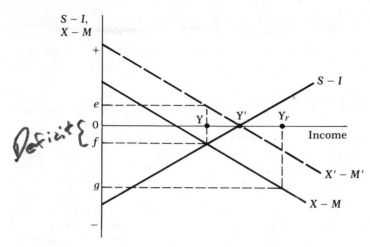

FIGURE 19.3   Effect of Devaluation on Income

> Devaluation shifts trade-balance schedule to $X'-M'$, raising
> income from Y to Y'. Final improvement in the trade bal-
> ance, Of, is less than the improvement that would have
> occurred without the expansion of income (ef).

balance schedule ($X - M$) and what we shall call the hoarding schedule ($S - I$). Intersection of these two schedules indicates an equilibrium level of income Y. This equilibrium corresponds, however, to a
deficit of Of in the balance of trade. We have thus depicted a case of
overspending, for by definition the excess of investment over saving
equals the excess of total expenditure over income.[4]

If the conditions for exchange stability are met, we know that a
devaluation improves the balance of trade. Exports (valued in domestic currency) rise and imports tend to fall. Both changes raise
the trade-balance schedule to a position such as $X' - M'$ in Figure
19.3, and the equilibrium level of income must rise. In fact, the
diagram illustrates a devaluation correctly calculated to restore
external balance *after* this induced increase in income. In the rigid-
prices model of Chapter 17, devaluation leads to an exogenous
injection into the income circuit of ef, the amount by which the
trade balance would improve *if no income expansion took place*. The

---

[4] See Chapter 4 (section 4.3) and Chapter 17 (section 17.1). You may wonder
how pure overvaluation could be shown in Figure 19.3. It results when production and spending plans are based on disequilibrium prices; the deficit
country spends more than its income, because of unplanned inventory investment. Figure 19.3 would describe this case if the functions indicated actual
or ex post rather than planned levels of expenditure. But we normally interpret
the $X - M$ and $S - I$ functions as describing planned behavior, and hence the
deficit of Of is more directly interpreted as the result of overspending.

increase of income from Y to Y' displays the multiplier effect of this injection.

Notice the implication of Figure 19.3 for the size of the devaluation. The change in the exchange rate was calculated to improve the trade balance by ef. That is larger than the devaluation indicated by the actual trade deficit, Of, because the higher level of income raises imports by Oe. But this increase of income raises saving by Of, and thus eliminates the overspending associated with the deficit.

Another important feature of this new equilibrium at Y' is that the internal balance after devaluation does not entail full employment (Y_F). "Overspending" refers to the conditions for external balance and *not* to the aggregate demand needed for full employment. As we learned in Chapter 18, restoring full employment as well as external balance would require a larger devaluation shifting the trade-balance schedule upward by Og, coupled with an increase in government spending (or investment) to make the $S - I$ schedule pass through Y_F.[5]

Devaluation and Planned Expenditure

The effect of devaluation on income, and the effect of their interaction on the necessary size of the devaluation, reveal no connections in the expenditure circuit that we have not already studied. However, devaluation might change planned saving — shifting the hoarding $(S - I)$ schedule of Figure 19.3 up or down, as contrasted to the movement along a stationary schedule already witnessed. These linkages depend on diverse circumstances — some appropriate to the rigid-prices model, some to flexible prices, some to both. Nonetheless, Figure 19.3 may be used to interpret each.

The possible shifts of the hoarding function are simple to outline. Consider Figure 19.4, which reproduces the principal features of Figure 19.3, including the devaluation-induced shift of the trade-balance function to $X' - M'$. Suppose that the devaluation somehow causes people to reduce their spending, or increase their saving *from any given level of income.* This increase implies an upward shift of the hoarding function to a position like $(S - I)'$. The devaluation then needed to repair an external deficit is smaller than if $S - I$ stays put. The associated increase in income is also smaller. Indeed, if the shift to $(S - I)'$ is as large as the one illustrated, income does not rise at all; a devaluation that improves the trade balance by Of and shifts the hoarding function to $(S - I)'$ leaves income unchanged at Y. On the other hand, suppose the devaluation causes people to increase their spending from any given level of income. The hoarding

---

[5] In terms of Figure 18.1, the initial situation shown in Figure 19.3 is described by a point like a, from which both devaluation and an increase in government expenditure are needed to restore external balance.

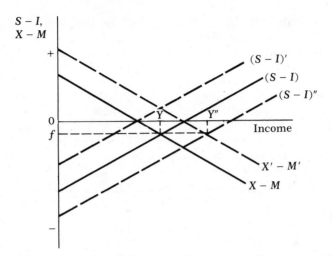

FIGURE 19.4 Effects of Induced Shifts in Hoarding Function
Following Devaluation

Devaluation shifts the trade-balance function to X'-M'.
It might induce an increase in saving (hoarding function
becomes $(S - I)'$) or a reduction in saving $(S - I)''$ from any
given level of income.

function shifts downward to $(S - I)''$. The increase in income associated with devaluation is enlarged. The effect of the devaluation on the
trade balance shrinks, however; should the hoarding function shift
as far as $(S - I)''$, the initial trade deficit of Of would not be reduced
at all.

With these possibilities outlined, let us consider the forces that
might induce shifts of net saving like $(S - I)'$ or $(S - I)''$. They all have
to do with changes in prices associated with devaluation. We have so
far neglected the domestic implications of the deterioration of the
terms of trade that results from devaluation. We are measuring income (on the horizontal axes of our Figures 19.3 and 19.4) in terms of
the country's exportable good.[6] The terms of trade effect of a devaluation reduces the purchasing power of any given income, and we must
allow for the economy's reaction to that impairment.

Terms of Trade and Saving. The most direct effect of the worsened
terms of trade should be on the portion of their incomes that households save after devaluation. At any given level of income, as measured in the export good (clothing), they can buy fewer exportables
and imports than they could before the devaluation. They may adapt

[6] In order to measure income in exportable goods, we have made the devaluing economy completely specialized.

to these straitened circumstances partly by reducing their saving. This reduction means a shift to $(S - I)''$ in Figure 19.4.[7]

Terms of Trade and Assets. The worsened terms of trade affect not only the purchasing power of current domestic output but also any wealth or assets valued in terms of exportable goods. Examples would be balances of domestic currency and securities whose yields are valued in domestic prices. As we noticed in section 16.5, consumption is thought to depend on wealth as well as income. When people's wealth is reduced, they curtail consumption in order to restore the desired relation of wealth to current expenditure. Saving out of any current income would rise, shifting the hoarding function toward $(S - I)'$.[8] This shift will not occur if people hold a lot of assets valued in terms of foreign goods, i.e., if the country is a heavy foreign investor.

Expectations. We have supposed that people always expect prevailing prices to continue into the foreseeable future. Before a devaluation they do not expect the price of imports to rise; afterward, they do not expect it to rise further. Yet expectations can affect the economy in many ways when devaluation has occurred, or is in the wind. When people expect devaluation, they buy things whose prices may rise. Foreign currency is certainly one of these — hence the well-known tendency for wealth to flee a currency when its devaluation is expected. But a flight to foreign goods can gain the same sort of advantage. Hence, when a country's external deficit raises fears of devaluation, savings may be reduced and real expenditure stepped up for speculative purchases of imports. Devaluation in this case may raise saving — a shift to $(S - I)'$ — by removing this incentive for speculation. On the other hand, if a timorous government devalues by too little and fails to remove the deficit, it could conceivably fuel the speculative fires and witness a decline in saving to $(S - I)''$ following devaluation.

Inflation. As people can act on the fear of devaluation, so can its occurrence change their expectations about future inflation. The public may get used to steadily rising prices and reduce their real rate of saving (if they have trouble finding inflation-proof forms in which to hold their wealth). They also try to reduce their cash balances, because holdings of cash depreciate although holdings of

---

[7] This substitution between saving and imports was emphasized by S. Laursen and L. A. Metzler, "Flexible Exchange Rates and the Theory of Employment," *Review of Economics and Statistics*, 32 (November 1950): 281–99.

[8] This is the mechanism that eliminates external imbalance in the flexible-prices model. When a trade deficit occurs, as we showed in section 16.3, cash balances are drained from the economy. This loss reduces spending until the deficit is gone. Devaluation, in this context, increases the domestic-currency prices of traded goods and hence the total cash outlay needed for the previous volume of consumer goods. This jolt further decreases the adequacy of cash balances and should cause transactors to cut their spending more.

Devat.

goods may not. Both forces can, at least temporarily, drive down the propensity to save. Devaluation must often be resorted to in such circumstances. If coupled with a financial stabilization that curbs the growth of domestic demand, it might assist in reducing over-spending — $(S - I)'$. But devaluation without any change in domestic spending patterns may be ineffective or may even reduce the saving rate — $(S - I)''$.

Evidence on Devaluation and Expenditure

Studies of devaluations confirm some of these propositions about devaluation, saving and expenditure. J. J. Polak and T. C. Chang studied a number of devaluations that occurred between World Wars I and II. They measured the change in the export prices of countries that devalued, in terms of *foreign* currency, and compared them to the simultaneous movements of export prices of countries with fixed exchange rates. If a devaluing country's exports are some-what specialized and lack close competitors, its terms of trade ought to worsen, as in our two-country model, and its export prices fall in terms of foreign exchange. Indeed, on our previous assumption that export prices are stabilized in *domestic* currency, they should fall by the full amount of the devaluation. (Perhaps not quite this much, if the exports embody imported raw materials and their foreign-cur-rency prices stay unchanged.) Polak and Chang found that countries with unemployment at home gained very large price advantages when they devalued. But countries with full employment and infla-tion won little or no price advantage. Devaluation failed to cut over-spending and in the end brought little improvement in their external balances.[9]

We also suggested above that devaluation itself, in the context of chronic inflation or overspending, might reduce saving and thus fail to promote either internal or external balance. This outcome is often feared by European policy-makers who contemplate devalua-tion, because interwar episodes seemed to justify the fear that one devaluation portends another, and the public memory can be long.[10] On the other hand, countries have occasionally acted with apparent success against inflationary overspending and used devaluation to mop up the residual overvaluation.[11]

[9] See J. J. Polak and T. C. Chang, "Effect of Exchange Depreciation on a Country's Export Price Level," *IMF Staff Papers*, 1 (February 1950): 49–70.

[10] Polak and Chang (*ibid.*) studied the results of four successive devalua-tions of the French franc during the 1920's and found that the advantage gained in export prices grew less each time. Apparently the French public was learning.

[11] For a case of success in combining devaluation with internal stabiliza-tion and other policy reforms, see Andreas S. Gerakis and Haskell P. Wald, "Economic Stabilization and Progress in Greece, 1953–61," *IMF Staff Papers*, 11 (March 1964): 125–47.

19.3 DEVALUATION AND OTHER POLICIES *(Expenditure − Switching)* FOR FINANCIAL BALANCE

We must relate section 19.2 to the more general problem of pursuing financial balance (outlined in Chapter 18). A common cause of an external deficit (and hence devaluation) is overspending, i.e.,

$$X - M = S - I < 0.$$

Overspending are thru deval.

A correctly calculated devaluation can eliminate the deficit (and the overspending). But the new internal and external balance might not occur at full employment. Attaining full-employment balance requires an additional policy instrument, such as fiscal policy.

Our outline of the possible side effects of devaluation on expenditure is thus important for either of two reasons. If there is no coordinated policy for attaining internal balance at full employment, the side effects tell us where devaluation leaves income and employment relative to this target. If another instrument is in use for attaining full-employment balance, they help us calculate the appropriate size of the devaluation as well as the fiscal (or other) policy shift needed to bring about full financial balance.

Expenditure Switching Policies

Other policy instruments are commonly used for achieving external balance, and in this section we shall analyze them in the same way. The basic function of devaluation is to cause people (at home and abroad) to switch their expenditure from foreign goods to domestic goods. Other policies for switching expenditure include import tariffs and nontariff restrictions, import deposit schemes, and restrictions on capital outflows. We shall compare the effects of each to those of devaluation. The comparison allows us to judge their performance for altering domestic expenditure. We will also notice their potential effects on economic efficiency, drawing on the analysis in Part 3.

Figure 19.5 illustrates an issue arising when we must choose an expenditure-switching policy. It closely resembles Figure 19.4. An initial deficit of Of can be remedied by either of two general classes of policies. Policies of type P' shift the trade-balance schedule to position $(X - M)'$; they also increase domestic saving (or reduce investment) at any given level of income, and hence shift the hoarding schedule upward to $(S - I)'$. A P'-type policy thus restores income equilibrium and external balance at Y'. Policies of type P'' shift the trade-balance schedule to $(X - M)''$; this greater shift is necessary, because P'' cuts saving or increases exogenous domestic spending and shifts the hoarding schedule downward to $(S - I)''$. Policy P'' thus restores income equilibrium and external balance at Y''.

Suppose that our only preference regarding policies P' and P'' was for the one that brought us nearer to full employment. The choice must then depend on the position of Y_F in relation to Y' and Y''. If it lies to the left of Y', so that either P' or P'' would generate overfull

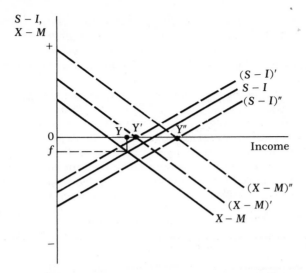

FIGURE 19.5 Expenditure-switching Policies with Positive and Negative Effects on Domestic Expenditure

Initial external imbalance is *Of.* Policy of type *P'*, which raises domestic saving, yields full balance at *Y'*. Policy of type *P''*, which cuts domestic saving, yields full balance at *Y''*.

employment and inflationary pressure, we prefer *P'*. If it lies to the right of *Y''*, so that neither policy eliminates unemployment, we prefer *P''*. If it falls between *Y'* and *Y''*, the choice depends on the closeness of the miss and our feelings about the respective evils of unemployment and inflationary pressure. We will now identify some expenditure-switching policies in terms of the *P'* and *P''* prototypes. We know from section 19.2 that this exercise cannot be entirely clean-cut; we found that the possible shifts of the hoarding function following a devaluation could run to either the *P'* or the *P''* prototype. Nonetheless, other policies bear systematic relations to devaluation in their effects on the hoarding function. The policies can thus be compared.

Import Tariffs and Export Subsidies. We saw in Part 3 the effects of tariffs that change the terms of trade on the allocation of resources and the level of real income. A tariff's effect on expenditure, like that of devaluation, makes the taxed imports more expensive and switches expenditure toward home goods. Likewise, an export subsidy would shift the supply curve of our exports downward and, making them cheaper to foreigners, shift expenditure in foreign countries toward the goods that we produce. Thus, both export subsidies and import duties cause switches of expenditure resembling those due to a devaluation. They also act as expenditure-increasing policies in the home market. During the 1930's, tariffs and related trade-control devices gained the epithet of "beggar-thy-neighbor" policies when used to increase employment, rather than to curb imports or raise exports; the relation of such policies to the open-economy multiplier was considered in Chapter 17.

However, tariffs and subsidies can, in principle, affect prices in the same way as a devaluation. Suppose we wanted a ten percent devaluation but were somehow forbidden to undertake it directly. A ten percent devaluation would in the first instance mark up the domestic prices of all imported goods by ten percent. Prices could be raised instead by a ten percent ad valorem duty on all imports. Likewise, the devaluation would discount the foreign prices of all our exports by ten percent. A ten percent ad valorem subsidy on all of our exports would bring the same result.

> Thus a devaluation of x percent is equivalent to an x percent tariff on all imports coupled with an x percent subsidy on all exports.[12]

Furthermore, the tariff-cum-subsidy has no adverse effects on the allocation of resources.

Quantitative Restrictions on Imports. We saw in Chapter 14 that we can equate the static effect of a quantitative restriction on an imported good to that of a tariff large enough to induce the same cut in imports. The proposition also applies here, and it identifies quantitative restrictions as another expenditure-switching device that, like import duties, affects only domestic consumers of the goods subject to the restrictions. Quantitative restrictions (QRs) may spill over to affect domestic expenditure differently than tariffs, however. This difference is important, because the General Agreement on Tariffs and Trade registers a preference for quantitative restrictions over tariffs when one is employed to deal with external imbalance.[13] And governments seem to prefer QRs when caught with a sudden external deficit in conditions of full employment or inflation.

The difference is that import duties raise tariff revenue which, if the government does not immediately spend it, leaks out of the income circuit and reduces the money supply. Tariffs are thus an expenditure-switching policy with a heavy clout for expenditure reduction. An increase in government saving raises the hoarding function of Figure 19.5 to a position like $(S - I)'$. QRs' effects may differ, however, if the quotas are doled out to domestic importers, or if

---

[12] The parallel extends to the monetary effect of devaluation and tariff-cum-subsidy. If both changes together just restore external balance, the tariff revenues collected will exactly equal the export subsidy bill, so there is no net fiscal leakage or injection.

[13] The political reasoning behind this provision of Article XII was that tariffs once imposed on this pretext would become permanent, whereas a country would more readily dismantle emergency QRs. For further discussion of the General Agreement see section 14.3.

imperfectly competitive foreign exporters will not raise their home-
currency prices (for fear of long-run adverse effects on their sales).
If the importers get the windfall profits permitted by the QRs, they
presumably spend them and thus recycle the purchasing power into
the domestic income circuit. If exporters simply fail to take advantage
of the chance to shove up their prices, the windfalls are handed over
to domestic consumers lucky enough to secure the rationed imports,
and frustrated buyers presumably channel their purchasing power
elsewhere in the domestic income circuit. QRs thus may perform an
expenditure-switching function, but they are more likely to increase
expenditure than are either import duties or devaluation. They are
thus a P''-type of policy in comparison to these alternatives.

3.)   *Advance Deposits on Imports.* A relatively new expenditure-
switching device is the requirement that the importer make an
advance deposit with the central bank of a sum related to the value of
the goods he wishes to import. Import-deposit requirements have been
imposed by a number of less-developed countries, especially in Latin
America, and have also been used in the industrial world. They are
expenditure-switching devices with strong expenditure-reducing
potential. The importer must leave his deposit with the central bank
for a specific period, such as six months, and he receives no interest
on it. The restrictive effect thus lies in the interest cost to the importer of having his funds tied up for this period. If all imports are
subject to the same deposit requirement, the system acts as a uniform
ad valorem special duty on imports. If the deposit were refunded only
after six months, the deposit equal to the value of the imports, and the
importers' cost of borrowing ten percent per annum, the deposit requirement would be equivalent to a five percent surcharge on imports.

This device is interesting theoretically because its expenditure-
reducing effect comes via monetary conditions. We have seen how the
money supply is ordinarily contracted by the amount of the *net
deficit* in the balance of payments. Import deposits, on the other hand,
reduce the money supply by the *gross* value of imports entering the
country during the period (e.g., six months) for which the deposits are
held. That is, when the scheme goes into effect, money in the hands of
the public (and the commercial banking system) is progressively
siphoned off so long as importers place deposits with the central
bank. When the first deposits are refunded, no more restriction takes
place, but the money supply in circulation remains below what it
would otherwise be as long as the scheme stays in effect. A deposit
requirement thus reduces cash holdings, drives up interest rates, and
reduces expenditure. A deposit scheme with expenditure-switching
power equal to a five percent tariff would reduce expenditure significantly, rather than increase it. Thus it is clearly a P' policy.

Import deposits are particularly attractive to less-developed countries where inflation may be politically endemic and control of the
money supply not well developed institutionally. They are handy

administratively, because both the duration of the deposit and its size relative to the value of the goods imported can be varied freely. They can also be varied between products to achieve the effects of different rates of duty. In Chile at one time the ratio of the size of the deposit to the value of the goods varied from 5 percent to 5,000 percent, depending on the "essentiality" of the product.[14]

Restrictions on Capital Exports. In the past decade a highly popular balance-of-payments policy among the industrial countries has been to restrict capital exports when in external deficit or to restrict capital imports when in external surplus. Capital flows inject a new dimension to our analysis, because they have been neglected so far in this chapter. From the principles of balance-of-payments accounting in Chapter 5, we know how to define external balance when a capital outflow occurs. The current-account balance must equal not zero but the capital outflow. In the terms of our illustrations, for external balance and income equilibrium we need:

$$X - M = S - I = \text{capital outflow}.$$

The economy depicted in Figure 19.6 would enjoy external balance and equilibrium in income flows (not necessarily at full employment, however) if capital outflows of Oc offset a current-account surplus and domestic underspending of the same amount. People are spending less than their incomes, but they use the excess to purchase foreign securities; foreigners spend the proceeds from the sale of securities, buying our net exports in an amount equal to domestic underspending.

Conversely, equilibrium could exist with capital inflows if an import surplus of the same amount has developed. This case relates directly to Figure 19.2, in which we first explained overspending. There we found that trade would be in balance except for the regular transfer of a quantity of clothing EG from the foreign to the home country. Yet if foreigners were simultaneously purchasing the home country's securities in amount EG, Figure 19.2 would depict external balance with an ongoing capital inflow.

Our concern here, however, is with the effect of altering financial capital flows, say, by a tax on the income that citizens receive from their foreign securities. Suppose that Figure 19.6 illustrates not an initial equilibrium but a deficit due to capital outflows in excess of the current-account surplus. Make the capital outflow (measured for convenience on the vertical axis) Ok, the export surplus Oc as before. An external deficit of $Ok - Oc$ exists. The government restricts the capital outflow in order to restore external balance. Let us suppose that capital exports are forbidden, so that Ok goes to zero. As we shall discuss in Part 5, the trade-balance and the hoarding

[14] For information on these controls see Jorge Marshall, "Advance Deposits on Imports," *IMF Staff Papers,* 6 (April 1958): 239–58; and E. A. Birnbaum and M. S. Qureshi, "Advance Deposit Requirements for Imports," *IMF Staff Papers,* 8 (November 1960): 115–25.

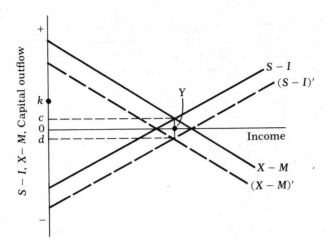

FIGURE 19.6   Effect of Tax on Capital Outflows

Eliminating capital outflow *Ok* shifts trade-balance schedule to $(X - M)'$ and hoarding schedule to $(S - I)'$. External balance improves only if $Od < ck$.

schedules are apt to be shifted by this change. Foreigners, deprived of the inflow of purchasing power, reduce their expenditure on all goods, including exports of the home country. A reduction in exports shifts the trade-balance schedule downward, perhaps to $(X - M)'$ in Figure 19.6. The domestic net savings, now blocked from transfer abroad, are apt to increase expenditure at home. We can think of this increased expenditure as increased investment, indicating a downward shift of the hoarding function, perhaps to $(S - I)'$. As Figure 19.6 shows, these shifts can change income in either direction; in the diagram it remains unchanged. The shifts definitely deteriorate the trade balance, by *cd*. The balance of payments has been improved by eliminating the capital outflow of *Ok* and worsened by the induced deterioration of the trade balance *cd*. In Figure 19.6 the net result is an improvement in the balance of payments; the new deficit, *Od*, is smaller than the old deficit, *ck*. But the new deficit need not be smaller; it could exceed *ck*.   *Od may be > ck*

We conclude that the control of capital outflows differs quite distinctly from the other policies we have examined. It may not increase income: it is more like the P' than the P'' model. More to the point, we cannot depend on it to improve external balance unless we have measured carefully the effect of a reduced transfer of purchasing power upon the trade-balance and hoarding schedules.   *Summary*

Deflation. For completeness, our list of policies should include reduction of domestic expenditure. We know from Chapter 18 that domestic deflation to attain external balance is a poor choice of policy if unemployment increases. Nonetheless, nations occasionally feel that they must resort to this expedient. In terms of Figure 19.5, a

(handwritten note at top: "Reflat. vfp: 6↓")

(handwritten margin note: "not usually exercised")

"deflationary policy" would decrease investment (or government spending) and thus shift the hoarding function upward until it intersects the trade-balance schedule $(X - M)$ on the horizontal axis. External balance is restored, but at the cost of unemployment unless full-employment income is less than Y.

Deflation is not an expenditure-switching policy. It merely reduces total expenditure until imports have fallen by the amount of the deficit, Of. Thus it differs fundamentally from the expenditure-switching policies previously listed, effecting no upward shift in $X - M$ and the maximum upward shift in $S - I$. It would make sense only in the context of flexible prices, or (with rigid prices) if the overspending that causes the external deficit just equals the planned excess of total expenditure over full-employment output.

19.4 THE UNITED STATES PAYMENTS DEFICIT: A REVIEW

The United States began running a serious balance-of-payments deficit in 1958. In 1971 its actions led to a 7.5 percent devaluation of the dollar (allowing for revaluations of other currencies). In between, many different remedies were tried, without substantial success. No general history of the problem can be provided here, only an outline of the major policies that have been used. Against the background of this chapter and Chapter 18 we can then suggest some judgments about these policies.[15]

The statistical record of the period appeared in Table 5.1 (p. 89). We shall mention the causes of the deficit only for a word of caution. During its early years, single-cause explanations abounded: the United States had too much inflation; other countries had devalued too much in 1949; American business was investing too much abroad; the United States government was giving away too much foreign aid. Such explanations by and large were disguised policy prescriptions rather than behavioral analysis. There ultimately emerged a general agreement that the deficit resulted from many broad historical forces, and, more important, that in any case its putative causes need not be connected to the appropriate remedies. For example, even if the deficit was partly due to increased capital exports, the fact alone did not prove capital exports should be reduced.

Monetary Controls

General macroeconomic policies were sometimes used for dealing with the deficit in its early years. During 1958–1960 the Eisenhower

[15] Although much has been written on this experience, the more extensive studies cover only the early years of the 1960's. See Henry G. Aubrey, *The Dollar in World Affairs* (New York: Praeger, 1964); Alvin H. Hansen, *The Dollar and the International Monetary System* (New York: McGraw-Hill, 1965); and Gottfried Haberler and Thomas D. Willett, *U.S. Balance of Payments Policies and International Monetary Reform* (Washington: American Enterprise Institute, 1968).

administration employed general deflationary fiscal and (especially) monetary policies. Selected more as checks on domestic inflation than from concern with the balance of payments *per se*, these policies nonetheless probably deserve some credit for the smaller deficit observed in the early 1960's. They imposed a high real cost in the form of increased unemployment, however. General deflationary policies can always be used to improve the balance of payments, but they can be economically costly when unemployment is created.

Some analysts urged the United States to follow the prescription for financial balance that we explored in Chapter 18. The country suffered both a deficit and unemployment. From Figure 18.1 we know that devaluation would have helped move the economy toward both goals. But it was ruled out then and for many years later as being "too drastic" or "a blow to American prestige," or (a stronger argument) as potentially ruinous to the world's structure of international reserves. With devaluation excluded, it was urged instead that fiscal and monetary policy be played against each other for internal and external balance in the way suggested in Figure 18.2. The combination of unemployment and a deficit indicated a restrictive monetary policy and an easy fiscal policy; interest-sensitive capital inflows should relieve the deficit, while fiscal ease combated unemployment.

This recipe never received general favor, however, because of its adverse implications for yet another policy objective — economic growth. Faster growth would result from low interest rates, whereas external balance called for high rates. There were thus too many policy goals (growth, full employment, external balance) for the usable policy instruments (fiscal and monetary). As a result, in 1961 the United States began an experiment called "Operation Twist" designed to generate the necessary third policy. High interest rates, demanded for external balance, were thought to affect mainly short-term international capital flows. The long-term interest rate, however, affects growth. Why not use monetary policy (and the management of the national debt) to raise short-term interest rates while keeping long-term rates low? This "twist" in the term-structure of interest rates was tried. It met with only limited success, for at least two reasons: domestic lenders and borrowers move freely enough between long-term and short-term securities that no substantial twist of the structure of market interest rates proved possible; although short-term capital was more mobile internationally than long-term capital, the latter was rapidly growing more accustomed to crossing national boundaries.

Taxes and Restrictions on Capital Flows

When the deficit survived this modest effort to deal with it through general policy instruments, attention switched to more specific controls. Many of these attacked international private capital flows. In 1963 the Interest Equalization Tax was imposed on United States purchases of foreign long-term securities. It was designed to wipe out the profit margin on foreign lending that resulted from long-term interest rates being lower in the United States than in other industrial countries. The less-developed countries were exempted, as was Canada because of her traditional heavy use of the American capital market.

The Interest Equalization Tax appeared to reduce capital exports, at least in the form of securities subject to the tax. In part, however, these capital outflows were simply transmuted into other forms. An increase began quite promptly in foreign lending via long-term bank loans. Later informal controls were imposed on these bank loans as well. Similar controls spread over direct investments abroad by American corporations. These at first affected only about 550 large nonfinancial corporations. Later they were extended to smaller corporations and converted into curbs on the net outflow of capital in all forms through these corporations.

These capital-flow controls raise several questions. First, did they actually reduce outflows of financial capital? Table 5.1 fails to give us an obvious yes answer. As the controls were elaborated and extended, borrowers and lenders kept finding alternative ways to accomplish the same transaction plans. Nonetheless, let us suppose that the controls did have a deterrent effect. Did they then improve external balance? As we suggested in section 19.3, the answer could be negative. They certainly could worsen the current-account balance, conceivably enough to leave the overall balance no better off than before. The evidence on this point also is unclear. The current account did worsen during the 1960's, but this decline reflected many other forces such as the domestic boom that began in 1965. Detailed studies suggest that controls on direct investment generated offsets in the current account large enough to yield little net improvement in the balance of payments.

Suppose the statistical record convinced us that capital-flow controls improved the overall balance of payments. Would they then efficiently deal with the problem? We generally expect controls on international capital flows to impose some cost in real economic welfare. When capital is kept at home to earn a lower rate of return than it could abroad, this difference between its domestic and its potential foreign earnings provides a rough estimate of the welfare cost involved. It is not clear that any balance-of-payments improvement from restricting capital outflows was worth its welfare cost.

Restrictions on Government Expenditure Abroad

The United States government also tried to restrict its own payments abroad. One way was expanding a previous "Buy American" policy in government procurement, so that domestic suppliers of defense goods could win orders even when their prices exceeded those of foreign suppliers by fifty percent. By this rule the government essentially imposed an ad valorem duty of fifty percent on its own imports of defense goods. We noticed in section 19.3 that a *uniform* import tariff and export subsidy could efficiently deal with an external deficit. *Nonuniform* tariffs such as this one, however, impose the welfare costs identified in Part 3.

The government also implicitly taxed foreign aid by "tying" the funds to the purchases of United States goods and services. Such a requirement reduces the real value of a dollar's worth of aid to the recipient. A dollar is worth less to you if you must spend it in a given store, than if you can shop at stores that might offer some goods at lower prices. The tying of foreign aid thus probably did switch some expenditure toward United States goods and services, but it reduced the real value of aid dollars. It extracted an efficiency cost similar to the "Buy American" policy or any other tax on trade lacking specific justification.

A review of the United States' management of its external deficit suggests that the policies used up to 1971, if they were effective at all, incurred a significant welfare cost. This cost took the form of either higher unemployment than would otherwise have prevailed, or lower real income due to controls that distorted international transactions. Devaluation was finally brought about through a complex process begun in August 1971. Most economists felt that the devaluation would end the deficit at last. Does devaluation impose real costs? It does, because the terms of trade are turned against the United States (as shown in Figure 19.1). But the cost should nonetheless fall short of those imposed by other policies — if they had been pushed far enough to wipe out the deficit. Creating unemployment to cure the deficit means throwing output away entirely, which is worse than selling it at a slightly lower price. Imposing special taxes and restrictions turns the terms of trade against *some* American outputs (or factor services) more than against others. Besides a terms of trade cost for the country as a whole, these special restrictions imposed an extra burden by distorting the prices of American outputs relative to one another. It is hard to avoid concluding that devaluation was the least costly remedy, and should have been used earlier.

As a wild alternative, could the United States have run a deficit forever? After all, for more than a decade it purchased more abroad than it sold.[16] This deficit forced it to borrow continually abroad, its debts measured by the dollar hoards accumulating in the international reserves of foreign countries. In the next chapter we shall consider international reserves as a device to allow temporary overspending.

19.5 SUMMARY

This chapter studied devaluation and related policies for external balance when internal balance need not prevail. Devaluation turns

---

[16] We are counting purchases and sales of securities, as well as of goods and services.

the terms of trade against the devaluing country. We can distinguish between external deficits due to overvaluation (where the only distortion is inappropriate relative prices) and those due to overspending (where an excess of expenditure over income has become built into people's transaction plans). Devaluation corrects an overvaluation disturbance directly, but its aptness for overspending depends on what happens to the overspending.

Actually, devaluation itself is apt to alter the level of spending relative to income. In the rigid-prices model (Chapter 17), it raises net exports and thus provides an injection into the income stream. Domestic income and expenditure rise via the multiplier process, but expenditure rises less due to increased saving. A correctly calculated devaluation can restore external balance after this multiplier process works itself out, although the devaluation must be greater than if income failed to increase. In addition to this multiplier effect, devaluation can also alter real income by shifting the amount that people save (or spend) at any level of income. This effect works in various ways through the effects of devaluation on prices, or on expectations about prices.

Devaluation moves expenditure (home and foreign) toward the goods of the devaluing country. Nations also employ other expenditure-switching policies, which can be compared to devaluation on the basis of their likelihood of raising income and employment. A uniform ten percent export subsidy and import tariff would in fact have the same effect as devaluation on both external and internal balance. Quantitative restrictions having the same incidence would probably raise expenditure by a larger amount. Requiring that importers place no-interest deposits with the central bank, on the other hand, would be strongly deflationary. (Any of these trade controls impose real costs on the economy if their incidence is not uniform on all goods.) Restrictions on capital exports may not improve overall external balance. If they succeed, they increase income and employment by less than a devaluation that also attains external balance. Finally, external balance can be restored purely by deflating expenditure (which involves no switching of expenditure, if prices are rigid). Income and employment must fall in this case.

The United States deficit since 1958 provides a case study in the application of policies such as these. During the years 1958–1963 general instruments of fiscal and monetary policy were applied, but insufficiently to attain external and internal balance along the lines suggested in Chapter 18. Heavy reliance was then made on the restriction of international capital flows and of expenditure abroad by the United States government. These policies entailed some real costs. The devaluation finally undertaken in 1971 imposes the real cost of worsened terms of trade, but this cost should be less than those of other possible remedies that either create unemployment or selectively worsen the terms of trade for some transactions.

SUGGESTIONS FOR FURTHER READING

Cooper, Richard N. "The Balance of Payments," *Britain's Economic Prospects,* ed. R. E. Caves. Washington: Brookings Institution, 1968, chap. 4. Case study of Britain in the 1960's.

Fieleke, Norman S. *The Welfare Effects of Controls over Capital Exports from the United States.* Essays in International Finance, No. 82. Princeton: International Finance Section, Princeton University, 1971. Welfare costs vs. balance-of-payments gains in controlling capital flows.

Haberler, G., "The Market for Foreign Exchange and the Stability of the Balance of Payments: a Theoretical Analysis," *International Finance,* ed. Richard N. Cooper. Harmondsworth, England, and Baltimore: Penguin, 1969, chap. 5. A partial-equilibrium approach to devaluation more traditional than that presented in this volume.

Hansen, Alvin H. *The Dollar and the International Monetary System.* New York: McGraw-Hill, 1965. Early years of the United States payments deficit.

Johnson, Harry G. "Towards a General Theory of the Balance of Payments," *International Finance,* ed. Richard N. Cooper, chap. 11. Presents a classification of policies for internal and external balance similar to that used in this volume.

Polak, J. J., and T. C. Chang. "Effect of Exchange Depreciation on a Country's Export Price Level," *IMF Staff Papers,* 1 (February 1950): 49–70. Study of price effects of some actual devaluations.

Tew, Brian. "The Use of Restrictions to Suppress External Deficits," *Manchester School,* 28 (September 1960): 243–62. Problems with use of trade controls to suppress monetary imbalance.

Supplement to Chapter 19: Alternative Models of Devaluation

In Chapter 19 we assumed that currency devaluation was equivalent to a change in the terms of trade. This assumption was possible because we also assumed that each country pursued a monetary policy geared to stabilizing the own-currency price of its export commodity. For some cases this assumption is not appropriate. A small country cannot do much to affect the terms of trade of commodities that bulk large in trade flows of other countries. And yet small countries have been known to alter their exchange rates. A different theory must explain such a devaluation. We shall sketch this theory out first.

THE SMALL-COUNTRY CASE: DEVALUATION AND NONTRADED COMMODITIES

Assume that in addition to imported and exported commodities, a country produces commodities that are consumed only at home and not obtainable from abroad. These are *nontraded* commodities — goods and services (such as haircuts, housing, and most retail services) that by their very nature, or the high natural costs of transport, are precluded from entering into international trade. If the country is too small to affect the world prices of its imports and exports, as we assume, the terms of trade remain insensitive to any policy changes undertaken at home. But there is a relative price that can be altered, the relationship between the price of nontraded commodities, on the one hand, and traded commodities, on the other.

A diagrammatic presentation in two dimensions is made possible by the fact that with the world price of importables and exportables given, these two classes of commodities can be lumped together into one class: the class of tradeable commodities. Of course with changes in incomes and/or changes in the price of nontraded goods, the composition of "the" traded commodity can easily change — e.g., a rise in income may cause local consumption of importables to rise by more than exportables. But we can neglect these changes and concentrate instead on the bundle of traded commodities, the relative price of whose separate ingredients is locked by the given terms of trade.

Figure 19.S.1 illustrates a bowed-out transformation schedule, TT', between traded goods and nontraded goods.[1] It also illustrates a set of indifference curves for these two classes of commodities. The initial *balanced trade* situation is shown by point A and the price of nontraded goods (relative to traded goods) by the slope of line 1. Quantity OE of the nontraded good is produced and consumed. Distance AE represents both some mixture of production of exportables and importables, and some mixture of consumption of exportables and importables. These mixtures are not the same, assuming that some trade takes place, but the value of each (in units of one of the traded goods) is equal to AE. Trade is initially balanced.

Suppose, now, that for some reason the price of nontraded goods should rise, as shown by a steeper price line — line 2 or line 3. These prices are *disequilibrium* prices: resources are shifted into nontraded goods and away from traded goods, as shown by the movement from A to B. On the other hand consumers respond by shifting demand from the higher-priced nontraded goods to tradeables — the move from A to C. There is excess supply of the nontradeable good — shown by FB. There is also a balance of trade *deficit,* shown by CF. This deficit reflects the fact that with traded goods priced too low, consumption (at C) exceeds production (at B).

Suppose that the government at home is alarmed by the inability of local demand to support the production of nontradeables shown by B and, to forestall unemployment, allows domestic spending to rise (e.g., through running a budget deficit by cutting taxes). At the given prices this increased spending falls partly on traded goods and partly on nontraded goods. The ray OCD is intended to show how demand responds to increases in spending. Only when spending has increased to the level shown by line 3 will demand and supply for the nontraded commodity be in line. (Point D lies vertically above point B.) With consumption at D and production at B the nontraded goods market is cleared but the balance of trade deficit has increased, as shown by distance DB.

By working backward we can show that this balance of trade deficit reflects a combination of the country's *overspending* plus an *overvalued* exchange rate. The overspending is reflected in the country's attempt to consume a greater aggregate value of commodities (shown by D) compared with its production (shown by B). The difference is the trade deficit (DB in units of traded

---

[1] This kind of diagram was used some years ago by W. E. G. Salter, "Internal and External Balance: The Role of Price and Expenditure Effects," *The Economic Record,* 35 (August 1959): 226–38. If the country produces positive quantities of exportables, importables, and the nontraded commodity, each with the use of only two factors of production (say labor and capital) as in the Heckscher-Ohlin Model of Chapters 8 and 9, there *may* be flat stretches along the transformation schedule. This does not alter the analysis with which we are concerned above, and is therefore ignored.

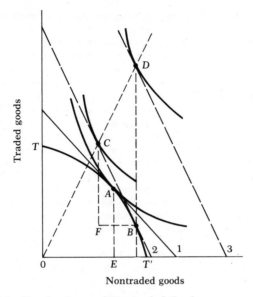

Nontraded goods

FIGURE 19.S.1   Devaluation and Nontraded Goods

Suppose the relative price of nontraded goods (compared with the fixed world prices of traded goods) is shown by the slope of lines 3 or 2. If consumption is at *D* and production at *B*, the trade deficit is *DB*. This deficit can be cured by a cut in spending (to line 2), reducing the deficit to *CF*, coupled with a devaluation, which flattens the budget line to 1. Trade is balanced at point *A*.

goods). A *cut* in spending is clearly in order. But suppose spending is reduced by this amount — as shown by a shift of the budget line from 3 to 2. This cuts the trade deficit from *DB* to *CF*, but does *not* eliminate it entirely. Nontraded goods prices are still too high, reflecting an overvalued exchange rate. If the price of nontraded goods cannot be altered, the local currency price of traded goods can be raised by the appropriate *devaluation* because *world* prices of traded goods are fixed. The budget line would be flattened, to that of line 1, reducing demand for the now higher-priced tradeables and shifting resources into exports and import-competing goods. The cut in spending, coupled with the devaluation, restores trade balance at point *A*.

THE MONETARY APPROACH TO DEVALUATION

In the supplement to Chapter 16 we observed that money balances greater than the local demand in a country can spill over to raise expenditure on commodities above the value of incomes earned in production. This effect implies that such a country runs temporary balance of trade deficits until higher price levels allow the higher monetary stocks to be matched by the transactions demand for money, with some of the initial increase in money at home flowing abroad to match the trade deficits. A similar story can be told about currency devaluation. This essentially monetary approach to devaluation enjoys a recent popularity among economists, and deserves a few brief remarks in this supplement.[2]

The key element is the notion that when a country devalues its currency it instantly lowers its monetary stock's ability to handle the transactions that cover imported commodities whose local-currency price has risen and local consumption of exportables, whose domestic price has been stimulated by an increase in foreign demand. As a consequence the devaluing country contracts expenditures relative to income in an attempt to accumulate the required increase in monetary stocks for transactions. Abroad, in mirror-image fashion, there is a tendency to overspend in response to some of their prices (the devaluing country's exports as well as their own exports) softening either as a direct consequence of devaluation in the home country or indirectly by the induced fall at home in demand for foreign commodities. The tableau is familiar from the account of changes in a country's monetary stock in Chapter 16. Two points are worth emphasizing: the devaluing country tends to run surpluses in its trade account (or eliminates preexisting deficits) as a consequence of its attempt to accumulate money balances — coupled with dishoarding abroad; and this effect is *temporary*. The deficits and surpluses triggered by the devaluation reallocate the world's monetary balances toward the devaluing country. Once monetary stock equilibrium in all countries is achieved, the motivation for the devaluing country to hoard and foreigners to dishoard vanishes.

In the supplement to Chapter 16 we remarked that a monetary change could set in motion a *transfer* of spending from one country to another that, during adjustment, would affect the terms of trade in proportion to each country's propensity to spend out of income. This effect was made more explicit in Chapter 19 and will receive direct treatment in Chapter 22. The point that deserves emphasis here is that the monetary approach to devaluation focuses upon the changes in aggregate expenditure patterns effected in each country by devaluation, which disturbs the relationship between the demand for money and preexisting supplies.

THE ROBINSON-BICKERDIKE-METZLER EXPRESSION

No account of the effects of devaluation on a country's balance of trade is complete without mention of a classic formula known as the Robinson-Bickerdike-Metzler expression.[3] If the condition shown in 19.S.1 is satisfied, a devaluation improves a country's balance of trade:

$$\frac{\eta\eta^*(e + e^* + 1) + ee^*(\eta + \eta^* - 1)}{(\eta + e^*)(\eta^* + e)} > 0. \qquad (19.S.1)$$

The η's are demand elasticities for imports in each country and the e's are supply elasticities of exports.

---

[2] To cite two recent contributions: Harry G. Johnson, "The Monetary Approach to Balance-of-Payments Theory," *Journal of Financial and Quantitative Analysis* (March 1972): 1555–72, and Rudiger Dornbusch, "Devaluation, Money and Non-traded Goods," *American Economic Review,* forthcoming. Emphasis on the monetary factors at work in balance-of-payments disequilibria is evident in the writings of Robert A. Mundell. *International Economics.* New York: Macmillan, 1968.

[3] A reference to this expression is found in the 1948 survey article by Lloyd Metzler, "The Theory of International Trade"; reprinted American Economic Association, *A Survey of Contemporary Economics.* Philadelphia: Blakiston, 1948, vol. 1, chap. 6.

This formula is complicated. It rests on some highly dubious assumptions.[4] Notice that if each country tries to maintain a constant local-currency price for its exports, which can be interpreted as saying that export supply elasticities, e and e^*, are infinite, $\eta + \eta^*$ exceeds unity. This is like the Marshall-Lerner condition for market stability discussed in Chapter 3. At the other extreme, completely *in*elastic supply response ($e = e^* = 0$) reduces the left side to unity, thus guaranteeing an improvement in the trade balance with a devaluation. This response highlights a peculiar characteristic of the expression: sufficiently *small* values for supply elasticities can guarantee a favorable balance of trade response to a devaluation.[5]

A sketch of a proof can illustrate the glaring assumptions upon which most derivations of the formula rest. Suppose that the demand for imports in each country depends only upon the local currency price of imports and the supply of exports likewise depends only upon the local currency price of exports. Allow both the import and export markets to be cleared before and after a devaluation. A change in the exchange rate alters the relationship between any commodity's price expressed in one country's currency and that of the same commodity expressed in the other country's currency. That is, the home country's demand for imports, when related to the foreign country's price, would shift downward with a devaluation of the home currency, as would the home country's supply curve of exports. Thus the quantity and foreign price of imports falls while the quantity of exports rises (but foreign price falls). Foreign currency expenditure on imports falls, but foreign exchange receipts from exports may or may not rise. Much depends on the values of the elasticities of demand and supply for imports and exports. This dependence is what formula 19.S.1 intends to convey.

This account is glaringly at odds with our analysis wherein *relative,* not *absolute,* prices guide consumer and producer behavior. Furthermore, no allowance is made for the real income changes that accompany a devaluation and a change in relative prices. However, by introducing a third category of commodities — nontraded goods — we can closely approximate formula 19.S.1.[6] Our purpose here is not to pursue this analysis, but rather to warn the reader against an uncritical acceptance of this formula and the implications that have been drawn from it.

---

[4] A fairly simple diagrammatic analysis was provided by Gottfried Haberler in "The Market for Foreign Exchange and the Stability of the Balance of Payments: A Theoretical Analysis," *Kyklos,* 3 (1949): 193–218.

[5] Compare this with the expression obtained in the supplement to Chapter 6 for the elasticity of the home country's offer curve: $\epsilon = \eta + e$. The *higher* is the supply elasticity, e, the greater the value of ϵ, and the more likely that the Marshall-Lerner stability condition, $\epsilon + \epsilon^* > 1$, will be satisfied.

[6] A critical account of the Robinson-Bickerdike-Metzler expression for a two-commodity model can be found in R. W. Jones, "Stability Conditions in International Trade: A General Equilibrium Analysis," *International Economic Review,* 2 (May 1961): 199–209. A more recent reappraisal of the formula, based upon an explicit treatment of nontraded commodities, is given by R. W. Jones, "Trade with Nontraded Goods: The Anatomy of Interconnected Markets," unpublished.

20 Reserves and Liquidity: External Balance from an International Viewpoint

In the previous four chapters we discussed the use of policies for internal and external balance. External balance was defined throughout as equilibrium in the foreign-exchange market. The simple test for external balance, when the exchange rate is pegged, is that the authorities do not need to buy or sell foreign currency in order to maintain the desired market rate. For many reasons, countries fail to attain continuous external balance. They must use foreign currency to meet an excess demand, when in payments deficit, or acquire it when in surplus. On the average they hold some "international reserves," reflecting past surpluses and anticipating deficits.

During the past decade countries have loudly debated over the amount and form of international reserves. They have finally agreed on the means of creating new reserve assets. In this chapter we shall first consider the factors that determine a desired quantity of reserves, then survey the forms and sources of international reserves and the debate over their reform.

20.1 THE DEMAND FOR INTERNATIONAL RESERVES

Our goal in this section is to show what determines the total quantity of reserves demanded by the trading countries of the world. We shall approach it by a devious path. First, we can describe the single-country's demand for reserves as a rational exercise in policy planning. Then we shall explore (drawing on Chapters 16–19) the way in which countries' policies for external balance interact, and we shall discover that this dependence influences their demands for reserves.

Finally, we shall put this information together to suggest some reasonable tests for the adequacy of world reserves.

A Single Country's Viewpoint

A country's demand for international reserves in some ways resembles a household's demand for cash balances. The paycheck comes in at the end of the month, but the family's purchases are spaced out irregularly over the month. Hence it is both handy and prudent *on the average* to keep some cash balances, even though these may dwindle to nothing when the next paycheck is due. Countries likewise hold reserves to see them through alternating periods of surplus and deficit; we shall try to explain this long-term average level that they desire. It will depend on the *economic events* impinging on a country's foreign-exchange market, the *automatic adjustment mechanisms* responding to payments disturbances, and the *economic policies* used to bring the market into equilibrium.

In the short run the demand and supply curves in the foreign-exchange market need not intersect at the official exchange rate. The forces that determine each class of international transactions are apt to shift from time to time, pulling the demand-supply balance in the exchange market back and forth. Some of these disturbances may be regular or cyclical. A country that has a heavy seasonal tourist business may find its balance of payments regularly strong during the tourist season and weak in the off-season. Some of the forces affecting the balance are transitory shocks, while others represent a permanent new state of affairs. A crop failure creates a one-shot deficit in the balance of a country heavily dependent on this primary export; the development elsewhere of a cheaper synthetic substitute may cause a persistent deficit.

These forces combine to explain the historic pattern of disturbances in a country's exchange market and foretell the sizes of the shocks it can expect in the future. The reserves needed to finance the resulting deficits will depend, however, not just on these disturbances but also on the automatic adjustment mechanisms restoring equilibrium when external balance is upset. In Chapters 16 and 17 we saw that adjustment mechanisms involving cash balances, the price level, and real incomes theoretically will push a disturbed external balance back toward or to equilibrium. A deficit sets these mechanisms to work. Whenever the adjustment remains incomplete, however, reserves continue to flow out. Thus the more quickly these mechanisms work, the smaller is the total imbalance resulting from a disturbance, and the smaller the cumulative change in reserves needed to finance it. Hence we can say that the average reserves a country needs to hold will be smaller, if the corrections brought by automatic mechanisms of adjustment are speedier.

Furthermore, the demand for reserves depends on the policies chosen to eliminate an imbalance once it occurs. If the policies discussed in the preceding chapters could be used promptly and freely to deal with disturbances, no reserves would be needed. But no country can apply its policies for external balance with such precision, for a number of reasons. Policy instruments need time to take effect. A government often prefers to delay, following the onset of a disturbance, before shifting its policies; perhaps this delay results from honest uncertainty about the permanence of the disturbance, perhaps from a natural tendency to procrastinate and hope that the winds of chance will turn favorable. The application of a policy for external balance is always a political decision for a democratic government; one group will invariably see its interest harmed and often will delay action. Finally, there may be no effective policy for some transitory disturbances, and the best policy hence may be to "finance" the imbalance through a change in reserves rather than to shift policy to correct it.

Figure 20.1 suggests the combined effect of disturbances, adjustments, and policy actions on the demand for international reserves. Curve A shows the deficits and surpluses in a country's balance of

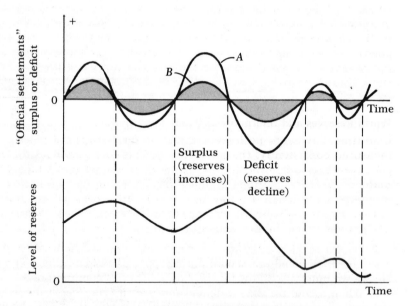

FIGURE 20.1   Relation among Payments Disturbances,
              Automatic and Policy-induced Adjustments,
              and Changes in Reserves

              Level of reserves rises during periods of surplus in "official
              settlements" balance, falls during periods of deficit.

payments caused by the disturbances striking it if no adjustment takes place. Curve *B* shows the residue of deficits and surpluses that might remain after automatic market adjustments and the best available economic policies have been effected.[1] The areas between this latter curve and the base line show the cumulative gains in reserves associated with surplus (the hills) and the cumulative losses due to deficit (the valleys). The demand for reserves of a nation anticipating such a pattern would be related to the *maximum* drawdown that it expects. In the lower part of Figure 20.1 we have arbitrarily started the country out with only enough reserves to finance its worst net payments deficit over a period of time. Presumably its preferred level of reserves will be the amount that permits it to cope with the most dire contingency it expects to face.

In discussing a country's demand for reserves we have concentrated on what we can call the *transactions* demand. We have left out a separate motive for holding reserves — one we can call the *precautionary* demand. When the exchange rate is fixed officially, the government can never forget that the public, watching the level of its reserves during a period of deficit and cumulative decline, may grow fearful that a devaluation is imminent and switch their assets into foreign currencies. Such a speculative flight of liquid capital, trying to avoid the capital loss resulting from a devaluation, would augment the independent forces producing the deficit. It could force on the country an otherwise unneeded devaluation or other inefficient policy to defend the market value of the currency. A nation's demand for reserves will thus allow for the cushion needed to keep at bay those holders of its currency who otherwise would speculate against it.

World Reserves and International Policy Coordination

Countries' payments positions depend on one another. If they are measured consistently, the payments deficits and surpluses for all countries sum algebraically to zero. The deficit in one country is matched by a net surplus of all other countries. Considering this interdependence, can we calculate the world's demand for international reserves by adding up the demands by individual countries? Unfortunately, no, for two reasons:

1. Countries can decrease payments imbalances, and hence the reserves they need, by coordinating policies among themselves. Hence we must also allow for the extent of policy coordination.

2. When a country runs a deficit and uses its reserves, the rest of the world is condemned to run a surplus. Reserves are claim checks

---

[1] Notice that we give the government the benefit of the doubt by assuming that it always moves the balance in the right direction. Wrong measures, or wrongly timed ones, could make curve *B* lie outside of *A* and increase the quantity of reserves needed.

that can be used at any time to draw on other countries' resources. Hence each nation will care how many of them other countries hold.

International coordination of policies can help countries to secure external balance because, acting jointly, they gain fuller control over their flows of international payments. Suppose that the home country plans to manipulate its interest rate and fiscal policy to secure internal and external balance, as described in Figure 18.2. It lowers its interest rate from $5\frac{1}{2}$ to 5 percent, assuming that the interest rate in the foreign country will continue to be $5\frac{1}{2}$ percent. But the foreign country, planning its own short-term policy adjustments, is contemplating an increase to 6 percent. Both may fail to gain their policy objectives. International capital flows depend on differences between national interest rates, and the appearance of a gap of one percentage point is likely to cause a large outflow of capital from the home country to the foreign — more than either nation's officials expected. Advance consultation about each other's plans and needs might have led to a smaller interest-rate differential (with compensating changes in other domestic policies), and hence to a smaller disturbance in international payments. Thus if countries allow for this interdependence and coordinate their policies, the expected payments imbalances and the necessary reserves should be reduced.[2]

The industrial countries have taken tentative steps toward coordinating their financial policies. Limited and informal consultation seems to take place through such international agencies as the Organization for Economic Cooperation and Development and the Bank for International Settlements. Too often, however, the evidence suggests that nations do not align their policies but rather compete and work at cross-purposes with one another.

There is a second reason for the interdependence of reserves needs. Either deficit or surplus countries can act to eliminate external imbalance. If neither acts (and automatic mechanisms fail to extinguish it), reserves flow from the deficit to the surplus country. The surplus country can remain passive if it wishes, but declining reserves eventually goad the deficit country into action. The smaller the volume of international reserves, the sooner a deficit country must seek external balance. Conversely, abundant reserves thrust the job of restoring external balance upon the surplus countries, if they find continuation of the surplus unwelcome.

Because the quantity of reserves determines how the burden of adjustment is shared among deficit and surplus countries, the adequacy of world reserves becomes a political question on which each country's views depend on its actual or expected external balance. The reserves available to *every* country affect the management of

[2] See Richard N. Cooper. *The Economics of Interdependence.* New York: McGraw-Hill, 1968, chap. 6. We shall discuss short-term capital flows and their influence on policies for external balance in Chapter 24.

financial balance of *any* country. This effect explains the second reason that the demand for world reserves cannot be calculated mechanically by adding up the demands of individual countries.

Let us explore these political interests of deficit and surplus countries more closely, because they have dominated the debate over monetary reform. Deficit countries feel that the burden of adjustment falls disproportionately upon them: the surplus countries may passively accumulate reserves, whereas a deficit country's loss of reserves sooner or later impels it to act. Furthermore, deficit countries find insult added to injury when surplus countries cloak themselves in moral superiority, gaining a political advantage whether or not the deficits rest on profligate spending by the deficit nations. We saw in Chapters 16–19 that the deficit country can choose from a variety of expenditure-switching and expenditure-reducing policies to regain external balance. In practice, deficit countries reluctant to change their exchange rates have often argued that they are unfairly and inappropriately driven to expenditure-reducing policies that create unemployment. Hence they hold that inadequate reserves impart a "deflationary bias" to the adjustment process.

To understand how surplus countries see the situation, recall that a payments deficit involves ex post a loan from the surplus to the deficit country. The deficit country secures a net inflow of goods (or securities) from the surplus country, which it pays for with international reserves. Reserves thus are claim tickets on the resources of the surplus country. The surplus country can duck the obligation to lend by adjusting to get rid of the surplus, of course. But such a correction may be costly or disagreeable in the light of its other objectives. Hence it pleads that large international reserves let other countries force upon it an unwanted choice between lending and adjustment. Countries in strong positions of external surplus hence have often opposed major enlargements of international reserves — the United States at the close of World War II, France in the mid-1960's.

Even if countries agree on a change in the total quantity of reserves, they inevitably conflict over its distribution. The extra units must wind up in *someone's* hands. Their allocation hence invokes the inevitable conflict between the deficit and surplus countries of the moment. We shall see this conflict illustrated below when we review recent international negotiations over international reserves.

Demand for Reserves in Practice

Recognizing these problems of prediction and coordination, how can we measure the demand for reserves? Estimating it for a single country is no snap, even before we worry about reconciling countries' conflicting interests in the world total. The transactions demand for reserves often seems likely to grow with the value of a country's imports, or the precautionary demand with its domestic money supply. This method of forecasting demand is rough and ready: why should disturbances to the trade balance, the correct indicator of the transactions demand, grow proportionally with the total value of imports? But in practice it is hard to do better.[3]

When proposals for international cooperation to change the quantity of reserves are discussed, the world total, not just the quantities demanded by individual countries, is important. We saw that nations are bound to disagree on world reserve levels, because the costs and benefits of reserves are not equal for deficit and surplus countries. Can the social scientist judge the adequacy of world reserves, or must the question be left to the statesmen? Many people feel that rough judgments, at least, can be made about whether reserves are too small — creating adjustment problems for the deficit countries. Inadequate reserves can cause capital flight forcing a country to devalue or to impose inefficient emergency controls on its external trade and payments. Counting such actions in countries that otherwise manage their economic affairs competently helps us to judge whether reserves are becoming adequate.

Is there a parallel test for a possible excess of reserves? When surplus countries sell abroad more than they buy, they must either tolerate inflationary pressures or ply their expenditure-reducing policies to hold down expenditure at home, forcing "underspending" to match the overspending in the deficit countries. Evidence that the surplus countries are forced to take such restraining actions would suggest that reserves are excessive.

The recent application of that test by the Managing Director of the International Monetary Fund is interesting:

> In the 1950's and early 1960's there was little doubt as to the adequacy of global reserves. These were years of great expansion in production and international trade and great progress in the liberalization of international transactions. . . . After about 1964, the signals supplied by the basic criteria of reserve adequacy became conflicting. Judged by the criterion of world demand conditions alone the period from 1965 to the present could scarcely be considered one of reserve inadequacy. World output and international trade expanded rapidly in these years; domestic prices rose rather fast. . . . The main indications of reserve inadequacy in these years lie in the increased reliance on restrictions on international transactions and the increased recourse to international financial assistance, bilateral and multilateral, for the purpose of meeting payments deficits and sustaining reserves. Liberalization of trade has continued but its momentum has slackened. Temporary balance of payments restrictions have been imposed on trade and tourism in several major countries. . . . Above all, measures to restrict, attract, or occasionally repel capital flows have been applied or intensified for payments reasons in many countries, large and small.[4]

[3] For an interesting attempt at quantitative estimates for individual countries, see H. R. Heller, "Optimal International Reserves," *Economic Journal,* 76 (June 1966): 296–311.

[4] Managing Director, International Monetary Fund. *Allocation of Special Drawing Rights for the First Basic Period.* Washington, D.C.: International Monetary Fund, 1969, pp. 6–7.

20.2 SOURCES OF RESERVES IN THE POSTWAR PERIOD

We have examined the demand for international reserves without paying much attention to the substance demanded, or to the mechanism supplying it. We saw that a country's reserves must consist of foreign currencies that can be used to defend the value of its own currency in the exchange market, or of assets quickly and reliably convertible into such currencies. In fact after World War II countries evolved a system called the *gold-exchange standard,* whereby gold and some currencies have become the principal international reserves. In 1946 they also created the International Monetary Fund, an institution to regulate some aspects of countries' pursuit of external balance and to lend them additional reserves.

The Gold-Exchange Standard

Both logically and historically, the gold-exchange standard can be viewed as an outgrowth of the gold standard that prevailed before World War I. (This standard was described in section 16.4.) Under the gold standard, gold had been (nearly) the sole form for international reserves, and exchange rates were defined in terms of gold. An obvious potential difficulty with the gold standard is that the supply of gold for international reserves need not relate to the reserves that nations wish to hold. If money prices were freely flexible (as in the model explored in Chapter 16), this independence would present no problem: prices could simply adjust, setting the value of international trade consistent with the gold available for monetary reserves. Indeed, some scholars have suggested that world prices during the late nineteenth century reflected fluctuations in the output of newly mined bullion, as "gold rushes" came and went. If money prices are inflexible, however, and national currencies are pegged to gold, severe difficulties can arise if the demand for reserves somehow outruns the supply of monetary gold. Countries desiring more reserves tend, when they run payments surpluses, to avoid any inflation of their own price levels, although countries with payments deficits are forced into deflationary policies. Average world unemployment is apt to rise, because the surplus countries have no less and the deficit countries have more.

This dilemma faced the principal trading countries after World War I, because prices and the money value of trade had risen greatly during and since the war while the supply of monetary gold had not. The gold-exchange standard was discussed at that time, as a device for economizing on monetary gold, and was recommended at the Genoa Conference of 1922 on postwar financial reconstruction. The gold-exchange standard requires only the willingness of some countries to hold as international reserves, instead of gold, the currencies of nations that hold reserves of gold. The "reserve-currency countries" whose currencies are held by others continue to follow the rules of the gold standard, by standing ready to exchange gold for their own currencies. They thus become bankers to the nonreserve-currency countries. A principal consequence of the system is that gold, although still regarded as the ultimate reserve asset, is economized: currency reserves can be erected on the base of the reserve-currency countries' gold holdings. Indeed the superstructure of currency reserves can exceed the size of the base on which they are erected, as long as the official holders of currency reserves stay confident of their ability to redeem their holdings in gold.

The creation of the gold-exchange standard requires no conscious international planning. It takes only a country's decision to hold its reserves in currency rather than gold, plus the passive behavior of the reserve-currency country in keeping its money pegged to gold. The system failed during the Great Depression and World War II. However, it was reborn after World War II and continued up to the monetary crisis of 1971.

The United States' role as a major reserve-currency country evolved only since World War II, and initially reflected the exigencies of post-war reconstruction. Immediately after the war, the United States was the only major industrial nation not to have suffered massive destruction of her productive capacity. The United States dollar hence was prized for its power to purchase the goods needed to keep consumption at a tolerable level in the European countries while they rebuilt their economies. Dollars were carefully conserved by European treasuries, and their use closely controlled. From this experience the use of the dollar as a principal reserve medium was natural, because the success of European recovery was measured, during the 1950's, by the ability of countries to retain and augment their holdings of dollars.

Table 20.1 shows changes in the growth and composition of reserves since 1951. The growth of total reserves has not been particularly rapid, averaging only 2.1 percent annually during the years covered by the table. (During the 1960's, the value of world exports grew by $8\frac{1}{2}$ percent annually; here we see the basis for the worries over the quantity of total reserves, mentioned in the preceding section.) Furthermore, the composition of reserves has shifted rapidly. Currencies — mainly dollars and sterling — grew fairly rapidly at 3.7 percent annually. The contribution of the International Monetary Fund (discussed below) grew at a faster 8.5 percent but remained a small portion of the total. Monetary gold, however, increased at only 0.8 percent. As a result, the ratio of currency reserves to gold rose steadily from 0.45 to 1 in 1951 to 0.72 to 1 in 1969. Credit facilities, measured in the final column, have grown faster than total owned reserves; they are explained below.

The significance of this rise in the "exchange" component of the gold-exchange standard comes clear when we consider the position in which it places the reserve-currency countries, as the bankers of the system.

TABLE 20.1 Levels of International Reserves and Credit
Facilities, 1951–1969 (billions of U.S. dollars)

End of year	Gold	Foreign exchange	Reserve positions in IMF	Total reserves	Unused credit facilities
1951	33.9	15.1	1.7	50.7	6.5
1953	34.3	16.9	1.9	53.1	7.1
1955	35.4	18.4	1.9	55.7	7.9
1957	37.3	18.4	2.3	58.0	7.2
1959	37.9	17.9	3.2	59.0	12.9
1961	38.9	20.8	4.2	63.8	14.5
1963	40.2	23.6	3.9	67.7	15.5
1965	41.9	24.2	5.4	71.4	16.3
1967	39.5	26.7	5.7	71.8	23.5
1969	39.1	29.1	6.7	75.0	31.3

Source: International Monetary Fund. *Annual Report of the Executive Directors for the Fiscal Year Ending April 30, 1971.* Washington, 1971, p. 19.

External Balance and Reserves Quantity. The only way for the rest of the world to increase its net holdings of foreign-exchange reserves is for the reserve-currency countries to run deficits. As we saw in Chapter 5, the deficit of the United States (official settlements basis) is indeed *measured* by the increase in dollars held as official reserves (along with reductions in the United States monetary gold stock).[5] What, then, is the right position for the United States balance of payments? Should we aim for external balance? If we do, other countries are denied what Table 20.1 shows to be their principal recent source of additional reserves. If we do not, the reserve-currency country faces the problems of external imbalance.

The problem is no less vexing for the nonreserve countries, who must run surpluses to build up their reserves. Only accidentally will such surpluses square with their needs for internal balance. Furthermore, in running surpluses they must by definition sell abroad more than they buy. They must transfer purchasing power — implicitly, lend — to the reserve-currency country. The need to lend to the wealthy Americans in order to accumulate dollar reserves has galled many countries.

Confidence and Reserves Quality. The amount by which a commercial bank can expand its deposits (in the course of lending to its customers) depends on the liquid reserves it must keep to satisfy those who wish to cash in their claims. The bank does not keep a dollar of

[5] An obvious exception may have occurred to you: could the United States simply swap dollars with another government for another reserve currency, such as sterling, without running a deficit in the exchange market? In fact, such temporary swaps have had an important though supplementary role during the last decade. They are discussed below.

reserves for every dollar of deposit liabilities. However, even without laws setting minimum reserve ratios, the prudent banker keeps enough to protect himself against a collective loss of confidence by his customers — a "run on the bank." The same problem confronts a reserve-currency country supplying a reserve-hungry world. The larger its cumulative deficit, the greater are its liquid liabilities in the form of its currency or short-term securities held as official reserves by foreign countries. Because the reserve-currency country's gold hoard is its ultimate means of payment, the gold hoard must stay large enough, relative to these liquid liabilities, to maintain the confidence of the depositors. Suppose that gold hoard stays constant in size. The reserve-currency country with generous deficits supplies the world with abundant foreign-exchange reserves, which may be needed and desired. But in doing so it undermines the confidence of external holders in its currency, and impairs the "quality" of the reserves it creates. Conversely, if the reserve-currency country sternly maintains external balance, its currency may be prized as a reserve asset, but an overall shortage of reserves may arise. If the quality of currency reserves is good, the quantity may be inadequate — and vice versa.

These theoretical hazards of the gold-exchange standard match all too closely the experience of the last two decades. Both reserve-currency countries, but primarily the United States, have run recurrent deficits in their balance of payments, financing the moderate growth of currency reserves that we mentioned above (3.7 percent annually). But they have run into recurrent losses of confidence in their ability to meet their external liabilities, as the size of these liabilities grew relative to their gold reserves.[6]

Finally, in August 1971, speculative pressure against the dollar became too much. Both private and official foreign holders feared a devaluation of the dollar and capital losses on their dollar assets. The United States had to suspend sales of gold to foreign central banks, in order to avoid a run on its gold stock. The gold-exchange standard temporarily collapsed. Without a guarantee that they could convert their dollar holdings into gold, nations were left to make their own decisions about continuing to hold dollars or attempting to switch to another reserve asset. Temporarily, at least, most countries were on a "dollar standard" rather than a gold-exchange standard. The prophets of doom who predicted the failure of the gold-exchange standard were all too accurate.

In section 20.3 we shall present some proposals for avoiding these hazards of the gold-exchange standard.

---

[6] In mid-1970 the ratio of the United Kingdom's total reserves to the value of liquid sterling liabilities held abroad was just under one-quarter; it fluctuated between one-third and one-fifth over the last two decades. For the United States the ratio in 1970 was 0.4, having declined over two decades from 2.7. These figures refer to total external liabilities, not just to official holders.

The International Monetary Fund

The International Monetary Fund, born of the Bretton Woods Conference in 1944, began business in 1946 as an international organization to lend deficit countries additional reserves and to promote the removal of restrictions on international payments and the orderly adjustment of exchange rates. As we have mentioned previously, Fund members are committed to maintaining fixed exchange rates and making substantial changes only after consultation with the IMF.

In the supplement to this chapter we shall describe the rules that govern the volume and use of the IMF's loanable resources. The IMF holds a pool of currencies and gold contributed by its members and draws on the currencies to make temporary loans to members needing to supplement their foreign-exchange reserves.

The IMF got off to a slow start in the 1940's. Would-be borrowers just after World War II needed not short-term credit but long-term loans or gifts. These needs were filled in some measure by assistance from the United States under the Marshall Plan and other programs, and the Fund in essence sat out the period of postwar reconstruction. Borrowings from the IMF increased sharply around 1956, however, and the Fund has done a brisk business since. Gross new borrowings have recently run over $2 billion annually. The Fund has also scored high marks for institutional innovation.

Stand-by Arrangements. One difficulty commonly plagues the IMF and its members when they either borrow from the Fund or consult it about changes in their exchange rates. The former action is taken often, and the latter invariably, under the pressure of speculative attack on the member's currency. The Fund lacks time for adequate consideration of the request, and the member suffers seriously from uncertainty about the credit available to him. In 1952 the Fund developed the stand-by arrangement. Worked out with a member before his payments problem becomes critical, it sets in advance the terms of a drawing from the Fund, which can then be made on very short notice within the next six or twelve months. Uncertainty is thus removed, and the IMF staff has time to review the member's situation. Since 1952 over 300 stand-by arrangements have been approved.

General Arrangements to Borrow. The Fund has a limited stock of useful currencies — no more than $15 billion — and it might not have access to sufficient currencies to help all worthy borrowers at one time. To escape this threat, in 1962 ten leading IMF members agreed to lend the Fund jointly a maximum of $6 billion of their currencies when needed by any of the ten. Through fiscal 1969/70 a (gross) total of $2,155 million had been drawn under the arrangements. Thus they have provided an important supplement to the Fund's lending resources.

Compensatory Financing of Export Fluctuations. In 1963 the Fund added a facility for special lending to countries, usually less-developed, whose export value fluctuated. Such "compensatory financing" of temporary sags in exports, ordinarily limited to fifty percent of the member's quota, is additional to the member's regular borrowing privileges at the Fund. From 1967 to 1970, 17 countries made (gross) drawings of $303 million. The volume of business naturally fluctuates, rising in years of widespread crop failures.

Although the Fund was a successful innovator in these areas, it has failed in another. Its role as provider of international reserves holds value only while the gold-exchange standard operates smoothly. Smoothness here depends upon countries' willingness to change their exchange rates when serious disequilibrium is present, or to use only efficient adjustment mechanisms to restore equilibrium by other methods. Many economists feel that the system failed on both counts. Collaboration in developing adjustment mechanisms took place only outside of the Fund, and in the 1960's inefficient controls over capital flows were heavily used to suppress disequilibrium.

20.3 THE DEBATE OVER REFORM

During the 1960's a vigorous debate raged, first among economists, then central bankers and other government officials, over the weaknesses of the world's system of international reserves. Plans for reform trod on each other's heels as each draftsman tried to add his favorite features to the preceding plans. Out of this jostling have come several major changes in the postwar reserves arrangements described in the preceding section.

Issues in the Debate

A number of economists, led by Robert Triffin,[7] began pointing to both short-run and long-run weaknesses in the emergent gold-exchange standard. These weaknesses they felt could reverse the liberalization of controls over trade and payments that had occurred during the 1950's and threaten nations' internal balance as well. The diagnoses centered on the interrelated difficulties of the gold-exchange standard that we mentioned above: either it would not provide adequate growth in the quantity of reserves, or it would produce reserves of impaired quality and hence doubtful stability.

Quantity. Triffin and others noticed that the ratio of reserves to the major indicators of the need for reserves had been falling steadily.[8] Furthermore, the gold-exchange standard did not increase reserves at a reasonable rate in the long run. The stock of monetary gold was growing by less than 1 percent annually. Currency reserves depended on the payments deficits of the reserve-currency countries, which could not be counted on to continue. Countries would have to scramble

[7] See his *Gold and the Dollar Crisis.* New Haven: Yale University Press, 1960.
[8] Robert Triffin. *The Evolution of the International Monetary System: Historical Reappraisal and Future Perspectives.* Princeton Studies in International Finance, No. 12. Princeton: International Finance Section, Princeton University, 1964.

for reserves through panicky adjustments to avert external deficits or create surpluses: restrictions on imports and capital outflows, and deflationary pressure on domestic economies.

Stability. Some critics were concerned less about the quantity of reserves than with the stability of their composition. The gold-exchange standard depends on countries' collective willingness to hold gold and one or more foreign currencies in their international reserves in more or less stable proportions. Each reserve medium has its advantages to a country: gold is not expected to depreciate, but it yields no interest to the holder; currencies risk capital loss if they are devalued, but they pay interest when held as treasury bills. Countries need not all hold gold and currencies in the same proportions, the critics suggested, but their preferred proportions had to remain stable. Otherwise, switches from one reserve currency to another, or from reserve currencies into gold could drive the reserve-currency countries, and perhaps others, into exchange control and deflation. These fears were realized in 1971.

The two lines of criticism, despite their differing emphases, leveled their fire at the same basic properties of the gold-exchange standard and anticipated the same ills from its unmodified operation. Several devices were proposed to attack these difficulties.

Raise the Price of Gold. The quantity of international reserves could be increased "at the stroke of a pen" by raising the price of gold. This increase would revalue monetary stocks and increase the value of newly produced monetary gold flowing into reserve holdings. If the quantity of gold produced responds positively to its price (i.e., its supply is elastic), its physical output would also rise. The principal objections to this proposal turned on the uneven benefits of the resulting capital gains: some countries hold their reserves all in gold, others all in currencies. Also, the principal gold-producing beneficiary, the Republic of South Africa, is unloved by many.[9]

Standardize the Composition of Existing Reserves. Countries might agree on the proportions of gold and currencies in which they would hold their reserves, to keep shifts in the composition of official reserves from causing or aggravating a flight from one of the reserve currencies, or into gold. The objection to such an agreement typically was that, by itself, it did not provide for the growth of reserves.

Create New Reserve Assets. Various schemes were suggested for creating new types of reserves under international agreement. At the simplest, new currencies could come into international-reserve status; e.g., if the United Kingdom and United States should run surpluses, they could accumulate reserves of German marks and French francs, rather than force Germany, France, and other countries to decrease their holdings of dollars and sterling. Other proposals called for artificial assets to be created and distributed. Under the Stamp

[9] In 1972 the United States raised the dollar price of gold from $35 to $38 an ounce, but its price was not increased in relation to most other important currencies.

Plan, for example, new reserve certificates would be created by international agreement and doled out initially to the less-developed countries. Those nations would then spend them in the industrial countries for their development needs, receiving a one-shot injection of foreign aid in the process. The industrial recipients would hold the certificates as reserves, transferring them when necessary to other industrial countries in order to secure foreign exchange. These proposals ignored the "quality" or stability of reserves and, indeed, assumed that another asset could be added to reserve portfolios without worrying whether it would be held with currencies and gold.

Create a World Central Bank. Proposals for a world central bank went beyond those for the creation of new reserve assets by placing control over their supply in an expanded Monetary Fund (or other world institution), giving it power over the volume and distribution of new reserves. Triffin, for example, proposed that the IMF should not only enjoy some discretion over the rate at which new reserves were created from year to year, but also that it place them among nations following deflationary policies on account of their external payments situation to encourage more expansionary domestic policies among them. Many people are, of course, unwilling to give such power over national policies to an international organization.

The Coming of Reforms

At first these plans fell on deaf official ears. Many of the prophecied disasters occurred, however, starting in 1960. These threatening episodes have prodded nations into adopting at least three major changes to shore up the gold-exchange standard and enlarge the role of the International Monetary Fund.

Swap Arrangements. A simple and flexible way to increase reserves is for two countries whose currencies are broadly traded (hence usable for financing a payments deficit) to swap equivalent amounts of their own currencies. Starting in the early 1960's, the central banks of the major trading countries began negotiating extensive lines of credit with each other. These lines of credit permit either partner, on short notice, to secure foreign exchange by swapping an equivalent amount of his own currency for that of the partner country. These swaps are normally repaid within three to twelve months. This short term is not a serious limit on their usefulness, because the private capital movements they are designed to offset are usually reversed within a few months. In Table 20.1 swap lines and similar credit arrangements comprise 46 percent of the "unused credit facilities" listed in the last column. (The rest is in IMF credit facilities.) They became an important defense of the stability of the gold-exchange standard.

Two-Tier Gold. If the stock of monetary gold only grew as fast as world's demand for reserves, making the gold-exchange standard work smoothly would become much easier. Claims on the gold-holding reserve-currency countries could increase no faster than their gold reserves and still supply the world's reserve needs without raising the chances of a run on the bank. In some years the central banks of the world have had to reduce their gold holdings in order to satisfy industrial and speculative demands. When the world's monetary gold fell by $1.58 billion in 1967, the result of feeding a massive speculative demand, the central banks worked out the so-called two-tier gold system. Since 1968 the private market for gold has been segregated from gold transactions among central banks. The banks continue to trade in gold among themselves at a fixed price (since 1972, $38 an ounce), and the private market's price fluctuates in response to supply and demand. This system keeps the speculators from raiding official gold holdings and removes one source of instability from the gold-exchange standard.

Special Drawing Rights. The most important result of the debate over international monetary reform has been the agreement that the IMF shall issue a new form of reserve asset — Special Drawing Rights (SDRs).[10] Often called "paper gold," SDRs held by members of the IMF can be used for various purposes. A country can transfer them to another Fund member for foreign exchange needed to combat a deficit. It can use them to buy back hoards of its own currency accumulated by a nation with a payments surplus. It can turn them over to the IMF to repay past borrowings from the Fund's regular credit facility. Inaptly if diplomatically named, they are a new form of owned reserves (rather than credit) with its value guaranteed in terms of the central banks' price of gold. "Debtors" who have drawn on their SDR allocation pay interest; "creditors" who have received SDRs from others receive it. Countries can in principle spend all of their SDR allocation, but they must limit their average borrowing through use of SDRs over a period of years. The creation of SDRs, unlike gold, uses up none of the world's scarce resources; unlike the accumulation of currency reserves, it requires no disequilibrium in international payments between reserve and nonreserve countries. SDRs are created annually through the IMF at rates agreeable to the Fund's Board of Governors, and are allocated to participating members in proportion to their IMF quotas. For the three years 1970–1972 it was decided that $9.5 billion of SDRs should be created, an annual increase of over four percent in the stock of international reserves.

Status and Prospects

How do these important changes in the international monetary system match up to the charges made by its critics during the last decade? How do they score on the appropriate tests of economic efficiency?

[10] For an account see Fritz Machlup. *Remaking the International Monetary System: The Rio Agreement and Beyond.* Baltimore: Johns Hopkins Press, 1968.

Important gains have been won on several fronts. The two-tier gold system appears to end the threat of financial disruption due to a flight of private hoarders from reserve currencies into gold. The swap arrangements bolster the resources available to central banks for handling sudden changes in short-term private capital flows. SDRs provide a way to increase the stock of reserves over the long run. Nonetheless, two major problems remain.

Stability. As the events of 1971 and 1972 showed all too clearly, nations can still suddenly change the composition of their reserves, and thereby destabilize the gold-exchange standard. The threat of foreign official holders to cash massive quantities of their dollar reserves for gold at the United States Treasury lay behind the United States decision in August 1971 to "suspend convertibility" — i.e., to curtail this privilege. Such instabilities in official reserves can either cause or result from speculative private capital flows; one instability feeds the other. Many economists have argued with renewed vigor for an agreement among countries to limit such destabilizing switches in the composition of reserve assets. A popular suggestion is that countries reluctant to hold their reserves in dollars be allowed to swap them for SDRs with the International Monetary Fund. The Fund and the United States could then work out an arrangement for converting the dollar balances into a long-term United States liability to the IMF.

Efficiency. Somewhat lost in the concern over short-term crises in international reserves has been the question of whether or not our present reserve arrangements promote efficiency in the use of resources. When a country with a deficit uses its international reserves, we saw that it borrows from the countries that are in surplus. This borrowing gives its citizens (and their government) a claim to foreigners' resources, as a man may borrow from his neighbor. For a government to make an efficient decision to let a payments deficits run, it must be aware of the borrowing involved. Hence, many economists argue, the use of reserves should cost it something like a market rate of interest — the current price for borrowing resources. A country that uses its SDRs pays a modest interest charge. So does a nation in deficit that draws down its balances of reserve currencies, because it loses the interest it formerly received through holding them in the form of treasury bills. Both interest rates may be low, however, because a deficit country's borrowing is not obviously short-term. The use of gold to finance a deficit entails no sacrifice of opportunity cost of interest, and hence fails this test for efficiency.

Another aspect of efficiency in reserves arrangements relates to the precautionary motive for holding reserves — that, besides needing to *use* reserves, countries must *hold* them to convince speculators of their ability to sustain the exchange values of their currencies. In this case no opportunity cost need be involved, because the ability to run deficits is the question, not actually running them. On this test SDRs score well, because nations incur no cost in acquiring them and neither pay nor receive interest for merely holding their initial allotment. Both reserve currencies and monetary gold fail this test, however. The gold producer incurs real costs in wresting the metal from nature, and the official purchaser in turn pays (transfers real resources) when he buys the gold. Likewise, when reserves of foreign currencies are built up, the country acquiring them must run a surplus and transfer (or at least lend) resources to the reserve-currency country, for which the interest rate on that nation's treasury bills may or may not be reasonable compensation. The point is that reserves can be created (as through SDRs) without this resource transfer.

In summary, at least two major problems remain with the international monetary system: countries still depend on a shaky mutual trust regarding the stability of their reserves; although SDRs score better than the traditional reserve assets, no reserve asset perfectly meets the efficiency test of no opportunity cost to hold, but a market interest rate to use. A reliable system of fixed exchange rates cannot be restored and efficiently maintained unless these problems are solved.

20.4 SUMMARY

A country with a fixed exchange rate holds reserves to tide it over fluctuations in its balance of payments. The size of the reserves it wishes to hold should depend on the size of the disturbances affecting its external payments, the speed and effectiveness of the automatic mechanisms that eliminate imbalances, and its willingness to use discretionary policy instruments (including exchange-rate changes) to restore equilibrium. These factors determine its transactions demand for reserves; in addition, it should hold a precautionary margin to convince speculators of its ability to defend its exchange rate.

Because every payments imbalance has its counterpart in the rest of the world, the collective demand for reserves also depends on countries' cooperation in eliminating imbalances. Furthermore, the reserves held by the rest of the world are a matter of policy concern for a country, because they represent a potential claim on its own resources. Hence countries in external surplus will voice concern over measures to expand the quantity of reserves, just as deficit countries may feel that they bear an unfair share of the costs of adjustment and demand larger quantities. A reasonable test for deficient reserves, in the aggregate, is the widespread application of inefficient measures to prevent payments deficits. Views differ on whether or not inflation indicates excessive reserves.

The system for creating and using reserves employed since World War II is called the gold-exchange standard: some countries hold their reserves in gold, which they buy and sell at a fixed price, and other countries employ the currencies of these reserve centers for their own reserves. Apart from the supply of new monetary gold, this system depends for the growth of reserves on payments deficits run by the reserve currency countries. Over the past two decades, reserve currencies have comprised a rising portion of total reserves, and the ratio of dollars in official reserves (United States liabilities) to America's gold stock (United States assets) has risen drastically. A "run on the bank" became a serious and, in 1971, an imminent, threat.

A heated debate over reform of the system of international reserves has occurred during the past decade. Critics emphasize two short-comings: the lack of a mechanism for expanding the quantity of reserves as the value of international transactions increases; and the potential instability of the system due to speculative flights from reserve currencies into other currencies or gold. The many reforms suggested can be grouped roughly under the following proposals: (1) raise the price of monetary gold; (2) standardize the composition of reserves, to avert destabilizing shifts in official holdings; (3) create new reserve assets; (4) empower an international institution to ex-pand reserves in line with the world's needs. Changes have included elements of all four. Swaps of currencies among principal countries give each government ammunition to use in staving off a sudden imbalance. The loss of monetary gold into private hoards has been blocked. Most important, countries have agreed on a process for creating a new reserve asset — Special Drawing Rights — at a rate consonant with the growth of international transactions.

SDRs (although not other reserve assets) score well in economic efficiency. A nation that uses its reserves implicitly borrows resources from abroad, and should pay a market rate of interest. The holding of reserves (to stave off the speculators) need not involve the use of resources, however, and thus should not incur an opportunity cost.

SUGGESTIONS FOR FURTHER READING

Baldwin, R. E., and J. D. Richardson, eds. *Selected Topics in International Trade and Finance: A Book of Readings.* Boston: Little, Brown, 1973. Part IV includes several useful papers on international reserves.

Grubel, Herbert G. "The Benefits and Costs of Being the World Banker," *National Banking Review,* 2 (December 1964): 189–212. Analysis of the position of the United States as a reserve currency country.

Horsefield, J. Keith, ed. *The International Monetary Fund, 1945–1965.* Washington: International Monetary Fund, 1969, vol. 2 (Analysis). Contains papers describing the IMF's operations in detail.

Krause, Lawrence B. *Sequel to Bretton Woods: A Proposal to Reform the World Monetary System.* Washington: Brookings Institution, 1971.

League of Nations. *International Currency Experience: Lessons of the Inter-War Period.* Geneva: League of Nations, 1944. Classic study by Ragnar Nurkse of international monetary relations in the interwar period.

Machlup, Fritz. *Remaking the International Monetary System: the Rio Agreement and Beyond.* Baltimore: Johns Hopkins Press, 1968. Special Drawing Rights and their relation to the international monetary system.

Salant, Walter S. "International Reserves and Payments Adjustment." Re-print No. 175. Washington: Brookings Institution, 1970. Relation between reserve needs and adjustment mechanisms.

Triffin, Robert. *The Evolution of the International Monetary System: Historical Reappraisal and Future Perspectives.* Princeton Studies in International Finance, no. 12. Princeton: International Finance Section, Princeton University, 1964. Long-run perspective and survey of approaches to reform.
Triffin, Robert. *Gold and the Dollar Crisis.* New Haven: Yale University Press, 1960. Critique of gold-exchange standard.

Supplement to Chapter 20:
Operation of the International Monetary Fund

To understand how the IMF provides extra reserves, we should start with the concept of the *quota* assigned to each of the 124 countries that (as of 1972) belong to the Fund. The quota fills three primary functions. It defines:

1. The maximum amount of reserves the member can ordinarily borrow from the Fund.
2. The resources that the member must itself contribute to the Fund's loan assets.
3. The member's voting strength in the IMF Executive Board.

Figure 20.S.1 will help to show how the quotas define the IMF's principal loanable resources and how members borrow from the Fund. First, a member must ordinarily contribute, when he joins the Fund, an amount equal to his quota. The composition of this contribution is shown in the upper bar of the diagram: 25 percent gold, 75 percent his own currency. Thus the IMF's basic resources consist of the proceeds of these quota contributions — gold amounting to a quarter of the sum of all national quotas, a mixture of currencies making up the rest.

The quota also defines the member's right to borrow from the Fund foreign exchange that he may need to supplement his "owned" reserves and tide himself over a deficit in his external payments. His borrowing rights are defined in terms of *tranches*, or shares, of his quota, each tranche being equal to one-fourth of quota. (The scale at the base of Figure 20.S.1 is marked in quarter-of-quota units.) The more he wishes to borrow, at one time, the higher is the interest charge he pays (to a maximum of 5 percent) and the more closely does the Fund scrutinize his policies for internal and external balance. The first fourth of a nation's quota is referred to as its *gold tranche* (because it equals the country's gold contribution to the Fund); under present rules the member can borrow within the gold tranche with no questions asked. Beyond the gold tranche his borrowing can proceed through four successive *credit tranches* — again, each equal to one-fourth of his quota. Thus, without a special waiver, the member's borrowing is restricted to 125 percent of his quota.

Borrowing foreign exchange from the Fund is actually called a *purchase*, because the member deposits an equivalent amount of his own currency. (Notice that the member controls the supply of his own currency, so the opportunity cost of this deposit is negligible.) Conversely, when the member repays a loan by returning foreign exchange to the Fund, he is said to repurchase his own currency. His maximum ordinary indebtedness to the Fund is described in terms of the Fund's holding of his own currency: 200 percent of his quota. You can easily see that 200 percent of the quota equals the sum of the member's initial currency contribution (75 percent) and his maximum

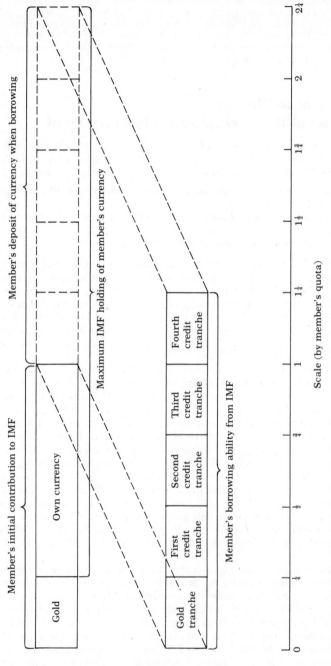

FIGURE 20.S.1   Member Country's Contribution to IMF, Borrowing Rights from IMF, and Mechanics of Drawing from IMF

borrowing ability (125 percent). This sum is shown in the upper part of Figure 20.S.1.

A member's quota is determined by his national income, international reserves, level of imports, the variability of his exports, and the size of his exports relative to national income. This formula does not define quotas rigidly; rather, it is a basis for negotiation. Quotas have often been increased for individual countries. Furthermore, they are reviewed every five years, and quotas have thrice been increased all around. These increases raised total quotas by 54 percent in 1959, 33 percent in 1965, and 35 percent in 1970, to a total of $28.9 billion.

The total amount of members' quotas in the Fund corresponds to the amount of resources — gold and currencies — available for supplementing members' reserves in times of deficit. The Fund's gold is only a second-line resource for aiding members who need foreign exchange to cope with deficits. The Fund can use its gold to buy more of a currency that has become particularly scarce, and many transactions in gold have been devised that increase the general flexibility of the Fund's resources. The Fund's holdings of currencies are its first line of assets for aiding its members. Not every currency in the vault is equally useful, however. The currencies of many smaller and less-developed countries are elaborately controlled and are not widely traded outside their own borders, and hence are useless to another member needing to stabilize its currency in terms of foreign exchange. In the IMF's 1970/71 fiscal year only 18 countries' currencies were drawn. These countries are large, of course, and their quotas total about three-fourths of all IMF quotas. Nonetheless, the Fund's normal holdings of their currencies, about $15.4 billion, are just over half of the Fund's total resources.[1]

In relation to member countries' reserves, the IMF's lending facilities comprise "credit" rather than "money." Other things equal, credit is less desirable than cash in hand (for the nation as for the individual), because credit may be unavailable when it is needed. Critics of the IMF used to argue that it had actually *reduced* international reserves, absorbing gold (one-fourth of quotas) and giving no equally sure access to credit in return. The Fund tried to meet this charge by making credit freely available to a country up to the amount of its gold tranche. Furthermore it urged each country to count as part of its international reserves its "IMF net position," equal to its quota minus the IMF's actual holdings of its currency. The sum of such positions appears in Table 20.1. The IMF net position of a country will equal its gold tranche if it has done no net borrowing, and if none of its currency has been loaned by the Fund to other nations.[2]

---

[1] A great deal of information about the Fund's operations can be found in its *Annual Report* and in J. Keith Horsefield, ed. *The International Monetary Fund, 1945–1965,* vol. 2 (*Analysis*), Washington, D.C.: International Monetary Fund, 1969, especially Part 4.

[2] If a country has not borrowed, and its currency has been sold by the Fund in its lending operations, its net position exceeds its gold tranche. The excess called a "super gold tranche" and increases the member's automatic borrowing privileges at the Fund.

21 External Balance, Flexible Exchange Rates, and Optimum Currency Areas

Maintaining a fixed exchange rate is not a small chore. As we have shown in the preceding chapters, securing both external and internal balance — when the government cannot depend on automatic mechanisms of adjustment — requires accurate diagnosis of the nation's economic problems and the adroit use of multiple instruments of policy. These requirements cause the market for foreign exchange to clear at an arbitrarily chosen price. Why go to all this trouble when we could simply let the exchange rate fluctuate as needed to clear the market? The simplicity of that solution to the problem of external balance is the core of the case for flexible exchange rates. Yet there is surely an advantage to fixed exchange rates — an advantage we take for granted when we assume that a United States dollar earned in Massachusetts will always be worth exactly one United States dollar in Connecticut. In this chapter we shall explore the advantages and disadvantages of fixed exchange rates. As we shall see, this quest can become a search for the criteria of an "optimum currency area": how much economic activity should be linked by a single currency and hence subject to permanently fixed exchange rates?

21.1 FLEXIBLE EXCHANGE RATES FOR A SINGLE COUNTRY

The case for flexible exchange rates can be put in two ways, relating respectively to the models of flexible and fixed prices developed in Chapters 16 and 17.

Flexible Domestic Prices

In a theoretical model where all prices are flexible, automatic market adjustments can secure internal and external balance. As we saw in Chapter 16, full employment should prevail under a fixed exchange rate even without the active assistance of public policy. Following a disturbance, external balance is won by net changes in the country's money supply that alter its price level and (temporarily) the level of real expenditure to restore equilibrium. If external balance could be obtained, in principle, with so little trouble when the exchange rate is fixed, why let it fluctuate? The answer suggested by Professor Milton Friedman and others lies in finding the least costly way to bring about the necessary adjustments.[1]

A disturbance occurs — let us suppose a reduction in demand for the home country's export good. It causes an external deficit, and ultimately requires worsening our terms of trade to restore equilibrium in exchange. This adjustment could come about in either of two ways. With the exchange rate fixed, the monetary mechanism of adjustment could take its course, forcing all money prices and factor payments within the country to be bid down. Alternatively, the average level of domestic money prices could stay unchanged, and the adjustment could come about through a change in a single price — the exchange rate. Is it not simpler to change one price, rather than thousands of domestic money prices? The choice has been compared to the adoption of daylight saving time in the summer months. If we all wish to shift our activities one hour earlier in relation to the sun's daily cycle, is it not simpler to set the clock forward an hour rather than reschedule every event to take place an hour earlier by the clock? The lower "transactions costs" of changing the clock correspond directly to the advantages of changing the exchange rate, rather than all the domestic prices linked to prices abroad by the exchange rate.

Fixed Domestic Prices

When domestic prices are rigid, or even sticky in the short run, we enter the world described in Chapters 17 and 18 where interventions of public policy are periodically necessary to maintain both internal and external balance. We saw that, in theory, these two objectives could be attained if the nation possesses two policy instruments — fiscal and monetary policy, fiscal policy and changes in the pegged exchange rate, etc. — which it can deploy freely. Owning the two

---

[1] Milton Friedman, "The Case for Flexible Exchange Rates," *Essays in Positive Economics,* in *Readings in International Economics,* ed. R. E. Caves and H. G. Johnson (Homewood, Ill.: Richard D. Irwin, 1968), chap. 25. Also see Harry G. Johnson, "The Case for Flexible Exchange Rates, 1969," *Approaches to Greater Flexibility of Exchange Rates: The Bürgenstock Papers,* ed. G. N. Halm. Princeton: Princeton University Press, 1970, chap. 8.

instruments is not enough, of course. Perfect measurement and foresight are needed to use them correctly. There must be no constraints on the use of these instruments. No delays must occur while skeptical legislators are being convinced of the wisdom of the changes. Clearly our ideal prescription for attaining internal and external balance denies many of the realities of policy formation.

From this observation springs the second basic defense of flexible exchange rates, due to Professor James Meade.[2] Were the exchange rate not fixed, the market for foreign exchange (described in Chapter 5) would adjust to disturbances, continuously setting and revising the exchange rate to equate demand and supply. By fixing the price of foreign exchange we hamstring this market, and thereby take up the burden of a new policy target — external balance. Conversely, by switching from a fixed to a flexible rate the country reduces the tasks required of its available policy instruments. It potentially frees itself from the need to make unsatisfactory compromises that perpetuate internal imbalance as the cost of maintaining a tolerable state of external balance.

This argument for flexible rates also draws force from our study of international reserves and policy coordination among countries. We saw that a deficit financed by reserves transfers real resources to the deficit country from those in surplus, and that the switch only accidentally moves them from less to more productive uses. A flexible rate removes the need for a government to spend its foreign-exchange reserves and thus to initiate such transfers. The government can occasionally spend or acquire reserves, if it chooses, without voiding the response of the exchange rate to market forces. The point about flexible rates is that such involuntary transfers of resources between countries are no longer a necessary part of the policy landscape. In Chapter 20 we noticed the potential usefulness of international coordination of financial policies with fixed exchange rates, as well as some of the problems it entails. If flexible exchange rates were in general use, the need for international coordination of monetary policies would be reduced, and their enslavement to external balance ended.

Will a Flexible Exchange Rate Work?

Although many economists favor flexible exchange rates, practical men who manage international monetary affairs generally oppose them. It is hard to assess the reasons for this persistent split in opinion. The practical man who understands the intricacies of the par-value system and functions within it is surely intellectually interested in its persistence. And he may dislike stretching his imagination to contemplate life with another exchange-rate regime. On the other

[2] J. E. Meade, "The Case for Variable Exchange Rates," *Three Banks Review* (September 1955): 3–27.

hand, the issue may be one of political power and policy objectives, as we shall see in the next section. Whatever the reason, we need to mention briefly some of the questions that are raised over whether or not flexible exchange rates would work in practice.

Many objections to flexibility ultimately boil down to fears that a flexible rate would be highly unstable — that considerable changes would be needed to restore equilibrium after modest disturbances. The theory of exchange markets identifies the issue involved, but we can settle it only by resorting to the facts. Hence we shall refer to Canada in the 1950's — the one industrial country with a long period of recent experience with flexible rates.[3]

One factor that could make flexible rates relatively unstable is low (absolute) values of the price elasticities governing the flows of traded goods. Even if the requirements for stability in the underlying commodity exchange model (set forth in Chapter 3) are met, the margin might be small. Then the exchange rate — and the equilibrium terms of trade — would have to fluctuate widely to adjust to disturbances. The height of these elasticities is a factual question, of course, and the answer will vary from country to country. The evidence mentioned in section 3.2 suggests that they are reasonably high for industrial countries. That would not be the case, however, for a nation that is the specialized sole producer of a product facing a price-inelastic demand in the rest of the world.

Those who fear the instability of a flexible exchange rate often have in mind not the trade balance but speculative capital flows. What will happen when the holders of a country's currency see its market-determined price begin to fall? Will they not rush to convert their liquid assets into foreign exchange, and thereby drive the exchange rate down further? Similarly, will not speculative rushes amplify the appreciation of an exchange rate? Speculation thus could make a flexible rate wildly unstable. Nonetheless, there are several good reasons for discounting this outcome:

1. Imagine a currency whose price is market-determined, with its average equilibrium value constant in the long run, but its actual value subject to periodic upward and downward disturbances. Would speculation amplify these disturbances? If so, the speculators would be buying when the price is high, and selling when it is low. Their speculative activities would be unprofitable in the long run, and they would ultimately have to desist. Just what this argument proves is uncertain, because it is not hard to find other examples of persistent

[3] For a good brief summary of Canada's record, see A. F. W. Plumptre, *Exchange-Rate Policy: Experience with Canada's Floating Rate.* Essays in International Finance, no. 81. Princeton: International Finance Section, Princeton University, 1970; and also S. C. Tsiang, "Fluctuating Exchange Rates in Countries with Relatively Stable Economies: Some European Experiences After World War I," *IMF Staff Papers*, 7 (October 1959): 244–73.

unprofitable speculations.[4] But it does cast some doubt on the view that speculation will generally be destabilizing.

2. The fear that speculation would destabilize a flexible exchange rate probably draws erroneous support from countries' experience with fixed exchange rates. Speculating on a change of a fixed rate is quite a different game from speculating on the movement of a flexible rate. When a country has persistently lost international reserves and faces continued pressures to devalue its currency, a bearish speculator selling the currency can hardly lose. If the government fails to stave off devaluation, he wins a quick profit. If the government weathers through and no change occurs, the speculator at worst makes no profit; there is little or no chance that a currency will be revalued (inflicting a loss) when the general public thinks it likely to be devalued. By contrast, a flexible exchange rate responds continuously to pressures in the foreign-exchange market. If persistent forces push a currency in one direction (downward, let us suppose), speculators may indeed swing into action and try to profit by anticipating the final extent of the depreciation. In doing so they would push the rate to its new equilibrium value sooner than otherwise. Eventually, however, the speculators bet against one another. They run out of the one-way option for speculative profit that is supplied by a fixed rate on the verge of change, and cannot discount the possibility that the currency has been oversold and will appreciate somewhat. Hence, the fact that profit-maximizing speculators tend to "destabilize" the maintenance of a fixed exchange rate at a disequilibrium value fails to prove that they would likewise destabilize a flexible rate.

3. A lot of empirical evidence has accumulated on the effects of speculation when exchange rates have been freed. When exchange rates are freed in a crisis, wide swings due to speculative movements sometimes occur. But these swings should in all likelihood be blamed on the crisis conditions rather than on the innate destabilizing potential of speculation. In more tranquil cases such as the Canadian dollar in the 1950's, speculation appears to have been stabilizing. Speculators bucked movements in the price of the Canadian dollar and pushed it back toward its average or trend value.[5]

Does a Flexible Rate Have Disadvantages?

A flexible exchange rate has disadvantages. Some will be mentioned in the next section. Here we shall consider one of general significance. Two classic functions of money are as a "unit of account" and a "store of value." It performs these functions better if the general price level of the goods and services bought with money

---

[4] Furthermore, there are important limitations to the theoretical argument. See W. J. Baumol, "Speculation, Profitability, and Stability," *Review of Economics and Statistics*, 39 (August 1957): 263–71.

[5] Paul Wonnacott. *The Canadian Dollar, 1948–1962.* Toronto: University of Toronto Press, 1965, esp. chap. 8.

remains constant. Uncertainty about future transactions is reduced. People can more easily plan transactions that will maximize their profits or utility, and are likely to make fewer mistakes. We often think these advantages of monetary stability hold for a price level that is stationary over time. Yet they have a spatial dimension as well: the wider the scope of economic activity over which money's average value is stable, the greater are the advantages to the holder. Clearly a business firm in the United States benefits from knowing that a dollar will always be worth a dollar anywhere in the country. For instance, in deciding whether to erect a new plant in Ohio or Illinois, the entrepreneur need not devote his energies to weighing the chances that Ohio's currency unit will shift in value against that of Illinois. Thus the certainty provided by a single currency promotes the integration of economic activity across an area, making competition more effective and decisions on the allocation of resources more rational.

These advantages accrue in greatest measure to the use of a common currency within a country. But keeping exchange rates fixed between currencies provides similar if lesser gains in certainty, rationality, and the integration of markets. Notice that to secure these advantages countries must not just eschew flexible exchange rates. They must also avoid changing their pegged exchange rates. The advantages are those of monetary integration and permanent fixity of exchange rates, and not advantages of the "adjustable peg" over flexible rates.[6] Notice also that this advantage is greater for the small and specialized nation that consumes mostly imported goods and services, and little of its domestic produce. If the nation produces only coffee for export (coffee comprising a small portion of domestic household budgets), its citizens would benefit more if the monetary unit is stable in terms of imported goods and services than if it is stable in terms of coffee. For this nation a fixed exchange rate would stabilize its currency's purchasing power in terms of foreign goods and services, whereas a flexible exchange rate would allow it to be stabilized in terms of coffee.[7]

21.2 NATIONAL POLICY SYSTEMS AND GAINS FROM FLEXIBILITY

How do we weigh this advantage of fixity against those of flexibility outlined above? Each country must choose among ways to attain external balance, of course. The analysis makes it plain that the gain a

---

[6] Many observers have winced over the paradox that governments defending fixed exchange rates — in the name of economic certainty — often employ special tariffs and restrictions on capital flows that impair the certainty of international transactions just as fundamentally as does changing the exchange rate.

[7] This point is made by R. I. McKinnon, "Optimum Currency Areas," *American Economic Review*, 53 (September 1963): 717–24.

country can derive from a flexible rate depends both on its economy
and on the way it manages its economic policy. Here we shall show
how various features of a nation's economic policy system can affect
its potential benefits from exchange-rate flexibility.

The Source of Disturbances

The gains from flexibility are influenced by the source of disturbances
to a national economy — whether they originate in its own expenditure circuit (e.g., changes in investment, or shifts in consumers'
purchases of durable goods) or in its international transactions
(demand for exports, or level of international capital flows). In Chapter 17 we saw that disturbances from either source, in the fixed-
price model, cause changes in expenditure and employment, through
the open-economy multiplier. Adopting a flexible exchange rate
changes the extent to which these disturbances are multiplied,
however, and the change is not the same for domestic disturbances as
for those of foreign origins.

Suppose that a disturbance takes the form of a recession abroad,
cutting the demand for the home country's exports. With the exchange rate fixed, the analysis of Chapter 17 suggested that domestic
real income and employment are lowered by the amount of the reduction times the open-economy multiplier — $1/(s + m)$ if we neglect
foreign repercussions. If domestic expenditure also responds to net
outflows of cash balances, we saw that the reduction in real income
becomes larger still — the disturbance times $1/m$. With the exchange
rate fluctuating freely, however, and no changes occurring in private
capital flows, we expect no reduction in income and employment at
all! The fall in exports drives down the demand for the country's currency on the foreign exchanges and reduces its price. Imports become
more expensive at home, its exports cheaper abroad; throughout the
world, this shift of relative prices causes home goods to be substituted for foreign goods. The depreciation of the exchange rate proceeds until the trade balance is restored to equilibrium. No net
disturbance arises in the trade balance. If the value of exports falls,
its effect on the domestic income stream is just offset by a switch of
domestic expenditure from imports to home goods. Hence, ideally, a
flexible exchange rate completely insulates an economy's income
stream from expenditure disturbances originating abroad.[8] An additional advantage of flexible exchange rates thus lies in their power to
insulate the domestic income circuit from external disturbances. A
nation would value this virtue more, the larger and more frequent the
foreign disturbances impinging on its trade balance.

At the other extreme, suppose that a nation's trade flows undis-

[8] The completeness of this insulation is subject to some qualifications. See
S. Laursen and L. A. Metzler, "Flexible Exchange Rates and the Theory of
Employment," *Review of Economics and Statistics,* 32 (November 1950):
281–99.

turbed, but major fluctuations in private investment chronically upset its domestic income circuit. Suppose also that its policy instruments are inadequate to control or offset these fluctuations. Is it then better to let the exchange rate fluctuate, or should it be fixed? With a fixed rate, induced changes in income again are governed by the open-economy multiplier, $1/(s + m)$. If the exchange rate were flexible, however, the multiplier would be larger, and wider swings in income and employment would be induced. When investment declines, spending on imports is pulled down along with total income. The reduced demand for foreign exchange causes the country's currency to appreciate, switching world expenditure away from its exports and precluding the rise of a trade-balance surplus. The import leakage is blocked, and the value of the open-economy multiplier (for domestic disturbances) raised from $1/(s + m)$ to $1/s$. The flexible rate in effect denies the country the opportunity to export some of its unemployment, and supplies a selfish argument for a fixed rate when a country suffers uncontrollable income disturbances of domestic origin.

The Domestic Instruments Available

A country's preferred system for managing its exchange rate would also be affected by any constraints on the policy instruments available for maintaining internal balance. Every student of introductory economics learns how fiscal and monetary policy can be used alternatively (in the closed economy) to secure full employment. Yet political constraints often limit a country's use of one tool or the other. In the United States, the need for agreement between the legislative and executive branches on any change in taxes or expenditures shackles fiscal policy; in the British parliamentary system, by contrast, major fiscal changes can be put into effect almost immediately. On the other hand, some less-developed countries find monetary policy unusable because their domestic money markets are undeveloped, or because the money supply is tied by statute or convention to foreign-exchange reserves. If a country must count on only fiscal policy, or only monetary policy, to maintain full employment at home, it needs to know whether fixed or flexible exchange rates make its available policy instrument work better.

In section 21.1 we mentioned, as a basic argument for flexible rates, that letting the rate float relieves the country of the need to use its scarce policy instruments to sustain external balance. On this ground a nation with an impaired supply of policy instruments would prefer flexible rates. The matter is not so simple, however, when capital is highly mobile internationally. We ordinarily think of monetary policy affecting aggregate demand and employment through a change in the rate of interest. If capital flows into or out of the country whenever the rate of interest rises or falls, one's hunch would be that the ability of monetary policy to affect employment is changed substantially. Indeed, when the exchange rate is flexible and capital highly mobile, monetary policy is an effective tool for altering aggregate demand, but fiscal policy is fettered. (We shall explore the reasons for this in section 23.2.) Hence, a nation blocked from using monetary policy for internal balance should think twice before adopting a flexible exchange rate in a world where capital is highly mobile.

Inflationary Pressures — reason for fixed rates

One popular argument for fixed exchange rates holds that they are necessary (for some countries) to prevent runaway inflation. The competing claimants for the real income flow — workers, farmers, pensioners, shareholders, etc. — jointly demand more than 100 percent of the pie. A democratic government can keep their demands from leading to unreasonable inflationary pressures only by a political gambit: it must elevate the protection of its (fixed) exchange rate to top-priority status and justify curbing inflation by its adverse effects on the balance of payments. If one accepts the view that income demands can be quelled in no other way, this argument for a fixed exchange rate deserves some weight. But a government in this position adopting a flexible exchange rate does not obviously wield a weaker club. It can point to the "disgraceful" depreciation of a flexible exchange rate subject to inflationary pressures, to warrant attacking them.

This nail-the-flag-to-the-masthead argument for fixed rates has another weakness. The country that tolerates inflation while maintaining a fixed exchange rate may simply "export" part of its inflation by running a trade deficit. That deficit must be matched by a net surplus in the rest of the world, which could be inflationary for other countries.

21.3 ADJUSTMENT IN AN INTEGRATED MONETARY AREA

We have seen that countries in some situations might rationally prefer fixed exchange rates: if uncontrollable income disturbances arise from internal sources, if only fiscal policy is available for attaining internal balance, or if preserving a fixed exchange rate is the only defense against inflationary pressures at home.[9] These findings lead to a more basic question: how far can we extend the advantages of an integrated monetary area? How large is an "optimum currency area," a region united by a common currency unit so that exchange-rate changes become impossible? Should all 50 United

---

[9] For a more complete survey of these pros and cons, see T. D. Willett and E. Tower, "Currency Areas and Exchange-Rate Flexibility." *Weltwirtschaftliches Archiv,* 105 (no. 1, 1970): 48–63.

States employ the same currency unit, or would some regions benefit by declaring monetary independence? Should the members of the European Economic Community proceed with their plans to establish a common currency and monetary area? To answer these questions, we need evidence on how adjustments take place among the regions of a single country. One hears no complaints about external imbalance from the State of Wyoming or the County of Durham. Do such imbalances occur? Are they automatically corrected? Or are they simply not noticed?

Regions do suffer from external imbalance, often very seriously. But they see the problem — quite reasonably — as one of adjusting to whatever *real* imbalance underlies the imbalance in net payments. A region by definition lacks control over its own money supply, and cannot bring external imbalance upon itself through unwarranted monetary policies. It may be subject to real disturbances, however, which leave it in external disequilibrium: "overvaluation" or "overspending" disturbances, as defined in Chapter 19, or their opposites. A common source of regional payments disturbances is a change in the fate of a major regional industry. New England suffered an external deficit when manufacturers in the South discovered that they could produce textiles at lower cost than the Yankees, and expanded output. New England's textiles came into excess supply at the current terms of trade; the rest of the nation's goods came into excess demand. When the mountain states exhaust deposits of nonferrous metal ores (which they sell competitively at the world price), once again the area's factor services are in excess supply and the rest of the nation's goods in excess demand. The region is likely to spend more than the real income it can now command.

One reason that a region does not believe its adjustment problems involve external imbalance is that it holds no official "interregional reserves" to allow itself to run an exchange-market deficit. Thus there can be no ex post deficits measured in the way described in Chapter 5. But the many sources of internal disturbance to a region can easily provoke ex ante external imbalance, and one can often spot symptoms of adjustment to this imbalance even if no deficits become visible ex post. Let us explore some of the ways in which regional imbalances are financed in the short run, or corrected in the long run, within a national area such as the United States. We suppose that the country's demand shifts away from a major export of the region. At least in the short run, prices are sticky, so that resources become unemployed rather than permit a drop in their rates of pay.

Private Accommodating Capital Flows

Consider the adjustment burden faced by such a region, if the adverse demand shift is permanent. It must pay the adjustment costs of moving some of its factors to other activities where they can earn the highest reward now obtainable. And it may wish to consume more than its income, temporarily, to cushion the shock of shifting to a permanently lower level of real income and consumption. Hence adjustment is easier if the region's owners of factor services readily can borrow externally in order to finance these adjustments. This ease is greater, the more fully the region is integrated into a national capital market.

By ease of borrowing, we refer to several traits of an integrated capital market. Many of the securities held by individuals will be widely traded outside the region, so they can be sold to finance short-run overspending without any decline in their price.[10] The region's banking system is likely to have access to an external wholesale market in short- and medium-term credit. Hence a heavy contraction of bank credit need not be forced when the external imbalance causes the region's banks to lose reserves — a likely manifestation of external imbalance. Finally, apart from these special links, if the region's capital market is more integrated, it will be less likely to pay a heavy risk premium for short-term borrowing, and substantial borrowings will be less likely to drive up the rate of interest it must pay.[11] Hence an integrated private capital market, by easing short-term transitional borrowing, helps to mask external imbalance for a region. This private borrowing in a sense substitutes for the accommodating capital flows reflected by changes in the official reserves of a nation in external imbalance.[12]

Official Transfers in a Federal Fiscal System

Membership in a federal fiscal system can smooth a region's internal and external adjustments considerably. A region's citizens pay taxes into a central treasury, and public expenditures within the region are determined by a central authority. The outflow of tax payments from the region need not equal the inflow of expenditures from the federal treasury, in either the short or long run. Whether the region is a net donor or a net recipient of transfers in the long run, its position in the short run will shift when internal and external imbalances arise. We assumed that, because of price rigidities, the decline in demand causes regional unemployment in the short run, and reduces incomes. Important taxes, especially personal and corporate income taxes, vary with the level of incomes, and regional tax payments fall when unemployment increases. In addition, some government ex-

[10] We noticed this element in monetary adjustment in section 16.5.

[11] We are abstracting from the influence of the size of the region relative to the capital market into which it is integrated. (In a larger region, a given proportional rate of borrowing would more greatly increase the rate of interest of the nation as a whole.) Rather, we refer to the interest premium that would be demanded in a less integrated capital market by lenders asked to hold more securities of a "foreign" region in their portfolios. See section 23.2.

[12] For an interesting case study see J. C. Ingram, "Some Implications of Puerto Rican Experience," *International Finance,* ed. R. N. Cooper. Harmondsworth, England, and Baltimore: Penguin, 1969, chap. 4.

penditures are likely to rise — unemployment insurance and related welfare payments, any public works projects that are designed to combat unemployment, etc. The region's receipts from the central government rise and its payments fall; this net increase in inward transfer payments helps to finance the trade deficit that reflects the initial disturbance. Like the private borrowings described previously, it provides a transitional contribution to maintain expenditure levels and cover the costs of reallocation.

Factor Migration

The difficulties facing a region in which the demand for its export has declined would be only transitional if resources could be shifted to other industries within the region where they could earn the same rewards. For reasons set forth in Chapter 8, however, at least some factors of production are likely to be worse off after all readjustments have been made within the region. Rather than settle for lower rewards, they may instead migrate to other regions. The outward movement of labor, for instance, should relieve the external imbalance of a region, as well as the unemployment that reflects its internal imbalance. When a worker leaves a region, regional income goes down by the amount of his marginal product, and regional expenditure by the amount of his consumption. As we saw in Chapter 5, the region's trade balance (in the absence of capital flows or transfer payments) must equal the difference between these. The unemployed worker's marginal product is zero, whereas his consumption (sustained from personal savings, unemployment compensation, or borrowing) remains positive. Hence his departure should help to restore external balance. The same conclusion would follow even if he had not become unemployed, but the decline in demand for his output renders the market value of his marginal product less than his current level of consumption. Hence the easy interregional movement of factors of production provides the region in an integrated national economy with another cushion for adjustment to external imbalance. However, this mobility may leave stranded any complementary factors of production that are immobile between regions. An important difficulty faced by "declining regions" is the burden placed on immobile resources; they cannot protect their real incomes, and they may fail to lower their money wages (either through price flexibility or a downward adjustment of the region's exchange rate) to gain any remaining employment opportunities.[13]

These adjustments suggest the conditions needed for a country to

[13] In principle, the argument of this paragraph pertains to the long-run allocation of real capital as well as of labor. One must distinguish between the short-run advantages of a region in borrowing from outside in order to finance adjustments, and the best long-run alternative, which may be a permanent net export of capital from the region. We shall take up the relation between real and financial flows of capital in Part 5.

benefit from permanently locking its exchange rate. Its factor markets should be integrated with those of other countries, so that private capital can assist in financing transitional difficulties, and labor and capital can migrate to avoid severe and prolonged adverse swings in their incomes. It would benefit greatly from membership in a fiscal union as well, to secure the cushioning benefits of transfers of federal funds. Fiscal unification is also needed to secure high factor mobility, because otherwise differing tax structures and regulations governing factor payments impede mobility. Finally, the region fixing its exchange rate must in effect abandon an independent monetary policy. As we saw in Chapter 18, divergent movements of national price levels will ultimately be inconsistent with equilibrium at the initial exchange rate; and the size of the imbalances resulting from unequal rates of inflation increases as markets become more tightly integrated.

Can the European Economic Community's members, or any such group of sovereign nations live with exchange rates permanently fixed among themselves? Significant monetary and some fiscal integration are planned by the EEC, but many observers doubt that they will be accomplished soon or easily. The preceding analysis suggests that for a country to benefit from joining a currency area — permanently fixing its exchange rate — it must also take part in an integrated system for planning financial policy. Will the nations of the EEC place their macroeconomic policies in the hands of the Community's central authorities, to the degree indicated? Is the EEC an optimum currency area?[14] Does *any* optimum currency area extend beyond the borders of an established nation-state? These questions remain open.

21.4 OTHER WAYS TO MANAGE RATES

Fixity and flexibility of exchange rates each seem to enjoy some advantages. Hence people have sought devices that would combine the chief advantages of each, or at least eliminate some major disadvantages. In this section we shall examine two of the principal compromise proposals to see how they try to combine the pure systems of fixed and flexible rates.

The Band Proposal

From World War II until 1971, members of the International Monetary Fund committed themselves to exchange rates fixed not at a single point value but within ±1 percent of their announced parities. In

---

[14] Stephen Marris. *The Bürgenstock Communiqué: A Critical Examination of the Case for Limited Flexibility of Exchange Rates.* Essays in International Finance, no. 80. Princeton: International Finance Section, Princeton University, 1970, chap. 3.

principle, a nation's exchange rate could remain flexible and market-determined so long as its equilibrium value stayed within these limits. The international monetary upset of 1971 and the events leading up to it convinced nations of the need for somewhat greater flexibility of exchange rates. As a result, many have now agreed to maintain their rates within a wider "band" of $\pm 2\frac{1}{4}$ percent. In fact, most countries failed to utilize the full flexibility allowed by the former ± 1 percent band; their use of the wider limits remains to be seen.

The acceptance of enlarged limits for exchange-rate fluctuations effected what has been called the *band proposal* for increased flexibility. Its proponents have usually called for widening the band, say, to ± 5 percent of the announced parity. An exchange rate could then change as much as 10 percent. The proposal dates back to nineteenth-century discussions of "gold points" — the margins for exchange-rate fluctuation under the gold standard that result from the transactions costs of shipping gold from one country to another.[15]

The band proposal claims the flexible rate's advantage of relieving the government of the need to use its policy instruments in pursuit of external balance. Within the generous limits of the band, the exchange rate would respond freely to market forces. Policy must be managed to keep the rate within these limits, of course, but a preoccupation with external balance is no longer necessary. At the same time, limits on the band, which the government is firmly committed to defend, would reduce the uncertainty otherwise associated with a flexible exchange rate. If the government made clear its determination to keep the equilibrium rate within the band, persons planning long-term international transactions (for example, establishing manufacturing subsidiaries in foreign countries) would know the maximum loss they could incur from exchange-rate variation. Exchange-rate risks would deter them less from undertaking transactions that, on the most likely outcome, would be profitable and socially productive. Furthermore, any tendency for speculators occasionally to take flight and thus destabilize a purely flexible rate would be curbed.

In evaluating the band proposal, one should notice that as a currency's market value approaches the upper or lower limit of the band, the government finds itself in the same position as a surplus or deficit country under the adjustable-peg system of Bretton Woods. In its pure form, the band proposal aims to relieve the constraint of external balance on policy formation in the short run, but offers no help for securing any cumulative long-run changes in exchange rates that may be needed.

[15] For a good introduction, see George N. Halm. *The "Band" Proposal: The Limits of Permissible Exchange Rate Variations*. Special Papers in International Economics, no. 6. Princeton: International Finance Section, Princeton University, 1965.

The Crawling Peg

In some ways the opposite of the band proposal is the *crawling peg*, sometimes also called the gliding parity. Rather than undergo discrete changes of 5 to 15 percent (the typical range nowadays), exchange rates would be changed (when necessary) by much smaller amounts, but at much more frequent intervals. Thus, nations might agree to change their pegged rates by no more than two percent annually, and to make such shifts through periodic tiny changes, perhaps $\frac{1}{26}$ percent each week.[16]

The chief aim of the crawling-peg proposal, as a modification of the present system of pegged rates subject to occasional large changes, is to avert the pressure of speculative capital flows. When a rate changes overnight by 15 percent, a speculator correctly foreseeing the move can make a handsome profit on his funds. The smaller the exchange-rate change that he expects within a period, however, the smaller is this rate of speculative profit. Suppose that a country in external deficit wishes to devalue its currency by the maximum two percent a year via the crawling peg, and that the (short-term) interest rate prevailing in the rest of the world is five percent. If it announces its plan for a crawling devaluation, and at the same time puts its own interest rate at seven percent, it destroys the incentive for speculators to move their funds outward. The two percent capital loss they can avoid by exporting their funds for a year is just offset by the two percent they would then forego in higher interest earnings at home. And transactions costs deter them from moving funds just to benefit from the weekly changes. By deescalating the size and significance of changes in the exchange rate, proponents claim that the crawling peg would also permit more rational planning of exchange-rate changes within countries and better coordination among nations.

Would the crawling peg really dispatch the threat of speculative pressures to orderly changes in exchange rates? In the short run, its effectiveness depends on the credibility of each country's commitment to change its rate at no more than the indicated speed. This credibility depends, as with the present fixed rates, on the adequacy of the international reserves that the country owns or can borrow. In the long run, the crawling peg can work only if the underlying market equilibrium exchange rate moves no faster than the maximum crawl of the pegged rate.[17]

[16] See John H. Williamson. *The Crawling Peg*. Essays in International Finance, no. 50. Princeton: International Finance Section, Princeton University, 1965, and Marris. *The Bürgenstock Communiqué*, chaps. 4, 6.

[17] In principle, of course, nations could choose a faster rate of crawl. But a faster rate would require wider displacements of their short-term interest rates in order to deter speculative capital flows. Most economists implicitly believe that as the "assignment" of monetary policy to this role grows more vexatious, interest rates must become more displaced from their conventional levels.

Unlike the band proposal, the crawling peg leaves a country with the policy system of fixed exchange rates. External balance must still be consciously and continuously pursued. The leverages of policy instruments on domestic aggregate demand (see section 21.2) would remain those of the fixed-rate system. The band proposal by contrast would switch the economy to those of the flexible-rate system when the rate floats within the band, but they would flip back (for changes in one direction) to those of the fixed-rate system when it lies at the floor or ceiling. The crawling peg concentrates on removing a principal inhibition to changes in exchange rates under the Bretton Woods system, with the goal of allowing more prompt and rational changes in pegged rates.

In summary, one might say that the crawling peg naturally appeals to those who prefer the policy system of the fixed exchange rate, but are worried about securing adequate room for long-run changes in exchange rates. The band proposal, on the other hand, appeals to those who prefer the policy system of the flexible rate, but are worried about the play of speculative forces and the cost imposed by the risk of large exchange-rate changes.

21.5 SUMMARY

Allowing the exchange rate to fluctuate freely in response to market forces has potential advantages that a country can view in two ways. When restoring exchange-market equilibrium requires changing the level of its prices relative to external prices, altering the exchange rate is easier and less costly than changing each domestic money price. Alternatively, letting the rate float removes external balance as a policy objective and allows use of the nation's scarce supply of policy instruments for other purposes. Fixed exchange rates claim the advantage of reducing the risks to international transactions — if they are permanently, and not just temporarily pegged.

The weight of these competing claims will vary for a country, depending on its policy system. (1) If disturbances to its income circuit stem mostly from external sources, flexible exchange rates insulate its income and employment level from them; if disturbances are internal, fixed rates let it foist the adjustment burden partly on other countries. (2) With capital highly mobile internationally, monetary policy becomes an effective tool for internal stabilization when the rate is flexible, fiscal policy when it is fixed; this fact could influence the choice for a country constrained in its use of one instrument or the other. (3) Some people argue for fixed rates as a political help to a government fighting inflationary pressures.

The question of a fixed or a flexible rate can be generalized to the question of what constitutes an "optimum currency area," within which the rate is permanently fixed, and between which it floats. Adjustments taking place in regions of a single country reveal the conditions necessary for a nation to benefit from belonging to such a currency area. They include high levels of interregional (international) factor mobility, membership in an integrated federal fiscal system, and willingness to abandon an independent regional (national) monetary policy. It is difficult to see how a nation could gain from joining a larger currency area without at the same time subordinating itself to a federal government.

Devices have been proposed for combining the advantages of fixed and flexible rates. The band proposal would allow the rate to fluctuate freely within a fixed floor and ceiling. The crawling peg would keep the rate fixed but adjust it (when necessary) by tiny amounts at frequent intervals. Coupled with appropriate management of monetary policy, it would allow exchange rates to change without disruption by speculative pressures.

SUGGESTIONS FOR FURTHER READING

Cooper, Richard N. *The Economics of Interdependence: Economic Policy in the Atlantic Community.* New York: McGraw-Hill, 1968. In Chapter 7 Cooper summarizes the evidence on the adjustment of interregional payments imbalances.

Friedman, Milton. "The Case for Flexible Exchange Rates"; American Economic Association, *Readings in International Economics.* Homewood, Ill.: Richard D. Irwin, 1968. Flexible rates are viewed as a device to improve performance of markets.

Halm, George N. *The "Band" Proposal: the Limits of Permissible Exchange Rate Variations.* Special Papers in International Economics, no. 6. Princeton: International Finance Section, Princeton University, 1965. Allowing exchange rates to adjust flexibly between fixed limits.

Johnson, Harry G. "The Case for Flexible Exchange Rates, 1969," *Selected Topics in International Trade and Finance: A Book of Readings,* ed. R. E. Baldwin and J. D. Richardson. Boston: Little, Brown, 1973. Sophisticated summary of case for flexible rates.

McKinnon, R. I. "Optimum Currency Areas," *American Economic Review,* 53 (September 1963): 717–24. Fixed rates are analyzed in terms of optimum currency areas.

Plumptre, A. F. W. *Exchange-Rate Policy: Experience with Canada's Floating Rate.* Essays in International Finance, no. 81. Princeton: International Finance Section, Princeton University, 1970. Canada's experience with a floating rate in the 1950's.

Williamson, J. H. *The Crawling Peg.* Essays in International Finance, no. 50. Princeton: International Finance Section, Princeton University, 1965. Adjustment of fixed rate by small periodic changes.

Fixed : crawling peg

Flex. : band proposal

PART FIVE **International Factor Movements**

22 The International Mobility of Factors

The traditional account of international trade and production that was discussed in Chapters 6–9 of Part 2 is based on a strict and partially unrealistic dichotomy between commodities and productive factors. Commodities can be traded between countries at zero transport costs, whereas factors of production — especially labor and capital — are assumed to be immobile internationally. This assumption is certainly convenient and powerful, and the theory that it supports casts light on the manner in which the international exchange of commodities can to some extent compensate for international differences in resource endowments and technology. However, some international mobility of factors does exist in the real world. This fact both alters some of the conclusions based on earlier models and poses new problems for economic policy.

This chapter provides an overview of the significance of international factor mobility. The discussion begins in section 22.1 with the classic analysis of the "transfer problem." This term refers to the consequences, especially for the terms of trade and the balance of payments, of having one country transfer purchasing power to another in the form of reparations, grants, or loans. Such a transfer of purchasing power is one type of international "capital" movement, although the real transfer of capital may be more indirect, with the receiving country able to free some of its own resources for the accumulation of capital. In section 22.2 we shall face this issue by analyzing the transfer of productive factors from one country to another. The significance of factor mobility for the efficiency of world production is the subject of section 22.3.

Although the international movement of capital involves a greater accumulation of real capital in the receiving country, ownership of this capital often remains vested in residents of the other country. This is the case of direct foreign investment, and it poses policy problems both for the government of the host country and for the government of the country that owns the capital. As we shall reveal in section 22.4, arguments for government intervention are similar to those encountered in Part 3 in our discussion of commercial policy interfering with the free flow of commodities. In section 22.5 we shall turn to some aspects of the international migration of labor.

This chapter is succeeded by two others that probe in depth the phenomena of long-term and short-term international capital flows, emphasizing their importance in the present world trading community.

22.1 THE TRANSFER PROBLEM: PURCHASING POWER

Consider the following case: The home country is obligated to make a gift or reparations payment to the foreign country. It could be France after the Franco-Prussian War in 1870–71, or Germany after World War I. To broaden the possible categories we could consider a different kind of "gift" — the Marshall plan whereby the United States sent aid to Europe after World War II. For analytic purposes we should also include international lending and borrowing, but we shall ignore the future problems of repaying loans (a reverse transfer). All these cases have something in common: the home country transfers purchasing power to the foreign country.

Transfer and the Terms of Trade

We may begin our discussion by referring to the simple model of commodity exchange discussed in Chapter 2. As you recall, the home country exchanged some of its fixed endowment of clothing for food, which was in excess supply in the foreign country. To discuss the transfer problem we may either (1) assume that the home country makes a gift of clothing and food from its commodity endowment, or (2) assume that the home country transfers purchasing power abroad by cutting its own consumption below the level of its endowment income, enabling the foreign country to consume the same amount above its endowment income. Either assumption leads to the same conclusions — for ease of exposition we have chosen the second.

The immediate question is the effect of such a gift or reparations on the commodity terms of trade. Figure 22.1 illustrates the initial equilibrium for the commodity imported by the home country, food. World demand equals world supply at a relative price of food (the terms of trade) shown by OA. A transfer of purchasing power does not alter the world totals of food and clothing, so that the world supply curve in Figure 22.1 does not shift. But if tastes differ at home and abroad the world demand curve will shift, leading to new equilibrium terms of trade.

To ascertain whether the relative price of food rises or falls with

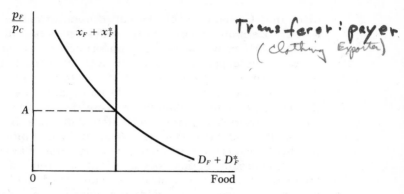

Handwritten annotation: Transferor : payer (Clothing Exporter)

FIGURE 22.1 World Demand and Supply for Food

transfer, we must determine whether the world demand schedule, $D_F + D_F^*$ in Figure 22.1, shifts to the right or to the left. In the home country aggregate spending is reduced by the amount of the transfer, and a fraction of this, m (the marginal propensity to import), represents the reduced demand for food at the initial terms of trade, OA. Thus the D_F curve shifts leftward by amount m times the amount of the transfer. This shift may be more or less balanced by the increased demand for food abroad as their demand curve, D_F^*, shifts rightward by their marginal propensity to consume food times the amount of the transfer. But this marginal propensity is just one minus their propensity to import clothing, m^*. Thus the aggregate world demand curve for food shifts to the right if and only if $(1 - m^*)$ exceeds m. More formally, a transfer turns the terms of trade against the transferor (in our case, the relative price of food rises as the home country pays reparations) if and only if the sum of the two countries' marginal propensities to import falls short of unity.[1]

If the sum of the marginal propensities to import is less than unity, we speak of the "secondary burden" of the transfer in acknowledgement of the fact that price changes create an international redistribution of income additional to the initial loan or grant. Between the two world wars a number of eminent economists were concerned with the practical importance of this issue. John Maynard Keynes eloquently argued that the reparations payments imposed by the Allies on Germany after World War I underestimated the true pay-

Handwritten margin notes: $\Delta D_F \downarrow$ $\Delta D_F^* \uparrow$ Donor country worsens its TOT if $m + m_2 < 1$ (Secondary Burden of the Transfer)

[1] Recall the income effects of a change in the terms of trade that we introduced in Chapter 3. We found that any rise in the relative price of a commodity causes real income to fall in the country that imports the commodity and to rise in the exporting country. That is, any change in the terms of trade *transfers* real income from the net importer to the net exporter of the commodity that has risen in price. In other words, the concept of a transfer payment and its effect on world demand has already been encountered in our earlier discussion of the exchange model. The novel element introduced in this chapter is the consideration of an explicit income transfer at the initial terms of trade — in the form of a gift, reparations payment, or loan.

ment that Germany would be called upon to make.[2] According to Keynes, German export prices would have to fall considerably, coupled perhaps with a rise in its import prices, in order for Germany to create the export surplus that is the counterpart of the financial transfer. In reply to Keynes, Bertil Ohlin proposed that the transfer itself, by lowering spending in Germany and raising spending in the recipient country, could bring about the required export surplus without requiring a change in the terms of trade. By thus focusing on the effects of income changes, Ohlin ironically anticipated some of the theory that is now associated with the name of Keynes. Ohlin was more "Keynesian" at this early stage.[3] In any event tracing the adjustments that the German reparations required is difficult, for this period was characterized by an additional reverse transfer in the form of private loans and capital movements from the United States to Europe.

Of course the terms of trade will shift in favor of the paying country if the sum of the marginal propensities to import exceeds unity. Each country's taste pattern might be biased heavily toward the commodity that it imports — perhaps explaining the pattern of trade. (Recall our discussion in Chapter 2 of how both supply *and* demand differences between countries contribute to the export-import pattern.) In such a case the home country's cutback in spending on foreign goods with transfer, coupled with the increased demand for the home country's export commodity as spending rises in the foreign (recipient) country, could substantially improve the home country's terms of trade. What are the limits to such a "secondary blessing" of the transfer payment? Could the terms of trade turn so much in favor of the transferor that its real income gains on this account outweigh the initial loss due to the transfer? As long as commodity markets are stable they cannot.

To see why the answer must be no, consider Figure 22.2. The initial terms of trade are shown by *OA*. Suppose that *OB* represents the relative price of imports in the home country at which the gains in real income at home (represented by the improvement in the terms of trade in going from *OA* to *OB*) would exactly balance the direct loss of real income represented by the transfer itself. If, after transfer, the terms of trade should settle at *OB*, real income in each country would remain what it was before the transfer with terms of trade, *OA*. The question is: could there be zero or negative excess demand for food at price *OB* after the transfer? Clearly not, because with real incomes unchanged, the drop in food's relative price in going from

---

[2] John Maynard Keynes, *The Economic Consequences of the Peace* (New York: Harcourt, Brace and Howe, 1920).

[3] See the exchange between Keynes and Ohlin: Keynes, "The German Transfer Problem," *Economic Journal*, 39 (March 1929): 1–7 and B. Ohlin, "The Reparation Problem: A Discussion," *Economic Journal*, 39 (June 1929): 172–73. Both are reprinted in American Economic Association, *Readings in the Theory of International Trade*.

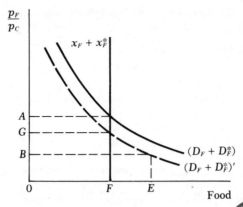

FIGURE 22.2   Transfer and the Terms of Trade

A transfer may improve the terms of trade of the transferor, as shown by the drop in food's relative price from *OA*
to *OG* when the home country (the importer of food) makes
a transfer. *OB* represents such an improvement in the home
country's terms of trade that its real income is unaffected
by the payment. Therefore at price *OB* world demand must
exceed world supply, because only substitution effects are
involved in demand.

OA to *OB* must induce only a substitution effect in each country —
toward a greater demand for food than initially at *OA*. The new world
demand for food must exceed the fixed world supply at terms of trade
OB — shown by distance *FE* in Figure 22.2. Therefore the new equilibrium relative price of food must be higher than *OB*, say at *OG*. The
paying country can never improve its terms of trade so much that it
actually gains by giving.

Having established that the direction of the movement in the terms
of trade depends on the comparison between $m + m^*$ and unity, is
there any presumption as to the direction of the inequality? On the
basis of the exchange model considered here, relatively little can be
said.[4] But if the "transfer" involves resources as well as purchasing
power we may argue that the terms of trade will probably turn in

[4] The issue of "presumption" as to the movement of the terms of trade with
transfer was exhaustively analyzed by Professor Paul Samuelson in 1952:
"The Transfer Problem and Transport Costs: The Terms of Trade when Impediments are Absent," *Economic Journal*, 62 (June 1952): 278–304. Samuelson concluded that in the model analyzed above there was little presumption
one way or another. More recently, one of the authors of this book has argued
that there may be a presumption that the terms of trade turn in favor of the
transferor. The argument depends on the fact that a country's trade pattern
need not be independent of its tastes and that, more often than not, a country
may import the commodity for which it has a taste bias. R. W. Jones, "The
Transfer Problem Revisited," *Economica*, 37 (May 1970): 178–84.

favor of the paying or lending country. This presumption will be taken up in section 22.2.

Transfer and the Balance of Payments

The transfer described above must result in a trade surplus for the home country amounting to the value of the transfer, which we call T. That is, in the new position of equilibrium,

$$p_C M^* - p_F M = T.$$

Suppose such a transfer takes place, and consider the initial effect before any prices change or the exchange rate alters. Because of the rise in incomes abroad (by amount T), the home country's exports rise by $m^* \cdot T$. Similarly, imports at home are reduced by $m \cdot T$. On both counts a balance of trade surplus is created for the home country. How does this surplus compare with the eventual required surplus, given by T? Adding up the increase in home exports and the reduction in home imports suggests that the transfer will be *undereffected* if $(m^* + m)T$ falls short of T. Obviously this question involves the same criterion that we have discussed. If the sum of import propensities is less than unity, additional steps must be taken to effect the transfer. The home country's exports might have to fall in price and perhaps its exchange rate devalued.

The point of this discussion is that there are two ways of describing the consequences of a transfer: (1) By concentrating on commodity markets we can ask what change, if any, is required in the terms of trade to clear markets that are thrown out of equilibrium by the initial transfer. (2) By concentrating on the balance-of-payments equilibrium condition we can ask whether the income effects of the payment can create a sufficient trade surplus for the transferor. If it cannot, we speak of the transfer as being undereffected, requiring further measures to stimulate the appropriate excess of exports over imports. On the other hand, if $(m + m^*)$ exceeds unity, the transfer is "overeffected" and may be accompanied by an improvement in the terms of trade of the transferor or, perhaps, an appreciation of its exchange rate.

22.2 THE TRANSFER PROBLEM: REAL RESOURCES

A transfer in the form of a gift, a loan, or reparations often involves more than a redistribution of purchasing power. Real resources may be moved from one country to another. This movement may be direct, such as in the stripping of German capital equipment at the end of World War II and its relocation in Eastern Europe and the Soviet Union. Or the process may be more indirect: a country such as Canada may borrow on the New York market, causing a greater investment in new capital equipment in Canada and perhaps less new capital equipment in the United States. In this section we shall investigate the possible repercussions on the terms of trade and real incomes of a transfer of real capital from one country to another.

To analyze the effect of such a real transfer on the terms of trade we should reconsider the logic used in the previous section. In a stable market the relative price of a commodity will rise only if the transfer creates an excess world demand for that commodity at the original price. The world supply schedule in our previous analysis was un-affected by transfer — no new commodities were created in the exchange model. But if productive resources are involved in the transfer, the world supply pattern, as well as the demand pattern, may be affected. We shall now consider three extreme possible responses of production to a transfer of resources.

The Heckscher-Ohlin model of trade discussed in chapters 8 and 9 illustrates one possibility. Both countries share the same technology, and let us assume that each is incompletely specialized in the production of the same two commodities, food and clothing. A transfer of real capital equipment from the home country to the foreign country contracts production of the capital-intensive commodity at home and expands the production of the capital-intensive commodity abroad. If there are no factor-intensity reversals, this commodity is the same in both countries. We do not need to go into such details as the fact that production of the labor-intensive commodity would actually expand in the country losing capital and contract in the receiving country. The important point is that if technology is identical in the two countries, and if both countries produce the same two commodities, there is *no* change in the world supply of either as a result of the transfer of real resources. The effect of transfer of resources on the terms of trade in such a case depends only upon differences in taste patterns between countries — just as in the preceding analysis. By assumption the countries have identical technology and would use an increment in resources, of whatever composition, in the same way.

Turn, now, from this extreme case to another. Suppose each country specializes in producing its export commodity. As was illustrated in Chapter 9, this outcome is possible even in the Heckscher-Ohlin model with identical technologies if factor endowments are sufficiently different between the two countries. If the home country transfers resources to the foreign country, production of the commodity exported at home must fall, and the supply of the home country's import commodity on world markets must rise. There is no question as to which way the terms of trade will be altered. The relative price of exports in the home country must improve, thus alleviating to some extent the decline in its real income represented by the initial transfer.[5]

---

[5] You may wonder if the improvement in the terms of trade could make it worthwhile for the home country to give resources to the foreign country in such a case. The answer is quite possibly yes, in contrast with our analysis

The two extreme cases considered above make the general point that much depends on the use to which each country would put extra resources. To round out this discussion consider a "neutral" case in which a transfer of resources from the home country to the foreign country causes a proportional fall (in the home country) and rise (abroad) in the quantity of all commodities that would be produced at the initial terms of trade. This case is illustrated in Figures 22.3a and b. The initial free trade equilibrium is shown by production points A and A^* and consumption points B and B^*. The home country (Figure 22.3a) imports food, and its demand for imports matches the foreign country's exports. (The line segment BA is parallel and equal in length to A^*B^*.) The assumption here is that a transfer of resources from the home country to the foreign country causes the home country's transformation schedule to shrink uniformly toward the origin and the foreign country's T^*T^* schedule to expand uniformly in the same proportion to $T^{*'}T^{*'}$. Such a transfer in resources also changes incomes and spending at the initial terms of trade. We assume that in the home (paying) country consumption of both commodities is cut proportionally from B to D, while in the foreign (receiving) country consumption expands uniformly from B^* to D^*. This ensures that the line segment DC in Figure 22.3a is shorter than segment D^*C^* in Figure 22.3b, or, to phrase this differently, that at the initial terms of trade the paying country's demand for imports (of food) shrinks, while abroad the net import demand for clothing rises. Because segment BA initially equaled segment B^*A^*, the world market for food and clothing cannot be in equilibrium at the old terms of trade after the transfer. The emergent excess world supply of food at the old terms of trade must improve the home country's terms of trade. There is no "secondary burden" of the transfer. Instead, the alteration in world demand and supply must, in this idealized case, mitigate the net effect on real incomes of such a transfer.

In this discussion we have dealt with the transfer of resources in rather simple models of trade to show that if the receiving country applies its resources in a different manner than they would have been employed in the paying country, the terms of trade are apt to change. If each country puts new resources into the commodity in which it possesses a comparative advantage, such a transfer of resources must improve the terms of trade of the transferor.[6] Of course this

---

in section 22.2 in which no aggregate world supply changes were involved. To probe further at this point is to anticipate our discussion of the phenomenon of "immiserizing growth" in Chapter 25 whereby an increment in the resource base of a country may, through deterioration in the price that its exports can command on world markets, make the country worse off than it would have been without growth.

[6] Recently Professor Samuelson has argued in the opposite vein, in what might be termed the "Avis" school of transfer. Suppose the receiving country responds to the transfer by increasing leisure instead of production, while the transferor compensates for its loss of purchasing power by cutting back on

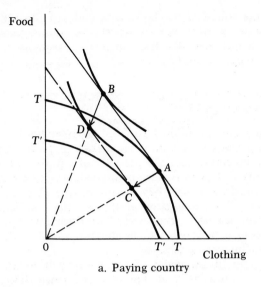

a. Paying country

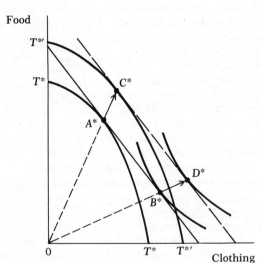

b. Receiving country

FIGURE 22.3 Transfer of Resources: The Neutral Case

If a transfer of resources shrinks production and consumption uniformly toward the origin in the paying country and outward in the receiving country, the terms of trade must improve for the paying country.

result need not follow if the borrowing country allocates its newly acquired resources to bolster its import-competing facilities. More will be said about this allocation in our subsequent discussion of economic development in Chapter 26.

22.3 FACTOR MOBILITY AND THE EFFICIENCY OF WORLD PRODUCTION

The first important lesson derived from the model of pure exchange in Chapter 2 pointed to the gains from trade if pretrade price ratios differed between countries. The existence of different prices signaled the profitability of buying where commodities are cheaper for consumption in markets where they are more expensive (i.e., evaluated relatively highly). A comparison of the returns that factors of production earn in various markets would similarly indicate the profitability and gains in efficiency to be derived from the international mobility of productive factors.

The Heckscher-Ohlin model of two-country trade (discussed in Chapters 8 and 9) is a convenient point of departure. In that model we proved that if both countries engage in free trade in commodities, and produce both commodities with the same technology, factor prices will be equalized between countries although factors are (in that model) completely immobile internationally. Free trade in commodities completely substituted for the international mobility of factors; with factor prices equalized internationally, no economic incentive remains for labor or capital to migrate even if barriers are removed. Notice furthermore that if resources are transferred between countries, world outputs would not change — as we found in the previous section. This finding supports our contention that gains in potential efficiency in production are signaled by a discrepancy between what a factor can earn in one region and another. A world of factor price equalization as a consequence of trade in commodities is a world in which factor mobility itself would be unnecessary in further expanding world output.

These remarks are not intended to suggest the unimportance of international factor movements. Instead, they should indicate that factor mobility could be significant when commodity trade does not completely equalize factor returns internationally. As we discussed in Chapter 9, even in the Heckscher-Ohlin model with technology identical throughout the world, one or both countries could be specialized in production if factor endowments are sufficiently dissimilar. In such a case free trade would not equalize factor returns from one

leisure and working harder. If each country is specialized to its export commodity, such a transfer must worsen the terms of trade for the transferor. See P. A. Samuelson, "On the Trail of Conventional Beliefs About the Transfer Problem," *Trade, Balance of Payments, and Growth*, eds. J. Bhagwati et al. Amsterdam: North Holland, 1971, chap. 15.

country to another, and if capital, say, could migrate from the region in which returns were low to the country where capital earns higher returns, the efficiency of world production would be improved.

Figure 22.4 illustrates these points. Two transformation schedules are drawn — each showing the locus of maximum *world* outputs in a model in which each country has the same technology. The inner locus, *TT*, shows the possible world outputs of food and clothing if labor and capital in each country are efficiently utilized, and if free trade guarantees that producers everywhere face the same (world) commodity prices — but factors of production are not allowed to move from one country to another. The range *AB* corresponds to world outputs of the two goods where each country produces both food and clothing. The stretch northwest of *A* along *TT* has one country specialized in food, and the *BT* section of *TT* southeast of *B* has one country specialized to clothing production. Along both these stretches factor returns are not equalized between countries, so that once factors are free to migrate, world output would expand. The dashed curve, *T'T'*, shows possible world outputs when factors can move from one country to another.

The gains to world production from international factor mobility can considerably exceed those shown in Figure 22.4 if countries have different technologies and if these differences are not rooted in the superiority of the factors of production. This latter proviso is important. If, say, the typical American worker is better trained and

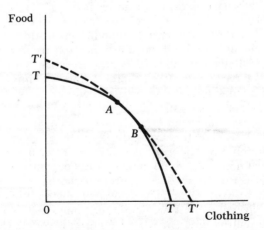

FIGURE 22.4   The World Transformation Curve with International Factor Mobility

The *TT* locus of production possibilities for the world assumes that factors are immobile internationally. The expanded locus, *T'T'*, results if factors can move across national boundaries in response to differential rewards.

educated than the typical Andorran, a higher American wage rate to attract the Andorran would be the wrong signal. Only if differential returns to factors geographically represent the contribution to efficiency of other factors or technology will a migration of that factor yield increased output.

22.4 FOREIGN INVESTMENT AND COMMERCIAL POLICY

Policy decisions are rarely made with international welfare in mind. Rather, a nation typically pursues its own gains. Our discussion of commercial policy in Part 3 amply demonstrated that a single country may gain by interfering with the free flow of commodities although from a world point of view such interference causes inefficiencies.

The same considerations guide a nation's stance toward the outflow or inflow of capital. In this case we have in mind not a gift or reparations, or even a sale of physical capital equipment. A different form of capital outflow often occurs in international transactions: Investment in foreign securities that may or may not grant effective control. This investment gives residents in one country a claim on earnings of physical capital in another. The important feature of this arrangement, for policy, is that either the lending or the borrowing country can, through interfering with this international flow of capital, affect the rate of return on capital at home and abroad. And this interference can affect real incomes.

Perhaps we can see this effect most easily by pointing to the analogy with tariffs or export taxes. If a country is not of negligible size compared to others it can raise the relative price of its exports (i.e., lower the relative price of its import commodity on world markets) by restricting trade by means of tariffs and/or export taxes. Suppose a country has followed a policy of noninterference with its own residents as they have accumulated capital abroad yielding an income (in the form of dividends and interest payments) that is repatriated. In such circumstances a tax levied on earnings of investments abroad will cut back the capital outflow. That is, such a policy makes capital artificially scarce abroad, driving up the rate of return to capital on previous foreign investments. This higher rate, in turn, increases real income at home, as would an export tax or import duty by raising the relative world price of a country's exports. In both cases the phenomenon at work rests upon a country's being important enough in foreign markets so that artificial (i.e., policy-induced) restrictions increase the relative price of what a country is selling (in the case of commodity exports) or lending and investing (in the case of foreign investment).

This argument seems geared to policy choices for a country whose residents have established a net flow of capital abroad. But it works as well for the "host" or borrowing country. If the home country is borrowing, and if it taxes foreigners on their investments at home, rates of return to capital at home will be raised. However, this policy also lowers the rate of return to capital secured from abroad (because foreigners now keep more capital in their own country). You may think that taxation of earnings of nonresidents would in both cases raise the rate of return on capital in the borrowing country and lower it in the lending country; that is correct. But if the borrowing country levies the taxes, its government collects the tax revenue. Thus restriction on capital flows can appeal not only to the lending country but also to the borrowing country.

This argument has ignored the interaction between capital markets and commodity markets. Quite aside from the direct effect of a nation's restrictions on the international flow of capital is the use of that capital in producing commodities and the consequent effect on the terms of trade. Any nation that engages both in export-import transactions and international borrowing or lending must be aware of the consequences of these capital flows on commodity markets. And these may either harm or help. For example, a nation's foreign investment may be focused toward developing increased supplies of commodities that it imports. In such a case, any argument for restricting outflows of capital must balance, as well, the consequences of such policies in worsening the country's terms of trade. On the other hand, countries such as the United Kingdom have engaged in capital exports that have established foreign sources for commodities such as textiles that competed directly with British exports. Restrictions on these exports of capital could have been considered as a device to prevent the British terms of trade from deteriorating.

The connection between commodity markets and capital markets is not as one-sided as this discussion suggests, with its emphasis on the feedback to the terms of trade of policies designed to affect international investment flows. International capital mobility in turn questions the desirability of commercial policy that is aimed directly at commodity markets. In brief, what is involved is the possibility that a tariff or other interference in commodity markets may affect the rate of return on foreign invested capital. It is all a bit reminiscent of the joint problem of maintaining internal and external balance in Part 4 — any policy aimed at one target usually spills over to affect the other.

22.5 INTERNATIONAL LABOR MOBILITY

In our discussion of the international mobility of factors of production we have concentrated on capital flows. But labor may cross international boundaries as well. In some cases this flow has been striking: the large emigration of European labor (and, to a lesser extent, Asiatic nationals) to the United States in the late nineteenth and early twentieth centuries; the flow from East to West Germany from the end of World War II to the time of the Berlin Wall; the huge influx

of labor into Israel after 1948; in Europe today the provisions made
for labor flows between countries in the Common Market.

The effect of immigration of foreign nationals upon the well-being
of already-established residents at home is often questioned. Fears
are sometimes expressed that if such immigration is allowed, and if
the newly arrived workers bring with them, on the average, less
wealth or capital per head than that possessed by local residents,
the living standards of the original community will deteriorate. No
doubt such immigration will cause a redistribution of factor incomes
among laborers, capitalists, and landlords.[7] But the question usually
goes beyond this effect in asking about the welfare of the community
as a whole.

Some insight into this problem can be gained by considering a
simple model in which all residents at home own the same bundle of
two factors of production, say labor and capital. Suppose, furthermore, that the country produces only one commodity, and does not
exchange goods with other countries. The situation is illustrated in
Figure 22.5. The original inhabitants possess the factor endowment
combination shown by point A, and the factor price ratio is given by
the slope of line BB tangent to isoquant Q_1 through A. The community
consumes what it produces, quantity Q_1. Suppose now that immigration is allowed, and that the new entrants bring with them, on average, less capital per man than the original group possesses. The new
aggregate capital-labor bundle is a point such as C, with the enlarged
community producing quantity Q_2 and the capital-poor immigration
reflected in the lower wage/rental ratio shown by the slope of the Q_2
isoquant at C. The question first raised concerns the fate of the
original inhabitants. At the new factor prices the capital-labor bundle
A, their endowment, is worth the same as bundle D. But D can produce quantity Q_3, which is greater than Q_1. In short, the original
inhabitants can now consume more of the single commodity produced
than they could before immigration.[8]

This argument is not new. It is a rehash of our account in Chapter 2
of the gains to be derived when a community can trade at prices different from those originally prevailing at home. The novel element
is that there is only one commodity, and the new prices are factor
prices. The original inhabitants, whose factor endowment bundle is
shown by point A in Figure 22.5, are viewed as trading *factor services*
with an outside community at "terms of trade" for factors that would
differ from those at home before immigration. As long as immigrants
possess a different factor endowment bundle from the original inhabitants, thus causing a change in the wage/rental ratio, the original
community will gain.

[7] This redistribution can be significant. Why are European capitalists and
American workers up-in-arms about United States direct investment in
Europe?

[8] The foregoing argument was suggested by Harry G. Johnson in "Some
Economic Aspects of Brain Drain," *The Pakistan Development Review*, 7
(August 1967): 379–411.

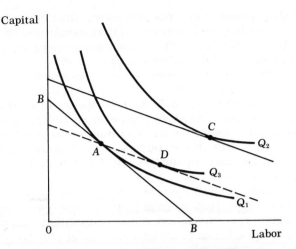

FIGURE 22.5 Immigration Benefits Home Residents

The community owns the labor and capital shown by bundle *A*. Preimmigration factor prices are given by the slope of line *BB*. Immigration alters factor prices, allowing owners of bundle *A* now to trade factor services to command output Q_3 at *D*, greater than initial Q_1.

This result may be surprising. It is predicated, however, on the assumption that no international exchange of commodities takes place, allowing us to neglect the effect of migration upon the terms of trade. For example, the original community might export the labor-intensive commodity and the influx of immigrants embodying an even higher labor/capital ratio than at home might worsen its terms of trade. Although this effect is possible, it is not necessary. It ignores the fact that the immigrants come from a region in which they were also producing commodities. Indeed, our remarks about the Heckscher-Ohlin model with two countries producing two commodities with common technology illustrated that no change in world outputs or the terms of trade need be implied.

22.6 SUMMARY

In this chapter we have sketched some ways in which a world where commodity exchange is supplemented by loans, reparations, or factor movements differs from the "classical" models in which each country relies on its own internationally immobile resources. Transferring factors of production or purchasing power from country to country is apt to disturb commodity markets. On the demand side this transfer entails a comparison of taste patterns, and the terms of trade will change according to whether the sum of import propensities exceeds or falls short of unity. This result is merely the international expression of the basic proposition that any redistribution of purchasing power and spending will shift the composition of aggregate demand if tastes differ between the gainers and the losers.

To the extent that real resources are also mobile internationally, aggregate world supply changes also influence the effect of factor mobility on the terms of trade. Our discussion in section 22.2 suggested that the initial effect of a transfer on welfare would be mitigated by a movement of the terms of trade in favor of the lending, or paying, country. But this secondary effect depends on the circumstances, and the reader should be warned that in this area economists' opinions differ widely.

More agreement can be reached on the view that greater mobility of factors is better from a world point of view than lesser mobility. The argument relied upon here is basic: any differential in returns to factors from one locale to another is a signal that productive gains may be obtained by allowing factors to move from regions where their return is low to areas where it is greater. As section 22.4 revealed, however, national and international perspectives can differ. From one country's point of view limiting international factor movements — especially of capital — may be rational. Labor mobility presents its own problems. In addition to the arguments cited in section 22.5 there must be mentioned the concern of some countries about the departure of especially talented citizens in response to more lucrative employment possibilities abroad. This departure has sometimes been referred to as the "brain drain." We leave as an open question whether it is in any country's interest to impose controls over the movement of peoples across national boundaries.

SUGGESTIONS FOR FURTHER READING

Johnson, Harry G., "Some Economic Aspects of Brain Drain," *The Pakistan Development Review,* 7 (August 1967): 379–411. A discursive treatment of some problems of labor mobility.

MacDougall, G. D. A., "The Benefits and Costs of Private Investment from Abroad: A Theoretical Approach," *Economic Record,* 36 (March 1960): 13–35. The analysis of foreign investment in a simple model of specialization.

Samuelson, Paul A., "The Transfer Problem and Transport Costs: The Terms of Trade when Impediments Are Absent," *Economic Journal,* 62 (June 1952): 278–304. A thorough analysis of the classical transfer theory.

Supplement to Chapter 22:
Transfer, Capital Flows, and Welfare

At two points in Chapter 22 an algebraic account based on the supplements to Chapters 3, 12, and 13 can usefully verify or extend our discussion of transfer and capital flows.

THE TRANSFER PROBLEM

First we shall consider a transfer of purchasing power from the home country to the foreign country that was the subject of section 22.1. Before any transfer takes place the value of imports at home (pM in units of clothing) equals imports abroad (M^*). A transfer of purchasing power, of amount T expressed in units of clothing, causes imports at home to fall short of imports abroad by the transfer:

$$pM = M^* - T. \tag{22.S.1}$$

Differentiating totally, and dividing every term by pM (which initially equals M^* when the transfer is zero) yields:

$$\hat{p} + \hat{M} = \hat{M}^* - \frac{dT}{pM}. \tag{22.S.2}$$

Recall that a ^ over a variable indicates a relative change, so that $\hat{p}$ is dp/p, etc.).

Imports into each country change for two reasons: (1) At unchanged terms of trade the transfer of purchasing power produces an income effect in each country. $\partial M/\partial T$ is given by $-m/p$, where m is the marginal propensity to import at home; $\partial M^*/\partial T$ is *plus* m^*, the foreign marginal propensity to import. (2) A change in the terms of trade causes imports to adjust along the offer curve. The elasticities, ϵ and ϵ^*, capture these changes. Putting them together we find:

$$\hat{M} = -\epsilon\hat{p} - m\frac{dT}{pM} \tag{22.S.3}$$

$$\hat{M}^* = \epsilon^*\hat{p} + m^*\frac{dT}{pM}. \tag{22.S.4}$$

With the decomposition of each country's imports thus available in these two equations, we can substitute into 22.S.2 in order to solve for $\hat{p}$ in terms of dT:

$$\hat{p} = \frac{1}{\Delta}(1 - m - m^*)\frac{dT}{pM}, \tag{22.S.5}$$

where

$$\Delta \equiv \epsilon + \epsilon^* - 1 > 0.$$

The denominator, Δ, is positive by virtue of the Marshall-Lerner conditions for market stability. Therefore a transfer of purchasing power from the home country adds a "secondary burden" in the form of a deterioration of the home country's terms of trade if the sum of import propensities is less than unity. This result was obtained by less formal means in section 22.1.

CAPITAL FLOWS AND WELFARE[1]

In section 22.4 we found that a country's policy toward foreign investment would be guided by some of the same considerations that are relevant to tariff policy. This formal similarity comes out clearly in the algebraic breakdown of the influences on a country's real income that we developed in the

[1] This section is based on R. W. Jones, "International Capital Movements and the Theory of Tariffs and Trade," *Quarterly Journal of Economics,* 81 (February 1967): 1–38.

supplements to chapters 12 and 13. In particular it is equation 12.S.6, re-written below as 22.S.6, which provides the basis for comparison:

$$dy = -Mdp^* + (p - p^*)dM. \tag{22.S.6}$$

Recall that the first term, $-Mdp^*$, is the familiar terms of trade effect while the second term, $(p - p^*)dM$, is the *volume* of trade effect. This latter effect states that if a tariff raises the home price of importables above their world level, any policy that cuts imports (e.g., a further tariff rise) results in a loss in real income because imports are valued more highly at home (as shown by p) than it costs to obtain them abroad (as shown by p^*).

To heighten the similarity let us assume that foreigners have invested a quantity of real capital (call it k^*) in the home country. They earn a return on this capital, dictated by prevailing rentals on capital equipment at home (call this r, measured not in dollars but in units of clothing). Assume the home country has levied a tax on these earnings, raising r above the foreign return to capital, r^*. *Net* of tax the home country is borrowing capital from abroad at rental r^*. Allowance for these payments must be made in the home country's budget constraint, as some of the incomes earned in production belong to foreign-owned capital. Thus:

$$D_C + p^*D_F = x_C + p^*x_F - r^*k^*. \tag{22.S.7}$$

At world prices the value of aggregate home demand equals the value of production less the amount (r^*k^*) that foreigners repatriate after payment of the tax.

Now follow the procedure we adopted in the supplements to Chapters 3, 12 and 13 and differentiate this totally to obtain:

$$(dD_C + p^*dD_F) = (dx_C + p^*dx_F) - Mdp^* - r^*dk^* - k^*dr^*.$$

In the left-hand expression in parentheses subtract and add pdD_F; in the right-hand expression in parentheses subtract and add pdx_F. Thus:

$$(dD_C + pdD_F) = (dx_C + pdx_F) + (p - p^*)dM - Mdp^* - r^*dk^* - k^*dr^*.$$

The expression in parentheses on the left is now, by definition, the change in real income at home, dy. The expression $dx_C + pdx_F$ would reduce to zero if there were no change in foreign investment, for it would represent a movement along the home country's transformation schedule. But if k^* changes — say it increases — the home country's transformation schedule shifts outward. That is, the new foreign capital would raise the aggregate value of home production. We do not have to specify the composition of this change; we notice only that the aggregate value of home production would rise by the marginal productivity of capital at home — and in a competitive market this is given by r[2]. Thus $dx_C + pdx_F$ would equal rdk^*.

Inserting these simplifications yields 22.S.8 as the basic result:

$$dy = -Mdp^* - k^*dr^* + (p - p^*)dM + (r - r^*)dk^*. \tag{22.S.8}$$

The home country imports food, whose relative world price is p^*, and, as well, "imports" or "borrows" capital, where r^* indicates the rental that must be paid abroad for capital services. The first two terms are thus both "terms of

---

[2] If the underlying production structure is characterized by the Heckscher-Ohlin model, we know from Chapters 8 and 9 that at constant prices the output of the capital-intensive sector will rise and output in the other sector fall, by virtue of the Rybczynski theorem.

trade" effects. An increase in p^* lowers welfare by an amount proportional to the volume of imports. In similar fashion for any increase in r^* the home country pays more to obtain its foreign capital, lowering welfare by an amount proportional to the preexisting stock of foreign capital invested at home, k^*. The last two terms are "volume of trade" effects. We have already described $(p - p^*)dM$. The term $(r - r^*)dk^*$ indicates that any restriction on foreign investment (a negative dk^*) must lower welfare at home if an interference with capital flows (a tax on foreign earnings at home) has raised the rate of return at home (r) over the cost of obtaining funds abroad (r^*).

Given the possible interconnections between foreign investment and trade patterns, the policymaker's task is clearly not easy. For example, the tax on foreign investment may be raised in the hopes of gaining from the "terms of trade" effect, $-k^*dr^*$. But this increase would involve a countervailing loss through the "volume of trade" effect, $(r - r^*)dk^*$. This is exactly analogous to the problem discussed in Chapter 12 in devising an optimum tariff. The present situation is more complicated because a restriction of foreign investment may, through its effects on the world pattern of production, change the *commodity* terms of trade (p^*) as well. As we will discuss in Chapter 23, this link may be strong because much foreign investment is channeled directly into a country's export- or import-competing industries. This account is clearly only the beginning of the story, even in theoretical terms, for the interconnections between capital flows and commodity production depend heavily on the underlying productive structure. Many possibilities could be spelled out. Our concern here is to develop the analysis only as far as equation 22.S.8, which provides the basic breakdown of the effect of commercial and investment policies on welfare.

23 Long-Term Capital Flows:
Portfolio and Direct Investment

In this and the following chapter we shall examine the principal forms of international capital transfers taking place about us. One purpose is to explore the practical side of the theory of international factor movements set forth in Chapter 22. We shall discover, for instance, that each type of capital movement is apt to affect domestic expenditure differently. Hence, when we ask whether a transfer of capital from A to B is requited, we must always specify the form of capital flow. We shall also find that each type of capital flow raises its own problems, when we try to explain its behavior and evaluate policies that nations employ toward it.

23.1 TYPES OF INTERNATIONAL CAPITAL TRANSFERS

Economists, practical men, and balance-of-payments statisticians agree on dividing capital flows into three types. First, we shall sort them into short-term and long-term flows, on the basis of the time expected to elapse before a loan is repatriated. The strictly arbitrary dividing line identifies long-term flows as those maturing after more than a year. We shall discuss short-term flows in Chapter 24. Next, we shall divide the long-term flows into *portfolio* and *direct* investments. Direct investment by one country in the economy of another gives its citizens control over the economic activity in which they invest; portfolio investment does not. The direct investor typically holds common shares in an enterprise abroad; foreign ownership today is usually by a multinational corporation, although it can arise simply through control of a majority of shares by foreign households. Bonds, preferred stocks, and common shares insufficient to gain control are the instruments of portfolio investment.

474

TABLE 23.1   Sources and Destinations of Long-Term
International Capital Flows, 1961–1964 [a]
(millions of U.S. dollars)

| Country | Direct investment | | | Other net long-term | Total |
	Outflows	Inflows	Net		
United States	−3,210	310	−2,900	−1,180	−4,080
United Kingdom	−670	480	−190	0	−190
France	−100	280	180	350	530
Germany	−220	200	−20	280	260
Italy	−170	350	180	−270	−90
Netherlands	−120	60	−60	60	0
Other industrial Europe	−60	110	50	240	290
Canada	−100	360	260	360	620
Japan	−90	80	−10	200	190
Semi-developed nations	0	510	510	370	880
Latin America	0	280	280	310	590
Africa/Middle East	0	250	250	40	290
Other Asia	0	90	90	220	310
Net errors of measurement [b]			−1,380	980	−400

Source: Marcus Diamond, "Trends in the Flow of International Private
Capital, 1957–65," *IMF Staff Papers,* 14 (March 1967): table 2.

[a] Negative figures represent outflows. See original source for qualifications
concerning the measurement of certain flows.

[b] Columns of net figures fail to add to zero because of errors in measuring
individual flows, inconsistencies in nations' definitions of flows, and omission
of some small countries. The large net outflow of direct investment results in
part because countries fail to count retained earnings of foreign subsidiaries
as inflows of direct investment.

You should realize that the divisions between these forms are not
only arbitrary but difficult to draw in practice. When one buys a
foreign bond with an original term to maturity of 30 years, the transaction will typically be classed as a long-term capital flow. Yet if the
bond was in fact issued more than 29 years ago, the purchaser surely
regards it as a short-term asset, and it should be so classed. Likewise,
passing control to foreigners, the distinguishing trait of direct investment, is hard to ascertain in practice. Suppose a United States corporation buys 30 percent of the outstanding common shares of a
Canadian company. If the remaining 70 percent of the shares are
dispersed in small holdings, this block may convey effective control.
Yet it is not the legal control conveyed by a majority ownership.

These capital movements are not the only forms of international
transfer of purchasing power. The principal exceptions are gifts
rather than loans. In the private sector, migrants' remittances are an

important transfer for some countries, because emigrants often send large sums to the relatives whom they left behind. (There is, of course, the reverse tradition of the "remittance man" — the black-sheep off-spring who is pensioned off to a remote pasture.) Important transfers of purchasing power such as foreign aid take place between governments. Reparations are transfers extracted by the victor from the vanquished after a war.

Because international capital flows are less visible to the ordinary citizen than are flows of merchandise trade, we show in Table 23.1 the flows of portfolio and direct investment between leading countries or groups. These data, averaged for the years 1961–64, were collected from the nations' individual payments statistics. They reveal the United States as the principal lender, but not the only one. Several countries are net lenders in one form, net borrowers in another. This fact suggests the wisdom of scrutinizing the types of capital flow among countries, rather than lumping them all together. Finally, the leading industrial countries experience both large inflows and large outflows of direct investment; we shall try to explain this two-way traffic in section 23.3.

23.2 PORTFOLIO CAPITAL AND THE TRANSFER PROBLEM

Long-term bonds are typically sold on the international market by borrowers who plan long-lived physical investments with low risks attached to their real productivity. The life span of the bonds usually matches somewhat the life span of the project because the borrower prefers to make his future revenues (or other benefits) from the investment project more or less match his future payments of interest and repayments of principal. The low-risk proviso is necessary if lenders are to take the bonds without demanding a forbidding risk premium. (If a project is spectacularly successful, the bond buyer gets no more interest; if it flops and the borrower defaults, he gets less. Because risk affects him asymmetrically, the bond buyer naturally demands a compensating increase in interest payments for a more risky project.) The only borrowers exempt from these patterns are central governments with strong taxing powers. They can raise revenues to meet their debt obligations even if the debt was incurred for no economically constructive purpose (e.g., fighting a war).

Because of these factors, which mark domestic as well as international capital markets, portfolio capital finances some types of projects more than others. Private enterprise borrows to finance large-scale durable investments such as transportation facilities, electricity generating plants, and plant and equipment in large-scale capital-intensive industries. Governments, especially local governments, borrow to finance what economists call "social overhead capital" — highways, schools, and the like. Governments of less-developed countries borrow heavily to finance major development projects.

These links between the capital flows and the use to which the funds are put are critical for the "transfer process," and are discussed below. We shall also study the forces that induce flows of portfolio capital, for these also affect the behavior of the economy and the working of economic policy.

Portfolio capital is a less important component of international capital flows now than in the past, and so we shall take an historical view of the subject. Although international bond sales have revived since World War II, they have not recaptured the relative importance which they enjoyed in the late 19th century, or even (fleetingly) in the 1920's. For instance, in the years 1900–1913, when Great Britain's net national income was about £1,900 million, new foreign investment (mostly portfolio) averaged over £150 million annually, about equal to her gross capital formation at home. Over the longer period 1880–1913 her accumulated foreign investments yielded annual earnings averaging £100 million, of which about £60 million were used to finance an import surplus and the balance plowed back into additional foreign investments. Whatever its status today, portfolio investment in the past transferred massive amounts of capital from country to country.

The Transfer Process in Practice

In section 22.1 we set forth a formal approach to analyzing the adjustment following a transfer of financial capital. That approach identifies the changes in the trade balance that should be associated with spending and financing a capital transfer, and compares the net reduction in the current-account demand for the borrower's currency with the increase in the capital-account demand for his currency due to the transfer. We saw that this comparison can fall in either direction. The model tells us how to predict the effect of a particular transfer on external balance (the terms of trade and equilibrium exchange rate), but not the direction of that effect. Such predictions are often very important for economic policy. For instance, during the 1960's the United States restricted outflows of both portfolio and direct investment in order to improve its balance of payments. Such measures could be sensible means to this short-run goal only if the forbidden transfers would have been undereffected, and it is not clear that American policy-makers assured themselves that this was the case.[1]

In this section we shall explore the transfer process, in less abstraction than in Chapter 22, for both portfolio flows and direct invest-

---

[1] Even if such measures improved the balance in the short run, they could impose real costs on the economy in the long run that would make them inefficient. See section 19.3.

ment — they do not differ greatly in this regard. We shall consider the link between the financial capital transfer and the trade balance in two stages: (1) how the financial capital transfer alters total expenditure; (2) how the change in total expenditure affects the trade balance.

Financial Transfer and Real Expenditure. A portfolio transfer generally begins with the purchase of a bond, giving the borrower purchasing power in this amount, and removing a corresponding amount of loanable funds from the capital market of the lending country. Likewise, when a corporation makes a direct investment abroad its domestic liquidity is reduced and the funds available for investment in or by its subsidiary increase. The first step in exploring the transfer process is to estimate the total change in expenditure in each country. Now, in a simple neoclassical model, one simply assumes that a dollar borrowed is a dollar spent. But this assumption is not necessarily true in the short run, and it is not necessary at all in the fixed-prices or Keynesian world that we explored in Chapter 17.

Consider the effect of a portfolio transfer on the capital markets of the lending and borrowing countries. A bond issued in the borrowing country is sold in the lending country. Had the transfer not occurred, the interest rate would have been higher in the borrowing country, and vice versa in the lending nation. The primary differences in real expenditure in the two countries are whatever results from these differences between the actual and hypothetical alternative levels of the interest rate. In a flexible-price model (Chapter 16), the mutual adjustment of interest rates, saving, and investment would have to proceed until the change in expenditure in each country equaled the transfer.[2] In the short run, however, investment may not be responsive enough for this result to occur. That is, the lower interest rate due to the transfer in the borrowing country need not tempt forth an equivalent net increase in investment, and the higher rate in the lending country need not compel an equivalent restriction. If we merely assume that capital markets take time to adjust, the short-run changes in spending can fall short of the amount transferred.

On the other hand, the real investment spending associated with borrowing from abroad can exceed the borrowing. This is especially clear for direct investment in a Keynesian model, where we recognize that investment depends on intangible factors of "confidence," and where an expansion of investment spending from one source need not raise the cost or lower the return to any other investment. A corporation establishes a subsidiary and builds a plant in the borrowing country. The plant's construction might induce complementary

---

[2] If saving responds to a change in the interest rate, part of the difference in expenditure in each country would be due to a change in consumption. E.g., in the lending country the lower interest rate in the absence of the transfer would correspond partly to higher consumption (lower saving), partly to higher investment.

investments: suppliers of inputs, or users of the plant's output, might expand their facilities; local governments might build more roads or other "social capital." The total increase in expenditure associated with the direct investment could then exceed the financial transfer made by the corporation.

Thus we see that the change in expenditure in the borrowing country could be either more or less than the amount of the transfer. Symmetrical possibilities exist for the contraction of expenditure in the lending country. Neither expenditure change thus must equal the other, nor must it equal the amount of the financial transfer.

Real Expenditure and Trade Balance. The theoretical analysis of Chapter 22 identifies the marginal propensities to import of the two countries (at pretransfer terms of trade) as the theoretical links between the change in expenditure, associated with a transfer, and the change in the trade balance. These propensities are not the same for each type of expenditure that might be increased in the lending country, or reduced in the borrowing country. Suppose that the borrower indeed spends the proceeds to build a factory (or other physical capital). If much of the expenditure falls on labor and heavy building materials, the import content (and thus the effective marginal propensity to import) is apt to be small. On the other hand, if the borrower imports his machinery, it could be large. Symmetrical possibilities pertain to the reduction of expenditure in the lending country. Of course, the reduction in spending in the lending country might be made by consumers, who increase their saving in order to invest profitably abroad. Then the relevant propensity to import would be that of the savers.

Policy-makers, we assume, are interested in the short-run responses of expenditure and the trade balance to changes in capital transfers. Hence, they often want to know not whether the transfer will be requited by income effects after everything has worked itself out, but rather how far along it will be after a period of time. Thus, one study of long-term capital transfers to Canada (a heavy borrower abroad) found that portfolio inflows would stay underrequited for at least a year. Hence an increase in portfolio inflows should improve the Canadian balance of payments (if its exchange rate is pegged) or drive up the price of the Canadian dollar (if it fluctuates freely). Direct investment inflows, however, are often overrequited within a year, if the Canadian economy is at or near full employment. Thus, an increase in direct investment would worsen the Canadian balance of payments (or depress the price of the Canadian dollar).[3] The difference between direct and portfolio inflows in this case depends partly on the complementary domestic investment accompanying projects that direct investment typically finances in Canada.

[3] R. E. Caves and G. L. Reuber. *Canadian Economic Policy and the Impact of International Capital Flows.* Canada in the Atlantic Economy, no. 10. Toronto: University of Toronto Press, 1969, chap. 2.

The Transfer Process and Economic Growth

Economic historians have noticed that transfers of portfolio capital in the nineteenth century were bound up with economic growth in various parts of the world economy. The rapid expansion of the regions settled by European emigrants — North America, Australia, New Zealand, South Africa, Argentina — reflected the emigration of European capital as well as European labor, and the rapid growth of their capital stock depended heavily on borrowing abroad. But capital transfers were also caused by the rhythm of economic growth. That is to say, they were not a strictly exogenous force in the expansion of these regions. Rather, movements of the capital account and current account both reflected fluctuations in the underlying pace of economic growth.

Professor J. G. Williamson studied this dependence on United States economic growth during the nineteenth century. He accepts the view that "long cycles" of 15 to 20 years can be found in the rate of economic growth, affecting both aggregate income and such major components of the capital stock as construction and railway building. When growth rates were high, the heavy demand for imports pushed the trade balance into deficit. But the peak growth periods also lured large quantities of capital from abroad. Indeed, the swings in capital imports were even stronger than those in the current account. As a result, the country was in external surplus during periods of peak growth and in deficit when growth slowed down (and the current account improved).[4] Viewed over the course of a long cycle, these movements of capital and the current-account balance resemble the transfer process at work: the current account moves in the right direction, but not enough to effect the transfer. Yet the dependence of both capital and current balances on the domestic growth rate explains the whole process more fully.

23.3 ENDOGENOUS CAPITAL FLOWS AND ECONOMIC POLICY

The dependence of capital flows between countries on conditions in their national economies has far-reaching implications for economic policy as well as economic behavior. Of course, the notion that capital movements between countries should depend on conditions within their economies also comes as no surprise. If lenders try to place their funds where the expected returns are highest, and borrowers to secure them from the cheapest source, capital will flow from areas where its price — the rate of interest — is low to where it is high. In the extreme, it might be perfectly mobile between countries.

[4] Jeffrey G. Williamson. *American Growth and the Balance of Payments, 1820–1913: A Study of the Long Swing.* Chapel Hill: University of North Carolina Press, 1964, esp. chap. 7.

Then the interest rate would be the same everywhere, and any country too small to influence the "world" interest rate could borrow or lend any amount it wished at that rate.

As with other commodities bought and sold, we can measure the responsiveness of international capital flows to changes in the rate of interest. We shall roughly equate a situation in which capital mobility is high to one in which the elasticity of portfolio capital flows to changes in the interest rate is high.[5] Much statistical evidence shows that the elasticity of capital flows among the industrial countries has risen to dramatically high levels since the late 1950's. This is true not only for long-term bonds but also for many short-term capital movements that will be discussed in Chapter 24, and the analysis of this section thus pertains to short-term flows as well. We cannot quite say that there is now just one interest rate in the world; imperfections in capital markets, transactions costs, and uncertainties about exchange rates and government policies still separate comparable interest rates in different countries. Furthermore, these wedges between rates are not constant in size. However, an interest rate does not appear to change significantly in one major country without visibly disturbing rates in other countries.

Countries have at times viewed this sensitivity of capital flows as a nuisance for the management of their domestic policies. The United States in 1963 put into effect an Interest Equalization Tax, designed to eliminate the advantage the European countries enjoyed by borrowing in the United States at lower interest rates than prevailed abroad. As we noticed in section 19.4, this action allowed the United States to maintain low interest rates (on account of unemployment at home) and still control its balance-of-payments deficit. Yet it imposed a real cost by preventing United States lenders from earning higher returns by placing funds abroad. In Chapter 24 we shall explore further the ways in which countries have struggled against the constraint imposed by international capital mobility on their domestic interest rates and economic policy.

As we saw in Chapter 18, however, their frustration is unnecessary. By wielding the proper combination of economic policies, both full employment and external balance should be attainable. Even if they wish to avoid changing the exchange rate when international payments are imbalanced, they can employ both fiscal and monetary policy in ways which ideally will secure full financial balance. Yet this message has been little taken to heart, and hence it is important to understand what happens when a country neglects it.

Consider the United States in the early 1960's, suffering from unemployment and wishing to ease monetary policy to reduce it. Assume that capital flows are perfectly elastic in response to changes

---

[5] We shall ignore until the next subsection some reasons that this elasticity is not constant over time — reasons that would not apply, say, to the elasticity of demand for apples or shoeshines.

in its rate of interest: any depression of the rate finds an unlimited amount ready to flow abroad. The central bank, neglecting this fact, applies its open-market policy and buys bonds, trying to place more cash in the hands of the public and to drive down the rate of interest (which is the same as driving up the price of bonds). Now, we expect that the public and the nation's financial institutions hold settled views on the money and bonds they wish to own, at any current rate of interest.[6] After the central bank makes its purchase, they find themselves with more cash and less bonds than they prefer. They buy bonds, trying to restore their portfolios to the desired mix. Now, if capital were not mobile internationally, these efforts would drive down the rate of interest and accomplish the bank's goals. With capital internationally mobile, however, an unlimited supply of bonds can be bought abroad at the current price (interest rate). Hence the asset holders' efforts to restore their portfolios simply replace from abroad the bonds bought up by the central bank. The cash injected by the central bank's bond purchase is spent to buy bonds abroad. But the exchange rate is fixed, and this extra demand for foreign exchange requires the government to step into the exchange market, selling foreign exchange and taking up the excess supply of domestic currency. The central bank's cash injection winds up back in the government's pocket again! Neither the public's cash holdings nor the domestic interest rate have changed at all, and monetary policy only creates (or worsens) an external deficit.

Although we shall not develop the argument here, it can be shown that this frustration will not apply to fiscal policy. A cut in taxes or an increase in government expenditure could stimulate total spending in the way described in the simple theory of fiscal policy.[7] Hence the government can stimulate employment at home if it picks the right policy.

Paradoxically, the effects of international capital mobility on the usefulness of policy instruments for full employment reverses completely if the nation adopts a flexible exchange rate. Monetary policy then effectively manages internal balance, and the frustration falls

---

[6] This behavioral assumption and some of its implications were discussed in section 16.5.

[7] In fact, capital mobility helps the application of fiscal policy. When the government tries to stimulate spending through fiscal measures, it increases its own deficit. It must sell bonds to finance this deficit, and the bond sales would ordinarily drive up the interest rate and partially offset the stimulus of the government deficit. With capital perfectly mobile, however, the extra government bonds face a perfectly elastic demand abroad, and can be sold without driving up the domestic interest rate or unleashing this offset. For a fuller account see R. A. Mundell. *International Economics.* New York: Macmillan, 1968, chap. 18; and R. I. McKinnon and W. E. Oates. *The Implications of International Economic Integration for Monetary, Fiscal, and Exchange-Rate Policy.* Princeton Studies in International Finance, no. 16. Princeton: International Finance Section, Princeton University, 1966.

upon fiscal policy. Let us trace the consequences of a monetary injection, now, with capital perfectly mobile but the exchange rate flexible. The story proceeds as before, until the public tries to buy bonds abroad to replace those bought by the central bank. With no government agency stabilizing the exchange rate, their extra demand for foreign exchange (to purchase foreign bonds) pushes up the price of foreign exchange, i.e., depreciates the country's currency. The inflow of bonds from abroad still keeps the interest rate from falling, so monetary policy is again denied its usual direct influence on interest and investment spending. However, the depreciating exchange rate changes the nation's balance of trade. Its goods grow cheaper abroad, and importable goods more expensive at home. The trade balance improves. As an expenditure stimulus for cutting unemployment, this favorable shift in the trade balance is just as good as an increase in domestic investment spending. Hence monetary policy works, under these conditions, if by a rather roundabout channel.

Fiscal policy would, by a process we shall not describe, become ineffective in the same circumstances of exchange-rate flexibility and capital mobility. Once more, we conclude that *one* policy instrument remains available to secure domestic policy objectives when capital is highly mobile internationally. Policy-makers must understand that high capital mobility, although it does not preclude successful management of domestic policy, does impel careful choice of a policy instrument. As we suggested in section 21.2, if an instrument is unavailable because of political or other constraints, the nation's choice between a fixed and a flexible exchange rate may be affected.

How much difference does the mobility of capital make in practice for the choice of policy instruments? The elasticities of capital flows may be high and rising, but they could still take effectively less than the infinite values assumed in the theoretical analysis. Table 23.2 reports the results of an attempt to calculate the effect of capital mobility on the effectiveness of policy instruments for the Canadian economy. During 1951–62, the period on which this study is based, Canada was closely exposed to sensitive international capital flows. Hence her experience may shed light on the situation in which the other industrial countries were more recently placed by the rising interest-sensitivity of capital flows.

The table shows estimates of the effect of fiscal policy (expenditure increase) and monetary policy (money supply increase) on gross national product in Canada. After these policies are changed, GNP starts to adjust to its new equilibrium value. The lines of the table reveal its deviation over the next five three-month periods from its previous value. Thus you can view the lines as empirical estimates of the multiplier effects described in elementary macroeconomic theory. The table confirms the theory set forth above about the effect of capital mobility on the relative strength of these multiplier effects.

TABLE 23.2   Effect of Changes in Canadian Policy Instruments
on Gross National Product in Succeeding Quarters,
with and without Capital Mobile, and with
Fixed and Flexible Exchange Rate
(millions of Canadian dollars)

| | | Number of quarters elapsed since policy change | | | |
Policy change	1	2	3	4	5
A. With exchange rate fixed:					
1. Increase government expenditure by $100 million					
a. Capital mobile	101	105	113	130	151
b. Capital immobile	97	98	103	117	136
2. Increase rate of growth of money supply by 1 percent					
a. Capital mobile	4.3	3.3	5.0	4.9	4.5
b. Capital immobile	8.4	5.6	8.7	8.5	7.8
B. With exchange rate flexible:					
1. Increase government expenditure by $100 million					
a. Capital mobile	77	81	91	115	144
b. Capital immobile	110	111	120	143	173
2. Increase rate of growth of money supply by 1 percent					
a. Capital mobile	63.8	7.1	13.1	17.1	18.8
b. Capital immobile	9.7	6.4	10.1	10.4	10.3

Source: R. E. Caves and G. L. Reuber. *Canadian Economic Policy and the Impact of International Capital Flows.* Canada in the Atlantic Economy, no. 10. Toronto: University of Toronto Press, 1969, table 9.

When the exchange rate is fixed (top half of the table), capital mobility raises the effectiveness of fiscal policy and lowers that of monetary policy. When the exchange rate is flexible (bottom half), the opposite shifts are observed. The differences are quite large, at least after a few quarters. Governments would ignore the effects of capital mobility, when calculating how far to pull the levers of policy, only at their peril.

Capital Mobility and Portfolio Adjustment

If the interest rate in Belgium remained higher than in the other countries of the world, would all the world's capital rush to Belgium? Would lenders of every nation hold nothing but Belgian bonds? Economists have recently investigated an important constraint on international capital movement — "portfolio balance." It arises in the following way.

Lenders place their capital on the basis of the returns they expect to receive on various assets. They are interested, however, not just in the size of the return, but also in the riskiness of the investment — the chances that their earnings from it might differ from their expectations. The wealthy individual (or financial institution) hence selects assets, not on the basis of the highest possible return, but rather for what he considers the best package of (high) return and (low) risk. The investor usually includes in his package a combination of assets — e.g., some common stocks likely to yield high returns but with high risk, and also some "gilt-edge" bonds yielding a low return but with low risk. If the expected return on the common shares of one company increases, investors will try to add more of it to their portfolios, but not to the exclusion of all other assets. Thus the demand for a security does not appear to be perfectly elastic in response to a change in its yield.

This practice of balancing portfolios for the best combination of return and risk holds important implications for international capital flows. Consider the lender choosing among bonds and stocks issued in several countries. A mix of countries will be represented in his portfolio, for at least two reasons:

1. One risk for the international lender is that of a change in the exchange rate between his currency and the one in which his assets are denominated. In order to cut the exchange risk to his portfolio, he would hold assets denominated in several currencies.[8]

2. The financial fates of companies (and, for that matter, local governments) within a country are often tied together. The nation's rate of growth, its ability to maintain full employment, its political stability, etc., affect the financial results of all its business firms in roughly the same way. That is, the levels and fluctuations of their profits, and the chances that they will meet payments schedules on their bonds, all move together. Because of this, the investor starting to diversify his portfolio gains less from adding new assets from the same country than from adding new assets from different countries. By "buying into" the growth and cycle patterns of different national economies, he may cut his risks quite effectively.[9]

---

[8] Of course, borrowers may prefer to take the exchange risk upon themselves, issuing obligations in a foreign currency in order to secure a lower interest rate. The bulk of Canadian bonds issued in the United States are denominated in United States currency, so the Canadian borrower loses if the price of the Canadian dollar falls and gains if it rises. Borrowers in European capital markets have issued bonds payable in "packages" of currencies, or in alternative currencies at the option of the lender, in order to secure the best combination of exchange risk and capital cost for themselves. For examples, see J. O. M. van der Mensbrugghe, "Bond Issues in European Units of Account," *IMF Staff Papers*, 11 (November 1964): 446–55.

[9] Herbert G. Grubel, "Internationally Diversified Portfolios: Welfare Gains and Capital Flows," *American Economic Review*, 58 (December 1968): 1299–1314.

If lenders heed these considerations in building their portfolios, several interesting implications arise for the pattern of international flows of portfolio capital. Interest rates could differ between countries without causing capital flows; the risk characteristics of securities emanating from the high-yield country could make investors unwilling to add enough of its securities to their portfolios to eliminate the difference in interest rates. On the other hand, capital could flow between two countries even if their interest rates are the same. Differences in risk could make investors want to hold securities of both countries; their expected returns would stay constant when they diversify in this way, but the riskiness of their overall portfolio is diminished. Notice that capital in this case would not flow only into or out of a country; securities would be swapped back and forth in both directions.

Finally, portfolio balancing tells us that differences in the sizes of countries can affect the direction of capital flows between them. Suppose that the current market value of the total portfolios of financial assets in country A is ten times as large as that of country B. No capital flows have taken place between them in the past, but both A's and B's investors now become conscious of the potential gains from diversification. If most lenders wish to hold assets from both countries, the *net* capital flow would probably run from large country A to small country B. The value of B securities which citizens of A try to add to their giant (aggregate) portfolio will probably exceed the value of A securities sought in order to balance the relatively tiny B portfolio. The United States is a heavy net lender to Canada, and the sizes of their respective portfolios differ in at least a ratio of 10 to 1. Yet the proportion of United States securities held in Canadian portfolios appears to be larger than the proportion of Canadian securities held in United States portfolios. Perhaps portfolio balancing and the different sizes of these two nations help to explain this pattern of capital flows. Notice, however, that it cannot be the *only* explanation, because Canadian interest rates do continue to lie above those in the United States.

23.4 DIRECT INVESTMENT

Direct investment is a distinctive form of capital transfer, and one that has become deeply controversial, especially in the borrowing (host) countries. Its distinctiveness lies in two traits:

1. Direct investment represents a capital movement, but the capital involved is entrepreneurial or risk-bearing. It does not merely finance the construction of plant and equipment. In its entrepreneurial role, direct investment is usually linked to the transfer of managerial skills and knowledge from one country to another. The corporation establishing or expanding a subsidiary abroad is the typical agent of direct investment.

2. It is strongly *industry-specific.* Its economically significant traits arise not so much from the transfer of capital from country *A* to country *B*, as from *A*'s *x* industry to *B*'s *x* industry. Specifically, direct investment flows along two industrial channels. *Horizontal* investment occurs when a firm producing a product in the source (lending) country establishes a subsidiary to produce the same good in the host country. *Vertical* investment occurs when it establishes a subsidiary to perform the next stage forward, or the next stage backward, in the fabrication and sale of its product. Many small foreign subsidiaries only distribute and sell the parent company's products in the host country; we shall largely ignore these cases of "forward" vertical integration. Much more important, in terms of the capital involved, are "backward" vertical integrations into producing a raw material or input in the host country used by the parent in the source country.

Because of these traits, an understanding of the causes and effects of direct investment is best gained by leaving the simple general-equilibrium models, usually so helpful in international economics, and turning to models of individual industries and markets. The models of imperfect competition and the analysis of technological factors presented in Chapter 11 are especially useful here.

Causes of Direct Investment

Why should a firm invest in production facilities abroad? It does not know the language, the laws, the customs, the local markets. The foreign government may not be its friend. There must be a general explanation for profit-maximizing firms, at least in certain industries, establishing foreign subsidiaries in the face of these obstacles. The following explanation concentrates on horizontal investments.

We can start with a factual observation: foreign investment is seldom undertaken by a company before it becomes an established, substantial seller in its domestic market. At this stage it has acquired managerial know-how, patents, trademarks, and other such intangible assets. These assets allow it to earn at least normal profits on its invested capital. Having been acquired while the firm built a position in the domestic market, they are now available for use elsewhere, if a profitable opportunity can be found.[10] At this point, foreign markets are apt to fall under its gaze.

Direct investment is sometimes an effective way to use these assets profitably abroad. Consider the company producing consumers' durable goods. It has discovered how to devise and modify features of

---

[10] These forms of intangible capital comprise what economists call "public goods." When a technique or an idea is put to productive use in the United States, there is no less of it available for employment in Britain. The productive capacity of a machine obviously does not share this property. See Harry G. Johnson, "The Efficiency and Welfare Implications of the International Corporation," *The International Corporation,* ed. C. P. Kindleberger. Cambridge: MIT Press, 1970, chap. 2.

its products to attract a significant share of those demanding such goods. Its products have attained a reputation for satisfactory durability and service. Its trademarks, patents, innovative and marketing skills, and (to a degree) its reputation with customers can be transplanted to foreign markets when it establishes production facilities abroad through direct investment. Furthermore, owning local production facilities aids it greatly in penetrating foreign markets. They make it easier to design its products for the special requirements of foreign markets, and to modify the new product as information on consumer acceptance feeds back. They may improve its performance in servicing its products.[11]

The firm described in this tale clearly does not sell in purely competitive markets. Indeed, the marketing assets that make its foreign investment profitable describe *product differentiation* as a characteristic of markets. We also described the firm as a large seller in its market. The marginally successful firm is not likely to have either the intangible assets or cash resources for profitable foreign investment; furthermore, gathering the information to start a foreign subsidiary is itself costly, and likely to appeal only to a firm willing to stake a large investment abroad. Hence we deduce oligopoly as another trait likely to mark the industrial setting of firms making direct investments. If firms investing abroad must be both large and prominent in their home markets, their number in those markets must be few.

When we notice the industries drawing the most direct investment, the pattern strongly supports this analysis. American firms producing automobiles, other consumer durables, rubber, and pharmaceuticals are very likely to have subsidiaries abroad. Firms producing primary metals, paper, and textiles are not. The same holds in other countries as well: in Canada, England, or other countries that have received large inflows of direct investment, foreign subsidiaries are likely to be important producers in the former's industries.

A firm is apt to become multinational at a certain stage in its growth. It has built up its research capacity and its product innovations. It has already expanded far enough in its base industry to make it look elsewhere for continued growth. When it goes abroad, its organizational structure must become suitable for new problems. Finally, its subsidiary undergoes a life cycle of its own, typically starting with a few activities under close supervision from the parent, gradually developing greater independence and a broader purview of its own.[12]

The causes of foreign investment are quite different for subsidiaries supplying raw materials needed by their parents. The explanation of

[11] This account is closely related to the "product cycle" explored in section 11.2. For such an interpretation, see Raymond Vernon. *Sovereignty at Bay: the Multinational Spread of U.S. Enterprises.* New York: Basic Books, 1971, chap. 3.

[12] See Vernon. *Sovereignty at Bay,* chap. 4.

these investments at first seems obvious: how can a rubber company produce tires without crude rubber? The more interesting question, though, is why the raw material source is developed by a subsidiary of the company that will process it, rather than by independent firms in the country where the raw material is found. The gain from this vertical direct investment seems to be the reduction of risk. Few companies in the world refine and fabricate copper. Important deposits of copper ore occur in only a few locations. If independent firms produced and refined the ore, both would be forced to commit funds to the construction of large fixed facilities without any guarantee about the bargain they could strike with the other party. What could the ore producer do if his smelter customer convincingly threatened to drop his business? What could the smelter do without an ore supply? "Vertical integration" in any industry reduces uncertainty. Because the firms extracting raw materials must be located where the resources are, and the firms processing and selling them where the markets are, foreign investment must be involved. We shall return to foreign investments of this type in Chapter 26 to consider their effects on the host country.

Direct Investment and Other Forces in the International Economy

Because of its distinctive character, direct investment interacts with other forces in the international economy in ways that distinguish it sharply from other types of capital flow. Let us consider some of these:

Exports and Absolute Costs. When the firm sees potential profits in markets abroad, exporting and direct investment often are alternative strategies for capturing them. They are not close alternatives always, or in all respects. Exporting may prove clearly superior when the firm's foreign sales are not yet large enough to utilize an overseas plant of efficient scale. Also, the firm that has established a producing subsidiary may continue to ship substantial exports to the same market, using its subsidiary as a marketing agent. However, we would always expect to find some companies close to the margin, with no clear preference for exporting or producing abroad.

This proposition implies an important contrast between direct investment and other capital movements: it is sensitive to the exchange rate.[13] When the home currency depreciates (or is devalued), the foreign-currency cost of producing at home and exporting falls while the foreign-currency cost of producing abroad (via direct investment) stays unchanged. Hence direct investment should fall and exports expand. Variations in direct investment should be one source

---

[13] Any capital movement is affected by an anticipated change in the exchange rate, of course; $100 invested in a currency just before it is revalued yields the same windfall gain, no matter what the investment. Direct investment, however, is related to the *level* of the rate as well as to its expected change.

of elasticity in the demand for foreign exchange. When the outflow of direct investment from the United States was particularly heavy during the years 1958–1965, with the dollar in external deficit, some argued that appropriate changes in exchange rates would help restore balance partly through cutting the flow of direct investment.

Tariffs in Host Countries. The choice between exporting and direct investment should reflect the producer's desire to serve a foreign market at the lowest cost. If the exchange rate potentially affects his choice, so should the level of tariffs surrounding the foreign market. Tariffs raise the cost of importing and tilt the decision toward direct investment. Surveys of foreign subsidiaries in host countries show that they were often founded when the parent had been serving the market by exports that were slapped with an increased tariff. Countries have often used tariffs to lure direct investment.

The response of direct investment to tariffs often contains an element of poetic justice. Protection results from political agitation by import-competing producers who would prefer to compete with fewer imports. When the tariff induces their foreign rival to establish local production facilities, their leap from the frying pan may land them in the fire.

The formation of the European Economic Community (discussed in section 15.3) illustrates the effect of tariffs on direct investment. The members of the Common Market did not raise the average level of their external tariff, but they did enlarge their internal market by eliminating tariff frontiers among their members. Consider the American firm that was exporting to the EEC countries, because none of their national markets seemed large enough to utilize the output of an efficient plant abroad. The EEC's formation left unchanged the tariff disadvantage to exporting, but sharply mitigated the small-scale disadvantage to European production. We would expect a flurry of efforts to "get inside the Common Market," which is just what occurred.

Net Versus Gross Flows. We expect capital to flow from the country where the profit rate is low to where it is high. The industry-specific character of direct investment clouds this simple prediction. The corporation invests abroad because no domestic use for its funds offers a higher expected return. But the firm does not consider investment in *every* other home industry as an active alternative to investing abroad. International differences in profits within an industry are more likely to be influential. Thus, direct investment could be flowing from, say America to Britain in the automobile industry while moving from the British to the American petroleum industry. Indeed, such crosshauls could even occur in the same industry when firms use direct investment to invade each other's markets. Hence we expect major industrial countries to both export and import direct investment, and this expectation is confirmed in Table 23.1.

The multinational corporation is popularly thought to be an American invention, and American managerial techniques and research and development outlays are both bountiful sources of the intangible capital that is profitably used through direct investment. Yet the explanation developed here establishes no reason that the United States should be the exclusive source. Although the data are deficient, they suggest that the American share of the total book value of direct investment in the industrial countries may not greatly exceed its share of their combined national incomes.

Competition in Product Markets. Direct investment occurs, we argued, in industries with market structures of differentiated oligopoly. This pattern should hold for both the source and the host country. Does direct investment make them more competitive than they would be in its absence, or does it reduce competition? With oligopoly, the answer is almost always, "anything can happen." Let us consider some of the possibilities. Sometimes a foreign subsidiary is started from scratch; sometimes the parent buys out a domestic firm in the host country. The former course surely is more likely to increase competition. Buying out a domestic firm means that direct investment does not raise the number of sellers in the host country's market. If the once independent firm competed with exports shipped by its new foreign parent, competition is reduced by its capture. On the other hand, a newly founded subsidiary may increase the competitiveness of the domestic industry. Natural forces often inhibit the entry of new firms into oligopolistic industries, and the established foreign firm may be a valuable aid to keeping markets reasonably competitive. Many people in countries that host large inflows of direct investment worry deeply lest the international corporation prove too competitive and drive all its domestic rivals to the wall. An efficient newcomer may often cost the life of an inefficient established firm, of course. The evidence has not been analyzed closely, but it does not seem to support the view that multinational corporations often monopolize host-country markets through predatory actions.

Benefits from Direct Investment and Their Distribution

The significance of direct investment for economic welfare is a matter of fierce controversy. On the one hand, its supporters laud it for transferring to the host countries not just capital but also technology and managerial skills. On the other, its critics charge it with exploiting the host economy, impairing its sovereignty, and frustrating its economic policies. In few countries hosting a visible number of foreign subsidiaries is their control out of political controversy. Hence we shall carefully define the benefits of foreign investment and explore their division between the source and host countries.

The primary gain (if any) from relocating productive resources is measured by the net increase in the value of output. This increase in turn should be reflected in the extra reward they receive in the new location. The extra profits an enterprise earns on its foreign investment, over the best domestic alternative, thus on certain assumptions measure the social benefit of the investment. The same goes for any rents accruing to its managerial talent or other assets utilized abroad. For intangible capital — patents, trademarks, know-how — the *gross* rewards measure gain, because its use abroad does not preclude use at home.

Measuring these extra rewards in practice is forbiddingly difficult. The parent corporation usually engages in many sorts of transactions with its subsidiary — selling it semi-finished components, charging it for managerial services, etc. The prices charged on these intrafirm transactions need not be market prices. Indeed, the firm may face strong incentives to manipulate them in order to minimize its overall tax burden. Shifting a "transfer price" on an intrafirm transaction affects the amount of the firm's total (global) profits that pop up in any one country, and may in turn change its tax liabilities. General evidence on the financial results of foreign investment leave little doubt that it yields generous profits over opportunity costs to many firms, but precise measures of its payout to the world as a whole are lacking.

Because the chief policy question is not whether foreign investment benefits *somebody,* but whether it benefits the host countries, let us concentrate on the possible gains to them. If the parent company captured the total net product of the capital and other resources it invests in the host country, the host would by definition gain nothing from the transaction. The host does enjoy one important benefit, however, because of the way countries levy the corporate profits tax. The general rule is that the host country is first to tax the subsidiary's profits, and the company's tax payments to the host country are then offset against its tax liability to the source country when those profits are repatriated. An example shows what is involved. Suppose that both source and host countries levy a corporate profits tax of 50 percent, and that a company earns a rate of profit (before tax) of 20 percent in the host country, whereas it could have earned only 16 percent had it invested the same funds at home. When the 20 percent is earned, the host country's tax authorities get 10 percent. The corporation keeps the remaining 10 percent; when it repatriates these profits, they become liable for taxation in the source country, but the credit for taxes paid to the host nation just offsets this. Had the direct investment not occurred, the corporation would have earned 8 percent after a tax payment of 8 percent to the source country. The real net return to the foreign investment of 4 percent (20 − 16) exceeds the net gain to the corporation of 2 percent (10 − 8). However, the host country gains more than the real net return (10 percent, compared to 4 percent), and the source country loses on the transaction; the corporation and the tax authorities together garner 16 percent from the domestic investment, but only 10 from the foreign. Thus corporation tax practice not only guarantees the host country a cut of the primary gains, but can even award it more than the extra real product.[14]

The host nation may also derive important "spillover" benefits from actions by the subsidiary that raise the productivity of its own factor stock. The subsidiary may show its local suppliers how to achieve better quality control, or its way of distributing its output may improve the general productivity of the distribution sector. Some of the knowledge comprising the intangible capital of the multinational corporation may leak out to its local competitors as they seek to emulate its success (or resist its competitive pressure).[15] The size of these gains — indeed, whether they are substantial at all — will vary from subsidiary to subsidiary, and from host country to host country. Subsidiaries of manufacturing firms operating in developed countries like Australia and Great Britain have been found to extend significant productivity benefits of this sort. At the other extreme, a capital-intensive subsidiary operating in a less-developed country and making few transactions with local enterprises may have few secondary benefits.

Policy Issues in Host Countries

Our analysis suggests that the host countries are apt to derive significant benefits from direct investment. Why then does it arouse such ire? Do hidden costs more than offset these benefits? Or are significant economic misunderstandings involved? Let us explore some host-country complaints.

High Profits. Subsidiaries' profits are "too high." There is no doubt that international corporations win high profits. This is hardly a surprise. They operate in industries where elements of oligopoly permit more than a competitive level of profits. Furthermore, the profit records that are observed and complained of naturally belong to subsidiaries that survive and prosper; the failures are ignored. Finally, within their industries the international corporations are the more efficient and hence the more profitable. Considering these explanatory factors, where does the complaint about high profits point? A good case can be made for procompetitive (or antitrust) policies bearing on subsidiaries and home-owned firms alike. Such a policy should be superior to one often proposed: tying the hands of subsidiaries and thereby awarding more monopoly power to their domestic rivals.

Research and Development. Subsidiaries undertake most of their research in the source country and thus deny research and develop-

---

[14] Lawrence B. Krause and Kenneth W. Dam. *Federal Tax Treatment of Foreign Income.* Washington, D.C.: Brookings Institution, 1964, chap. 4.

[15] For a survey of these effects in Australia, see Donald T. Brash. *American Investment in Australian Industry.* Canberra: Australian National University Press, 1966, chap. 8.

ment activities to the host country. The multinationals usually centralize their basic research activities in their home country and undertake research in the host countries primarily to develop and adapt their products to local conditions more efficiently. (Even so, evidence shows that in some countries they undertake more research than do their home-owned competitors.[16]) Frequently, as in this instance, it is hard to grasp what alternative practices the complainers would prefer. Should the multinational corporation decentralize its research, perhaps losing some efficiency? It would still capture the profits from its discoveries (and incur the losses from its failures). A greater demand for host-country nationals in research jobs would be felt, but the reason for a nation's gains from research (as opposed to other skilled or professional activity) is not clear. People often treat science and research as "consumption goods," as if the nation's benefit depended on the number of its citizens wearing white coats and shaking test tubes, rather than upon its access to the fruits of research (wherever carried out). The ease with which research results travel across national boundaries suggests that this attitude is not rational.

Exports. Capitalist countries seldom resist taking a mercantilist attitude toward their foreign trade. Hence they often berate subsidiaries for failure to export and thus to aid the nation's balance of trade. Actual export performance seems to be diverse, but we should not be surprised if subsidiaries were typically not heavy exporters. We saw that they are often created to get into an import-competing industry behind a tariff wall. The subsidiary's activity in such cases is not one in which the host country enjoys a comparative advantage. To develop a net export position would be a triumph indeed. The multinational is suspected of "reserving the privilege" of exporting for its head office. Why it should do this, if its subsidiary could produce exportable goods more cheaply, is far from clear. Hence, one doubts that converting a subsidiary to domestic ownership would often lead to a significant rise in exports.

Submission to Public Policy. Because of its international connections the subsidiary enjoys alternatives not open to home-owned firms, and it can often take successful evasive action when the screws of public policy are applied. For instance, confronted with new social legislation that raises production costs, it may channel any expansion of capacity to another country. Its ease of lending and borrowing internationally may frustrate the use of direct macroeconomic controls for internal or external balance. Does this freedom warrant restricting its activities? Here again the question of the alternative arises. A policy that causes a subsidiary to move its activities elsewhere might simply put a home-owned firm in the same straits out of business. A government whose policies fight market

---

[16] A. E. Safarian. *The Performance of Foreign-Owned Firms in Canada.* Montreal: Canadian-American Committee, 1969, chap. 5.

forces should ask whether it is using the most effective possible policies. As we saw in section 23.2, the answer may be no. Even if its policies must clash with the market, it is hardly clear, as a general proposition, that reducing firms' sensitivities to market forces improves economic welfare overall.

5. *Vulnerability to Foreign Government Pressure.* The subsidiary is the servant of two political masters — the government of the country in which it dwells, and the government sovereign over its parent. Here lies a fundamental conflict of sovereignties, for which no easy remedy has been found. Efforts by the United States government to pressure foreign subsidiaries through their American parents have aroused more rancor than any purely profit-seeking actions by the subsidiaries themselves. A famous episode occurred in 1957 when the Ford Motor Co.'s Canadian subsidiary was exploring the possibility of a large sale of trucks to Mainland China. At that time Canada's policy permitted and even encouraged an expansion of trade with China, while the United States sought to prohibit trade altogether. Washington voiced its displeasure, and parent Ford laid a restraining hand on its errant Canadian offspring, to the great displeasure of many Canadians.[17] There is no doubt that the source-country government can get at the subsidiary through the parent; to a lesser degree, the host-country government can affect the parent through the subsidiary. No resolution exists short of an agreement of governments to keep hands off.

The multinational corporation also channels another form of governmental influence, which should be distinguished from this one. Among its interferences with capital markets to protect its balance of payments in the 1960's, the United States included a campaign to prod its multinational corporations to borrow abroad. This they did, driving up interest rates in other nations and raising outcries of interference with their domestic policies. Affected though these countries doubtless were, one can feel only limited sympathy. Insofar as a general tightening of monetary policy was an appropriate policy for the United States in the face of its deficit, market forces would have reduced its foreign lending and raised its borrowing from abroad in any case, and foreign capital markets would have been tightened even if no multinational corporation had lifted a finger. The problem really lies in the general interdependence of nations' economic policies (see sections 23.2 and 24.4). The multinational corporation draws the wrath because it personifies this interdependence, which policy-makers often wish would go away.

6. *Structure of Political Forces.* Business managers comprise an important interest group in any political system. Managers of foreign subsidiaries do not behave the same way politically as do domestic entrepreneurs. Some complaints about foreign investment simply assert a preference for a political system without foreign business-

---

[17] See L. A. Litvak and C. J. Maule, "Conflict, Resolution, and Extraterritoriality," *Journal of Conflict Resolution,* 13 (September 1969): 306–15.

men. In its usual form, this plaint stresses the possibility of foreign influence intruding on the national political scene and frustrating the sovereign will of the nation's own citizens. However, A. O. Hirschman has complained (from the perspective of Latin American politics) that foreign businesses are too timid; he would prefer assertive domestic entrepreneurs, as a counterweight to domestic political groups of whom he disapproves.[18]

These complaints about the foreign firm have been arranged to move from the purely economic to the purely political. To evaluate them broadly, they identify no systematic and severe economic costs of direct investment to the host country, although they certainly reveal offsets that must be chalked against the benefits conveyed. They do raise, however, the problem of national sovereignty pervading international economic policy. A nation would be most sovereign if it could mold its economic policy without heed to the economic or political reactions of the rest of the world. Yet perfect sovereignty is hardly conceivable without perfect isolation from the rest of the world. Hence, gaining the benefit of specialization and exchange means tolerating economic and political links to the rest of the world that create both constraints and opportunities for policy-making, but in any case cannot be prudently ignored. Economists are prone to urge policies designed to get the best of both worlds — to secure the benefits of international exchange and to use the leverage for policy provided by international sensitivities rather than fighting it. But this is not a complete answer to the nationalist who would rather ignore the existence of the rest of the world, even at some cost of real income to himself.

23.5 SUMMARY

Portfolio capital flows are distinguished from direct investment by the legal control over the enterprise obtained by direct investors. To analyze in practice the "transfer process" associated with movements of portfolio (or direct) investment, we shall break it into steps. (1) How does the transfer influence spending in the borrowing and lending countries? (2) How does that expenditure in turn affect the balance of trade? In practice, a transfer of $1 need not change expenditure in the lending and borrowing countries by just that amount. When we study the transfer process, we should remember that capital flows themselves may depend on countries' incomes.

In stable conditions, portfolio capital flows (and also flows of short-term capital) become highly sensitive to differences between interest rates in different countries. This sensitivity affects the ability of a country to use fiscal and monetary policy to achieve external balance

---

[18] Albert O. Hirschman, *How to Divest in Latin America, and Why.* Essays in International Finance, No. 76. Princeton: International Finance Section, Princeton University, 1969.

at full employment. With the exchange rate fixed, capital mobility blocks the effectiveness of monetary policy. On the other hand, if the exchange rate is flexible and market-determined, fiscal policy becomes ineffective. Lenders often include a mixture of securities among their assets, in order to minimize the risks they face in earning any given rate of return. Portfolio balancing has important implications for international capital flows.

Direct investment typically involves the creation of a subsidiary abroad by a corporation. It is thus industry-specific, and usually occurs in certain market structures. Some companies invest abroad to obtain sources of raw materials or other inputs (backward vertical integration); others acquire subsidiaries that produce the same product line as the parent (horizontal integration). Horizontal investment is an alternative to exporting, and thus direct investment (unlike other long-term capital flows) should be sensitive to the exchange rate. It is also influenced by the host-country's tariffs. A principal benefit to the host country derives from taxes on the subsidiary's net revenues. The political issues that embroil the subsidiaries in host countries can be better understood by asking what course of action maximizes profits for the multinational corporation, and how such actions influence the real incomes of the source and host countries.

SUGGESTIONS FOR FURTHER READING

Baldwin, R. E., and J. D. Richardson, eds. *Selected Topics in International Trade and Finance: A Book of Readings.* Boston: Little, Brown, 1973. Part III deals with the multinational corporation.

Brash, Donald T. *American Investment in Australian Industry.* Canberra: Australian National University Press, 1966. Survey of effects on one host country.

Caves, Richard E. "International Corporations: the Industrial Economics of Foreign Investment," *Economica*, 38 (February 1971): 1–27. Implications of "industry-specific" direct investment.

Caves, Richard E., and Grant L. Reuber. *Canadian Economic Policy and the Impact of International Capital Flows.* Toronto: University of Toronto Press, 1969. Empirical study of the transfer problem.

Grubel, Herbert G. "Internationally Diversified Portfolios: Welfare Gains and Capital Flows," *American Economic Review*, 58 (December 1968): 1299–1314. Implications of "portfolio balancing" for capital flows.

Kindleberger, Charles P., ed. *The International Corporation.* Cambridge: MIT Press, 1970. Papers on various aspects of direct investment.

Vernon, Raymond. *Sovereignty at Bay: the Multinational Spread of U.S. Enterprises.* New York and London: Basic Books, 1971. Survey of evidence on behavior of United States subsidiaries abroad.

Whitman, Marina v. N. *International and Interregional Payments Adjustment: A Synthetic View.* Princeton Studies in International Finance Section, Princeton University, 1967. Model of endogenous capital flows.

24 Short-Term Capital Flows, Forward Exchange Markets, and Economic Policy

Short-term capital flows raise more questions than their long-term brethren about the management of economic policy for internal and external balance. Capital flows that are sensitive to the short-term interest rate affect the leverage of fiscal and monetary policy as do interest-sensitive long-term flows. But most countries regard the short-term interest rate as a more flexible domestic policy device than they do the long rate, and are less ready to yield its determination to the international capital market. As a result, the problems of living with interest-sensitive capital flows keep continuous company with the policy-makers.

In the first section of this chapter we shall scrutinize the monetary consequences of short-term flows and relate them to the transfer process. Then we shall consider the forward exchange market, which is closely linked to short-term capital movements. We can then analyze the effects of short-term capital movements on economic policy for both external and internal balance, in theory and practice.

24.1 CAPITAL FLOWS, MONETARY CONDITIONS, AND THE TRANSFER PROCESS

A short-term capital outflow typically involves the acquisition of a claim on foreigners. The nature of this claim and the method by which it is purchased determine its effects on expenditure in the paying and receiving countries. Many actual short-term capital flows reflect the efforts of holders of liquid funds to maximize the rate of return earned on them through the purchase of alternative money-market instruments. Hence the banking system is important, always as an intermediary and sometimes as an initiator of these transactions. We thus shall study the effect of short-term transfers on monetary conditions in the paying and receiving countries, as well as their direct effects on real expenditure. These monetary effects can be present for any capital transfer, but they assume greater importance here because of volatility as well as the short duration of these flows.

Monetary Conditions

Whatever the short-term claim purchased, someone in lending country *A* must reduce his cash balances — generally a bank deposit — by the same amount. At some stage this cash payment must be converted into the currency of the receiving country *B*, where it adds to bank deposits. With the exchange rate fixed (as we shall assume), the central monetary authority of either country accommodates this disturbance to the exchange market, increasing its holdings of *A*'s currency and reducing its holdings of *B*'s. The monetary effect of the transfer depends on the possible net outcomes of these transactions.

Let us consider the effects on their banking systems of a transfer from *A* to *B* of $1,000,000, used to purchase a short-term liability of *B*. The purchaser's bank (the Bank of *A*) loses deposit liabilities and cash assets equal to $1,000,000 (we suppose the dollar is *A*'s currency). If the cash reserve ratio against deposits kept by *A*'s banks is ten percent, the initial change in the balance sheet of the Bank of *A* will appear as follows:

BANK OF A

Assets		*Liabilities*	
Required reserves	− $100,000	Deposits	− $1,000,000
Loans or free reserves	− $900,000		
Total assets	− $1,000,000	Total liabilities	− $1,000,000

To see the possible implications for monetary conditions in *A*, you should recall the process of credit creation through a fractional-reserve banking system. Monetary contraction could greatly exceed the initial outpayment of $1,000,000; indeed, it ultimately reaches $10,000,000 if the banking system was fully "loaned up." On the other hand, if the $900,000 portion of the cash drain not financed from reduced reserve requirements flowed from idle balances (free reserves), the contraction would be limited to the initial $1,000,000.

The associated initial effect in *B*, when its banking system gains the local-currency equivalent of $1,000,000, might be as follows (all changes valued in *A*-currency):

BANK OF B

Assets		*Liabilities*	
Required reserves	+ $200,000	Deposits	+ $1,000,000
Loans or free reserves	+ $800,000		
Total assets	+ $1,000,000	Total liabilities	+ $1,000,000

We have assumed that B imposes a higher reserve requirement on its commercial banks than does A — twenty percent. Thus the maximum expansion of bank deposits in B would be $5,000,000. It would be less, of course, if B's banking system already had excess reserves, or if loans fail to expand to utilize the new excess reserves.

These examples show that the contraction of the money supply in A, and its expansion in B, are both larger when (1) the required reserve ratio is lower, and (2) the banking system is more fully loaned up.[1] In the short run, the monetary expansion in B need not equal the contraction in A, even though the initiating disturbances were the same size.

This story remains incomplete because we must allow for the reaction of the A and B central banks to the transfer. Viewing the transfer in isolation, we suppose that it disturbs an initial equilibrium in the market for foreign exchange, and thus forces one of the monetary authorities to intervene to avert a change in the exchange rate. Suppose that A's authorities intervene, selling foreign exchange or gold to maintain the external price of A's dollar. A's external reserves thus fall. If its central bank followed the rules of the gold standard, it would reduce its liabilities (which are the assets of the commercial banking system) in response to the decline in the country's international assets. This response prompts a further credit contraction in A, beyond that traced above. (Had B intervened instead of A, B's reserves would have increased, and the gold-standard rule would have called for an expansion in the liabilities of B's central bank.)

Of course, A's (or B's) central bank may not follow the gold-standard rules, which are designed to use monetary policy to secure external balance. Instead, it may try to stabilize the domestic economy. This goal would call for action in the opposite direction by either central bank. A's central bank, to offset the contraction of commercial-bank deposits in A, would expand rather than contract its liabilities. This expansion is equivalent to *sterilizing* changes in its international reserves, a practice defined in Chapter 16. Depending on what rule it follows, the central bank can thus either augment or offset the change in monetary conditions that results from a short-term capital flow.

One more feature of central-bank policy should be considered. We have treated actions by the two central banks as independent of one another. Yet they may not be independent. Suppose that A's dollar is a principal "reserve currency," used throughout the world by B and other countries as the medium in which international reserves are held. B's monetary authorities now acquire dollars in their efforts to offset the disturbance to their exchange market. Whatever way B's central bank reacts to the situation, A's central bank finds its liabilities to foreign holders of its currency increased. Will it react to

[1] You may wish to review credit creation within a fractional-reserve banking system, as it is described in any textbook on introductory economics or money and banking.

this increase in its liabilities in the same way as it would to a decrease in its (foreign-exchange) assets? Will it react as strongly?

Important properties of the gold-exchange standard depend on the answers to these questions. As we saw in Chapter 20, a reserve-currency country that is as sensitive to the growth of its liabilities as to the shrinkage of reserves would be inhibited from allowing its currency to become a reserves medium. It would take restrictive action whenever other countries gain reserves of its currency. On the other hand, an absence of concern about its growing official liabilities can, some observers have argued, lend an inflationary bias to the gold-exchange system when the reserve-currency country is suffering a sustained payments deficit (whether due to short-term capital or other causes). The central bank of reserve-currency country *A* suffers no contraction in its foreign-exchange assets, and hence does not shrink its domestic monetary base. *B*'s central bank gains foreign assets, which expand *B*'s money supply.

Short-Term Flows and Real Expenditure

The analysis of the possible monetary consequences of short-term capital flows leads naturally to the "transfer problem" they may pose. We have already seen that the changes in the lending and borrowing countries' money supplies need not be the same. Changes in the levels of expenditure associated with these monetary forces could diverge correspondingly. The next question is how the proceeds of the transfer might be spent in the borrowing country, and what sorts of expenditure contraction might occur in the lending nation. The range of possibilities is without limit. The extra funds in the borrowing country might finance extra imports, or they might support expanding domestic inventories. The operative marginal propensity to import thus might range between one and zero. (A secondary expansion of the borrower's credit base expands real expenditure in general, and hence in a more typical way; thus we may more easily predict the amount of extra spending, due to the secondary credit expansion, that will fall on imports.)

We can only conclude, alas, that predicting the transfer process resulting from a change in short-term flows is not an easy task. Most flows in practice involve general money-market instruments, such as bank time deposits or Treasury bills. We may surmise the effect of movements of deposit funds on general credit conditions in the lending and borrowing countries, but we ordinarily know nothing specific about the ways in which the proceeds of extra bank loans are spent. The same holds for international transactions in government short-term debt, such as Treasury bills: the borrower is well defined, but a government denied short-term financing through international flows enjoys many options other than cutting its expenditure.

The problem of predicting the pattern of real transfers associated with short-term capital flows in fact cuts even deeper than this.

Governments generally regard monetary conditions, including the
short-term interest rate, as a tool of stabilization policy. When the
short-term rate is regulated for purposes of economic policy —
whether to stabilize aggregate demand or external payments — short-
term capital flows lose their status as an exogenous force affecting
the balance of payments and the level of real expenditure. Instead,
they become an induced variable in the national policy system — as
they were in our models of policy for internal and external balance
(Chapter 18). Sometimes short-term flows are thus manipulated by
public policy as a consistent part of an overall design for achieving
balance. Policy-makers often treat these induced short-term flows as
an incidental nuisance rather than as a normal part of the policy
system that they control, and correspondingly devise their strategies
to fend off changes in these flows rather than to use the leverage they
provide. We shall return to this policy stance.

   If short-term capital flows become chiefly dependent on the decisions of policy-makers, can we suppose that they improve the allocation of the world's resources, moving capital from where its marginal
product is low to locations where it is high? It is easy to see that "inefficient" capital flows can result from the short-run manipulation
of policy tools, as when a capital-rich country like the United States
becomes a heavy short-term borrower due to a credit crunch imposed
by monetary authorities to halt inflation. Yet one also witnesses sustained net flows of short-term funds to countries like Japan and Italy,
where (as among industrial countries, anyhow) capital seems gen-
uinely scarce. The efficiency of the international capital market thus
appears blunted but not destroyed.

24.2 SHORT-TERM CAPITAL AND
FORWARD EXCHANGE RATES

Economic theorists assume that most people — except those who
like to gamble — prefer to avoid taking risks. International capital
movements expose lenders or borrowers to various risks, notably that
the exchange rate may change after the funds are committed but
before the loan matures. Actually, a market exists in which the short-
term lender can relieve himself of this risk, the "forward market" for
foreign exchange to be delivered in the future. In this section we shall
investigate hedging exchange risks in the forward market, then we
shall explore in full the determinants of the forward exchange rate.
   International short-term lending, when hedged against exchange-
rate risks, is called "covered interest arbitrage." The term "arbitrage"
refers to any transaction involving a movement from a cheap market
to a dear one, tending to equalize the prices in the two. A short-term
capital movement undertaken to earn higher interest becomes
"covered" if the lender hedges it against exchange-rate risk.

Arbitrage

Forward markets exist for foreign exchange, just as they do for many commodities, to allow traders to relieve themselves of uncertainty about future prices. An American expects to receive a definite sum in British (sterling) currency three months hence. He feels certain about the sterling receipt, but he may also want assurance about its worth in United States dollars. That, however, will depend on the spot exchange rate three months hence. He can provide this certainty — perhaps at a cost — by contracting now to sell his sterling proceeds on receipt at a preagreed exchange rate for United States dollars. He becomes a seller in the forward market for sterling. Our man's future sterling receipt might stem from his ownership of a United Kingdom short-term security, but he might also acquire it as an exporter who has sold goods to a British buyer, on terms calling for a future payment in sterling by the customer. Other transactors in the market will have bound themselves to make sterling payments in the future, and will enter the market as buyers of forward sterling, to assure themselves of the dollar cost of their future liability. Obviously, a utility-increasing trade can be arranged between someone holding a future sterling receipt and fearing that the price of sterling will fall, and another faced with a future sterling payment and fearing it will rise. But the forward market also contains pure speculators who are willing to buy or sell forward sterling, knowing that on the day their forward contracts mature they must enter the spot exchange market to cover their commitments. They thus bet on the relation between the forward exchange rate now prevailing for a future date, and the spot rate that the market will set on that day. Thus we can sort the principal traders in the market for forward exchange into the following classes:

1. Interest arbitragers, seeking assurance about the value of future foreign-exchange receipts or payments.
2. Commercial traders — buyers and sellers of goods and services — seeking assurance about the value of future foreign-exchange receipts or payments.
3. Speculators, willing to bet on the relation between forward and future spot exchange rates.

We described the forward market as a market for foreign currency. Yet, in a two-currency world, a buyer of forward sterling is perforce a seller of forward dollars. Just as with the spot exchange market (see Chapter 5), the market for forward dollars is the mirror image of the market for forward sterling; there is only one market.

Covered Interest Arbitrage

Forward markets and covered interest arbitrage are not complex in principle, but their mechanics are hard to remember, involving as they do price ratios which can be stated in different ways. Hence we must carefully define our terms and examples. We shall concentrate on two countries, the United States and United Kingdom, and on capital flowing from the United States to the United Kingdom. We shall define the exchange rate as the dollar price of the pound sterling (r in previous chapters), and give to the spot exchange rate the symbol rs. The forward rate rf is the price of sterling for future delivery. In practice forward markets exist for contracts of varying maturities, but we shall assume that all forward contracts call for delivery 90 days hence. Thus (once the forward market reaches equilibrium) only one forward rate exists. We noticed above that the spot and forward markets for dollars are the mirror image of those for sterling; the price of the dollar in these markets is $1/rs$ and $1/rf$ respectively. When the price of sterling for future delivery exceeds its spot price $rf > rs$), we say that sterling trades at a forward premium; simultaneously, the dollar would be traded at a forward discount ($1/rf < 1/rs$).

The American interest-arbitrager is influenced by interest rates in the United States and United Kingdom, as well as by exchange rates. To show how they determine his profitable course of action, we express short-term interest rates not in percent per year, but percent per 90 days or quarter-year, the duration of the standard forward contract. We denote American and British rates respectively as iu and ik. Now, an American lender willing to accept the risk of a change in the exchange rate would invest in the United Kingdom if $ik > iu$. To avoid exchange risk, however, he must calculate the outcome of a more complex series of transactions. He could purchase a United States Treasury bill, which after 90 days would yield him dollar proceeds of its original cost plus interest, $1 + iu$. He chooses this transaction unless a higher dollar return is available through covered interest arbitrage. To make a covered investment in a United Kingdom Treasury bill, he first converts the same initial amount of dollars into sterling (at exchange rate $1/rs$), buys a United Kingdom bill in that amount, and simultaneously makes a forward sale of the sterling proceeds he will receive in 90 days; the proceeds are $1 + ik$ and would yield him $(1 + ik)rf$ when his forward contract is executed. For the covered interest arbitrage to be more profitable than a United States Treasury bill investment, it is necessary that

$$1 + iu < (rf/rs)(1 + ik). \qquad (24.1)$$

Another way to put the condition,

$$\frac{1 + ik}{1 + iu} > \frac{1/rf}{1/rs}, \qquad (24.2)$$

may be clearer because it can be given an easy verbal interpretation: covered arbitrage is profitable if the (proportionally) higher interest yield on a sterling bill exceeds the (proportional) premium on the forward dollar.[2]

Equation 24.1 or 24.2 reveals some important features of covered interest arbitrage. First, for short-term investments to be profitable abroad, the foreign interest rate does not have to exceed the domestic! Should the pound be traded at a forward premium (perhaps because speculators expect the dollar to depreciate), interest arbitragers might profit by exporting capital from the United States even when $ik < iu$. Second, if circumstances reverse the inequality in either equation, covered arbitrage from America to Britain will become unprofitable, but arbitrage from the United Kingdom to the United States would yield positive profits. Whenever market conditions fail to yield equality between the two sides of equation 24.1 or 24.2, short-term capital movements are profitable in one direction or the other — or would be, except for the small margin of transactions costs encountered in practice.[3]

Because we want to demonstrate below the determinants of the forward exchange rate, we illustrate in Figure 24.1 the (excess) demand curve for forward exchange for covered interest arbitrage. To fix this demand curve we must accept the other factors controlling the profitability of covered arbitrage. Once the interest rates and spot exchange rate are known, we can calculate (from equation 24.1) that value of the forward rate, rfa, which would render interest arbitrage unprofitable in either direction. The excess demand shown by curve AA thus is zero at this value. If the forward rate rises above this value, capital flows from the United States to the United Kingdom, and arbitragers offer a net supply of forward sterling; if $rf < rfa$, however, capital would flow the other way, and arbitragers selling

---

[2] You may find it helpful to work through a numerical example. Suppose that $rs = \$2.40$ and $rf = \$2.39$; thus, sterling is at a forward discount, and the dollar at a forward premium. Suppose that the American and British interest rates are respectively 6 and 8 percent on an *annual* basis, or 1.5 and 2.0 percent quarterly. Suppose (to make the arithmetic easy) a United States Treasury bill costs \$240; 90 days later it will yield the investor $\$240(1.015) = \$243.60$. A United Kingdom Treasury bill would also cost an initial \$240 in United States currency if its face value is £100, because $£100 = \$240(1/2.40)$. The proceeds of £102, when sold forward at \$2.39, would yield $(£102)(2.39) = 243.78$. Hence the covered interest arbitrage is profitable. We would reach the same conclusion by plugging these values into either formula given in the text, e.g.:

$$1 + 0.015 < (2.39/2.40)(1 + 0.02),$$

when the right-hand side of the inequality works out to be 1.01575.

[3] For movements between the United States and Britain or Canada, these transactions costs have been estimated at 0.18 percent per annum. See W. H. Branson, "The Minimum Covered Differential Needed for International Arbitrage Activity," *Journal of Political Economy*, 77 (November/December 1969): 1028–35.

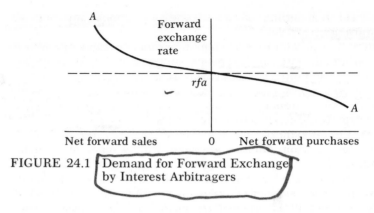

FIGURE 24.1 Demand for Forward Exchange by Interest Arbitragers

forward dollars would demand forward pounds. Hence this schedule slopes downward.

Some economists have argued that this schedule would be highly elastic over a wide range, indeed elastic enough to lock rf at rfa rendering capital movements in either direction unprofitable. But other forces also impinge on the forward rate. There is no guarantee that the supply of funds available for interest arbitrage will be un-limited in the short run. Hence we have drawn the schedule AA in Figure 24.1 highly elastic only over a limited range.

As a concluding exercise, let us notice how changes in the American or British interest rate would influence the position of this curve. A rise in iu reduces the attractiveness of covered arbitrage to the United Kingdom, and a larger forward premium (or smaller discount) on the pound would be necessary to offset it. Hence it would shift the curve in Figure 24.1 upward, and tend to raise the price of forward sterling. A rise in the British short-term rate, ik, would have the opposite effect; the forward premium on sterling must fall if covered arbi-trage to Britain is not to become more attractive than before.

Other Transactors in Forward Exchange Markets

Exporters and importers are a second group of traders who may take part in the forward exchange market. Foreign-trade contracts often call for payment months later, usually in the currency of one party. Either the exporter or the importer thus faces an exchange risk. The exporter receiving a known amount of (spot) foreign exchange at a future date may want to hedge by selling it forward; if the trans-action is in the exporter's currency, the importer may buy forward exchange to cover his future payment. To simplify, suppose the im-porter always faces the exchange risk. The expense of forward cover is one of his business costs: at the spot exchange rate when he arranges his transaction, a higher forward rate for the currency he must buy means a greater total cost of the goods to him. Hence he will purchase a smaller quantity of imports—and of forward exchange. The demand for forward sterling by American importers will hence be negatively sloped.

Recall that a premium on the forward pound implies a discount on the forward dollar. If forward cover is expensive for American importers, it must be cheap for British importers. Their purchases of American exports may be encouraged, and their supply of pounds sterling to the forward market thus increased. The behavior of both trading groups together implies a downward sloping excess demand curve for forward sterling, such as that shown in Figure 24.2.

Unlike the case of interest arbitrage (Figure 24.1), we can say nothing about the forward-rate value *rft* that would yield no net demand from the traders. This value depends on additional factors, such as the relative values of exports and imports (the trade balance between the two countries) and the extent to which traders hedge their exchange positions.

The final group of transactors in the forward exchange market is the speculators. A speculator's profit depends wholly on the relation between the forward rate *rf* at which he buys or sells and the *future value of the spot rate* prevailing when his contract matures. He ties up no capital (except perhaps for margin requirements) because he buys and sells at the same instant. But he does carry the full risk of exchange-rate fluctuations, in part absorbing it from the arbitragers and traders desiring forward protection. How do speculators as a group conjecture about the future spot rate? The process must be subjective. Current and past values of the spot rate surely supply the basis for their prediction, but to cook them into a forecast each speculator must be his own chef.

Still, we should feel some confidence about the slope of the function describing the speculators' behavior. If the spot exchange rate is

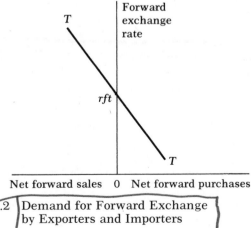

FIGURE 24.2 Demand for Forward Exchange by Exporters and Importers

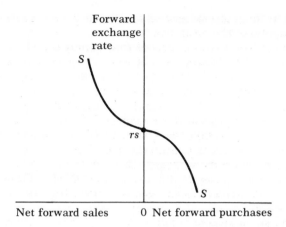

FIGURE 24.3 Demand for Forward Exchange by Speculators

pegged, and the peg generally expected to hold in the near future, a forward rate much below the spot rate is likely to attract net speculative purchases, and one much above net speculative sales. Hence this excess demand curve should be downward sloping, like those of the other two groups. Such a schedule is shown in Figure 24.3, where schedule SS shows no net demand when the forward rate equals the spot rate. This might occur when the spot rate is rather confidently expected to prevail in the future, but you should keep in mind that the SS schedule can readily shift and change its shape as the speculators detect governmental intents, trends, rumblings, etc.[4]

The actors in the forward exchange market have now been described (with one exception, to be noted), and we can consider the process whereby the equilibrium forward rate is determined. We are used to saying that a market reaches equilibrium when a price is established at which demand equals supply. Ordinary demand and supply schedules are not convenient tools for analyzing the forward market, however. Each group of transactors is a net buyer at some forward rates, a net seller at others, and hence we have to employ excess-demand schedules. But "net excess demand equals zero" is the exact equivalent of "supply equals demand." We must find the forward rate at which the positive excess demand of one (or two) of

---

[4] The SS schedule might take any shape, depending on circumstances. The one shown in Figure 24.3 can be rationalized in this way. Suppose the exchange rate rs is generally expected to persist in the future. When the forward rate deviates moderately from it, speculators' expectations about the persistence of the present spot rate are not disturbed, and their excess demand function is relatively elastic. Greater deviations from the spot par value, however, portend more uncertainty about future spot rates in general, and speculators eventually become unwilling to expand their commitments further.

our three trading groups just offsets the negative excess demand (or excess supply) of the other two (or one).

This process is less complicated than it may sound. We can visualize the solution in Figure 24.4. Suppose the speculators and traders become net buyers of forward sterling, the arbitragers net sellers. We can translate the schedules already presented in Figures 24.1, 24.2, and 24.3 by the following steps: (1) to the speculators' excess demand *SS* we add that of the traders, *TT* (both are shown only as dashed lines), and derive their total, *STST*; (2) we can turn the arbitragers' excess-demand function into an excess-supply function *A'A'*, which is simply the mirror image of *AA* in Figure 24.1 (with net sales shown on the right side of the origin, not the left); (3) we notice that schedules *A'A'* and *STST* intersect at forward rate *rfe*, which becomes the equilibrium rate.[5]

Working out a qualitative description of the equilibrium shown in Figure 24.4 is a good exercise. The arbitragers are net sellers when forward sterling trades at a discount (*rfe < rs*), and so we know that the British short-term interest rate must lie above the American. (Alternatively, we say that the interest differential in favor of Britain more than offsets the forward premium on the United States dollar.) Speculators are net buyers of forward sterling, presumably expecting that something like the spot rate *rs* will still prevail when their contracts mature. Traders are also net buyers of forward sterling, perhaps because the United States runs an import surplus, perhaps merely because American importers make greater use of forward cover than do British importers.[6]

How do forward markets behave in practice? Although governments may intervene to affect the forward rate, it is never "pegged" like the spot exchange market. We can explore the record of shifts in the forward rate to learn which group of transactors described above carries the most weight. We noticed that casual opinion often classes the arbitragers as the dominant group determining the forward rate.

[5] Here are further hints on how we locate this rate. We know the forward rate at which each group's own excess demand would be zero: *rfa*, *rft*, and *rs* respectively. As you can see from the vertical axis of Figure 24.4, we arbitrarily assumed that *rft* is the highest of these, then *rs*, then *rfa*. From this fact we know that the traders must be net buyers, the arbitragers net sellers. Hence we picked the arbitragers' excess demand curve for conversion to an excess-supply curve, and aggregated the other two as excess-demand curves. If the speculators had turned out to be net sellers, *rfe* would have been above *rs* rather than below.

[6] This theoretical analysis of forward markets draws upon S. C. Tsiang, "The Theory of Forward Exchange and Effects of Government Intervention on the Forward Exchange Market," *IMF Staff Papers*, 7 (April 1959): 75–106; and especially Herbert G. Grubel. *Forward Exchange, Speculation, and the International Flow of Capital.* Stanford, Calif.: Stanford University Press, 1966. For more institutional description of the forward-exchange market, see Paul Einzig. *A Dynamic Theory of Forward Exchange.* London: Macmillan, 1961.

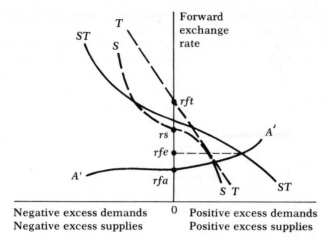

FIGURE 24.4   Equilibrium in the Forward Exchange Market

> Excess demands of arbitragers, traders, and speculators
> must sum to zero. Arbitragers' excess supply ($A'A'$) is shown
> equal to sum of traders' and speculators' excess demands.
> Equilibrium forward rate is *rfe*.

This proposition is in fact easy to test. Knowing the levels of short-term interest rates and the spot rate, one can calculate the forward rate for curbing the flow of short-term capital (*rfa*, above). If the actual forward rate closely matches the rate needed to wipe out the profit on covered interest arbitrage, we can say that the arbitragers dominate the forward market. They need not do so, however. When speculative flurries occur, the speculators' excess-demand curve can shift sharply. In terms of Figure 24.4, it can then carry the equilibrium point into one of the inelastic ranges of the $A'A'$ curve and drive the market forward rate far away from the one that would make further covered arbitrage unprofitable. Herbert Grubel calculated the gap between these two rates over a period of years for six pairs of currencies. Most of the time, the margin was very small, implying that arbitragers indeed dominate the forward rate. When the newspapers were reporting speculative fears of an impending devaluation or revaluation, however, he found that the speculators took over and drove the forward rate to a substantial margin above or below what the arbitragers would have set.[7]

24.3 CONTROLLING SHORT-TERM CAPITAL
FOR EXTERNAL BALANCE

We noticed in section 24.1 that short-term capital flows theoretically need cause no special difficulty for economic policy. Policy-makers

[7] Grubel, chap. 10.

equipped with sufficient instruments can simply allow for and use them as part of a systematic pursuit of internal and external balance. Reality is not so obliging, however, and present-day policy-makers often find them a special hazard to be coped with, rather than merely another feature of the structural situation to be controlled. In this section we shall explore the special problems they pose for maintaining external balance with a fixed exchange rate, using the model of covered interest arbitrage and the forward exchange rate developed in section 24.2. In section 24.4 we shall turn to their consequences for the pursuit of internal balance.

Speculators' actions in the spot exchange market can either help or hinder authorities' efforts to defend a fixed rate. Recall that usual practice until 1971 (sanctioned by the IMF Articles of Agreement) was to hold a pegged rate not at a single value but within a maximum range of ±1 percent; now it is slightly enlarged. During tranquil times, when the market equilibrium value of the spot rate lies within these limits, speculators are apt to assist monetary authorities by selling foreign exchange when its price veers toward the upper limit and buying when it sags toward the lower one. On the other hand, when the market rate presses upon its upper or lower limit and the public counts a change in the peg likely, speculators are apt to bet against the authorities, speeding the loss of reserves if they foresee a devaluation, building reserves massively if a revaluation looms.

We have reviewed these possibilities simply to show that the speculator's transactions by definition constitute international short-term capital flows, because they involve a change in either domestic holdings of foreign exchange or foreigners' holdings of domestic currency.[8] In practice they are often bound up with other functional short-term flows.

Trade Credit

Importers often purchase on credit extended either directly by banks or by the exporters. We saw in section 24.2 that importers can, and often do, avoid exchange risks by hedging their foreign-currency obligations as of the date payment is due. Some, however, secure the exchange they need in the spot market. Because they are assuming the role of speculators, they rationally try to guess movements of the spot rate in deciding when to pay their creditors. Suppose that speculators widely expect the price of the pound sterling to rise. American importers rush to pay their outstanding sterling debts lest the cost rises. British importers, however, delay paying their dollar debts as long as possible, in hope that the dollar will cheapen. These actions amount to a short-term capital inflow for Britain — her loans are reduced but her liabilities preserved. They also increase the (excess) demand for sterling on the spot exchange market — American import-

---

[8] These features of the balance-of-payments accounts were discussed in section 5.3.

ers demand more than usual, British importers supply less. This form of speculative capital flow is called "leads and lags in commercial payments."

Short-Term Bank Loans

Whether for foreign trade or other purposes, short-term borrowers may be influenced by exchange-rate expectations. Suppose that American and British interest rates are identical and, once more, the public expects sterling to be revalued. British borrowers facing the same interest cost in both New York and London become eager to acquire dollar liabilities rather than sterling liabilities, because of the possible speculative profit if the sterling cost of dollars falls before repayment is due. Once again, "legitimate" international short-term capital flows are combined with the function of speculation against the pegged exchange rate being sustained.

Speculative Currency Holdings

The simplest form of international capital flow, in context of an expected sterling revaluation, occurs when an American acquires liquid sterling balances and holds them in hopes of revaluation. The increased holding of foreign exchange of course constitutes a capital flow to Britain and a speculation against the pegged value of sterling. Such a transaction involves an opportunity cost for the speculator, however: interest on the funds he holds in purely liquid funds. This is why pure speculators are attracted to the forward market where, as we saw in section 24.1, they can place their bets on future exchange rates without tying up any capital.

These speculative capital flows, when destabilizing, can create enormous difficulties for a country clinging tenuously to its current pegged exchange rate. They can lead to changes in reserves many times larger than what would be needed to sustain the imbalance on longer-term transactions. Furthermore, if the authorities trade currencies in the spot market with the speculators and *then* change the exchange rate, the government transfers real income from the public to the speculators (some of whom probably are its own nationals, but the rest are foreigners). If it devalues after a speculative run, the speculators get the foreign exchange — an asset that is about to be revalued; if the country under attack revalues, its monetary authorities will hold the depreciated foreign currency. These real (opportunity) losses, as well as the desire to avoid changing an exchange rate when underlying real forces may not require it, have prompted governments to intervene in the forward exchange market to relieve pressure on the spot market. Let us see how that may be done.

Official Transactions in the Forward Market

Return to Figure 24.4 and consider its implications for the British authorities trying to maintain the external value of sterling. In that example, market forces cause sterling to trade at a forward discount. Although this was by our assumption due to nothing more sinister than a high British interest rate (leading arbitragers to supply large quantities of forward sterling), the United Kingdom government might worry lest the discount on the forward pound stir speculation that spot rates will slip in the future, and devaluation occur. The British government can keep the forward market from flashing this signal if it is willing to buy forward sterling. Unless either the *A'A'* or the *STST* function in Figure 24.4 is perfectly elastic — and we expect neither to be — governmental purchases of forward pounds drive up the price, and the forward discount can potentially be eliminated.

What does the government accomplish by dealing in the forward market? To answer this question, we must notice a feature of the forward market that we neglected in section 24.2, namely, its interrelation with the spot exchange market. When the British government buys forward sterling and drives up the price, it discourages some would-be buyers of forward sterling and encourages potential sellers. But these affected buyers and sellers, unless they are pure speculators, can change their transactions in the spot market for sterling when the government's actions induce them to alter their forward transactions. Let us follow these linkages, in the situation described in Figure 24.4.

1. When the government purchases forward sterling and drives up its price, it encourages the net movement of short-term capital toward Britain. This additional short-term lending involves more sales of forward pounds, but correspondingly additional purchases of spot pounds (in order to make the initial investment). Hence the government supports the spot market for sterling indirectly, through the effect of its purchases of forward pounds on the arbitragers' demand for spot pounds.

2. The equilibrium shown in Figure 24.4 identifies the speculators as net buyers of forward pounds, because the forward rate lies below the pegged spot value. When the government buys forward pounds, it displaces some private speculative buyers. This displacement itself is not useful. However, many have argued that intervention in the forward market can powerfully influence speculative transactions in the *spot* market. The speculator is always a soothsayer, telling the future from signs that seem apt. One of the best objective signs of the future level of a spot exchange rate is the currency's forward rate. The speculators are not the only group affecting the forward rate. However, knowing nothing about the situation except that the forward rate lies below the spot, you would believe that speculators expect the spot rate to fall. That hunch could lead you to sell pounds spot, or reduce your purchases, if such a speculative maneuver lies open to you. Conversely, if government purchases in the forward market raise the rate and extinguish this signal of a possible de-

preciation, speculative net demand for the spot pound would increase. Hence, government intervention in the forward market also stabilizes the spot market, as speculators change their posture in the spot market on the basis of what is happening to the forward rate.[9]

3. Governmental purchases in the forward market increase the cost of forward cover to American importers of British goods and lower its cost to British buyers of American goods. Hence the forward-market intervention will worsen the British trade balance. This effect does not alter the conditions in the spot market *today*, however, because traders who hedge their future commitments do not use the spot exchange market. The higher price of forward pounds might cause an American importer to enter the spot market now, of course, to purchase sterling to cover his future obligations. But he would then take upon himself the role of speculator.

We conclude that government intervention in the forward market helps to support the spot market through its effect on arbitragers, and may also help through its effect on speculators. Thus it gains a short-term advantage. The support entails no loss of reserves, until its forward contracts mature and the government must disgorge reserves of foreign currency in order to fulfill its commitments to purchase sterling. One reason for intervening in the forward market, then, is to postpone the loss of reserves. This advantage may not be trivial for a country that is hard-pressed, because the market is apt to take a reported loss of reserves as a sign that the currency's value is likely to fall, and increase its speculative sales.

Besides, more than a short-term advantage might be gained if support of the forward rate deters speculative sales of sterling in the spot market. Bearish speculators in the spot market for sterling potentially drain British reserves. If forward-market intervention keeps them from appearing, the reserves may permanently lie higher than otherwise.[10] Thus, a country stabilizing its exchange rate may definitely gain from official intervention in the market for forward exchange, as either an adjunct to or a substitute for stabilizing the spot market directly.

24.4 CONTROLLING SHORT-TERM CAPITAL FOR INTERNAL BALANCE: THE EURO-DOLLAR MARKET

We shall now turn to some problems of coping with internal balance when there are interest-elastic flows of short-term capital. As we

[9] For a model of spot and forward markets that emphasizes this speculative connection, see J. L. Stein. *The Nature and Efficiency of the Foreign Exchange Market*. Essays in International Finance, no. 40. Princeton: International Finance Section, Princeton University, 1962.

[10] A controversy has occurred over whether or not a country gains from intervening in the forward market if it in fact is driven to devalue its currency. See B. J. Cohen. *Balance-of-Payments Policy*. Harmondsworth, England, and Baltimore: Penguin, 1969, pp. 81–87.

saw in Chapter 18 and section 23.2, the proper assignment of policy instruments renders such flows merely a datum rather than a conundrum for policy-makers. However, governments have seldom felt free to follow this recipe. A common posture among the industrial countries has been to ply both fiscal and monetary policy in the direction demanded by internal balance. Occasionally, when external imbalance becomes too blatant, monetary and perhaps fiscal policy are diverted to cope with the situation, often supplemented by direct controls over certain international transactions.

Rather than spin out abstract cases, it is instructive to draw upon recent international monetary developments, notably the rise of the Euro-dollar market and the devices employed by several European countries to blunt its effect on their domestic policies. Because the Euro-dollar market helps to perfect international short-term capital markets, we also consider it as an instrument for reallocating capital resources.

The Euro-Dollar Market

The Euro-dollar market deals in time deposits denominated in United States dollars but placed in banks located outside of the United States. The banks (which are often European branches of major American banks) accept these deposits and employ them to make short-term loans to borrowers who may be of any nationality. This market is like any other for bank deposits and bank loans except that the transaction is not denominated in the currency of the country in which it takes place. We shall ask shortly why such a market should arise. We should understand first, however, when its operations involve international capital movements.

Because Euro-dollar banks stay fully "loaned up," we need notice only transactions between depositors and ultimate borrowers, intermediated by the banks. When a Euro-dollar deposit changes hands between citizens of different nationalities, the depositor's country experiences a short-term capital outflow to the borrower's country. When their citizenship is the same, no international flow occurs. The fact that the currency denominating the transaction may be foreign to one or both parties is not significant, although the depositor's hoard of dollars must reflect a net outflow from the United States in the past if he is not an American citizen.

Now let us consider the traders in this market. They include United States corporations who can earn a higher return on their liquid balances in the Euro-dollar market than at home. But they also include many non-Americans who acquire liquid dollar balances, or choose to hold their funds in dollars rather than another currency. Corporations abroad, including subsidiaries of American firms, often transact large amounts of business and hold their liquid balances largely in dollars. Central banks, likewise interested in maximum returns on their international reserves, have placed large amounts of dollar balances in this market. Indeed, among the most important early lenders in the Euro-dollar market were central banks of the Soviet bloc countries, which hold dollar balances but were revolted at the prospect of placing them at short-term on Wall Street, that bastion of capitalism!

The prominence of non-American depositors in the Euro-dollar market vividly demonstrates the role of the dollar as a "vehicle currency" in international commerce. Even if traders try to maximize their profits (or income) only in terms of their national currencies, they will still hold balances of foreign exchange, particularly the most widely used foreign currencies. The convenience of transactors would be best served if only one currency existed in the world, ending the costs and risks of exchange conversion, just as communication would be eased if everyone spoke the same language. Lacking this utopia, traders as a group still benefit when a major currency comes into use for denominating transactions not even involving the country that sired the currency. The dollar and sterling both play this role.[11] Thus, one can identify many willing non-American lenders of Euro-dollars even without reference to sheiks fearful of the stability of their nation's currency — or the rapacity of their nation's tax collectors.[12] The use of such vehicle currencies by central banks as a medium for transactions and store of value was similarly explained in Chapters 5 and 20.

Borrowers in the Euro-dollar market can include anyone seeking large amounts of short-term funds. As we shall see, United States banks become heavy borrowers when credit conditions are tightened by the Federal Reserve System. It should be stressed, though, that the borrower in the Euro-dollar market is typically interested in short-term credit, and not in borrowing dollars per se. For instance, an important group of borrowers are local government units in Britain, which of course transact their business in sterling. When they borrow Euro-dollars, they (or their banks) "swap" the dollar proceeds into sterling for the duration of the loan. The "swap" involves only a simultaneous spot purchase and forward sale of sterling, to cover the borrowers against exchange risk. Thus, such a Euro-dollar borrowing represents the same covered interest arbitrage that we described in section 24.2, except that the switch of currencies is initiated by the borrower rather than the lender.

We thus see why an international market in short-term capital can be denominated in United States dollars (and other chief "vehicle currencies"). You may still wonder why this business should flow through non-American banks, rather than through American banks,

---

[11] Thus transactions in United States dollars comprise 47 percent of the business done in the French foreign exchange market, although only one-twelfth of France's trade is with the United States.

[12] This argument is developed in more detail by A. K. Swoboda. *The Euro-Dollar Market: An Interpretation*. Essays in International Finance, no. 64. Princeton: International Finance Section, Princeton University, 1968.

for which the dollar is native financial ground. The answer to that question shows how the Euro-dollar market helps to perfect international markets in short-term capital. First, foreign banks take Euro-dollar business because it is profitable. They face no significant exchange risk, because they can match the dollar assets and liabilities maturing at any date. And they can pay interest rates that attract lenders, yet charge rates that lure borrowers. They are thus taking business away from United States domestic banks. Perhaps they are more competitive than the United States banking system, in that the latter holds out for a higher margin of "price" over "cost" of short-term capital. The main reason, however, is surely the effect of United States government restriction on the maximum interest rates that banks can pay on time deposits (Regulation Q) and perhaps on the minimum reserves that must be held.

But the Euro-dollar banks do not compete just with other banks lending dollars, but with any financial institutions extending bulk short-term credit in any currency. The Euro-dollar market competes (and intermingles) with national banking systems throughout the world. Thus, for an Italian corporation, borrowing Euro-dollars in London (and swapping them into lire) is an alternative to borrowing directly from an Italian bank. By its use of the dollar as a vehicle currency the market brings together lenders and borrowers situated in many different countries, increasing the sensitivity of short-term capital flows to differences in interest rates and undercutting imperfections in competition in national banking systems. It is no wonder that fluctuations in short-term interest rates in the major countries quickly spread to the Euro-dollar market and then to the home-currency capital markets of other countries.[13]

Monetary Policy and the Euro-Dollar Market

Countries with pegged exchange rates often try to use monetary policy to attain internal balance, despite its inefficiency when capital is highly interest-elastic. A country might, of course, find itself in a situation where a shift of monetary policy would move it toward both internal and external balance, as when it initially suffers unemployment and a payments surplus, or inflation and a deficit. But only accidentally will a twist of the monetary knob just attain both objectives. Hence countries often find their pursuit of internal balance through monetary policy frustrated by what they see as its undesirable side-effects on external balance.

By increasing the international mobility of short-term capital, the

[13] For further information, see F. H. Klopstock. *The Euro-Dollar Market: Some Unresolved Issues.* Essays in International Finance, no. 65. Princeton: International Finance Section, Princeton University, 1968, and H. W. Mayer. *Some Theoretical Problems Relating to the Euro-Dollar Market.* Essays in International Finance, no. 79. Princeton: International Finance Section, Princeton University, 1970.

Euro-dollar market has enlarged these side-effects. Furthermore, the market's development may have been inflationary overall, thus augmenting the pressures on countries for tight money policy to curb inflation.[14] Let us see how several countries have coped with flows of interest-sensitive capital.

Germany. Germany has experienced payments surpluses regularly since the early 1950's, along with internal conditions which the German authorities felt required restrictive financial policies. A 1961 revaluation was too small to restore equilibrium. The German central bank (Bundesbank) faced the problem of maintaining high interest rates without thereby worsening the external surplus through short-term capital inflows. In 1960 the authorities discouraged borrowing abroad by German commercial banks by establishing discriminatory reserve requirements and prohibiting the payment of interest on deposit liabilities to foreigners. The German banks were thus unable to compete in the Euro-dollar market. The Bundesbank also operated on the forward market for German currency, although not by the straightforward method of driving the Deutsche mark to a forward discount (which, at the current interest rates, would encourage covered outflows and discourage inflows). Instead, the commercial banks were offered a special favorable "swap" rate, or premium on their sales of forward foreign currency, to make covered loans in the Euro-dollar market profitable for them. This policy developed a loophole. It drove down Euro-dollar interest rates by expanding the supply of funds, and German nonbank borrowers simply retrieved these funds from the Euro-dollar market. In 1964 the Bundesbank tried to avert this leakage by making its special forward rate available to the banks only for the purchase of United States Treasury bills. Such investments would be much less likely to encourage offsetting German private borrowings abroad.[15]

United Kingdom. Before the devaluation of 1967, the management of financial policy in Britain was regularly hampered by problems of

---

[14] Mayer, *Some Theoretical Problems,* mentions several reasons for this pressure. The market obviously moves funds from countries where the banking system is not fully loaned up to those where it is; to this extent, expansion in the borrowing country is not matched by contraction in the lending country. More important, when the United States lends Euro-dollars, often no domestic credit contraction results. Suppose an American places a Euro-dollar deposit in a London bank, which loans it to an Italian company. The company swaps its dollar proceeds for lire, and Italy's official reserves are enlarged by this amount. The United States banking system's deposit liabilities stand unchanged if Italy holds its reserves in dollars, but the liabilities and assets of the Italian banking system are increased. (Cf. section 24.1.)

[15] For an interesting study of the experience of Germany and other countries, see Samuel I. Katz. *External Surpluses, Capital Flows, and Credit Policy in the European Economic Community, 1958 to 1967.* Princeton Studies in International Finance, no. 22. Princeton: International Finance Section, Princeton University, 1969.

external imbalance, due perhaps less to actual deficits than to a low level of reserves that subjected sterling to recurrent panics. Domestic borrowings of Euro-dollar funds augmented the United Kingdom's exposure to speculative pressures, in a special sense: she could lose through Euro-dollar outflows no more than the reserves she had gained through Euro-dollar inflows, but these funds could decamp in a moment of panic and augment other speculative forces. Unlike Germany, the Bank of England tried to influence the forward exchange rate. At times this attempt apparently involved enormous commitments to purchase sterling forward, in order to ward off speculative outflows of funds (including Euro-dollar repatriations). John Spraos calculates that in late 1966 these forward commitments reached a staggering magnitude, equal to all of the nation's owned reserves plus much of what she probably could have borrowed.[16] As we mentioned in section 24.3, if devaluation is averted such commitments can easily be covered in the spot exchange market when they mature. Had devaluation intervened, however, the Bank would have suffered a substantial capital loss.

United States. The increased mobility of short-term capital has posed a recurrent dilemma for the United States during the past decade, especially during periods of domestic unemployment. With interest rates below those in the Euro-dollar market, any change in monetary policy designed to aid employment (by cutting interest rates) would worsen the capital outflow and external deficit. In general, the United States sought to deal with the problem through suasion or direct controls on banks and corporations to deter them from placing funds abroad. In 1968 and 1969, however, a different problem arose. Monetary policy was tightened sharply to curb a domestic boom. The commercial banks, in a credit crunch, found that they could secure additional reserves by borrowing from the Euro-dollar market — often from their own foreign branches. Such borrowings did not necessarily evade the Federal Reserve's policy of credit contraction. A bank might simply acquire a liability to its own branch and replace a deposit liability to a former holder of a Euro-dollar deposit. If the American banks' enlarged demand for Euro-dollars caused foreigners to buy more dollars from their own central banks, however, the credit contraction was averted; the United States banking system would gain reserves to offset the effort of the Federal Reserve to tighten credit. Because Euro-dollar borrowings thus could be frustrating its policies, the Federal Reserve imposed a reserves requirement on bank liabilities to their foreign branches. This requirement (on liabilities above a certain level), initially set at 10

---

[16] John Spraos, "Some Aspects of Sterling in the Decade 1957–66," *The International Market for Foreign Exchange,* ed., R. Z. Aliber. New York: Praeger, 1969, pp. 158–76; see also pp. 86–91.

percent, then raised to 20 percent, effectively taxed the net profits banks could earn by borrowing and relending Euro-dollars, and reduced this leakage in credit-control policies.[17]

Two broad lessons emerge from the development of the Euro-dollar market and countries' reactions to it. First, men and institutions constantly develop ways to move capital from places where its return is low to where its return is high; the Euro-dollar market exemplifies this process. Second, a government can sometimes escape a dilemma of economic policy by devising additional instruments of policy. When its goal is to sever the links between national capital markets, however, it needs ingenuity to stay ahead of the devices found by the market to circumvent its policies.

24.5 SUMMARY

The effect of short-term capital flows on expenditure — and thus on the transfer process — depends on their effect on the money supply. This effect should be larger when a banking system is fully loaned up, and varies with the reserve ratio. Central-bank policy is also apt to intervene. A central bank following the rules of the gold standard would contract its deposit liabilities (and thus the money supply) when a capital outflow causes a loss of reserves. One stabilizing the domestic money supply would react in the opposite direction. The transfer process following a change in short-term capital flows depends heavily on these features of monetary conditions and monetary policy.

Short-term capital exports are often covered by selling the expected proceeds in the forward exchange market. Interest arbitragers thus comprise one of the groups of transactors in the forward market, exporting capital and selling foreign exchange forward when its price is high enough to offset any differential between foreign and domestic short-term interest rates. Commercial traders (exporters and importers) also enter the forward market to avoid risks associated with future receipts or payments in foreign exchange. Finally, speculators enter the forward market, betting on the relation between the forward rate and the spot rate that will prevail when their contracts mature. The equilibrium value of the forward exchange rate sets the net excess demand of these three groups equal to zero.

Authorities who must maintain external balance under fixed exchange rates are preoccupied with short-term capital flows, because these embody speculative transactions. Speculative transactions can help the authorities when the public expects the current exchange

[17] Before this requirement went into effect, the transfer and reborrowing of United States funds through the Euro-dollar market was inflationary, because it lowered the banks' net reserve requirements. See Milton Friedman, "The Euro-Dollar Market: Some First Principles," *Morgan Guaranty Survey* (October 1969): 4–14.

rate to prevail in the future, but can magnify disturbances massively when the public expects a change in the pegged exchange rate. Speculative capital flows can occur through changes in trade credit ("leads and lags in commercial payments") as well as bank loans and foreign-exchange balances. Each class of transactions is potentially affected by the forward exchange rate as well as the spot rate. By intervening in the forward market, the government can affect spot-market transactions without actually changing its reserves (until the forward contracts mature).

Countries' efforts to control short-term capital movements have been frustrated in part by the growth of the Euro-dollar market. This market is for bank (time) deposits denominated in currencies other than that of the country in which the bank is domiciled. For large transactors the Euro-dollar market provides increased competition both with United States banks and with native banking systems dealing in foreign currencies, because the proceeds of Euro-dollar loans can readily be "swapped" into other currencies. Countries have attempted market interventions and direct controls on their banking systems to offset the rising interest-elasticity of capital flows associated with the growth of the Euro-dollar market.

SUGGESTIONS FOR FURTHER READING

Baldwin, R. E., and J. D. Richardson, eds. *Selected Topics in International Trade and Finance: A Book of Readings*. Boston: Little, Brown, 1973. Part V contains papers by Friedman and Klopstock on the Euro-dollar market.

Cohen, B. J. *Balance-of-Payments Policy*. Baltimore: Penguin, 1969. In Chapter 2 Cohen summarizes the case for government intervention in the forward market.

Einzig, Paul. *A Dynamic Theory of Forward Exchange*. London: Macmillan, 1961. Practical approach to forward exchange markets.

Grubel, Herbert G. *Forward Exchange, Speculation, and International Flow of Capital*. Stanford: Stanford University Press, 1966. Theory and evidence on forward exchange markets.

Katz, Samuel I. *External Surpluses, Capital Flows, and Credit Policy in the European Economic Community, 1958 to 1967*. Princeton Studies in International Finance, no. 22. Princeton: International Finance Section, Princeton University, 1969. Financial policies and short-term capital flows.

Stein, J. L. *The Nature and Efficiency of the Foreign Exchange Market*. Essays in International Finance, no. 40. Princeton: International Finance Section, Princeton University, 1962. Forward markets and speculative crises.

Swoboda, A. K. *The Euro-Dollar Market: An Interpretation*. Essays in International Finance, no. 64. Princeton: International Finance Section, Princeton University, 1968. Analytical treatment.

PART SIX Growth, Trade, and Development

25 The Effects of Growth on Trade

We live in a changing world. That statement is perhaps too pessimistic. For many countries and many time periods the dominant thrust of change is *growth*. Much of our preceding discussion of international trade and payments has sidestepped this issue by treating countries as if the resource base and technology were invariant. In this concluding part of the book we shall turn to the phenomena of growth, trade, and development.

In this chapter we shall assume that a country is experiencing growth and we shall examine the consequences for the pattern and gains from trade. In the next chapter we shall turn things around by focusing, instead, on how trade interacts with the growth process, especially for countries at early stages of development. In so doing questions similar to those posed in Parts 3 and 4 are raised, dealing with the appropriate commercial and financial policies for development.

25.1 POSSIBLE SOURCES OF GROWTH

We need to define growth or, more accurately, to specify what is growing. In what follows we shall be concerned with cases in which the community's production-possibilities schedule is shifting outward over time. But there are other kinds of change. Suppose foreign demand for the home country's export commodity grows. Even without any change in the factor endowment base or development of technology the home country's terms of trade will steadily improve and its real income will grow over time. There may be changes in production along the transformation schedule, but there need be no outward shift of the schedule. Of course if unemployed resources exist, then the export boom can increase the effectively used factor base of the economy. Or, as is pointed out in Chapter 26, the increased demand for the exports of the home country may stimulate exploration of resources and/or technical breakthroughs that would shift the community's production possibilities curve outward.

In this chapter we shall assume that the home country grows in one or more of three basic ways.

Growth in Population and the Labor Force

In most countries population is growing, and with it the supply of labor for productive activities. This expansion is certainly a source of growth and will shift the transformation schedule outward, especially in the direction of the labor-intensive commodity in a two-factor Heckscher-Ohlin model. What is peculiar about this source of expansion is that on a per-capita basis the community may be made worse off by growth. Incomes per head are rarely raised merely by an increase in the number of heads. An important distinction must be made between a community's aggregate output, which may be a prime determinant of the terms of trade, and its output per capita, which is more directly linked to welfare comparisons. This distinction is less necessary for other sources of growth.

Capital Accumulation

Whereas in our earlier treatments of the Heckscher-Ohlin model the factor of production, "capital," was assumed to be fixed, in real life capital goods are produced by other factors of production (including capital). If such production (or possibly imports) exceeds the current rate at which capital goods are depreciating, the community's net stock of capital rises, and with it the schedule of commodities that can currently be produced. In courses on economic growth capital accumulation is fundamental in developing models of the economy in which today's production affects tomorrow's resource base and thus tomorrow's production. We can easily construct models in which the pattern of growth over time is thus determined by a few simple features such as the rate of savings (which indicates the level of current capital accumulation) and some exogenous rate of population expansion.

Our task here is different. We shall forego constructing a dynamic model of growth in favor of considering the effect of growth on trade. This stance is somewhat modified in Chapter 26 where we shall remark on the feedback effect of trade on elements such as the rate of savings which is crucial in determining the rate of growth itself. Capital accumulation and labor-force expansion can both enlarge the flow of commodities that the community can produce. But in contrast to the growth of labor, net growth in the stock of capital promises as well to increase incomes per capita.

Technological Change

A preliminary study of the sources of growth in the American economy suggested that much less than half of the increment in per-capita production possibilities could be attributed to capital accumulation. Left out of account is the tendency for technology itself to develop over time.[1] If the same bundle of resources can yield a greater output than previously, growth in production possibilities can occur.

Advances in technology not only allow greater levels of output, they may alter the proportions in which labor and capital are employed and thus affect the composition of output in a manner that is similar to changes in the community's factor endowment proportions. A classification of three types of technical progress is illustrated in Figure 25.1 for the home country's clothing industry. In each diagram the initial point of cost-minimization along the unit isoquant is shown by point A. The original wage/rental ratio is depicted by the slope of the line at A, and the (a_{LC}, a_{KC}) input-output coefficients per unit of clothing are those that minimize unit costs among all the possible combinations (to produce one unit of clothing) shown by the unit isoquant. Technical progress is shown by the shift of the unit isoquant toward the origin — implying lower labor and capital requirements per unit of output. If wages and rents remain unchanged, the new optimal techniques are shown by the points labeled B in Figure 25.1. Case a illustrates *neutral* technical progress: the capital and labor input coefficients are each reduced proportionally (line AB extended would pass through the origin). Case b illustrates technical progress in the clothing industry that would cause the labor input coefficient to be reduced relatively more than the capital coefficient at the same factor prices. This is termed *labor-saving* progress. The opposite bias is shown by case c: the capital coefficient has fallen more than the labor coefficient so that with *capital-saving* technical progress, the capital/labor ratio would be reduced even if factor prices remained unaltered. In the last two cases we could have illustrated a more extreme bias. For example, in case c the new isoquant, after technical change, might have been tangent to the dashed line at point D, in which event the change economizes so much on capital that the labor coefficient is actually raised.[2]

Clearly the effect of technical change on production possibilities depends on the relative extent of technical change in each industry, and on the nature of the bias in technical change.

---

[1] See Robert M. Solow, "Technical Change and the Aggregate Production Function," *Review of Economics and Statistics*, 39 (August 1957): 312–20.

[2] This three-way classification of the bias in technological change is called *Hicksian,* in honor of the original discussion by J. R. Hicks in *The Theory of Wages.* London: Macmillan & Co., 1932.

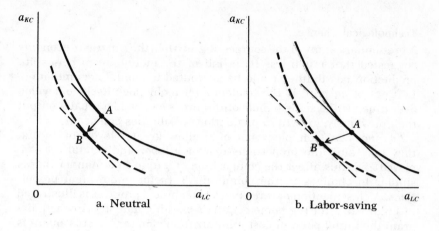

a. Neutral   b. Labor-saving

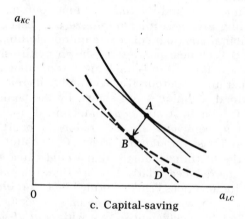

c. Capital-saving

FIGURE 25.1   Types of Technical Progress

Three types of technical progress in the clothing industry
are illustrated. In each case the unit isoquant is shifted
toward the origin. The cases differ depending upon whether
at the same factor price ratio the labor coefficient is reduced
the same proportional amount (a.), greater (b.), or less than
(c.) the capital-coefficient.

25.2 FACTOR GROWTH AND PRODUCTION POSSIBILITIES

The link between factor accumulation, whether predominantly of
labor or capital, and the transformation or production-possibilities
curve has already been developed in the analysis of the Heckscher-
Ohlin trade model in Chapters 8 and 9. Figure 25.2 will help review
this material. Units of capital are shown on the vertical axis and units

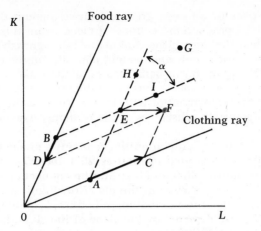

FIGURE 25.2   Labor Growth and Output Changes

> Given the endowment point at *E*, only if both capital and labor grow (within the α-cone) will it be possible, at constant prices, to increase output in both sectors of the economy.

of labor on the horizontal; the home country's initial factor endowment bundle is shown by point *E*. Two rays are drawn from the origin. The slope of the steeper ray shows the capital/labor ratio that would be employed in the food industry at the wage/rent ratio prevailing in the economy. We shall assume this wage/rent ratio remains constant in order to explore the effect of growth *at constant prices* on outputs. (Later we shall analyze the effect of growth in changing prices). The flatter ray depicts the capital/labor ratio that would be employed in the clothing industry at these factor prices. As before, we shall assume food to be produced by more capital-intensive techniques than clothing. Output levels for each commodity can be measured along these rays. Given the endowment bundle shown at *E,* only the output combination *OB* of food and *OA* of clothing leads to full employment of both factors. (The line *AE* is parallel to *OB* and *BE* is parallel to *OA*.)

Suppose the home country's labor force grows with no concomitant change in the supply of capital. That is, the endowment point moves from *E* to *F*. Completing the new parallelogram, we can see that the output of the labor-intensive sector, clothing, must expand (from *OA* to *OC*) to absorb the addition to the labor force. Furthermore, with factor prices (and therefore input-output techniques) assumed constant, the expansion of clothing requires more capital, which can only be obtained from the food industry. Output of food must contract, from *OB* to *OD*.

Notice how an uneven growth in the factor resource base (in this case labor growth positive and capital growth zero) leads to a magnified disparity in the growth of outputs at constant prices (clothing production rises by an even greater relative amount than the labor force and food production declines). Indeed, from this argument it should be clear that only if the capital and labor growth is sufficiently balanced so that the new endowment point lies in the cone α in Figure 25.2 will expansion in both sectors of the economy be possible at the given prices. A special case would be represented by *balanced growth*. If the endowment of both factors rises in the same proportion (say to point G), all sectors of the economy expand at this uniform rate.[3]

The effect of factor growth on the economy's production-possibilities schedule is illustrated in Figures 25.3 and 25.4. These two alternatives, perhaps suffice to illustrate the connection. In each case the original factor endowment bundle (E in Figure 25.2) and technology support the transformation schedule TT. Suppose that the terms of trade are depicted by the slope of line 1 so that initial production is at point A. If these prices are held constant, the movement in Figure 25.3 from A to B illustrates growth only of the labor supply, such as the movement from E to F in Figure 25.2. A new transformation schedule, $T'T'$, corresponds to this new factor endowment bundle, and it has a slope equal to the given terms of trade at position B where output of the labor-intensive commodity, clothing, has expanded while food production has actually contracted. The $T'T'$ schedule in Figure 25.4 corresponds with a hypothetical endowment move from E to H in Figure 25.2. That is, the economy experiences both capital and labor expansion, in the proportions required by the capital-intensive food industry. At the techniques dictated by the initial factor prices, the entire increment in resources is exactly absorbed in food production so that point B, in Figure 25.4, lies vertically above point A. In both diagrams the transformation schedules are bowed out from the origin, suggesting that alternative output combinations are possible, but only at increasing opportunity costs.

This brief account illustrates some consequences of factor growth on production possibilities. Before turning to the effect of growth on the terms of trade and welfare, we shall consider the effect of technological advance on the transformation schedule.

25.3 GROWTH INDUCED BY TECHNICAL PROGRESS

Technological progress in one or both industries also enlarges the combinations that the economy can produce, but the analysis of the outward shift in the transformation curve is more complex than in the case of factor growth. There are basically two reasons for this: As our discussion surrounding Figure 25.1 revealed, in any industry several different types of technical change are possible, depending on the bias that the improvement in techniques implies for the use

[3] We are, of course, adhering to the constant-returns-to-scale technology assumed earlier in discussions of the Heckscher-Ohlin model.

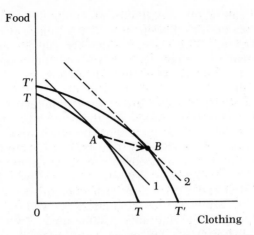

FIGURE 25.3 Labor Growth and the Transformation Schedule

An increase in the labor endowment, with no change in the capital stock, yields a higher clothing output and lower food output at the same prices. Clothing is labor-intensive.

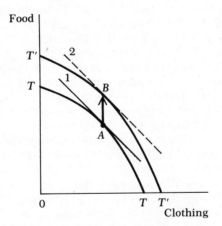

FIGURE 25.4 Capital and Labor Growth in the Proportions Required in Food

The shift in the transformation schedule corresponds to the movement of both capital and labor in Figure 25.2 from point *E* to point *H*, in the proportions required by food. This increased bundle is absorbed completely by the food industry, shifting output from *A* to *B* at constant prices.

of labor and capital. As well, improvements may be taking place in both industries but at different rates. The number of possible cases one might wish to explore escalates quickly, and can easily degenerate into a taxonomic approach, which we wish to avoid. The second reason that the analysis of technical progress is inherently more complicated than that of factor growth is that if technical progress takes place at different rates between the two industries, the relationship between factor price ratios and the commodity price ratio will be altered. We shall illustrate both these reasons with a few examples.

Consider, first, the possibility that *neutral* technical progress, illustrated in Figure 25.1a, occurs in the home country's export industry, clothing. This unbiased improvement in techniques implies that at the initial factor price ratio both labor and capital coefficients are reduced uniformly, so that no change takes place in factor proportions. The slope of the clothing ray in Figure 25.2 would not change at the initial factor prices, but the scale of output as it is measured along the clothing ray would increase. For example, before technical progress the distance OA may have measured 60 units of clothing. A 50 percent neutral technical advance in the clothing industry would imply that the input bundle shown by point A would now correspond to an output of 90 units of clothing. With the endowment point constant at E, the old transformation schedule would show an output of OB units of food and 60 units of clothing at the given wage/rent ratio, while the new transformation schedule would, at the same level OB of food, show an increased output of clothing of 90 units. In short, neutral technical progress in one industry will shift the production-possibilities schedule by a uniform percentage (the rate of technical progress) outward in the direction of the industry experiencing technical change. This shift is illustrated in Figure 25.5 for the case of a uniform 50 percent neutral advance in clothing.

A slightly different way of viewing this may prove helpful. The old output combination shown by point A in Figure 25.5 in the TT schedule can, after technical progress occurs in the clothing industry, be produced with a smaller aggregate labor and capital endowment bundle. That is, technical progress *releases* productive factors and is, on this count, equivalent to an expansion of the community's resource base. Reconsider Figure 25.2. If neutral technical progress in clothing is like an expansion in the endowment bundle, E, by 50 percent of the resource base initially used in clothing, it is as if the endowment point, E, expands to point I (EI is 50 percent of OA). From our earlier analysis of the effect of factor growth on outputs, a movement from E to I in the endowment base in Figure 25.2 would leave food production unchanged and increase clothing production by 50 percent, as shown in the movement from A to B in Figure 25.5.

The seeming equivalence between technical progress and factor growth stressed in this account is misleading in that it ignores the relationship between factor and commodity prices. In Figure 25.5 the

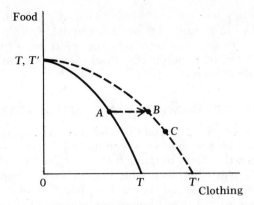

FIGURE 25.5 Neutral Technical Change in Clothing

A 50 percent neutral technical change in clothing shifts *TT* to the right, to *T'T'*, by 50 percent.

movement from *A* to *B* would occur with neutral technical progress in the clothing sector if the factor price ratio is unaltered. But notice that the *T'T'* curve at *B* must be flatter than *TT* at *A*. In other words, technical progress in the clothing industry would, at unchanged factor prices, lower the relative cost of producing clothing. The point on *T'T'* that has the same slope as point *A* on *TT* is *C*, southeast of *B*. That is, at a given *commodity price ratio* (or terms of trade), neutral technical advance in clothing increases clothing production and *reduces* food output. The production response at given *commodity* prices is like the output change (from *A* to *B* in Figure 25.3) consequent to an increase just in the factor of production used intensively in clothing.

To sum up: any technical progress alters outputs at given *factor* prices by amounts dictated by the released factor requirements. In this sense technical progress is just like factor accumulation. We examined *neutral* technical change in clothing. Consider, briefly, the case illustrated in Figure 25.1b, of *labor-saving* technical progress in clothing. It is as if the economy had more capital and more labor, but primarily an increase in labor, even relative to the proportions employed initially in the labor-intensive (clothing) industry. Therefore at unchanged factor prices the output of the labor-intensive commodity would expand, and the capital-intensive commodity contract. At given *commodity* prices this altered composition of outputs is accentuated. The output of the industry experiencing technical progress must rise in order to raise costs (along the transformation schedule) sufficiently to balance the initial cost reduction (at original factor prices) that is reflected by the technical progress itself. For example, in the neutral case pictured in Figure 25.5, progress in the clothing industry has cut the relative cost of producing clothing in going from *A* to *B*. To raise this cost back to the level shown at *A*, it is necessary to release more resources into clothing — the movement from *B* to *C* — because increased output of clothing can be obtained along *T'T'* only at increasing opportunity costs.

25.4 GROWTH, THE TERMS OF TRADE, AND WELFARE

So far we have concentrated on the effects of various types of growth on the production-possibilities schedule. More precisely, we have asked how growth affects outputs at the initial terms of trade. To the extent that growth expands production, welfare is improved — subject to the proviso that an increase in population may cause per capita incomes to fall even though the aggregate value of outputs is expanding. A final judgment as to the effect of growth on real incomes in an open economy, however, must take account not only of the growth of outputs but the effect on the terms of trade. As our entire discussion of welfare in the context of either an exchange model (Part 1), a production model (Parts 2 and 3), or a model in which factors are somewhat mobile internationally (Part 5) revealed, a change in the economic environment that causes a country's terms of trade to deteriorate will, on that account, depress welfare. The task confronting us in this section is to trace the effects of the various types of growth previously considered on the terms of trade.

The broad outline of the results is clear. Any source of growth that expands production of the country's export commodity more than that of its import commodity will, unless outweighed by other factors, depress that country's terms of trade. Consider some of the cases we have already examined. If growth takes place primarily because of an expansion in the community's supply of the factor of production that is used intensively in exports, the relative supply of exports will rise in world markets and the terms of trade will deteriorate. An extreme case involves the expansion of just one of the factors of production. This was illustrated for the case of labor growth in Figure 25.3. At constant terms of trade the output of the capital-intensive commodity, food, was reduced from *A* to *B*. If food is not an inferior commodity, the local demand for food will rise with growth at constant terms of trade. Putting these together, the home country's excess demand for food must rise as the home country grows, and unless countervailing forces are operating in the foreign country, the relative price of food must rise in world markets. That is, the terms of trade for the home country must deteriorate. A neutral technological change in the export clothing industry, illustrated in Figure 25.5, also must involve a deterioration in the terms of trade because at constant *commodity* prices output of the imported commodity, food, drops while the expansion of income raises local demand. This effect would be more pronounced if technical progress in the clothing industry were marked by a labor-saving bias (as in Figure 25.1b), as this bias will further expand the output of the labor-intensive exports, clothing.

Of course technical change may, instead, expand production of the country's import-competing commodity. Or the home country, an exporter of labor-intensive clothing, may control population growth and accumulate capital over time. This, as well, would expand its production of the import-competing capital-intensive food industry at the expense of clothing and thus improve its terms of trade.

Although growth can therefore affect the terms of trade in either direction, there is a sense in which growth itself will on balance worsen the terms of trade. By this remark we refer to the consequence in an open economy of balanced expansion in outputs and consumption. This case is illustrated in Figure 25.6. Initially at terms of trade given by the slope of line 1 production takes place along *TT* at point *A*, line 1 is the budget line, allowing consumption at point *B*, with imports of food equal in value to exports of clothing. Balanced growth is represented by the uniform expansion of the transformation curve to *T'T'*, so that at the initial terms of trade, shown also by the slope of line 2, production would expand proportionally from *A* to *C*. If the higher incomes result in a uniform expansion in demand (from *B* to *D*), distance *DC* must exceed distance *BA*. The *structure* of the

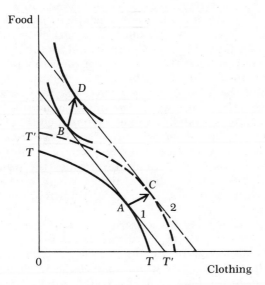

FIGURE 25.6 Uniform Growth at Given Terms of Trade

If the transformation schedule shifts uniformly outward, and if all demands expand uniformly at constant prices, growth must worsen the terms of trade by increasing the demand for imports.

home country's economy is identical before and after growth, but the increase in size spills over to increase the absolute quantity of food demanded as imports and clothing offered as exports. If the rest of the world is not experiencing growth (at least at this rate), there is pressure set up for the home country's terms of trade to deteriorate. The sheer act of growing more than other countries will increase the demand for imports and thus induce a deterioration in the terms of trade that to some extent may erode the gains from growth.[4]

If the terms of trade deteriorate as a consequence of growth, it is natural to ask whether the deterioration can outweigh the direct benefit of growth. This possibility, which is described as a case of *immiserizing growth,* cannot be ruled out. An illustration is provided in Figure 25.7. Initially the terms of trade are given by the slope of line 1, with the home country's production at A and consumption at B. Growth in some form that favors the nation's export industry, clothing, shifts the transformation schedule outward from TT to $T'T'$. As a consequence we assume that the relative price of clothing in world markets drops to the level shown by the slope of line 2. The home country adjusts its production to point C and, at the new terms of trade, maximizes its real income by consuming at point D. But its real income after growth, as indicated by the y_1 indifference curve, is lower than the original real income shown by indifference curve y_0. Economic growth has made the country worse off.

Two basic factors could contribute to produce this result. (1) Growth primarily increases capacity and output in a nation's export industries. (2) Demand elasticities throughout the world for the country's export commodity are quite low. The first factor ensures that the major effect of growth in world markets is the increased supply of the nation's exports, while the second suggests that the terms of trade must deteriorate sharply to raise world demand enough to clear commodity markets. If a country like Brazil has a bumper coffee crop, the world price of coffee might fall so much that Brazil loses real income as a consequence of the good crop. The argument has validity as well for groups within a country. Agriculture provides the prime example. Many nations attempt, on behalf of their farmers, to encourage crop restriction programs to keep farm prices from falling in the face of inelasticity in demand.[5]

In this abstract account of the consequences of growth on trade you may detect a prescription for developing countries: channel new investments toward import-competing industries and away from the export sector. This argument has indeed been popular in many countries, and in the next chapter we shall attempt to appraise its

[4] The reader may recall that this argument about balanced growth was used in Chapter 22 where we discussed the effect of uniform expansion in the receiving country and contraction in the paying country of a transfer of productive resources. See Figure 22.3.

[5] In the supplement to this chapter we shall develop explicit conditions required for the possibility that growth could be immiserizing.

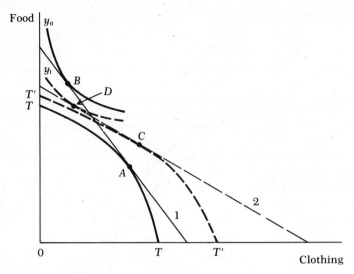

FIGURE 25.7 Immiserizing Growth

> Growth biased towards the nation's export industry (clothing) can reduce real income by so worsening the terms of trade (from line 1 to line 2) that consumption (at *D*) ends up on a lower indifference curve than initially (at *B*).

validity. At the present level of abstraction, however, notice that such a case for import substitution can be made only if the developing country is important enough in world markets to affect the terms of trade. If it is not, then interference with the allocation of newly acquired resources makes no more sense than did the argument for tariff protection in the small-country case; in Chapter 12 we showed that the optimal tariff rate is zero if the terms of trade cannot be altered.

Suppose that a country too small in world markets to affect the world terms of trade nonetheless has provided tariff protection for its import-competing industry. Furthermore, suppose that growth is taking place, in this instance biased toward the import-competing sector. (This may be the consequence of natural forces or it may reflect a deliberate governmental policy of channeling new resources into production that competes with imports.) It may sound surprising, especially in view of our emphasis above on the possibly damaging effect of growth in the export sector on a country's welfare, that in this case as well growth may lower the community's real income. First we illustrate the possibility and then dissolve any semblance of paradox with a more general account of the forces influencing real income.

The home country initially produces at point *A* along its transformation curve, *TT*, in Figure 25.8. Two sets of price ratios are shown: the

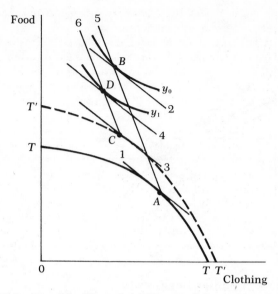

FIGURE 25.8   Possible Harmful Effects of Growth with Protection

The home country, too small to affect the terms of trade, has
levied a tariff on food imports. Before growth it produces at
A and consumes at *B*. Although growth, biased toward the
import-competing food sector, raises the value of production
at domestic prices (*C*), it lowers the value at world prices
and results in a loss of real income (compare *D* with *B*).

slope of lines 5 and 6 represents the relative *world* price of clothing,
while the slope of 1, 2, 3, and 4 reflects price ratios behind the tariff
wall in the home country. We shall assume that the tariff rate on food
imports, which is the wedge separating the slope of 1 and 5, is kept at
the same level during growth and that the home country cannot affect
the world terms of trade. Initial consumption at home is shown by
point *B*, where indifference curve y_0 is tangent to domestic price line 2.
Line 2 is parallel to line 1 — both producers and consumers respond
to prices behind the tariff wall — and is higher by the amount of the
tariff revenue.[6] Of course at world prices production point *A* and consumption point *B* have the same value — they both lie on line 5.

We shall assume that growth shifts the transformation schedule
outward to $T'T'$, heavily biased toward resources (both new and old)
being channeled into import-competing food production and away
from the clothing export sector. The same domestic prices prevail,
as by assumption the tariff rate is unaltered and the country is too
small to affect world prices. The new production point is at *C* and the

---

[6] Recall from Figure 12.3 how a tariff is illustrated in a diagram showing a
transformation schedule and indifference curves.

consumption point at D, which lies on a *lower* indifference curve, y_1, than the pregrowth consumption point on y_0.[7]

The reason that growth has lowered welfare in this case has nothing to do with our previous example in which the terms of trade deteriorated. Instead, it depends on the existence of a tariff separating home and foreign prices. Notice that the new production point, C, on the higher $T'T'$ curve has a *higher* value than does A at domestic prices (line 3 lies above line 1), but a *lower* value at world prices (line 6 through C lies below line 5 through A). Growth has been so biased in favor of the commodity (food) that is artificially high priced at home that the seemingly higher valued production point C (compared with A at domestic prices) represents an actual loss at world prices. This phenomenon clearly could not arise except for a policy of protection to the import-competing sector.

With these examples in hand we can state in more general terms the effect of growth on an open economy's real income: (1) As growth has been defined, the transformation schedule shifts outward so that at original domestic prices a greater aggregate value of goods and services is produced. This shift raises real incomes.[8] (2) The sources of growth affect the composition of the expanded output, helping to determine the extent, if any, in the change in the terms of trade. Growth that is concentrated in a nation's export sector generally worsens the terms of trade, and thus leads to a deterioration in welfare that must be set against the directly favorable effect of growth at given terms of trade. For a small country the terms of trade effect is so negligible that it can be ignored. (3) If tariffs or trade taxes exist, the cost to the community of obtaining imports on the world market (given by the terms of trade) falls short of the value at home of this commodity (given by the domestic relative price of imports). In such a situation any change in the volume of imports that is brought about by growth must affect welfare. In the case illustrated in Figure 25.8, growth has greatly reduced the community's imports (DC is smaller than BA), thus forcing a reduction in net purchases of a commodity that is cheaper to obtain abroad than it is worth at home. Conversely, should growth have been concentrated in the nation's export sector, the consequent increased reliance on foreign sources of supply for imports could increase the gains in welfare beyond the direct effects described in (1). Unlike the terms of trade argument discussed in (2), the argument that a change in the volume of protected imports can affect welfare is applicable to small countries as well as large.

---

[7] This argument is based on Harry G. Johnson, "The Possibility of Income Losses from Increased Efficiency or Factor Accumulation in the Presence of Tariffs," *Economic Journal,* 77 (March 1967): 151–54.

[8] Once again a qualification must be made for the possibility that real income *per capita* may fall even as aggregate output rises if growth is attributable to an increase in population that exceeds the extent of capital accumulation and technological progress.

25.5 GROWTH AND THE BALANCE OF PAYMENTS

Growth can affect the balance of payments in a number of different ways, and in briefly discussing some of these we shall depart from our two-commodity, full-employment, Heckscher-Ohlin model. Economists have disagreed on this question, and there is no clear evidence that consensus is being achieved currently. First let us consider the more extreme views:

Economic Expansion Leads to Trade Deficits

One of the strongest cases for this point of view can be found in the models described in Chapter 17 where we discussed balance-of-payments problems in a world of sticky prices and Keynesian unemployment. Growth is synonymous with putting more resources to work; whether these resources are new or previously unemployed is beside the point. The effect on the balance of trade stems largely from the effect of increased incomes on the demand for imports. If a country's exports are determined by foreign demand, and if growth abroad proceeds at lower rates than at home (or is nonexistent), the growing country must suffer a balance of trade deficit, leading, in a world of sticky prices, either to a prolonged loss of reserves or to an eventual devaluation of the exchange rate in the absence of direct controls over imports.

This argument can be made more secure if we consider a model in which commodities that can neither be exported nor produced abroad and imported are considered. Call these "nontradeables" or "home goods." For some countries these are a large part of the gross national product — commodities such as services, construction, and other items for which international transport costs are prohibitively high. If domestic growth is centered primarily on these activities, incomes at home rise, along with an induced increased demand for imports, without necessarily any significant concomitant rise in production of import-competing commodities or exportables. This is the classic case of growth being synonymous with balance-of-payments difficulties, made perhaps more severe by any tendency of domestic growth to raise factor prices and push up costs, thus shrinking export markets and switching local spending onto imports. Government policy, in turn, may focus on preventing a balance-of-payments crisis by dampening the sources of growth — until the consequent rise in unemployment forces attention onto this problem. As a caricature of Britain's stop-go policies in the 1960's, this may not be far off the mark.

Economic Growth Strengthens the Balance of Payments

The strongest version of this argument points to growth that finds its nourishment in technological progress in either the export sector or import-competing sector of the economy. Going beyond the two-commodity Heckscher-Ohlin model, this argument cites, on the export side, the case in which a country leads in developing new products that establish the country temporarily as the unique source of supply in world markets. Although imitation in lower-cost countries can eventually erode this position, new products may emerge to keep a country's export position strong. In short, we have the phenomena of the "product cycle" and "technology gap" theories of trade that we elucidated in Chapter 11.

As opposed to the payments pessimists' view of growth as leading to income rises and spillovers that expand imports, the optimists stress the innovational aspects of growth and the benefits of not only new products but cost-reductions for existing lines that foster exports and enhance import-competing production. Obviously, much depends on the assumption made about prices. In previous sections of this chapter we found that growth from any source may put pressure on the terms of trade; the direction of the pressure depends upon the nature of growth. If prices are sticky, growth that leads to an excess demand for imports could be translated into growth that leads to balance-of-payments deficits. This was the same analogy cited in Chapter 22 where we discussed the transfer problem. If prices are flexible, so that commodity markets are cleared, balance of trade deficits or surpluses must in the last analysis reflect underspending or overspending. This was the message of Chapter 4 and the discussion of balance-of-payments problems in Part 4.

To round out this discussion we shall consider two aspects of the growth process that have been neglected so far in this chapter. The first refers to the possible effect of growth on monetary equilibrium. In Chapter 16 we noticed the importance of the demand for money based on the expected volume of transactions, and the tendency for a community to hoard (i.e., cut its spending below the level of its income) in the event that monetary stocks fall short of the quantity of money demanded for transactions. In a growth context what emerges is the possibility that if monetary stocks (and especially foreign exchange reserves) do not keep pace with increased monetary demand (tied to increased incomes and spending generated by growth), the community will hoard in order to build up its reserves with temporary trade surpluses. This view puts monetary factors foremost in defending the position that strong balances of payments are more apt to be found among growing countries (Germany, Japan) than countries with low rates of growth (the United States, Great Britain).[9] It is a view that needs to be expanded to consider the source of growth. If a country's high rate of growth is based largely on its success in expanding its export markets, it should not be surprising to find growth synonymous with trade surpluses.

The other neglected aspect of the growth process is the possibility that growth induces changes in the capital account of the balance of

[9] One variant of this argument has been presented by Robert Mundell in *International Economics*. New York: Macmillan, 1968, chap. 9.

payments. Basically what we have in mind is the connection between growth and domestic rates of return on capital. To the extent that rates of return are driven up with high rates of growth (either as cause, or effect, or some mixture), foreign capital may be attracted. The capital inflow allows a trade deficit without putting pressure on the balance of payments overall.[10]

25.6 SUMMARY

We began the chapter by discussing various sources of growth. To expand levels of output a community must either increase the supply of one or more of its productive factors or alter techniques so that fewer factor inputs are required per unit of output. The effect of growth on commodity markets and the terms of trade depends on the nature of growth and the sector in which it is concentrated. The terms of trade may either improve or deteriorate. In search of presumptions we found that "balanced" growth, whereby all demands and outputs expand proportionally, implies a rise in the relative price of imports. Implicit in this argument is the assumption that the country under consideration is growing relative to the rest of the world, so that its "balanced" expansion in reality entails an increased net demand for the commodity it imports. To this extent the benefits of growth in one country spill over and favorably affect other countries through changes in their terms of trade.

Partly through the terms of trade effect growth was seen to pose dangers for an open economy. We illustrated a case in which world demand was so inelastic that export-biased growth led to such a fall in the world price of exports that the country would have been better off without the growth. (In the example cited in the text, Brazil might benefit by burning some of its coffee.) Although protectionist policies can be employed to encourage new resources to be devoted to the import-competing sector, the wedge thus driven between world and domestic prices may signal that such growth, which cuts down on imports, entails a real income loss in restricting purchases from lower-cost sources abroad. The chapter concluded with a more generally based discussion of the effect of growth on the balance of payments. This theme is picked up again in the next chapter.

SUGGESTIONS FOR FURTHER READING

Findlay, Ronald, and H. Grubert, "Factor Intensities, Technological Progress and the Terms of Trade," *Oxford Economic Papers,* N.S. 11 (February

---

[10] For a model that incorporates this effect on the balance of payments see Harry G. Johnson, "Some Aspects of the Theory of Economic Policy in a World of Capital Mobility," *Essays in Honour of Marco Fanno,* ed. T. Bagiotti. Padua: Cedam, 1966, and Ronald W. Jones, "Monetary and Fiscal Policy for an Economy with Fixed Exchange Rates," *Journal of Political Economy,* 76 (July/ August 1968): 921–43.

1959): 111–21; reprinted ed. Jagdish Bhagwati. *International Trade.* Baltimore: Penguin, 1969, chap. 14. A basic paper on biased technical progress.

Johnson, Harry G., "The Possibility of Income Losses from Increased Efficiency or Factor Accumulation in the Presence of Tariffs," *Economic Journal,* 77 (March 1967): 151–54. How growth may lower welfare in a small country.

Johnson, Harry G., "The Theory of Trade and Growth: A Diagrammatic Analysis," *Trade, Balance of Payments, and Growth,* eds. J. Bhagwati et al. Amsterdam: North Holland, 1971, chap. 7. A full diagrammatic account of growth and trade.

Meier, Gerald M. *International Trade and Development.* New York: Harper & Row, 1963, chap. 2. Presents a discussion of the effect of growth on comparative costs.

Supplement to Chapter 25:
Growth and Welfare

Growth may be a mixed blessing. This fact was underscored in Figures 25.7 and 25.8 in which growth led to a loss in welfare. Both of these examples are amenable to the analysis of welfare changes that has been discussed in the supplements to Chapters 3, 12, 13, and 22. The reader patient enough to follow through those exercises will be pleased to find that only a slight variation is required to handle the growth cases with which we are now concerned. First we shall look at a country large enough to affect the terms of trade by its growth but following a policy of free trade. With no distinction necessary between home and foreign prices, the change in real income is:

$$dy = -Mdp + (dx_c + pdx_F). \qquad (25.S.1)$$

This decomposition, showing the terms of trade effect, on the one hand, and the change in the aggregate value of output, on the other, is equivalent to equation 3.S.5. Indeed, in the supplement to Chapter 3 we have worked out the case of growth in the exchange model where only the endowment of the home country's export commodity, clothing, expanded. The effect on real income, shown there as equation 3.S.14, is reproduced below as 25.S.2:

$$dy = \left[\frac{\epsilon + \epsilon^* - (1 + m)}{\Delta} \right] dx_c. \qquad (25.S.2)$$

Δ, as before, is the Marshall-Lerner stability expression ($\epsilon + \epsilon^* - 1$), which must be positive. But the numerator could be negative, in which case growth so deteriorates the terms of trade that welfare is reduced.

With this expression as a point of reference two additional comments can be made. (1) If growth is so biased toward the export commodity that at constant prices the production of import-competing goods would fall, the deterioration in the terms of trade will be even more pronounced and the possibility of immiserizing growth correspondingly enhanced. Pure expansion in the labor force in a Heckscher-Ohlin setting (Figure 25.3) is an example. (2) Even if growth is less skewed, so that at constant prices some expansion in import-competing goods takes place, immiserization remains a possibility. The crucial thing is that at constant prices growth in the home country presents the rest of the world with a net increase in the supply of the home country's exportables. Low demand elasticities at home and abroad can then produce the result.

In the second example (illustrated in Figure 25.8) there is a tariff wedge, but with the terms of trade assumed constant (the small-country case) we can ignore the $-Mdp^*$ term that usually is present in the decomposition of dy. With this in mind, differentiate the budget constraint expressed in foreign prices:

$$D_c + p^*D_F = x_c + p^*x_F \tag{25.S.3}$$

to obtain

$$dD_c + p^*dD_F = dx_c + p^*dx_F.$$

As before we wish to subtract and add pdD_F on the left-hand side. By itself this yields:

$$dy = (p - p^*)dD_F + (dx_c + p^*dx_F) \tag{25.S.4}$$

because dy is defined, as always, as $\{dD_c + pdD_F\}$. An alternative form for this expression follows if the term pdx_F is subtracted and added on the right-hand side:

$$dy = (p - p^*)dM + (dx_c + pdx_F). \tag{25.S.5}$$

Consider both 25.S.4 and 25.S.5 in the context of Figure 25.8. That diagram showed a loss of welfare in moving from point B to the post-growth point D. The value of output at domestic prices has grown; $dx_c + pdx_F$ in equation 25.S.5 is positive. (Line 3 is higher than line 1 in Figure 25.8.) But imports have been drastically reduced — the line DC being shorter than BA. With a tariff wedge, $(p - p^*)dM$ in equation 25.S.5 is therefore negative, and, in Figure 25.8, outweighs the value of growth in production at domestic prices.

Equation 25.S.4 is, in a sense, more precise. With domestic prices constant throughout, only income effects operate to change the demand for food. Therefore,

$$dD_F = \frac{m}{p}dy.$$

But the expression $(p - p^*)/p$ is the fraction $t/(1 + t)$, where t is the tariff rate on food imports. Therefore dy is given by 25.S.6:

$$\left(1 - m\frac{t}{1 + t}\right)dy = (dx_c + p^*dx_F). \tag{25.S.6}$$

This equation tells us that growth by a small country that protects imports *reduces* welfare if and only if the value of production at *world* prices falls. This effect was shown in Figure 25.8, with line 6 through D lying below line 5 through B.

26 Effects of Trade on Growth and Development

Economic growth affects international trade, in ways considered in Chapter 25. But a country's pattern of growth and development also reflects changes in the trading opportunities presented to it by the international economy. More important for economic policy, the country may be able to manipulate its trade controls to alter its economic development.

The history of international commerce is studded with apparent paradoxes concerning the effect of trade on growth. On the one hand, trade appeared to be an "engine of growth" for many nations settled and developed during the nineteenth century, with gains from trade playing a crucial role in expanding their real incomes. On the other hand, many countries that remain underdeveloped today have long been active exporters of primary products, and yet have seen the gap between their own real incomes and those of the industrial countries widen relentlessly. Many less-developed countries now ruthlessly restrict foreign trade in the hope of promoting economic development.

What do the lessons of history really teach? Has trade been "good" for the development of some countries, "bad" for others? Do these broad historical patterns provide much information for the country trying to decide whether to channel resources toward the export sector or toward the replacement of imports by domestic production? Does the desire to promote growth lead us to select controls on trade different from those we would pick in order to maximize real income? In this chapter we shall move through this series of questions from historical analysis to the policy choices facing less-developed countries today.

26.1 TRADE CHANGES AND PRODUCTION POSSIBILITIES

The international economy presents a constant stream of disturbances to the member economy. Foreign demand for its exports rises
or falls because of the business cycle or variations in growth rates
abroad. The relative world prices of individual commodities rise or
fall in response to shifts in external demand and supply. We can
describe each of these disturbances as a shift in the offer curve that
the country faces (if it is large enough to affect world terms of trade)
or in the terms of trade themselves (if it is a small country). Take the
small nation affected by an external disturbance that increases the
relative price of its export good. In Part 2 we saw that this change
increases its real income and the proportion of resources devoted to
production of its export good. But what of growth?

If we assume that the country's production possibilities are described by a fixed transformation function, improved trading opportunities can lead to growth only in the sense of greater gains from
trade. Trade expansion affects growth more fundamentally, however,
*if an improvement in the terms of trade shifts the economy to a
permanently enlarged transformation curve,* and thus increases
its production and consumption possibilities. This effect is illustrated in Figure 26.1, a diagram of the type first introduced in Chapter

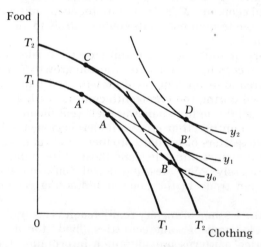

FIGURE 26.1   Effect of Improved Terms of Trade
on Production Possibilities

Static gains from trade raise income from y_0 to y_1 when
terms of trade improve from AB to $A'B'$. Dynamic gains from
this improvement shift production possibilities to T_2T_2, raise
income to y_2.

6. The country exports food, initially at terms of trade AB. With the production possibilities supplied by T_1T_1, it produces output combination A and by trade obtains consumption bundle B and real income y_0. Now the terms of trade improve to $A'B'$, perhaps as a result of population growth and increased demand for food abroad. Without any expansion of production possibilities, real income y_1 could be obtained. Previously we have allowed only this effect: a movement along the given transformation curve. Suppose now that this improvement in the terms of trade expands the production set to T_2T_2. Production would be located at C, consumption at D, and real income y_2 could be obtained. If the production set remains permanently expanded to T_2T_2, no matter what now happens to the terms of trade, we can credit the improvement for causing growth which can be measured by the increase of income from y_1 to y_2.

So far, we have merely depicted the effect of improved trading opportunities on growth, without explaining how growth might be induced. Several hypotheses about this effect can be advanced, along with the historical evidence that suggested them. An expansion of trade may increase the utilization of a country's factor stock. It may enlarge that factor stock. Or the increase of export production may generate external effects that raise the economy's output capacity all around.

Improving Factor Utilization

In many countries trade has brought into use factors of production that had gone unused or underemployed. These include both natural resources and, in indigenous societies newly exposed to trade, labor.

The early development of resource-rich countries such as Canada has been marked by the discovery and development of a sequence of "staples," or products exported as lightly processed natural materials. Improved terms of trade bestir the discovery of these resources, or convince people to make investments needed to put them to use. The economy's capacity to produce them is then permanently expanded. Referring to Figure 26.1, "food" might be such a staple, its production expanded through the extension of frontier settlement and clearing of new land. The transformation schedule would then shift upward, in that more food could be produced for any output of cloth. (If cloth requires little land, however, the maximum output of cloth might stay unchanged, anchoring the transformation curve at T_1 on the horizontal axis.)

This pattern of export-led growth has apparently repeated itself often in Canada's economic development. Resources exploited in response to favorable shifts of reciprocal demand include codfish, timber, beaver fur, grain, and nonferrous metals. Similar waves of growth marked by the expanded discovery and use of natural resources occurred in other countries settled during the nineteenth century, such as Australia, New Zealand, Argentina, and South Africa.[1]

Many of the still less-developed countries were drawn into international trade while using previously underutilized resources. Their uncultivated agricultural land was often such a resource, but so was underutilized peasant labor. Think of the transformation function in Figure 26.1 as reflecting the production possibilities of a self-sufficient peasant economy, in which "food" represents an exportable agricultural staple (such as rice) and "clothing" stands for a bundle of home and artisan manufactures and services. In the absence of trade, a peasant society is apt to divide its labor services between these bundles of goods and share the resulting outputs on the basis of traditional status patterns. Labor may be underutilized, partly because the individual's consumption results from a customary share of the community's product and not necessarily from the marginal product of his own labor services (as in a market economy).

Now offer this peasant economy the chance to exchange its food output for manufactured goods. The manufactures may serve the same wants as the community's handicraft output. They are qualitatively different, however, and thus open a new range of consumption choices. The peasant economy is apt not only to reallocate resources toward food production but also to increase its total input of labor services, sacrificing some leisure in order to consume a larger and more varied bundle of goods. This increase would be shown in Figure 26.1 by a movement from production point A to C; the exchange of food for manufactures, however, cannot be illustrated because the foreign manufactures are not directly comparable to native handicraft production.

Historical research has documented this pattern for such countries as Thailand and Burma, where rice cultivation expanded and peasant handicraft contracted in response to improved terms of trade for rice on world markets. The associated increase in real income did not, however, always promote qualitative development of these peasant economies. The rice growers were presumably better off for having a wider choice of goods available,[2] but they did not learn to become manufacturing entrepreneurs; nor did transportation facilities or other broadly useful forms of social capital always spring up. Furthermore, the pretrade social organization of the peasant economy some-

[1] For references to some of the historical literature, see R. E. Caves, "Export-led Growth and the New Economic History," in *Trade, Balance of Payments, and Growth,* ed. J. Bhagwati et al. Amsterdam: North-Holland Publishing Co., 1971, esp. pp. 419–38.

[2] Actually, the real-income gains from resource-based exports may not accrue to the laborers at all unless they own agricultural land. If the country's labor supply is perfectly elastic — through immigration, or a high birth rate — the whole gain from such an export boom goes to the owners of the natural resource.

times suffered significant disruption as it responded to new market incentives.[3] As we shall discover below, promoting economic development can point to different policies than maximizing real income in the short run.

Expanding Factor Endowments

Improved terms of trade or trading opportunities can also promote economic growth by raising the nation's stock of factors of production. The enlargement can stem from either an inflow of mobile factors from abroad or the creation of additional stock at home.

Theory tells us to expect factors of production — labor and capital — to move internationally when they can earn higher incomes thereby. The incomes in question are *expected,* so the critical influences raise anticipated returns abroad. During the nineteenth century, the migration of labor and capital from the European countries to the newly settled areas overseas was clearly if roughly related to periods of booming exports from these regions to the European center. The factor movements expanded not only the export capacities of new regions but also their transport and service sectors and a wide range of other economic activities. A large share of Europe's foreign investment was attracted to the recently settled areas (including the United States): on the eve of World War I, they had drawn two-thirds of Britain's total foreign investment. Expanding trade and induced factor inflows thus played a major role in placing these regions among the fastest-growing countries of the nineteenth century.[4]

A favorable shift of trading opportunities may also induce expansion of a country's native factor endowment — especially its capital stock. New investment opportunities raise the expected rate of return and thus may increase the portion of income that is saved. In the two decades following World War II, the European countries with the most rapidly growing exports also seemed to show the highest rates of capital formation and saving. Their less favored neighbors meanwhile experienced lower investment and saving, slower growth, and more inflationary pressure. It is easy to see why strong prospects for export sales should encourage heavy capital formation, by making large expansions of capacity in the export industries appear profitable. Without corresponding increases of saving, however, the investment and export booms would have choked themselves off through inflationary pressure. Capital imports provided some of the extra resources, but so did increases in domestic saving rates. These increases

---

[3] For brief case studies, see S. A. Resnick, "The Decline of Rural Industry Under Export Expansion: A Comparison among Burma, Philippines, and Thailand, 1870–1938," *Journal of Economic History,* 30 (March 1970): 51–73.

[4] For a good brief account of this experience see Ragnar Nurkse. *Equilibrium and Growth in the World Economy.* Cambridge: Harvard University Press, 1961, Chap. 11.

were apparently caused by temporary redistributions of income due to rapidly growing exports. Business profits gained, and a high proportion of these were plowed back into investment. The general public also saved more, perhaps because its consumption standards did not adjust upward as fast as personal incomes were rising. These high saving and investment rates may not have been permanent for any of the countries enjoying rapid export growth, but they were a strong temporary link between improved trading opportunities and rapid economic growth.[5]

Trade, Linkages, and Growth

These cases show that expanding trade can enlarge a country's production possibilities. But not every export boom has generated broad or sustained growth in that country. A glaring example is the oil refinery or aluminum smelter in a less-developed country producing for export markets. Highly capital-intensive, it employs imported capital and managers and creates few jobs for the country's nationals. It adds little to the country's stock of labor skills. It provides nationals with few opportunities to become entrepreneurs. It does not induce the establishment of complementary industries that would supply its inputs or purchase its outputs for further processing. Gains from trade still accrue, usually in the form of rents to native owners of the natural resources used in process. But little cumulative development is nurtured.[6]

Conversely, different export specialties might generate a wide range of these "spillover" effects, instilling labor skills, inducing the creation of complementary industries and transportation facilities, encouraging entrepreneurship and raising the rate of saving. It all depends — on the traits of the economy where the export growth occurs, but also on the input requirements and the production process for the export good in question. A country's growth may be strongly affected by luck — whether or not a principal export turns out to encourage complementary development in other sectors of the economy.[7]

But these differences between the developmental effects of export specialties really shift our attention to the policy questions facing countries consciously promoting economic development. A country cannot easily alter its broad pattern of comparative advantage, so far as that pattern rests (in Ricardian fashion) on its physical endow-

[5] See A. Lamfalussy. *The United Kingdom and the Six*. Homewood, Ill.: Richard D. Irwin, 1963, esp. chap. 9.

[6] H. W. Singer, "The Distribution of Gains between Investing and Borrowing Countries," *American Economic Review,* 40 (May 1950): 473–85; reprinted American Economic Association, *Readings in International Economics*. Homewood, Ill.: Richard D. Irwin, 1968, chap. 19.

[7] Robert E. Baldwin, "Patterns of Development in Newly Settled Regions," *Manchester School,* 24 (May 1954): 161–79; also his case study, *Economic Development and Export Growth: A Study of Northern Rhodesia, 1920–1960*. Berkeley and Los Angeles: University of California Press, 1966.

ment: it either possesses or lacks crude petroleum reserves; its climate either does or does not permit tea plantations. On a smaller scale, however, it can modify its pattern of production and trade by the taxes and subsidies discussed above in Part 3. Indeed, the presently less-developed countries employ a bristling arsenal of devices to promote the substitution of home production for imports or to encourage the expansion of selected exports. We shall now turn to these policies for controlling trade in the name of swifter economic development.

26.2 TRADE PESSIMISM IN THE DEVELOPING COUNTRIES

If a favorable shift in trading opportunities can further economic growth, a country's best interest might still lie in restricting trade and promoting substitutes for imports. It could be driven to this finding by two conditions: (1) it does not expect a markedly favorable turn in the trading opportunities for its principal exports; (2) it finds its development goals better served by restriction of trade. Strictly speaking, one can contribute little to wise policy-making for one less-developed country (LDC) by reciting prospects for the relative prices of the goods which LDCs export as a group. What matters for Brazil is whether a higher social rate of return will result from investing resources in another coffee plantation or a transistor radio factory; long-term trends in the price of crude rubber have no bearing on the choice.

Nonetheless, we should notice some of the sources of the LDCs' pessimism about trade as an engine of growth, if only to understand their eagerness to restrict imports. Their discontents gave rise to the United Nations Conference on Trade and Development (UNCTAD), which has stirred extensive discussion of many of the issues considered in this chapter.[8]

Unsatisfactory Terms of Trade

Many of the complaints lodged by the LDCs about their role in international commerce have to do with the terms at which their exports — mostly primary products — exchange for the manufactured goods that they principally import from the industrial countries. The complaints have to do with both the level of these terms and their movement over time.

The level of their terms of trade, the LDCs claim, is adversely affected by the monopoly power of the industrial countries. Monopoly gains are taken in two ways. First, many manufacturing industries are imperfectly competitive, so that manufactured imports can be purchased only at prices in excess of marginal costs. Manufacturing

[8] A basic document is *Towards a New Trade Policy for Development: Report by the Secretary-General of the United Nations Conference on Trade and Development.* United Nations, 1964.

industries, as we noted in Chapter 11, behave somewhat more competitively in export markets than in their national home markets.
Nonetheless, they surely glean some monopoly returns from their
exports to the LDCs. A second source of monopoly extractions lies in
the tariffs imposed by the industrial countries, which render the
LDCs' terms of trade less favorable than otherwise. The incidence of
these tariffs is in fact rather uneven. Many products of tropical agriculture do not compete with close substitutes made in the industrial
countries, and hence have generally escaped protective tariffs (though
they sometimes face revenue tariffs). On the other hand, LDC exports
competing with temperate-zone agriculture or with low-skill manufacturing industries in the industrial countries often meet moun-
tainous tariff barriers.

The LDCs have occasionally attempted to exert some monopoly
power of their own by means of marketing boards, international
commodity agreements, and similar devices to control the sale of their
primary exports. These usually proclaim a loftier motive of stabilizing
prices or bringing them up to a fair level. Motives aside, they often
have attempted to control supply and secure a higher price than otherwise. The long-run success of these arrangements for most products
of tropical agriculture has been quite limited. They usually founder on
the same rock as many other attempts to monopolize a market: lacking the adherence of all potential producers, any success the members
enjoy in raising prices by the restriction of sales simply draws new
producers into the market and costs the members part of their market
share.[9]

Worsening Terms of Trade

Apart from these forces affecting the LDC terms of trade, some LDC
spokesmen have claimed that the terms of trade for primary products
have systematically worsened for many decades and — worse yet —
must continue to do so. The historical side of this charge has not with-
stood the test of empirical research very well. Over the eighty-year
period from the late 1870's to the late 1950's, we perceive no trend one
way or another in the terms of trade between manufactures and
primary products. Given the changes occurring in the composition
and character of manufactured goods over such a long period, the
meaning of any long-term price trend is unclear; in any case, the
hypothesis of secular worsening of primary-products prices is not
confirmed.

World output and world trade of manufactures and primary products have not grown at the same rate, however. From 1900 to 1960
production and trade of manufactures per capita grew fourfold, pro-

[9] See J. W. F. Rowe. *Primary Commodities in International Trade.* Cambridge: Cambridge University Press, 1965, part 4; and Harry G. Johnson.
Economic Policies Toward Less Developed Countries. Washington: Brookings Institution, 1967, chap. 5.

duction and trade of primary products only about 50 percent.[10] The world's income elasticity of demand for manufactures evidently has been much higher than that for primary products. Other studies also show that the price elasticity of demand for most primary products is low. Still a further complication is the stream of technical discoveries that have replaced primary exports of the LDCs with synthetic substances produced in the industrial countries (natural rubber is an example). These facts establish a significant danger for the LDCs, that rapid expansion of primary-products output could be immiserizing, and indicate a general limit on the growth of these outputs.[11] If the LDCs based rapid growth on expanding outputs of primary products, their terms of trade would systematically deteriorate.

Instability of Export Earnings

A third complaint of LDCs about the economic results of concentrating on exporting primary products is that their export earnings are less stable than those of sellers of manufactures. The reasons for this instability lie in the low price-elasticities of demand and supply for primary products on world markets. Consider a product such as coffee, for which world demand is relatively price-inelastic. The crop fails one year in a major producing country, and supply is markedly decreased. The price must be greatly increased to eliminate excess demand in the market. The fact that supply is quite inelastic in the short run rules out mitigation. Hence world wholesale coffee prices and export earnings are high in years of crop failure and low in years of bumper crops. Another factor that expands the possibilities of instability is the long lag in the supply response of many primary products to a price change. A short coffee crop causes a high price this year, and induces the planting of more coffee trees; the trees take years to reach bearing age, however, and the factors causing the temporary high price might then be long gone.

Indexes of instability can be calculated in many ways. The one quoted below represents, roughly speaking, the average percentage

---

[10] Data from A. Maizels. *Industrial Growth and World Trade.* Cambridge: Cambridge University Press, 1963, chap. 4. Also see W. Arthur Lewis. *Aspects of Tropical Trade, 1883–1965.* Wicksell Lectures. Stockholm: Almqvist & Wicksell, 1969.

[11] An argument popular among LDC spokesmen a decade ago, originating with Professor Raul Prebisch, deduced worsening terms of trade for primary producers from the assumption that productivity gains in the LDCs led to lowered money prices of their exports, whereas productivity gains in manufactures led to higher money wages for industrial-country factors of production. This argument is logically invalid unless one assumes the low price- and income-elasticity values mentioned above. Once these values are assumed, however, the difference in price flexibility asserted by Prebisch has no effect. See M. June Flanders, "Prebisch on Protectionism: An Evaluation," *Economic Journal,* 74 (June 1964): 305–26.

year-to-year change in export earnings, corrected for a trend factor.
Here are some sample values, calculated for the years 1946–1958[12]:

Average instability index, 45 LDCs:		23.1
Iran (highest)	73.8	
Argentina	41.3	
India	16.2	
Panama (lowest)	9.9	
Average instability index, 18 rich countries:		17.6
Japan (highest)	31.0	
Switzerland (lowest)	6.2	

The export earnings of the LDCs thus are more unstable — although
not *much* more unstable — than those of the industrial nations.
Furthermore, their earnings instability reflects price movements
quite heavily, whereas the instability for the rich countries more
often reflects fluctuations in quantities.

Most people dislike uncertainty about the incomes their labors (or
investments) will earn, and hence avoid activities yielding variable
or risky returns. Economic theory suggests that people will insist on
a higher average expected income from a risky activity than from one
yielding a risk-free income. On this ground, one would expect LDCs
to shun the expansion of primary export activities yielding risky but
low returns. Export fluctuations are thus cited by LDC spokesmen as
another general reason for eschewing the expansion of primary-
product exports as a principal strategy for growth.[13]

26.3 THE CASE FOR IMPORT-SUBSTITUTING
INDUSTRIALIZATION

The bases for trade pessimism outlined in the preceding section provide an LDC's planners with a general warning against unverified
optimism about the rate of return to resources used to expand the
production of exportable primary products. They do not, however,
yield any specific information about the best investment of extra
productive resources. Solving that problem is the essence of development planning. We can say little, here, about planners' methods
of forecasting prices or commercial rates of return. There is much to
say, however, about countries' methods of evaluating these forecasts

---

[12] From Joseph D. Coppock. *International Economic Instability: The
Experience after World War II.* New York: McGraw-Hill, 1962, chap. 4.

[13] Oddly enough, statistical analysis has failed to show that countries suffering from high export fluctuations seem overall to grow slower than those with
modest fluctuations. Perhaps the reason lies in the response of investment to
price fluctuations: if people take each upward fluctuation as the sign of a
protracted favorable trend, but view each downward change as a temporary
aberration, investment in the long run will be higher with unstable than with
stable export earnings. See A. I. MacBean. *Export Instability and Economic
Development.* London: George Allen and Unwin, 1966.

and any proposals for restricting or subsidizing trade. We know from section 25.4 that a country's domestic growth can lower its real income either if it restricts trade insufficiently (in the face of inelastic foreign demand) *or* if it restricts trade excessively (in the face of highly elastic foreign demand). We shall now expand the analysis of Chapter 13 to consider trade restriction in a developing country. Then we shall notice the patterns of trade restriction actually used by the LDCs, and some evidence of their effects.

Arguments for Trade Restriction

Several arguments for trade restriction introduced in Chapter 13 are asserted with special force for developing economies. As each argument is presented we shall ask whether it identifies trade restriction as the best policy under the circumstances, or whether instead it is a needlessly expensive, or "second-best," choice.

Saving and Distribution of Income. A principal policy goal of development planners is to raise the rates of domestic saving and thus capital formation. We saw (section 13.2) that restricting — or subsidizing — international trade can redistribute income from one factor of production to another. Suppose that the factors differ in their average propensities to save; owners of the factor used intensively in the import-competing sector save ten percent of their incomes, say, whereas the factor used intensively in exportables saves only five percent. A restriction of trade would (subject to conditions mentioned in section 13.2) then redistribute income toward the thriftier group and raise the average rate of saving. Many LDCs apparently believe that incomes earned by landowners from producing primary exports are not invested — or at least not invested in activities the government favors. If one makes that assumption, the most efficient policy is to tax landowner incomes directly. Export taxes, however, are often used as a second-best substitute.[14]

Saving and Consumer Expenditure. The personal income tax is seldom well developed or enforced in an LDC. Hence another popular strategy of trade control, as a substitute for progressive income taxation, is to restrict the importation of luxury consumer goods. The planners hope that consumers deterred from luxury spending will save instead. Even if this assumption is correct, the use of a tariff is inefficient when a tax on consumption of the luxuries is really desired. The policy is once more "second-best," as we explained in section 13.3. If the assumption is wrong, the policy has the undesired side effect of promoting domestic production of luxury consumer goods (such as fancy urban housing).

Wage Levels and the "Dual Economy." An important resource misallocation often found in developing economies — and industrial

---

[14] Export taxes and import taxes are symmetrical in their tendency to restrict the level of trade.

ones — results from a difference in the marginal product of labor in the agricultural and industrial sectors of the economy. Some students of LDCs have argued that the marginal product of labor in traditional agriculture is usually less than the income the worker receives, because of traditional distribution arrangements in the peasant economy (see section 26.1). Hence, in order to tempt him from agriculture into industry, he must be paid a wage in industry that exceeds his marginal product in agriculture. The marginal product of labor in industry would equal this higher wage, and hence labor's marginal product would not be equalized between different sectors of the economy. The same effect is achieved by the generous — extravagant? — social legislation that inflates industrial wage costs in some LDCs and further increases the discrepancy between sectoral marginal products of labor.

Again, the ideal device to combat this misallocation would not be a tariff. Instead, labor should be subsidized in the industrial sector. Even a general subsidy to industrial production would probably be better than restricting industrial imports, although it would encourage industry to overuse factors of production other than labor. A tariff on industrial imports needlessly distorts domestic consumption of industrial goods, and thus becomes "third best." Nonetheless, LDC governments often lack sources of tax revenue, and thus cannot judge subsidies and taxes equally. Hence they often prefer import duties.[15]

Infant Industries and Externalities. The infant industry case for tariff protection (discussed in section 13.5) is about as old as the subject of international economics, and its popularity is not dimmed by the austere list of assumptions necessary for its validity. To warrant the social cost of protection a young industry must not only become competitive at free trade prices; it must further become productive enough to repay the cost of subsidizing its infancy. Although infant industry protection may be special, its conditions are much more likely to be met in an LDC than in an industrial nation. The LDC is typically very short of rudimentary industrial skills, including both entrepreneurship and many labor skills. Some of these (notably entrepreneurship) can be learned only by experience. Others could be purchased on the market — e.g., instruction in welding, or running a lathe — but recently urbanized peasants will surely underinvest in them. In this setting the first industrial enterprises may face heavy initial costs of on-the-job training (and entrepreneurial first-time mistakes). Most important, individual enterprises cannot recoup all the benefits of labor skills provided to the work force, in that workers must be paid the market wage that their new skills command, or they

---

[15] This argument for protection is developed by E. E. Hagen, "An Economic Justification of Protectionism," *Quarterly Journal of Economics,* 72 (November 1958): 496–514.

will switch to other employers.[16] The value of the skills created by some industries — at one stage of development — hence may exceed the returns earned by the firms that provide them. These conditions provide a valid temporary case for infant industry protection until enough labor skills are built up. Once more, however, protection is an inefficient way to attack the problem; a subsidy to on-the-job training would avoid incidental distortions of production and consumption patterns.

Promoting Capital Inflows. In the pure Heckscher-Ohlin model outlined in Part 2 of this book, tariff protection may not raise the rate of return to capital in the import-competing sector, because capital's reward in the economy generally rises only if capital is used most intensively in the import-competing sector. If industries are not purely competitive, however, and exhibit the elements of entry barriers and product differentiation that we considered in Chapter 11, tariffs are likely to be a sustained profit stimulus in import-competing industries. The stimulus in turn allows tariffs to induce an inflow of capital through foreign direct investment.

Studies of the multinational corporation show that a tariff often causes it to invest in a country. Previously it has exported to the market in question, investing in advertising and customer good will but not in physical production facilities. When its imports to the market are struck with a tariff, direct investment becomes more attractive than the only alternative — writing off the firm's investment in good will and leaving the market entirely.

Actual Patterns of Trade Restriction

The general thrust of these tariff arguments is to justify some import restriction as part of a development program — at least if we grant that "first-best" policy instruments are often unavailable, and trade controls must be used instead. The question is: how much trade restriction can be justified? Let us consider some evidence on trade restriction by LDCs and ask what claim it has to maximizing their welfare and promoting their growth.

The LDCs use the same trade controls as the industrial countries, only more so. Tariffs and quantitative restrictions are commonly applied. Some countries tax their exports of primary products, especially where demand or supply of these products is thought to be price-inelastic. Other protective devices, not often found in the industrial countries, are also in use:

Multiple Exchange Rates. LDCs often employ foreign-exchange control, meaning that all exchange earned must be surrendered to the government, and purchases of exchange must be made from it. When it monopolizes the foreign-exchange market the government

[16] One possible solution is for the firm to charge its workers implicitly for their training by paying them a very low wage until it is acquired. In practice, however, they probably can seldom bear the full cost.

can discriminate in its exchange transactions, paying or charging different prices for exchange earned in or used for different activities. Suppose the domestic currency unit is the *erg,* and a free-market exchange rate of ten ergs to the dollar would clear the foreign-exchange market. The importer required to pay 11 ergs per dollar for his exchange requirements is effectively paying a 10 percent ad valorem tariff on his purchases; likewise, the exporter who receives only 9 ergs per dollar for his exchange earnings is effectively taxed 10 percent. Multiple exchange rates thus substitute for (or supplement) conventional tariffs. Many LDCs have built up complex systems of protection by installing at various times tariffs for protection and also exchange control to deal with crises in external payments.

Domestic Content Requirements. Manufacturing establishments, especially foreign subsidiaries, must often secure a minimum of the inputs for their final product from domestic sources. The purchaser must then buy his supplies from high-cost local sources and forego lower-cost imports. Thus the effect is in general the same as that of tariffs on the imported components.

We can secure a general idea of the structures of tariff protection in LDCs from a detailed study of six of them, undertaken at the International Bank for Reconstruction and Development (World Bank).[17] The countries studied — Brazil, Chile, Malaya, Pakistan, Mexico, and Philippines — have made some headway with economic development. Table 26.1 presents average rates of protection for several broad economic sectors in those countries. Two important features of these tariff rates should be noticed. First, they are *effective* rates of protection as they were defined in Chapter 13. That is, they represent rates of duty on individual economic processes, and take into account the fact that the domestic prices of inputs needed at a processing stage may or may not be elevated by tariffs on those inputs. Second, they allow for suppressed disequilibria in the foreign-exchange markets of these countries. The latter adjustment is particularly important for LDCs, which often maintain exchange rates (prices of foreign exchange) too low to ration demand to supply. The percentage overvaluations for the countries studied by the IBRD ranged from 68 percent for Chile and 50 percent for Pakistan down to 4 percent for Malaya. An overvalued exchange rate provides negative protection for import-competing industries, by making the domestic price of imports lower than it would be in equilibrium.[18]

---

[17] Bela Balassa et al. *The Structure of Protection in Developing Countries.* Baltimore: Johns Hopkins Press, 1971.

[18] Suppose the erg is overvalued when 9 exchange for $1, and that 10 to the dollar would be needed to clear the exchange market without controls. The world price of gadgets is $1, and the import-competing producer enjoys a 10 percent tariff. He can set an erg price of 9.9 on his output without being undercut by imports. But this price is (approximately) the same as the price (10 ergs) he could set if he received no protection and the erg exchange rate were in full equilibrium.

TABLE 26.1 Rates of Effective Tariff Protection, Selected Commodity Groups, for Six Developing Countries (percentages)[a]

Industry group	Brazil (1966)	Chile (1961)	Mexico (1960)	Malaya (1965)	Pakistan (1963–64)	Philippines (1965)
Agriculture, forestry, fishing	15	-6	-3	17	-46	16
Mining and energy	-34	2	-20	-12	-14	-21
Processed food	52	111	10	3	219	65
Construction materials	41	51	-13	5	45	36
Intermediate products[b]	127	76	43	20	82	42
Nondurable consumer goods	151	138	33	15	71	28
Consumer durables	204	33	70	-9	307	58
Machinery	52	17	27	2	40	8
Transport equipment	-42	-79	19	n.a.	n.a.	-15
Total manufacturing	79	54	21	7	92	34

Source: Bela Balassa et al. *The Structure of Protection in Developing Countries.* Baltimore: Johns Hopkins Press, 1971, Table 3.2.

[a] Effective rates of protection calculated after adjustment for disequilibrium values of the countries' exchange rates. Input-output coefficients calculated at free trade prices were employed.

[b] Figures are given in the source for two heterogeneous groups of intermediate products. The figures shown here cover textile fabrics, wood and paper products, rubber and plastic goods, chemical products, steel products, and metal castings and manufactures.

Table 26.1 shows that these countries all give heavy protection to their manufacturing industries, especially consumer goods, and impose negative protection on their primary product sectors. (Negative protection can occur, for example, when the output is sold at world prices but the prices of some inputs are inflated by tariffs.) The table confirms the impressions of observers that many LDCs have since World War II gone through a first phase of promoting import substitutes, eliminating or severely restricting imports of nondurable consumer goods requiring only unskilled and semiskilled labor. These domestic industries will usually take root behind moderate tariff protection. The larger LDCs have also pressed into advanced import substitution in which they establish the production of consumer durable goods, basic industrial materials, and machine tools.[19] Such heavy protection has certainly extracted a cost in economic welfare foregone. The question is, have its dynamic benefits to development made this cost worthwhile?

Many observers of tariff-protected industrialization in LDCs report fairly gloomy assessments. The most compelling theoretical arguments for protection, among those listed above, stress dynamic infant industry benefits stemming from temporary protection. But these benefits flow from the early development of such an industry, and are of dubious worth unless the industry later becomes efficient enough to compete without protection. However, few LDC manufacturing industries have matured to this competitive status, or seem likely to do so. The infant industry justification, after the event, is not clearly tenable.

Instead, these heavily protected industrial sectors reveal some unwelcome results of their sheltered status. Insulated from foreign competition and often beset by few domestic rivals, firms are free from competitive pressure for efficiency. As the World Bank study showed, they "tend to follow a policy of low turnover and high profit rates and have little incentive for product improvement and technical change . . . Product quality has often deteriorated and firms have been reluctant to assume the risk associated with the introduction of new products, production methods, and innovating activity in general."[20] High levels of excess capacity are often found, for such reasons as difficulties in securing imported raw materials through the import-control machinery.[21] The domestic markets of many LDCs are small enough that many lines of manufactures must be inefficient due to

[19] For a descriptive account for Latin America, see Joseph Grunwald, "Some Reflections on Latin American Industrialization Policy," *Journal of Political Economy,* 78 (supplement to July/August 1970): 826–56.

[20] Balassa et al. *The Structure of Protection in Developing Countries,* p. 79 and chap. 4 generally.

[21] G. C. Winston, "Capitalisation in Economic Development," *Economic Journal,* 81 (March 1971): 36–60.

small-scale production. This problem becomes especially severe when import substitution is pushed beyond simple consumer nondurables into durables and industrial materials, or beyond assembly operations (e.g., automobiles) into the manufacture of major components (e.g., engines and transmissions). Profligate insulation of the domestic market helps to load the dice against any manufacturing industries becoming exporters and thereby ducking the small-scale problem; we shall consider in the next section the prospects for LDC exports of manufactures.

But, one might argue, the alternative to inefficient industries perhaps was no industries. Without protection, the factors of production might be under-employed (e.g., agricultural labor) or might not even exist (e.g., capital, if saving would otherwise not have occurred). This defense implies that countries using heavy tariff protection have not diverted resources from their export sectors but instead have enlarged their economies overall. The evidence fails to support this possibility. The countries that have heavily promoted import substitution seem to have pulled resources away from their primary export sectors and reduced their shares of traditional export markets. Furthermore, the growth of import-substituting industrial sectors has not corresponded to an expansion of exports of industrial goods. According to the World Bank group, manufactured exports seem to have done better in countries that have employed less extreme and comprehensive promotion of import substitutes.

The ideal extent of trade restriction in developing countries remains controversial. On the one hand, profligate import restriction seems to have done more harm than good. On the other, the case for *some* conscious promotion of industry seems strong. The trick is to choose the right amount. In recognition of this problem the interests of many LDC spokesmen have shifted in recent years toward the promotion of more efficient manufacturing sectors by choosing sectors for encouragement more carefully and using export markets more. We shall now turn to that possibility.

26.4 OUTWARD-LOOKING INDUSTRIALIZATION AND EXPORT PROSPECTS

Industrialization is natural and desirable for LDCs that have attained the minimum requisites of human resources and social overhead capital. The high income elasticity of demand, the world around, for manufactures (and services) relative to food and other primary products points toward increasing resources in industry — in both less-developed and mature economies. Thus the real policy question for LDCs is how to proceed efficiently along this route — not whether to take it. To escape the inefficiencies of industrialization through steep tariffs, industrialization policies have been urged to be more "outward-looking" and industrial markets to keep in touch with the structure of world prices.[22] This means promoting manufacturing industries with an eye to their export possibilities and — more broadly — paying heed to the principle of comparative advantage and encouraging only industries that can prospectively meet the test of world competition.

An outward-looking industrialization policy would escape many of the inefficiencies found in heavily protected industrial sectors. World price competition penalizes outright inefficiency and forces firms to pay attention to innovation and quality control. They must be more attuned to signals from the world market. As Donald Keesing argues: "A close link exists between communication and competition. Whether someone receives a signal intended for him, and whether he acts upon it, depend in part on his attention and motivation. He will tend to pay close attention and spring into action if his survival, advancement and success depend on this behavior."[23] In heavily protected sectors, on the other hand, the relevant signals are domestic political ones relating to subsidies, controls, and the like. And the prize skills are apt to be those of political maneuver rather than entrepreneurship.

A problem of efficiency potentially soluble through exporting is that of small-scale diseconomies in LDCs' home markets. Although domestic markets of many LDCs are quite small, all the available scale economies in any relevant industry could be achieved by winning a very small share of world exports.

Are there manufacturing industries in which the LDCs are likely to enjoy a comparative advantage? Have LDCs found and exploited these activities? A study by Hal B. Lary[24] suggests a clear affirmative answer to the first question, on grounds familiar from the Heckscher-Ohlin model developed above in Chapters 8 and 9. Suppose that the relevant factors of production are capital — both physical capital and human skills — and "raw" (unskilled) labor. Suppose that we can rank all production processes by the ratios of total capital to labor required. Suppose, finally, that there are no factor-intensity reversals among manufacturing industries: if industry X is more capital-intensive than Y at United States factor prices, it is also more capital-intensive at India's factor prices. Then industries could be ranked from the most to the least capital-intensive, and we would expect the LDCs' comparative advantage to lie in the latter, that of the industrial countries in the former. Lary's research shows that these assumptions broadly hold true in practice, and points to a set of industries as supplying both the base for outward-looking in-

[22] E.g., D. B. Keesing, "Outward-Looking Policies and Economic Development," *Economic Journal*, 77 (June 1967): 303–20.

[23] *Ibid.*, p. 312.

[24] *Imports of Manufactures from Less Developed Countries.* New York: National Bureau of Economic Research, 1968.

dustrialization by the LDCs and also the basis for a mutually profitable division of labor with the industrial countries.

Has this division of labor been developing? Exports of labor-intensive manufactures from the LDCs have been growing fast — about 13 percent annually 1953–1965 — but remain small in total volume. In 1965 the United States imported only 4 percent of its consumption of labor-intensive manufactures from all foreign sources, and only 0.7 percent from the LDCs. Even so, it accounted for 41 percent of all industrial-country imports of these products from the LDCs. Furthermore, the LDC sources of these goods were quite concentrated, with tiny Hongkong accounting for no less than 28 percent, and the whole of Latin America less than one-fifth.[25] Clearly the industrial and LDC worlds have not divided much labor between themselves. Why not, and what can be done about it?

A serious constraint on the expansion of this division of labor has clearly been the tariffs and other trade controls imposed by the industrial countries. As we saw in Chapter 14, the United States has imposed the heaviest tariff protection on the small-scale and labor-intensive industries that are naturally the potential export specialties of the developing nations. Although systematic evidence is not available, the same pattern seems to mark the tariff structures of other industrial countries. It is hard to believe that these trade restrictions serve even the selfish interests of the industrial countries. An optimal tariff (see Chapter 12) still permits some imports. In any case, considerations of world welfare strongly support the expansion of LDC exports of manufactures. But these labor-intensive industries involve the greatest problems of readjustment in the industrial countries, when faced with increased import competition, and hence most clamorously demand sustained and expanded tariff protection.

What policy measures can be devised to attack this political impasse? If all-around trade liberalization by the industrial countries is unavailable, second-best measures must be considered. Two have received extensive attention:

Customs Unions among LDCs. Perhaps the developing countries could consciously take in each other's washing. *A, B,* and *C* form a customs union. *A* establishes industry *x, B* establishes *y,* and *C* establishes *z.* The demand in each country for each product will grow, and a more or less balanced expansion of preferential trade could take place among them if each develops his own export specialty. Although the general idea of preferential arrangements has been popular among the LDCs (as we stated in Chapter 15), many political difficulties have inhibited their success. Economically, such unions can easily be second-best choices and promote less than efficient division of labor among the member countries. Furthermore, they offer similar possibilities for inefficiency in "hothouse" pro-

---

[25] Figures from Lary. *Imports of Manufactures,* chap. 4.

tected markets as does heavy protection within a single national market. Nonetheless, they allow an LDC to develop an industrial sector without the crippling drawbacks of small-scale production.

Tariff Preferences by Industrial Countries. A proposal far more popular among LDCs is that industrial countries levy lower tariffs, or none at all, on manufactures imported from the LDCs, while maintaining their present tariffs on the same goods imported from other industrial countries. If the LDCs were given tariff-free access to industrial-country markets, they could expand their exports when their costs were below the (tariff-protected) domestic prices in the industrial countries. Without such preferences, their costs would have to lie below the world price. Thus a tariff preference offers an export opportunity to potential exporters whose costs lie above world prices by the industrial countries' margins of protection — often 20 percent or more. The effect of tariff preferences on LDC outputs of manufactures would thus be rather like that of the LDCs' own tariffs, except that the preference against foreign competitors now comes in a foreign market rather than in the LDC's home market.

Trade preferences do have serious disadvantages. They bear a cost for the industrial countries. When a preference is created, LDC exports will ordinarily displace exports from other sources. There is no reason to expect the domestic price to fall in the industrial country, and so its consumers are no better off. Its customs office, however, loses the revenue it formerly collected in the displaced imports from other sources, and this is a net loss to the industrial country. Tariff preferences thus can be looked at as a special — and inefficient — form of foreign aid. They convey other disadvantages. The countries whose exports are displaced will normally be the poorer industrial countries — Japan, Italy, Ireland, etc. The favored imports would probably be subject to quotas, and thus to all the difficulties of quota administration mentioned in section 14.4. The same awkward conclusion emerges as before: when a second-best remedy is proposed, we can seldom judge it on the basis of qualitative pros and cons.[26]

26.5 SUMMARY

A country's growth may be stimulated by foreign trade when the offer curve it faces shifts outward. Such a shift improves the country's terms of trade. It may also encourage the growth of its factor endowment, rate of utilization of that factor stock, or level of technology, and thus shift its production possibilities outward. The expansion of trade has often induced the discovery or development of previously idle natural resources, and thus expanded production possibilities. It has caused expansion of total labor inputs in the developing coun-

---

[26] For a fuller analysis see Johnson. *Economic Policies Toward Less Developed Countries,* chap. 6.

tries. The capital stock may increase because domestic saving rises, or capital is imported from abroad. Expanding export industries in some cases improve skills and technology for the country as a whole, but that improvement depends on the traits of its export sectors.

The less-developed countries (LDCs) have been discontented with their role in international trade, for several reasons. They argue that industrial monopolies in the mature countries charge them high prices for manufactures. They claim that the terms of trade tend in the long run to turn against their exports; this is in fact unclear, but world demand for their primary-product exports certainly grows less rapidly than it does for industrial products. They complain that their export earnings are relatively unstable, and this is clearly the case.

Careful analysis is required, however, to determine the extent to which the LDCs can improve their lot by restricting trade, as they have extensively done. Several of the arguments for tariffs popular in the LDCs are second-best: tariffs can change the income distribution (but direct taxation would be better); tariffs can curb luxury imports (but may simply stimulate luxury-goods production at home); tariffs can lure labor from the traditional agricultural sector (but a subsidy to industrial employment would be more efficient). The infant industry argument is valid but justifies only temporary protection. Actual trade restrictions in LDCs are quite heavy, taking such forms as multiple exchange rates and domestic content requirements as well as tariffs and quotas. Studies of protected industrialization find heavy costs of inefficiency, excessive capital-intensity, and the like.

Concentration on import-substituting industrialization may cause countries to overlook the potential gains from expanding international trade, especially the export of manufactured goods. The evidence suggests that it would be efficient for the LDCs to expand their exports of simple manufactures requiring labor-intensive fabrication. Alas, heavy tariff protection on such items by the industrial countries has minimized this mutually beneficial division of labor. Proposals to circumvent this drawback include customs unions among the LDCs themselves and the granting of tariff preferences by the industrial countries.

SUGGESTIONS FOR FURTHER READING

Balassa, Bela, and Associates. *The Structure of Protection in Developing Countries.* Baltimore: Johns Hopkins Press, 1971. Detailed studies of six LDCs.

Johnson, Harry G. *Economic Policies Toward Less Developed Countries.* Washington: Brookings Institution, 1967. Tightly argued survey of policy issues.

Keesing, D. B. "Outward-looking Policies for Economic Development," *Economic Journal,* 77 (June 1967): 303–20. Case for export-oriented industrialization in LDCs.

Levin, Jonathon V. *The Export Economies: Their Pattern of Development in*

Historical Perspective. Cambridge: Harvard University Press, 1960. Case studies of exports and growth.

Lewis, Arthur W. *Aspects of Tropical Trade, 1883–1965.* Wicksell Lectures, 1969. Stockholm: Almqvist & Wiksell, 1969. Stimulating quantitative approach to history and policy.

Meier, Gerald M. *The International Economics of Development: Theory and Policy.* New York: Harper & Row, 1968, esp. chaps. 7–9. Extended treatment of many issues discussed in this chapter.

Myrdal, Gunnar. *An International Economy: Problems and Prospects.* New York: Harper & Row, 1956. Pessimistic view of development prospects through trade.

Rowe, J. W. F. *Primary Commodities in International Trade.* Cambridge: Cambridge University Press, 1965. Summarizes experience with international commodity agreements.

United Nations. *Towards a New Trade Policy for Development: Report by the Secretary-General of the United Nations Conference on Trade and Development.* United Nations, 1964. Statement of issues from LDC viewpoint.

Index